INDOOR PLANTS

George B. Briggs
University of Nebraska

Clyde L. Calvin
Portland State University

Illustrated by
Michele Angle Farrar

JOHN WILEY & SONS
New York   Chichester
Brisbane   Toronto   Singapore

Cover drawing by Lynn Shaler
Cover and interior design, Dawn L. Stanley
Production Supervisor, Pamela Pelton

Library of Congress Cataloging-in-Publication Data

Briggs, George B.
    Indoor plants.

    1. House plants.   2. Indoor gardening.   I. Calvin,
Clyde L., 1934-   II. Title.
SB419.B72   1987   635.9′65   86-4070
ISBN 0-471-03298-0

Printed in the United States of America

10 9 8 7 6 5 4 3 2 1

The grass withers, the flower fades,
But the word of our God stands forever.

ISAIAH 40:8

contents

PART FIVE
A GUIDE TO THE IDENTIFICATION
AND CULTURE OF
THE TOP 150 INDOOR PLANTS 377

preface

Back in the late 1970s as I began teaching another quarter of plant propagation in the Virginia Tech Horticulture Department, a gentleman entered the class and seated himself. I discovered after that first class that his name was Dr. Clyde Calvin, a botany professor at Portland State University who was in temporary residence at Virginia Tech as a visiting professor. Clyde attended my course the entire quarter, often staying after class to discuss some particular aspect of the subject. We formed a mutual respect for each other's professional interests—Clyde's botanical and agronomical expertise and my horticultural and landscape architectural training.

Also at that time, Clyde was in the midst of writing a vegetable gardening textbook, which has since been published. Partly because of my frustration at the lack of a credible text for the indoor plants classes I was teaching and because of Clyde's book involvement, we began to discuss the need for a well-developed textbook in the indoor plant area. We polished our idea, submitted it for consideration to John Wiley & Sons, and received a most favorable response. We set out to work, embracing the motto "Quality before Speed." This finished product is the result of several years of research, writing, and editing. We feel it represents the most comprehensive and thorough indoor plant treatment in the academic area, both from a botanical and a horticultural point of view.

This text is designed for students of indoor plant classes at the college level. Although intended for beginning students, its subject matter is also suitable for horticulture majors and upper-level high school courses. The listing of the 150 top plants at the rear of the book includes most of the plants in the current FFA Indoor Plant competition.

The study of indoor plants is both a visual and an academic endeavor. Consequently, we have made a major commitment to the artistic quality of the book. The pen and ink illustrations, numbering over 300, were prepared by Michele Angle Farrar, the former art director of the Nebraska Game & Parks Commission. She has illustrated the award-winning *Nebraskaland* magazine for over 12 years, thus establishing a formidable reputation as a free lance artist specializing in botanical subjects. We are fortunate, indeed, to have had her deft hand interpret the beauty and intricacies of the indoor plant world.

Three prominent authors were selected to write chapters in their area of expertise. Dr. Charles Conover, director of the Agricultural Research Center in Apopka, Florida, is perhaps America's foremost research scientist on the subject of the indoor acclimatization of plants. He is the author of numerous books and research articles on indoor plants. Karen Solit, former botanist of the U.S. Botanic Garden in Washington, D.C., prepared the chapter on plant disorders. Recently, she completed another book on living indoor green gifts. The interior design chapter was written by Robert McDuffie, landscape architect and professor of landscape horticulture at Virginia Tech. This diversity of expertise and perspectives gives *Indoor Plants* an unusual credibility among texts.

The overall purpose of the text is to present a comprehensive view of the nature, culture, and utilization of plants indoors. We begin with the basics of plant identification and nomenclature, plant growth and development, and propagation. We then move into the cultural aspects of indoor plant growth, with such topics as fertilization, soils, the indoor climate, and pests and diseases. The concluding chapters deal with special aspects of cultivation, special plant groups, and the most popular indoor plants. The chapters form a logical progression, giving the student a comprehensive awareness and understanding of the diverse factors that are necessary for successful plant growth inside. We have intended to maintain that delicate balance between technical complexity and practical application.

GEORGE B. BRIGGS

acknowledgments

No textbook is the product of one person alone; certainly this one is no exception. The glue holding the preparation process together has been Don Deneck, editor of natural resources, with John Wiley & Sons. He has kept progress moving forward through an adept mix of gentlemanliness and forcefulness.

Regardless of the precision of an author, the person who types a manuscript either makes the process run smoothly or causes additional steps of proofreading. We have been exceptionally fortunate in having three caring typists who greatly expedited the process—Vickie Firtion and Vickie Klaff at Virginia Tech and Marilyn Peterson at the University of Nebraska. Working on the book in its later stages, Marilyn Peterson also contributed a sound organization in compiling the complete manuscript and keeping accurate track of the illustrations as they were completed. Without her cheerful and diligent contributions, the task would have been much more difficult to complete.

On a more personal level, George Briggs would like to acknowledge his gratitude to his wife, Sara, and children, Lash, Hunt, and Anna for their loving support and the sacrifice of time with Dad that any effort of this magnitude entails. Also, George would like to give thanks for his parents, Howard and Lucy Briggs, who planted the seeds of plant loving at an early age.

Clyde Calvin would like to express his gratitude to the many teachers and colleagues who are indirectly the source of many of the views expressed herein. Foremost among them is his wife, Carol, whose constant companionship, encouragement, and intellectual interaction make it difficult for him to distinguish her thoughts from his own. Also, Clyde would like to extend thanks to his children, Stephen, Carolyn, Christopher, and Jeremiah, for their mature willingness to give up times together so that this task could be completed.

Much of the photography is the product of Douglas Hindman who has lent artistic value and clear communication to even the simplest of subjects.

An expression of thanks is certainly in order for Campbell's Nurseries and Garden Centers, Tyrell's Flowers: A Special Kind of Place, and Oak Creek Plants and Flowers in Lincoln, Nebraska, for their unselfish sharing of plant materials for our illustrations. Each was exceptionally trusting and helpful to us in locating plants and providing a place to work on the drawings.

The text has also been blessed with excellent reviewers. Dr. Charles Conover made superb recommendations throughout, whereas Dr. David Bradshaw of Clemson University and Dr. Jay Fitzgerald of the University of Nebraska-Lincoln made suggestions on more specific parts of the text. We would also like to thank the following reviewers for their contributions: Jay Holcomb, Penn State University; Thomas C. Weilor, Cornell University; Robert Lyons, Virginia Polytechnic Institute and State University, Blacksburg; and Barry Eisenberg, University of Illinois, Urbana.

We wish also to thank Luann Finke, education director of the Nebraska Statewide Arboretum, for her diligent and thorough proofreading and the Florida Education and Research Foundation, Inc. for their helpful assistance with providing resources and publications.

G. B. B. / C. L. C.

The author and illustrator are indebted to the following publications as valuable general references:

BYRD GRAF, Alfred, *Exotica*, 10th edition (Series 3), January 1980. Roehrs Company, Inc., East Rutherford, N.J., 1976.

KROMDIJK, G., *200 House Plants in Color*, translated by A. M. H. Speller. Herder and Herder, New York, 1974. Zomer en Keuning Boeken B.V., Wageningen, Holland, 1967. English translation, 1968 by Lutterworth Press. Printed in The Netherlands.

NICOLAISEN, Age, *The Pocket Encyclopedia of Indoor Plants*, Editor of the Americal Edition, Jerome Eaton. Macmillan Publishing Company, Inc., New York. First published in the English edition, 1970, English text, Blandford Press Ltd., London. World copyright 1969, first American edition, 1970.

SOCIETY OF AMERICAN FLORISTS, *Care and Handling of Flowers and Plants*. Merchants Publishing Company, Kalamazoo, Mich., 1976.

chapter one
introduction

The term "indoor plants" means different things to different people. To the college student, it refers to plants that will thrive within the confines of an apartment or dormitory room. A townhouse dweller's definition might include plants that will do well in a container on a patio, whereas a homeowner with an attached greenhouse might have an even broader definition. Who is right? They all are for their particular situation.

The scope of this book will include plants that thrive in the domain of the living area, that is, that area where most people usually display and care for their plants. Since a patio is most certainly outside and a greenhouse's conditions are not typical of the light, temperature, and humidity limitations imposed on plants living with people, these aspects of plant culture will not be the focus in this book. Rather, **indoor plants** are defined as plants that, with a reasonable amount of care, lend beauty of flower or foliage to interior human living areas.

This text will also use the term "house plant" interchangeably with "indoor plant," as well as the somewhat more specific term "foliage plant." Although, admittedly, the foliage plant designation is misleading in that it seems to exclude plants whose primary value is flower or fruit effect, it still has gained wide acceptance as a label for all

indoor plants. As a matter of fact, the most common name applied to the indoor plant trade is the "foliage industry" or the "foliage plant industry." We might add that another vernacular synonym is "green plant," but we will refrain from its use because of its ambiguity.

GETTING THINGS INTO PERSPECTIVE

The study of indoor plants is generally considered to be a branch of **floriculture**—the culture of plants that bear commercially important flowers such as cut roses, carnations, and chrysanthemums. Obviously, indoor foliage plants do not fit this definition, so there is still some difference of opinion as to whether they fall under the jurisdiction of the floriculture industry, the nursery industry, the landscape industry, or whether they would best be considered an autonomous industry. The problem is not lessened by the fact that foliage plant writings are found in the literature of several industries and disciplines.

It is under floriculture that the indoor plant industry seems to fit most comfortably in spite of the arguments otherwise. Floriculture, in turn, is one of the disciplines of **horticulture**—the art and science of cultivating fruits, vegetables, and ornamental plants.

The use of plants indoors, like other horticultural pursuits, is both an art and a science. It is an *art* in that indoor plants, having the potential of enhancing a living area with their great diversity of color, form, and texture, hold the commanding position as major elements of interior design. Selection of the proper plants to complement a room's arrangement and accentuate the color and texture of finishes and fabrics demands an awareness and understanding of artistic principles such as unity, harmony, contrast, balance, rhythm, and dominance. Using plants to make a room an artistic composition can be an exciting means of creative expression, an important consideration as our living spaces become smaller and our lives more confined.

On the other hand, growing indoor plants is also a *science*. Successful cultivation must rely on proper conditions of light, humidity, temperature, soil composition and moisture, and nutrition. These factors—thanks to years of research, study, and experience—are now well-understood and take most of the guesswork out of growing plants. We understand the factors of plant growth, such as how light quality and intensity affect plant growth, how nutrients enter plants and stimulate growth, and why pinching off stem tips encourages development of dormant buds. Research has also explained the relationships among the various environmental and cultural factors—how temperature changes humidity levels, how pH can alter nutrition, and how soil moisture can influence soil aeration and the prevalence of plant diseases. Plant culture has become easier as scientific knowledge has increased, and the unknowns are constantly becoming fewer and fewer.

THE GREEN THUMB. Although most of the guesswork has been removed from plant culture, a frequent misconception among many beginning indoor plant students is that growing healthy plants is so much an art that one must have some sort of special knack to be successful. Perhaps the ancient reference to better gardeners as "green thumbs" contributes to this belief, indicating that innate factors are just as important as scientific knowledge in caring for plants. Recent developments, such as the quite dubious theories advocating conversation and music for plants' growth, have only aggravated the problem. Regardless of the underlying causes, the fact remains that many beginning students are inhibited and unconfident because they have been led to believe that there is a good chance that they do not possess the natural talent to become a successful indoor gardener.

It is important for the novice to realize from the beginning that anyone, regardless of innate abilities, can grow plants well if he or she adequately understands the cultural and environmental factors that affect plant growth. Granted, some cultural techniques such as potting, pruning, and pest control require judgment and a certain degree of skill, but study and practice will quickly enable one to perform these tasks with assurance. Learning to care for plants is a rewarding and enjoyable pursuit; enter it enthusiastically and with the expectation of developing a life-long interest. But expect some casualties along the way!

LOOKING BACK:
A HISTORICAL SKETCH

Our current affinity for plants indoors is a relatively recent development, but the idea of cultivating foreign and unusual plants in pots, its predecessor, is anything but new. The origins of the practice, 3500 years old and revealed by stone carvings, lie with the Sumerians of Babylonia and the Egyptians. The most prominent example is the Hanging Gardens of Babylon, built around 605 B.C. and one of the seven wonders of the Ancient World. These gardens existed in the form of a large pyramid with a square or rectangular base, and were constructed with arch-supported terraces on which were planted trees, shrubs, and flowers. Stone vessels were also used for displaying individual plants.

THE GREEKS. The ancient Greeks were more interested in the arts and philosophy than gardening, but they did continue the development of pot gardening. Not only did they use pots for starting plants, but they also originated the idea of using potted plants to decorate their surroundings. A yearly festival was held to worship Adonis, the mythological god of the growing world who was believed to die in the autumn and disappear into the earth, only to be saved in the spring by Aphrodite and brought back to earth. Most Greeks celebrated the spring arrival of Adonis by decorating his statue with seeded pots of fast-growing plants such as lettuce and barley, believing that their germination represented Adonis' return to earth, and that their death in late summer indicated Adonis' departure. Having spread to most areas of the Mediterranean and still practiced in many of these locations even today, the Adonis Garden thoroughly established pot gardening as an ornamental technique (Figure 1.1).

ROME AND THE MIDDLE AGES. The practice of pot culture continued intermittently through succeeding centuries. The Romans, who enjoyed the cultivation of unusual plants and fruit, cultivated them using stone containers in the inner courtyard, or peristyle, of their homes. These unroofed, open-air rooms served as the garden and were often heated by flues carrying hot air. The hothouse or greenhouse, made of thin sheets of talc or mica and later of glass, was put to use by the Romans for the cultivation of exotic plants and forcing roses into bloom.

After the fall of the Roman Empire in 476 A.D., the growth of horticultural knowledge stagnated, kept alive primarily in the monasteries during the Dark Ages. The monks continued the use of earthenware pots in

FIGURE 1.1 This fifth century B.C. vase marks the longevity of pot gardening, showing Eros, god of love, giving seedlings to a girl who is celebrating rites for Adonis. *Source:* Crockett, J.U., *Flowering House Plants,* New York: Time-Life Books, 1971, p. 44.

their cloister gardens, not as a mythological or ornamental practice, but rather for the cultivation of medicinal and culinary herbs, as well as for establishing new plants that were acquired during pilgrimages and from travellers. The decorative use of pots was also practiced during medieval times in southern Spain by the Moors, who developed a patio style of gardening that featured water for its cooling effect and abundant potted plants to decorate steps and other architectural features. The late medieval period, known commonly as the Age of Chivalry, saw the introduction of potted plants into castle gardens where they were used to decorate walls, benches, and flower beds (Figure 1.2).

FIGURE 1.2 During the late medieval years, pots became common as wall decorations.

RENAISSANCE DEVELOPMENT. The Renaissance period of the fifteenth and sixteenth centuries, an era of revived learning, brought about gardening as an art form and an intensified interest in exotic plants. Columbus' discovery of America in 1492 was also important in that his expeditions introduced the cactus, the agave, and the pineapple to Europe. The expansion of trade by the southern Europeans led to the discovery of Java and India around the beginning of the sixteenth century and resulted in tropical plant introductions from both the East and West Indies. Plant collections became a popular hobby for wealthy merchants; Padua, Italy, opened the first Botanic Garden in 1545. In northern Europe during the sixteenth century, particularly in France and England, there arose among the aristocracy a preference for exotic flowering plants and trees to brighten the often foggy, drizzly climate. The Germans, though not with the fanfare of Italy, France, and England, also made an important contribution during the Renaissance. It became the custom, particu-

larly among average citizens, to decorate windows with decorative plants growing in clay pottery. Here lies the most direct historical link to our current practice of indoor gardening.

The Renaissance movement also brought the garden pot into focus as a major garden element, particularly in Italy, France, and England. As gardens grew in size during the Renaissance, so too did the size of pots in order to accommodate the trend of displaying orange and lemon trees in formal rows and arrangements. A new development also occurred in northern Europe that led one step closer to indoor plant culture. In trying to copy Italy's lead in displaying potted citrus fruit, some northern European countries including England and France found that these plants could not survive their colder winters. As a solution to the problem, gardens began to display these large plants during the colder months in an **orangerie,** a long decorative building with a glass front through which the plants could be viewed from the garden. Some of these were gigan-

FIGURE 1.3 The orangerie, for the winter protection of exotic plants, was the precursor of the greenhouse.

tic, such as the Orangerie of Louis XIV at Versailles. Built in 1683, it could overwinter 1500 citrus trees and palms. The concept of the orangerie led to the development of **conservatories,** large all-glass buildings to house collections of exotic plants. The development of cheaper methods of producing flat glass around 1700 opened the way for the dramatic greenhouse proliferation of the eighteenth century (Figure 1.3).

VICTORIAN PURSUITS. Beginning at the end of the eighteenth century and continuing through the Victorian Era (1841–1903), English interest in exotic plants reached its peak. The emphasis was on growing flowers, particularly those that displayed bright and pure colors. Since these colors were usually only available in semitropical and tropical plants, the practice of **bedding-out** became necessary, that is, exotic plants were grown under glass during the winter and "bedded-out" for the growing season (Figure 1.4).

This fascination with exotic plants resulted in an intensive world-wide search for plants that were suitable for bedding-out. By 1820, the now-famous Kew Botanic Garden in England had 8000 species and its director was convinced that this was far too few, thus opening the way for Kew to become one of the largest plant collections in the world. The early nineteenth century was characterized by a flood of horticultural and botanical periodicals, most of which were graced by large plates of exotic plants recently introduced into the country by the increasingly large number of explorers. Most plant hunters were hired by Kew or large nurseries to travel to all parts of the world in search of new plant species. Many of our common house plants today are the direct result of these efforts in such places as China, the Indies, and South America. Some of the most notable plant collectors and explorers were medical doctors who had an interest in botany by hobby or a need for medicinal purposes. Ornamental plant collection was

FIGURE 1.4 Bedding-out tender flowering plants became the Victorian means of gardening.

also often incidental to trips for herbs and spices.

Even now, explorations in foreign countries occasionally yield new plants for indoor use (Figure 1.5). Plant importation, however, is not easily accomplished due to strict inspection standards by the U.S. Department of Agriculture to prohibit introduction of foreign, potentially harmful pests and pathogens.

Although plants continued to stream into Europe during the early eighteenth century, it was not until around the middle of the century that explorers were able to overcome the plant losses that occurred during the long ocean voyages. Heat, salt spray, poor cultural care, disease—all cut deeply into the numbers of live plants collected in tropical areas and transported back to Europe.

Like many other significant historical discoveries, the solution to the problem of plant losses was accidental. In this case, Dr. Nathaniel Ward, a London surgeon, conducted an experiment in connection with his hobby of natural history. The year was 1829. Placing the cocoon of a sphinx moth on moist soil in a sealed jar to observe the hatching of the adult, Ward was delighted to find that a fern he had unsuccessfully tried to grow in his garden had germinated and was thriving along with some grass. Fascinated with this development, he continued to experiment with plant growth in sealed containers until he achieved the significant feat of sending plants around the world in large glass containers. His results were published in 1842 and the glass containers, dubbed then as **Wardian Cases** and more commonly known now as **terrariums,** made it possible to export rare and tender plants to Europe with great success. Though the results of an unanticipated side effect, Ward's efforts have had a great impact on today's indoor gardens. Not only did the Wardian case expand the selection of plants available for cultivation, but it was probably the single-most reason for the rise in the popularity of terrariums within contemporary interior environments.

FIGURE 1.5 One of the more notable plant hunters of the nineteenth century was Dr. Joseph Dalton Hooker who, as director of Kew Gardens, traveled the world in search of exotic plants. He is shown here in the Himalayas. *Source:* Coats, A., *The Plant Hunters*, New York: McGraw-Hill, 1969, p. 186, plate 14. Courtesy of The British Library.

It was during the Victorian era that indoor gardening came to America. The English fad of parlor gardening crossed the Atlantic and even those of meager means acquired large tropical plants for their parlor, front hall, or drawing room (to which guests withdrew after dinner). Palms and the Boston fern were the two most popular plants for these purposes and were often placed in theatre and hotel lobbies.

RECENT DEVELOPMENTS. The next major step in indoor gardening did not develop until years later—around the late 1930s. At that time in California, an outdoor garden style, developed by a new group of landscape architects, emerged that provided direct access between house and garden. Outdoor space was now designed for outdoor entertaining, children's play, and other family activities. In other words, the outdoors was to be as functional and beautiful as the indoors.

Frank Lloyd Wright, the twentieth century architect whose primary architectural objective was the integration of nature and man, carried this a step further by using glass walls and cantilevering to break down the barrier between building and garden (Figure 1.6).

What do these developments have to do with indoor plants? They broke down the formerly invincible concept of separate indoor versus outdoor space and opened the way for the migration of plants inside. Just as people were no longer considered to be solely indoor dwellers, plants were no longer confined to the outdoors.

FIGURE 1.6 Since the 1930s the increased use of glass and spatial manipulation has removed many of the visual barriers between American homes and their gardens.

FOREIGN INFLUENCES. Along the same lines, landscape architectural trends of other countries also had an impact, particularly those of Japan and the Scandinavian countries. The Japanese influence was one of sensitivity (Figure 1.7). Developed over hundreds of years and bearing great religious significance, the Japanese garden is a composition of texture and shape, using stone, water, sand, and plants as the artistic medium. The oriental garden's trademark was thoughtful use of space, that is, the creation of a naturalistic theme in a small area. As a result of this appreciation for form, the Japanese precipitated Western awareness for the artistic expression of foliage. Unlike the gardens of Victorian England, Japanese gardens were sound compositions year-round: Flowering effect was an added, but unnec-

essary, benefit. Likewise, the Scandinavians also increased interest in the form and leaf shape of house plants through their design trends that initiated what we now think of as contemporary design.

THE INDOOR PLANT BOOM
The preceding historical sketch describes the underpinnings of today's methods of indoor gardening. However, the recent growth in popularity of foliage plants has not been a continuous gradual ascent, but rather a slow climb that suddenly skyrocketed in North America and Europe in the early 1970s. Since the boom started, the indoor plant industry has expanded at a rapid rate.

WHAT CAUSED THE BOOM? A number of factors seem to be involved, many of which social scientists are still trying to sort out. The first and perhaps the most important factor is what we might call the symbiotic (mutually beneficial) person/plant relationship that has always existed but that has been stifled by recent events. During the early 1900s, most of our society was rural, making a living from agricultural pursuits. As time progressed, a major shift of population from rural areas to cities and suburbs occurred, leaving us today with a society that is mostly urban and further removed from the green world of nature. Coupled with this has been the relatively new architectural trend of cluster housing, wherein dwellings are sited in high-density groupings with green and parking space situated among the clusters. Individual apartment or townhouse yards are confined to a small, usually fenced plot of about 200 square feet—hardly enough space for a small traditional garden. Hence, our population is being pushed further and further away from the outdoors and an association with nature. But there have been some recent books dealing, excellently, with small space gardening and terrace gardening to address this situation.

FIGURE 1.7 Japanese gardens, with their careful attention to composition and texture but restrained use of flowers, have created an appreciation for the artistic value of foliage and plant form.

In response to the crowding and pollution that has followed, society adapted itself to types of stress—physical, psychological, and sociological. The ecology movement of the 1970s made us well aware of the adverse physical effects of water, air, and noise pollution, but we are just beginning to identify the adverse psychological effects of our added stress. One effect is offered by E. Stainbrook, University of Southern California School of Medicine:

Having lived through eons with nature, organisms including man are genetically programmed to biological rhythms paced by sun, moon, and seasons. Hence, we are often out of phase with modern situations—with artificial lighting, central heating and air conditioning, with work organizations and other social institutions structuring wakeful activity around the clock, with distressingly high and insistent daily input of complex information demanding sleep-disturbing attempts at mastery, with rapid travel through time zones. Fatigue and inefficiency—and perhaps more subtle impairments of adaptation and biological responsiveness—may be the price we pay for the disharmony between the body's innate rhythms and the artificial surroundings and demands that press upon us.

As continued stress increases our frustrations, we, as a society, have become suddenly aware of the need for the reestablishment of this connection to our environment. The turning to indoor plants is but one manifestation of our reaction. A dramatic increase in vegetable gardening activity, more concern for landscaping to conserve energy and to subdue harsh urban surroundings, more interest in outdoor recreational sports such as camping, golf, and tennis, and indeed the interest in ecology and conservation all point to our desire for a renewed kinship with nature. The indoor plant boom is perhaps one of the most conspicuous moves to nature because of the direct association with plants, per se.

Some doctors and sociologists feel that the association between plants and people, as previously described by Stainbrook, is our major reason for gardening outdoors. This link is so strong that the therapeutic and rehabilitative qualities of plants are now receiving much more attention, particularly from doctors in rehabilitation medicine such as A. Barber of the Menninger Institution who says

Germination of seeds, vegetative growth, flowering, and maturation have close parallels in the basic concepts of human development. Common gardening tasks such as watering, fertilizing and protecting plants from bad weather have human connotations. The physical structure of a greenhouse has been likened to a mother's womb and provides an atmosphere of security.

FASCINATION versus ATTENTION. This sense of security generated by indoor gardening is also closely linked with another important effect—that of fascination. Psychologists distinguish between fascination (involuntary attention) and voluntary attention. Whereas voluntary attention requires effort and is not easy to maintain, fascination is effortless. Since indoor gardening (and gardening in general) is usually performed through fascination, it relieves one of the effort required for the voluntary attention of the workday and, by excluding competing thoughts, diverts one from those daily worries and cares that might otherwise be the mind's sole occupant. Indoor gardening, by giving a close-at-hand bit of diversion, is a natural way to cope with the increasing stresses and strains on modern society. As these stresses have come on strong, so also has the indoor plant boom.

Along with these innate traits of the human mind, other factors also help to explain the plant revolution. The most prominent cause is improved technology. Home heating and cooling systems have become more reliable, without the temperature fluctuations that were so detrimental to the indoor gardening efforts of our ancestors. New developments in lighting have also made the home a much more conducive place for plants to grow. Improved containers, fixtures, and effective soil mixes have eased the task of the indoor gardener. Improved plants with greater tolerance for seemingly dismal interior conditions like low temperatures and poor light are constantly being introduced.

Not only are products better, but also they range in design from contemporary to traditional and from hanging varieties to stationary planters. The new selection of styles and foliage has stimulated the use of plants as an interior design element. Home furnishing publications, and even television and newspaper advertising, are taking advantage of the asthetic appeal of foliage and their accompanying paraphernalia (Figure 1.8). Indeed, even various types of plant accessories have resulted in popular trends at one time or another, such as macrame hangers, sand sculpture in glass containers, and lighted plant shelves. There is no doubt that technology has been a big impetus to the boom.

And finally, the contribution of horticulture within the mass media cannot be overlooked. More books have entered the marketplace on the subject of indoor plants recently than almost any other subject. Most newspapers include daily or weekly gardening columns answering readers' questions or providing information on gardening "know-how."

More and more popular magazines are including articles or special sections on plants and their care, decorating ideas for foliage, and new plants on the market. Garden journalists are even becoming permanent fixtures on radio and television, where they often discuss or display plants and highlight tips for their proper care.

One unfortunate aspect of the surge in writing is that many books have appeared on the market that are quickly constructed by unqualified writers who are more interested

FIGURE 1.8 Advertising now employs foliage plants to soothe the consumer. This "studio shot", provided by Bassett Furniture Industries, uses plants to enhance the eye appeal of this furniture grouping.

in royalties than accurate information. Consequently, indoor gardeners must now examine potential book purchases carefully, checking the reliability of the publisher and the credentials of the author.

Surely, these are not all of the reasons behind the plant revolution; more than one person has called for research to decipher the underlying reasons so that the industry can better adapt itself to the wants and needs of its clientele.

The Indoor Plant Industry

Few economic enterprises have risen to prominence as quickly as the foliage plant industry. During the period from 1959 to 1970, the wholesale value of foliage plant sales in the United States increased $3 million, from $24.1 million to $27.1 million. After 1970, the wholesale value of sales grew dramatically each year, with increases ranging from $10 million in 1971 to $73.7 million in

1975. The wholesale value of foliage plant sales was a whopping $236 million in 1976. Hence, the production industry mushroomed to a level over 850 percent of its 1970 level in just six years. In 1983, the last year for which government figures were available at the time of this writing, the value had reached an estimated one of $364.1 million, representing a 13-year increase of nearly 1340 percent! This probably represents a higher rate of increase than for any other major American agricultural crop over the same time period. At retail, foliage plants accounted for consumer expenditures of over $1 billion in 1983, and in the process, a whole new service profession of interiorscaping arose.

Until the recent expansion, the industry was about equally divided among ten states. According to the U.S. Department of Agriculture (U.S.D.A.), the nation's top producer of foliage plants in 1981 was Florida with almost 50 percent of the market (Table 1.1).

TABLE 1.1 THE VORACIOUS APPETITE AMONG AMERICANS FOR INDOOR FOLIAGE IS DEPICTED BY THIS GROWTH PATTERN IN THE INDUSTRY

| | PRODUCERS, PRODUCTION, AND NET SALES FOR FOLIAGE PLANTS | | |
Year	Number of Producers	Square Feet in Production (× 1000 sq. ft)	Wholesale Net Sales (× $1000)
1971	835	36,476	$ 37,586
1972	898	38,836	48,066
1973	854	46,088	67,982
1974	1061	63,936	111,289
1975	1489	87,201	184,898
1976	1685	116,299	235,768
1977	1879	119,678	275,300
1978	1979	122,523	298,998
1979	1710	121,314	283,928
1980	2053	145,733	312,968
1981	2086	154,105	329,160
1982 (est.)	2173	166,567	346,190
1983 (est.)	2129	173,507	364,100

SOURCE: Crop Reporting Board, Economics and Statistics Service, U.S.D.A., 1973–1981. There has been some change in the reporting base during the last 10 years.

Much of Florida's production is centered near the city of Apopka that considers itself the foliage capital of the world. California holds about 23 percent of the market; these two states are by far the country's largest producers. For example, the next three highest producing states are Texas, Ohio, and Hawaii with 8.9, 4.2, and 2.1 percent, respectively, of the national market. Recently, Puerto Rico, with an excellent climate for foliage production, has increased its production. Although far below Florida or California in sales, Puerto Rico is thought to have the potential to be a major center of production when technical assistance becomes available through research and university extension channels. Most of the technical knowledge in Puerto Rico is now directed toward the agricultural products of the country—sugarcane, coffee, tobacco, and pineapples.

One of the interesting aspects of the foliage industry's expansion in the United States is its relationship to the value of the related industries producing roses, chrysanthemums, and carnations as cut flowers. In 1970, the value of foliage plants was considerably less than the value of roses, carnations, or mums. By 1974, the foliage value had increased to 2.5 times that of carnations, 2 times pompon and standard mums, and 1.5 times roses. All of this adds up to an impressive statistic: The value of the foliage plant wholesale industry now exceeds the value of the combined domestic carnation, standard mum, pompon, and cut rose industries. Remarkably, foliage moved from near the bottom of the floriculture industry to a commanding lead in just five years (Figure 1.9). In fairness, some of the impact here has resulted in the increasing importation of cut flowers. Ironically, there is a recent trend to add color (flowering pot plants, cut flowers) to the "greened" interior so one development

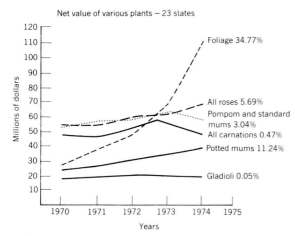

Net value of various plants – 23 states

Foliage 34.77%
All roses 5.69%
Pompom and standard mums 3.04%
All carnations 0.47%
Potted mums 11.24%
Gladioli 0.05%

Millions of dollars

Years: 1970 1971 1972 1973 1974 1975

FIGURE 1.9 The dramatic increase in foliage plant sales is displayed in graph form. Note that these figures are based on U. S. domestic production and do not reflect either imported cut flowers or the value of the interiorscaping service industry. (Redrawn from Jensen and Kirschling, "The Foliage Plant Boom: Is It Here to Stay?", *Florists' Review*, May 13, 1976)

(indoor green plant consumption) can be viewed as leading to another (indoor flowering plant and cut flower consumption).

Is It a Fad?

The logical concluding question is "how long will the boom last?" Emerging with the foliage industry have been numerous market analysts who keep a finger on the pulse of the industry, and who make projections as to the direction foliage will go. Most agree that the boom in indoor plants is not a passing fad that will quickly erode once interest has subsided. The consensus is that the current growth rate is far too rapid to endure and that the rates of increase will begin to plateau into a reasonable year-to-year expansion. Of course, no one can accurately predict the future of such a mushrooming enterprise, but it is reasonable to expect that, if the reasons behind the boom are valid, there will be a continuing bright future for the foliage industry.

It appears then that the interest in indoor gardening is more than a passing fancy.

Although the growth of the industry has been spectacular, it is leveling off into a more normal, year-to-year growth pattern. Dollar values of sales are continuing to increase, but a greater share of the market is large commercial interiorscaping stock than in earlier years. With plants being used so extensively for business and pleasure, the chances that the interest and the industry will decline dramatically are slim indeed.

FOR FURTHER READING

Allan, M. *Plants that Changed Our Gardens.* North Pomfret, Vt.: David and Charles, 1974.

Berrall, J. *The Garden.* New York: Penguin Books, 1966.

Brookes, J. *Room Outside.* New York: Viking Press, 1971.

Clifford, D. *A History of Garden Design.* New York: Praeger, 1963.

Coats, A. *The Plant Hunters.* New York: McGraw-Hill, 1969.

Colvin, B. *Land and Landscape.* John Murray, 1970.

Conklin, E. "Man and Plants—A Primal Association." *American Nurseryman* **136**, 9 (1972).

Elbert, G. "A Look at the Reasons Behind the Indoor Plant Revolution." *Florists' Review* (May 6, 1976).

"Flowers and Foliage Plants." Crop Reporting Board, U.S.D.A., Washington, D.C., March 1977.

Hyams, E. *Capability Brown and Humphrey Repton.* J. M. Dent and Sons, Ltd., 1971.

Jensen, F., and P. Kirschling. "The Foliage Plant Boom: Is It Here to Stay?" *Florists' Review* (May 13, 1976).

Joiner, J. *Foliage Plant Production.* Englewood Cliffs, N.J.: Prentice-Hall, 1981.

Kaplan, R. "Some Psychological Benefits of Gardening." *Environment and Behavior* **5**, 2 (1973).

Kayatta, K., and S. Schmidt. *Successful Terrariums.* Boston: Houghton Mifflin, 1975.

Laurie, A. "Alex Laurie's Changing Times." *Florists' Review* (December 11, 1975).

Laurie, M. *An Introduction to Landscape Architecture.* New York: American Elsevier, 1975.

Lewis, C. "Horticulture as a Therapeutic and Rehabilitative Discipline." A talk presented at the Horticulture Therapy Symposium Horticultural Society of New York, April 16, 1974.

Lewis, C. "Plant People Interaction." A talk presented at Horti-therapy Workshop, Clemson University, Clemson, South Carolina, June 13, 1974.

Manaker, G. *Interior Plantscapes*. Englewood Cliffs, N.J.: Prentice-Hall, 1981.

Newton, N. *Design on the Land*. Cambridge, Mass.: Belknap Press of Harvard University, 1971.

Rathmell, J., Jr. "Puerto Rico, Apopka—Which Will Be the Foliage Center?" *Florists' Review* (December 11, 1975).

Smith, C., et al. "An Economic Overview of the Tropical Foliage Plant Industry." *Foliage Digest* (April 1982).

Stainbrook, E. "Man's Psychic Need for Nature." *National Parks and Conservation Magazine* **47**, 9.

White, M. *Pots and Pot Gardens*. New York: Abelard-Schuman, 1969.

PART ONE

GETTING STARTED WITH INDOOR PLANTS

As we begin this venture into the world of indoor plants, our first steps involve getting acquainted with the ways indoor plants are named and identified, how they grow and function, and how new plants are begun.

At our disposal are specific systems that make the calling of plants by name consistent and easily understood. In the physical sense, plants exhibit a myriad of characteristics that are useful in distinguishing the species and individual variations within a species. It is important to learn early the typical configurations of leaf shapes, hair, leaf arrangement, and so forth that plants display. This knowledge makes establishing an acquaintance with the various members of the indoor plant family both easier and more memorable.

Along similar lines, our success at culturing specific plants is based on a general knowledge of how plants grow and function. How plants take in water and nutrients, how they proceed through their life cycle, how they flower, and other similar issues are essential to a successful experience with growing even one specimen. The understanding of plant processes makes the cultivation of plants a more interesting and meaningful experience as well.

And finally in Part One, we present the

fascinating process of starting new plants. There are many different ways of doing this, and each plant may require one of several methods. This practice not only expands plant collections but provides a fascinating pastime for both the hands and the mind.

chapter two
plant names
and faces

Recognizing plants and remembering their names are much like making new acquaintances with people—our memory must store the name and face before we can absorb very much about the person. With plants, discussion of cultural care and other peculiarities is also meaningless unless we know the name and appearance beforehand. Fortunately, **plant taxonomy,** the science of identifying, naming, and classifying plants, assigns scientific names that often relate to some characteristic of the plant, making for an easier association between a plant and its name. For example, *Peperomia obtusifolia,* the blunt-leaved peperomia, is named for its blunt leaves: obtuse (blunt) and folia (leaf). Obviously, a knowledge of this plant's name helps one with its identification.

Likewise, identifying plants is also based on scientific principles that will be discussed further later in this chapter. Such items as leaf arrangement on the stem, leaf shape, and textural characteristics have been classified and named and are quite useful in making identification decisions. Often, the only difference between two plants that look alike will be the presence or absence of hair on the leaves or some other characteristic that the untrained eye might overlook. Since many indoor plants are conspicuously colored, textured, or otherwise unique, their identification can usually be determined

much easier than exterior landscape plants. There are those, however, that share similarities at first glance.

The purpose of this chapter is to explain naming procedures and to discuss the many methods by which plant identification is achieved.

THE BASICS OF PLANT NAMES

Common Names
Plant names that have gained wide acceptance but that usually do not have scientific origins are known as **common names.** The imagination is often responsible for their coinage and they can vary from locale to locale. These names can be important to horticulture and are a useful and easy way to describe many plants. A number of these names are so common, in fact, that they are recognized by most people regardless of one's interest in plants. Geraniums are good examples of this. They are also good examples of why common names are not as reliable as scientific names. Two common house plants are the house geranium and the strawberry geranium. Which of these is a true geranium? Neither. The plant known simply as geranium is *Pelargonium × hortorum* and the strawberry geranium, *Saxifraga stolonifera.* Therefore, these com-

FIGURE 2.1 Carolus Linnaeus (1707–1778) was responsible for developing the binomial system of nomenclature, which we still use as our system for naming plants. *Source:* Fuller et al., *The Plant World*, New York: Holt, Rinehart, and Winston, Inc., 1951. Reprinted by permission of CBS College Publishing.

mon names, though widely recognized and accepted, are misleading and incorrect botanically.

Another problem with common names is that the same plant may have several. The strawberry geranium, mentioned above, is also commonly called beefsteak geranium, strawberry begonia, creeping sailor, and mother-of-thousands. Common names are easy to remember and widely used, but they frequently make discussion of a particular plant quite difficult and confusing.

Scientific Names

For years, the confusion of common names has inspired botanists to devise one con-sistent nomenclature, or naming, system. Prior to the eighteenth century, some species of plants had a one-word name, others had long descriptive phrases consisting of as many as a dozen names. This inconsistency of naming was both inconvenient and awkward.

The situation was remedied by the work of a great Swedish naturalist, Carolus Linnaeus (1707–1778), whose work formed the basis for our present classification and nomenclature systems (Figure 2.1). Linnaeus wrote extensively on the classification of both plants and animals during the first half of the eighteenth century and categorized plants according to size and number of flower structures. This system became popular and stimulated interest in botanical studies, leading later botanists to recognize that some groups of plants were more similar to one another than to other groups based on structure and mode of reproduction.

One of Linnaeus' major contributions to botany was the **hierarchial system of classification.** His system involved the use of increasingly specific categories to which plants belong. Kingdoms, classes, orders, genera, and species were the basis of his naming system; the division, subclass, and family categories were added to the system later. Table 2.1 explains the use of this system. Note that each category of the hierarchy is a collective unit containing one or more groups from the next lower level of the hierarchy.

Although our main interest centers around the more specific categories of classification (family and below), it is important that the student understand broader taxonomic levels. Briefly, the plant kingdom is comprised of several divisions representing the algae, fungi, mosses and liverworts, ferns and their allies, **gymnosperms** (plants whose seeds are borne naked on the surface of a scale, for example, pine trees), and **angiosperms** (plants whose seeds are enclosed within an ovary borne in a flower). According to one

TABLE 2.1 OUR PRESENT HIERARCHIAL CLASSIFICATION SYSTEM, WITH THE MAPLE-LEAF BEGONIA (*BEGONIA OLBIA*) AS AN EXAMPLE OF ITS USE

Category	Description	Example
Kingdom	Plant or animal, but recently three other classifications have been recognized for such organisms as fungi, protozoa, bacteria, and viruses.	Plantae
Division	Tracheophyta (ferns and their allies that reproduce by spores and plants that reproduce by seeds); algae, fungi, and mosses are included in other divisions.	Tracheophyta
Class	Three classes are of concern in tracheophyta: ferns and their allies; gymnosperms (seeds borne on the surface of a scale); and angiosperms (seeds enclosed within an ovary borne in a flower).	Angiospermae
Subclass	Angiosperms form two subclasses: dicotyledonae (plants with two or more cotyledons or seed leaves in the embryo) and monocotyledonae (plants with one seed leaf).	Dicotyledonae
Order	Related plant groups within the above subclasses. Order names usually end with -*ales*.	Violales
Family	Composed of plants sharing certain characteristics of flower, fruit, and sometimes of leaf, but differing among themselves such that they can be recognized as lesser units or genera. Family names are usually composed of the ending -*aceae* attached to the root of a common genus within the family. Violaceae = Viol (violet genus is *Viola*) + the ending -*aceae*.	Begoniaceae (the begonia family)
Genus	One or more species that can be arranged in subordinate units.	*Begonia*
Species	Plants that resemble each other more than they do other plants.	*olbia*

established system of classification, indoor plants fall within a single division, the **tracheophyta.** The common characteristic shared by all members of this group is the presence of specialized conducting (vascular) tissue: xylem and phloem.

The tracheophyta is divided into a number of **subdivisions,** among which three more or less distinct plant groupings are recognized (Table 2.2). The so-called **lower vascular plants** include the ferns and their allies. Members of this group reproduce by sexual means, but none has seeds or fruits. In contrast, both the gymnosperms and angiosperms, comprising the **higher vascular plants,** produce seeds, but only the angiosperms, the flowering plants, produce true flowers and fruits.

The above vascular plant groupings make varying contributions to our indoor plant resources (Table 2.2). Among the lower vascular plants, the ferns and selaginellas play an important role, contributing numerous and diverse, primarily shade-tolerant forms. Relatively few gymnosperms find their way into the home, the Norfolk Island pine (*Araucaria heterophylla*), the Buddhist pine (*Podocarpus macrophyllus*), and cycads such as the sago palm (*Cycas revoluta*) being three of the more familiar types for home use. Incidentally, the common name of all of these plants is misleading—none is actually a pine or a palm! The angiosperms, on the other hand, contribute a vast number of indoor plants. The maple-leaf begonia exemplified in Table 2.1 is just one of the hundreds of flowering plants utilized in the foliage plant industry.

In addition to providing us with a comprehensive and organized system of classification, Linnaeus also added simplicity to the naming of plants and animals by

TABLE 2.2 GROUPINGS WITHIN THE DIVISION TRACHEOPHYTA, DESCRIBING CERTAIN PLANT CHARACTERISTICS AND FOLIAGE PLANT CONTRIBUTION

Groups within the Tracheophyta	PLANT CHARACTERISTIC			Use as a Source of House Plants	House Plant Examples
	Vascular Tissue	Seeds	Fruits		
Lower vascular plants	+	−	−	Moderate	Rose of Jericho (*Selaginella lepidophylla*)
					Boston fern (*Nephrolepis exaltata* 'Bostoniensis')
Gymnosperms	+	+	−	Low	Sago palm (*Cycas revoluta*)
					Norfolk Island pine (*Araucaria excelsa*)
					Buddhist pine (*Podocarpus macrophyllus*)
Angiosperms	+	+	+	Very high	Jade plant (*Crassula argentea*)
					Christmas cactus (*Schlumbergera bridgesii*)
					Spider plant (*Chlorophytum comosum* 'Vittatum')
					Maple-leaf begonia (*Begonia olbia*)

developing the **binomial system of nomenclature.** Each species was given a name consisting of two words: the genus (pl. genera) to which the plant belongs followed by a specific epithet for that particular species. Hence, the scientific name for the example in Table 2.1 is *Begonia olbia* consisting of the genus name and specific epithet. Other species in the genus *Begonia* have the same first word in their name, but each species has its own individual designation (for example, *corallina*, *cubensis*, and *foliosa*). It is important to notice that the species name is *olbia*, but the combination of the genus and the specific epithet, *Begonia olbia*, is the complete scientific name.

Species are commonly subdivided into either botanical or horticultural subdivisions. The primary botanical subcategory of importance to indoor gardeners is the **variety,** a group of plants within a species that occurs in nature and that shows minor but consistent variation of structure or form that is not related to geographical or ecological distribution. When the variation is related to geographical or ecological distribution, the subcategory is known as a **subspecies.** The most important horticultural subcategory

is the **cultivar,** a short form of the term *cultivated variety.* The cultivar, as defined in the *International Code of Nomenclature of Cultivated Plants*, is "an assemblage of cultivated plants which is clearly distinguished by any characteristics (morphological, physiological, cytological, chemical, or others), and which, when reproduced (sexually or asexually), retains its distinguishing characters." The basic difference between a variety and a cultivar, then, is that the variety occurs naturally, whereas the cultivar is perpetuated through cultivation by man. Both varieties and cultivars may have horticultural importance.

The botanical or scientific names of plants are governed by the *International Code of Botanical Nomenclature*, a set of internationally accepted rules. Accordingly, no two species of plants have the same name and the form of plant names is strictly regulated by specific rules with which the indoor gardener should be familiar. As mentioned previously, common names are not governed by a formal code of nomenclature and can be assigned by anyone.

Botanical names are either Latin or consist of Latinized words. The generic name may

TABLE 2.3 EXAMPLES OF PLANT NOMENCLATURE, SHOWING HOW THE GRAMMATICAL FORM OF THE PLANT NAME IS USED TO DESCRIBE THE SPECIES, SUBSPECIES, VARIETY, AND CULTIVAR DESIGNATIONS

Species	*Philodendron selloum*
Subspecies	*Philodendron scandens* subsp. *oxycardium*
Variety	*Philodendron pedatum* var. *palmatisectum*
Cultivar	*Dracaena deremensis* cv. Warneckii
	or
	Dracaena deremensis 'Warneckii'

be an ancient Greek or Latin name, an adaptation of an ancient real or mythological person's name, or it may indicate some characteristic of the plant itself. The specific epithet following the genus may be taken from any source, but it is usually an adjective that further describes the plant and thus has a Latin ending that agrees with the gender of the generic noun. Both the genus and species names are written in italics in print or underlined if typed or handwritten. The initial letter of the genus name is always capitalized, whereas the initial letter of the specific epithet is lowercase. It has been the practice of many botanists to capitalize specific epithets taken from former generic names, common names, and the names of people. This practice is still permitted, but for the sake of uniformity, it is now recommended that lowercase letters be used consistently.

Subcategories of species are also treated uniformly depending on their nature. Botanical varietal epithets are written like the specific epithet—in italics and with the initial letter lowercased. The term "var." (variety), without italics or quotation marks, may be placed before the varietal epithet to denote its rank. A subspecies is written exactly like a varietal name, except "subsp." is used to denote the rank rather than "var." The horticultural cultivar name is treated differently to distinguish it from the varietal epithet. It is not written in italics and its initial letter is capitalized. In addition, it is further designated either by the inclusion of the unitalicized

term "cv." (cultivar) before the cultivar name or by enclosing the cultivar name in single quotation marks. This precision of form not only ensures consistency of naming, but also it makes the name more descriptive of the nature of the plant. Table 2.3 illustrates the correct nomenclature form for the various plant types.

Botanical plant names may also be accompanied by other descriptive information. In reference material, plant names are often followed by a name or an abbreviation consisting of one or several letters, without italics. This is indicative of the author of that particular name. Linnaeus was, of course, one of the most prolific namers of plants, so it is common to see plant names written with the abbreviation of his name: *Begonia* L. The particular reference in which such abbreviations are used will generally provide an appendix for their interpretation.

Plants that are hybrid in origin, that is, the result of the sexual reproduction between two genera or species, are denoted by the inclusion of the multiplication sign ($\times$) with the name. The location of the "$\times$" is indicative of whether the genus or species is a hybrid. A hybrid genus, written with the $\times$ before the generical name ($\times$ *Fatshedera lizei*), is formed by the sexual crossing of two plants from separate genera. *Fatshedera* was formed by a cross between the two genera *Fatsia* and *Hedera*. If the species is of hybrid origin, the $\times$ is placed just before the specific epithet (*Begonia* $\times$ *erythrophylla*).

Here, the example is a cross between the species *Begonia hydrocotylifolia* and *Begonia manicata*. In pronouncing such hybrid names, note that the multiplication sign is not pronounced as the letter "*x*" or as "cross," but rather as "the hybrid genus" or "the hybrid species." Hence, × *Fatshedera* would be described as the hybrid genus *Fatshedera*.

The genus of a species name is often abbreviated when it is obvious as to what plant one is writing about. For example, if a list of *Begonia* species were to be listed here, they might be written: *Begonia corallina*, *B. rex-cultorum*, and *B. cubensis*. Or if this paragraph were to continue discussion of *Begonia* × *erythrophylla*, mentioned in the previous paragraph, it would be referred to now as *B.* × *erythrophylla*.

One aspect of scientific plant names that usually occurs with regularity and can be a source of frustration to indoor gardeners is change. A number of plants have changed names in recent years, some even several times. The common philodendron, which is now known as *Philodendron scandens* subsp. *oxycardium*, was recently changed from the name *P. oxycardium*. Still earlier, it was known as *P. cordatum*. Another example is

the common Australian umbrella tree (*Brassaia actinophylla*) that has dropped the very familiar name of *Schefflera actinophylla*. Table 2.4 lists a few other plants that have also undergone recent name changes.

Why are such familiar and well-established names changed? First, the *International Rules of Botanical Nomenclature* state that the correct name for any species is usually the oldest validly proposed name, beginning with the publication of Linnaeus' *Species Plantarum* in 1753. Plant taxonomy, like all other sciences, is continually expanding its knowledge, and as botanical records and other historical information are researched, plant names are often found that were validly recorded prior to the name that is in use now. Therefore, under the rules of botanical nomenclature, taxonomists are obligated to assign the plant the older name.

A second reason for changes in plant names is the fact that classification systems do not exist in nature but are man-made organizational methods for a complex science. Plants have changed over time, producing variants of color, size, hardiness, and other characteristics. Hence, plants are not broken into neat categories in nature, but rather form a complex continuum of traits

TABLE 2.4 SEVERAL EXAMPLES OF INDOOR PLANTS THAT HAVE RECENTLY UNDERGONE NAME CHANGES

Common Name	Old Name	New Name
Barbados aloe	*Aloe vera*	*Aloe barbadensis*
Myers asparagus	*Asparagus meyeri*	*Asparagus densiflorus* 'Myers'
Asparagus fern	*Asparagus plumosus*	*Asparagus setaceus*
Sprenger asparagus	*Asparagus sprengeri*	*Asparagus densiflorus* 'Sprengeri'
Spotted dieffenbachia	*Dieffenbachia picta*	*Dieffenbachia maculata* 'Baraquiniana'
Rudolph Roehrs dieffenbachia	*Dieffenbachia roehrsii*	*Dieffenbachia maculata* 'Rudolph Roehrs'
Dracaena	*Pleomele reflexa*	*Dracaena reflexa*
Moses-on-a-raft	*Rhoeo discolor*	*Rhoeo spathacea*
Leather fern	*Rumohra adiantiformis*	*Polystichum adiantiforme*
Golden pothos	*Scindapsus aureus*	*Epipremnum aureum*
Rose periwinkle	*Vinca rosea*	*Catharanthus roseus*
Sago cycas	*Zamia furfuracea*	*Zamia pumila*

SOURCE: Adapted from Sheehan, T., "New Names for Old Plants," *Proceedings of the 1977 National Tropical Foliage Short Course*, p. 148.

that taxonomists are continually debating and trying to sort into categories. Plant names, then, often change because taxonomists feel that a particular group of plants should be transferred to an existing species or subcategory. Even though the change of name requires some extra effort on the part of indoor gardeners, the benefits of continuous upgrading in plant classification far tinuous upgrading in plant classification far outweigh the disadvantages. Certainly more confusing and less logical would be the practice of leaving plants misnamed or misclassified simply because of human habits.

Many students have a preconceived fear or apprehension about learning botanical names of plants. Perhaps the problem lies in the fact that Latin is used as the basis for names and that we occasionally hear of the rigors of learning a so-called dead language. Or perhaps in classes, students must memorize the names quickly rather than through the experience of working with them. Our opinion is that scientific names are usually remembered longer than common names. Students give us long looks of disbelief at this idea. It takes a while longer to learn a scientific name and its spelling than a common name. But, holding true to the concept that the forgetting curve is a mirror image of the learning curve, it takes longer to forget the Latin name. Also, as mentioned earlier, students find that the name, especially the specific epithet, often relates to a particular feature of the plant. Many specific epithets and root words are repeated for various species. The root word *-folia*, meaning leaf, is found in such names as *rotundifolia* (round leaf), *parvifolia* (small leaf), and *acerifolia* (maplelike leaf). Names such as *alba* (white), *crispum* (curled or ruffled on the margin), and *acuminata* (leaf tip a protracted point with convex sides) are used over and over (Figure 2.2). After reading the following section on identification characteristics and studying a few names, the reader will find that scientific names,

FIGURE 2.2 Like many plant names, the specific epithet of *Peperomia obtusifolia* (obtuse = blunt; folia = leaves) is quite descriptive of the plant.

once a source of apprehension, will become a very helpful tool for learning plants.

The use of scientific names is becoming more widespread among the public and plants-persons as their value continues to be discovered. More and more plants are being offered in the trade under common names that are simply generic names or a variation of them: aphelandra, monstera, watermelon peperomia, Chinese hibiscus, to name a few. As international interest and trade increase in indoor plants, it is evermore significant that scientific names are in one language, thus eliminating the great potential for confusion. Whether scientist or enthusiast, each party of a plant transaction, regardless of nationality, knows exactly what plant the other party is referring to when scientific names are used. Scientific names—consistent, universal, informative—are not a foe, but a friend.

PRONUNCIATION. The pronunciation of botanical names, though somewhat foreign and awkward to the novice, becomes more natural with practice. After learning the names of several plants, one discovers the systematic similarity among names and becomes able to master new pronunciations quickly. In fact, as time progresses, an appreciation of plant nomenclature usually develops because of the distinctive sound of well-pronounced Latin epithets.

The fact that plant names are Latin or Latinized words means that a pronunciation choice exists between the old Roman and the modernized Latin. Although numerous Latin scholars feel that we should not deviate from the rigors of old Roman Latin, the widespread acceptance of botanical names among gardeners indicates that the less formal modern usage is more practical for today's needs.

Modern usage lacks standard agreement on the rules of pronouncing plant names; hence, variation occurs depending on the individual speaking and where he or she lives. Just as "tomato" can be *to-may-to* or *to-mah-to*, so too can the Latin name *Maranta* be *Ma-ran-ta* or *Ma-rahn-ta*. Variation also occurs with the vowels *e* and *i;* some pronounce them with a short sound; others with a long. Both interpretations are perfectly acceptable.

There are pronunciation principles that most botanists agree should be followed. The ending of botanical family names, *-aceae*, is pronounced *ace'-ee*. The cactus family, for example, is pronounced *Cact-ace'-ee*. A common characteristic of Latin names is the presence of double vowels. Familiarity with the typical sounds of these combinations is helpful for effective pronunciation. Table 2.5 outlines the more frequently recurring pairs.

The pronunciation of consonants has changed over the centuries. Whereas the Romans consistently pronounced *C* like *K* and *G* like *g* (in gone), common usage now allows the soft pronunciation of certain situations. In front of *a*, *o*, and *u*, the hard sound still prevails for both (*Caladium*, *Gardenia*). But before *eae*, *ae*, *i*, *oe*, and *y*, *C* takes the soft *z* or *s* sound (*Citrus*), and *G* softens before *e* and *i* (*Geranium*).

TABLE 2.5 GUIDE TO THE PRONUNCIATION OF COMBINATIONS OF TWO VOWELS IN BOTANICAL NAMES

Vowel Combination	Pronunciation	Example
ae	keen	*Dracaena*
au	mouse	*aureus*
ei	eight (*ā*)	*Leiophyllum*
eo	creole (*ee-oo*)	*areole*
eu	erroneous (*eh-oo*)	*Coleus*
ie	variable (*ee-eh*)	*variegata*
iu	Julius (*ee-uu*)	*folius*
oe	ceiling	*Coelia*
oi	soy (*oh-ee*)	*agavoides*
ue	cruel (*uu-eh*)	*Ruellia*
ui	ruin (*uu-i*)	*Pinguicula*

Once Latin sounds are mastered, one must develop the ability to correctly accent the syllables of Latin words. The rule of thumb with words of two syllables (*Hoya*) is to stress the first syllable (*Hoy'-a*). The next-to-last syllable is accented in words of more than two syllables, with the exception of proper names such as those of people or geographical places. Here, the familiar dictates the pronunciation, with stress placed as it occurs in the name itself (*Saint paul'-i-a; vir-gin'-i-ca*).

IDENTIFICATION OF INDOOR PLANTS

Liberty Hyde Bailey, a famous American horticulturist, once wrote: "Nomenclature follows identification. The first problem then in clarifying the names of cultivated plants is to identify the plants to be named." Bailey's point is one that applies directly to those who wish to become acquainted with the substantial number of indoor plants now commonly used. Learning scientific names takes work and patience, but it is futile if one cannot associate names with faces.

Although it can be easy because of conspicuous leaves or coloration, indoor plant identification can be challenging when plants share similarities. Dumbcane and Chinese evergreen, as well as philodendron and pothos, are quite alike in appearance and are frequently confused, even in the plant trade. Therefore, effective identification requires an observant look beyond superficial traits. Like a doctor sorting symptoms, the indoor gardener must observe in a systematic manner, eliminating the obvious before proceeding to more obscure characteristics.

LEAF CHARACTERISTICS. The first phase of identification should be leaf configuration and coloration, since this is the most conspicuous aspect of house plants. In particular, attention should be focused on the shape and texture of **leaves** (the temporary, lateral appendages of the stem specialized for photosynthesis). The leaf is typically composed of the expanded **blade,** which may be with or without lobes, and the supporting stalk or **petiole** (Figure 2.3). In some cases, the petiole is absent and the blade base attached directly to the stem; such leaves are said to be **sessile.** The angle formed between the petiole or sessile blade is known as the leaf **axil,** which in angiosperms contains one or more buds. These **axillary or lateral buds** are the growing points along the stem, much like the terminal bud at the growing tip or apex of the stem. On some plants, leafy appendages known as **stipules** are found attached near the base of the petiole. If stipules are absent, **stipule scars** may remain at the same location.

LEAF ARRANGEMENT. The points along the stem where leaves attach are **nodes.** Typically, nodal regions are somewhat thickened as compared to the elongated stem areas between the nodes, the **internodes.** The arrangement of leaves at the nodes may take three basic forms (Figure 2.4). The most prevalent arrangement is **alternate,** in which one leaf is found at each node. If the leaves are paired at the same height, one on each side of the node, the arrangement is **opposite.** When more than two leaves are found at each node, they are **whorled** or **verticillate.** One variation that occasionally occurs is the **subopposite** arrangement in which the leaves are nearly, but not quite, opposite.

Leaves may be **simple** (composed of one blade) or **compound** (blade divided into two or more leaflets). The difference between the two is not always obvious. Since leaves have axillary buds and leaflets do not, this is a good test to use with the understanding that these buds may be hard to see—either sunken into the stem tissue or hidden by the base of the petiole. Careful observation is also

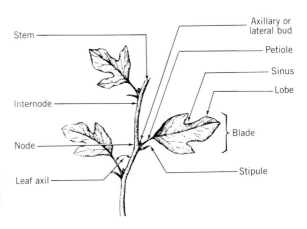

FIGURE 2.3 The structural configuration and terminology of a typical plant twig.

Stem

Internode

Node

Leaf axil

Axillary or lateral bud

Petiole

Sinus

Lobe

Blade

Stipule

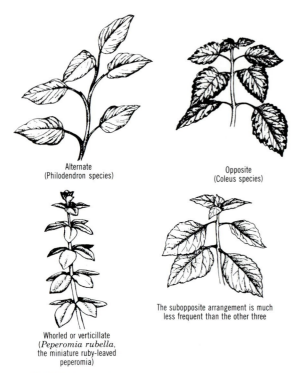

FIGURE 2.4 Leaf arrangement on the stem can be a helpful identification tool.

Alternate
(Philodendron species)

Opposite
(Coleus species)

Whorled or verticillate
(*Peperomia rubella*,
the miniature ruby-leaved
peperomia)

The subopposite arrangement is much
less frequent than the other three

Anatomy of a compound leaf

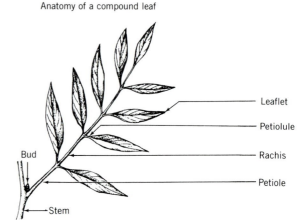

Leaflet

Petiolule

Rachis

Petiole

Bud

Stem

FIGURE 2.5 The terminology associated with a compound leaf.

necessary when a simple leaf is deeply cut or indented, such as is the case with the tree philodendron. In compound leaves, the portion of the leaf axis extending beyond the lowest leaflet is termed the **rachis.** The individual leaflets making up a compound leaf are attached to the rachis by means of a short stalk termed a **petiolule** (Figure 2.5).

Compound leaves are described according to the arrangement of the leaflets on the rachis (Figure 2.6). If the leaflets radiate from the tip of the rachis, like fingers around a hand, the arrangement is **palmate.** When the leaflets are arranged along the side of the rachis, usually opposite from one another, the arrangement is described as **pinnate. Bipinnately compound** leaves possess leaflets that are also pinnately divided. In certain ferns, the leaves (fronds) may exhibit several levels of leaflet division. Some plants, such as grape ivy (*Cissus rho-*

mbifolia), have compound leaves that possess three leaflets. Leaves of this type are described as **trifoliate.**

Leaves are shaped in numerous ways, with a particular shape usually consistent for a species. When the leaf is lobed, the shape is described according to the outline produced by running an imaginary line around the tips of the lobes. Table 2.6 illustrates the most common shapes of indoor plant leaves. Leaves, on rare occasion, may be imposters or disguised. On the asparagus fern, for example, the "leaves" are not leaves at all, but are actually flattened or needlelike

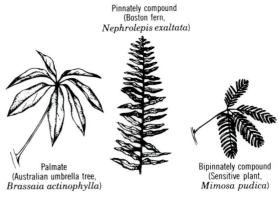

Pinnately compound
(Boston fern,
Nephrolepis exaltata)

Palmate
(Australian umbrella tree,
Brassaia actinophylla)

Bipinnately compound
(Sensitive plant,
Mimosa pudica)

FIGURE 2.6 Compound leaves are arranged in one of several distinct configurations.

TABLE 2.6 LEAF SHAPES OF INDOOR PLANTS

ACICULAR Needlelike; very slender, long, and pointed Ex: *Podocarpus macrophyllus* (Buddhist pine)	SCALELIKE Small sharp-pointed leaves broadened at the base Ex: *Araucaria heterophylla* (Norfolk Island pine)
LINEAR Narrow with approximately parallel sides; a number of times longer than wide Ex: *Sansevieria trifasciata* (Snake plant)	OBLONG Longer than broad, with sides nearly parallel Ex: *Aspidistra elatior* (Cast-iron plant)
ELLIPTICAL Shaped like a football; broad at center and sloping to a point at both ends Ex: *Episcia cupreata* (Flame violet)	LANCEOLATE Lance-shaped. Widest about one-third the distance from the base with narrowed ends; several times longer than broad Ex: *Spathiphyllum* spp. (Peace lilies)
ORBICULAR Circular in outline Ex: *Pellaea rotundifolia* (Button fern)	RHOMBOIDAL Diamond-shaped; with equal sides but unequal angles Ex: *Cissus rhombifolia* (Grape ivy)
OVATE Egg-shaped, with the broadest part near the base Ex: *Coleus* spp.	CORDATE Heart-shaped Ex: *Philodendron scandens* subsp. *oxycardium* (Common philodendron)
DELTOID Triangular; shaped like the Greek letter delta Ex: *Oxalis regnellii* ("Rubra Alba" Oxalis)	SPATULATE Broadly rounded at tips but tapering to narrow base; narrower than obovate[a] Ex: *Peperomia obtusifolia* (Baby rubber plant)

[a]The prefix *ob-* refers to the inverse arrangement; therefore, obovate has the broadest part near the base.

SOURCE: *Textbook of Dendrology*, Harlow and Harrar, 1969, McGraw-Hill Book Co. Reprinted by permission of McGraw-Hill Book Co.

branchlets (stems) called **cladodes.** On the other hand, spines and tendrils (discussed on p. 33), although quite different in appearance than foliage, are often modified leaves.

JUVENILITY. Special mention should be made here of the juvenile-to-adult change that some plants exhibit. This phenomenon is important among indoor plants because the appearance of some species changes dramatically with the transition to the adult phase of growth. A change in leaf shape usually marks the transition from juvenility to adulthood, but included also may be initiation of flowering, loss of thorns, and reduced growth vigor. The best example of this phenomenon is presented by the swiss-cheese plant, *Monstera deliciosa*. The adult form bears large (up to three feet wide) leaves that are perforated with large, oblong holes on either side of the midrib. But as a juvenile, the plant has smaller uncut leaves that resemble the philodendron's, so much so that the juvenile form has been confusingly and improperly named *Philodendron pertusum* in horticultural usage. Another example, though not confused by multiple names, is the Australian umbrella tree (*Brassaia actinophylla*) that has palmately compound leaves as an adult but may have simple leaves as a juvenile. The point here is that although leaves are usually consistently characteristic for a species, factors exist that cause changes (Figure 2.7).

Aside from juvenility, light may also play an important role in determining leaf shape.

Adult leaf   Juvenile leaves

FIGURE 2.7 The Australian umbrella tree (*Brassaia actinophylla*) demonstrates how different the adult and juvenile foliage can be on the same species.

In poor lighting, small leaves and elongated internodes give the plant an appearance that varies from the norm. Lighting may also affect leaf color. Plants under insufficient or no light, for example, will become bleached or whitened in time, a process known as **etiolation.** Similarly, variegated plants usually display much less coloration in poor light. Inspection of leaves for identification purposes must include an awareness of these possibilities for deviation. Since leaves vary so much in form, it is easy to see why plants are botanically classified according to sexual structure rather than leaf shape.

The leaf **margin,** or edge of the blade, varies in characteristic ways and is also an important aid to identification. Likewise, the apex of the leaf (the end farthest removed from the petiole) and the base take on common shapes. Table 2.7 outlines the various configurations.

LEAF VENATION. Two main types of leaf venation exist among angiosperms or flowering plants: the **parallel** or **closed** and the **reticulate** or **open** system. The parallel typical of monocotyledonous plants such as palms, consists of veins that run nearly parallel to each other along the entire length of the leaf. These are connected by transverse veinlets, thus creating a closed system. Reticulate venation, on the other hand, is characteristic of dicotyledons and is a system of interlacing veins, some of which may end blindly in the leaf, forming the basis for the "open" designation. When three or more veins branch from the base of the leaf, the leaf is **palmately veined.** If there is a midrib extending the length of the leaf and secondary veins branching off it at intervals, the venation is **pinnate** (Figure 2.8).

Flowers and Fruits

Chapter Three will treat flowers and fruit in their role as the sexual reproductive mechanisms of the plant and will explain their structure and functions in detail. Our pur-

TABLE 2.7 CHARACTERISTIC LEAF MARGINS, APICES, AND BASES

L E A F M A R G I N S	ENTIRE—smooth, without lobes or teeth.
	UNDULATE—slightly wavy.
	SINUATE—deeply or strongly wavy.
	LOBED—divided into lobes separated by sinuses that extend from one-third to one-half of the distance between margin and midrib.
	CRENATE—with rounded or blunt teeth.
	SERRATE—finely toothed like a saw, with teeth pointing toward apex.
	DENTATE—with coarse teeth, pointing outward from margin.
L E A F A P I C E S	ACUTE—shaped like an acute angle (less than 90°) with straight or convex sides.
	ACUMINATE—shaped like an acute angle with convex sides.
	OBTUSE—bluntly tipped, with sides forming an angle greater than 90°.
	ROUNDED—apex forming a round outline.
	TRUNCATE—as though abruptly cut off transversely at the end.
	MUCRONATE—abruptly tipped with a short, narrow, hairlike projection.
	CUSPIDATE—tipped with a sharp and stiff point.
	EMARGINATE—with a shallow notch at the tip.

(continued)

TABLE 2.7 (Continued)

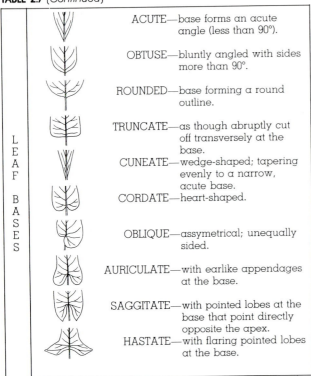

ACUTE—base forms an acute angle (less than 90°).

OBTUSE—bluntly angled with sides more than 90°.

ROUNDED—base forming a round outline.

TRUNCATE—as though abruptly cut off transversely at the base.

CUNEATE—wedge-shaped; tapering evenly to a narrow, acute base.

CORDATE—heart-shaped.

OBLIQUE—assymetrical; unequally sided.

AURICULATE—with earlike appendages at the base.

SAGGITATE—with pointed lobes at the base that point directly opposite the apex.

HASTATE—with flaring pointed lobes at the base.

SOURCE: *Textbook of Dendrology*, Harlow and Harrar, 1969, McGraw-Hill Book Co. Reprinted by permission of McGraw-Hill Book Co.

pose here is to examine these two plant parts regarding their typical forms and their use in plant identification. A majority of indoor plants are grown for their leaf qualities, but all produce flowers and most fruit, even if inconspicuously, giving strong clues of identity.

A knowledge of typical flower and fruit structure is important, particularly since the classification of plant families is dependent on flower structure. A good case in point is the Aroid family (*Araceae*) that has an inflorescence composed of two basic parts: (1) an upright, elongated central axis, called the **spadix,** which is densely covered with minute, petalless flowers and (2) the **spathe,** a leaflike bract (modified leaf) that is attached at the base of the spadix and is so showy that it is mistakenly considered the petal of the flower.

FLOWERS. Like buds, flowers may be axillary or terminal. Many plants have single flowers, others have clusters of flowers to form a floral arrangement known as an **inflorescence.** When the flower at the terminus of the central flower stalk (**peduncle**) blooms slightly before the adjacent flowers, the inflorescence is **determinate.** The **cyme,** an inflorescence consisting of a central rachis bearing a number of pedicelled (stalked) flowers, is the most common determinate type (Figure 2.9).

Indeterminate flowering occurs when the flowers open progressively from the base of the inflorescence upward. Several indeter-

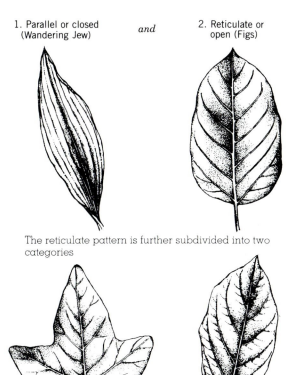

1. Parallel or closed
(Wandering Jew)   *and*   2. Reticulate or
open (Figs)

The reticulate pattern is further subdivided into two categories

(a) Palmately veined
(English ivy)

(b) Pinnately veined
(Anthuriums)

FIGURE 2.8 The two basic leaf venation patterns.

minate arrangements exist. A **spike** consists of a central axis that bears a number of sessile (stalkless) flowers. A similar inflorescence with flowers on **pedicels** or stalks is the **raceme.** The **panicle** is simply a raceme with compound or branched pedicels. Unlike the raceme and panicle with pedicels of nearly equal length, the **corymb** consists of a central axis with a number of unbranched or branched pedicels, the lower ones much longer than the upper, resulting in a flat or somewhat rounded flower cluster. If the pedicels arise from the same point of attachment, the structure is flat-topped or rounded much like a corymb, but is called

an **umbel.** A final indeterminate inflorescence is the **head** that consists of a number of sessile flowers clustered on a round or flat-topped receptacle or base. The members of the composite family, such as the velvet plant (*Gynura aurantiaca*) and chrysanthemums, produce heads that have two flower types, central small disk flowers and elongated, straplike ray flowers (Figure 2.9).

FRUIT. The female sexual organ of the flower, the gynoecium, is generally composed of the pollen-receiving **stigma,** the typical stalklike **style,** and the basal **ovary** in which the seeds develop (see Figure 3.14). The **fruit** is defined as a developing or mature ovary, with or without closely associated floral parts.

Only occasionally, such as with cacti, citrus, *Aglaonema* species, and Jerusalem cherry, are fruits decorative on indoor plants. Many are rather unattractive and are usually removed from the plant just after the flowers fade, before their development can draw growth energy away from the plant or reduce subsequent flowering. Therefore, since fruit is not usually used as a means of identification unless it constitutes a conspicuous attraction of the plant, this fruit section will provide the reader with only a brief look at the basics of fruit classification.

Fruits are usually classified as simple, aggregate, or multiple and may be dry or fleshy. **Simple fruits** develop from one or several united carpels, the organ in angiosperms that encloses the ovules. (See Chapter Three.) When the fruit develops from separate carpels in the same flower, it is termed an **aggregate** fruit, a type not found among common house plants.

Compact clusters of simple fruits traceable to the carpels of separate flowers and usually borne in a head are known as **multiple** fruits. The pineapple (*Ananas comosus*) is such a fruit, with each "bump" representing the developed ovary of one flower.

Dry fruits may be woody, leathery, or

The inflorescence may be determinate:

or indeterminate:

Spike   Raceme   Panicle

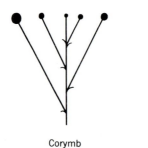

Corymb   Umbel   Head

FIGURE 2.9 The compound flower structure, or inflorescence, may be arranged in a number of ways. *Source:* Calvin and Knutson, *Modern Home Gardening*, New York: Wiley, 1983, p. 68

papery in texture and may mature in one of two ways. If they split along sutures to release their seeds, they are **dehiscent.** An example would be the **capsule,** which is found on the popular winter-flowering amaryllis, and formed from a compound pistil that splits along two or more sutures at maturity. The sensitive plant (*Mimosa pudica*), which responds to the touch by temporarily wilting, produces a **legume** or "pod," the product of a simple pistil splitting along the two lines of suture. A similar fruit to the legume is the **follicle,** not common to indoor plants, which differs in that it splits along a single suture line. Dry fruits, such as nuts, that do not split at maturity to release the seeds are **indehiscent** fruits. These are rare among indoor plants.

Fleshy fruits do not open at maturity. The most common of these among indoor plants is the **berry,** a several-seeded (rarely one-seeded) fruit with fleshy outer and inner walls and the seeds imbedded in the pulpy mass. Berries occur on cacti, avocado, *Aglaonema,* and kaffir lily. Although berries are usually thought of as an edible fruit, some, such as those of the Jerusalem cherry (*Solanum pseudocapsicum*), are poisonous if eaten. A specialized type of berry with a thick outer rind, known as a **hesperidium,** is borne by members of the citrus family, several of which are grown indoors. A fleshy fruit that contains a **stone** or hardened inner ovary wall is known as a **drupe.** The abundantly fruited coralberry (*Ardisia crenata*) is a good example. The fourth type of fleshy fruit, the *pome* (such as the apple and pear), does not occur on indoor plants.

Miscellaneous Identification Features

The aforementioned plant characteristics—leaves to a great extent and flowers and fruit to a lesser—are the primary indicators of plant identity. Other features can be just as helpful. The form of the plant, for example, should be observed by noticing the nature of the stem. **Aerial stems** grow above the soil and may be erect, climbing, or prostrate in growth habit. Stems also may be **woody** in texture or **herbaceous,** that is, soft, succulent, and usually green like those of coleus and geraniums. Many stems are spotted or streaked with corky **lenticels,** areas of loosely arranged cells that permit the exchange of gasses between the stem's internal tissues and the atmosphere. **Aerial roots,** often a conspicuous display, are frequently produced by climbing vines like philodendrons and **epiphytic** plants such as orchids that grow on other plants but do not derive nourishment from them. Other climbing stems produce **tendrils** that are curled, threadlike projections by which the plant grasps and clings to a support. Grape ivy (*Cissus rhombifolia*) and other members of

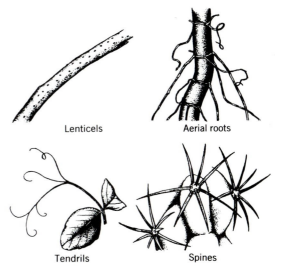

FIGURE 2.10 Miscellaneous features that often are helpful with identification.

the grape family bear tendrils. Cacti, as well as numerous other plants, bear **spines** that are sharp, rigid projections from the stem (Figure 2.10).

Not all plants produce aerial stems. Numerous plants are **acaulescent** or rosette, with the leaves emerging or appearing to emerge from the soil; the stem is actually present, but lies below the soil surface or is very short. The cast-iron plant (*Aspidistra elatior*) and many ferns are good examples. There are numerous types of underground stems that will be discussed in Chapter Four under plant propagation.

THE PLANTS WE GROW INDOORS

The centuries of exploration for exotic plants have yielded an immense number of plants. Whereas Linnaeus and his colleagues knew 85,000 species, we now recognize approximately 350,000 species of flowering plants alone, belonging to some 12,500 genera. In addition, there are over 9000 kinds of ferns.

Plant Appearance versus Culture

A plant's physical appearance is often indicative of its region of origin, as well as its cultivation requirements. Succulent plants, such as the aloes and the jade plants (*Crassula*), having acquired the ability to store water in thick or **coriaceous** leaves, can reasonably be assumed to have developed in arid surroundings. Succulence, however, is not always made obvious by leaf thickness. The ponytail palm (*Beaucarnea recurvata*), for example, stores its water in a thick, fleshy stem rather than modified leaves. Most of these plants come from the arid, sunny grasslands of South Africa and, as such, need to be cultivated with dryness between waterings and bright light.

On the other hand, plants such as the spider plant (*Chlorophytum*), having thin or **membranous** leaves that cannot store water and which respond quickly to moisture stress by wilting, usually inhabit regions where rainfall and soil moisture are rather regular. The spider plant is also from South Africa, but from the moist areas around the Cape of Good Hope. As a result, it must be watered regularly. Understanding the relationship between physical appearance and environment can be a critical aspect of successful plant culture.

Where Do They Come From?

The plants of indoor use come from all over the world but are concentrated in the tropical and subtropical belt that lies an average of 3000 miles to the north and south of the equator. The division between the tropical zone and the subtropical zone is the Tropic of Cancer to the north and the Tropic of Capricorn to the south, imaginary lines that are about 1600 miles from the equator (Figure 2.11). One of the best references on the subject of indoor plant world habitats is Alfred Byrd Graf's *Exotic Plant Manual*, one of our primary sources for the treatment of this subject.

THE CLIMATES. Understanding the tropical climate is quite beneficial to the cultivation skills of the indoor gardener. Although elevation, ocean current patterns, and rainfall may vary from place to place in the tropics to cause various climatic patterns, each area shares a common denominator: a relatively uniform mean monthly temperature during each month of the year. This regularity is in strong contrast to the significant thermal changes between seasons in the temperate regions of the world.

LOWLAND FORESTS. Because of climatic uniformity, there are important similarities among many of the tropical plants. Inhabitants of the tropical lowland forests are quite sensitive to temperature changes. Therefore, when placed in an indoor location where cold drafts from doors and windows cross their foliage, they suffer from the abrupt chill, for example, *Dieffenbachia*. On the other hand, it is important not to confuse temperature sensitivity with a preference for heat; plants of the tropical zones, especially at high elevations, often experience temperatures as low as 50°F (10°C.). Some orchids, such as the cymbidium, for example, are cultivated in a cool greenhouse, such as one with a night temperature around 50°F.

Light intensity and relative humidity are important considerations also. In tropical areas, the larger trees of the forest cast a dense shade onto the smaller understory plants. Hence, such shade-loving plants as philodendron and spathiphyllum are popular because they can tolerate the darker corners of rooms without great difficulty. Tropical humidity is very high and is quite difficult to duplicate in the average home. Consequently, plants that enjoy high levels of humidity often develop marginal leaf browning or other leaf disorders when placed indoors and must frequently be placed in the moisture of a greenhouse or terrarium to be grown successfully.

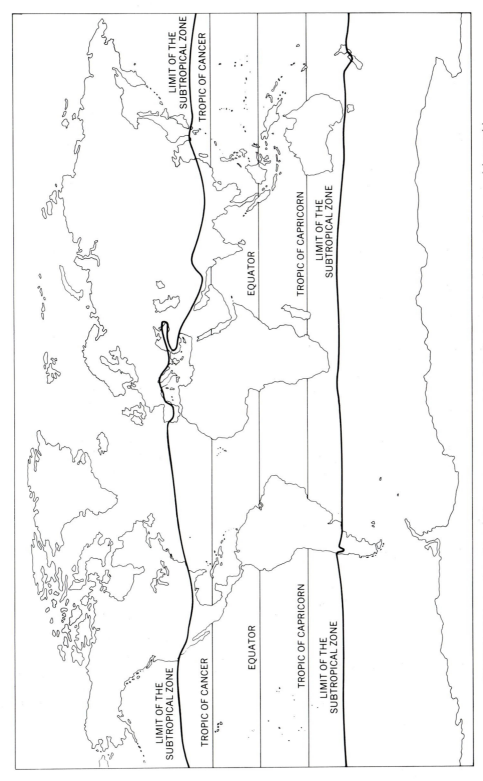

FIGURE 2.11 Most indoor plants of the temperate zones originate in the tropical and subtropical areas of the world.

A final characteristic of the tropical environment is the soil: moist and well drained. In growing plants in pots, we do not always get optimal drainage, so for many plants we commonly allow the soil to dry somewhat between waterings to ensure sufficient soil aeration and to inhibit the development of root and stem diseases.

DESERTS. At the other end of the climatic scale, we cultivate plants such as cacti and succulents that are native to the harsh condition of deserts. The unusual configurations of many of these plants are a response to environmental adversity. Living in areas where rainfall is scarce, these plants have the ability to absorb water quickly and to store it in their thickened tissue. To protect that stored water from the thirst of other desert creatures, spines are found on many of the cacti. Succulents, such as *Lithops* or living stones, exhibit a physical appearance similar to rocks that disguises them from their predators. And finally, the fiery heat of the desert day coupled with the extreme cold of night have created plants that are able to stand extreme and rapid temperature changes.

Plants such as cacti that inhabit a climatic zone with fluctuating and rigorous temperatures adapt more easily to home temperatures than many tropical plants that are accustomed to high humidity and constant temperatures that can only be created in a greenhouse. It is important to realize, however, that plants are adaptable and that they can often become acclimated to the less favorable conditions of the home. In many cases, this situation is actually desirable because the plant is much slower to outgrow its design situation.

The Major Foliage Plant Regions of the World

WESTERN HEMISPHERE. The majority of our indoor plants are native to the Western Hemisphere. The Amazon Basin of South America, with an estimated 60,000 species, is one of the most densely populated plant regions of the Western world. One of our major plant groups, the Aroid family—including *Philodendron*, *Dieffenbachia* (dumbcane), and *Spathiphyllum* (spathe flower)—comes to us from the American tropics. Other dependable and famous plants also arise in the Western Hemisphere: orchids, bromeliads, and cacti to name a few. Others are listed in Table 2.8.

AFRICA. Northern, southern, and eastern Africa are primarily dry grassland or desert, abounding with succulent plants that are adapted to the lack of water. Although cacti are absent in Africa, such familiar plants as *Saintpaulia* (African violet), *Sansevieria* (snake plant), and *Lithops* (living stones) grow there. Central and western Africa is mostly rainforest, with *Dracaena* being the most conspicuous representative. Table 2.8 lists other native plants of Africa.

EAST INDIES AND ASIA. The East Indies, consisting of Southeast Asia, the Philippines, and Indonesia, along with the other tropical and subtropical Asiatic regions, offer numerous indoor plants including many ferns and orchids. The monsoon rainfall pattern of many areas produces abundant moisture and humidity that complement the warm temperatures to produce colorful plants such as *Codiaeum* (croton), *Coleus*, and *Hibiscus*. The cooler areas of southern China and Japan have produced such plants as bamboo, *Podocarpus* (Buddhist pine), and *Aspidistra* (cast-iron plant). The list of Asian contributions is expanded in Table 2.8.

AUSTRALIA AND NEW ZEALAND. One final area of the world that deserves comment of its plant wealth is the area around Australia and New Zealand. One of the most bountiful zones of fern inhabitation, this area also produced *Brassaia*, formerly called *Sche-*

TABLE 2.8 REPRESENTATIVE INDOOR PLANTS FROM THREE OF THE WORLD'S FOUR MAJOR TROPICAL REGIONS

The Americas

Amaryllis (*Hippeastrum*)	Hen-and-chickens (*Echeveria*)
Arrowhead vine (*Syngonium*)	Lady's eardrops (*Fuchsia*)
Begonia	Monkey-faced pansy (*Achimenes*)
Bloodleaf (*Iresine*)	Nerve plant (*Fittonia*)
Carpet plant (*Episcia*)	Palm (*Chamaedorea*)
Century plant (*Agave*)	Prayer plant (*Maranta*)
Columnea	Radiator plant (*Peperomia*)
Elephant's ear (*Caladium*)	Stonecrop (*Sedum*)

Africa

Belladonna lily (*Amaryllis*)	Heath (*Erica*)
Calla lily (*Zantedeschia*)	Jade plants (*Crassula*)
Cape primrose (*Streptocarpus*)	Kaffir lily (*Clivia*)
Geranium (*Pelargonium*)	Orchids
Groundsel (*Senecio*)	Spurge (*Euphorbia*)

Asia

Aglaonema	Copperleaf (*Acalypha*)
Aluminum plant (*Pilea*)	Japanese Fatsia (*Fatsia*)
Aucuba	Pothos (*Epipremnum*)
Azaleas	Sago palm (*Cycas*)
Begonias	Wax vine (*Hoya*)

SOURCE: Graf, Dr. A. B., *Exotic Plant Manual*, East Rutherford, N.J.: Roehrs Company.

fflera (the umbrella tree), *Dizygotheca* (the false aralia), *Araucaria* (the Norfolk Island pine), and *Cordyline* (the ti plant).

Wherever in the world plants grow, they have an abundance of some natural element: sunlight, humidity, rainfall, soil rich with organic matter and nutrients from decomposed leaves, air circulation, or appropriate temperature. The average home or office cannot supply these conditions without special design or equipment. The indoor gardener must, therefore, realize that to bring the plant inside and away from its natural habitat is to protect the plant from some of the rigors of the outdoors and to expose it to a hostile environment. He or she is expecting it to adapt to conditions far inferior to those that the species experiences in its natural habitat. It is in this way that many indoor gardeners fail in their attempts to grow plants—by purchasing plants unsuitable for their home or by not adjusting temperature, humidity, light, or other cultural practices to the plant's minimal standards. Part Two of this text will examine these environmental factors and how they relate to plant growth.

FOR FURTHER READING

Bailey, L. *How Plants Get Their Names*. New York: Dover Publications, 1963. Republication of the 1933 version by the Macmillan Company.

Barden, J. A., and G. Halfacre. *Horticulture.* New York: McGraw-Hill, 1979.

Graf, A. *Exotic Plant Manual.* 3rd ed. East Rutherford, N.J.: Roehrs Company, 1974.

Graf, A. *Exotica.* 7th ed. East Rutherford, N.J.: Roehrs Company, 1973.

Harlow, W., and E. Harrar. *Textbook of Dendrology.* New York: McGraw-Hill, 1968.

Hartman, H., and D. Kester. *Plant Propagation: Principles and Practices.* Englewood Cliffs, N.J.: Prentice-Hall.

Hortus Third. Staff of the L. H. Bailey Hortorium. New York: Macmillan, 1976.

Keeton, W. *Biological Science.* New York: W. W. Norton & Co., 1967.

Rayle, D., and L. Wedberg. *Botany: A Human Concern.* New York: Saunders College/Holt, Rinehart and Winston, 1980.

Taylor, J. *Growing Indoor Plants.* Minneapolis, Minn.: Burgess Publishing Co., 1977.

chapter three
how plants grow
and function

Now that we have learned how to identify and name plants, it is time that we explore how they grow and function. After all, these activities give plants their utility and value. In the living plant, the many activities of growth occur in an integrated and systematic way within and among the different plant organs. For convenience of discussion, however, we will divide the subject material of this chapter into four categories, (1) the reproductive cycles of plants; (2) vegetative growth of stems, roots, and leaves; (3) sexual reproduction in plants; and (4) other important life processes.

THE REPRODUCTIVE CYCLES OF PLANTS

The successful management of plants, indoors or outdoors, requires a thorough understanding of plant life cycles. Both sexual and asexual cycles are recognized (Figure 3.1). The **sexual cycle** involves the formation of cones or flowers and the ultimate production of seeds. This designation is quite appropriate because the formation of seeds generally depends on the fusion of sexual cells known as **gametes.** The **asexual cycle,** on the other hand, makes use of vegetative propagules (cuttings, divisions, etc.) to produce new plants; a union of sex cells is not involved. An important distinction between the two reproductive cycles is that new

plants produced by sexual methods typically show genetic variation from their parents, whereas plants produced by asexual means are typically identical with the parent plant. Recent research, however, has produced asexual methods of stimulating variation. Both reproductive cycles are of concern to the indoor gardener and need to be explored in more detail.

Relationships between the Sexual and Asexual Cycles

SEED FORMATION. The sexual cycle begins with the germination of a seed and the growth of a new plant by the elongation of roots and stems and by the initiation and development of leaves. Frequently, as mentioned earlier, vegetative growth encompasses a transition from a juvenile to an adult form. Regardless of changes in form, however, growing plants eventually reach a point where they will form flowers in response to flower-inducing stimuli, or cones in the case of gymnosperms. The production of flowers signals the beginning of the reproductive process in the plant. Within the flower, gametes form that eventually fuse to form a **zygote,** the first cell of the next generation. The zygote undergoes a period of development to become the embryo in a mature seed, a seed that, when exposed to

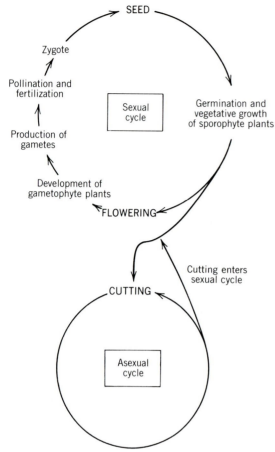

SEED

Zygote

Pollination and
fertilization

Production of
gametes

Sexual
cycle

Germination and
vegetative growth
of sporophyte plants

Development of
gametophyte plants

FLOWERING

CUTTING

Cutting enters
sexual cycle

Asexual
cycle

FIGURE 3.1 Reproduction in higher vascular plants
includes both sexual and asexual cycles. A vegetative
phase of growth occurs in each cycle.

the proper environmental conditions, will
usually germinate to begin yet another
sexual cycle.

INTERRUPTIONS IN THE SEXUAL CYCLE. In
nature, plants progress through the sexual
cycle relatively undisturbed, but man, inten-
tionally or unintentionally, often interrupts
the sexual process in a number of ways. For
example, plants often fail to flower because
they are not exposed to the proper flower-
inducing stimuli. Although many conditions
influence flowering, the effects of day length
are most familiar. Some plants flower only

under short days, others long days. Poinsettias, *Gardenia*, and the Christmas cactus are
all plants that will flower after they have
been exposed to a certain number of short
days, but these day length requirements are
not always met in the home. In other cases,
such as with caladium and coleus, flowers
are generally removed as they appear because they detract from the overall appearance and vigor of the plant. The removal of
flowers, of course, interrupts the sexual process also.

The sexual cycle is also interrupted when
plant growth is channeled into the asexual
cycle (Figure 3.1). Indoor gardeners commonly employ asexual methods, as when
they propagate plants by cuttings or other
vegetative propagules. Basically, **cuttings**
are vegetative plant parts—leaf, stem,
root—that can be used to start new plants.
Shoot tip cuttings of plants such as
Aglaonema, Coleus, and *Dieffenbachia,* for
example, readily form new roots. The rooted
cuttings then undergo a period of vegetative
growth before flower formation occurs. But
cuttings can be taken from these new plants
before they flower, and in this way, the
growth and multiplication of plants without
the intervention of a sexual process can
continue indefinitely. These relationships between the two reproductive cycles—sexual
and asexual—are illustrated in Figure 3.1.

As you have no doubt guessed by now,
the propagation of plants by asexual, as
opposed to sexual methods, has important
consequences. We have already said that
plants produced by asexual means are typically identical in genetic makeup to the
parent plant. The variation usually inherent
in individuals produced by sexual means
does not occur often because no sexual
activity is involved in their asexual propagation. Many other advantages, and some
disadvantages, are accredited to asexual
propagation. Both the sexual and asexual
methods of propagation are discussed in
detail in Chapter Four.

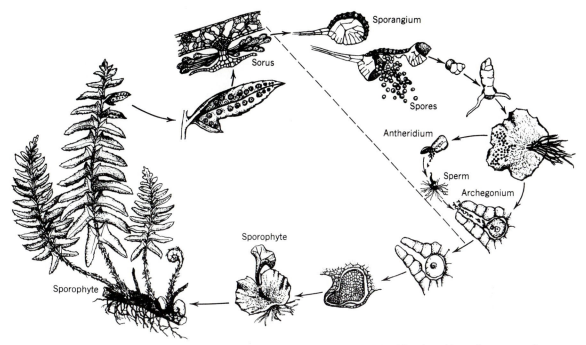

FIGURE 3.2 Fern life cycle. The sporophyte generation is shown to the left of the dotted line; the gametophyte generation to the right. Redrawn by permission of Carolina Biological Supply Co.

A Different Twist: The Ferns

Thus far, our discussion of vascular plant life cycles has centered around higher vascular plants. But what about the ferns? We are often led to believe that they reproduce by a different and even somewhat mysterious process. A common statement describing the sexual cycle in the two groups is that ferns reproduce by means of spores, whereas higher vascular plants reproduce by means of seed. Let us briefly examine this statement.

The fern **sporophyte** (spore-producing plant) produces spores within sporangia that occur in clusters on the lower side of leaves, or **fronds** as they are commonly called (Figure 3.2). **Spores,** unlike gametes, can develop into new plants without fusing with another cell. True to this definition, the fern spores, after liberation from the sporangium, germinate and develop into new, small plants about the size of your thumb nail.

These small, green plants are termed **gametophytes,** and they produce gametes that fuse to form zygotes. Zygotes, over a period of time, give rise to new sporophytes to complete the sexual cycle. (Ferns can, of course, also be propagated asexually.)

SPORES AND HIGHER PLANTS. With regard to higher vascular plants, a logical first question is this: Do these plants produce spores? The answer is an emphatic yes! They do indeed produce spores that, like those of ferns, develop directly into new gametophyte plants (Figures 3.3 and 3.4). Furthermore, these gametophyte plants produce gametes—eggs and sperms. These fuse to form zygotes that, as discussed earlier (Figure 3.1), develop into new sporophyte plants capable of producing spores. Compare the life cycle of a fern (Figure 3.2) to that of a gymnosperm (Figure 3.3) or an angiosperm (Figure 3.4). Can you identify

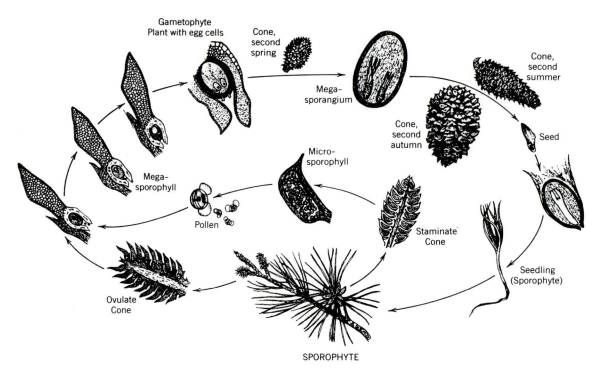

FIGURE 3.3 Gymnosperm life cycle as exemplified by pine. *Source:* Modified from Carolina Biological Supply Co., Burlington, North Carolina, 1977.

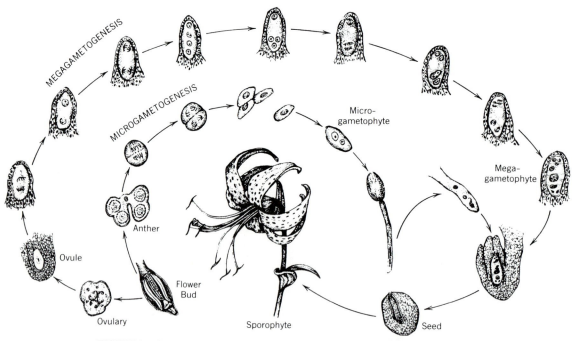

FIGURE 3.4 Angiosperm life cycle as exemplified by lily. *Source:* Modified from Carolina Biological Supply Co., Burlington, North Carolina, 1977.

the spore, gametophyte, gamete, and sporophyte stages in each of these life cycle types?

We have pointed out some features common to the life cycles of the three groups, but what are the differences? The major difference is simply this: In the ferns, spores germinate to form gametophytes *after liberation* from the sporangium, whereas in higher vascular plants, the spores are retained and undergo development *within* the sporangium. The retention of spores within the sporangium is an advance that led to the development of the seed. Another difference between the two groups is that in higher vascular plants, two kinds of spores are produced, each in separate sporangia, and these develop as unisexual gametophytes (Figures 3.3 and 3.4). The male gametophytes, known as **pollen grains,** or simply as pollen, are liberated from their sporangia after development, but the female gametophytes are retained indefinitely. In nearly all ferns, the gametophytes are bisexual. A final difference is this: The retention of spores within the sporangium of higher plants created a natural tendency for smaller gametophyte plants to develop. This tendency reaches its extreme in the angiosperms where the male gametophytes (pollen) consist of only two cells and the female gametophytes of less than one dozen cells each.

We encourage you to study the sexual cycles of the plants illustrated until you have a good comprehension of them. After all, you may be working with these plants for 50 or more years. A small effort now can pay big dividends later, because skillful propagation techniques require a thorough understanding of life cycle basics.

Life Cycle Patterns

Thus far, we have given no indication of the time intervals required to complete a single plant life cycle. As it turns out, plants *in nature* show definite time patterns in their vegetative and reproductive development. On this basis, three distinct plant groups are recognized—annuals, biennials, and perennials—each having a characteristic life cycle (Table 3.1). **Annuals** are plants that naturally complete their sexual cycle—from seed to seed—in a single growing season. Seeds of desert annuals may lie quiescent in the sand for long periods of time. When a rain comes, the seeds germinate, plants grow vegetatively, produce flowers, set seeds, and die; often within an interval of only a few weeks. Many vegetables and garden flowers are annuals. **Biennials** normally complete their life cycle over two growing seasons. During the first year, growth is entirely vegetative, with a cluster of leaves known as a **rosette** radiating out from near ground level. Near the beginning of growth the second year, after surviving the winter, the biennial will **bolt,** sending up an elongated flowering stalk. After setting seeds, the plant will die. Numerous vegetables (beet, carrot, onion) and garden flowers (hollyhock, pansy) are biennials. **Perennial,** from the Latin word *perennis*, meaning enduring or perpetual, refers to plants that live for more than two years. In some cases, perennials produce flowers and seeds during the first year of growth, but many grow for several years before sexual reproduction occurs. Perennials may be either **herbaceous** (developing predominantly soft, fleshy tissue) or **woody.** In temperate regions, herbaceous perennials die back to ground level each fall. When conditions are again favorable for growth, new shoots arise from underground structures such as bulbs, crowns, or rhizomes. Woody perennials may be either **deciduous** (lose their leaves each fall) or **evergreen** (retain their leaves for several years). Our hardwood and coniferous trees serve as conspicuous examples of these perennial types.

Indoor Effect on Life Cycle Patterns

In our discussion of life cycle types, we have referred specifically to plants growing in

TABLE 3.1 THE LIFE CYCLE PATTERNS OF ANNUALS, BIENNIALS, AND PERENNIALS

ANNUALS, BIENNIALS, AND PERENNIALS IN SUMMER AND WINTER

	Summer	Winter	Summer	Winter	Summer	Winter
Annuals			—	—	—	—
Biennials					—	—
Herbaceous Perennials						
Woody Perennials						

SOURCE: Modified from Taylor, J. Lee, *Growing Plants Indoors*, Minneapolis, Minn.: Burgess Publications, 1977, p. 8. Reprinted by permission.

nature. When plants are moved indoors (or outdoors), their life cycle patterns can change drastically. To illustrate, the very popular garden geranium acts as an annual when grown outdoors in temperate regions. When grown indoors, however, the geranium behaves as a perennial, reflecting the growth habit it displays when at home in the more tropical regions. Likewise, *Coleus* and certain begonias can be grown outdoors in temperate regions as annuals, but when grown indoors, they express their true perennial nature. As you may have guessed by now, the vast majority of our indoor plants are perennials. As mentioned earlier, most originated in the tropics or subtropics, zones in which there was not a strong selection pressure for the shortened types of life cycles

found in colder climates. Consequently, our tropical and subtropical foliage plants blend readily into the environment of the home where conditions provide for year around growth.

Superimposed over the perennial life cycles of most foliage plants are growing and resting (dormant) cycles that repeat themselves on a yearly basis. Often, the growing period corresponds to a time of plentiful rainfall and warm temperatures, and the resting period to a time of sparse rainfall and cool temperatures. Many cacti and succulents, for example, have their period of active growth during spring and summer, with a gradual onset of dormancy during fall and winter. These plants must be kept warm and moist during their period of natural growth and cool and dry during their dormant period. Certain other succulents, such as the living stones (*Lithops* species), are native to the Southern Hemisphere (South Africa) and have their growing and dormant seasons reversed from those of the Northern Hemisphere succulents. These plants may, after some time, switch over to the summer (rather than our winter) growing season, signs of which must be discerned by the successful grower. These two examples are given simply to reinforce the point that knowledge of each plant's growing and rest cycles is prerequisite to quality plant care.

Our discussion so far has centered around the sexual and asexual cycles of higher plants, and variations in the time that plants require to go through a sexual cycle from seed germination to seed production. We also commented that a large portion of the sexual cycle, to say nothing of the asexual cycle, is devoted to vegetative growth. Indeed, an extended period of vegetative growth is required to create an extensive plant body with enough food reserves to fulfill the energy requirements related to the production of seeds and fruits. But how does vegetative growth occur in plants? Let us explore this important topic.

VEGETATIVE GROWTH OF STEMS, ROOTS, AND LEAVES

We can begin our discussion of vegetative growth at the same point we began our discussion of the sexual cycle, namely, with the seed. Seeds vary greatly in size, shape, internal structure, germination requirements, and longevity, but regardless of these differences most seeds share certain common features. Seeds typically have three basic parts: an embryo, a reserve of stored food, and an outer protective covering known as the seed coat (Figure 3.5). After seed germination, the growth of the new plant takes place by the elongation of roots and stems, as well as by the initiation and development of leaves.

Generally, the elongating root is the first structure to emerge from the seed, eventually producing a network of roots that form one of several typical configurations. In some plants, growth of the **primary** (or tap) root is dominant over the **secondary** (or branch) roots (Figure 3.6) and a deep **tap root system** develops. In other plants, strong development of laterals occurs and a shallow, spreading **fibrous root system** results. Among cultivated plants, whether of indoor or outdoor use, the fibrous arrangement is

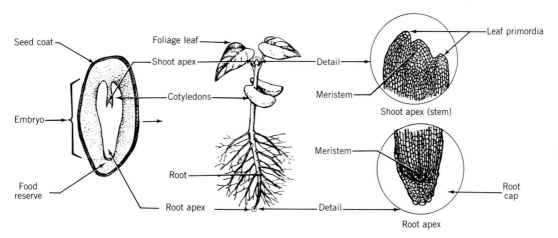

FIGURE 3.5 A seed and the seedling that develops from it upon germination. *Source:* Reprinted with permission of Wadsworth Publishing Company, Inc. from William A. Jensen and Frank B. Salisbury, *Botany: An Ecological Approach.* © 1972 by Wadsworth Publishing Co., Inc.

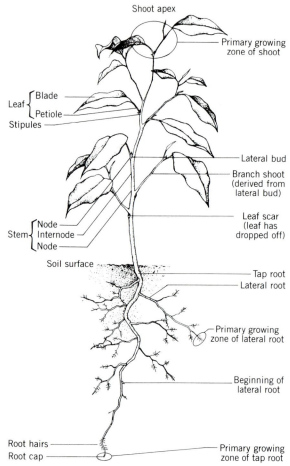

Shoot apex

Primary growing zone of shoot

Leaf { Blade
Petiole

Stipules

Lateral bud

Branch shoot (derived from lateral bud)

Leaf scar (leaf has dropped off)

Stem { Node
Internode
Node

Soil surface

Tap root

Lateral root

Primary growing zone of lateral root

Beginning of lateral root

Root hairs

Root cap

Primary growing zone of tap root

FIGURE 3.6 Diagram of the primary plant body illustrating mode of growth and external morphology of shoots and roots.

preferable due to the increased root surface and an associated ability to absorb water and nutrients more effectively, as well as the relative ease of transplanting. In containers, where a tap root cannot develop fully, plants prone to tap root development form modified root systems of a more fibrous nature. Consequently, indoor plants typically possess the more desirable fibrous arangement, whether due to a natural tendency or pot culture, and are usually not seriously disrupted by repotting.

Shoot (stems plus leaves) growth becomes

evident shortly after root emergence. Both of these emergent structures have the potential to elongate rapidly, and in both the mechanisms for elongation are similar.

Meristematic Tissue

In the apical regions of both roots and shoots, there are present tissues known as **meristems,** where new cells are constantly being produced by cell division. This division of cells in the meristem does not bring about organ elongation directly, but it does give a supply of cells that elongate as they mature, bringing about increases in the length of both roots and shoots.

It should be stressed that meristems are rather unique collections of cells. Cell divisions can, and do, occur throughout the plant body, but in meristems there is found an organized mass of cells dividing in a systematic pattern. The individual cells within meristems are sometimes called **initials.**

Shoot versus Root Meristems

The shoot and root meristems, as mentioned above, have in common an organized collection of initials. There are differences, however, between the two kinds of meristems (Figure 3.5). In roots, the meristems not only produce derivatives to the inside to add to the plant body, but they also yield derivatives to the outside to form a root cap. The **root cap** is a protective structure that acts to shield the meristem of the root as the root tip advances through the soil. During root elongation, the root cap is constantly sloughing off cells at the outside, while at the same time, new rootcap cells are being formed from the interior meristem. In shoots, on the other hand, derivatives are produced only inwardly. Another difference between root and shoot meristems is that lateral appendages of the root—branch roots and root hairs—arise some distance back from the apex, whereas in shoots, the lateral appendages, the leaves, are initiated in close proximity to the apex (Figure 3.5). The clustering of rudimentary leaves, known as **leaf primordia,** around the apex tends not only to protect this vital region from injury, but also it obscures the apex from view. The non-visibility of shoot apices can present problems to the indoor gardener because the apex may not be at the physical tip of the shoot. With monocotyledons such as wandering Jew (*Tradescantia*), for example, the actual apex is some distance back from the physical tip of the shoot, and if care is not taken in pruning, the meristem may not be removed.

Primary and Secondary Growth

Thus far, we have talked of meristems and their derivatives, and how derivatives enlarge and mature to carry out a number of specific functions. Activity from these *terminal* meristems, termed **primary meristems,** is said to give rise to the primary plant body. The primary plant body has all of the normal plant organs (Figure 3.6). It can also produce flowers, fruits, and seeds and is thus regarded as a complete and functional entity in itself. In many plants such as trees and shrubs, additional increments are added to the plant body. This additional growth comes from a *lateral* meristem known as the **vascular cambium.** Since growth from a vascular cambium can occur only after the primary plant body is present, the vascular cambium is regarded as a **secondary meristem.**

Growth from the two forms of meristems—primary and secondary—can be distinguished by the fact that growth from primary meristems contributes mainly to increase in *length*, whereas growth from secondary meristems is growth in *diameter*. Primary growth gives a plant body complete with root, stem, and leaves. Secondary growth merely adds additional yearly increments of stoutness to the existing plant body. Many perennial house plants have at least a small amount of secondary growth, but some, such as the jade plant and the weeping fig, show considerable secondary thickening of their axes.

Tissue Differentiation in Plants

We have outlined in general terms the mode of growth of plants. But what are the developmental changes associated with the **differentiation**—the gradual process of maturation—of cells, tissues, and organs, and how do these changes relate to function? As it turns out, the sequence of differentiation in roots and shoots is quite similar—although the arrangement of mature tissues in the two organs is different—and can be visualized to occur as illustrated in Figure 3.7. As shown, cells of the apical meristem give rise to cells that become visibly different from the cells of the apex and each other. These partially differentiated cells, which still have a high **meristematic** (dividing) potential, form the three **primary meristematic tissues**—protoderm, ground meristem, and procambium—of the plant body (Figure 3.7b). At still older levels of stem and root, the primary meristematic tissues become the **mature primary tissues** of the plant—primary phloem, primary xylem, pith, cortex, and epidermis (Figure 3.7c).

FORMATION OF EPIDERMAL TISSUE. The cells of the **protoderm,** as shown, mature as the **epidermis,** the outermost, protective layer of root, stem, and leaf. On aerial plant parts, the epidermis is covered with a surface layer of waxy material termed **cutin,** which forms a layer known as the **cuticle** (see Figure 3.12). Different plants have different quantities of cutin. The shiny appearance often apparent on aerial parts is due to these surface waxes. This covering drastically reduces the loss of water from plant surfaces, a feature of great importance in the relatively dry environment of the home.

In addition to the ordinary cells present in the epidermis, several kinds of specialized cells are formed. On stem and leaf, nonglan-

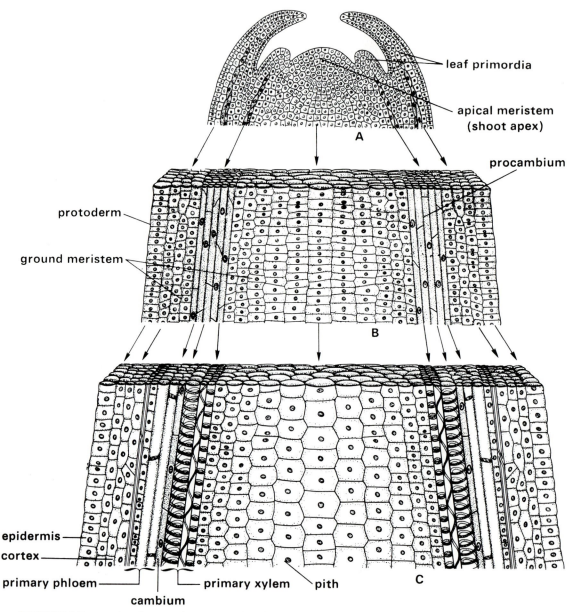

leaf primordia

apical meristem
(shoot apex)

procambium

protoderm

ground meristem

A

B

epidermis

cortex

primary phloem

cambium

primary xylem

pith

C

FIGURE 3.7 Progressive changes during growth in the terminal portion of a dicotyledonous stem as seen in longitudinal section. *Source:* Wilson, Loomis, and Steeves, Botany, 5th ed., New York: Holt, Rinehart & Winston, 1971, p. 160. Reprinted by permission of CBS Publications.

dular and glandular hairs, each comprised of one or more cells, may occur. These hairs, technically known as **trichomes,** are often abundant, as in the velvet plant (*Gynura aurantiaca*). In one important indoor plant family, the bromeliads, the leaves are characterized by elaborate trichomes, particularly on their lower surface (Figure 3.8). These trichomes are implicated in protection, moisture absorption, gas exchange

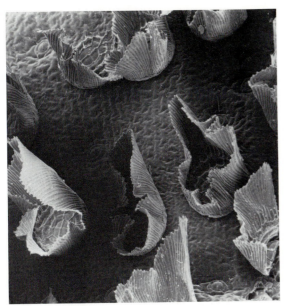

FIGURE 3.8 Scalelike trichomes on the leaf surface of *Tillandsia ionantha*, a bromeliad. Ordinary epidermal cells and stomates are also visible. *Source:* Courtesy of Dr. D.H. Benzing.

regulation, light reflectivity, and reduction of water loss from leaf surfaces. Another important specialized cell type is the **guard cell,** which occurs in pairs to comprise the **stomates** (Figure 3.9). The paired guard cells of the stomates have unequally thickened walls that allow for an opening, or pore, to form

between the pair when water enters the guard cells. These openings allow for the exchange of gases between the external environment and the internal tissues of stem and leaf. We will say more about this important feature of stomates later.

In roots, the most important specialized epidermal cells are the **root hairs** (Figure 3.6). The presence of root hairs vastly increases the absorbing surface of roots and thereby enhances water and mineral uptake.

CORTEX AND PITH FORMATION. The **ground meristem** gives rise to the tissue comprising the **cortex** of stems and roots and the **pith** region of stems (Figure 3.7). The predominant type of cell present in these two tissue regions is a relatively unspecialized cell termed **parenchyma** (Figure 3.10). The living parenchyma cells function in storage, food manufacture, energy release, aeration, and support. Parenchyma cells perform functions directly related to the activities of the indoor gardener. For example, when stem cuttings are taken from a plant, it is parenchyma cells that undergo the formative responses related to the initiation of roots. In summary, the parenchyma tissue is a vital, living tissue that carries out a number of important plant functions. It also

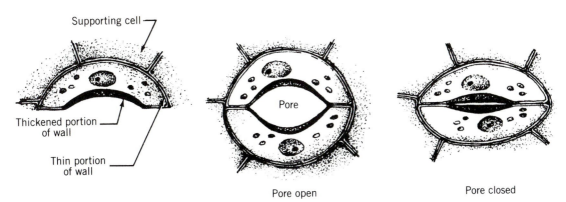

FIGURE 3.9 Open and closed stomates as they appear in surface views of the epidermis. Each guard cell has an unevenly thickened wall, which causes a pore to form as water fills the cells. *Source: Principles of Plant Physiology,* Bonner and Galston, W.H. Freeman and Co. © 1952.

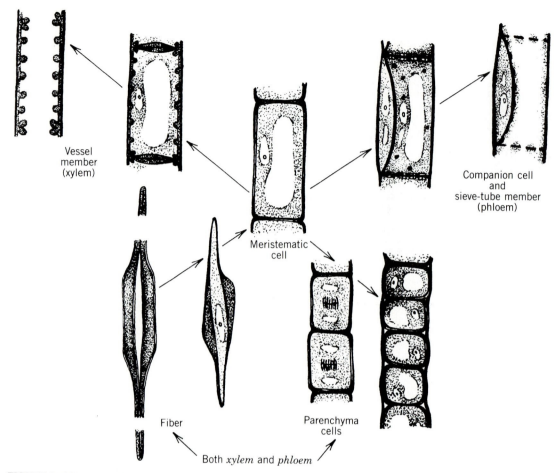

Vessel member (xylem)

Meristematic cell

Companion cell and sieve-tube member (phloem)

Fiber

Parenchyma cells

Both *xylem* and *phloem*

FIGURE 3.10 Diagram illustrating some of the basic cell types derived from meristematic cells of the procambium. Certain cell types, such as parenchyma, are also derived from the ground meristem. *Source:* Redrawn from Raven, P., Evert, R., and Curtis, H., *Biology of Plants*, 3rd ed., New York: Worth Publishers, 1981, p. 403.

forms the basic ground tissue of stem and root in which the vascular, or conducting, tissues are embedded.

THE VASCULAR TISSUES. The parenchyma tissue of plant organs is classified as a **simple tissue,** because it is composed of just one cell type, the parenchyma cell. In contrast, the vascular tissues—xylem and phloem—are regarded as **complex tissues,** because each is comprised of several different kinds of cells, as follows:

XYLEM	PHLOEM
Parenchyma cells	Parenchyma cells
Fibers	Fibers
Vessel members	Sieve-tube members
Tracheids	Companion cells

A given cell of the **procambium** can give rise to any one of the above cell types depending, of course, on its location within a vascular strand (Figure 3.10). In roots, the vascular tissue occurs as a solid central core, whereas in stems the vascular tissue is in the

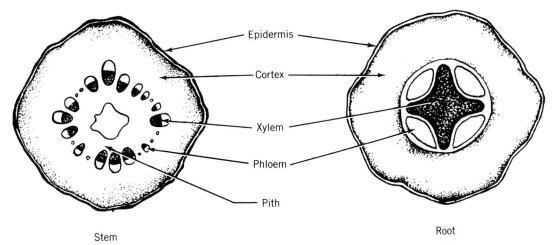

FIGURE 3.11 Cross sections of stem and root to illustrate their general anatomical features.

form of separate bundles arranged either in a single ring (most dicotyledons) or scattered throughout the stem (most monocotyledons). The basic arrangement in a dicotyledonous stem and root is shown in Figure 3.11. Note that in a given vascular bundle of the stem, the phloem tissue occurs near the periphery, the xylem to the interior. In roots, the xylem and phloem have an alternating arrangement.

We have said that differentiation in the xylem and phloem gives rise to several cell types. In both tissues, parenchyma cells and fibers are found. The **fibers** are elongate cells with thickened walls especially adapted to a support function (Figure 3.10). In the **xylem** of angiosperms—the water- and mineral-conducting tissue of the plant—two unique cell types are found, the **tracheids** and **vessel members** (Figure 3.10). In contrast, conifers and most lower vascular plants have no tracheids. The two cells are similar in structure except that at maturity the end walls of the vessel member are lost. As a result, long columns of continuous vessel members can form open tubes known as **vessels.** Interestingly, both the tracheid and the vessel member are dead at maturity;

that is, they are specialized to such a degree that they can carry out their primary functions only after a loss of cellular contents. Obviously, these two cells have lost any meristematic potential and could not dedifferentiate to participate in the formation of new plant organs. The living parenchyma cells of the xylem can, however, become meristematically active.

In the **phloem**—the food-conducting tissue of the plant—specialized cells are also found. The cell designed for conduction purposes is the **sieve-tube member,** or **sieve element,** as they are sometimes called. Sieve elements always occur in association with one or more specialized parenchyma cells known as **companion cells** (Figure 3.10). Like vessel members, sieve-tube members can join end to end to form long files known as **sieve tubes.** Unlike vessel members, however, the sieve elements do not lose their cellular contents at maturity, although they do become highly modified. For years, numerous researchers have been busy trying to characterize the cellular features of sieve elements and to relate these features to cell function. Though the story is far from complete, it can be said that the form of cellular contents is quite unusual as compared to a typical cell and that even though sieve elements are definitely alive, they lack certain features that characterize living cells. As you might expect, these highly specialized cells, and the companion cells associated with them, lack the ability to resume meristematic activity.

Leaf Structure and Diversity

Although we have alluded briefly to the leaf, we have basically excluded it from our discussion so far. This was done because the leaf, although arising from the same three primary meristematic tissues as the stem and root, differs markedly in structure. This differing structural adaptation is related in no small way to the primary function of the leaf, photosynthesis. Although there are numerous good definitions of photosynthesis, one that is especially vivid states simply that **photosynthesis** is the process whereby plants create themselves out of water, carbon dioxide, and minerals with the help of light. The physiological aspects of this remarkable ability of plants to manufacture food substances, such as carbohydrates and

proteins, from raw materials in the presence of sunlight is discussed later in the chapter. Here, we wish to examine leaf structure as it relates to this life-sustaining process.

ANATOMICAL FEATURES OF THE LEAF.

Although stems and roots are basically elongated, rounded organs, leaves are typically flattened. Variations in leaf form can be considerable: leaves can be simple or compound; sessile or petiolate; glaborous or pubescent; entire, toothed, or lobed, just to mention a few of the possible morphological variations. In spite of these numerous differences, most leaves display a similar anatomy (Figure 3.12).

Each side of the leaf is limited by a cuticle-covered epidermis containing numerous stomates. In a majority of species, the stomates are confined almost entirely to the lower epidermis, in others they are present in both, and in a few plants where the leaves float on water, they are confined to the upper surface. The vascular tissue in these flattened organs is a ramifying network embedded within the parenchyma tissue of the leaf, the **mesophyll.** Because of the extensive branch-

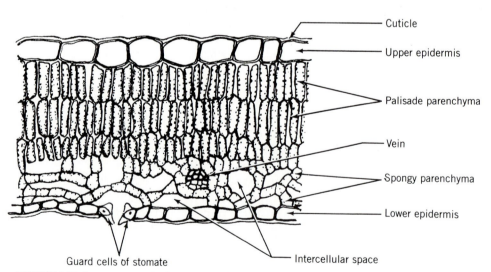

Cuticle

Upper epidermis

Palisade parenchyma

Vein

Spongy parenchyma

Lower epidermis

Guard cells of stomate

Intercellular space

FIGURE 3.12 Cross section of a leaf (apple) illustrating anatomical features. *Source:* Calvin and Knutson, *Modern Home Gardening*, New York: Wiley, 1983, p. 35.

ing of the vascular tissue, no cell in the mesophyll is more than a few cells removed from the conducting tissue.

In many plants, particularly dicotyledons, the mesophyll contains two distinct kinds of parenchyma. Near the upper surface, barrel-shaped **palisade parenchyma** cells stand both end to end and side to side. Although these cells appear to be tightly packed together, each is in contact with a great deal of air space. Near the lower surface of the leaf occurs the **spongy parenchyma,** the other type of mesophyll tissue. In a cross-sectional view of the leaf, the two parenchyma types join near the center of the leaf, at about the same level as the veins. Consequently, the veins are in direct contact with both forms of parenchyma tissue.

It is important to emphasize the presence of stomates on leaves and the extensive intercellular air system. These features, coupled with the flattened shape, make the leaf an extremely effective photosynthetic factory. As if these anatomical features were not

adequate, leaves of many plants also have the ability to position themselves in relation to each other for maximum interception of the sun's rays.

DIVERSITY OF LEAF FORM. In our discussion of root, stem, and leaf—the basic plant organs—we have confined our examples to those most typical of temperate region plants. As you are well aware, however, many house plants are far from this temperate region norm. To illustrate, consider the vast array of cacti and other succulents. In many of these plants, the stems are modified for photosynthesis and storage (including water), and the leaves are modified as slender, nonphotosynthetic structures termed **spines.** In others, such as the spineless Christmas cactus (*Schlumbergera bridgesii*), the flattened branches often resemble leaves (Figure 3.13). In still others, such as the little zebra plant (*Haworthia subfasciata*) and split rock (*Pleiospilos bolusii*), the leaves are modified as the fleshy

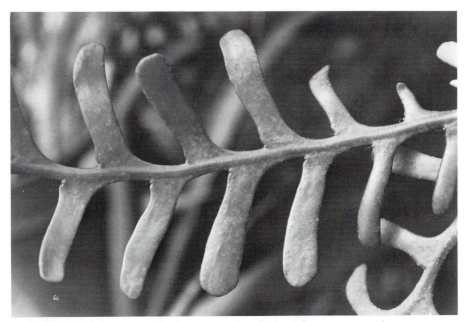

FIGURE 3.13 The "leaves" of St. Anthony's rick-rack plant, *Cryptocereus anthonyanus*, are actually stem tissue.

photosynthetic organs and the stem is reduced to a compressed crown. These examples illustrate some of the characteristic diversity of vascular plants. Although our discussion has, due to space limitations, overlooked much of this diversity, you should now be in a better position to make botanical interpretations of your own.

Leaves arise close to the apex, and their development is closely correlated with that of adjacent stem tissues. The first leaves produced may display a juvenile form, but later, leaves having the characteristics of the adult plant are formed. As stem growth continues, most plants begin to form new kinds of modified leaves along the stem axis, given the proper stimulus. The first of these modified leaves are leaflike in appearance but later-formed members have little or no superficial resemblance to the foliage leaves typical of the plant. These modified leaves and the shortened stem axis on which they occur compose the flower. The flower represents the crowning achievement in vascular

plant development. It is fair to say that the angiosperms owe much of their success to the efficiency with which the process of sexual reproduction is carried out within the flower.

THE PROCESS OF SEXUAL PLANT REPRODUCTION

Flower Structure

The **flower,** in this new sense, can be defined simply as a stem bearing modified leaves. The modified leaf appendages occur in a particular sequence within the flower (Figure 3.14). The **sepals,** collectively called the **calyx,** make up the lowermost whorl. These are typically green and somewhat leaflike. The **petals,** collectively called the **corolla,** constitute the next whorl. These are usually leaflike in form but brightly colored. The calyx and the corolla together comprise the **perianth.**

The perianth parts are important additions to the flower. The brightly colored petals

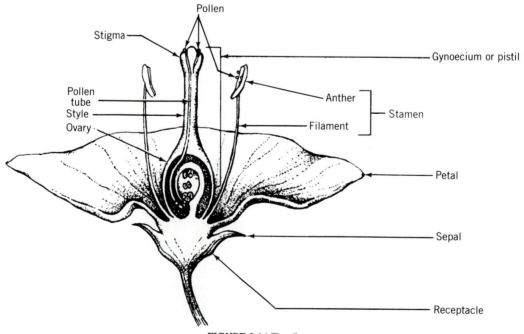

FIGURE 3.14 The flower.

often serve to attract pollinators such as bees to the flower, and once the pollinator has arrived, they may serve as a landing platform on which the pollinator can rest while doing its job. Coincidentally, we humans have made flowers an important part of our lives primarily because of the sensual delights created by perianth parts. In spite of these many virtues of the perianth parts—sepals and petals—they are not, in a strict sense, required for sexual reproduction.

THE SEXUAL FLOWER PARTS. The floral parts directly involved in the sexual process are the stamens and the carpels.

The **stamens** occur just above the petals. Typically, each stamen consists of two distinct parts, a **filament,** or stalk, and a terminal **anther** (Figure 3.15). It is within the anther that the sporangia occur and in which spores are produced. The spores, as you may recall, on germination give rise to miniature gametophyte plants known as pollen grains (Figure 3.4). Each pollen grain has the potential to form two **sperm cells,** or male gametes. The **carpels,** collectively known as the **gynoecium,** constitute the uppermost whorl of the flower. Each carpel, or the fused carpels, consists of three parts (Figure 3.15). The uppermost part, the **stigma,** is the specialized, pollen-receptive area. Connecting the stigma to the ovary below is a more or less elongate, tubular-shaped **style.** The basal **ovary** contains one or more **ovules.** These ovules also contain highly modified sporangia that produce spores. These spores germinate to produce small plantlets or cells termed the **female gametophytes** (Figure 3.4). Each female gametophyte has the potential to produce a single **egg cell,** or female gamete. Upon union of sperm and egg cells, a zygote is formed. Because of their direct involvement in the sexual process, the stamens and carpels are said to be the essential parts of a flower but do not necessarily occur in the same flower.

FLOWERS WITHOUT ALL THE PARTS. Thus far, we have painted a rather simple picture of flower structure, but much variation from the general scheme presented above occurs. For example, although the flower shown in Figure 3.14 contains four kinds of appendages—sepals, petals, stamens, and carpels—many flowers lack one or more of these structures. If a flower contains all four kinds of floral appendages, it is described as being **complete.** If *any* of the four is lacking, the flower is **incomplete.** We said earlier that of the four different flower parts, only two—stamens and carpels—are directly involved in sexual reproduction. If a flower contains both of these essential parts, it is described as **perfect,** whereas if one or the other is missing, it is **imperfect.** It is clear from these descriptions that a number of different floral conditions can occur. Some possible combinations are as follows:

FLORAL PARTS PRESENT	COMPLETE OR INCOMPLETE	PERFECT OR IMPERFECT	
S + P + St. + C	Complete	Perfect	
S + St. + C	Incomplete	Perfect	
S + St.	Incomplete	Imperfect	

Perfect flowers are said to be **bisexual,** whereas imperfect flowers are **unisexual.**

You may recognize by now another set of floral variations. In plant species having unisexual flowers, there exist both staminate and carpellate flowers. In plants such as the

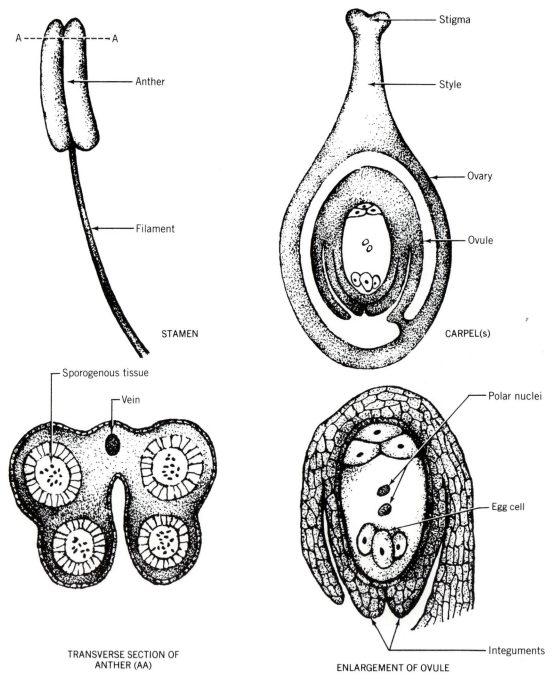

FIGURE 3.15 Diagrammatic representation of the stamen and carpel, the essential parts of a flower. *Source:* Modified from Jensen, W., and Salisbury, F., *Botany: An Ecological Approach*, Wadsworth, 1972.

wax begonia (*Begonia* × *semperflorens-cultorum*), these different kinds of flowers occur on the same plant. When this condition is prevalent, the plant is said to be **monoecious.** In many plants, such as the gold dust tree (*Aucuba japonica variegata*), the essential flower parts occur not only in separate flowers, but also these flowers are on separate plants. When this condition occurs, the plant species is said to be **dioecious.** The terms monoecious and dioecious also are applied to nonflowering plants such as the gymnosperms. The familiar sago palm (*Cycas revoluta*) and other cycads are strictly dioecious. All of the conifers, although they also do not flower, are considered to be either monoecious or dioecious as exemplified by the dioecious Norfolk Island pine (*Araucaria heterophylla*) and the monoecious ponderosa pine (*Pinus ponderosa*).

As an exercise to improve your awareness of flower structure, examine the flowers of a number of house plants to see if they are perfect or imperfect. (Remember, an imperfect flower is always incomplete, but an incomplete flower may well be perfect.) If an imperfect condition is found, then try to determine if the plants are monoecious or dioecious. In making your search to determine flower and plant type, you should recall that the flowers of a plant frequently occur in groups known as **inflorescences.** Sometimes, an entire inflorescence can take on the appearance of a single flower, as, for example, in the crown of thorns (*Euphorbia splendens*). In the flowerlike inflorescences of this plant, the brightly colored "petals" are actually bracts (modified leaves) surrounding a group of rather inconspicuous flowers. In the closely related poinsettia (*Euphorbia pulcherrima*), the large red (or pink, white, etc.) upper leaves surrounding the inflorescence are even more showy.

FUSION OF FLOWER PARTS. The sepals, petals, stamens, and carpels are usually numerous within a flower, but certain members—especially the carpels—may occur singly. It is often hard to distinguish the exact number of flower parts, however, because they may fuse or unite in various ways. Two distinct forms of fusion are recognized. Like parts may unite, as petals to petals in gloxinia, a condition known as **coalescence,** or unlike parts may fuse, as stamens to gynoecium in orchids, a condition known as **adnation.** Often, both coalescence and adnation occur in a single flower. It is not uncommon, for example, to find flowers in which the stamens are adnate to a corolla formed of united petals (e.g., azalea).

SYMMETRY. In flowers of many plants, such as those of burro's tail (*Sedum morganianum*) and other sedums, the sepals and petals are similar in size, shape, and orientation. Flowers displaying this condition are said to be **regular.** In other flowers, such as those of the lipstick plant (*Aeschynanthus lobbianus*), the petals (less often the sepals) are dissimilar in form and orientation. Flowers of this type are described as **irregular.** Regular flowers display **radial symmetry,** also termed **actinomorphy.** Most irregular flowers display **bilateral symmetry** or **zygomorphy.** Flowers of this latter type can be divided into two equal halves along only a single plane. Characteristics of symmetry are widely used in plant classification systems.

The Reproductive Process

Although an understanding of flower morphology is important and interesting, the primary role of the flower is in the sexual process and the production of spores. In brief, you will recall that stamens and carpels of the sporophyte plant contain sporangia. Each stamen has four sporangial regions, while each carpel contains one within each ovule (Figure 3.4). Within these sporangia, spores are produced that on germination give rise to small gametophytes that produce gametes. When gametes fuse, a zygote is formed. This basic cycle can be summarized as follows:

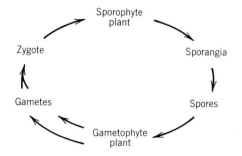

An important point to note here is that gametes *fuse*, or join together, to form zygotes.

THE ROLE OF CHROMOSOMES. In every organism—plant or animal—the hereditary information is carried by the **chromosomes,** occurring in pairs, in the nucleus of the cell. Further, for every organism, the number of chromosomes remains constant (26 in figs, 46 in man, for example). But how can this constancy of numbers persist through countless generations, when cells and their nuclei fuse once in each generation? The union of gametes causes a doubling of the chromosome number in the zygote. A constancy of chromosome number is retained in each generation because in the two divisions giving rise to spores, the chromosome number of each cell is halved. That is, each spore contains only half the number of chromosomes as the parent cell from which it was derived. The specialized division whereby the chromosome number of nuclei is halved

is termed **meiosis.** At fertilization, the fusion of **haploid** (having half the normal chromosomes) nuclei simply reestablishes the chromosome number characteristic of the species. These features can be added to our basic cycle to exemplify lily as shown at the bottom of the page.

In summary, through meiosis, the chromosome number is halved, and through fertilization, it is doubled back to the original number. As a consequence, the robust sporophyte plant has the doubled, or **diploid,** number of chromosomes in its body cells, whereas the diminutive gametophyte has the haploid number. The halving of chromosome number in cells and the subsequent random fusion of gametes creates the genetic variability characteristic of sexually producing populations. Genetic variability, in turn, is the basis for plant adaptation in ever-changing environments.

At this point you may be wondering what, if anything, happens to chromosome numbers during the multitude of divisions that comprise vegetative growth in both sporophyte and gametophyte plants.
The answer is that the normal division of body cells, termed **mitosis,** retains a constancy of chromosome number in that each new daughter cell of a division gets a copy of each chromosome present in the parent cell. This constancy of chromosome numbers requires, of course, that the genetic material in the nucleus be faithfully duplicated, or replicated, prior to each mitotic division, a phenomenon that is well documented.

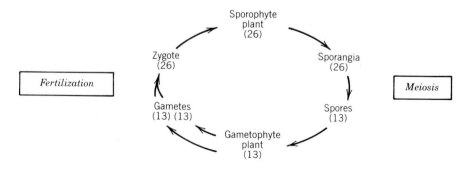

**TRIGGERS INITIATING THE REPRODUC-
TIVE PROCESS.** In our discussion of the
flower, we have spoken only in passing of
the stimuli that induce plants to flower rather
than continue their vegetative growth.
But what are these stimuli, and how are they
perceived by the plant?

Photoperiod. One phenomenon that
puzzled scientists for decades was the nature
of the stimulus that brings about the initial
transformation of an apex producing typical
leaves to one that produces floral appendages. Little progress was made in solving
this puzzle, however, until the early 1920s
when two U.S.D.A. scientists, W. W. Garner
and H. A. Allard, published the results of
their work with tobacco. Most cultivars
of tobacco flower in the summer, but a newly
developed cultivar, 'Maryland Mammoth,
flowered only in the greenhouse during the
late fall. The two scientists tried several
common techniques to induce earlier flowering in the new cultivar, but all failed. Finally, they attempted a number of new approaches, including varying the length of
day, or **photoperiod.** They soon found that,
in the Maryland Mammoth cultivar, short
days were required to trigger flowering.

As you might surmise, the work of Garner
and Allard stimulated many other investiga-
tors to study the flowering response in a
wide range of plants. From these numerous
studies, it soon became apparent that a
great many plants responded, or failed to
respond, to variations in day length. Among
the many plants studied, three distinct patterns emerged as follows:

Short-Day Plants: Initiate flowers only when
the day length is less than a species-
specific critical number of hours.

Long-Day Plants: Initiate flowers only when
the day length exceeds a species-specific
critical number of hours.

Day-Neutral Plants: Initiate flowers independent of day length.

Subsequent research has shown that the

situation with regard to flowering is more
complex than suggested above. For example, it turns out that plants respond to the
length of the dark period rather than the
light period. That is, short day plants require
an uninterrupted dark treatment *longer* than
some critical length in order to flower.
In essence, short-day plants are really long-
night plants. This concept is illustrated in
Figure 3.16 for a short-day plant, such as the
Christmas cactus (*Schlumbergera bridgesii*).
Note that if the night length is interrupted,
even by a light period of less than one
minute in duration, the short-day plant will
not flower. Conversely, long-day plants,
such as *Calceolaria*, require a dark period
shorter than some critical length for flowering. In essence, they are short-night plants.
When a typical long-day plant is grown
under a regime of 10 hours light and 14
hours of darkness, it will not flower. If, however, the dark period is interrupted by a brief

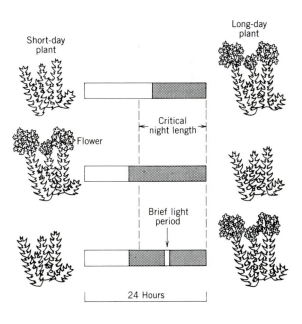

FIGURE 3.16 The length of the dark period in relation to
the flowering of short-day and long-day plants. *Source:*
Calvin and Knutson, *Modern Home Gardening*, New
York: Wiley, 1983, p. 70.

light period, the plant will flower (Figure 3.16) because the continuous dark period has become shorter than the critical length.

Other Flower-Inducing Stimuli. Several other factors play a role in the flowering process. For example, in the Christmas cactus referred to above, temperature variations can influence or override the photoperiodic response. To illustrate, the short-day photoperiod that normally induces flowering is largely ineffective if night temperatures are maintained above 80°F. Conversely, the plant will flower, regardless of photoperiod, if provided with cool temperatures at night. In other words, although the Christmas cactus is a short-day plant, it is not obligatorily so. To complicate matters even more, the plant will reportedly form more flower buds if under moderate water stress during the fall period when flower buds are being formed. Great care must be taken when using this technique to enhance flower production, however, because if the water stress is too

great, the plant may not even be alive on Christmas day! Most day-neutral plants are insensitive to day length—as their designation implies—and appear to flower only when a certain physiological maturity has been reached. Finally, many plants that have specific day length requirements for flowering tend to lose these as they become older and larger.

Reception of the Flower-Inducing Stimulus. What part of the plant actually perceives the flowering stimulus? A logical choice would seem to be the shoot apex as this is where the flowers will develop. As it turns out, however, it is the leaves, not the apex, that are the receptors of the stimulus to flower. This has been shown experimentally and is illustrated diagrammatically in Figure 3.17. As shown, a short-day plant, when subjected to long days, remains vegetative, whereas under short days (and long nights), it flowers. Alternately, a short-day plant growing under a long-day regime can have

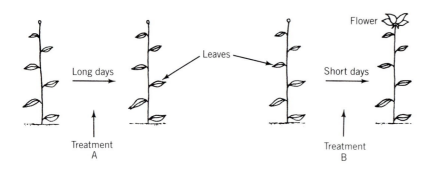

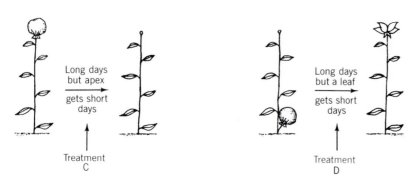

FIGURE 3.17 Leaf perception of the photoperiod by a short-day plant.

its apical region subjected to short days by enclosure in a light-proof bag. When this treatment is given, the plant remains vegetative. If, however, even a single leaf is subject to short-day treatment, while the plant as a whole is growing under long days, it will flower. Thus, it must be concluded that the leaves are the receptors of the stimulus to flower. Furthermore, the stimulus, once received, must be transmitted to the site of flower formation—the apical meristems.

Transmitting the Stimulus. It would seem logical that the message to form flowers is transmitted from the leaves to buds by some sort of chemical messenger. Indeed, there are in plants a group of chemical substances that, in low concentrations, regulate physiological processes. These chemical substances, known as **growth regulators** or **hormones,** generally move within the plant from a site of production to a site of action. The apparent behavior of the flowering stimulus fits the general pattern of hormonal action in plants. As a matter of fact, the substance that promotes flowering, presumably a plant hormone, has been given a name commensurate with its action—**florigen.** Unfortunately, florigen remains only a name; it has never been isolated. There is, however, evidence that florigen exists. We saw earlier (Figure 3.17) that if a short-day plant is grown under long days with only one leaf subjected to a short photoperiod, the plant will flower. Later experiments have shown that flowering will not take place if the leaf is removed immediately after the short-day treatment; it must be left on the plant for a few hours. It has also been shown that the hypothetical hormone can cross a graft union between two plants. In one experiment, a closely related long-day plant and short-day plant were joined together by grafting. Under these conditions, the short-day plant will induce flowering in the long-day plant when the graft partners are subjected to short days. The reverse also holds true. Moreover, a short- or long-day plant induced to flower can transmit the stimulus to a day-neutral plant when the two are grafted. It seems that florigen, if it exists, is the same in all three flowering groups.

OTHER IMPORTANT LIFE PROCESSES

Perception of the flowering stimulus by the leaves, its transmittal through the plant, and its action in changing drastically the kinds of lateral appendages produced at shoot apices are just three of many important physiological processes occurring in plants. Although it is beyond the scope or space limitations of this text to discuss all of these many processes, it is important that we look briefly at those that have a major bearing on our success as indoor gardeners.

Photosynthesis and Respiration

PHOTOSYNTHESIS. Earlier in the chapter, we described photosynthesis as the process whereby plants make themselves out of water, carbon dioxide, and minerals in the presence of light. It should be added that in the photosynthetic process **oxygen**—the atmospheric gas required by all higher forms of animal life (including man)—is produced as a by-product. The essentials of the photosynthetic process are summarized in Figure 3.18. For convenience, the process is often described in chemical terms as follows:

$$6CO_2 + 6H_2O \underset{\text{Chlorophyll}}{\overset{\text{Light}}{\rightarrow}} C_6H_{12}O_6 + 6O_2$$

(Carbon Dioxide + Water) →
(Carbohydrates + Oxygen)

Note from the illustration that the source of carbon dioxide (CO_2) is the atmosphere and that water and minerals are provided by the soil solution. One *product* of photosynthesis, oxygen (O_2), is released into the atmosphere.

It is virtually impossible to overemphasize the importance of photosynthesis, because it is this process that sustains all other forms of life. Life as we know it could not exist without

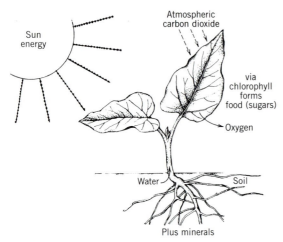

Atmospheric
carbon dioxide

Sun
energy

via
chlorophyll
forms
food (sugars)

Oxygen

Water

Soil

Plus minerals

FIGURE 3.18 The essentials of photosynthesis. *Source:* Graf, A., *Exotic Plant Manual*, East Rutherford, N.J.: Roehrs Company, 1974, p. 12.

green plants. Through photosynthesis, plants convert raw materials into **foods**—carbohydrates and other essential molecules (proteins and fats)—that they utilize for their own growth. Fortunately for us, they normally manufacture more food than they can consume in maintenance and growth. This surplus food is stored in roots, tubers, seeds, fruits, and other plant parts. These storage sources can be tapped directly by man and other animals. We also tap plant

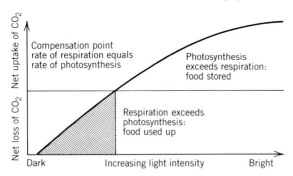

Net uptake of CO_2

Net loss of CO_2

Compensation point
rate of respiration equals
rate of photosynthesis

Photosynthesis
exceeds respiration:
food stored

Respiration exceeds
photosynthesis:
food used up

Dark

Increasing light intensity

Bright

FIGURE 3.19 The relationship between photosynthesis and respiration in the daily cycle of a plant. *Source:* Rayle, D., and Wedberg, L., *Botany: A Human Concern*, New York: Saunders College/Holt, Rinehart & Winston, 1980. Reprinted by permission of CBS College Publishing.

sources indirectly as, for example, when we eat beef, pork, or chicken—animals that lived and grew at the expense of plants.

Respiration

We have seen that photosynthesis is an energy-storing process that takes place in light. Another process, one that occurs around the clock in all living cells—plant and animal—is respiration. **Respiration** is an energy-releasing process that can be summarized in chemical terms as follows:

$$C_6H_{12}O_6 + 6O_2 \rightarrow 6CO_2 + 6H_2O + Energy$$
$$(Carbohydrates + Oxygen) \rightarrow$$
$$(Carbon\ Dioxide + Water + Energy)$$

Note that the basic reaction for respiration is just the reverse of that given earlier for photosynthesis. Note also that O_2 is required in respiration. The dependency of animals on O_2 mentioned earlier is directly related to its use in the respiratory process.

THE COMPENSATION POINT. Since photosynthesis is an energy-storing process and respiration is an energy-releasing process, plants must produce more in photosynthesis during the daylight hours than is broken down in respiration around the clock if they are to increase in size (grow). This close relationship between the energy-producing and energy-yielding processes is shown in Figure 3.19. In darkness, plants respire with a net consumption of O_2 and a net evolution of CO_2. As the light of the early morning increases, respiration continues and photosynthesis begins, consuming the CO_2 produced in respiration. Soon, a point is reached where the amount of CO_2 consumed in photosynthesis just equals that liberated in respiration. At this point, known as the **compensation point,** the rate of photosynthesis exactly equals the rate of respiration. As light intensity increases still further, the rate of photosynthesis increases even more, resulting in a net uptake of CO_2 and, of course, a net production of O_2.

Thus, during the daytime hours when there is a net uptake of CO_2, a plant adds "credits" to its energy account, whereas below the compensation point, "debits" occur.

FACTORS INFLUENCING PHOTOSYNTHETIC AND RESPIRATORY RATES.

For luxuriant plant growth, the indoor gardener must strive to maximize energy credits while minimizing debits. To do this effectively, we need to understand the factors influencing the rates of the two vital metabolic processes.

LIGHT AND TEMPERATURE.

We have said that light—natural or artificial—is required for photosynthesis. At least one reaction in the photosynthetic process is light driven. A characteristic of such reactions is that they proceed in light *independently* of temperature. Dr. Benny Tjia, a horticulturist at the University of Florida, has provided an analogy that helps us to understand light reactions. His analogy, which relates to exposing film in a camera, states that "regardless of where a picture is taken, in South Florida or the North Pole, as long as light intensity is equal, the same exposure is used." This is so because light reactions are not temperature dependent. Conversely, many additional reactions in the photosynthetic process have been shown to proceed in the absence of light. These dark reactions, in contrast to the light reactions, are driven by enzymes that are quite sensitive to temperature. The entire series of reactions comprising respiration can, obviously, proceed in the dark also. An important characteristic of these temperature-dependent dark reactions is that over the range of temperatures at which biological reactions occur, their rate is directly proportional to the temperature. In general, for each 10°C (18°F) rise in temperature, the reaction rate approximately doubles.

What does all of this mean to the indoor gardener? Since both photosynthesis and respiration involve temperature-dependent

reactions, the rate at which these processes occur is somewhat under our control. Examples will illustrate the practical value of this. A plant placed on a windowsill where the light intensity is high but the temperature low, say 50°F, could carry out the light reactions of photosynthesis, but the overall rate of the process would be low because the dark reactions of photosynthesis are temperature dependent. At this same low temperature, respiration rates would be low also. Or, consider a plant on a southern windowsill exposed to high light intensity and comfortably high temperatures. Under these conditions, photosynthesis could proceed unabated. If the same high temperature carried over to the night, however, much of the food manufactured during the daylight hours would be utilized in respiration. Lowering of respiration rates is a major reason for providing indoor plants with lower night temperatures.

GAS EXCHANGE AND WATER RELATIONS.

The rate of photosynthesis depends not only on light intensity and temperature, but also on other factors including CO_2 supply, water availability, and nutrient status of the plant. The CO_2 necessary for photosynthesis diffuses into the leaves from the external atmosphere mainly through the stomates (Figures 3.9 and 3.12). The amount of CO_2 in the air is quite low (0.03% or 300 parts per million) and can become limiting under certain conditions.

Consider a very large plant in a home. If the plant happens to be in a quiet corner of the house, the windows are tightly closed, and people are not moving about, a pool of stagnant, CO_2-depleted air can build up around the plant, limiting photosynthesis. Many commercial growers, because greenhouses are much tighter environments than homes, install CO_2 generators in their greenhouses, increasing CO_2 levels by as much as five times. Under these conditions, photosynthetic rates will increase, provided the process is not limited by some other factor. On the other hand, if our windowsill plant is too near the window pane on a sunny day, it may **wilt** (become flaccid, or limp, due to abnormal loss of water from cells) because temperatures near the glass can get quite high. As the plant wilts, the stomatal pores become greatly constricted or closed. In this condition, the exchange of gases and the water milieu needed for photosynthesis are in short supply. As a result, the process of converting light energy into chemical energy slows or stops altogether.

NUTRIENTS AND PHOTOSYNTHESIS. About 16 nutrient elements are required by the plant for normal growth, as discussed in Chapter Seven. A majority of these are provided by the medium in which the plant grows. If any of these nutrients are in short supply, the rate of photosynthesis will be limited, even if all of the other requirements are present in excess. Consider the element magnesium, for example. Magnesium is needed by plants in only small amounts, yet its presence is absolutely essential because it is a vital part of the chlorophyll molecule. When magnesium is limiting, chlorophyll synthesis is lessened, and, of course, photosynthesis is reduced.

A CLOSER LOOK AT CHLOROPHYLL.
Granted that the light-absorbing pigment chlorophyll is required for photosynthesis, you might ask what is the relationship of chlorophyll to the plant as a whole. Most above-ground parts contain chlorophyll as manifested by their green color. The highest concentrations of this molecule normally occur in the leaves. But where? Figure 3.20 shows one leaf mesophyll cell and parts of several associated cells. Within the whole cell are several smaller, somewhat dense bodies known as plastids, or more specifically as **chloroplasts.** Each chloroplast contains an elaborate membrane network consisting of membrane stacks known as **grana** and

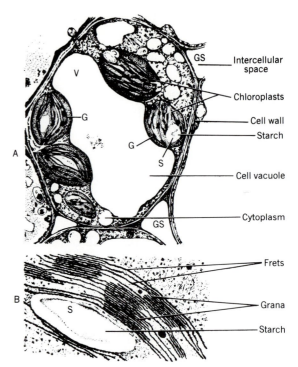

FIGURE 3.20 Leaf mesophyll cell with chloroplasts. *Source:* Redrawn from Rayle, D., and Wedberg, L., *Botany: A Human Concern,* New York: Saunders College/Holt, Rinehart and Winston, 1980, p. 48.

interconnecting membranes known as **frets.** It is within these membrane systems that the chlorophyll and other molecules required for photosynthesis are located. It is important to note that abundant intercellular space surrounds the mesophyll cells (Figures 3.12 and 3.20), a necessity for the efficient exchange of gases essential to photosynthesis. Note also that within each chloroplast are starch grains. **Starch** is a storage form of fixed carbon. At night, much of this storage carbohydrate is converted to sugar and moved to other parts of the plant. A concept as to how this sugar is moved will be discussed later in this section.

Chloroplasts are remarkable cellular structures whose ability to carry out photosynthesis is enhanced by several factors. First, they are self-perpetuating bodies containing their own genetic material and capable of division. This is a great asset because they are able to maintain or increase their numbers within cells. Second, chloroplasts are capable of motility. They are in a constant state of movement within cells. This motion enhances the ability of chloroplasts to acquire needed raw materials from their environment. Third, chloroplasts (like leaves) are able to position themselves with respect to light. This positioning allows the chloroplast to intercept weak light more effectively or reduce its exposure when the light is too intense. This remarkable ability of chloroplasts to regulate light absorption by arranging themselves in particular positions can be carried one step further. As light intensity increases, the efficiency of the chloroplast in using the light energy gradually decreases. At some point, photosynthetic rates may actually decrease with increased light intensity because of the decreased efficiency of light absorption. To the plant, these adjustments provide a mechanism for surviving in hostile environments. High light intensity adjustments normally are not a major concern of the indoor gardener because of the low light intensities of the home environment. Nevertheless, foliage plants having relatively low light intensity requirements, such as the cast-iron plant (*Aspidistra elatior*) or holly fern (*Cyrtomium falcatum*), can easily receive too intense light, resulting in a poor-quality plant.

Transport of Materials in Plants

At least brief mention should be made of the mechanisms of movement of (1) water and dissolved minerals and (2) food materials within the plant.

MOVEMENT OF WATER AND MINERALS.

An abundant supply of water and minerals is essential to normal plant functions. In the usual course of events, water and minerals are taken up from the soil solution by the roots and transported via the xylem (or **wood**) tissue to aerial parts of the plant. What drives this process?

Root Pressure. In certain cases, when the soil is saturated with water and atmospheric humidity is high, water and minerals may actually be pushed into aerial parts by pressures originating in the roots. You have probably observed this phenomenon because of plant adaptations that allow excess water to be expelled from leaves. In leaves, special openings termed **hydathodes** are found at tips and margins. When conditions favorable for root pressure occur, dewlike droplets of water exude through these openings. In essence, this **water of guttation** is being forced out of the leaves by the pressure originating in the roots.

Water of guttation can be distinguished from dew by its regular distribution and the larger size of the droplets. Indoors, of course, dew is not a factor, but the plant grower can encounter problems related to water of guttation.

Guttation fluid carries with it mineral salts. Eventually, the water droplets evaporate, but the mineral salts remain. These salts can build up to toxic levels, killing portions of the leaf. **Necrosis** (death) near leaf margins or tips, areas where guttation fluid accumulates, is a manifestation of this phenomenon. It can only be avoided by periodic cleaning of the susceptible areas.

Cohesion. A majority of the time water is not pushed upward by root-originating pressures, but rather pulled upward by shoot-originating tensions. A mechanical apparatus will aid our understanding (Figure 3.21). First, a porous clay pot is filled with water and attached to the end of a long glass tube also filled with water. The water-filled tube is then placed with its lower end below the surface of a volume of water. As water evaporates from the pores in the pot, it is replaced by water pulled up from below in a continuous column through the narrow glass

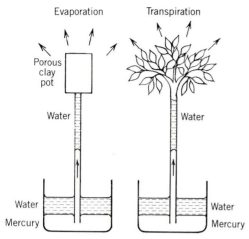

Evaporation   Transpiration

Porous
clay
pot

Water   Water

Water   Water
Mercury   Mercury

FIGURE 3.21 A simple physical apparatus that demonstrates the upward pull of water created by evaporation from the surface of a porous clay pot. A similar mechanism, driven by transpiration operates in plants. *Source:* Raven, P., Evert, R., and Curtis, H., *Biology of Plants,* 3rd ed., New York: Worth Publishers, 1981, p. 564.

tube. In other words, the evaporation of water creates the driving force for pulling water upward. The ability of water molecules to stick together, termed **cohesion,** allows pull over long distances.

Similarly, it has been demonstrated that the loss of water from plant surfaces, termed **transpiration,** creates a negative pressure in the piping (xylem) of the plant. Furthermore, the tensions created have been shown to be great enough to lift water to the tops of even the tallest trees. Although the transpirational loss of water is essential to the operation of the system just described, it also means that much of the water taken up by plants is merely transpired into the atmosphere. As a matter of fact, it has been shown repeatedly that plants transpire several hundred units of water for each unit of dry matter produced. This high loss is related to the presence of natural openings in the leaf—stomates—essential to effective exchange of gases. Transpiration is sometimes called the "necessary evil" of the plant kingdom, but even

evils have their advantages. For one, transpirational water losses create the negative pressures needed for water uptake.

Then also, the transpired water vapor around the leaves acts as a coolant on leaf surfaces during the heat of the day.

FOOD MOVEMENT. The carbohydrates manufactured in photosynthesis are moved throughout the plant in the phloem tissue, specifically in the sieve elements. While this movement is visualized to be predominantly downward to roots and storage organs, elaborated foods (often termed **assimilates** by plant physiologists) move upward to young leaves that are not yet exporting assimilates. That food material moves downward in the phloem can be demonstrated by removing a ring of bark completely around a stem, a treatment known as **ringing.** (The **bark** is the tissue outside the xylem or wood of a stem and contains the phloem.) When a tree is ringed, the portion below the ring no longer receives nourishment, and the tissue just above the ring becomes swollen, presumably due to the accumulation of assimilates. A modification of this procedure is used by the indoor gardener when he or she practices certain forms of asexual propagation (Chapter Four). In making leaf cuttings, for example, it is a common practice to cut or sever the larger veins. These cuts stop the downward movement of assimilates at the cut and result in the accumulation of food materials and growth hormones, substances necessary for the formation of a new plant.

What is the mechanism of transport of assimilates in the phloem tissue? While this question has not been completely answered, great strides have been made in this century toward understanding phloem movement. Perhaps, we should list the "knowns" first. These include the following: (1) assimilate, mainly sucrose, moves in sieve elements; (2) the rate of movement can approach 100 centimeters (a little over a yard) per hour; (3)

the major direction of flow is from sites of manufacture, known as **sources,** to sites of utilization, termed **sinks.** The most widely accepted theory used to explain this movement is the **pressure-flow** mechanism illustrated in Figure 3.22. According to this concept, the sugars manufactured in the leaf enter sieve tubes in quantity. This causes water, which always moves toward sites of relatively lower concentration, to enter the sieve tube, increasing turgor pressure. At the other end of the line, at sinks, sugar is removed from sieve tubes to be utilized in respiration or stored as starch. As a result, water leaves the sieve tubes and turgor pressure falls. As a result of the pressure differential at the two ends of the line (source and sink), the sugar solution flows through the sieve tube toward the sink. In Figure 3.22, a root is designated as sink, but developing leaves, shoots, and fruits can also be sinks.

MOVEMENT OF OTHER MATERIALS. Many additional materials, including the growth hormones mentioned earlier, move throughout the plant. Do these substances move within the xylem or phloem? If not, what is known about their movement? As it turns out, the first growth hormone discovered, auxin, appears to move mainly outside of the vascular tissues. Furthermore, its movement shows rather unusual features. In essence, auxin is known to move from the tips of shoots (sites of production) toward the base of the plant (sites of use). Experimentally a shoot tip can be removed and placed on an agar (a gelatinlike substance) block (Figure 3.23). When this is done, auxin will flow into the agar. If the agar block with auxin is now placed on a properly oriented stem segment, the agar will flow through the segment to the block below. If, however, the agar block is placed on an inverted stem segment, the auxin will not move through. In other words, the substance moves from the apex to the base, but not the reverse. This polarity of

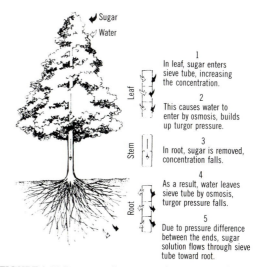

FIGURE 3.22 Diagram illustrating the pressure-flow mechanism for transport of sugar in the phloem. Source: Ray, P., *The Living Plant*, New York: Holt, Rinehart, and Winston, 1972, p. 76.

movement is just one manifestation of complex biological organization.

Currently, auxin is believed to move in the ground tissues of the stem rather than the xylem and phloem. The transport process is thought to involve an interaction between auxin and the limiting membranes of plant cells. Although the mechanism of auxin movement remains somewhat obscure, much is known about the role of auxin in the plant.

The Importance of Auxin to Plants

Long ago, the eminent biologist, Charles Darwin, and his son, Francis, studied the nature of movement in plants. In an early experiment, this father and son team discovered that the natural curvature of seedlings toward light could be prevented if the tip of a seedling was covered with a lightproof collar. If the collar was placed below the tip, the characteristic curvature took place. Correctly, the two Darwins concluded that, in response to light, an "influence" that causes bending is transmitted from the seedling tip to the area below, where bending normally

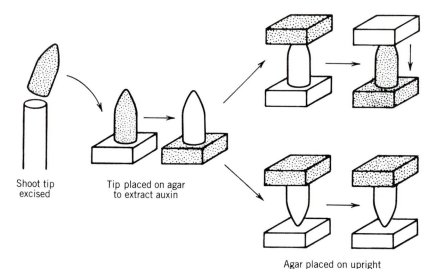

Shoot tip excised

Tip placed on agar to extract auxin

Agar placed on upright (above) and inverted (below) stem segments to show polarity of movement

FIGURE 3.23 Illustrations to show the nature of auxin movement. (Stippled areas indicate the presence of auxin.)

occurs. Many years passed before the nature of Darwin's stimulus was established. In the early 1920s, an ingenious Dutch botanist, Frits Went, discovered that if one placed seedling tips on agar blocks, a substance would move into the block that could promote bending in decapitated seedlings. Went called the substance **auxin.** Later, the substance was determined to be a chemical named indoleacetic acid.

Since the pioneering work of the Darwins and Went, much work has been done with auxin. It has been shown, for example, that auxin can induce a variety of responses in plants, including the following:

1. Promote curvature of stem and root.
2. Cause shoots to elongate.
3. Stimulate or inhibit root growth.
4. Influence leaf abscission (drop).
5. Promote the growth of fruits.
6. Influence the differentiation of vascular tissues.
7. Stimulate cambial activity in woody plants.
8. Inhibit the growth of lateral buds.

It should be stressed that in addition to auxin, a variety of additional plant hormones are now known, including the gibberellins, cytokinins, abscissic acid, and ethylene.

It should also be stressed that the action of a hormone can be stimulatory or inhibitory and that in the living plant, these substances act not alone, but in concert with one another. Finally, it should be added that the plant hormones, particularly auxin, have found widespread use by both commercial growers and home gardeners.

COMMERCIAL ROOT-PROMOTING SUBSTANCES. Appearing on garden center shelves today are various brands of substances that are employed for their ability to promote rooting of cuttings. The major ingredient of these compounds is auxin, either extracted from plants or produced synthetically. These products vary in their composition, but are made up principally of one or more of three auxins: (1) IAA (indole-3-acetic acid), identified in 1934 as a naturally occurring auxin that is produced in the terminal bud and small developing leaves of the stem and moves down the stem in the direction of the roots; (2) IBA (indole-butyric acid); and (3) NAA (naphthaleneacetic acid). These latter two auxins were found around 1935 and are synthetic materials that are, ironically, even more effective at root initiation than the naturally occurring IAA. We now know that the presence of auxin, either natural or synthetic, is required for the cell division that initiates adventitious roots on stems.

Auxins, like other growth hormones, operate in very low concentrations. In fact, an excessive concentration may inhibit root formation or damage the tissue to which it is applied. Several of the available products come in many concentrations for cuttings with varying degrees of rooting difficulty. The highest concentration, for difficult-to-root woody plants, contains less than 1 percent active ingredient and over 99 percent of inert matter such as talc. The weakest concentration, recommended for most indoor plant cuttings, contains about one-tenth of 1 percent (0.1 percent) active ingredient. Using a higher concentration than the label specifies for indoor plants will not speed rooting, but will generally damage the cutting tissue and delay or prohibit rooting. The principles and techniques used to make cuttings and other vegetative propagules are the subject of Chapter Four.

FOR FURTHER READING

Esau, K. *Anatomy of Seed Plants.* New York: Wiley, 1977.

Galston, A., P. Davies, and R. Satter. *The Life of the Green Plant.* Englewood Cliffs, N.J.: Prentice-Hall, 1980.

Graf, A. *Exotic Plant Manual.* East Rutherford, N.J.: Roehrs Company, 1974.

Nicolaisen, A. *The Pocket Encyclopedia of Indoor Plants.* New York: Macmillan, 1970.

Raven, P., R. Evert, and H. Curtis. *Biology of Plants.* 3rd ed. New York: Worth Publishers, 1981.

Ray, P. *The Living Plant.* New York: Holt, Rinehart, and Winston, 1972.

Rayle, D., and L. Wedberg. *Botany: A Human Concern.* New York: Saunders College, Holt, Rinehart and Winston, 1980.

Salisbury, F., and C. Ross. *Plant Physiology.* Wadsworth, 1978.

Tjia, B. "Photosynthesis and Respiration." Proceedings of the 1977 National Tropical Foliage Short Course, Florida Foliage Association, 1977.

Weier, T., C. Stocking, M. Barbour, and T. Rost. *Botany an Introduction to Plant Biology.* New York: Wiley, 1982.

Wolfe, S. *Biology of the Cell.* Wadsworth, 1981.

chapter four
plant
propagation

Plant propagation, the practice of reproducing plants by seeds, spores, or plant parts, is for many people the most fascinating aspect of indoor gardening. Begun in ancient times as a means of more easily acquiring food, propagation has progressed through the centuries into a specialized and rapidly growing science. Developments such as the greenhouse, the use of plant hormones to stimulate rooting, and the intermittent mist system have opened the way to the propagation of more and more plants that previously could not be reproduced asexually (Figure 4.1). These developments and our increased knowledge of plant nutrition and pathology have enabled scientists to find methods of propagation that seemed incomprehensible just a few decades ago. For example, it is now possible to produce as many as 1,000,000 orchid plants in one year from a block of cells just 1 millimeter across! Moreover, each little orchid has the same **genotype** (exact genetic constitution) and **phenotype** (physical characteristics) as the parent plant. The same process is also being used for the rapid production of some foliage plants.

Fortunately, most indoor plants can be started by methods much less complicated and more accessible to the indoor gardener. But to be successful at propagation and to appreciate the underlying principles, one should have some exposure to several basic principles. First, the information presented in Chapter Three regarding basic elements of plant structure and function is imperative. It helps us to know how to remove bromeliad offsets properly from the parent plant and why we worry about getting the proper end up when placing cuttings in the propagation medium. Second, a familiarity with the diverse propagation techniques and skills demands not only study, but also practice for mastery. With some techniques such as air layering, irreparable damage to the new plant-to-be can occur with a single slip of the knife. And third, one must understand the environmental requirements of a seed or cutting such as temperature or water, and how such things as the propagation medium can affect these. The point here is that anyone can stick a sprig into a glass of water, but true enjoyment and the ability to handle unexpected problems do not develop fully until one understands the basic principles of propagation.

As seen in Chapter Three, plants may be reproduced by sexual means, that is involving the union of gametes, or by asexual means when a union of gametes does not occur. This division based on the two broad types of reproductive cycles is the most convenient manner in which to discuss plant propagation.

FIGURE 4.1 The use of intermittent mist systems in commercial operations has promoted faster rooting, less wilting, and better environmental control of propagation beds.

SEXUAL PROPAGATION

The Advantages of Seed Propagation

Stated simply, sexual propagation entails reproducing plants by means of seeds or spores, a method that has both advantages and disadvantages in comparison to asexual techniques. The first advantage is that many seeds, namely, those that are capable of enduring a winter or dry season of unfavorable germination condition, can be kept for long periods prior to germination. Consequently, such seeds can tolerate transportation and storage that stem cuttings, for example, cannot. Many foliage plant seeds, however, have a very short life. Second, seeds are a combination of genetic material from both parents; thus, they can produce variable offspring that may exhibit enhanced growth characteristics, known as hybrid vigor. This is desirable for the development of

plants with new or more desirable traits, but undesirable when uniformity is preferred. It is possible, however, to produce uniform offspring from seeds by self-pollinating lines, groups of plants that maintain a high degree of genetic uniformity from generation to generation. Third, seeds are usually available. That is, by looking in gardening publications, one can locate seed companies that retail indoor plant seeds, whereas finding the live plant or a cutting from it may be difficult locally. And finally, seeds are inexpensive and allow the production of large numbers of plants more easily and in less space than asexual methods.

But sexual propagation has its disadvantages. Seeds represent the slower method of obtaining mature plants, so they are not as practical as cuttings when only a few plants are needed and live sources of cutting material are available. They also must be raised with more care due to their susceptibility to damage from disease agents and environmental factors. And finally, when propagating from local sources of plants, seeds are only present for a short period each year. The great majority of indoor plant production, both commercially and at home, is performed by asexual methods (Figure 4.2).

The first step in successful seed germination is to purchase the seeds from a reputable source. The names and addresses of mail-order seed companies abound in garden periodicals, and even companies specializing in vegetables and flowering outdoor plants frequently offer indoor plant seeds as well. Ordering by mail is advantageous in that a wide selection of species is available, including obscure plants that only collectors would care to purchase. An added benefit is that most mail-order establishments provide catalogs that are informative, well illustrated, and require no more effort to place an order than returning a postcard. In urban areas where garden centers are conveniently located, the advantage may swing to local buying. The shipping costs, delay, and slow rectification of problems associated with mail-ordering can be avoided with this method. Although there are advantages to both means of acquiring seeds, either one will work quite well so long as the buyer selects reputable firms.

Seed Production

As described in Chapter Three, sexual propagation begins with the induction of flowering, a physiological readying of the plant for the physical development of the flowers. Once the flower is produced, **pollination** (the transition of pollen to the surface of the stigma) must occur for further sexual development to take place. On pollination, the pollen grain germinates, producing a **pollen tube** that grows down through the style of the pistil and finally to the ovule, one or more of which are contained in the ovary (Figure

FIGURE 4.2 The indoor plant industry relies heavily on dependable asexual propagation methods for much of its production.

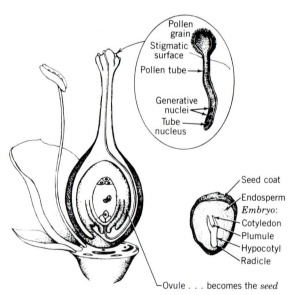

FIGURE 4.3 Diagram showing the structure and growth pattern of the pollen tube to the ovule (left) and the typical components of a seed (right). *Source:* Hartmann/Kester, *Plant Propagation*: Principles and Practices, © 1983, Reprinted by permission of Prentice-Hall, Inc., Englewood Cliffs, New Jersey.

4.3). There is one **generative nucleus** contained in the pollen tube that divides to yield two male gametes. One of these unites with the polar nuclei of the ovule (Figure 3.15, ovary structure) to form the **primary endosperm nucleus,** the eventual food storage organ of the seed, and the other male gamete unites with the egg to form the **zygote,** the diploid cell that develops into the embryo of the seed. The seed coat is formed from the **integuments** (Figure 3.15, ovary structure) or outer walls of the ovule; it is not the direct result of **fertilization** (the fusion of two gametes to form a zygote). Often occurring in multiples and in conjunction with other tissues, the ovary expands into the fruit structure.

When the seed separates from the parent plant, its rate of metabolism is very slow and there is essentially no growth activity. The seed coat protects the inner parts of the seed by its hardness, impermeability to water, and/or its production of chemical germination inhibitors. If internal factors prevent germination, the seed is said to be **dormant.** On the other hand, if the seed were not internally inhibited and would germinate on exposure to favorable environmental conditions, it is **quiescent.**

The Three Requirements for Germination

VIABILITY. The most basic requirement for germination is that the embryo must be alive and capable of developing into a mature plant, that is, it must be **viable.** Tropical seeds that are exposed to intolerably cold temperatures or which have been allowed to dry out before planting may contain dead embryos within relatively healthy-looking seed coats. Even when the seeds have survived storage or adverse conditions, the **vitality** or growth vigor may be reduced, resulting in stunted seedlings on germination. Many indoor species produce seeds that are quick to dry out; hence, these should be planted relatively soon after removal from

the plant. Seeds of this type usually do not stand storage well unless they are kept cool and moist, or warm and moist with some seeds. To ensure both viability and vitality, seeds should be obtained from reputable seedsmen who store and handle seeds by professional standards.

QUIESCENCE. In addition to viability and vitality, the seed must also be free of physical or chemical barriers to germination. Some plant seeds, such as the asparagus ferns, should be **scarified.** In other words, their hard or impervious seed coats must be altered by cracking, scraping, or soaking to allow water to enter the interior portions of the seed. Small numbers of seeds can be filed, sandpapered, or cracked with a knife or hammer; large-scale scarification utilizes mechanical scarifiers. The seeds of many temperate plants, particularly those produced in the fall, remain dormant until the chilling temperatures of the winter stimulate physiological changes that allow germination. This can be done artificially by a process known as **stratification** wherein the seeds are kept moist and exposed to temperatures just above freezing. Since tropical plants do not experience winters as such, they generally do not require stratification. Most tropical plant seeds fall into two categories: (1) those that must be planted shortly after removal from the parent plant and (2) those that are able to be stored for long periods but that germinate on exposure to favorable environmental conditions. Consequently, the best rule of thumb is to plant tropical seeds as soon as they are mature if specific information on storage characteristics is not known.

ENVIRONMENT. The third general requirement for germination to occur successfully is a set of several rather exacting environmental conditions (Figure 4.4). The initial step in germination is the imbibition of **water** into the dry seed. This hydrates the inner tissues, causing them to swell and help break the

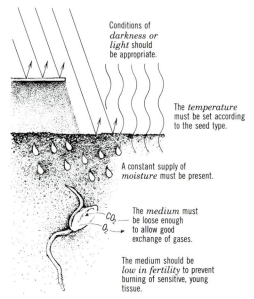

Conditions of *darkness* or *light* should be appropriate.

The *temperature* must be set according to the seed type.

A constant supply of *moisture* must be present.

CO_2

O_2

The *medium* must be loose enough to allow good exchange of gases.

The medium should be *low in fertility* to prevent burning of sensitive, young tissue.

FIGURE 4.4 The five critical environmental aspects of seed germination.

seed coat. More important, hydration activates the various enzymes and substances that control the metabolism of the cells. Water, then, is essential for the life processes to occur and its supply must not be interrupted during germination or death of the seedling will occur.

After imbibition, the resulting enzymatic activity digests the food stored in the endosperm and cotyledons. These digested compounds are transported to the growing points of the embryo, stimulating and supporting cell division and growth. This growth process is accompanied by a steady increase in respiration, creating a constant increase in the demand for oxygen. Due to this need for oxygen and the necessity for removal of carbon dioxide and other by-products of respiration, germinating seeds require a second major environmental condition, **aeration.** This is accomplished by providing a loose, well-drained propagation medium.

The third aspect of the environmental requirement is **low fertility of the propagation**

medium. As described above, the seed provides most of the nutritional needs of the developing embryo and young seedling. A small amount of external fertilization is necessary for proper growth of the seedling after germination occurs, but too much fertility can be detrimental to the seedling's development by burning the new and sensitive tissues of the growing points. Stunting or death of the seedling may result.

The metabolic process of the germinating seed is **temperature** *dependent.* If temperatures are too cold or hot, these processes slow down or stop, thus injuring or killing the plant tissue. Of course, this results in a stunted or dead seedling. Most seeds have a range of temperatures in which germination occurs. The **optimum temperature,** usually close to the upper temperature limit, produces the fastest germination and seedling growth. Deviations in temperature from the optimum result in slower germination until finally, the upper or lower limit is reached and germination will not occur. Although not necessary for adequate germination in most cases, many seeds also respond favorably to diurnal, or day–night, variations in temperature, the most favorable being a difference of about 18°F (10°C). A temperature rule of thumb is difficult to formulate since seeds are so variable in their temperature needs, but most tropical plants germinate best between 80 and 90°F (26.5 and 35°C). After germination occurs, the temperature should be reduced to a 65 to 75°F range (18 to 24°C) to harden off the seedlings for transplanting and reduce the chances of disease problems.

The fifth and final critical environmental condition necessary for germination is the presence or absence of **light.** For germination to occur, light is the least important of the factors listed here for seeds of foliage plants. Almost all will germinate in a wide range of light conditions if the other conditions are favorable. Light sensitivity and inhibition are means by which some plants regulate the time and place of their proliferation. Light-sensitive seeds that require light for germination are usually small and cannot emerge from a great depth in the soil. Hence, they lie dormant until they are near the surface, at which time the increased light level triggers germination, enabling the small seed to begin photosynthesis quickly. A similar situation occurs when dispersed seeds fall close to an established plant that would compete unfavorably with a new seedling for nutrients, light, and water. Here, the reduced light under the larger plant would discourage germination in such adverse conditions.

Seeds whose germination is inhibited by light are typically produced by plants native to arid regions. The absence of water near the soil surface is detrimental to shallow germination, thus light-inhibited seeds lie dormant until they reach the cooler and more moist soil depths.

Although most foliage plant seeds may either be germinated in darkness or left exposed to the light, it is usually critical that light be supplied to the young seedlings as soon as they reach the soil surface. The normal process of above-ground seedling development is light dependent (Figure 4.5). A good example is the geranium, whose germination pattern is comparable to a majority of the indoor plants that can be started with seeds. During its growth through the soil, the elongating seedling is **etiolated,** that is, possesses small, unexpanded leaves and a white or yellowish color resulting from the absence of chlorophyll. When the hypocotyl "hook" reaches the light at the soil surface, the growth-regulating auxins migrate to the darker underside of the hook, causing faster cell elongation there and the resultant straightening of the plant axis. (The plant hormones that are involved in root initiation, cell elongation, and other plant functions will be discussed later in this chapter.)

There is another reason why light must be

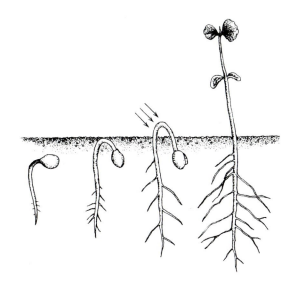

Light strikes the seedling "hook" as it emerges from the soil. The resulting migration of auxin to the dark undersurface of the hook, causing rapid elongation of the cells there, may be responsible for the change to erect growth. (Some scientists, however, believe that auxins are destroyed on the sunny side, rather than migrating to the dark side. Other research indicates the growth response to be under the control of light quality and ethylene.)

FIGURE 4.5 The role of light in the growth response of an emerging geranium seedling.

supplied to emerging seedlings. Having used much of the seed's stored food for the initial stages of germination, the new seedling must begin photosynthesis as soon as possible to produce food for further growth. Therefore, once the seedling shoot is free from the soil, normal growth takes place. The leaves turn green and expand, and the rate of shoot elongation decreases so that internodes are short. Thus, a compact plant form results. Whenever seedlings—or established plants—are grown at low light levels, the photosynthetic rate is reduced, the leaves remain small, and leaf spacing increases. This occurrence of extended internodes and a more open, spindly habit is termed **legginess.** The indoor gardener must constantly be on the lookout for legginess as an indication of insufficient light. The subject of lighting is discussed in Chapter Eight.

Preparation for Planting

Seed propagation works best when sowing follows conscientious planning and preparation. As mentioned earlier, the seeds must be viable. If seeds are to be stored for later planting, storage in a sealed container placed in the refrigerator is the most convenient and effective method. If seeds are improperly collected, handled, and stored, the propagation effort is doomed from the start.

The best container for seed propagation is one that is shallow and offers a relatively large surface area. Commercial growers typically use **flats,** 2 to 4-inch-deep metal or plastic trays that measure approximately 1 by 2 feet. For home use, an excellent container is the type of flowerpot known as the pan. Twice as wide as deep, the pan holds many seedlings and is not upset easily because of the wide bottom. Other containers that are often available around the home are square, wide-mouth jars placed on their side, milk cartons, plastic dairy product containers, or polyethylene bags. Regardless of the type of container used, it should be sterilized prior to planting by soaking in a solution of 95 percent water and 5 percent chlorox. This procedure helps to prevent diseases that can rapidly kill new seedlings.

If garden soil or sand is used for germinating seeds, precautions must be taken to rid these media of harmful disease organisms, insects, and weeds. Either sterilize, thus killing all organisms, or pasteurize, killing only the harmful organisms. These procedures can be done in the home oven using one of the following schedules:

SOIL TEMPERATURE	TIME	RESULTS
140°F	30 minutes	Kills most harmful fungi and bacteria
160°F	30 minutes	Also kills soil insects
180°F	30 minutes	Also kills most weed seeds

The soil to be treated should be moistened slightly and placed in a shallow container. Care should be taken that the entire soil mass attains the desired temperature for the prescribed time; otherwise, harmful organisms may survive within the interior soil areas that are slower to heat. Effective heating can be ensured by using a meat thermometer inserted into the middle of the soil, and beginning the timing once the thermometer records the desired temperature. On the other hand, the soil should not be overcooked because of the danger of soil minerals being released in toxic quantities. If clay containers are to be used, the medium and container can be heated in one operation. Plastic containers require the Chlorox soak method to avoid melting.

The medium should also be: (1) loose enough to avoid physically inhibiting the emergence of the seedling; (2) low in fertility to prevent chemical damage to the young, sensitive tissues; (3) wet enough to provide constant moisture for the germination process; and (4) sufficiently aerated to allow adequate gaseous exchange around the seed. Various soil mixes, such as equal parts of soil, sand, and peat moss, have commonly been used in the past. More popular in recent years have been single or combined artificial media, such as perlite or vermiculite. These are convenient materials to use since the intense heat required in their manufacture ensures sterility. These media should be initially supplemented with a low application of nutrients, or carefully fertilized shortly after germination occurs. More specific information on media types is found in Chapter Six.

Other handy materials when sowing include wooden or plastic labels to identify the kind and variety of seed being sown and the planting date. The label might also include the expected date of germination that the seed packet often provides. A plastic or glass sheet, a polyethylene bag, newspaper, or paper towels should be on hand to cover the container during the time before seedling emergence. You will also need a sink or large vessel of water for subirrigating your seed container. If watering will be from above, a sprinkling water vessel is needed.

Planting and Transplanting

Two steps are commonly involved when growing plants from seeds: (1) sowing in a suitable medium for germination to occur and (2) transplanting into a container and soil mix more conducive to further growth.

SOWING THE SEEDS. The first step in seed planting is to fill the container to the rim with medium, gently tamping it down to expel large air pockets and to leave about ½ to ¾ inch between the medium surface and container rim for easier watering of the seedlings. Next, the medium should be moistened by sprinkling from above or soaking from below until the medium surface is moist. The medium is then marked into rows with a label or other suitable instrument for sowing. Rows are preferable to broadcasting the seeds randomly over the surface for several reasons: (1) proper spacing of the seeds is easier to accomplish; (2) rows allow the systematic planting and labeling of numerous seed types in one container; and (3) the superior air circulation helps prevent damping-off. We will discuss damping-off in greater detail following this section (Figure 4.9).

The depth of the row depends on the size of the seed. Small seeds, such as begonias, should be placed on the surface of the medium and tamped gently to provide good seed-to-surface contact. The rule of thumb for larger seeds is to plant them two or three times their smallest diameter. For example, long and narrow seeds, such as marigolds, would be planted according to their width. Planting depth information is often provided on the seed packet. The best method of sowing the seeds along the row is to squeeze the seed packet so that the end flap becomes

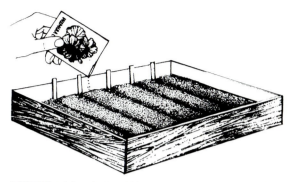

FIGURE 4.6 Seeds should be sown in rows and directly from the seed packet as shown.

a V shape. While moving the packet slowly along the row, tap its side causing the seeds to fall, one by one, into the row (Figure 4.6). Space the seeds evenly along the row, remembering that each seed will become a young plant and leaving about ¼ to ½ inch between the seeds. Spacing can be much closer, but damping-off and stunting of the seedlings are more likely to occur.

The seed packet often gives two other helpful bits of information. The **germination percentage** tells how many of the seeds can be expected to germinate in a lot. A percentage of 90 percent means that, on the average 10 percent of the seeds are not viable, indicating a 10 percent closer spacing in the row. Also stated might be the number of seeds per ounce or in the packet, which is also included in some of the mail-order seed catalogs. If you purchased a ¹⁄₃₂-ounce packet and there are 640 seeds per ounce, you can calculate that there are about 20 seeds in your packet. The 90 percent germination percentage reduces this to 18 seeds. With this information, you can more accurately calculate what portion of the packet you wish to sow to obtain the desired number of desired number of new plants.

After sowing, larger seeds should be covered with dry medium. This is easier to work with than moist material, and it will soak up water from the moist medium around it. If additional water is necessary, avoid disturbing the sown seeds by subirrigating or using a fine mist. Label each group of seeds.

Maintaining proper moisture is critical during the germination process. The medium surface must neither dry out nor become so wet that damping-off is encouraged. This can be accomplished by covering the newly sown and watered container with a plastic sheet or piece of glass, or by misting frequently. If a clear material is used, avoid placing the container in direct sunlight where high temperatures will result, damaging the young seedlings. Seeds that will germinate without light can be covered with moist, opaque material such as newspaper, paper towels, or cardboard, but if used dry, these papers will also pull moisture from the upper surface of the medium. The radicle normally emerges, anchors, and begins water absorption before the young shoot is pushed through the soil surface. Keeping the container covered ensures constant moisture for this root development. When the shoots appear, the covering should be removed to allow uninhibited emergence from the medium, stimulate light-initiated growth responses (Figure 4.5), increase air circulation, and allow photosynthesis to begin. Less water and cooler temperatures are recommended following shoot emergence to "harden" the seedlings for transplanting.

TRANSPLANTING. Seedlings growing in close proximity compete with each other for light and nutrients, and eventually a slowdown in growth occurs. **Transplanting,** the moving of seedlings from the propagation medium to individual containers and a more fertile soil mix, is the remedy for this.

The first leaves that develop on a seedling, called the **cotyledons** or **seed leaves,** contain stored food that is utilized during initial seedling development. These are usually rounded and somewhat fleshy. The **true leaves** develop from the plumule and have the characteristic leaf shape of the plant. When one or two true leaves or sets of leaves

FIGURE 4.7 Transplant seedlings when one or two true leaves or sets of leaves have developed, being careful to handle the plants by the cotyledons or leaves rather than the stem.

have developed and are carrying out photosynthesis for food production, the seedling is ready for transplanting (Figure 4.7).

Care must be exercised in handling the seedling during transplanting. The cotyledons or true leaves should be used as the "handle" because damage to the vascular tissue of the fragile stem can be fatal. Seedlings should not be pulled from the medium, but rather gently lifted out from below with a label or pencil while exerting a gentle tug from above. Older seedlings may have such extensive root systems that removal of the entire soil mass from the container will make separation of the individual plants easier and less damaging to the roots.

Transplanting may be into individual small pots or trays divided into cells. These should be filled level with a slightly moistened soil mix consisting of equal parts of soil, peat moss, and sand or perlite. Soil that is too dry will not hold its shape well enough for making a hole, and wet soil becomes **puddled** or devoid of air spaces during handling. If the soil will form a ball when compressed in the fist, but breaks apart easily, the moisture level is correct. The medium should be tamped lightly and **dib-**

Step 1. Using a dibble or pencil, make a deep hole in the soil mix.

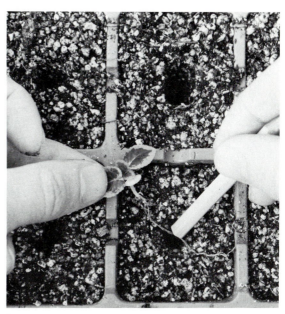

Step 2. Holding the seedling by the cotyledons or leaves, use the dibble to push the roots deeply into the hole.

Step 3. Placing the plant somewhat deeper than its original growing depth, firm the soil gently around the roots.

Step 4. Apply water, either by fine spray or subirrigation, to settle the soil around the roots.

FIGURE 4.8 Transplanting seedlings.

bled (a hole made) with a pencil or **dibble**. Hold the seedling by the leaves and place the roots down into the dibbled hole, ensuring that they go deeply and do not "ball up." Plant the seedling slightly deeper than its original growing depth and firm the soil around it (Figure 4.8). Placing the newly transplanted seedling in a cool, shaded location for several days will help to overcome the shock commonly associated with transplanting.

DAMPING-OFF. Special mention of this disease problem is necessary here since it is so prevalent and devastating among seedlings. It is caused by several fungal organisms, most notably *Pythium*, *Rhizoctonia*, *Botrytis*, and *Phytophthora*. These organisms may reproduce by the threadlike, vegetative strands, called *mycelia*, or by spores. These may be carried by soil, water, or infested plant parts.

The disease may occur at any stage of the seedlings' development. It may be a pre-emergent rotting of the seed or, more visibly, rotting of the seedling stem near the soil surface. Spreading quickly, the seedlings fall over in succession (Figure 4.9). Occasionally, seedlings will remain alive and upright, but the stem will wither, causing stunting and

FIGURE 4.9 Damping-off must be controlled as soon as it appears to prevent severe damage to the seedling flat.

eventual death. This latter condition is commonly known as **wire stem**.

The most effective means of prevention is good sanitation. This not only includes pasteurization of containers and media, but also such actions as the fast removal of dead or dying plant matter, use of clean tools during transplanting, and using uncontaminated water for watering. It can be disastrous, for example, to catch the runoff from one watering for use on another seedling container. If subirrigation is used, the water should be changed frequently or contain a fungicide.

Favorable growing conditions and vigorous plant growth also play important roles in avoiding damping-off. Care should be taken to use only fresh seeds, or those that have been stored properly, since seedlings of strong vitality grow faster and are more resistant to disease than slow-growing seedlings. Also, the temperature of the propagation area can be used to inhibit fungal organisms without affecting seedling growth. Damping-off fungi are most active between 68 and 86°F (20 to 30°C), whereas many tropical plants can be germinated at the warmer range of 90 to 95°F (32 to 35°C). After the seedlings are well developed, the temperature may be reduced to 65°F (18.5°C) for hardening prior to transplanting, again a range that is unfavorable to damping-off organisms. Water is critical as well—its proper availability is one of the primary determinants of damping-off incidence. Overwatering, poor drainage, and excess humidity are factors that cause damping-off and are to be avoided. And finally, poor air circulation is a contributing factor to the disease. Adequate air movement, perhaps provided by the use of open windows or a fan, is the last line of defense in combating damping-off.

Where damping-off infests seedlings, the objective is to stop its spread as soon as possible. This can be done by removal of the infected plants and medium, as well as a 1-inch band of adjacent material, or preferably, by treating the infested area with a fungicide.

ASEXUAL PROPAGATION

The Physiological Basis

A plant grows and develops based on cell division (**mitosis**) that produces two daughter cells of genetic identity to the original cell. Consequently, every cell in the plant, having resulted indirectly from the single-celled zygote, contains the same genetic information.

Asexual (or vegetative) propagation—the reproduction of a new plant from a vegetative plant part—utilizes the process of mitosis to produce an offspring plant that is identical genetically to the parent plant. When a stem cutting is taken for rooting, the new growing points on the cutting are the terminal and lateral buds that continue their natural mitotic development. A leaf cutting, with no buds present, develops new shoots from cells that revert from a mature state back to the **meristematic condition**—capable of active mitotic division. Regardless of the asexual method used, the same principal generally holds true: *Each new propagated plant is genetically identical to its parent.* This is the most important advantage of asexual propagation.

The Clone

Asexual propagation produces **clones,** groups of plants that have three characteristics: (1) they originated from the same plant directly or indirectly; (2) they are genetically uniform; and (3) they are produced by vegetative means such as cuttage, layerage, division, or grafting. If cuttings from a philodendron are taken from a single parent plant and placed in a glass of water to root, the new rooted plants will be in the same clone as the parent since all three clonal characteristics are present. By the same token, cuttings that are subsequently taken from the new rooted cuttings, as well as from any other descendent of the original parent, will also be clonal members since they satisfy the first clonal characteristic through indirect descent. Any cultivar, such as *Nephrolepis exaltata* 'Bostoniensis' (Boston fern), is a clone.

Although clones must be perpetuated by vegetative propagation, the converse is usually true, but not always, that is, vegetative propagation does not always result in the perpetuation of a clone. One of the most conspicuous exceptions to this generally accurate horticultural principle is the variegated snake plant (*Sansevieria trifasciata* cv. Laurentii) (Figure 4.10). If this plant is propagated by leaf sections, the common asexual method for snake plants, we could say that two of the three clonal conditions are satisfied—vegetative propagation and indirect origin from the original variegated snake plant. However, a variegated snake plant leaf section yields a green, unvariegated offshoot that is not a member of the clone because it lacks genetic identity. Perpetuation of the clone is only possible through division of the underground rhizomes, which maintain the variegated characteristic.

Many of the plants in the foliage industry are clones. This means that if one plant is susceptible to disease or insects, can be propagated in only one way, or will not tolerate certain cultural conditions, the same characteristic applies to all members of the clone. Clonal members may even share awards given to other members, such as those given by orchid societies. For example, if an orchid is awarded a prize at a show in Europe, all of the other plants in the clone all over the world also share the prize.

HOW CLONES ORIGINATE. In most cases, our new plants come either from selected

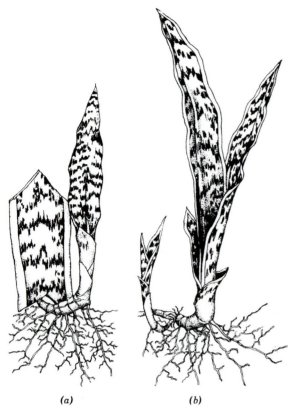

FIGURE 4.10 The variegated snake plant (*Sansevieria trifasciata* 'Laurentii') may or may not perpetuate the clone depending on how it is propagated: (a) By leaf section and (b) by division of the rhizome.

seedlings or a **bud sport,** a branch of a plant that is unique in appearance and can be asexually reproduced. Seeds often produce seedlings with unusual characteristics; unfortunately, the unusual ones are generally unimpressive and rarely worthy of cultivation. Bud sports usually arise as the result of a mutation in a cell when a change in chromosomal makeup occurs. Mitotic division follows the mutation and a branch is produced that displays the new phenotype or outward appearance. When a desirable seedling or bud sport is observed, it is grown on and used as a stock plant for subsequent propagation.

PLANT PATENTS. Displayed in most indoor plant shops are usually several plants that are tagged "patented." The U.S. government, in a 1930 amendment to the U.S. Patent Law, now allows individuals to patent new plant forms that they discover or are able to develop through plant breeding. As you might expect, this monetary benefit has been a great impetus for the prolific introduction of new cultivars not only in the indoor plant industry, but also in the areas of fruit and landscape plants as well.

Not all new plant forms qualify for patents. The law states that patents are available for "any distinct and new variety of plant, including cultivated sports, mutants, hybrids, and newly found seedlings, other than a tuber-propagated plant or a plant found in an uncultivated state." In addition, the plant must also prove to be capable of asexual propagation on a commercial scale to qualify for a patent. It was not until 1970 that patent protection was made available for some sexually propagated plants whose genetic uniformity can be maintained through lines.

A patent is granted to the originator of a cultivar for a period of 17 years. With it, the originator has the sole right to the propagation and sale of the new cultivar in the United States and its possessions. The patent does not necessarily indicate a plant of superior quality, although this is often the case, only that it is "distinct and new" in some characteristic such as growth habit; foliage shape or color; flower color; resistance to pests, drought, or poor cultural conditions; ease of propagation; and so on.

CHIMERAS. If the mutation affects only a part of the growing point, the resulting condition in which there are layers or segments of mutated tissue next to normal tissue is known as a **chimera.** The most familiar examples are variegated plants that have normal green tissue interspersed with segments of leaf tissue that cannot produce chlorophyll. Since the mutated areas contain no chlorophyll, they become white or yellow and produce the striped or mottled foliage variegation. Chimeras are responsible for much of the unusual coloration found in indoor plants (Figure 4.11).

The chimera concept explains the peculiarities of propagating the variegated snake plant (refer back to Figure 4.10). The mutated yellow tissue is confined to the epidermal or outer layer of leaf cells. When a leaf section is taken and placed in a medium, roots and a shoot originate in the internal tissue of the leaf and emerge from unmutated tissue at the base of the leaf section.

Hence, the new offshoot will have a normal green epidermis. On the other hand, division of variegated snake plants maintains the clone since the rhizome (thick underground stem) that produces the new plant emerges through the variegated epidermis, thus carrying the variegated appearance to the new plant.

Adventitious Structures

Plants typically can be propagated asexually if they have the ability to produce **adventitious** roots or shoots, that is, structures that arise on an unusual part of the plant. These occur when a new growing point is initiated on a stem, leaf, or root. Many plants exhibit adventitious structures under normal conditions (Figure 4.12). Adventitious roots may be in the form of aerial roots on a growing plant or as roots that develop on a leaf or stem during propagation. Likewise, adventitious shoots are those that develop on root tissue or stem areas, such as the internode, where new stems would not ordinarily arise. When plants like peperomia or sansevieria

FIGURE 4.11 The variegated snake plant is an example of a chimera. Note how the new shoot to the right retains the coloration of the parent plant.

FIGURE 4.12 Many plants, such as philodendrons, produce adventitious roots without any natural provocation.

are propagated by leaf cuttings, both adventitious roots and shoots must be produced in order to form the new plant.

Not all plants or plant parts are propagated by the same vegetative means, and it is not always obvious from the plant's appearance what method to use. For example, peperomias can be propagated from a leaf with its attached petiole, but not so with philodendrons, which require a stem section be included. The begonias and snake plants, on the other hand, are unlike most plants in that they can be propagated by a section of a leaf. A few plants, including the Boston fern, are now multiplied in large numbers by a technique known as **micropropagation.** Here, a small plant part, known as the **explant** and which may consist of only a few cells, is cultured under sterile conditions in a nutrient medium. The text that follows will describe the various procedures and how they are performed; the last section of the book (Part Five) identifies the commonly used propagation techniques for the more common house plants.

The Advantages of Asexual Propagation

The maintenance of genetic uniformity is by far the most significant benefit of asexually propagating plants. Most of our indoor plants are popular because they exhibit such physical characteristics as interesting foliage form and color, flower size and color, and growth habit. The loss or decline of these characteristics through sexual variation could render the plant less marketable. For this reason, indoor plants are asexually propagated.

A second advantage of asexual propagation is that plants that produce seeds infrequently or not at all can be multiplied. In individual circumstances, light intensity and duration, as well as temperature, can inhibit flowering and make seeds unavailable. The Christmas cactus, for example, flowers in response to short days at certain temperatures as outlined in Chapter Three but may flower sporadically or not at all in overly warm temperatures. The African violet and many other plants will fail to flower in low-light conditions. Under such adverse conditions, seeds are not produced, making asexual methods the only alternative.

Third, larger plants can be obtained more quickly in most cases. Large begonia cuttings root easily and develop quickly into mature plants, whereas the dustlike seeds take much longer periods to become established.

A final advantage is that cuttings are less susceptible to diseases such as damping-off than seedlings. These problems can occur, however, particularly when the propagation method involves sectioning a plant part and creating wounds through which disease organisms can enter. But the chances of disease occurrence in these situations can be substantially reduced by such treatments as **suberization** whereby the plant part is allowed to dry out prior to insertion in the propagation medium. The exposure to air of the wounded cells at the cut stimulates the formation of a waxy coating of **suberin** that seals the surface. This method is used on leaf and stem cuttings of succulents, tuber sections, and pineapple crowns.

General Considerations in Asexual Propagation

ROOT FORMATION. As noted in Chapter Three, at the time leaves and stems are developing on a plant, cells are undergoing **differentiation,** or specialization, into specific tissue types such as phloem, xylem, cambium, or otherwise. Many of these differentiated cells have the capacity to return to the meristematic condition, that is, they are able to undergo **dedifferentiation.** In their meristematic condition, these cells are able to contribute to the production of new roots, shoots, or both. This striking ability of plant cells to retain meristematic potential is the basis of asexual propagation. Although new adventitious roots or shoots may arise from various types of stem, leaf, or root tissue, this diversity of origin does not generally influence the genetic quality of the new plant since all cells of the parent plant, regardless of function, are genetically uniform. Chimeral plants, such as the variegated snake plant mentioned earlier, are exceptions since they are composed of two genetically distinct tissues.

The process of adventitious root formation is a gradual one in which three distinct phases are recognized: (1) the dedifferentiation of mature cells and the initiation of meristematic cells, which are termed the **root initials;** (2) differentiation of the meristematic cells into immature roots or **root primordia;** and (3) the development of the new root and its emergence through the outer tissue of the stem or leaf. Figure 4.13 illustrates the typical points of origin for new roots in both herbaceous and woody stems.

Not all foliage plants wait until asexual propagation techniques are performed to develop adventitious roots but **develop preformed root initials** in early stem development, which lie dormant until conditions are right for growth. Several plants, including some of the philodendrons, orchids, and English ivies, develop aerial roots

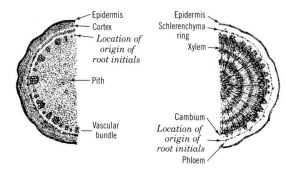

FIGURE 4.13 The location of adventitious root initials in herbaceous (left) and woody (right) stem tissue. *Source:* Hartman/Kester, *Plant Propagation:* Principles and Practices, © 1983, Reprinted by permission of Prentice-Hall, Inc., Englewood Cliffs, New Jersey.

from these latent initials. As a rule, plants with preformed root initials can be propagated more quickly than plants without them. The spider plant (*Chlorophytum comosum*), for example, produces aerial plantlets complete with roots, making the new plantlets essentially ready to pot and grow immediately after division from the parent.

APPLICATION OF ROOT-PROMOTING COMPOUNDS. Root-promoting compounds (auxin) should not be applied routinely to all cutting types. Where buds or shoots are present on the cutting, auxins in proper concentration will stimulate roots without inhibiting the buds. If the cutting has no bud and must develop one from meristematic tissue, such as with *Begonia*, *Peperomia*, or *Sansevieria* leaf or leaf section cuttings, the application of auxin can modify the natural balance of internal hormones in such a way that roots form readily, but shoots are inhibited. In other words, with cuttings that lack buds, the indoor gardener may be better off to avoid the use of auxins unless experience dictates otherwise.

Auxins usually come in powder form but may be purchased in crystalline form for dissolving into liquid dips. The former is far more convenient for home use. The compound is applied by dipping the base of the cutting into the powder and tapping the cutting to remove excessive material. A slit or hole should be made in the rooting medium prior to insertion as a means of avoiding rubbing the powder off the stem. It is advisable to place a small amount of powder into a small dish, throwing away the excess after treating the cuttings, rather than to stick the cuttings into the original container. This helps to prevent the spread of disease via the auxin material. In addition, auxins should also be kept cool, dry, and closed as much as possible since light, moisture, and warm temperatures can be detrimental (Figure 4.14).

It is important to note that cuttings of most houseplants do not require auxins for rapid rooting. In fact, many are damaged by auxin application. Also auxin works in concert with other substances in very complex ways. Roots will not always appear just because auxin has been applied.

POLARITY. An interesting attribute of hormone movement in plants is that it occurs in prescribed directions, resulting in a phenomenon known as **polarity.** Consequently, stems have a proper orientation that is not affected by gravity. Stem cuttings form shoots at the **distal** end (away from the crown) and root cuttings form shoots at the **proximal** end (the end toward the crown). In a similar fashion, stem cuttings produce roots at the proximal end and root cuttings form roots most prolifically at the distal end (Figure 4.15). These points of origin occur regardless of the orientation in which stem or cuttings are placed in a propagation medium. This interesting occurrence is related to the movement of auxin in the plant. When a cutting is made, the auxin accumulates at the proximal end of the stem or the distal end of the root, resulting in root initiation there. Though not as well substantiated, it is reasonable to surmise that cytokinins have

FIGURE 4.14 A number of root-promoting products in varying strengths are now offered for sale.

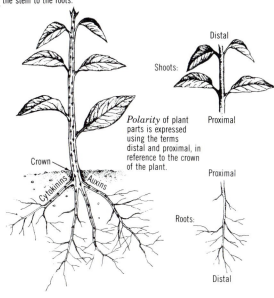

Auxins are produced in the apical meristem and young, developing leaves, moving down the stem to the roots.

Shoots:

Distal

Proximal

Polarity of plant parts is expressed using the terms distal and proximal, in reference to the crown of the plant.

Crown

Cytokinins   Auxins

Roots:

Proximal

Distal

FIGURE 4.15 The polarity found in plants is directly related to the movement of growth regulators throughout the plant.

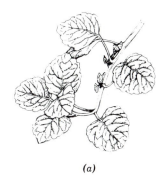

(a)

(b)

FIGURE 4.16 Polarity is not always easy to ascertain on a cutting. Swedish ivy (a) shows how the lateral buds can be used to determine polarity, whereas snake plant leaf sections (b) can be difficult to interpret.

similar movement but in an opposite direction in the cutting. Because of the polarity phenomenon, it is important to realize that cuttings placed in a medium upside down will not develop properly; they will either not root or will produce roots at the aerial proximal end, resulting in the eventual death of the cuttings. Some plants, such as trailing vines, often produce leaves that curl back up the stem and make it difficult to determine the proper polarity by leaf appearance. The most reliable method is to observe the lateral bud locations—they always are situated on distal side of the leaf petiole (Figure 4.16). Another polarity problem exists with snake plants. After sectioning the leaves, it is often difficult to distinguish proper polarity. This situation is remedied by cutting each section with a "V" cut so that the 'V' points toward the crown of the plant. The sections are then placed in the medium with the pointed end down (Figure 4.16).

WOUNDING AND CALLUS FORMATION.

With woody, hard-to-root cuttings from some of the foliage plants, wounding the basal portion of the cutting can be beneficial to rooting for several reasons: (1) auxins and carbohydrates (food) tend to accumulate around the wound; (2) the wounded tissue produces ethylene, which promotes rooting; (3) the wound can absorb applied auxins more readily; and (4) more water can be absorbed into the cutting.

Wounding is best accomplished by two methods. The most common way is to remove roughly the lower leaves, creating small points of stem damage where the leaves were attached. The second method is to make a 1-inch-long slit down both sides of the cutting base, penetrating the bark and barely into the woody xylem tissue.

CALLUS. When placed in the propagation medium under proper environmental conditions, the basal end of woody cuttings often develops **callus,** a mass of unspecialized vegetative cells that sometimes forms at a plant wound. Roots may grow through the callus mass and appear to arise from it, but they are initiated in the stem tissue. Two plants (sedum and adult English ivy) are exceptions to this, developing their roots from the callus mass. Although callus is not

Plant Propagation **87**

usually the source of root development, it does not inhibit root formation. Furthermore, callus removal could result in damage to young roots that may be growing through it.

Techniques of Propagating Plants Asexually

CUTTAGE. Propagation of plants by cuttings involves removing a portion of the parent plant's stem, leaf, or root and placing this cutting in proper environmental conditions for the formation of roots, shoots, or both. The cutting eventually becomes a new plant, typically genetically identical to the parent. Cuttage is one of the most efficient and convenient ways to start indoor plants, being inexpensive and requiring no special skills to perform.

Stem Cuttings. The most important type of cuttage, stem cuttings are usually 2- to 5-inch stem sections, which contain terminal and/or lateral buds that on rooting will develop into new shoots. Two types are common: (1) **terminal** or **tip** stem cuttings taken from the stem apex and containing the terminal bud; and (2) **medial** stem cuttings that are taken from the central or lower shoot and do not contain a terminal bud. Almost all foliage plants with stems above the soil surface root well from either type of stem cutting.

The procedure for taking cuttings is simple (Figure 4.17). A sharp knife or scissors should be used to take cuttings. Removing cuttings by pinching may: (1) damage the stem near the cut surface; (2) increase the chance of disease; (3) reduce root response; and (4) leave unattractive stubs on the parent. For cuttings, stems should be selected that are growing vigorously, have a healthy color, and are without disease or pest problems. The cut to remove the cutting from the plant should be made about ¼ inch above a node. This eliminates internode stubs on the parent that die back unattractively and can become a site for disease. The resulting internode at the bottom of the cutting should

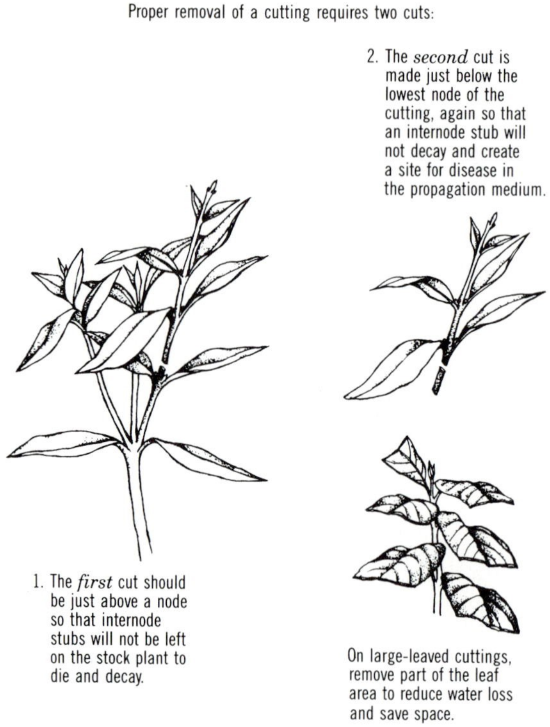

Proper removal of a cutting requires two cuts:

2. The *second* cut is made just below the lowest node of the cutting, again so that an internode stub will not decay and create a site for disease in the propagation medium.

1. The *first* cut should be just above a node so that internode stubs will not be left on the stock plant to die and decay.

On large-leaved cuttings, remove part of the leaf area to reduce water loss and save space.

FIGURE 4.17 Proper removal and preparation of stem cuttings.

be removed since roots generally occur near nodes. If not removed, the internode usually rots during propagation and increases the chances for disease in the propagation medium.

Remove enough lower leaves from the basal 1 to 2 inches of the cutting so that it will stand up well in the medium. If not removed, these leaves would decay and become a site for disease infection. The amount of foliage to be left on the upper portion of the cutting varies with the conditions of propagation (Figure 4.18). You will remember from Chapter Three that leaves both manufacture food and transpire water. If the propagation conditions are such that transpiration will be low, that is, if the cuttings are under mist or in a moist container such as a terrarium, then the more foliage that can be left, the better. However, if the conditions are dry

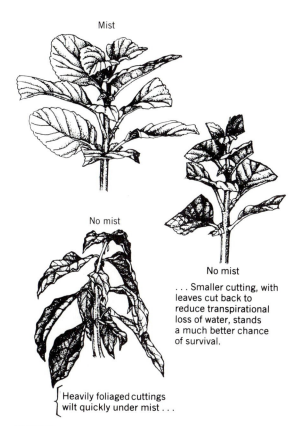

Mist

No mist

No mist

... Smaller cutting, with leaves cut back to reduce transpirational loss of water, stands a much better chance of survival.

Heavily foliaged cuttings wilt quickly under mist ...

FIGURE 4.18 Cuttings to be propagated under mist or in the moist confines of a terrarium may retain more food-producing foliage than cuttings that will experience water-stress during propagation.

and water stress may occur, reducing the foliage mass will result in perhaps slower, but more successful rooting. A balance is in order here; maximize photosynthesis and food production, while avoiding loss of the cuttings through wilting.

On some large-leaved plants such as dumbcane (*Dieffenbachia*) and Chinese evergreen (*Aglaonema*), the leaf area may be reduced by cutting off the terminal half of each leaf. This procedure can be followed even under mist conditions as a means of saving space. Incidentally, cuttings with reduced older leaves are more successful under water-stress conditions than tip cuttings with small, immature leaves. The cells of an older leaf, being more mature and

hardened, are less likely to dessicate than those of tender young leaves. Rooting benefits may also be derived from using terminal cuttings with the terminal bud and young leaves attached, but the rooting time of most indoor plant cuttings is so short that medial cuttings are only slightly less rapid to develop roots.

When placing the cuttings in the medium, the node at the bottom of the cutting and preferably an additional node should be under the medium surface. Roots will occur at the nodes. If a rooting compound is used, care should be taken to select the proper concentration since most indoor plant tissues are especially subject to damage from overapplication. Likewise, a powder of the proper concentration should be applied lightly for best results. Placement of the cuttings should be followed by firming the medium around the cutting bases and watering well to further settle the medium.

The humidity around the cuttings should be kept high by covering them with clear plastic or placing them under a mist system. Bright light, but not direct sun, should be present to encourage photosynthesis. Room temperature is satisfactory for most plants, and if desirable, heating cables can be placed below the medium to encourage faster rooting.

The most common mistake made in cutting propagation is removal of the newly rooted cuttings from the medium by pulling them up. If the new, brittle roots have begun to develop and anchor themselves to the medium, improper extraction will break them off. When checking cuttings for root development or removing them for transplanting, insert a label or pencil down under the root system, loosen the medium as much as possible, and pry the cutting up while pulling it gently by the top. When the roots are approximately 1 to 2 inches long, the cutting is ready for transplanting into its own container of fertile soil. Leaving the cutting in the infertile medium for long periods will have a stunting effect due to the lack of nutrients.

It is usually a good practice to pinch out the stem tips at or shortly after transplanting. The reason for this is that auxins produced in the stem tip inhibit the development of lateral buds, a phenomenon known as **apical dominance.** By removing the apex, the auxin supply is reduced and the lateral buds develop into shoots, resulting in a fuller, more compact plant. (In scientific fairness, some scientists believe that apical dominance may also be the result of other factors, such as nutrient diversion, other hormonal involvement, and even anatomical considerations.) Tips should be pinched just above the point where one wishes new shoots to arise, since the nodes just below the pinch will usually be the ones to flush out most rapidly. Therefore, if a plant has been allowed to become overgrown and leggy before transplanting, it is advisable to cut it back severely to remove the leggy growth. If just the tips of the stems are removed, then the undesirable situation of compact shoots arising at the ends of leggy shoots would occur. The plant would still be leggy, but just a bit more strange in appearance!

Plants vary in their degree of apical dominance; some species will form a bushy habit, if we assume environmental conditions are acceptable, when no pinching is exercised, whereas other species, such as the India rubber plant (*Ficus elastica* 'Decora'), develop long, straight, unbranched stems. As a matter of fact, even when the India rubber plant is pinched, it will rarely produce more than two or three lateral shoots below the pinch, and it will frequently produce only one, defeating the purpose of the pinch.

Leaf-Bud Cuttings. An abbreviated type of stem cutting consisting of only one node and the attached leaf or leaves is the **leaf-bud cutting.** This is used for many plants, including vining philodendrons, pothos, and coleus, and has the advantage over stem cuttings of yielding larger numbers of new plants from the propagation material. Leaf-bud cuttings have the disadvantage, however, of taking longer to develop into mature plants. They are particularly used when a detached leaf will produce roots but no shoot, because the lateral bud at the base of the leaf provides the new shoot.

Leaf-bud cuttings may be **single-eye** (one lateral bud per node) or **double-eye** (two lateral buds at each node), depending whether the leaf arrangement is opposite or alternate. Plants such as coleus with two leaves and buds at each node (an opposite leaf arrangement) can be made into double-eye cuttings that will produce two shoots, or into single-eye cuttings by slicing the stem longitudinally between the nodes. Following the possible application of a root-promoting substance, the cuttings should be placed in the medium with the bud(s) about ¼ to ½ inch below the surface. Plants with succulent stems should be allowed to suberize for several hours prior to insertion in the medium. Cuttings should be transplanted after the root system has been established and the new shoot is well above the medium surface. Remove the "parent" leaf or leaves when they begin to decay, or, if they remain healthy, when the new plant has developed several mature leaves.

Cane Cuttings. An even more abbreviated type of stem cutting is used on several plants that develop large, leafless stems, such as dumbcane (*Dieffenbachia*) and Chinese evergreen (*Aglaonema*). These stems, or canes, contain adequate food supplies to allow the propagation of each node with its associated latent lateral bud. These leafless cuttings are prepared by slicing the cane between each brown leaf scar, avoiding the bumplike lateral bud. The cutting should be allowed to suberize for several hours to lessen the chances of rotting. Cane sections should be placed horizontally in the medium with the bud facing up and just below the surface of the medium, or vertically with the proper polarity (Figure 4.19).

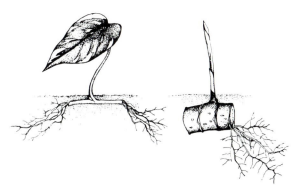

FIGURE 4.19 Leaf-bud and cane cuttings are actually modified stem cuttings.

Leaf Cuttings. A number of plants have the ability to regenerate new plants from a leaf without the attached axillary bud. Leaves of this type must be able to regenerate by (1) shoots and roots from the specialized leaf tissue cells or (2) the leaf must contain immature embryos.

In species where the mature leaf cells have the ability to dedifferentiate back to the meristematic condition, several possibilities exist as to how the cutting may be prepared. First, the entire leaf blade and the attached petiole comprise the cutting, with the lower ½ inch of the petiole inserted into the medium (Figure 4.20a). New roots and shoots form at the base of the petiole to create the new plant. The leaf blade either withers over time or can be removed for repropagation. Examples of plants that can be started this way are begonias, African violets, and peperomias.

A second variation of leaf cuttings is used on plants with large leaves and prominent veins such as the Rex begonia. With this method, the petiole is removed and the large radiating veins are severed. The intact leaf is placed flat on the medium, with the lower leaf surface down, and anchored with soil or pinned down to ensure good contact of the severed veins with the medium (Figure 4.20b). A new plant forms on the distal side of the cut due to the accumulation of auxins and carbohydrates. The old leaf will eventually degenerate and the new plants can be potted into individual containers.

The third and final type of leaf cutting is the leaf section. Many of the begonias can be propagated by sectioning the leaves into triangular pieces, each of which contains a large vein that terminates at the bottom of the section (Figure 4.20c). The snake plant represents a different variation of the leaf section in that the leaf is cut into 3- or 4-inch sections along the length of the blade, with care taken to maintain the correct polarity (Figure 4.16). Some plants may be multiplied by more than one method. Begonias and African violets, for instance, can be started by using the leaf blade and petiole, the blade only, or sections of the leaves.

Only a few plants are capable of regenerating offspring from **leaf embryos,** groups of cells that have never ceased meristematic activity. The best known is the devil's backbone (*Kalanchoe daigremontiana*), which produces new plantlets along the leaf margin by means of embryos that develop in the leaf and lie dormant until conditions permit maturity. Another plant of the same principle, but of a different configuration, is the pickaback plant (*Tolmiea menziesii*). Plantlets are produced from embryos on top of the leaf at the point of petiole attachment. The plants appear on top of the growing leaves, giving rise to another common name—piggyback plant. Both the pickaback and devil's backbone are propagated by pressing well-developed leaves flat onto the surface of the medium (Figure 4.21).

Root Cuttings. This method is simple but seldom used for indoor plants because other methods are easier and faster. *Aralia,* geraniums (*Pelargonium*), kaffir lily (*Clivia*), glory-bower (*Clerodendrum*), and banana trees are plants than can be propagated this way. Variegated forms of these plants, having roots that originally arose from inner, nonmutated tissue, will not reproduce the

FIGURE 4.20 Leaf cuttings must generate both roots and shoots from a secondary meristem in order to provide a new plant. (a) Leaf-petiole method of leaf cutting propagation. (b) The severed vein method of leaf cutting propagation. (c) The leaf section method of leaf cutting propagation.

variegation in new plants made from root cuttings.

The preferable time for taking root cuttings is late winter or early spring before new growth starts and when roots are well supplied with stored food. The root pieces should be from the heavier roots in the system and cut into 1- to 2-inch sections. These may be placed horizontally an inch or two below the medium surface or vertically with the proximal end of the cutting just below the surface. It is advisable to cut the

(c)

FIGURE 4.20 *(continued)*

distal end with a slanting cut and the proximal end straight across so that polarity can be easily determined.

PROPAGATION BY SPECIALIZED STRUCTURES.

Many indoor species produce interesting structures with which they propagate themselves. These present the indoor gardener with numerous possibilities for expanding a plant collection.

Multiple Crowns. Some species, such as the spider plant (*Chlorophytum comosum*), emerald ripple peperomia (*Peperomia caperata*), and many ferns, spread by means of sending up new stems and/or leaves from below the soil surface (Figure 4.22). These new shoots, also described as *crowns*, may be divided from the clump. One multicrowned plant can produce a number of separate individuals. The old plant is removed from the pot and divided into portions by cutting or gently prying the clump apart with the thumbs. Less damage is done to the roots if the entire clump is halved and each succeeding clump halved until single crowns are obtained. Since each crown will have roots attached, these can bypass the rooting media and be potted immediately.

Runners. Most commonly associated with strawberries, **runners** (or stolons), are specialized stems that arise from the crown of a plant at the base of the leaves and produce plantlets at one or several of the nodes (Figure 4.22). The spider plant (*Chlorophytum comosum*), the Boston fern (*Nephrolepis*

FIGURE 4.21 Two common plants that develop new plantlets by means of primary meristems. (a) *Kalanchoe daigremontiana* (Devil's backbone or bryophyllum). (b) *Tolmiea menziesii* (Pickaback plant).

FIGURE 4.22 The various specialized structures by which plants can be propagated. (*a*) Crowns. (*b*) Runners or stolons. (*c*) Offsets. (*d*) Rhizomes. (*e*) Tubers. (*f*) Corms. (*g*, *h*) Bulbs (tunicate and scaly).

FIGURE 4.22 (continued)

FIGURE 4.22 (continued)

FIGURE 4.22 (continued)

exaltata 'Bostoniensis'), and the strawberry begonia (*Saxifraga stolonifera*) produce runners in such abundance that they create an interesting cascade effect when used in hanging baskets. Propagation can either be by removing the plantlet and placing it into a medium or by placing a pot under the attached plantlet, allowing it to root and establish itself before severing the runner.

Runner production is related both to day length and temperature, requiring 12 to 14 hours of light (long days) and warmth. If plants fail to produce runners, a change of location or a modification of the environment may stimulate production.

Offsets. Many plants with a rosette leaf arrangement produce lateral branches, called **offsets** or **offshoots,** from the base of the main stem (Figure 4.22). Typical offset-producing plants are bromeliads, screw

pines (*Pandanus*), *Agave*, and *Echeveria*. Offsets are severed close to the main stem with a knife and either potted if roots have developed or placed in a medium if rooting is necessary. With plants that produce few offsets, the main rosette of foliage with a portion of stem can be removed and placed in a medium for rooting. Since this action also interrupts apical dominance, new offsets will develop at the base of an old plant.

Rhizomes. A **rhizome** is a swollen underground or surface stem, each node usually producing a parchmentlike sheath or expanded leaf (Figure 4.22). These organs store food, produce roots, and possess prominent buds that eventually develop into new shoots. It is by the continued development of these buds that the plant spreads. Some rhizomatous plants are the snake plant (*Sansevieria*), the rabbit's foot fern (*Davallia*), the cast-iron plant (*Aspidistra*), ginger (*Zingiber*), and several begonias. Rhizomes are best propagated at the beginning or end of the growth period by dividing the very swollen types and transplanting them or by cutting the slender types into sections that contain at least one node and placing them horizontally (with the bud up) in a rooting medium.

Tubers. A **tuber** is a short, thickened stem, either aerial or underground, that is covered with buds but lacks a sheath (Figure 4.22). Tubers, like rhizomes, are food storage organs that can also be used for propagation. Although the rosary vine (*Ceropegia woodii*) produces tubers along its vinelike aerial stems, most plants bear underground tubers as illustrated by the caladium (*Caladium × hortulanum*). These are propagated by planting the entire tuber or sectioning the tuber into pieces, each including at least one bud. If sectioning is used, suberization is recommended to discourage rotting. If it does not work, the tuber may be dormant and you will have to try again.

Corms. A **corm** is the swollen base of a vertical stem that is covered by dry leaf bases (Figure 4.22). It also is used as a food storage organ and is replaced each year by a new corm that develops on top of the old one. The only common indoor species that produce corms are freesia and crocus. These small flowers are often forced year-round for indoor color. Like tubers, they are covered with nodes and can be propagated by planting the small **cormels** that are produced each year at the base of the new corm or by sectioning a large corm and allowing it to suberize before planting.

Tuberous Roots. **Tuberous roots,** unlike true tubers of stem tissue, are swollen roots (or hypocotyl) that store food and can produce adventitious shoots. Tuberous begonias are the only plants of indoor interest that are currently propagated this way, although dahlias may become popular as seasonal indoor plants. The roots are taken from the soil in the fall, stored over winter, and divided after the sprouts emerge in the spring.

Bulbs. Among the most interesting of plant structures is the **bulb,** a short, fleshy disk of stem tissue that is covered with fleshy leaf bases called **scales.** Near the center of the bulb are growing points that produce leaves and flowers. Bulbs are food-storage organs for the cold or dry dormant seasons, as well as a means of vegetative propagation. Two distinct types of bulbs exist (Figure 4.22). Daffodils, tulips, and hyacinths produce **tunicate** bulbs that are made of thick, continuous scales and are covered by a thin, dry, parchmentlike covering called the **tunic.** Lily bulbs, on the other hand, have individual, separate scales and no tunic. These are called **scaly** bulbs.

Propagation of bulbs by vegetative means is easy to do, but the small bulblets that develop take several years to reach flowering size, making it wiser for the indoor gardener to purchase mature bulbs for forcing. If propagation is desirable, several methods can be used. First, almost all bulbs, regardless of type, produce small **bulblets** at the base of the large bulb each year. These can be separated and transplanted during the dormant season. Second, since bulb scales are modified leaf structures with associated axillary buds, propagation can be by leaf or leaf-bud cutting. Tunicate bulbs are longitudinally sliced into about six sections and each section is divided into two or three parts, each part containing a segment of stem tissue and the attached fleshy scales. Scaly bulbs are propagated by simply pulling healthy individual scales from the bulb. Both types of cuttings are placed in the propagation medium with the base about $\frac{1}{2}$ inch below the medium. After several weeks, the lateral buds of the tunicate bulb cutting will swell into bulblets, where a bulblet will develop from the scale tissue of the scaly bulb cutting. Other propagation methods exist for both bulb types, but none is as easy to perform and practical as those described here.

LAYERAGE. When a plant is difficult to propagate by other methods, **layerage** (propagating plant parts that are still attached to the parent plant) may be a satisfactory method. The advantage of layering is that, by being attached to the parent during propagation, the propagule continues to receive moisture and minerals until it can develop a root system. Thus, the success ratio is generally higher with layerage than with cuttage, particularly with difficult-to-root species. Two layering methods are practical indoors.

Simple Layering. This is performed on plants that have stems pliable enough to bend downward. After the stem is bent, a short portion of stem beginning about 3 to 6 inches behind the stem apex is covered with soil. The apex may be staked up if you prefer, but this is not necessary for adequate rooting. Indoor species root so readily as a rule that wounding of the submerged stem is not necessary for good rooting. Wounding and application of a rooting hormone may hasten the development of slow-to-root plants. Simple layering can be used to add new plants to a pot or hanging basket by layering long stems back into the container and to rejuvenate plants, such as dumbcane (*Dieffenbachia*), which often becomes leggy and unattractive, by staking the stems into separate containers.

Air Layering. This method, also known as Chinese or pot layering, is one of the oldest techniques of propagation. By girdling (removing a ring of bark) or slicing the stem about half through, roots are encouraged to form on the distal side of the wound while the new plant (layer) is still attached to the parent plant. By leaving the layer attached, the xylem or woody tissue continues to supply water and nutrients in the uncut tissue, whereas carbohydrates, auxins, and perhaps ethylene accumulate near the wounded phloem or bark, stimulating ad-

ventitious root formation. Air layering can be practiced at any time of the year, but just after a plant has produced several new leaves is the preferred timing. It is frequently used on such large-leaved plants as rubber trees (*Ficus*), crotons (*Codiaeum*), *Monstera*, and scheffleras (*Brassaia*), which often become leggy with age. These are difficult to propagate by cuttings becuase of slowness of rooting and the large leaf surfaces. Unless foliage is drastically reduced or kept under mist, these plants lose so much moisture that wilting usually occurs before rooting is initiated.

Air layering begins with the selection of a healthy 6- to 12-inch shoot at the top of the stem (Figure 4.23). At the place where the wound is to be made, several leaves may have to be removed to provide working space. It is preferable to wound the stem by girdling if possible, removing a 1-inch-wide circle of bark and scraping the exposed woody tissue clean to remove any phloem or cambium tissue that might stimulate healing. Another method of wounding is to make an upward 45° cut about one-third to one-half of the way through the stem. The slit should be held open by insertion of a toothpick or plug of sphagnum moss to prevent healing. Care should be taken to avoid completely severing the plant. Once the wound has been made, it should be dusted lightly with a root-promoting compound and wrapped with a 3- to 4-inch ball of slightly moist sphagnum moss. A single layer of clear polyethylene plastic, wrapped snugly and folded at the seam, is used to enclose the sphagnum moss. Electrical tape or "twist-ties" are used to secure each end of the plastic securely, preventing evaporation of water from inside and the entrance of water from the outside. The sphagnum moss should be checked every few weeks to ensure a proper moisture content. If the sphagnum is too wet, the chances of stem rots are much greater.

The layer can be removed after roots are

Step 1. Remove leaves from stem area where the layering procedure will occur.

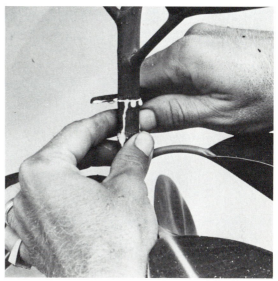

Step 2. Make two through-the-bark horizontal cuts around the stem about one inch apart. Connect these with one vertical cut.

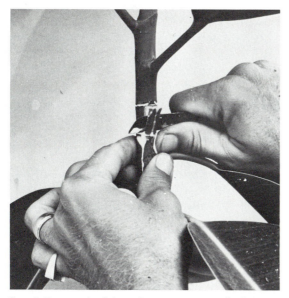

Step 3. Remove bark from the cut area to girdle the stem.

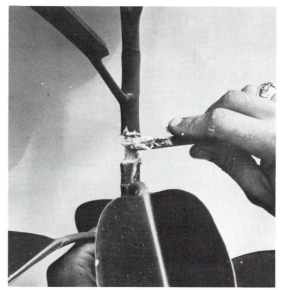

Step 4. Scrape away all bark residue from wound and apply root-promoting compound to the wound.

FIGURE 4.23 A step-by-step guide to air layering.

Step 5. Wrap damp sphagnum around the wound.

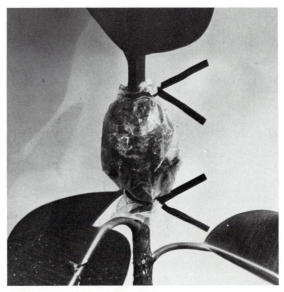

Step 6. Encase sphagnum with a plastic sheet and secure both ends of plastic with twist ties.

Step 7. After six to eight weeks, observe roots growing on outside of sphagnum moss.

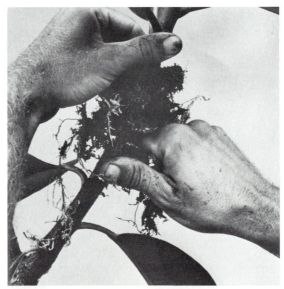

Step 8. Remove plastic and sever layer just below the moss ball. Pot the new layer, leaving the moss and root mass undisturbed except for gently spreading roots that are encircling the moss.

FIGURE 4.23 (continued)

observed growing through the sphagnum moss and around the inside of the plastic. At this time, the stem should be severed just below the sphagnum moss and the layer transplanted to an individual container. Since the foliage mass is out of proportion to the new root system, staking and some pruning of the top may be necessary. However, if the layer can be kept in a cool, humid environment until the roots are established, pruning usually is not needed.

In most cases, the decapitated parent plant will initiate new shoots and rejuvenate itself. If, after the layer has been removed, the old stem is tall and leggy, cutting it back to a lower height will result in a more attractive ultimate form. Make the cut just above a node to avoid leaving an unattractive stub of internode.

CONCLUSION

In this chapter, we have addressed the principles and techniques of propagation. The proper selection of containers and media is as important to success as propagation technique. For organizational purposes, we will include discussion of propagation containers in Chapter Five, and propagation media in Chapter Six.

Our hope is that these sections on plant propagation will equip the student with a sound theoretical and practical knowledge of the subject. With these tools, the art of propagation offers itself as a lifelong pursuit.

FOR FURTHER READING

Ball Red Book. 13th ed. George J. Ball, Inc., 1975.

Crockett, J. *Flowering House Plants.* New York: Time-Life Books, 1972.

Crockett, J. *Foliage House Plants.* New York: Time-Life Books, 1972.

Graf, A. *Exotic Plant Manual.* East Rutherford, N.J.: Roehrs Company, 1974.

Hartman, H., and D. Kester. *Plant Propagation: Principles and Practices,* 3rd ed. Englewood Cliffs, N.J.: Prentice-Hall, 1975.

House Plants Indoors/Outdoors. Ortho Book Series. San Francisco, Calif.: Chevron Chemical Co., 1974.

How to Multiply Your Plants. The John Henry Company, 1976.

International Plant Propagators' Society. *Combined Proceedings. 1951–present.*

Joiner, J. *Foliage Plant Production.* Englewood Cliffs, N.J.: Prentice-Hall, 1981.

Keeton, W. *Biological Science.* New York: W. W. Norton and Co., 1967.

McConnell, D. *The Indoor Gardener's Companion.* New York: Van Nostrand Reinhold, 1978.

Rayle, D., and L. Wedberg. *Botany: A Human Concern.* New York: Saunders College/Holt, Rinehart and Winston, 1980.

Taylor, J. *Growing Plants Indoors.* Minneapolis, Minn.: Burgess Publishing Co., 1977.

Wright, M. *The Complete Indoor Gardener.* New York: Random House, 1975.

PART TWO

GROWING PLANTS INDOORS

This section of the text will tackle a critical aspect of indoor gardening—the environment that confronts plants placed in homes, offices, malls, and other human enclosures. Although important, the home climate is misunderstood and miscalculated more than any other aspect of indoor gardening, often leading to the demise of plants and creating frustration in the mind of the individual. Though unsubstantiated, it seems that most gardeners who consider their thumb brown, or who have given up the idea of trying to grow plants inside, are reacting to problems associated with a lack of comprehension of home conditions.

In the first place, it is hard for us to realize that plants do not usually benefit from being our house guests. That is hard on our ego. But as you recall from the discussion of native habitats in Chapter Two, most of our plants come from regions of the world where environmental conditions are not like those of the interior of a home. For example, the amount of light to which plants are accustomed in their native setting may be as much as 50 times more than the average home can provide. The humidity of a home or office, particularly during the winter months when heat systems dry the air even more than usual, can fall to less than half the plant's optimum level. The indoor temperature level, set according to human comfort requirements, may be above, below, or less fluctuating than the temperature ranges in which our plants are adapted. Even factors such as water quality, watering methods, the restricted rooting space afforded by containers, and soil quality may also play a role detrimental to a plant's well-being.

In general, then, the climate we provide plants indoors is a sheltered one physically, but one which is usually hostile to the plant's best interests. Success with plants is only possible when this problem is approached realistically. The homeowner or designer has but two choices: (1) to select a plant that will tolerate the particular conditions of the place where the plant is to be placed and (2) to alter the conditions of the proposed site with additional artificial light, increased humidity, more appropriate temperature, and so on, thus accommodating the needs of the desired plant. Obviously, the second choice entails more work and expense, but can significantly increase the selection of plants available for use inside.

The interrelationship among the environmental factors that we will be examining in Part Two is an important concept to understand. Although the layout of our chapters will segregate each factor—nutrition, soil, climate, and so on—for the purpose of presentation, be aware that each of these factor's influences acts in conjunction with many of the others. For example, the quality of the soil in the container will affect fertilizer requirements, watering frequency, aeration of the root system, the acidity level, and so on.

Not only do these environmental factors affect each other, they also have a significant effect, individually, on plant growth—an effect that is so strong, an optimum level of other factors cannot compensate for the deficiency. This important relationship is demonstrated by the biological *Theory of Limiting Factors* that is illustrated by the Figure II-1 above. In our example, the factors that influence plant growth are represented

Level of plant growth (water level)

Et cetera · Soil moisture · Soil fertility · Soil acidity · Soil aeration · Disease and pests · Humidity · Temperature · Light intensity · Light duration · Light quality · Water quality · Watering practices · Et cetera

FIGURE II-1 The Theory of Limiting Factors explains how one negative cultural condition (light intensity) can negate many positive ones.

by the staves of our imaginary barrel. Just as the water level in the barrel can be no higher than the shortest stave, so also can the level of plant growth be no greater than the most limiting environmental factor. A common example for houseplants is a deficient amount of light. If a plant that requires 8 hours of 1000 foot-candles of light per day is placed in a 75-foot-candle location, the resulting poor growth rate of the plant will not be overcome by raising the humidity, changing the soil mix, raising the temperature, or any other alteration short of providing more light.

Another side of the limiting factor coin is that a low level of plant growth, caused by one or more limiting factors, may require a lowering of other factors to below optimum levels, particularly in the case of nutrition. When a plant is subjected to poor light, for example, and growing at a very slow rate, the appropriate rate of fertilization is much less than when the plant is grown under optimum conditions. Hence, the ordinary fertilization scheme may damage or kill the poorly lighted specimen.

These limiting factors are obviously critical to successful care of house plants indoors. Given that the home or office is a "hostile hostel" for plants and that growth is only as great as the worst of conditions, reality requires that we expect only so much from our plants inside. We cannot "push" a plant in poor light to grow faster or more attractively by adding more fertilizer or improving the soil. We can only try to alter the most limiting of factors or select plants that can tolerate those conditions over which we have no control.

Part Two is a detailed treatment of indoor environmental factors. Once you have completed study of this section of the book, you should understand the nature and importance of each factor and how it affects plant growth. Also included in the discussion will be means by which conditions adverse to plant growth can be lessened or overcome. With this information at hand, you should find that not only will your "plant sense" improve, but also the color of your thumb as well!

chapter five
containers
for growth
and aesthetic
appeal

During recent years while the indoor plant industry has been enjoying astounding growth, the industries that produce related products have also fared well. This is especially true of the container field, which has provided the indoor gardener with every container design imaginable. This chapter will discuss the fundamental considerations of pots and potting, as well as explore how the proper match is made between pot and plant. After looking at propagation and other specialized containers, we will suggest ways of making attractive planters at home as an alternative to purchasing commercial products.

CONTAINER BASICS

Pots vary greatly in design and material due both to functional and aesthetic factors. Knowledge of the basics for these variations helps the indoor gardener intelligently and creatively establish, maintain, and use plants to his or her best advantage. The following discussion will classify and analyze the wide variety of pots in an effort to establish a sound foundation for further discussion of cultural and aesthetic considerations of indoor plant growth.

Anatomy of a Pot

Most pots that are used for growing plants,

excluding the more decorative types, have several common anatomical characteristics (Figure 5.1). First and most important, they have holes in the bottom or near the bottom edge that ensure the uninhibited drainage of water. Second, the bottom of the container is designed with feet or rims so that air can circulate beneath the pot and excess water can freely flow away. As we shall see in the chapter on the growing medium (Chapter Six), air and water are equally important constituents of a good soil mix. Therefore, this design for drainage is intended to make certain that water does not become out of

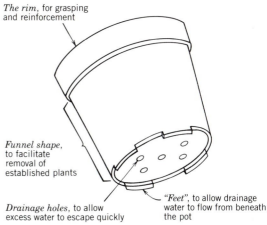

The rim, for grasping and reinforcement

Funnel shape, to facilitate removal of established plants

Drainage holes, to allow excess water to escape quickly

"Feet", to allow drainage water to flow from beneath the pot

FIGURE 5.1 Most plant pots have four basic design features in common.

balance with aeration, thus suffocating a portion or all of the root system. Third, pots are designed with a funnel shape, that is, the top is larger than the bottom. Since plants are growing organisms, their size increases over time and they must periodically be moved to larger containers. The funnel shape allows easy removal of the plant from the pot even after years of undisturbed growth, provided roots have not grown out the drainage holes. If pots were cylindrical or smaller at the top than the bottom, later removal would be most difficult, resulting in great disruption of the root system during repotting. And fourth, pots usually have a **rim**, a thickened collar around the upper circumference or lip. The rim, usually encompassing the upper inch or two of the pot, reinforces the pot against breakage and supplies the gardener a handle by which the plant can be grasped. Having examined the features that pots share in common, let us turn our attention to the other side of the coin—the diversity of pot shapes and materials.

Three Basic Pot Shapes

The most common pots for growing plants are made of clay or plastic, generally rang-

ing in top diameter from 2 to 12 inches, with larger sizes available. Three basic shapes are used: standard, azalea, and pan (Figure 5.2). The top diameter of a **standard pot** is equal to its height. This shape, probably the most common, is the deepest and allows for good vertical root penetration. The **azalea pot,** on the other hand, is sometimes called a "three-quarter" pot because its height is three-fourths its top diameter. Having a shorter height and wider bottom, it has the advantage of being less top-heavy than the standard pot and less inclined to tip over when containing a heavy-foliaged plant. Also, the stockier proportions are more appropriate for plants, like the azalea, that form a broad crown of foliage. Designed for shallow-rooted species such as the azalea, this pot is very suitable for most foliage plants. The third pot shape—the **bulb pan** or, more simply, **pan**—is approximately twice as broad as high and designed for bulbs that are planted shallowly to be forced into bloom. Though not suitable for most plants, the pan can be used to advantage in displaying fine-textured, ground-cover-like plants such as baby tears, as well as cacti and many other succulents. Pans also make excellent containers for the propagation of seeds, cuttings, and other plant parts.

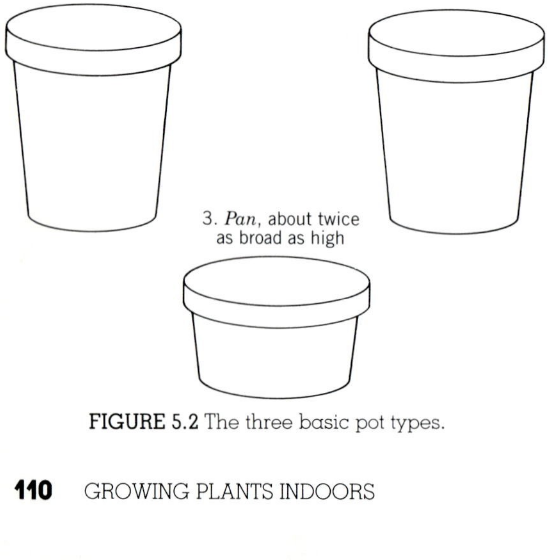

Material Differences Among Pots

Pots also vary in terms of the material from which they are made, each type having advantages and disadvantages in relation to the others (Figure 5.3). The following paragraphs summarize the pros and cons of these differences.

CLAY POTS. Porous clay pots, earthy red in color, are familiar to most people. The porosity of the clay allows evaporation of water through the sides of the pot, thus allowing its contents to dry out faster than impervious materials. New clay pots or those being removed from storage should be soaked in water for several hours; otherwise, the dry

1. *Standard*, top diameter and height approximately equal

2. *Azalea*, height about three-quarters the top diameter

3. *Pan*, about twice as broad as high

FIGURE 5.2 The three basic pot types.

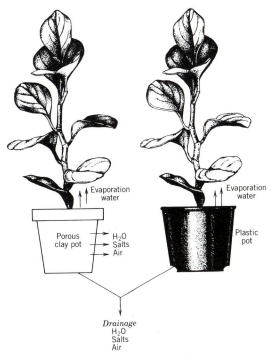

FIGURE 5.3 A comparison of clay and plastic pots in terms of water, air, and salt movement.

Additional characteristics of clay pots are that they are heavy, breakable, and not economical in terms of space because of their round shape. When they are broken, however, the pieces (**shards**) are useful for placement over another container's drainage holes prior to potting to allow water, but not soil, to escape the pot after watering. However, since shards are placed over the hole concave side-down, a moist space is created that may attract slugs, sowbugs, and other moisture-loving creatures. This is not usually a problem if the plant is located in the home but may be more serious with greenhouse or outside growing conditions. Heat sterilization may be successfully used on clay pots, but when soak sterilization is

walls of the pot will absorb moisture quickly from the newly planted specimen.

When clay pots have been in use for a number of weeks, a white coloration begins to appear on the outer surface (Figure 5.4). These are soluble salt deposits—usually made up of fertilizer minerals from tap water—that precipitate as the water evaporates from the pot wall. This is a normal phenomenon but may be a warning signal of soluble salts buildup, a topic that will be discussed in Chapter Ten. In addition to salts, algae will also form on the moist, rich walls. Clay pots must usually be soaked and scrubbed with each reuse to remove these salt and algae deposits. In contrast, the evaporation of water through clay pots yields the beneficial effects of increased aeration in the soil mass, higher humidity around the plant, and less chance of over-watering.

FIGURE 5.4 Only pots such as clay that allow movement of moisture through their walls will exhibit salt deposits.

used (as described next under plastic pots), a follow-up soaking in clean water is necessary to remove the toxic sterilant from the clay pores.

PLASTIC POTS. Being impervious to water, plastic containers do not "breathe," thus allowing less evaporation of water from the soil mass than clay pots. This is good in the sense that soluble salts and algae do not accumulate on the sides of plastic pots but disadvantageous in that the soil aeration and humidity around the pot are reduced in comparison to clay. The relative slowness of soil to dry out in plastic, as opposed to clay, containers increases the possibility of overwatering. Most plastic pots are equipped with several drainage holes, but in addition, one should use a light, porous, well-drained soil mix as well as care in watering. The watering interval with plastic pots is often considerably longer than with clay, all other conditions being equal.

Plastic containers are quite light in weight, less fragile than clay pots, and, unlike clay pots, are commonly available in two forms—round and square—the square being more space efficient if plants are being produced in mass. The lightness of plastic increases the convenience of handling and reduces the cost of transportation (that is why most plants today are purchased in plastic containers), but unfortunately, the light weight increases the likelihood that these pots will tip over. The size range of plastic containers is comparable to clay, but the wide range of plastic colors available allows for more design flexibility with their use (Figure 5.5).

Sterilization of plastic pots is usually done by a short soak in a weak disinfectant (1 part Clorox: 9 parts water), followed by a clear water rinse. Steam or high heat will melt plastic, but a quick 3-minute dip in hot water (158°F; 70°C) may be used when heat is desired.

FIGURE 5.5 Plastic pots exhibit a greater array of sizes, shapes, and colors than clay pots.

GLASS AND GLAZED EARTHENWARE.

Containers of this sort are typically decorative in nature and are impervious to water, being similar to plastic in their water relations. Most are without drainage holes, so gravel or other aggregate material should be placed in the bottom prior to potting as a reservoir for excess water. Proper watering is extremely critical since an overabundance will quickly damage the roots and perhaps kill the plant. A close eye must be kept on soluble salts through periodic flushes with water since salts are not flushed out of the pot with routine watering. It is usually advisable to include a tube with gravel on one side of the container during potting so that the plant can occasionally be tipped on its side and drained through the gravel runway. If the plant is too large or otherwise unsuitable for this treatment, the tube might contain a "dip-stick" dowel rather than gravel so that the water accumulation in the bottom of the container can be monitored (Figure 5.6).

FIGURE 5.6 Large glass, earthenware, or other containers without drainage holes may be potted with a "dip-stick" to monitor the level of drainage water that collects.

METAL. Metal is similar in cultural terms to plastic and glass, but the important distinction exists that some metals, such as copper, may be toxic to plant roots. However, since only the roots actually in contact with the metal will probably be damaged, there should be no appreciable reduction in the growth of most plants. More damage is likely to occur to the metal container. The salts, acids, and alkaline materials of the soil solution are likely to tarnish or corrode even galvanized metal over a period of time. For this reason, along with the fact that most metal containers have no drainage holes, clay or plastic pots should be used as the plant container, with the metal container being employed as a decorative covering. If this solution is not practical, the interior of the metal container may be lined with heavy plastic, an asphalt compound, or epoxy to prevent the detrimental corrosive effects.

SELF-WATERING CONTAINERS. Generally made of plastic, these containers are double-walled to form a reservoir of water that is used to supply water to the plant (Figure 5.7). In the bottom of the inner wall, a porous material or a wick allows water to enter the soil mass by capillary action. A cap is located near the top of the container that may be removed for refilling the reservoir.

This principle of watering is also used in the commercial production of potted plants, but in a different way. Soft mats, kept moist with small hoses that ooze water, cover the greenhouse benches and supply water to the pots that are placed on them. The self-watering concept has a great deal of merit, but an occasional watering from above followed by drainage of excess water is helpful in preventing an excessive concentration of

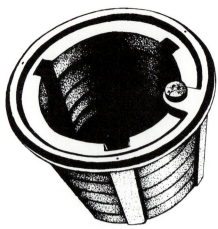

FIGURE 5.7 Self-watering containers are quite useful to frequent travelers or those who prefer less frequent plant maintenance.

soluble salts (see Chapter Seven on soil fertility problems).

TRANSLUCENT CONTAINERS: A PROBLEM.

An interesting aspect of translucent containers, such as those made from glass or light-colored plastic, has been published by the University of California Cooperative Extension Service. Studies have shown that the root systems of plants grown in translucent plastic pots may be inhibited by a sensitivity to light. Plants such as poinsettias, chrysanthemums, hydrangeas, certain palms and figs, schefflera, and the piggyback plant (*Tolmiea*) were shown to produce poor root systems in pots, whether clear or light in color, that allow a significant amount of light through the pot wall. When the roots reach the pot wall, they turn downward toward the darkness of the pot's bottom and show an absence of feeder roots compared to plants grown in opaque containers.

Propagation Containers

Any container is suitable for propagation if it holds the medium, provides good drainage, and is sterile. It need only be about 4 inches deep since cuttings are usually placed a maximum of 3 inches deep and transplanting occurs when the roots are about 1 inch long on most species.

CLAY AND PLASTIC POTS. As we have seen, these come in a variety of styles. The best for propagation is the shallow bulb pan shape that provides a large surface area in relation to the volume of medium used. Bulb pans have the added advantage of being very stable on the shelf because of their large base. If the medium must be pasteurized, both the medium and the clay pot can be put through the heat process at the same time.

Humidity and the moisture content of the medium can be made "automatic." A small 2-inch clay pot, with its drainage hole plugged with a cork, can be inserted down to its rim in the center of a larger, shallow container. The small pot is filled with water when the cuttings are inserted, and the slow loss of water through the small pot's clay wall will keep the medium moist. To maintain a high level of humidity, a plastic bag or cover can be placed in a tentlike fashion over bent coat hangers that form a "roof" over the entire container. The ends of the coathanger wires are inserted into the medium for support and the plastic is sealed with tape or a rubber band around the outside of the pot, or tucked under the pot. Two precautions must be taken: (1) the foliage should not touch the plastic, creating a place for water collection and fungal development, and (2) the container should not be placed in direct sun where temperatures during the day will cause the interior temperature to rise to dangerous levels.

PREMADE PROPAGATION BLOCKS AND CELLS. Many products are available to reduce the shock of transplanting new plants (Figure 5.8). Most can be grouped into (1) blocks into which seeds or cuttings are planted and which are transplanted intact

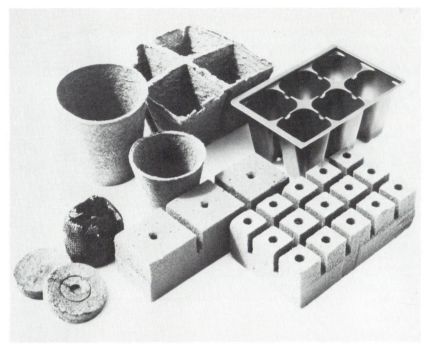

FIGURE 5.8 A sampling of the variety of propagation products available. Clockwise, beginning at the lower left are Jiffy Pellets® (compressed peat encased in a plastic netting), peat pots, peat strips, plastic cell packs, and Oasis® blocks.

with the plant and (2) cells that are temporary small "pots" removed from the plant before transplanting.

Blocks. Blocks of peat, wood fiber and peat, and Oasis® (foam-like material used in floral vases) are designed for cuttings or seeds to be planted in the top. Many are available with holes of varying size for seeds and cuttings of different dimensions. They are sterile when purchased. Upon rooting or germination, the roots grow through the block, allowing the roots, block, and all to be transplanted without disturbance of the root system. Some of the peat blocks are sold in a dry, compressed form and swell on being placed in water. Many of these products come with accompanying trays or fit conveniently into standard tray sizes.

Cell Packs. These are small pots, made of plastic or a combination of peat and wood

fiber, that are attached in units and fit standard tray sizes. Propagation occurs directly in the pots, or young seedlings are transplanted into them for further growth. The entire soil mass is eventually removed from plastic cells at final transplanting, but peat and wood fiber pots, being penetrated by the root system, are usually separated from the unit and planted intact.

DECORATIVE CONTAINERS. Propagation is not only a means of getting new plants, but it can be a unique decorating technique as well. In attractive pots and containers, vigorous cuttings or seedlings can be both a handsome addition to a room and a conversation piece. Containers are beginning to appear in plant shops and garden centers that are both functional and attractive. One such item is a glass or clear plastic bulbous container that has several holes at its top. Cuttings are inserted through the holes into a reservoir or water. Suspended from a string, the container creates an unusual and interesting means of adding interest to a bright window, as well as providing an out-of-the-way place to propagate plants.

Containers for Specialized Situations

The recent surge of foliage plant interest has also created an increase in the availability of containers that accommodate various uses of plants. Discussed here are several types that have proven most useful and popular.

HANGING BASKETS. A **hanging basket** is a container that displays trailing plants effectively by suspension from a bracket, the ceiling, or any other elevated point in the house. The better types for indoor use are of two styles. The first style is plastic containers that hang by means of three or four wires, plastic rods, chains, or cord. These are generally equipped with a plastic tray at the base for collection of excess drainage water. The tray, to be most effective, should detach for easy cleaning and not be so closely attached to the container that the reservoir capacity is inadequate. The second type for indoor use is constructed from the myriad of macramé styles (Figure 5.9). **Macramé** is the technique of using creative knotting to entwine various types of cord. Almost any kind of container can be used in these hangers, ranging from elaborate ceramic bowls with no drainage to simple clay pots with a tray underneath to catch water. The advantage of both types is that they are clean, attractive, and do not drip water.

Other types of hanging baskets are available, most notably wire, semispherical shells that can be lined with sphagnum or other kinds of moss, but these are only useful outdoors or in places indoors where their dripping and shedding of moss are acceptable. When the basket is to be hung onto a

FIGURE 5.9 Macramé comes in so many forms that it occasionally can be humorous. *Source:* Courtesy of W. H. Boserman.

wall, half-round models in plastic and wire are available, having a flat side that fits flush against the wall surface.

Hanging baskets offer the distinct advantage over other plant containers of requiring no table, shelf, or floor place. In smaller apartments or even in larger dwellings with a variety of bric-a-brac, space often becomes a limiting factor in the use of plants. Using vertical space effectively, hanging baskets generate new possibilities for plant placement. Also, the hanging of plants creates diversity of height, which in turn usually creates a more interesting and appealing room composition.

It is important to realize that hanging baskets often find themselves in hotter, drier conditions than most other plants, primarily because heat rises and hanging plants are positioned at higher levels in a room than other plants. This elevation of soil and foliage tends to increase both evaporation and transpiration, while making watering more difficult. Hanging plants also frequently find themselves placed near windows, under which are usually located radiators, heat ducts, or another form of heat source.

This direct heat and the additional natural heat if the window faces south or west tend to further enhance the problem. Consequently, it seems safe to assume that more hanging plants die of dryness than of overwatering. This temperature difference may also account for the problem occasionally encountered when healthy potted plants are propagated and experience difficulty in getting established as hanging specimens.

LARGE CONTAINERS. Pots are available, both in plastic and clay, that will nicely accommodate large plants or trees. Although relatively expensive, these give years of service with proper care. Since most have drainage holes, a water-catching tray must be provided to protect carpets and floors, and this must not be a clay tray since water will permeate these. To make watering and movement easier, a base with rollers can be built, into which is positioned the water tray and container.

Large ceramic containers are desirable since their inside walls are usually glazed and water-tight. Plants may be potted directly into these, or for more flexibility, a large pot may be set into the ceramic container. In the latter instance, props of wood should be used under the plant pot for elevation to the proper height, as well as to keep the pot base out of water that may accumulate in the ceramic container. Sphagnum moss or other mulch material may be used to disguise the inner pot.

STRAWBERRY JARS. Strawberry jars are small (one-pint) or large (several gallons) ceramic vessels, usually upright in form, that are wide-mouthed at the top and whose walls are covered with numerous pockets into which plants may be placed (Figure 5.10). Used historically in medieval times for the cultivation of herbs, strawberry jars are now used commonly as either indoor or outdoor planters.

Their unusual shape offers the indoor gardener several advantages. First, since most

FIGURE 5.10 Strawberry jars offer the opportunity for variety of textures, colors, and forms.

are unglazed, they breathe and allow the soil within to dry reasonably quickly. On the other hand, since the plants in each pocket may send their roots into the large central mass of soil, they are not as prone to death by dryness as a comparable plant growing in a small pot. Therefore, strawberry jars offer the best of both watering worlds—they help protect against overwatering by their porosity and against underwatering by containing a relatively large volume of soil that is slow to dry throughout.

Aesthetically, the strawberry jar provides height without using large plants. Also, infinite possibilities exist for combining plant colors, textures, and forms into pleasing arrangements. Since all the plants share the same pot, it is important to select species that have similar cultural preferences in terms of watering and light requirements. When this is difficult, the differences can be partially overcome by placing moisture-loving species in lower pockets where they can benefit from the slower-drying lower soil levels. A final aesthetic comment is that strawberry jars are usually more appealing to the eye when at least a few plants of loose, sprawling growth are included to lend grace and a sense of movement to the overall form.

Plant Pedestals

Initially popular during the Victorian era, in association with the Boston fern, pedestals for displaying ferns and other spreading or hanging plants are quite effective. These are tall (3 to 5 feet), slender wicker or wooden supports with an appropriate opening in the top for insertion of the plant container (Figure 5.11). A tray must be used for collecting

drainage water, and the base of the pedestal should be weighted or designed with spreading legs to provide stability.

Lighted Containers

For dark indoor settings, containers may be acquired that have a built-in source of light (Figure 5.12). These may or may not be satisfactory, depending on the type of light provided and how the container is used. If the container is designed to accommodate fluorescent tubes, then the fixture should be satisfactory, provided the light is of good quality and stays on 14 to 16 hours per day for most plants. However, if the light fixture uses only standard incandescent bulbs, the light quality and heat produced will be less desirable (see Chapter Eight on light).

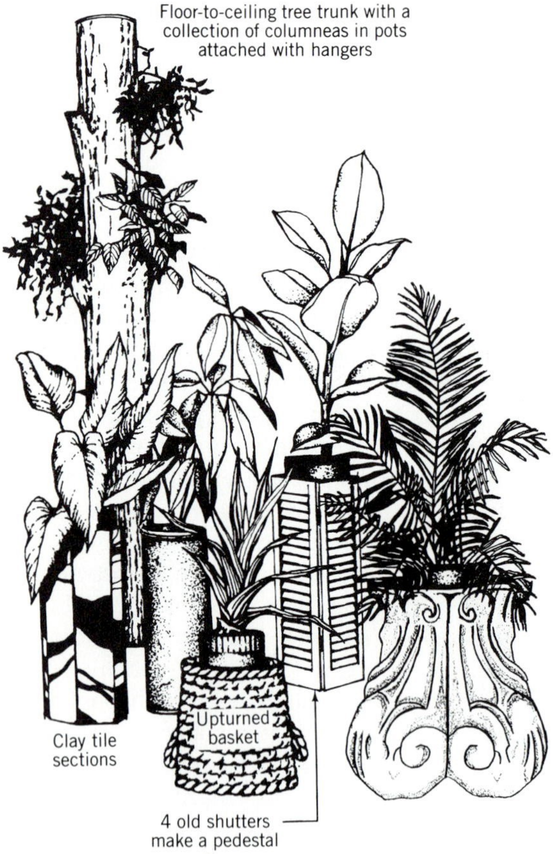

Floor-to-ceiling tree trunk with a collection of columneas in pots attached with hangers

Clay tile sections

Upturned basket

4 old shutters make a pedestal

FIGURE 5.11 A little imagination goes a long way in creating interesting pedestals. *Source:* Plants, Inc.

FIGURE 5.12 Commercially offered light stands come in a variety of styles, from tables to table models.

It is now possible to convert these incandescent fixtures to fluorescent lighting by using "screw-in" circular tubes designed to fit incandescent bulb sockets.

With the energy consumption of this method of growing plants taken into account, careful consideration should be given to the methods used. Predominant use of fluorescent tubes (one-half warm white plus one-half cool white, or the growth promoting types) is recommended because of their energy efficiency, light quality, low heat output, and longer bulb life. Also, lighted trays that house a number of plants are more energy efficient than individually lighted plants.

POTTING PLANTS INTO CONTAINERS

Potting plants is not a difficult task to perform, but one that requires care in several matters to assure proper development of the plant. An improperly potted plant may quickly become stunted or even die. This section will concern itself with the basic principles of the potting process, as opposed to considerations of repotting established older pots. Chapter Ten, "Care and Maintenance of Established Plants," will discuss the principles and practices of repotting.

Preparation of the Plant for Potting

Newly acquired plants that often need immediate potting are those growing in small plastic or clay pots, plastic trays or cell packs, and peat pots. Plants should be removed from these containers carefully to avoid injury to the root system. For plants in plastic or clay pots, tap the rim of the upside-down or tipped-over pot on a table corner, while holding the base of the plant stem between the index and middle fingers and the soil mass with the thumb and remaining fingers (Figure 5.13). This allows the soil mass to slide out of the pot gently without the detrimental effects of pulling on the top of the

Plants in clay or plastic pots usually pop out with a few taps on a solid surface.

FIGURE 5.13 Young plants should be removed from their containers with care to avoid disturbance of the root system.

plant. Removing plants from a cell pack simply involves pushing the bottom of each cell up to force the soil mass into a position where it can be grasped from above with the other hand. When several plants are growing in one individual tray, the soil should be cut into squares with a plant in the center of each one. The plants will recover from the resultant root damage.

Peat pots may be removed or left intact prior to potting. When the roots have begun significant penetration of the pot, it is advisable to leave the peat pot undisturbed to avoid damage to the roots. If the peat pot is potted intact, care must be taken to keep the plant well watered, because dry peat pots become rather hard and may restrict root development through the wall. In addition, the top edge of the peat pot should be broken down and covered by soil during potting. Otherwise, the exposed peat will create a wicking effect on the soil and result in rapid drying.

It is important to water young plants about to be potted prior to the operation. A wilted plant is far less apt to stand the shock of transplanting than a **turgid** (unwilted) one. Furthermore, a damp (but not wet) soil mass will not crumble as easily with handling and will slide out of the original container more readily.

If the plant that is to be potted has become **potbound** in the original container, that is, if the roots are significantly encircling the perimeter of the soil mass, these roots, if not prolific, should be gently pulled outward and spread prior to placement in the new pot. If the encircling roots are dense, several vertical cuts about ½ inch deep into the soil mass will cut the encircling roots, encourage development of new roots, and create a faster establishment of the newly potted plant by speeding the spread of new roots into the surrounding soil.

Potting Plants into Previously Used Containers

Most indoor gardeners eventually reach the level of affluence whereby they acquire a stock of previously used containers. Before these are used again, they should be scrubbed to remove soil, salt deposits, and adhering roots. After the pot is cleaned thoroughly, it should be sterilized as described in the preceding section.

Assuring Good Drainage

A critical concern during the potting process is the provision of an unrestricted movement of water away from the root system, thus reducing problems of poor root aeration and disease. Plastic and clay pots usually have varying numbers of drainage holes, depending on the pot size and type, to serve this purpose. Most small pots have one hole, whereas larger ones may have one or several. A pot with one hole usually requires steps to prevent erosion of soil through the hole and to ensure that the hole remains open, providing constant good drainage. Several

methods may be used at the outset of the potting procedure to protect the hole from blockage: (1) the already mentioned use of pot shards, concave-side down; (2) a layer of gravel on the bottom of the pot; (3) using a commercial "pot chip," which is a wafflelike plastic disc manufactured for this purpose; and (4) using a mesh material such as screen wire, nylon hose material, or another similar fabric that is fine enough to inhibit the erosion of soil but porous enough to allow the unrestricted passage of water. Pots with several smaller drainage holes require no special treatment to maintain good drainage, but it is a common practice to include a layer of gravel or to line the bottom of the pot with a mesh material to retard erosion of the growing medium.

Many of the decorative containers that are commercially available have no drainage holes for the escape of water. Holes may be easily drilled into plastic or wood, but not so with regard to ceramic materials. Without knowledge of the special techniques and materials required for drilling through ceramics, the indoor gardener is best advised to use the container as it was purchased, compensating for the drainage problem in other ways.

How to compensate for lack of drainage is a matter of controversy among horticulturists (Figure 5.14). On the one hand, a shallow layer of gravel at the bottom of the container is recommended by some as a reservoir for excess water. This procedure, they argue, allows water to collect in the bottom without keeping the soil mass constantly wet. The other side of the coin is to forego the gravel, using soil entirely, thus allowing the excess water to gradually evaporate through its capillary movement to the soil surface. Which method is preferable? The crux of the matter is not which method of potting is used, but how much water is applied to the established plant. Under either method, an overwatered plant will suffer. Our feeling is that either method works equally well if proper watering practices, as discussed in Chapter Ten, are followed.

Under any method of potting, determining the amount of water accumulating at the bottom of a large, closed container is difficult. Although the upper soil level may be dry, the lower area may remain soaked. There are two ways that one may overcome this quandry. First, before potting, a tube filled with gravel may be placed vertically along the side of the container, extending from the bottom to the soil surface. Once soil is added, the container may be periodically tipped onto its side, allowing the collected bottom water to escape through the tube. For situations when tipping would be difficult or inconvenient, a second method is more satisfactory and commercially available. Its operation is much like the first method, but a wick is enclosed in the tube, constantly transferring water from the bottom of the container to the atmosphere by means of capillary action and evaporation.

We should mention here that the word *soil* as we are using it may be at variance with the reader's interpretation. The following chapter will discuss soil for indoor plants at length, but suffice it to say here that a suitable **soil** for indoor use is a mixture of materials that provides a plant with proper nutrition, root aeration, moisture, drainage, and sanitation.

Even when a good soil mixture is used, poor procedures in potting may also inhibit drainage and root development. The soil used for potting should be moist, neither dusty dry nor muddy wet. A dry soil is difficult to use because it will not hold its shape well, and a wet soil is dangerous because it easily packs into a tight mass that becomes hard drying. In addition, care should be taken to avoid overpacking even the loosest of soil mixes during potting for the same reasons. Gentle firming with the fingers and a good watering will usually solidly anchor the plant without excessive compression of the soil. Such practices ensure that the soil

Without gravel reservoir   With gravel reservoir

FIGURE 5.14 Soil scientists point out that water does not move easily from a fine-textured soil mix down into gravel. Consequently, the presence of a gravel reservoir in the bottom of a container may actually increase problems of poor drainage above the gravel, particularly when watering practices are heavy handed.

mass is always well aerated and able to carry on the vital process of gas exchange.

Placing the Plant into the Pot
Plants beyond the seedling stage should be potted at the depth to which they are accustomed. It is also important to remember during potting that the upper soil level should be about ½ to 1 inch below the pot rim, depending on the pot size, to allow for easier watering. Therefore, the first step in potting is to place soil in the pot up to a level where the plant's root ball, when placed on this soil, will come up to this ½-inch-below-the-rim level. Firm this soil gently to avoid subsequent settling. Making sure that the plant is positioned properly, usually in the center of the pot, fill in soil around the sides until level with the top of the root mass. Again, this soil should be gently firmed into place. Using the thumbs

to compress the soil around the edge of the pot ensures a tight contact between soil and pot, thus helping to prevent water from escaping through that channel rather than penetrating the soil. After potting, the plant should be watered well to settle the soil into close contact with the root system. Periodic checking of drainage after potting is also necessary. Slow escape of drainage water or sluggish soaking of water into the soil mass indicates a problem that needs correction.

The soil ball should neither be higher nor lower in its new planting than it was originally growing, but plants such as African violets that are particularly susceptible to crown rots may be planted with the soil somewhat mounded up to the crown. Thus, the soil in the area of the crown is fast to dry after watering, if care is taken to avoid leveling the mound, thwarting the proliferation of moisture-loving rot organisms.

Aftercare of Newly Potted Plants

Until the roots establish themselves in the new medium, usually a period of 7 to 10 days, care should be taken in several areas. First, keep the plant out of warm areas to reduce the water loss through transpiration. Second, allow the plant to dry somewhat between waterings, discouraging rot organisms that might tend to infest the roots before the transplanting wounds are healed. And third, either do not fertilize or use dilute solutions (one-quarter to one-half strength), since full-concentration fertilizer applied immediately after potting may burn the roots or inhibit the growth of new rootlets.

CONTAINER CREATIVITY (CONTAINERS ARE WHAT YOU MAKE THEM)

Those who enjoy propagating young plants, and who prefer to grow large specimens rather than to buy them, find that providing containers for maturing plants can be expensive. Consequently, a collection of beautiful foliage plants may become less attractive by the use of inappropriate and inexpensive containers that distract the eye away from the foliage. Even for those indoor gardeners who can afford high-quality, commercially produced containers, a myriad of creative possibilities exists for one who is willing to invest a small amount of labor, materials, and skill. Several books are on the market that provide details of how to create attractive containers from a diverse selection of materials. Our purpose here is not to repeat the material covered in these books, but rather to summarize the common methods by which one can make containers at home and perhaps create an attractive, unique setting for one's indoor plants.

Selecting the Theme

Before selecting materials or methods of construction for containers, carefully consider the possible uses and placements for the container to be made. Will it be used indoors or outdoors, or possibly both? Is the setting formal, calling for a polished construction job and careful selection of materials, or would a rustic container be more in keeping with the environment? What colors must be matched or otherwise taken into consideration? Only when a careful survey is made of factors such as these will the design of a container be in harmony with its surroundings. Usually, after such thought is given to the existing situation, the materials and construction methods will be much easier to select since many unsuitable alternatives will be eliminated during the analysis process.

Creating Attractive Containers from Raw Materials

ACCOMMODATING SMALL PLANTS. Rooted cuttings or germinated seedlings, especially in larger quantities, may be transplanted into any household container that provides good drainage (Figure 5.15).

FIGURE 5.15 Young plants may be grown in large quantities at little expense if appropriate materials are saved rather than thrown away. Remember to create drainage holes.

The most suitable and economical items are the various styrafoam, plastic, or paper drinking cups. Paper and styrafoam cups simply need their bottoms pierced several times with a sharp pencil to provide drainage, and they will easily last until the plant outgrows them.

Clear plastic glasses have the additional advantage of durability. They can be cleaned and sterilized easily and used over and over so long as their brittle sides are not over-stressed and cracked. Drainage holes cannot be punched into these glasses without breaking the adjacent areas; an easy method of providing drainage is to use a heated knife to melt four or five evenly spaced holes around the basal rim.

Egg cartons are a good substitute for the plastic cell packs that commercial growers use to produce small plants. Seeds or small cuttings may be started and grown on in the carton, and the rounded shape of the individual sections facilitates easy removal of the young plants for transplanting. A hole punched in the bottom of each section is required for good drainage.

SPRUCING UP POTS. The easiest, least expensive, and least time-consuming method of creating containers is to face-lift clay pots in one of several ways. For fast color effects, these pots may be coated with a number of paint types, but preferably only after coating the surface with a sealer such as polyurethane. Unsealed pots allow water to permeate the wall, resulting in chipping or discoloration of the paint. With stencils or a small brush, designs may also be applied that give additional interest and perhaps relate to some textural pattern in the pot's surroundings. Only the outer surface of the pot should be painted, avoiding the possibil-

FIGURE 5.16 The simple cube jardiniere, constructed from cardboard or matboard, heavy tape, and fabric or contact paper, is inexpensive and easy to relate to its surroundings.

ity of damaging plants with the toxic effect of lead- or mercury-based paints.

Pots may also be decorated using waterproof glue and a variety of materials such as pieces of fabric, colored tissue paper, yarn, bark, and so forth. With materials such as fabric and yarn that can be easily stained by algae and the like, sealing the pot with clear polyurethane is also helpful before and after application of the decorative material. For a less permanent treatment, attractive pot coverings can be easily made from a piece of elastic or quilted fabric. These can be made with a minimum of sewing and in an infinite variety of colors and patterns. By making them fit standard pot sizes, they can quickly and easily be moved from pot to pot. With this method of pot decoration, take advantage of the opportunity of matching pot covers to fabrics found in draperies, furniture, or other room

furnishings. Cloth pot covers can be easily kept clean by an occasional washing or by construction with materials such as vinyl-coated cloth that repels water and can be wiped clean.

Like cloth pot covers, covered cardboard **jardinieres** (ornamental containers for plants) allow for frequent changes in decorating schemes. In this case, the plant's original container is simply masked by placing it in a larger, less permanent container (Figure 5.16). These jardinieres can be constructed from almost any material since they will not be in contact with moisture. The easiest method is to use a cardboard box or cylinder covered with some decorative material such as contact paper, wallpaper, fabric, photographs, or carpeting. Again, the possibilities for relating the design of the jardiniere to the decor of the room are numerous.

Natural Jardinieres and Containers

When natural or rustic materials are appropriate to the situation, several materials lend themselves quite well to serving as plant containers or jardinieres. Some require almost no preparation prior to planting, whereas others need some handiwork before use is possible.

DRIFTWOOD. Weathered pieces of wood can offer a great deal of character and interest to a room, particularly when their texture and form are accentuated by an associated plant. Driftwood has either a saltwater or freshwater origin, and the distinction is an important one. Freshwater driftwood is suitable for immediate use, but the salt content of ocean driftwood must be eliminated to avoid damage to the plant placed on it. A soaking for several days in fresh water is usually sufficient to correct the problem.

Although chicken wire, sphagnum moss, and soil mix can be used to facilitate direct plastering into a recessed area of the driftwood, this method is somewhat messy for indoor use. A better technique is the securing of a small pot to the rear of the driftwood, positioned so that the plant foliage protrudes through an opening in the wood or trails over the top. Including a drainage tray to catch excess water or making the pot easily removable from the driftwood will increase the convenience of watering. Furthermore, the driftwood can easily be made suitable for wall hanging by adding a screw-in hook to the back.

LAVA ROCK. Another natural material that is easy to find in plant stores and stone yards is pumic stone or lava rock, a lightweight stone that is the product of ancient lava flows, such as in the Sierra Nevada Mountains (Figure 5.17). Lava rock weighs about 80 percent less than comparably sized stones, is quite porous, and can be easily shaped and cut to fit the needs of the plant. With a hammer and chisel, holes suitable for plants can be cut into the stone and filled with a good potting medium. The plant is potted using normal planting procedures, and once established, the roots will penetrate the porous stone and firmly anchor the plant. Although its surface appears to be smooth, lava rock is actually quite sharp and its handling requires the use of gloves. Also, since it is so porous, watering is required rather frequently.

POTS FROM PLANTS. Some plants can provide containers for other plants, most notably the gourd and the coconut. Gourds come in a number of shapes and sizes, the larger types being the most suitable for planters because of the additional space they encompass for a soil mass. Figure 5.18 describes a process that may be used to prepare a gourd for planting. Gourds come in a variety of styles from long-handle types to simple, more rounded forms. Although usually small in size, decorative gourds offer interesting color and texture and may be prepared to accommodate small plant specimens. In this case, it is usually advisable to select plants

FIGURE 5.17 Lava rock or pumice stone is excellent when an unusual or rustic effect is desired. Handle with care!

without variegations or other extraordinary attractions, unless they accentuate a decorative quality of the gourd, so that a visual conflict of interest will be avoided.

Even though our main interest here is the artistic value of gourds, there is at least one functional benefit that this sort of container affords its associated plants. Since gourd walls contain cellular air pockets that serve as insulation, plants growing in them benefit from a relatively constant soil temperature.

Coconuts may be used in a similar fashion; their outer surface, however, requires no special treatment to make them attractive. Being much harder than gourds, their preparation is somewhat different. After a small knife is used to open the "eyes" of the coconut, the milk is poured out and one end cut off with a handsaw. The meat is then sliced thinly and carefully removed, leaving a clean inner surface that requires no waterproofing. The coconut may be used with macramé as it is; three holes may be drilled near the cut edge for attachment of hanging cords, or the end of the coconut as well as the end of the cutoff piece may be filed flat and joined together with glue and a small screw (Figure 5.19).

Step 1. Select an interesting gourd with sufficient soil holding capacity and a stem for hanging.

Step 2. If necessary soak overnight before sanding surface to remove residue.

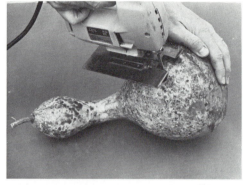

Step 3. After drilling a pilot hole, open a planting hole with a jigsaw, heavy knife, or comparable tool. Remove seeds and pulp.

Step 4. Attach decorative hanging cord, install plant, and locate in an appropriate setting.

FIGURE 5.18 With a minimum of effort, the common gourd can be transformed into an attractive container.

FIGURE 5.19 A carefully prepared coconut can provide food for the table and a feast for the eyes.

CLAY. If there is a ceramics dealer or school offering ceramics classes nearby, clay containers may strike your fancy, assuming that you can get access to a kiln for firing your finished products. Generally speaking, ceramic pots are turned on a wheel, a technique that requires training and skill. But a simpler, more foolproof method is available—constructing pots with clay coils. In this instance, a ¼-inch-thick disc of clay is rolled out, much like cookie dough, for the bottom of the container. A drainage hole, or sever-

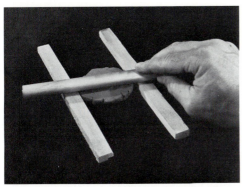

Step 1. Prepare the pot base by rolling out clay to a ¼-inch thickness and to the desired diameter.

Step 3. Add successive coils to the first, smoothing each coil into the one below it. Continue to add coils until the desired height is reached.

Step 2. Prepare coils of clay to be placed around the circumference of the base. Place one coil inside the first coil for added support of the pot wall.

Step 4. Finish the outside surface with the desired texturing and shape the rim. Allow to dry according to the clay instructions. Insert plant.

FIGURE 5.20 The coil method of ceramic construction requires almost no special skills or training.

al, should be cut. At this point, a number (depending on the pot size) of coils are rolled between the palms of your hands. These should be about ½ inch in diameter and about the same length as the circumference of the container bottom. A coil is then wound around the top of the bottom disc, adjacent to its edge. A second coil is wound around just inside the outer coil for reinforcement. These are then pinched together and smoothed out so that no crack remains. The inner coil should be shaped so that it forms a "ramp" between the bottom disc and the top of the outer coil.

Successive coils are then added to the wall, smoothing each one into the coil beneath it. The upper rim should also be reinforced and made easier to handle by flaring it or by making it thicker. Prior to firing, the container may be "dressed up" by creating textural patterns on it or by adding a glaze. If a glaze is used, you will recall, the container will loose its ability to breathe, but the problem of soluble salt accumulations on the outer surface will be eliminated (Figure 5.20).

WOOD. One of the most accessible of materials, wood can also be one of the most creative. It can be shaped, stained, and constructed rather easily and, if the proper power tools are accessible, grooved and joined in a multitude of ways. Since most indoor gardeners do not have easy access to such tools, we will discuss this aspect of container creativity using examples that can be made using ordinary hand tools.

Although wood offers so many alternative methods of design, there is one important aspect of its nature that must be considered to ensure a successful product: Most common woods will rot when exposed to moisture, giving containers constructed from them a short life. Therefore, one should use woods that are resistant to decay, such as cypress, cedar (except incense cedar), or redwood, or utilize woods that have been chemically treated with preservatives. If the preservative alternative is selected, care must be taken to avoid woods that have been treated with long-lasting plant-toxic materials such as pentachlorophenol, better known as "penta." Rather than purchasing wood that may have been treated with such products, it is preferable to purchase untreated wood and treat it with a nontoxic copper sulfate material that can be easily applied at home with a brush. By this method, a nontoxic finished product is guaranteed, but rot resistance is reduced. An additional precaution against decay is to use legs or blocks under wooden containers so that the bottom has air space and is not constantly moist from resting on the drainage tray.

Another important aspect of wooden container construction, regardless of the type of wood used, is that the pieces are joined together most commonly by metal screws or nails that may be susceptible to rust if not properly selected. Not only will the nails or screws become less apt to hold properly after rust proliferates, but also the adjacent wood may become stained unattractively. Therefore, it is advisable to use aluminum or galvanized nails and brass screws to construct containers that may be exposed to high humidity either from within or without, as well as to dampness from normal watering or rainfall.

For the purposes of indoor gardening, there are two basic means of building plant containers from wood, what we shall call the slat method and the box method. The slat method, as the name implies, is the creation of plant containers from slats, or small strips of wood such as lattice or 1 by 2's (inches). These are joined together by nails or wires into pot-holding configurations, most of which make excellent hanging containers.

The slats may be joined to one another in either a flat or vertical orientation. One of the simplest items using the flat orientation is a hanging pot holder that is simply a square or squares made from slats that support the rim of a clay pot (Figure 5.21). In this case, one measures the diameter of the pot just below the rim and uses slats, which may or may not be grooved at the intersections. The slats should be nailed or screwed together, and

FIGURE 5.21 The slat pot holder is one of the easiest wooden pot hangers to make.

FIGURE 5.22 The construction aspects of this container require precision of measurement and access to a power saw on which dado blades may be used. Some of the dimensions shown may require revision if dressed lumber is used.

Step 3. Drill four sets of holes down through all the squares as shown, being sure that each grooved bottom strip includes two of the four holes. Note wire in completed holes to maintain alignment during drilling.

Step 1. Cut 12 ten-inch strips of 1 x 2-inch wood as shown. The notches at each end are the same width as the strips and are cut halfway through the strip. Groove the bottom of two strips as shown to hold the lath bottom.

Step 4. Run wire through the four sets of holes, crimping the bottoms and hooking the tops.

Step 2. Assemble four squares, one incorporating the lath bottom.

Step 5. Attach decorative chain or cord, add a graceful plant, and enjoy an attractive homemade hanging planter.

Containers for Growth and Aesthetic Appeal **129**

holes drilled at each outside corner for insertion of the hanging ropes.

Another slat idea using square or rectangular slats piled on top of one another is a hanging container that completely disguises the pot it holds. If the slats are arranged in a vertical orientation, they should be grooved at each end so that they fit flush, and two of the bottom pieces should be grooved to hold the lath bottom pieces. Therefore, the pieces are fitted together to create the unified effect shown in Figure 5.22.

For more substantial planters, whether for hanging plants or large specimens such as trees, the box method is a better technique. It offers the advantage of camouflaging unsightly containers that may be quite large and heavy, as well as the ability to adapt to various plant sizes. As with the slat method, appropriate selection of wood and hardware is important. Nails work well for smaller containers, but screws or lag bolts are needed if the weight of a larger plant is involved. The number of ways pieces of wood can be cut and constructed into planters is limited only by our imagination.

When a simple box is to be constructed, identically cut four pieces of wood to the size you prefer. For the bottom, cut a square that is smaller than the side panels by the thickness of the wood you are using. For example, if you have cut four 10-inch squares out of 1- by 10-inch lumber, the bottom square should be 9 inches square (10 inches side square − 1 inch thickness = 9 inches bottom square).

To construct the box, be sure all parts fit satisfactorily, glue the edges together, and secure with finishing nails, screws, or lag bolts. If plants are to be placed directly into the planter, drainage holes must be added to the bottom. Also, wooden strips for air space or holes for hanging cords must be included depending on whether the box will be a table or hanging planter. If other, more complicated shapes are desired, one should draw sketches prior to construction or consult one of the several books listed at the end of this chapter that deal with ideas and designs for planters and containers.

In conclusion, we can say that it is the selection or construction of plant containers that offers the indoor gardener the flexibility to interject creativity and personality to the greatest extent. If horticulture is both an art and a science, this is one area in which art is just as important as science. Therefore, the indoor gardener can enjoy this avocation to the fullest by taking advantage of the great diversity of containers as a medium of expression of oneself. Having said this, we turn again to science. In the next chapter, we consider that all-important, unseen aspect of any container-grown plant, the medium in which it grows.

FOR FURTHER READING

Container and Hanging Gardens. San Francisco, Calif.: Ortho Book Series, Chevron Chemical Co., 1975.

Fitch, C. *The Complete Book of Houseplants.* New York: Hawthorne Books, 1975.

Fitch, C. *The Complete Book of Houseplants Under Lights.* New York: Hawthorne Books, 1972.

Graf, A. *Exotic Plant Manual.* East Rutherford, N.J.: Roehrs Co., 1974.

Hawkey, W. *Living with Plants.* New York: William Morrow and Co., 1974.

Langer, R. *Grow It Indoors.* New York: Saturday Review Press, 1973.

Manaker, G. *Interior Plantscapes.* Englewood Cliffs, N.J.: Prentice-Hall, 1981.

Park's Flowerbook. George W. Park Seed Co., Inc.

chapter six
understanding the growing medium

Soil in the field may be defined as the unconsolidated cover of the earth, made up of mineral and organic components, water, and air, and capable of supporting plant growth. This definition also seems appropriate for agriculturists, gardeners, and indoor plant enthusiasts because it includes the four major components of soils. It also stresses the most important capacity of soils—their ability to support the growth of plants. As a medium for plant growth, the soil performs four vital functions:

1. It serves to anchor the roots of plants.
2. It supplies water to plants.
3. It yields minerals required by plants.
4. It provides aeration to plant roots.

Those growing plants indoors, however, rarely use field soils alone. More often, they utilize soils to which amendments have been added or media entirely devoid of soil, the so-called synthetic media, or artificial media. In addition to the differences in basic physical composition, the growing media used by indoor gardeners have other unique features associated with their confinement in containers. The most obvious features of media in containers are (1) small volume, (2) shallow depth, and (3) direct exposure to the atmosphere both at the top (surface) and bottom (drainage level or drainage holes).

In spite of the significant differences between field soils and container media, they share many features in common. The four vital functions performed by field soils are also essential attributes of container media. Furthermore, the quality of both is based primarily on their ability to support the growth of plants. Soils in the field serve so well in this capacity that indoor gardeners attempt to duplicate field conditions within the confines of a container. To do so requires knowledge of the physical and chemical properties of soils, topics to which we turn our attention in Chapters Six and Seven.

PHYSICAL PROPERTIES OF SOILS

Soils may be broadly classified, on the basis of their organic matter content, as either organic or mineral. Mineral soils are those containing less than 20 percent organic matter. Typically, their organic matter content ranges between 3 and 5 percent, although a higher percentage of organic matter may be present on the soil surface. Organic soils, in contrast, have an organic matter content greater than 20 percent, and many are composed almost entirely of organic materials. Mineral soils are far more abundant on the earth's surface and our attention will center on them. We will not entirely neglect organic soils, however, because many plants, including the popular sundews (genus *Drosera*) and Venus fly-trap (genus *Dionaea*), thrive on organic soils.

The Major Components of Soils

The major components of mineral soils are (1) mineral material, (2) organic matter, (3) air, and (4) water. Mineral material occupies by far the greatest volume as is illustrated by the silt loam soil shown in Figure 6.1. The organic fraction, on the other hand, occupies the smallest volume, usually averaging 3 to 5 percent by weight of the topsoil. The mineral and organic components make up about 50 percent of the volume of a given soil. Together, they comprise the **soil solids,** and their combined characteristics determine the inherent fertility of soils.

Between the soil particles, a great deal of **pore space** occurs, space that can be occupied either by air or water. When the indoor gardener waters a container, air within pore space is replaced by water. Through use by plants, evaporation, and drainage, water is lost from the medium and air content again increases. Obviously, the volume occupied by each of these components is in a constant state of flux. Maintaining a favorable balance between air and water—a major problem in container situations—determines in large part the suitability of soils or other growing media for indoor gardening.

MINERAL MATERIAL. The mineral fraction of soils consists of inorganic particles of various sizes and types. These particles are classified according to size, without regard to their chemical composition, color, or weight. Three size classes are recognized as follows:

PARTICLE	SIZE RANGE
Sand	0.05 to 2.0 mm
Silt	0.002 to 0.05 mm
Clay	Less than 0.002 mm

All soils are mixtures of sand, silt, and clay, but in each soil the proportions vary. In the laboratory, the proportion of each is determined using a series of sieves, but the home gardener can make a rough approximation by rubbing moist soil between the thumb and fingers, using the guidelines given in Table 6.1.

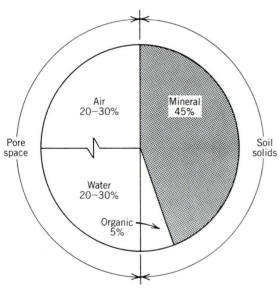

FIGURE 6.1 Mineral soils consist of four components in varying proportions. Mineral material and organic matter make up the soil solids; water and air fill the pore space. *Source: Brady, N., The Nature and Properties of Soils, 8th ed., New York: Macmillan, 1974, p. 13. Reprinted with permission.*

TABLE 6.1 GUIDELINES FOR APPROXIMATING THE MINERAL COMPOSITION OF FIELD SOILS BASED ON FEEL CHARACTERISTICS AND SUITABILITY FOR USE IN CONTAINERS

Kind of Soil	General Feeling	Suitability for Use in Containers
Sandy	Scratchy or gritty	Poor; low nutrient and water-holding ability, heavy
Silty	Smooth and slippery, but not sticky	Adequate if percentage of sand is high; best used in mixes
Clayey	Slippery and sticky	Poor; unfavorable aeration, contraction from container sides

SOIL TEXTURE. The proportions of the different particle sizes in a soil determine its **texture.** If a soil has moderate amounts of sand, silt, and clay, it is called a **loam.** If one particle is present in somewhat greater abundance, its name is added to the description; thus, there are sandy loams, silt loams, and clay loams. If a given particle class exerts an even stronger influence, the soil may bear the name of that textural class alone. These relationships are shown in Figure 6.2. Soil scientists recognize a total of 12 textural classes. While it is not essential that we know each of these classes, it is important that we have an understanding of the characteristics imparted to soils by sand, silt, and clay.

Soil particle size has a profound influence on water percolation, water retention, aeration, nutrient supply, and soil strength. In general, sandy soils allow faster water percolation and better aeration than finer textured soils, but their ability to hold water and supply nutrients is low. They also have less strength of aggregation and are easy to work (mix or cultivate). Loam soils combine all of the particle sizes in desirable proportions and because of this have favorable levels of water percolation, water retention, aeration, and fertility. Loam soils are versatile soils and, when properly managed, can be used successfully in containers. As the amount of clay (or sand) in a soil increases, the less versatile that soil becomes for growing plants and the more exacting are its management requirements for good plant growth. Heavy clay soils hold large amounts of water and have a favorable nutrient content, but because of a low degree of water percolation, these soils have poor aeration. Heavy clay soils are also sticky and difficult to work. For these and other reasons, they are entirely unsuitable for container use.

You may wonder why particle size has such a profound influence on soil properties. As it turns out, most available nutrients and water are adsorbed on the surfaces of soil

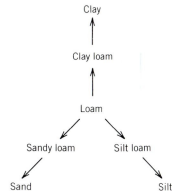

FIGURE 6.2 The relationship between soil particle size, distribution, and textural class.

particles. As particle size decreases, the total surface area of the soil volume increases proportionately. The relationships between particle size and surface area are illustrated in Figure 6.3. Clay has thousands of times more surface area than silt and about a million times more surface area than coarse sand. Because of its vastly greater surface area, clay has a far greater ability to enter into the physical and chemical reactions in the soil. The sand and silt are merely broken down rock fragments and when compared to clay are essentially inert, although they do have an important skeletal role. The minute clay particles, on the other hand, provide an enormous surface area. Furthermore, clay particles have an electrical charge (more on this in Chapter Seven) and therefore can adsorb and retain nutrients for use by plants. In essence, clay has a "dual character": It serves a positive role in water storage and nutrient retention. When too abundant, however, clay dramatically decreases soil aeration, resulting in poor plant growth.

SOIL STRUCTURE. As important as soil texture is in determining the characteristics of soil, it does not tell the whole story. Examination of the soil in your garden or yard will show that it is not composed of very small particles alone, but of **aggregates** of small

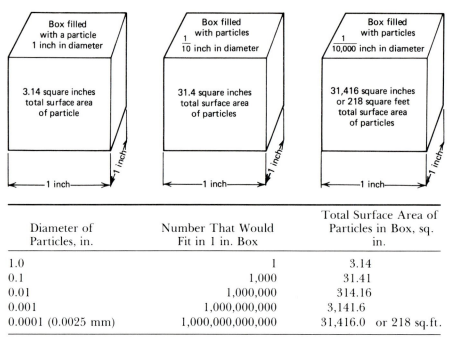

Diameter of Particles, in.	Number That Would Fit in 1 in. Box	Total Surface Area of Particles in Box, sq. in.
1.0	1	3.14
0.1	1,000	31.41
0.01	1,000,000	314.16
0.001	1,000,000,000	3,141.6
0.0001 (0.0025 mm)	1,000,000,000,000	31,416.0 or 218 sq.ft.

FIGURE 6.3 The relationship between particle size and surface area as illustrated by the number of round particles that will fit into a box 1 cubic inch in size.

particles (Figure 6.4). The term **soil structure** is used to describe these aggregates of soil particles. Several structural types are recognized in mineral soils. Their formation is promoted by the presence of clay colloids, high levels of organic matter, and the activities of living organisms, both plant and animal. Of the various types of soil aggregates, two—granular and crumb—are of importance to the indoor gardener. This is because granular and crumb-type structures are common to the surface soils and used in container situations.

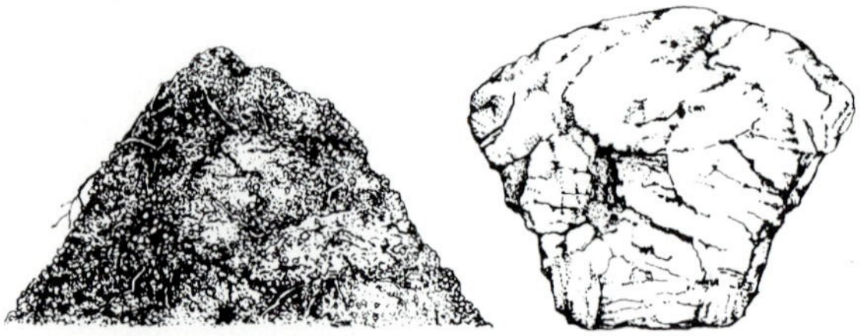

Soil structure, like texture, influences many soil properties including water movement, aeration, density, and porosity. Unlike soil texture, however, soil structure can be easily modified. Working clay soils when they are too wet causes a breakdown in soil structure and results in a condition known as **puddling.** Puddled soils are dense and compacted as evidenced by their crusted condition (Figure 6.4). Rain falling on such soils runs off much easier than it permeates the soil. The puddled condition also has an unfavorable influence on soil aeration. As a consequence of these factors, plant growth is poor.

ORGANIC MATTER. Of the major components of mineral soils, organic matter is present in the smallest amounts. But despite its small quantity, it has profound effects on

FIGURE 6.4 Granulated and puddled soils.

soil properties and thus on plant growth. Among the important attributes of organic matter, we have cited its beneficial effect on soil structure. Organic materials are also the main source of energy for the myriad of soil microorganisms, without which many important soil reactions would not occur. Organic matter is also an important source of nutrients used by plants. It contains from 5 to 60 percent of the total phosphorus, 10 to 80 percent of the total sulfur, and virtually all of the nitrogen. It also contains smaller quantities of other nutrients required by plants. Finally, organic matter influences the amount of water a soil can hold and the proportion of this water available to plants. When identical amounts of water are added to two soils—one low and one high in organic matter—the water penetrates a lesser volume of the high organic matter soil, revealing its greater water-holding capacity. Thus emerges the most remarkable feature of organic matter: Through its promotion of soil aggregation, organic material enhances soil aeration, while at the same time improving the ability of the soil to store water.

Two forms of organic materials are recognized: (1) newly added tissue and its partially decomposed derivative and (2) the humus. **Humus** is a dark, colloidal material of variable composition. It is a more or less stable breakdown product of organic debris. Added organic materials break down rapidly—in a matter of weeks or months—to humus, humus only slowly to again form the basic elements.

An understanding of the process of recycling of organic materials is of importance to the gardener, both outdoors and indoors. To illustrate, when an organic material such as cow manure is added to the soil, microorganisms rapidly begin decomposing it to humus. In early stages of decomposition, microorganism numbers increase greatly (Figure 6.5). This rapid growth of the microorganism population ties up much of the available nitrogen in the soil. As decomposition

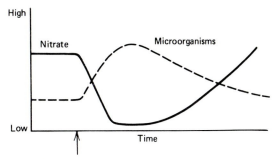

FIGURE 6.5 Changes in the amount of soil nitrate (solid line) and the activity of decomposer microorganisms (dashed line) when an organic material is added (at arrow) to the soil. *Source:* Chrispeels, M., and Sadava, D., *Plants, Food, & People,* San Francisco, Calif.: W. H. Freeman Co., 1977, p. 93.

nears completion, the microbe population decreases, releasing nitrogen in a form usable to higher plants. This pattern explains why the addition of organic residues to soils often results in the nitrogen deficiency of growing plants. The deficiencies can be prevented by adding additional nitrogen to the soil when high-carbon organic materials are incorporated. Alternatively, organic materials can be composted and the finished compost added to the soil.

SOIL AIR. Between soil particles, there are always many spaces of varying size, which collectively make up the pore space (Figure 6.1). The pore space comprises a fairly constant percentage of the total soil volume, ranging from 40 to 60 percent. This space is filled with water and air, the percentage of each depending on the moisture content of the soil. Sandy soils have less total volume occupied by pore space than do more finely textured soils, but the size of the individual pores is much larger. These large pores, called **macropores,** allow for faster movement of air and water through the soil, a process termed **percolation.** Thus, in a sandy soil, percolation may be quite rapid even though the total pore space is small, simply because of the greater pore size. These relationships are summarized in Table 6.2.

TABLE 6.2 THE RELATIONSHIP OF SOIL TEXTURE TO SIZE OF PORES, TOTAL PORE SPACE, AND RATE OF PERCOLATION

| | SOIL TEXTURE | |
	Sandy	Fine Textured
Size of pores	Large	Small
Total pore space	Low	High
Rate of percolation	Fast	Slow

Soil air is not merely an extension of atmospheric air. Indeed, the soil air does not form a continuum within the soil, but rather occupies a maze of spaces of varying sizes. Moreover, air composition varies from space to space as well as between soil and atmosphere. The relative humidity of soil air approaches 100 percent, a condition favoring the growth of soil organisms. Soil air commonly has more carbon dioxide—up to several hundred times as much—and less oxygen than atmospheric air. In general, there is an inverse relationship between the content of these two gases, with the oxygen decreasing as the carbon dioxide content increases.

The concentrations of both oxygen and carbon dioxide are related to biological activity within the soil by microorganisms, larger animals, and the roots of plants. Oxygen is essential in the respiratory process, and plant roots respire around the clock. A deficiency of oxygen to roots, even for a relatively short period, can severely retard plant growth. Deficiency symptoms may manifest themselves in unusual ways. For example, a deficiency of oxygen can slow nutrient and water uptake by plants. As a consequence, plants may show nutrient-deficiency symptoms on soils well supplied with the needed plant nutrients.

Soil oxygen levels are closely tied to soil structure. Soils with large aggregates have an abundance of macropores. Following a rain or irrigation, these pores are soon freed of water, thus allowing gases to move into the soil. A favorable balance of organic matter in the soil is the best way of assuring desirable structure.

SOIL WATER. Water is the solvent in which soil nutrients are dissolved. This mixture of water and nutrients, termed the **soil solution,** is the vehicle whereby nutrients are moved throughout the plant. The many chemical reactions that take place in the soil occur in water. Water also plays an important role in regulating soil temperatures and, as mentioned above, bears an intimate relationship to soil air.

Several categories of soil water are recognized. To illustrate, visualize a volume of soil that has just been deluged by water. At this point, all of the pores, large and small, are filled with water; the soil is completely **saturated** (Figure 6.6). This saturated condition will persist only until water begins to drain from the soil due to gravitational forces. The water in the macropores will then be replaced by air. When this weakly held gravitational water has been removed, the soil is said to be at **field capacity** (Figure 6.6). Plants can, of course, use gravitational water if they can capture it before it drains away.

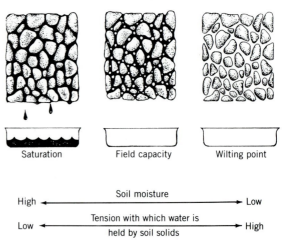

FIGURE 6.6 A soil at saturation, field capacity, and wilting coefficient. *Source:* Modified from Brady, N., *The Nature and Properties of Soils,* 8th ed., New York: Macmillan, 1974, p. 190.

Plants growing on our soil will absorb water, and water will be lost from the soil surface through evaporation. Finally, however, a point is reached at which the water is held so tightly by the soil particles that plants cannot obtain it fast enough to replace water lost by transpiration. As a result, the plants will wilt. The soil moisture content at this stage is called the **wilting coefficient** (Figure 6.6). In other words, the soil water available to plants is that present between field capacity and the wilting coefficient. This water is termed **available water.** It is important to add that soil at the wilting coefficient still has a considerable amount of moisture present; in fact, it still appears somewhat moist.

Available water moves from wetter to drier locations in the soil more or less independently of gravity. This movement, which can be up, down, or sideways, occurs through very fine pores, termed **micropores.** The diameter of micropores approximates that of hair and as a consequence, this water is called **capillary water,** from the Latin word *capilla* meaning hair.

PECULIARITIES OF CONTAINER CULTURE

The indoor plant boom has stimulated numerous investigations aimed at giving us a better understanding of container culture. In this section and the section to follow, we have drawn on the results of these investigations and, particularly, the innovative and detailed studies of L. A. Spomer, Department of Horticulture, University of Illinois.

Growing media in containers differ from field soils in two important ways: (1) they are small in volume and (2) they are shallow in depth. The effects of smallness are obvious. A medium of small volume can supply only a limited amount of water and minerals for plant growth. These limitations can be overcome by the frequent addition of plant nutrients and water, but as we shall see, frequent watering creates problems of its own. The effects of limited media depth are equally important but less obvious. To fully understand this parameter, we must first have an understanding of the unique properties of water.

Water, A Unique Molecule

Water is vitally important to plant survival and growth. The majority of mineral nutrients required by plants are dissolved in soil water. These nutrients move into and throughout the plant in a watery milieu. Likewise, the products of photosynthesis move from leaves to growing tips and roots in a watery transport medium. Water is a large part of the fresh weight of plants; a watermelon is over 90 percent water, whereas most plants grown indoors are between 60 and 80 percent water. Within living cells, water composes most of the protoplasm and provides a medium in which organelles can maintain their functional forms and relationships with one another. Water is under pressure in living cells, and this pressure gives form and rigidity to soft tissues. These are only a few of the vital roles of water in plants.

The water molecule has the chemical notation H_2O. This means that each molecule contains two atoms of hydrogen (H) combined with an atom of oxygen (O). The atoms are so arranged that the molecule is **polar,** that is, one end of the molecule has a positive electrical charge, the other end a negative charge. The polarity of the water molecule attributes to two important properties, adhesion and cohesion. **Adhesion** is the attraction of water molecules to other surfaces, **cohesion,** the attraction of molecules to each other. The cohesive force of water is much greater than its adhesive force, but both are important in terms of the movement of water in soils.

These forces can be illustrated by a simple physical apparatus. Imagine that we have a rack containing four 12-inch-long glass tubes with different inside diameters, as shown in Figure 6.7. If each of these tubes is immersed

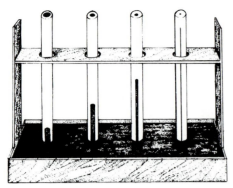

FIGURE 6.7 When glass capillary tubes are placed in colored water, the water rises in the tubes to a height inversely proportional to the diameter of the capillary. *Source:* Redrawn from Neel, P. L., "Soil and Water Relationships," Proceedings of the 1977 National Tropical Foliage Short Course, p. 95.

in a shallow layer of colored water, the water will rise up into each tube a certain distance. For each tube, this distance is inversely proportional to the internal diameter of the tube. Water rises due to its attraction to the walls of the tube and ceases upward movement at the point where the attractive force (adhesion) is balanced by the downward pull of gravity. Water rises higher in tubes of smaller diameter because the adhesive forces are stronger relative to the force of gravity. The force of gravity is still acting on the column of water, however, but cohesive forces keep the column intact. Thus, the water column in the tube is under tension. The phenomenon just described is termed **capillary action.**

The pores in the soil form an interconnecting network of capillary tubes in which water moves from wetter to drier regions due to adhesive and cohesive forces. When water is added to a soil, it enters the pores due to the combined effects of gravity and capillarity. The added water moves downward and sideways, replacing the stale air in the pores. With the continued addition of water, the length of the water-filled capillaries continues to increase until finally the soil mass is saturated with water. In a container, excess

water drains out the bottom holes; in the field, it continues to move downward to the water table.

Water Relations in Container Soils

Important differences exist in the movement of capillary water in container versus field soils. In field soils, the water-filled capillaries are so long that the pull of gravity is greater than the capillary force tending to hold the water within the pores. As a result, water tends to move downward pulling air from the surface down into the pores to replace the draining water. After about 24 hours, the water in the soil is at field capacity. Clay soils, due to smaller pores, hold water much more tenaciously than sandy soils with their larger pores. As mentioned earlier, the water held between field capacity and the wilting coefficient is the water used by plants.

When a field soil is placed in a container, the vertical length of the capillaries is reduced. Even when they are filled from top to bottom with water, the pull of gravity is not sufficient to counteract the capillary attraction in the pores. As a consequence, the pores remain filled and fresh air is not pulled into the pores from the top. Drainage is brought about not by gravity, but by the removal of water from pores by plant roots and evaporation. Thus, we see that a **perched water**

FIGURE 6.8 For a given soil in a container, water and air content following watering and drainage is a function of soil depth. The deepest soil is too dry, the shallowest too wet for good plant growth. *Source:* Redrawn from Spomer, L. A., "Soils for Interior Planters: Water Relations," Proceedings of the 1978 National Tropical Foliage Short Course, p. 109.

table (a water table above the general water table) is formed in containers. The shallower the container, the higher the water table. Said another way, for a specific soil used in a container, the water and air content of the pore space following watering and drainage is a function of soil depth. This relationship is illustrated in Figure 6.8.

As you might expect, soil water and air content also vary with soil textural class. If three containers of identical size are filled to the same height (depth) with soils differing texturally, the water and air content of the pore space varies dramatically (Figure 6.9). In general, when soil alone is used in containers, loamy soils are superior. Clay soil holds too much water resulting in poor aeration. Sandy soils, on the other hand, lose too much water from the upper strata and are too dry for good plant growth.

Clay soils display another undesirable feature when used in containers. Typically,

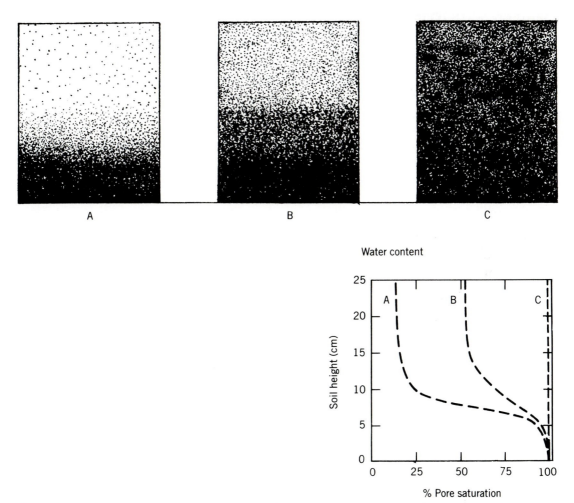

FIGURE 6.9 Soil water content following watering and drainage for container soils of uniform depth but differing texturally: A, a very coarse-textured sand; C, a silty clay loam; B, a mixture of A and C. Source: Modified from Spomer, L. A., "Soils for Interior Planters: Water Relations," Proceedings of the 1978 National Tropical Foliage Short Course, p. 108.

the soil mass contracts so much that a space develops between the soil and the pot (refer to Figure 10.3). Added water can move through this space and out the bottom of the container without wetting the whole mass of soil. This means that in clay soils, water coming out the bottom of the container is not a reliable indicator that the soil mass is uniformly wet. Soils high in organic matter may display similar characteristics, though less commonly.

AMENDING SOILS TO IMPROVE TEXTURE AND STRUCTURE

The above discussion suggests several reasons why soil alone is seldom suitable for plants in containers. Smallness and shallowness create the dilemma of a soil that contains an inadequate supply of water and minerals, yet this same soil may be too wet for the plant to absorb even these meager amounts. Frequent watering and fertilization appear as obvious remedies, but this will increase the frequency of poor aeration with its resulting negative effects on water and nutrient uptake. All is not lost, however. The solution lies in the use of soil amendments or soilless media. Before we evaluate some of the important and widely used soil amendments, we need some insight into the effects of these amendments on soil porosity.

Soil Amendment Basics

Many coarse-textured materials can be added to container soils to ensure adequate aeration and also favorable water retention. The more popular of these amendments are described in the next section. Here, we describe what happens when a coarse-textured sand with a narrow range of particle sizes is added to a natural soil. Although this is not the combination used most frequently by indoor gardeners, the principles illustrated herein apply equally well to other situations.

Figure 6.10 shows the effects of adding varying amounts of sand to a soil. In each case, the mixture volume is a constant 10 cubic yards, but media total (sand + soil) may exceed 10 cubic yards. Several features should be noted: First, if too little coarse-textured material is added, pore space and water retention actually decrease. Insufficient amendment (B, C) simply reduces soil volume without adding the large aeration pores characteristic of sand. As indicated in A to D, total porosity drops precipitously. Second, as additional sand is added, a point is reached at which the container is exactly full of the coarse-textured sand and the intervening pores are exactly full of soil. At this proportion, known as the **threshold proportion,** total porosity is at a minimum (Figure 6.10, see D). Even though a considerable amount of amendment has been added, this is the worst possible mixture for growing plants. Nevertheless, the threshold proportion is an important value. It represents not only the point of minimum porosity, but also the point at which the use of additional amendment begins to improve the quality of the medium for plant growth.

As amendment beyond the threshold proportion is added (or soil volume is decreased), porosity begins to increase (E, F). Pure sand (Figure 6.10, G) has approximately 36 percent pore space, whereas pure soil (Figure 6.10, A) has approximately 50 percent pore space. In general, the predominantly large pores in sand are air pores, the predominantly small pores in the soil are water pores. Pure sand is an unsuitable medium because of its poor water retention qualities, the soil because of its poor aeration qualities. A medium containing about half large aeration pores and half water retention pores is much more desirable for plant growth. This balance is reached when sufficient amendment has been added to reach the threshold proportion and additional amendment added to reach a level corresponding to Figure 6.10, E. The threshold proportion for common amendments such as sand, perlite, and vermiculite is approximately 5 volumes of the amend-

Amount of Sand, Soil and Pores (yd³ in ten yd³ mixture)

	A	B	C	D	E	F	G
Soil	10.	7.7	5.5	3.6	2.5	1.5	0.
Sand	0.	3.5	7.	10.	10.	10.	10.
Pores	5.	3.9	2.8	1.8	2.4	2.9	3.6

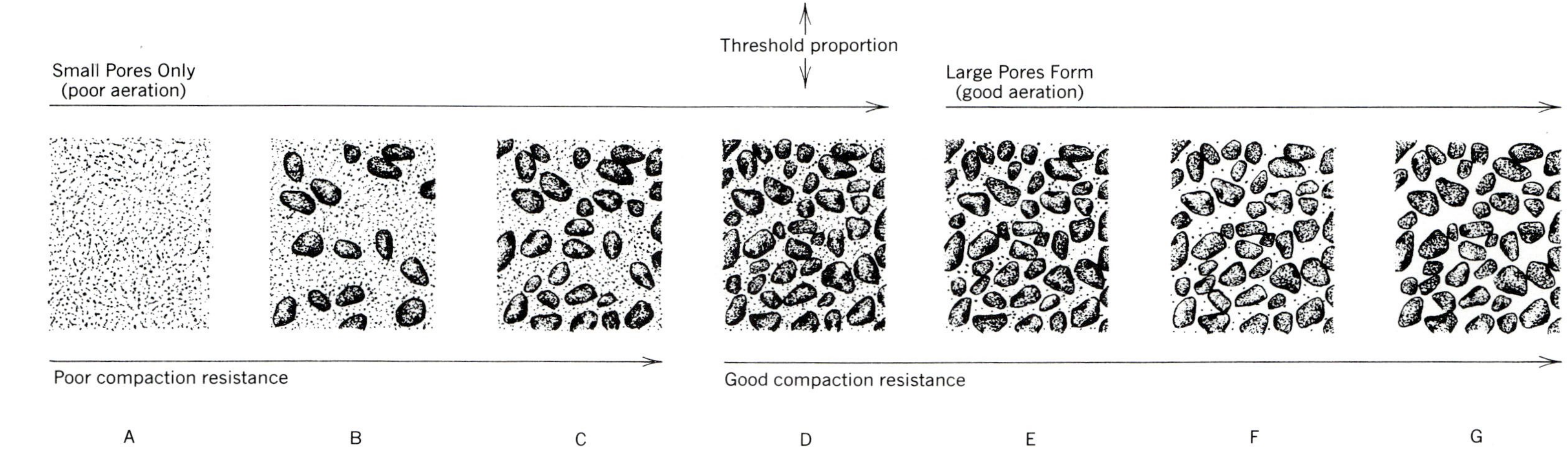

Small Pores Only (poor aeration)

Threshold proportion

Large Pores Form (good aeration)

Poor compaction resistance

Good compaction resistance

FIGURE 6.10 The effects of mixing a coarse-textured material (sand) with a fine-textured material (soil) on media volume, soil porosity, aeration, and compaction resistance. Total container volume was a constant 10 cubic yards. *Source:* Redrawn from Spomer, L. A., "Soils for Interior Planters: Water Relations," Proceedings of the 1978 National Tropical Foliage Short Course, pp. 105–113.

ment to 2 volumes of the fine-textured material. Therefore, a good container medium should contain about a 3:1 ratio of coarse-textured material to fine-textured material. Remember, all soils contain some coarse-textured material that must be considered in computing totals. Also, when organic materials such as peat or bark supply the coarse-textured component, lesser amounts are required in the mixture to reach the threshold proportion.

Commonly Used Soil Amendments

We have seen that soil alone is seldom suitable for container plants. Several amendments, when combined with soil, make excellent growing combinations. These are the most commonly used commercial amendments.

SPHAGNUM MOSS. This product is actually dried bog plants from the genus *Sphagnum* and may be purchased milled (ground into a fine texture) or unmilled and coarse (Figure 6.11). This material is unique in that it contains a natural antifungal substance that inhibits damping-off in seedlings. Pasteurization by heat, however, destroys the effectiveness of this disease protection. Sphagnum is light-weight, relatively sterile, and acidic, well aerated and can hold up to 20 times its weight in water. It contains only small amounts of nutrients and plants grown in it for any length of time will require supplemental fertilization.

PEAT MOSS. Peat moss is the accumulation of marsh mosses that have fallen under water and have been preserved there (Figure 6.11). Peat is dug from deposits in Canada, Europe, and some of the northern states (Michigan Peat being a common type). It varies in composition, depending on its geographic origin, plant deposits from which it originated, mineral content, and degree of acidity. All types of peat moss are lightweight and have high moisture and nutrient-holding capacities.

Peat moss is usually used with other coarse materials such as sand or perlite because of its unusual wettability characteristics. It is very hard to wet when dry. Water will run off dry peat moss and even when it penetrates, many particles are very slow to become wet. Once it is wet, it often becomes so wet that aeration is reduced. If ever allowed to dry out during its use, the problem of wettability arises again. Hence, the addition of sand or perlite loosens the peat moss to enhance aeration and water penetration.

PERLITE. Perlite is a sterile, light-weight material made by heating crushed lava from volcanic flows. Under the 1400°F furnace temperature, the water in the lava changes to pressurized steam, expanding the particles into puffy white pellets (Figure 6.11). The porous nature of the perlite gives it some ability to hold water, but the particles size (less than 1/8 inch) promotes good aeration and drainage. It contains no nutrients and is neutral in pH. This product is sterile, increases aeration in a mixture, and provides a lighter, more granular medium.

VERMICULITE. Known as well for its insulation uses as for its horticultural uses, vermiculite comes from deposits of micalike material in Montana and North Carolina. It is processed much like perlite, in 2000°F furnaces, but the steam-expanded, infertile, and sterile finished product is composed of expanded layers rather than pores like perlite (Figure 6.11). Spongy in texture and easily compressed, vermiculite is not recommended as a soil amendment when compression would destroy its effectiveness.

Vermiculite comes in four grades. The relatively coarse number 2 grade is best for starting cuttings, whereas the finer number 4 grade makes an excellent germination medium for seeds. Both grades are lightweight, hold water well, are neutral in pH, can store nutrients, and are well aerated.

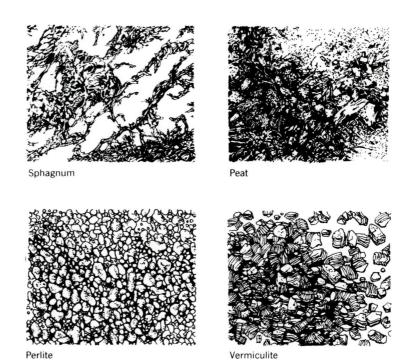

Sphagnum

Peat

Perlite

Vermiculite

FIGURE 6.11 Four popular soil amendments that are offered for sale by most garden shops.

SAND. Available from building supply and concrete dealers, sand is a satisfactory amendment. The coarse plasterer's sand is the most satisfactory grade to use. It drains well but must be watered frequently because it holds little moisture. Aside from being the heaviest material for growing plants, it has the additional disadvantages of being unsanitary and unable to hold nutrients. Like soil and peat, it should be pasteurized prior to use.

Selected properties of the above-described amendments are presented in Table 6.3, using soil as the standard for comparison.

MEDIA FOR GROWING PLANTS

To this point, we have discussed media only in general terms. Horticulturists and others working with plants recognize different categories of media, including (1) propagation

TABLE 6.3 SELECTED PROPERTIES OF COMMON SOIL AMENDMENTS AS COMPARED TO SOIL

Ingredient	Weight	Water-Holding Capacity	Drainage	Natural Fertility	Probability of Harmful Organisms	Requires Pasteurization Prior to Use
Soil	Heavy	Variable	Variable	Variable	High	Yes
Sphagnum moss	Light	High	Moderate	Low	Low	No
Peat moss	Light	High	Moderate	Low	Moderate	No
Perlite	Very light	Low	Excellent	Very low	Very low	No
Vermiculite	Very light	Moderate	Good	Low	Very low	No
Sand	Very heavy	Very low	Excellent	Very low	High	Yes

media and (2) potting media. In recent years, soilless or artificial media have become popular, and they too merit discussion.

Propagation Media

The **propagation medium** (pl. media) is that substance in which cuttings, seeds, and other propagation materials are placed for germination or rooting. For nurturing young plants that are very intolerant of environmental stress, the medium must consistently provide a number of conditions favorable for plant growth. First and foremost, there should be a constant supply of moisture. A medium should not hold so much water that rots occur or aeration is inhibited, nor should it drain so well as to necessitate frequent watering. Second, it should be loose enough to allow aeration of plant material to be propagated. This provides an adequate supply of oxygen and prevents a buildup of the by-product gases of respiration. Third, the medium should be of enough substance to support the seeds or cuttings but light and loose enough to allow removal of the young plants without damage of the root system. Fourth, it must be free of disease and insect pests and low in soluble salts (salts formed from fertilizers, hard water, etc.; see page 169). And fifth, it is generally helpful to rooting if the medium blanches (removes light from) the seeds or cuttings, although seeds of some species require light for germination. Most seeds respond well to darkness during germination. Let us look at two media commonly used for propagation and how well they fit these ideal criteria.

WATER. Ironically, water is the most frequently used and successful medium for indoor plant cuttings, but the one that least meets the requirements of a good propagation substance. It does not support a cutting, provide adequate aeration, or blanch the cutting. To be sure, however, it certainly does not need watering very frequently!

Water can get away with these shortcomings because most indoor plants root so well and so quickly that aeration (there is some oxygen in water) is not a limiting factor. The cutting is also supported by the glass or container holding the water, so support is not a problem either. Although not necessary for most indoor plants, blanching could be achieved by using darkly colored or opaque containers.

Water is so clean, convenient, and successful for indoor plants that its use cannot be discouraged. Once in a while, difficulty in adapting the water-produced root system to a soil mix is encountered, but this is usually not a serious problem. As a matter of fact, many plants can be grown in water for long periods if adequate plant nutrients are provided. This method of propagation is especially interesting to children, who enjoy watching the roots appear and fill the glass.

SOIL. Soil is popular for propagation because of its easy availability from the garden and lack of expense, but it may or may not be satisfactory for the job. As indicated earlier in the chapter, soils are extremely variable in their characteristics. Clay, the smallest inorganic particle present, stores nutrients, shrinks upon drying and expands upon wetting, holds water well, is poorly aerated, and drains poorly. Sand, on the other hand, is the coarsest constituent and drains well, does not hold nutrients, does not shrink and expand, and is well aerated. Silt is of intermediate particle size and has some of the qualities of both sand and clay.

Soils also usually contain about 3 to 5 percent of decayed organic matter (animal and plant tissue) or humus. This material has the ability, like clay, to hold nutrients, but also it can cement soil particles into aggregates to improve soil structure. An aggregated soil holds water in the aggregates but, due to the large pores among the aggregates, drains and aerates well.

For propagation then, a soil that meets the criteria for a good medium will be satisfactory. The critical factor is aeration, limiting the useful soil types to well-aggregated loams and sandy soils. The presence of too much clay inhibits drainage and aeration and creates problems of watering. An otherwise suitable soil, if it has been handled improperly, may be unsatisfactory. Soils that have been tilled while wet, for example, will be packed tightly and very poorly aerated.

Any soil that is taken from outside contains disease organisms, insect pests or their eggs, and weed seeds. To overcome these, the soil must be pasteurized by heating it to 140°F (60°C) for 30 minutes. Prepackaged soil mixes may be pasteurized and need no further treatment. Regardless of the type used, soil probably will not consistently be as successful as the combinations of materials given below.

DESIGNING PROPAGATING MEDIA. Since each of the common substances used in media has both advantages and disadvantages (Table 6.3), most growers prefer to mix materials, obtaining the best qualities and reducing the undesirable effects of each constituent. By far the most popular combination is peat and perlite. This mixture provides good drainage, good aeration, nutrient storage, and a loose, workable density. For the homeowner, the peat/perlite option is most practical since both components are readily available and relatively inexpensive. In addition, a number of products are appearing on the market, composed primarily of peat moss and vermiculite, that are sterile and come ready to use. These have proven to be as effective as other media in most cases, and some have the added advantage of being supplemented with low levels of standard or slowly releasing fertilizer.

Other effective materials or combination of materials and uses are as follows:

1. Sphagnum
   –Milled, seeds and spores.
   –Unmilled, air layering.
2. Perlite, cuttings.
3. Vermiculite
   –Coarse (No. 2 grade), cuttings.
   –Fine (No. 4 grade), seeds.
4. Sand
   –Coarse, seeds.
5. Perlite, one-third;
   Vermiculite, one-third;
   Peat moss, one-third: seeds, cuttings.

Potting Media

The **potting medium** or growing medium is that material in which well-established plants are placed for continued good growth. Potting media, like propagating media, should supply moisture, aeration, support, and a dark, disease-free environment.

Although potting and propagating media have similar requirements, they also differ in important aspects. The resistance of a mixture to change over time, particularly due to compaction, is especially important in potting soils that may be in place for several years. Vermiculite alone, for example, is often used in propagating. The material is spongy and easily compressed, however, and is not recommended for use alone or as an amendment in situations where compaction would reduce its effectiveness. In mixtures, compaction resistance is poor up to the threshold proportion then increases thereafter (Figure 6.10).

Fertility requirements in the two types of media also differ. Seedlings, cuttings, and other propagating materials are very intolerant of environmental stresses. In general, high levels of **soluble salts** (salts formed from fertilizers or present in hard water) are detrimental to the growth of these plant materials. In contrast, established plants not only tolerate but also require relatively high levels of fertility for optimum growth.

TABLE 6.4 SELECTED POTTING MIXTURES

	General		Cactus		Orchid		Bromeliads	Ferns	Bulbs	Carnivorous		Dish Gardens	Terrariums
Soil[a]	1/3	1/4	1/4					1/4	1/3			1/3	1/3
Peat	1/3	1/4	1/4		1/3		1/3	1/2	1/3	2/5		1/3	1/3
Sphagnum (unmilled)										2/5	1[d]		
Pine needles										1/5			
Bark					1/3	1[c]	1/3						
Vermiculite									1/3				
Perlite	1/3				1/3			1/4				1/3	
Sand			1/4[b]	1/2[b]			1/3						1/3
Manure			1/4										

[a]Loam or sandy loam.
[b]Perlite can substitute here.
[c]Some (most) do best in 100 percent bark.
[d]Many do well in 100 percent sphagnum moss.

Established, vigorous plants are also more resistant to disease organisms. As a consequence, the use of sterile media is not as critical as in propagation. Several potting mixtures are given in Table 6.4, and for many, soil is an essential ingredient. More likely than not, this soil will not require pasteurization. Only when problems are encountered or soil or mixtures are reused is pasteurization necessary.

Soilless Media

Many soilless mixes are available at garden centers and supermarkets. These offer certain advantages, as follows: (1) they hold moisture and plant nutrients well; (2) they provide good drainage and aeration; and (3) they are lightweight and convenient. Additionally, many of these mixes have been heat treated and thus are free of harmful organisms. Two of the most popular of the soilless mixes were developed at Cornell University and the University of California. These mixes are of similar composition, with the exception that the Cornell mix substitutes vermiculite for the fine sand used in the UC formula. The UC mix is marketed under such

trade names as Super Soil and First Step, and the Cornell mix as Jiffy Mix and Redi-Earth. Formulas for certain Cornell University soilless mixes are presented in Table 6.5.

A word of caution about packaged potting mixes is in order. The demand for these mixes was created by the indoor gardening boom. Many of the mixes on the market were formulated by commercial growers or university personnel. Others, however, have little or no growing experience behind them. As in any young industry, there is a shortage of guidelines or standards for manufacturers to follow, either in the production of mixes or their packaging and labeling. Furthermore, some manufacturers employ elaborate quality controls, others do not.

Thus, although the vast majority of packaged mixes are of high quality, problems have been encountered with some.

Chief among these problems are unfavorable levels of nutrients, unfavorable (usually low) pH, and the presence of toxic materials. The reader should not be overly concerned, however, because most mixes are of high quality. Also, when manufacturers have been apprised of deficiencies in their mixes,

TABLE 6.5 SELECTED SOILLESS POTTING MIXES (CORNELL UNIVERSITY PEATLIKE MIXES FOR 35 LITERS OR ONE BUSHEL)

Mix Component	Mix A[a]	Foliage Plant[b] (Mix B)	Epiphytic[c] (Mix C)
Sphagnum moss	17.5 liters (½ bushel)	17.5 liters (½ bushel)	11.7 liters (⅓ bushel)
Vermiculite	17.5 liters (½ bushel)	8.7 liters (¼ bushel)	—
Perlite (medium grade)	—	8.7 liters (¼ bushel)	11.7 liters (⅓ bushel)
Douglas fir bark (⅛ to ¼ inch)	—	—	11.7 liters (⅓ bushel)
Ground dolomitic limestone	74 ml (5 tbsp)	118.4 ml (8 tbsp)	118.4 ml (8 tbsp)
20 percent superphosphate	29.6 ml (2 tbsp)	29.6 ml (2 tbsp)	88.8 ml (6 tbsp)
10:10:10 fertilizer	44.4 ml (3 tbsp)	44.4 ml (3 tbsp)	44.4 ml (3 tbsp)
Potassium or calcium nitrate	—	14.8 ml (1 tbsp)	14.8 ml (1 tbsp)
Granular wetting agent	44.4 ml (3 tbsp)	44.4 ml (3 tbsp)	44.4 ml (3 tbsp)
Liquid wetting agent	4.8 ml (1 tsp)	4.8 ml (1 tsp)	4.8 ml (1 tsp)
Soluble trace element mix[d]			

[a]Mix A is recommended for general garden plants, vegetable seedlings, and flowers.

[b]Foliage Plant Mix B is recommended for those plants that need growing media with high moisture-retention characteristics. Plants having a fine root system or possessing many fine root hairs are included in this group. Some examples are *Amaryllis*, *Aphelandra*, *Begonia*, *Belo-perone*, *Buxus*, *Caladium*, *Cissus*, *Citrus*, *Coleus*, ferns, *Ficus*, *Hedera*, *Helxine*, *Maranta*, *Oxalis*, palms, *Pilea*, *Sansevieria*, and *Tolmiea*.

[c]Epiphytic Mix C is recommended for plants that require good drainage and aeration and have the ability to withstand drying between waterings. Plants having coarse, tuberous, or rhizomatous roots are included in this category. For example: African violets, *Aglaonema*, *Aloe*, bromeliads, cacti, *Crassula*, *Dieffenbachia*, *Episcia*, geraniums, gloxinias, *Hoya*, *Monstera*, *Nephthytis*, *Peperomia*, *Philodendron*, *Pothos*, *Syngonium*.

[d]Trace elements are needed in extremely small quantities. Overapplication can result in severe injury to the plant. Prepare a stock solution by dissolving 1 ounce of Soluble Trace Element Mix in 1 quart of water. Use ⅓ cup of stock solution added to sufficient volume of water (1 gallon) to obtain a good distribution in 1 bushel of mix. Do not add more than this amount. Do not repeat the application.

they have been quick to remedy the problem and to institute or upgrade quality control procedures.

TOPPING IT OFF WITH A MULCH

A mulch is created whenever the surface of the medium in which plants grow is modified. Mulches form an insulating layer or buffer zone between the medium surface and the atmosphere. When a mulch is present, surface evaporation occurs directly from the mulch, not the medium beneath. Likewise, when water is added to a container, it is first intercepted by the mulch layer. Mulches have been used effectively by outdoor gardeners for a long time, but they also offer advantages for use indoors with container plants.

Advantages of Mulching

Outdoor gardeners utilize mulching to regulate soil temperature, conserve soil moisture, control weed growth, and a number of lesser reasons. Mulches offer less versatility indoors in containers where they are employed chiefly to prevent rapid evaporation from the medium surface. A sphagnum mulch, for example, can decrease greatly the rate of evaporation, reducing the frequency with which plants must be watered.

Mulches are also used to protect the medium surface from the dispersing action of added water and for decorative purposes (Figure 6.12). When organic mulches are used, a moist environment develops at the medium–mulch interface that encourages the growth of microorganisms. These organisms slowly decompose the organic material.

Mulching Materials

A number of organic and inorganic mulching materials are utilized. Sphagnum is beyond doubt the most popular organic material. The coarse, unmilled material is preferable to the fine, which has been put through a hammer mill. Bark is also popular and enhances a container setting as well as retarding water loss. Sawdust and wood shavings are also used, but because of their alleged acidity and possible content of toxic materials do not find wide application. Other organic materials, such as peanut shells, ground corn cobs, and straw, can also be used as mulches. Though they are not particularly attractive, they can be as

FIGURE 6.12 Here, a mulch of sphagnum is used to retard the surface evaporation of water and enhance the appearance of a container plant.

effective as sphagnum in reducing surface evaporation. Inorganic materials include mainly assorted types of decorative rock and gravel. Materials such as black plastic and aluminum foil, which enjoy great popularity in the outdoor garden, are used infrequently indoors.

Problems Associated with the Use of Mulches

Earlier we described the effects of soil depth on water dynamics in container soils. Of particular interest was the formation of a perched water table in container situations. Instead of air being introduced by the downward movement of water, as in field soils, the introduction of air may depend on the use of water by plants and surface evaporation. In short, in shallow containers, the soil or other medium may stay wet too long following watering. In these situations, the use of a mulch can be detrimental, because the rapid evaporation of water from the surface enhances soil aeration.

Another common water-related problem associated with mulches is that often one cannot tell whether the medium needs water or not since the medium is hidden beneath the mulch. To remedy this problem, portions of mulch material such as sphagnum can be lifted up and the moisture content of the medium determined. Once proper watering schedules are established, this problem is largely eliminated.

When organic material is used as a mulch, microorganisms begin its decomposition to humus. As decomposition proceeds, microorganism numbers increase, tying up much of the available nitrogen in the surrounding medium (Figure 6.4). As a result, plants growing under organic mulch may show symptoms of nitrogen deficiency. Nitrogen deficiency can be prevented by adding additional amounts of nitrogen fertilizer when organic materials are utilized.

Another problem occasionally encountered when mulches are used is a buildup of particular pests. The mulch material provides an inconspicuous home to insects and other organisms. In some cases, the pest may already be present in the mulch material before use. Only clean, pest-free material should be used in mulching. Additionally, the gardener should examine in-place mulch occasionally for signs of pest infestation.

HYDROPONICS

Hydroponics is the science of growing plants on a soilless medium in which nutrients are supplied to the plant entirely by water. In hydroponics the nutrients, normally supplied by the soil, are instead added in the correct proportions to water. The nutrient solution can either bathe the root system continuously or be added and removed at intervals during the day. Gravel or other inert material provides the growing medium. Hydroponics is an old practice going back over 200 years. It has been popular in Europe and elsewhere for a long time and is gaining in popularity in America.

Hydroponics differs only in degree from the methods described earlier in the chapter. To illustrate, seedlings can be grown and cuttings rooted in a medium of perlite only. Normally, when these plant materials are established, they are transferred to a designed potting medium for continued growth. In theory, however, they could be retained in the perlite and continue normal growth so long as they are provided with the essential nutrients and other factors (light, temperature, humidity) required for growth. In short, they could be grown hydroponically. The growing procedures described below are simply refinements of this procedure.

Growing plants indoors, using hydroponics, is visualized to offer several advantages over traditional growing methods. The most commonly listed advantages are

- Produces healthier, longer-living plants.
- Reduces and simplifies plant maintenance.
- Reduces plant mortality due to

    –over or under watering.
    –over or under fertilizing.
    –soil borne diseases.
    –soluble salt buildup.

- Gives the gardener a greater appreciation for plant growth and development.

In short, it is a novel educational experience.

Hydroponic Methods

Success in hydroponic gardening requires an understanding of containers, media, plants, and nutrient supplies.

CONTAINERS. The types of containers used in hydroponics differ from those employed in traditional growing methods. In situations where plant roots are continuously bathed in nutrient solution, the requirements include a container that does not leak (or breathe) or corrode due to interaction with the nutrient solution. Specially designed plastic or glazed ceramic containers are ideal. The former offers the possible advantage of being lightweight. It is also helpful, if not essential, to have a way of determining the level of nutrient solution in the medium. When a daily cycling of nutrients is employed, a method for introducing and removing the solution must also be incorporated into the container design. A very simple procedure for doing this is illustrated in Figure 6.13. More elaborate systems can be designed, including some that are fully automated.

MEDIA. The main function of the medium is to provide support for the growing plant. The material selected should ideally be sterile (or easily sterilized), inert (so as not to supply nutrients or alter the nutrient solu-

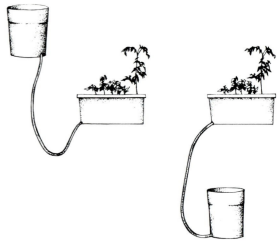

FIGURE 6.13 A simple procedure for introducing and removing the nutrient solution (in pail) from a small hydroponic garden. When the pail is raised, solution runs into the container by gravity flow. After a few minutes, the pail is lowered and the solution drains back. Solution level, pH, and nutrient content can also be easily checked.

tion), have a particle size ranging from approximately ⅛ to ⅜ inch in diameter to allow good aeration, hold plant roots firmly yet allow the entire root mass to be pulled without undue difficulty, and, finally, be recyclable. Several materials meet most or all of these criteria, including

Rock	Ground coke
Glass beads	Gravel
Perlite	Clay granules

In America, gravel is probably the most widely used medium, whereas in England specially treated granules formed from London blue clay are popular.

PLANTS. In general, it is best not to transfer an established plant grown in a standard potting medium to a hydroponic system. There are several reasons for this. First, removal of the root system from the medium causes a great deal of root damage unless extreme care is taken. Second, the root systems of established plants are adapted to the medium in which they have been grown. Roots growing in a standard potting medium are smaller in diameter and less succulent than roots growing in water. Thus, even if they could be successfully transplanted to hydroponic systems, their root systems would not be adapted. Generally, the period of adaptation takes from 6 to 8 weeks. In short, the earlier a plant can begin developing its root system in the environment in which it will mature, the better. Third, transplanting established plants from potting media often means transmittal of disease organisms as well. Starting hydroponic plants from seed largely eliminates disease problems.

Hydroponic plants can be started in several ways. Small-seeded types can be started in a separate propagation medium, such as that provided by Jiffy® pellets (Figure 6.14). Once a seedling is established in a Jiffy pellet, the entire pellet can be placed into the gravel or other medium. Care should be taken to see that the top of the pellet is covered by the medium. Otherwise, the exposed top will act as a wick, drawing water and nutrient salts to the surface. The salts left after the evaporation of water can have a corrosive effect on contacted plant parts. Large seed, the size of a pea, for instance, can be placed directly into the medium. Somewhat smaller seeds can be sown directly on the surface and will work their way into crevices where conditions are favorable for germination and seedling growth.

Vegetative propagules can also be utilized. Cuttings started in water or sand, for example, can be transferred to the hydroponic medium as soon as visible roots are present. Some plants, such as Yucca, regenerate new plants from root tissue. Here, individual root pieces can be placed directly in the medium. Success is usually greater if

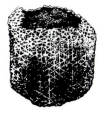

FIGURE 6.14 Common types of blocks and cell pots that are useful for propagation. *Source:* Jiffy® Products.

the root pieces are treated with a disinfectant before planting. Natural vegetative structures such as bulbs, corms, tubers, tuberous roots, rhizomes and runners, and offshoots can be set directly into the gravel or other aggregate and will initiate growth.

Nutrients

Plants require 16 mineral nutrients for growth (see Chapter Seven). Three of these come from water and air, the remaining 13 from the soil solution. In soils, most of these 13 are present in adequate amounts for good plant growth. A few must be supplemented when plants are grown in cultivation. In hydroponics, on the other hand, the indoor gardener normally starts with water containing little or no dissolved salts. To this solvent must be added the entire nutrient complement normally provided by the soil solids. This presents both problems and challenges. Each nutrient must be present in the correct form and proportion, and the resultant solution must have the correct acidity. Formulating complete nutrient solutions is a challenge that, once accomplished, gives the gardener a far greater appreciation of the requirements for plant growth and development.

The beginning hydroponic gardener may wish to purchase commercially prepared fertilizer mixes from which nutrient solutions can be quickly prepared. Later, as experience, interest, and time availability dictate, one may choose to prepare fertilizer mixes "from scratch." Table 6.6 gives nutrient formulas for some common fertilizers used in hydroponics. These formulas are only guidelines; a great deal of basic research is still needed to determine the proper levels and ratios of fertilizers for most foliage plants. As a rule of thumb, however, the ratios for nitrogen, phosphorus, and potassium—the mineral nutrients used in greatest abundance—should be approximately 3:1:2. Other plant nutrients are supplied in lesser quantities, and the nutrients used in smallest quantities, the micronutrients, may be present in adequate amounts simply as impurities in nutrient salts or water.

The theory of limiting factors, outlined at the beginning of Part Two, has an important bearing on hydroponic gardening indoors. To illustrate, it has been demonstrated that in commercial foliage production, the amount of nitrogen required for good plant growth is in the range of 100 to 125 pounds per acre per month. When foliage plants are grown in the home, however, the levels of light (and many other growth factors) are much lower. As a consequence, the level of nitrogen (and other essential nutrients) must be much lower as well, in the range of $1/10$ to $1/20$ that of production rates. Excessive fertilizer may damage or even kill poorly lighted specimens.

As mentioned above, plant roots can either be bathed continuously in nutrient solution, or the solution can be added and then drained one or two times daily. In either situation, nutrient content and balance of the solution, as well as its acidity, will change with time. The acidity can be checked using indicator paper, and corrections can be easily made. Nutrients are another matter entirely. To keep an adequate supply and balance of nutrients, the solution should be replaced periodically. Specific replacement times are hard to give due to lack of basic research in this area, but beginning replacement intervals of 2 to 3 weeks provide a starting point. Through experimentation, you can establish more precise intervals for specific plants and conditions.

TABLE 6.6 SOME REPRESENTATIVE NUTRIENT SOLUTIONS

	Concentration (mg/liter)
Major Nutrients	
Shive's solution	
Calcium nitrate	1060
Potassium phosphate	310
Magnesium sulfate	550
Ammonium sulfate	90
Ferrous sulfate	5
Hoagland's solution	
Calcium nitrate	1180
Potassium nitrate	510
Potassium phosphate	140
Magnesium sulfate	490
Ferric tartrate	5
Minor Nutrients[a]	
Boric acid	600
Manganese chloride	400
Zinc sulfate	50
Copper sulfate	50
Molybdic acid	20

[a]Add 1 cc of minor nutrient solution per liter of Shive's or Hoagland's solution.

Innovations in Hydroponics

The above discussion has dealt with the most basic aspects of hydroponics. In recent years, particularly in Europe, many refinements have been made in basic hydroponic techniques. Some of these innovations have been brought to America and deserve brief mention.

In Europe, designed hydroponic systems have been marketed for several years. All of these systems represent refinements of basic hydroponic technique. A popular system in England is hydroculture, in which a plant's roots are supported in designed containers by specially treated clay granules about ½ inch in diameter (Figure 6.15). The container is provided with an indicator to show when more water is required. The indicator apparatus is combined with a nutrient input tube. As shown in Figure 6.15, the nutrient solution covers only the bottom few inches of the container. The majority of plant roots are in the continually moist granules above the solution. As in other hydroponic systems, the rapid growth of plants is due in large part to the increased amount of oxygen available to the root system.

Another innovative system, having some of the characteristics of hydroponic systems, is the capillary watering system. In this system, a layer of aggregate at the bottom of the container is covered by a thin fiberglass mat. The mat, in turn, is covered by a soil or soilless mix, sand, perlite, or other material that acts as the growing medium for a plant or group of plants. A wick transfers the nutrient solution from the substrate below to the mat and so to the growing medium. This system is especially well adapted to the use of soil-grown plants. Capillary watering systems are being used commercially in Europe with great success. An apparent key to this success is the use of an open mix, providing good aeration throughout.

Systems such as those described above are ideal for office and home and lend themselves particularly well to minimum care situations. Purchase of one of these systems may include not only the container, medium, and nutrient supply source, but also a healthy, established plant. These represent but a few of the recent innovations and departures from traditional hydroponic gardening. Beyond doubt, concepts such as these will find widespread applicability in the future.

FOR FURTHER READING

Arnon, D. *The Water-Culture Method for Growing Plants without Soil.* College of Agriculture, University of California, Berkeley, Calif., 1950.

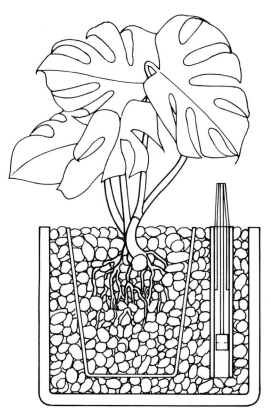

FIGURE 6.15 A sectional view of a hydroculture system showing a plant growing in a medium of clay granules. The horizontal line about one-third of the way up the pot represents the level of water in the container. To the right of the plant is an indicator to show when more water is required, combined with a nutrient input tube. *Source:* Rochford, T., *Houseplants*, Wisley Handbook 14, London: The Royal Horticultural Society, 1973, p.41.

Baker, K. (ed.). *The UC System for Producing Healthy Container-Grown Plants.* California Agricultural Experiment Station, 1957.

Brady, N. *The Nature and Properties of Soils.* 8th ed. New York: Macmillan, 1974.

Bridwell, R. *Hydroponic Gardening.* Woodridge Press, 1974.

Foth, H., and L. Turk. *Fundamentals of Soil Science.* New York: Wiley, 1972.

"Hydroponics—Grow and Sell Plants in a Soilless Medium." *Florist* (September 1975).

Kohnke, H. *Soil Science Simplified.* Published by author, 1953.

Neel, P. "Soil and Water Relationships." Proceedings of the 1977 National Tropical Foliage Short Course.

Poole, R. "Characteristics of Nursery Soils." Proceedings of the 1977 National Tropical Foliage Short Course.

Rochford, T. *Houseplants*. Wisley Handbook 14. London: The Royal Horticultural Society, 1973.

Spomer, L. "Principles of Nursery Container Soil Amendment." *American Nurseryman* (1975).

Spomer, L. "Soils for Interior Planters: Water Relations." Proceedings of the 1978 National Tropical Foliage Short Course.

Vosters, J. "Plant Availability and New Varieties." Proceedings from the Symposium on the Use of Living Plants in the Interior Environment, Society of American Florists, 1975.

chapter seven
soil fertility and
plant nutrition

In this chapter, we wish to explore several vital aspects of soil fertility and plant nutrition. Before we begin, however, we need to dispel one common misconception, namely, the concept of what constitutes a plant food.

If we go to a local supermarket to buy fertilizers for our plants, we will most likely find these products labeled as plant "food." In one survey, 40 out of 42 materials examined were labeled plant food rather than plant fertilizers. All of us know that there are three main kinds of foods used by humans: carbohydrates, fats, and proteins. These foods are used for growth and maintenance. Through the process of respiration, we have the controlled burning (oxidation) of carbohydrates with the release of energy to drive the processes of life. Plants derive energy for their life processes in exactly the same way, through the utilization of carbohydrates, fats, and proteins in metabolic processes. Plants, like animals, require oxygen for these life-sustaining processes. In short, plants and animals utilize exactly the same kinds of foods.

There is an important difference between plants and animals, however, with regard to food requirements. Animals and humans are described as **heterotrophic** in that they are *incapable* of manufacturing organic compounds (foods) from inorganic raw materials. Rather, they require organic compounds

from the environment. Plants are the source of these organic compounds. Plants are described as being **autotrophic** because they are capable of manufacturing organic compounds from inorganic raw materials. A small number of the raw materials utilized by plants in food manufacture come from the air and water directly. The remainder are mineral nutrients present in the soil solids. We call these nutrients **fertilizers.** It is these materials we buy in packaged form at plant stores and supermarkets. For the sake of accuracy, we will call these products fertilizers, not foods.

We will begin by examining the nutrients required by plants and discover how these are absorbed from the soil and moved throughout the plant. We will then look at the several kinds of fertilizers available to indoor gardeners and how these should be used. Finally, we will outline some of the problems associated with the shortage or overabundance of plant nutrients.

HOW PLANTS USE MINERALS

As mentioned, the bulk of nutrients used by plants come from the soil solids. The nutrient elements are present not only as a part of the soil solids, but also are found in the soil solution. Plants absorb nutrients from the soil solution as electrically charged particles termed *ions*. To understand how nutrients are absorbed by plants, we need to understand the nature of ions.

Ions: The Chemical Menu of Plants

The chemical **elements** are substances that cannot be broken into simpler substances by ordinary chemical means. The sugar sucrose ($C_{12}H_{22}O_{11}$) is not an element because our bodies and those of plants can break it down into carbon dioxide and water with the release of energy. Likewise, carbon dioxide (CO_2) can be broken down still further to give carbon and oxygen. The carbon and oxygen cannot be broken down, however, and thus fit our definition of elements.

Elements exist in the form of discrete units called **atoms.** Each atom of an element consists of a nucleus and one or more electrons (Figure 7.1a). The **nucleus** is the central core of an atom and carries a positive electrical charge. Surrounding the nucleus are the negatively charged particles known as **electrons.** Atoms as a whole possess no charge, because the number of positive charges in the nucleus is equal to the number of negative charges carried by the electrons. In the soil solution, however, atoms may either gain or lose electrons. When this occurs, they are no longer electrically neutral, but rather they become electrically charged particles termed **ions.**

CHEMICAL NOTATION. Chemists have given symbols to each chemical element. These symbols may represent abbreviations of the English name of the element, as in the case of nitrogen, N, oxygen, O, and hydrogen, H. Others represent abbreviations of the Latin, as the K for potassium whose Latin name is *kalium.* When designating ions, electrical charges are indicated. Some examples of positively charged ions are H^+, K^+, and Ca^{2+}. Negatively charged ions include Cl^-, NO_3^-, and SO_4^{2-}. Positively charged ions are termed **cations,** negatively charged ions **anions.** Note that most of the positively charged ions consist of only one element, whereas in many of the negatively charged ions, the crucial element is joined to other elements and these together form the structure of the total ion. The nitrate ion, NO_3^-, for example, consists of one atom of nitrogen and three atoms of oxygen and carries a single electrical charge.

The positively charged cations are attracted to and held by the surfaces of negatively charged soil colloids (Figure 7.2). Anions, on the other hand, are repelled by the soil colloids and occur mainly in the soil solution. As such, anions can be more easily leached from the soil by excess watering. Both cations and anions are taken up by the roots of plants, and for certain elements more than one ionic form may be utilized.

NUTRIENT UPTAKE BY PLANTS. The root system of a plant thoroughly permeates a given volume of soil. Dittmer's classic study of rye illustrates this point admirably (Table 7.1). As enormous as these figures are, they only begin to tell the story. Near the tip of each one of these millions of roots, vast numbers of root hairs are formed (Figure 3.6). Each root hair is an extension of an individual epidermal cell. It is estimated that the rye plant mentioned above had more than 14 billion root hairs with a total surface area of more than 4000 square feet. In total, the root system of the rye plant had a com-

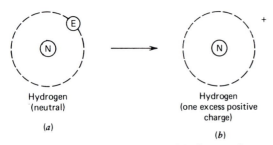

FIGURE 7.1 An atom of hydrogen (*a*), showing the nucleus N and surrounding electron E. The ionic form is also shown (*b*). *Source:* Calvin, C., and Knutson, D., *Modern Home Gardening,* New York: Wiley, 1983, p. 118. Reprinted by permission.

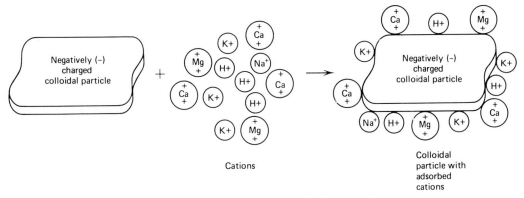

FIGURE 7.2 Negatively charged colloidal particles attract and hold the positively charged cations present in soil solutions. *Source:* Calvin, C., and Knutson, D., *Modern Home Gardening*, New York: Wiley, 1983, p. 119. Reprinted by permission.

bined surface area in excess of 6500 square feet, more than 130 times the total area of the shoots. But the volume of soil permeated by the root system comprised only about 2 cubic feet. These data leave no doubt as to the ability of plant roots to form a dynamic interface with the soil.

The innumerable root tips of a plant are continuously advancing through the soil. Just behind the region of elongation root hairs are formed, establishing an intimate and extensive association with the soil particles and the soil solution (Figure 7.3). The

TABLE 7.1 CHARACTERISTICS OF THE ROOT SYSTEM OF A SINGLE RYE PLANT 20 IN TALL WITH A CLUMP OF 80 SHOOTS

Kind of Root	Number	Total Length (feet)
Main roots	143	214
Branches of main roots (secondaries)	35,600	17,800
Branches of secondaries (tertiaries)	2,300,000	574,000
Branches of tertiaries (quarternaries)	11,500,000	1,450,000
Total	14 million	2 million (380 miles)

root hair region is only a few millimeters in length, and new root hairs are added nearer the tip at about the same rate as hairs are lost further back. In many plants, the life of a root hair is only a few days, but in others, such as cacti, individual root hairs may live for a prolonged period.

We have said that some of the nutrient ions in the soil, the cations, are attached to negatively charged soil colloids. Anions, on the other hand, are present primarily in the soil solution. At the interface between the soil colloids and the root hairs, activities occur that release positive ions into the soil solution. Basically, hydrogen ions from the root replace nutrient ions from the soil colloids. The less tightly held nutrient ions are forced into the soil solution where they can, along with negatively charged ions, be taken into the roots of plants. The process whereby hydrogen ions from the root system replace cations held by soil colloids is termed **cation exchange.** Cation exchange is an exceedingly important process. Any time nutrients are released from soil colloids, or any time nutrients are absorbed by roots, cations are exchanged.

MOVEMENT OF IONS THROUGH THE PLANT. The physical processes whereby water and minerals are taken up by plants

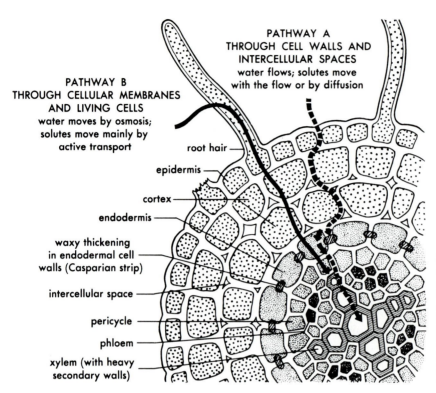

PATHWAY A
THROUGH CELL WALLS AND
INTERCELLULAR SPACES
water flows; solutes move
with the flow or by diffusion

PATHWAY B
THROUGH CELLULAR MEMBRANES
AND LIVING CELLS
water moves by osmosis;
solutes move mainly by
active transport

root hair

epidermis

cortex

endodermis

waxy thickening
in endodermal cell
walls (Casparian strip)

intercellular space

pericycle

phloem

xylem (with heavy
secondary walls)

FIGURE 7.3 Cross section of a root illustrating root hairs and the pathway of water and ions into the vascular cylinder of the root. *Source:* Ray, P., *The Living Plant*, 2nd ed., New York: Holt, Rinehart, & Winston, 1963, p. 56. Reprinted by permission of CBS College Publishing.

were described in detail in Chapter Three. Two different mechanisms were outlined. One mechanism is driven by forces originating in the roots themselves. These forces are created through the active uptake of ions by roots. Increased ion concentrations in cells of the root cause water to move into roots, and the resultant pressure actually pushes water and minerals into the shoot system of the plant. Water of guttation is nothing more than water (and minerals) forced out of specialized openings in leaves by pressures originating in the roots. The second mechanism is driven by forces originating in the shoot system. In essence, the evaporation of water from leaves creates a tension that pulls water upward through the xylem from the root system below. Both mechanisms operate in indoor plants. The root pressure mechanism is more likely to operate when the soil is saturated with water and atmospheric humidity is high. The tension mechanism operates when stomates are open and the plant is transpiring actively.

Water and minerals are visualized to move from the soil solution into the vascular cylinder of the root along two different pathways (Figure 7.3). One pathway of movement is entirely through living cells. The other pathway envisions movement of water and minerals along cell walls and through intercellular spaces until they reach the **endodermis,** the specialized parenchyma cells forming the innermost cortical layer. Here, the presence of a wall layer impervious to the passage of water and minerals, the **Casparian strip,** blocks further movement through the nonliving system of the root. As a result, the nutrient solution must now move into the interior of living endodermal cells. Thus, regardless of the pathway taken to the vascular cylinder of the root, water and minerals must move through the protoplast of endodermal cells. Once through the endodermis, water and minerals are carried mainly via the conducting cells of the xylem to the shoot system above.

The Elements of Plant Nutrition

The study of the elements required for plant nutrition has a long and exciting history. For many centuries, scientists believed that green plants derived all their nourishment from the organic materials of the soil. Finally, in about 1630, this concept, known as the **humus theory,** was shown by Belgian physician, Jean van Helmont, to be incorrect. In a classic experiment, van Helmont planted a 5-pound willow in a vessel containing exactly 200 pounds of dry soil. Then, for 5 years, he added only rain water to the soil. At the end of this period, he removed the willow, now grown large, and weighed it. All soil was carefully returned to the vessel. He found that the willow had gained 164 pounds and that the original soil mass had lost only 2

ounces during the 5-year period. Van Helmont concluded that the plant did not derive sustenance other than water from the soil. The 2-ounce loss in soil weight was attributed to experimental error.

Although the critical experiment of van Helmont demonstrated clearly the inaccuracy of the humus theory, his interpretation of results was only partially correct. For one thing, he did not know the role of carbon dioxide in the synthesis of organic matter. More to the point, we know now that the 2 ounces of material that the plant removed from the soil was absolutely essential to its growth. As we shall see, work over the last 100 years has added greatly to our knowledge in this area.

To date, plant scientists have shown that 16 elements are necessary for the normal growth of plants. Without any one of these elements, the plant cannot complete its life cycle. These 16 required elements are termed the **essential elements.** The essential elements come from different sources and are used by plants in varying amounts (Table 7.2). Three—carbon, hydrogen, oxygen—are obtained mainly from air and water. The remaining 13 elements come from the soil. Of these, six are used by plants

TABLE 7.2 THE ESSENTIAL NUTRIENT ELEMENTS, THEIR SOURCES, AND THE RELATIVE AMOUNTS NEEDED BY PLANTS

NUTRIENT ELEMENTS USED IN RELATIVELY LARGE AMOUNTS		NUTRIENT ELEMENTS USED IN RELATIVELY SMALL AMOUNTS	
Mainly from Air and Water	From the Soil Solids	From the Soil Solids	
Carbon	Nitrogen	Iron	Copper
Hydrogen	Phosphorus	Manganese	Zinc
Oxygen	Potassium	Boron	Chlorine
	Calcium	Molybdenum	
	Magnesium		
	Sulfur		

in relatively large quantities and are called **macronutrients.** The other seven are needed in much smaller amounts and are thus termed **micronutrients** (also called **trace** or **minor** elements).

THE MACRONUTRIENTS. The macronutrients are nitrogen, phosphorus, potassium, calcium, magnesium, and sulfur. Nitrogen, phosphorus, and potassium are the elements most commonly added to soils in agricultural fertilization programs. Thus, they are termed the **primary** or **fertilizer elements,** and any fertilizer that contains all three is said to be a "complete fertilizer." Calcium, magnesium, and sulfur are termed the **secondary elements.** They are also added to agricultural soils frequently, calcium and magnesium in the form of ground limestone and sulfur as a component of commercial fertilizers such as superphosphate and sulfate of ammonia. These elements are, of course, also present in organic fertilizers such as farm manure and fish emulsion.

THE MICRONUTRIENTS. The micronutrients—iron, manganese, boron, molybdenum, copper, zinc, and chlorine—are used by plants in very small amounts. They are present in organic fertilizers and occur as impurities in many commercial fertilizers. Field soils normally have an ample supply of these elements, but on soils cropped for many years, and in specific regions, one or more of the micronutrients may become deficient. One nutrient, cobalt, not listed in Table 7.2, has not been shown to be essential for a broad range of flowering plants, but it is essential for the nitrogen-fixing microorganisms. These microorganisms are vitally important in agricultural systems where in association with legumes (alfalfa, beans, clovers, peas, etc.), they fix vast quantities of atmospheric nitrogen, converting it into forms that can be used by higher plants. The importance of the nitrogen fixation process in nature, however, warrants the inclusion of cobalt as a micronutrient.

Functions of Minerals in Plants

Every essential element taken up by plants serves one or more specific roles within the plant body. Carbon, hydrogen, and oxygen are the basic elements of all organic molecules. Proteins contain, in addition, nitrogen and sulfur. Phosphorus is an essential component of cell membranes and is also involved in energy transformations within the cell. Calcium combines with pectic materials to form the middle lamella that cements plant cells together. Magnesium plays a central role in the structure of the chlorophyll molecule. Several of the trace elements are essential structural parts of enzymes or serve an indirect role as activators or regulators of enzyme actions. Boron somehow regulates calcium utilization, but other than that, its precise functions are unknown to date. A summary list of the essential elements, the forms in which they are taken in by plants, and their functional roles within the plant are given in Table 7.3.

Soil Reaction: Acids and Bases

Two classes of ionic compounds—acids and bases—have such a profound influence on soil properties that they merit special attention. Many definitions exist for acids and bases, but for our purposes, it can be said that a solution—such as the soil solution—is *acid* when it contains a preponderance of hydrogen ions (H^+) over hydroxyl ions (OH^-). Conversely, a solution is **basic,** or **alkaline,** when it contains more hydroxyl ions than hydrogen ions. When the two ionic forms are present in equal numbers, a solution is said to be **neutral** (Figure 7.4).

To illustrate, pure water is comprised of three components: water molecules, hydrogen ions, and hydroxyl ions. The number of molecules in a volume of water is very large, the number of ions very small. In pure water, the number of hydrogen ions equals exactly the number of hydroxyl ions and thus pure water is neutral. If something is now added to pure water that alters the relative con-

TABLE 7.3 A SUMMARY OF MINERAL ELEMENTS REQUIRED BY PLANTS

Element (and Chemical Symbol)	Forms in Which Absorbed	Approximate Concentration in Whole Plant (as Percentage of Dry Weight)	Some Functions
Macronutrients			
Nitrogen (N)	NO_3^- or NH_4^+	1–3%	Amino acids, proteins, nucleotides, nucleic acids, chlorophyll, and coenzymes
Potassium (K)	K^+	0.3–6%	Enzymes, amino acids, and protein synthesis; activator of many enzymes; opening and closing of stomata
Calcium (Ca)	Ca^{2+}	0.1–3.5%	Calcium of cell walls; enzyme cofactor; cell permeability
Phosphorus (P)	$H_2PO_4^-$ or HPO_4^{2-}	0.05–1.0%	Formation of "high-energy" phosphate compounds (ATP and ADP); nucleic acids; phosphorylation of sugars; several essential coenzymes; phospholipids
Magnesium (Mg)	Mg^{2+}	0.05–0.7%	Part of the chlorophyll molecule; activator of many enzymes
Sulfur (S)	SO_4^{2-}	0.05–1.5%	Some amino acids and proteins; coenzyme A
Micronutrients			
Iron (Fe)	Fe^{2+}, Fe^{3+}	10–1500 parts per million (ppm)	Chlorophyll synthesis, cytochromes, and ferredoxin
Chlorine (Cl)	CL^-	100–10,000 ppm	Osmosis and ionic balance; probably essential in photosynthesis in the reactions in which oxygen is produced
Copper (Cu)	Cu^{2+}	2–75 ppm	Activator of some enzymes
Manganese (Mn)	Mn^{2+}	5–1500 ppm	Activator of some enzymes
Zinc (Zn)	Zn^{2+}	3–150 ppm	Activator of many enzymes
Molybdenum (Mo)	MoO_4^{2-}	0.1–5.0 ppm	Nitrogen metabolism
Boron (B)	BO^{3-} or $B_4O_7^{2-}$ (borate or tetraborate)	2–75 ppm	Influences Ca^{2+} utilization; functions unknown
Elements Essential to Some Plants or Organisms			
Cobalt (Co)	Co^{2+}	Trace	Required by nitrogen-fixing microorganisms

SOURCE: Reprinted with permission of Worth Publishers, Inc. From Raven, P. H., Evert, R. F., and Curtis, H., *Biology of Plants*, 3rd ed., New York: Worth Publishers, 1981, p. 540.

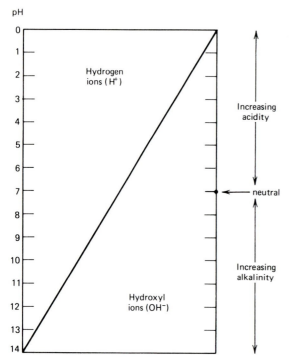

FIGURE 7.4 In an acid solution, hydrogen ions predominate. In a neutral solution, the numbers of hydrogen and hydroxyl ions are identical; and in an alkaline solution, hydroxyl ions predominate. *Source:* Calvin, C., and Knutson, D., *Modern Home Gardening,* New York: Wiley, 1983, p. 121. Reprinted by permission.

centrations of the two ions, the resulting solution will become acid or alkaline. The degree of acidity or alkalinity can, of course, vary. To express these variations chemists have devised a scale known as the **pH scale.** The pH scale goes from 0 to 14 with a pH of 7 being neutral (Figure 7.4). Solutions with a pH of less than 7 are acidic, while those with a pH greater than 7 are basic. Going in either direction from neutrality increases the acidity or basicity of a solution.

All of us deal with both acids and bases daily. Our drinking water is seldom, if ever, neutral, and the sour taste of citrus juices is due to their highly acidic contents. Common household products such as ammonia and lye are strongly basic in reaction. More to the point, however, is the fact that as indoor

gardeners, we are growing plants in media that vary greatly in pH. Furthermore, to these media, we add water and fertilizers that further alter the pH. These pH differences are of great importance, because they have a direct bearing on the availability of nutrients to plants.

SOIL pH AND NUTRIENT AVAILABILITY.

Soil pH directly influences the availability of plant nutrients, as shown in Figure 7.5. Above pH 5, the availability of iron, manganese, zinc, and copper show a marked decrease. The availability of molybdenum, potassium, calcium, and magnesium, on the other hand, increase above pH 5. Some of the nutrient elements have a rather broad range of maximum availability, but one, phosphorus, shows maximum availability over only a narrow pH range (Figure 7.5). This presents a serious problem because phosphorus is required in large amounts by plants, and even at its optimum pH—around

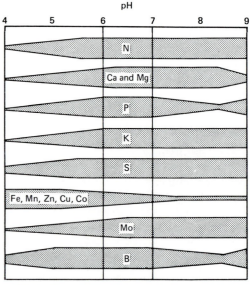

FIGURE 7.5 The relationships between the pH of mineral soils and the availability of plant nutrients. Overall optimal availability of the mineral nutrients occurs between pH 6.0 and 7.0. *Source:* Brady, N., *The Nature and Properties of Soils,* 8th ed., New York: Macmillan, 1974. Reprinted with permission.

6.5—is still only sparingly available. The key position of phosphorus in the nutrient availability scheme has prompted many soil scientists to recommend that the pH of mineral soils be maintained in the range of maximum availability of phosphorus, 6.0–6.5. This range not only helps assure an adequate supply of phosphorus, but also gives optimal availability of the other mineral nutrients. A few house plants thrive at a pH somewhat outside this range, but, for most, marked deviations lead to nutrient deficiencies or toxicities.

FERTILIZERS AND THEIR USE

In an earlier chapter, we indicated that there has been a veritable indoor plant boom during the past decade. To accommodate this tropical foliage plant boom, manufacturers have brought to the market a variety of "house plant fertilizers." These fertilizers vary strikingly in composition, nutrient content, and form. In this section, we explore many aspects of fertilizers, starting first with an overview of chemical and organic fertilizers, followed by an introduction to fertilizer terminology and arithmetic, and finally an examination of the numerous forms of fertilizers utilized by indoor gardeners.

Chemical versus Organic Fertilizers

Two broad categories of fertilizers are recognized—chemical (inorganic) and organic. Both types are used by indoor gardeners. **Chemical fertilizers** are commercially manufactured from inorganic materials. Some common examples include ammonium nitrate, superphosphate, and potassium nitrate. The **organic fertilizers** are materials normally derived from living organisms and include barnyard manure, fish emulsion, bone meal, and greensand. A few materials do not fit neatly into our scheme of classification. Sodium nitrate, for example, comes from natural deposits rather than commercial manufacture, but is inorganic in

composition. Urea, on the other hand, is synthesized commercially but is universally regarded as an organic material. A listing of selected chemical and organic fertilizers is given in Table 7.4.

Agriculturists and environmentalists debate heatedly as to the relative merits of organic and chemical fertilizers. In truth, each type of fertilizer has advantages and disadvantages. Among the advantages attributed to organic fertilizers are the following: (1) slow and continuous release of nutrients; (2) contain micronutrients as impurities; and (3) difficult to overapply. By comparison, the meritorious qualities of chemical fertilizers include the following: (1) rapid release of nutrients; (2) generally lower cost; (3) nutrient content tailored to any situation; (4) less bulky; (5) stable (organics are decomposing constantly); and (6) generally sterile. The stated advantages of chemical and organic fertilizers are not always clearcut, however. To illustrate, manufacturers are now producing slow release (timed release) chemical fertilizers. Furthermore, chemical fertilizers may contain micronutrients in specified amounts. Organic fertilizers, on the other hand, are being prepared in less bulky forms and at lower cost per unit of available nutrient materials. The ready availability, lower cost, and greater ease of transport and application have made the chemical fertilizers much more popular in commercial agricultural operations. For home gardeners, both indoors and outdoors, either type used alone or the two used in combination will usually provide excellent results.

Inasmuch as fertilizers are applied for the edification of plants, a legitimate question is this: What do plants "think" about (how do they respond to) these differing fertilizer sources? Earlier in the chapter, we pointed out that plants take up nutrients in ionic form. We have made no distinction between nutrients from inorganic sources and those from organic materials. We have not made a distinction, because there is none to be made!

TABLE 7.4 REPRESENTATIVE HOUSE PLANT FERTILIZERS AVAILABLE AT RETAIL OUTLETS WITH CHEMICAL ANALYSIS, TYPE OF FORMULATION, WEIGHTS AVAILABLE, AND SPECIAL FEATURES

Brand Name	GUARANTEED ANALYSIS		Type of Formulation	Weights (ounce or fluid ounce)	Special Features
	N–P–K	Other Elements			
1. Alaska					
Fish Fertilizer	5–1–1	Cl	Liquid concentration	16, 32, 128	Organic, no burning
Mor Bloom	0–10–10	—	Liquid concentration	16, 32	
2. Cole's					
House Plant Food	10–10–5	Fe, Zn, Mn	Liquid concentration	8	Contains soil penetrant
Bloom Plant Food	0–10–10	Fe, Zn, Mn	Liquid concentration	8	
3. Eleanor's VF–11	0.15–0.85–0.55	—	Liquid concentration	16	
4. Jobe's					
Plant Food Spikes	13–4–5	Cl	Spike	0.528	Slow release
Plant Food Spikes	10–10–4	Cl	Spike	0.528	Slow release
5. Lifeline Rich Cream Fertilizer	4–8–8	S, Fe, Cu, Mn, Mo, B, Zn, Cl	Liquid concentration	16	Controlled release N All micronutrients present
6. Ortho House Plant Food	5–10–5	Fe, Mn, Zn	Liquid concentration	8	Can be applied directly to medium
7. Osmocote Plant Food	14–14–14	—	Pellets	40	Controlled release of nutrients
8. Oxygen Plus					
Indoor Plant Food	1–2–1	—	Liquid concentration	8, 16	
African Violet Food	1–3–2	—	Liquid concentration	8	
9. Peters Professional Soluble Plant Food	20–20–20	—	Water-soluble powder	8	—
10. Plantabs House Plant Food	11–15–20	Fe	Tablets	2.9	Odorless, easy to apply
11. RA–PID–GRO Plant Food	23–19–17	—	Water-soluble powder	8	—
12. Schultz Instant Liquid Plant Food	10–15–10	—	Liquid concentration	5½, 12	—
13. Shelldance Bromeliad and Houseplant Food	12–4–6	Cu, Fe, Zn	Liquid concentration	16	—
14. Stern's					
Miracle-gro	15–30–15	Cu, Fe, Mn, Zn	Water-soluble powder	8	—
Liquid Miracle-gro	8–7–6	Fe	Liquid concentration	8	—

In the words of W. Schoonover of the University of California,

To a plant physiologist, the term organic has no meaning when applied to green plants. Plants grow and build organic matter by using ions of the essential elements. Whatever their source, the plant absorbs these ions in their inorganic forms. The plant does not distinguish between ammonia produced from fermentation in a manure pile and ammonia produced in a chemical factory or distilled from coal in coke manufacturing.

This is not to say, however, that organic fertilizers are of lesser value. To the contrary, their ability to improve soil structure, provide food for soil microorganisms, and help maintain an ecological balance in nature are legend. They are of unquestioned value, but for reasons other than a uniqueness in their nutrient contribution.

Fertilizer Terminology and Arithmetic

There are many different fertilizer formulations. Specific preparations may contain only one nutrient element, in which case they are called **fertilizer materials.** Or, they may contain two or more nutrients, in which case they are termed **mixed fertilizers.** Nitrogen, phosphorus, and potassium are the nutrients most commonly added to field soils. These macronutrients are used in relatively large quantities by plants and together are termed the **primary elements** or **primary fertilizer elements.** If a given fertilizer contains all three of these nutrients, it is said to be a **complete fertilizer.** This term is inaccurate inasmuch as 10 additional soil-borne nutrients would be required to make the fertilizer truly complete.

FERTILIZER ANALYSIS. By law, any material sold as plant fertilizer or "plant food" must list on its label the percentages of each of the nutrient elements it contains. These data constitute the fertilizer **analysis** and provide an important guide to determining the value of a specific fertilizer.

As indicated, the nutrients most commonly present in plant fertilizers are nitrogen, phosphorus, and potassium. The percentages of these nutrients are always presented in a specific manner. To illustrate, the labels for a selection of plant fertilizers may read as follows: 5-5-1, 5-10-5, or 14-14-14. In all three examples, these figures represent the amount of nitrogen, phosphorus, and potassium respectively in the fertilizer. Unfortunately, these figures do not represent, in a uniform manner, the amounts of each nutrient present. Thus, a label reading 18-6-12 has 18 percent of nitrogen (N), 6 percent of phosphorus pentoxide (P_2O_5) or its equivalent, and 12 percent of potassium oxide (K_2O) or its equivalent. It is planned that eventually all manufacturers of plant fertilizers will state the amounts of phosphorus and potassium in elemental form, as is now done for nitrogen. The amounts of elemental phosphorus and potassium in a fertilizer can be calculated, however, using the following formulas:

$$\%P = \% \ P_2O_5 \times 0.44$$
$$\%K = \% \ K_2O \times 0.83$$

In a bag of 10–20–10 fertilizer, 10 percent of its bulk supplies the nitrogen, 20 percent its phosphorus, and 10 percent its potassium. This means that 60 percent of its bulk is filler. In a 5-10-5 fertilizer, approximately 80 percent of its bulk is filler. Although the filler generally has little or no fertilizer value, it does serve to dilute the fertilizer ingredients, making them much easier to handle. In diluted form, rates of application can be controlled more accurately, and the possible caustic action of the fertilizer itself is overcome. The organic fertilizers usually have much lower analyses, because their nutrients are in less concentrated form. The nitrogen content of fresh cow manure (0.6) is only about one-fiftieth that of ammonium nitrate fertilizer (33.0).

LOW- AND HIGH-ANALYSIS FERTILIZERS. The total amount of nitrogen, phosphorus, and potassium in fertilizers varies greatly, ranging from less than 2 percent to more than 75 percent. Those with more than 30 pounds total nitrogen, phosphorus, and potassium per 100 pounds of material are termed **high-analysis** fertilizers, those with less than 30 pounds are **low analysis.** High-analysis fertilizers tend to be less expensive per unit of available nutrient but must be applied with greater precision. In general, organic fertilizers are low analysis, whereas chemical fertilizers fall into either category, depending on formulation.

FERTILIZER RATIOS. The fertilizer percentages stated in the analysis also represent ratios. The fertilizer **ratio** is the proportion of the primary elements present in the fertilizer. In a 10–20-10 fertilizer the ratio of the three nutrients is 1:2:1. Fertilizers with analyses of 10-20-10 and 5-10-5 would have the same ratios. A 50-pound bag of 10-20-10 fertilizer would have the same amount and proportions of nutrients as a 100-pound bag of 5-10-5. Both would contain 5 pounds of available nitrogen, 10 pounds of phosphorus (as P_2O_5), and 5 pounds of potassium (as K_2O).

An understanding of fertilizer ratios is as important as an understanding of nutrient content. This is because nitrogen, phosphorus, and potassium each fulfill specific roles in the plant and for best growth they must be present in favorable proportions. Although research data are scanty in this area, it is believed that, while there is no one single "best" ratio of the primary fertilizer elements in a house plant fertilizer, there are ratio limits. Research to date indicates that acceptable ratios include 1–1-1, 2-1-1, 2-1-2, 3-2-2, and 3-1-2. Fertilizers that do not fit within this range of ratios can, if used over an extended period of time, result in poor plant growth created by an imbalance of nutrients.

Unfortunately, many of the commercial fertilizers presently marketed do not fall within the ratio limits specified above. In one

survey, only 18 out of 42 fertilizers examined fell within the acceptable range of primary nutrient ratios. Phosphorus appears to be out of balance most frequently. In 15 of the 42 fertilizers surveyed, phosphorus occurred in the highest concentration. This, in spite of the fact that plants require phosphorus in approximately one-tenth the amount they require nitrogen and potassium. Furthermore, added phosphorus is only slowly leachable from container soils because of its low solubility. Its low solubility is, as a matter of fact, a major reason why it is acceptable in amounts equal to nitrogen (1–1-1, for example) and potassium (3-1-1, for example).

Forms of Fertilizers Used Indoors
Houseplant fertilizers come in several different forms, including

- Liquids.
- Powders.
- Tablets.
- Spikes.
- Granules.

Liquid fertilizers can be purchased in concentrated or dilute forms. Concentrates require further dilution in water before use, whereas the dilute forms are ready to apply. The ready-to-apply liquid fertilizers have a very low nutrient concentration. Thus, although the gardener is spared the inconvenience of preparing a dilute mix, the price per unit of available nutrient is high.

Several houseplant fertilizers are available in powdered form. Powdered fertilizers are generally less expensive than liquids per unit of available nutrient. On the minus side, powders are sometimes difficult to handle because of their light weight and tendency to blow away. Most powders are designed to be mixed with water and when prepared properly are useful for fertilizing house plants.

Pellet, tablet, and spike forms of fertilizers are widely used for fertilizing house plants. One distinct advantage offered by these fertilizer forms is that they can be "programmed" for a more or less controlled rate of release of nutrients. This is accomplished in several ways. One method is to include in the fertilizer a blend of several different chemical compounds. One of these compounds may release its nutrients immediately, whereas others require conversion or must be chemically broken down before they can be utilized by plants. Another method is to encapsulate the fertilizer in plastic or other material that releases available nutrients at a controlled rate. Slow-release fertilizers are usually somewhat more expensive than rapid-release types, but their convenience and efficiency of use generally far outweigh the added expense. The use of timed-release fertilizers is widespread in commercial operations.

MANAGING FERTILITY PROBLEMS

The nutrient needs of plants are complex. We have seen that 16 nutrients are required for normal, healthy growth. Three of these come from air and water, the other 13 come from the soil. Not only must these 13 essential nutrients be present in soils, but they must also be in forms available to plants at the proper pH at the time they are required. They must also be present in the proper proportions. To further complicate matters, plant nutrient needs vary during the season. Nutrient demands in a period of lush vegetative growth are far different than those associated with flowering and fruiting. The needs of a rapidly expanding root system differ strikingly from those of the developing shoot system. To manage fertilizer practices successfully, we need an understanding of nutrient utilization by plants, nutrient deficiency, and toxicity symptoms and how to deal with soluble salts that may accumulate in the course of the normal care of house plants.

Nutrient Utilization by Plants

The primary fertilizer elements, nitrogen, phosphorus, and potassium are the nutrients most frequently added to soils. We know that plant demands for these elements are high, but why? What are their important roles in growth?

As indicated in Table 7.3, nitrogen is a component of amino acids, the building blocks of proteins. Nitrogen is also present in the nucleic acids of DNA and RNA, in chlorophyll, and as a part of many enzyme systems, including the one needed to fix carbon dioxide from the atmosphere. In short, nitrogen is a vital part of the molecules of life. Small wonder then that succulent, actively growing portions of the plant have a high content of nitrogen. Said another way, ample nitrogen supports lush, luxurious vegetative growth, a shortage stifles it. With a constant supply of nitrogen, new leaves have a rich, deep green color; without it, they become **chlorotic** (having a pale yellow appearance).

But too much nitrogen or a nitrogen imbalance can also present problems. When nasturtiums are grown outdoors, for example, excess nitrogen encourages vegetative growth at the expense of flowers. Needless to say, these nasturtiums do not make a nice floral display. Likewise, nitrogen promotes vegetative growth in tomatoes. Too much nitrogen late in the season reduces greatly the production of fruits.

Phosphorus serves in many roles also. It is a component of cellular membranes and is intimately involved with energy transformations in cells. Phosphorus also promotes rooting in plants and is necessary for healthy stems. Plants lacking phosphorus may display an abnormally dark green-colored foliage, often developing red and purple colors.

Potassium also has a multitude of roles in plant growth. Potassium ions are implicated in the opening and closing of stomata, protein synthesis, and enzyme activation (Table 7.3). Although it is required in large quantities, it lacks known structural roles in plants. Abundant potassium promotes the development of healthy stems, flowers, and roots. In contrast, when the supply of potassium is inadequate, stems and leaf stalks may be slender, and spots of dead tissue may develop in leaves, usually at tips, edges, and interveinal regions near margins.

Our discussion by example has revealed several solvent features of nutrient relationships in plants. We have seen that the essential elements serve in specific roles and, as such, are in high demand at specific times in plant development. Further, too much as well as too little of an essential nutrient can present problems. Last, but not least, nutrient deficiencies (and toxicities) result in visual symptoms that can, if properly read, be used by the gardener as a basis for corrective actions.

Nutrient Deficiencies and Toxicities

The concepts of nutrient deficiency and toxicity can be better understood by examining a nutrient level scale (Figure 7.6). In the midregion of the scale, plants will respond to increases in fertility with better growth, although they do not show obvious deficiency symptoms. This condition has been termed *hidden hunger.* If we continue to add fertilizer to satisfy this hidden need, a point will be reached at which no further growth re-

sponse is evident, although the plant continues its nutrient uptake. This is termed **luxury consumption.** Finally, if the nutrient continues to be added, the plant will eventually *display* reduced growth due to a toxic reaction. One can safely assume that, as in the case of hidden hunger, a region of hidden toxicity precedes the visual expression of symptoms.

Toward the other end of the nutrient scale, we see that if the fertility level continues to decline through the hidden hunger range, a point is reached at which the plant begins to show *visible* signs of a nutrient shortage; that is, it displays nutrient deficiency symptoms.

NUTRIENT DEFICIENCY SYMPTOMS. Nutrient deficiency symptoms in plants fall into either of two broad categories; they occur first in older regions of the plant, or they show up on young tissues first. The location of the first visual symptoms of a deficiency is a reflection of the behavior of a specific nutrient in the plant. If the nutrient can be mobilized in mature tissues and transported to growing regions, then deficiency symptoms will be evident in these older tissues first. Conversely, if a nutrient cannot be mobilized for reuse, as is the case with the calcium incorporated into the middle lamella

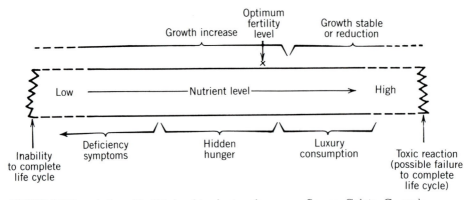

FIGURE 7.6 The relation of fertility level to plant performance. *Source:* Calvin, C., and Knutson, D., *Modern Home Gardening,* New York: Wiley, 1983, p. 131. Reprinted by permission.

cementing plant cells together, then deficiency symptoms occur in young tissues first. Nitrogen, phosphorus, potassium, and magnesium are very *mobile* elements in plants and in cases of deficiency will be transported to growing regions. It is easy to imagine, for example, the degradation of amino acids and chlorophyll in older tissues with the release of nitrogen and magnesium for transport and utilization elsewhere. As a result of the mobilization of magnesium through the breakdown of chlorophyll, older tissues become chlorotic, a major symptom of magnesium deficiency. Calcium, sulfur, and the majority of micronutrients are, in contrast, *nonmobile*. Thus, deficiency symptoms of these elements show up in younger tissues first.

A key to plant nutrient deficiency symptoms is given in Table 7.5. Note that the major dichotomy in the key (older or lower leaves mostly affected *versus* newer or bud leaves affected) is based on nutrient mobility. Study the key to become familiar with the deficiency symptoms characteristic of specific nutrient elements. Note that similar deficiency symptoms may occur for different elements; chlorosis, for example, characterizes both nitrogen and magnesium deficiency. Even though the pattern of chlorosis is somewhat different for the two elements, other diagnostic features may need to be taken into consideration in making nutrient deficiency determinations. Recall also that other factors can induce symptoms similar to those brought about by nutrient deficiencies. Overwatering, for example, may retard nutrient uptake and produce symptoms reminisent of specific nutrient deficiencies. The ability to accurately diagnose nutrient deficiency symptoms will allow you to take corrective actions, such as modifying the pH of the growing medium or adding the appropriate fertilizers, in a timely manner.

NUTRIENT TOXICITIES—A CASE OF EXCESS SALTS. Although it is important that

we be able to detect nutrient deficiences and take corrective actions should they occur, the problem of nutrient toxicities is much, much more common. Toxicities are caused by the buildup of salts in the medium, on its surface, or in the walls of the container itself (Figure 7.7). Most salt problems can be corrected easily, but to do this, we need an understanding of what salts are, where they come from, how they can be detected, and how they are eliminated.

What Are Salts? Acids and bases react to form chemical compounds termed *salts*. In the reaction shown below, sodium hydroxide ($NaOH$) and hydrochloric acid (HCL) react to form a salt, sodium chloride ($NaCl$), and water, $NaOH + HCl \rightarrow NaCl + H_2O$. In this reaction, one acid-forming ion, chloride, and one basic ion, sodium, combine in chemically equivalent quantities to form a neutral salt. Other common acidic ions include sulfate, nitrate, phosphate, and bicarbonate. Common basic ions include calcium, magnesium, potassium, and ammonium. Acidic and basic ions may combine in many ways; thus, a variety of salts may be formed. You may recognize the ions listed above as those essential to plant nutrition (Table 7.3) and therein lies the problem. In supplying plants with fertilizers, we are supplying them with salts useful for plant growth. As essential as these fertilizer salts are, they are harmful when amounts exceed the small quantities needed for growth.

Where Do Soluble Salts Come from? Salts may come from fertilizers, water, or the growing medium itself. By far the most important source of addition are plant fertilizers. Any fertilizer when used in excess presents problems. Chemical fertilizers, such as ammonium nitrate and potassium sulfate, are in the form of salts. Organic materials become mineralized through decay processes, and the nutrients are finally converted to salts. All domestic water supplies contain salts. Normally, these are present in small quantities, but in particular areas problems

TABLE 7.5 A KEY TO PLANT NUTRIENT DEFICIENCY SYMPTOMS

Symptoms	Element Deficient
1. Older or lower leaves of plant mostly affected; effects localized or generalized	
2. Effects mostly generalized over whole plant; more or less drying or firing of lower leaves; plant light or dark green	
3. Plant light green; lower leaves yellow, drying to light brown color; stalks short and slender if element is deficient in later stages of growth	Nitrogen
3. Plant dark green, often developing red and purple colors; lower leaves sometimes yellow, drying to greenish brown or black color; stalks short and slender if element is deficient in later stages of growth	Phosphorus
2. Effects mostly localized; mottling or chlorosis with or without spots of dead tissue on lower leaves; little or no drying up of lower leaves	
4. Mottled or chlorotic leaves, typically may redden, as with cotton; sometimes with dead spots; tips and margins turned or cupped upward; stalks slender	Magnesium
4. Mottled or chlorotic leaves with large or small spots of dead tissue	
5. Spots of dead tissue small, usually at tips and between veins, more marked at margins of leaves; stalks slender	Potassium
5. Spots generalized, rapidly enlarging, generally involving areas between veins and eventually involving secondary and even primary veins; leaves thick; stalks with shortened internodes	Zinc
1.′ Newer or bud leaves affected; symptoms localized	
2.′ Terminal bud dies, following appearance of distortions at tips or bases of young leaves	
3.′ Young leaves of terminal bud at first typically hooked, finally dying back at tips and margins, so that later growth is characterized by a cut-out appearance at these points; stalk finally dies at terminal bud	Calcium
3.′ Young leaves of terminal bud becoming light green at bases, with final breakdown here; in later growth, leaves become twisted; stalk finally dies back at terminal bud	Boron
2.′ Terminal bud commonly remains alive; wilting or chlorosis of younger or bud leaves with or without spots of dead tissue; veins light or dark green	
4.′ Young leaves permanently wilted (wither-tip effect) without spotting or marked chlorosis; twig or stalk just below tip and seedhead often unable to stand erect in later stages when shortage is acute	Copper
4.′ Young leaves not wilted; chlorosis present with or without spots of dead tissue scattered over the leaf	
5.′ Spots of dead tissue scattered over the leaf; smallest veins tend to remain green, producing a checkered or reticulated effect	Manganese
5.′ Dead spots not commonly present; chlorosis may or may not involve veins, making them light or dark green in color	
6.′ Young leaves with veins and tissue between veins light green in color	Sulfur
6.′ Young leaves chlorotic, principal veins typically green; stalks short and slender	Iron

SOURCE: McMurtrey, *Diagnostic techniques for soils and crops*, American Potash Institute, Atlanta, Ga., 1950.

FIGURE 7.7 Salt deposits have built up in this porous clay pot as evidenced by the white crystalline deposits on its outer surface.

medium surfaces, as when water evaporates leaving salty encrustations. Salts may also accumulate in and on the surface of porous clay pots (Figure 7.7) as a part of their "breathing" process. These deposits may cause rotting of leaves of African violets (*Saintpaulia*) that come into contact with the salt crust present on pot rims. Likewise, roots that come into contact with salt-encrusted pot surfaces may be injured or killed. Finally, salt deposits also occur on plant surfaces themselves and may be easily detected. You may recall from Chapter Three that under certain conditions plant roots push water into shoots. A manifestation of this pushing is the water of guttation that accumulates at the tips and margins of leaves in early morning hours. The warmth of day causes the water to evaporate, but the salts remain. Death of tissue at leaf tips and margins is generally a symptom of salt injury related to guttation.

Correcting Salt-Related Problems. Although the accumulation of soluble salts causes serious problems, most can be corrected easily. Salt deposits on aerial plant parts can be washed away by periodically spraying affected parts with water. Accumulations within the growing medium can be leached out by repeated watering in a short time period to flush the soil. Clay-encrusted pots can be soaked in water and scrubbed before reuse. Alternatively, plastic or glazed clay pots can be substituted. These do not breathe and, therefore, do not accumulate salts except on interior exposed surfaces (rims). Correcting for hard water is more problematic. The common water softening processes do not remove salts from the water; they merely substitute sodium for chemically equivalent amounts of calcium and magnesium. Whereas the "soft water" produced is better for doing the laundry and bathing, it is devastating to plants. Alternate wet and dry conditions should definitely be avoided. Any environmental factor that retards transpiration reduces the accumulation of salts in leaves.

may occur. Most of us are familiar with so-called "hard water." Such water contains sufficient quantities of calcium and magnesium salts to precipitate soap to an undesirable extent. In many field soils throughout Canada and the United States, soluble salts are in high quantity, frequently impairing plant growth. The container gardener, however, can *select* his or her growing medium and to this extent the medium should not present problems. Normally problems arise when, over time, the medium becomes contaminated with excess salts from fertilizers or water.

How Are Salts Detected? Soil scientists have devised elaborate methods to determine salt levels in field soils, but for the indoor gardener, the best method is to watch for visible salt deposits. These may occur on

While the methods described in the preceding paragraph will temporarily correct for soluble salt accumulations, one additional comment is required. At the beginning of this section, we introduced the theory of limiting factors. It bears repeating that this theory has a direct relationship to fertilizer practices. As indicated, a reduced level of plant growth, caused by one or more limiting factors, may require a lowering of other factors to below optimum levels. When a plant is subjected to low-light intensity, for example, and growing at a very slow rate, the appropriate rate of fertilization is *much less* than when the plant is grown under optimal conditions. The failure of indoor gardeners to reduce fertilizer applications accordingly is the major cause of soluble salt accumulations and overall reduction in desirable appearance.

FOR FURTHER READING

Baker, K. (ed.). *The UC System for Producing Healthy Container-Grown Plants.* University of California Agricultural Experiment Station, 1957.

Bienz, D. *The Why and How of Home Horticulture.* San Francisco, Calif.: W. H. Freeman and Co., 1980.

Brady, N. *The Nature and Properties of Soils.* 8th ed. New York: Macmillan, 1974.

Calvin, C., and D. Knutson. *Modern Home Gardening.* New York: Wiley, 1983.

Conover, C. "Fertilizer Systems—A Look at the Economics." Proceedings of the 1978 National Tropical Foliage Short Course.

Conover, C., and R. Poole. "Fertilization of Indoor Foliage Plants." Proceedings of the 1977 National Tropical Foliage Short Course.

Faust, J. *Book of House Plants.* New York: Quadrangle/The New York Times Book Co., 1973.

Henley, R. "House Plant Fertilizers—A Closer Look." Proceedings of the 1978 National Tropical Foliage Short Course.

Joiner, J. "Plant Nutrition." Proceedings of the 1977 National Tropical Foliage Short Course.

Poole, R., and C. Conover. "The Importance of Micronutrients in Tropical Foliage Production." Proceedings of the 1978 National Tropical Foliage Short Course.

Rice, L., and R. Rice. *Practical Horticulture.* Boston: Saunder College Publishing, 1980.

chapter eight
the climate
indoors*

Indoor gardeners must remember, when growing plants in interior locations, that their evolutionary development did not prepare them for a life indoors. In reality, then, it is all the more amazing that foliage plants can survive interior environments that would be lethal without a little help from their owners.

The climate indoors is characterized by low light levels, dry air, and temperatures that may be too high or too low. However, these and other climatic factors can be compensated for when one has a better understanding of how climate affects plant growth and survival.

ACCLIMATIZATION:
A PHYSIOLOGICAL PROCESS

Acclimatization is defined as "the adaptation of an organism, especially a plant, to a new environment." In the plant's natural environment, these adaptations may occur over extremely long periods of time, such as with southern and northern races of dogwood, *Cornus florida*, which will not flower and often will not even survive if planted too far from their original locations. Foliage plants, therefore, are not unique in their ability to acclimatize to a new environment.

*By Charles A. Conover, Director, Agricultural Research Center, University of Florida.

Means of Acclimatization

With foliage plants, however, we utilize and control these physiological processes of acclimatization during production or during the transfer period from production to final use area, increasing the likelihood of survival under interior environments. Consequently, a better understanding of acclimatization and its effects will aid the indoor plant grower in achieving greater satisfaction from plants already being grown, while improving the transfer of plants to their new growing environment.

Light Acclimatization

Of factors shown to be involved in the acclimatization of foliage plants, light has proven to be most important. Production of foliage plants (e.g., *Ficus benjamina*) under high light intensity yields a plant poorly equipped to grow and survive indoors, since it is adapted to survival in full sun. High light intensity induces physiological changes within plant cells and also causes the plant to produce smaller, somewhat thicker leaves that are closer together and often lighter green in color. These adaptive changes prevent cell damage from excessive energy absorption while a plant is under high light levels, but prevent maximum utilization of energy after placement under low light levels.

As explained in Chapter Three, light compensation point is the point at which food production, through photosynthesis, is equal to food utilization due to respiration, When a plant is existing at its light compensation point, it will neither grow nor die during the short term. However, unless it is somewhat above its light compensation point, the plant will not be able to produce new leaves to replace those lost through aging; thus, it will have to use stored food reserves. Plants at their light compensation point without stored food reserves will die as leaves age and become less efficient, since they will drop below the light compensation point and consume more food than they are capable of manufacturing. Leaves of different foliage plant genera have different life spans and this is one reason that some plants survive longer indoors even if they are below required light compensation points (Figure 8.1).

An example of light acclimatization and its effects on *Ficus benjamina* (weeping fig) is shown in Figure 8.2. When acclimatized and nonacclimatized plants are placed under a low light environment of 75 foot-candles, only the acclimatized plant is above the light compensation point. Therefore, under these conditions, the acclimatized plant will continue to grow, while the nonacclimatized

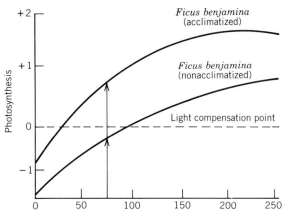

FIGURE 8.2 Comparison of acclimatized *Ficus benjamina* with shade leaves (upper line) with a nonacclimatized one with sun leaves (lower line). An acclimatized plant under an interior light intensity of 75 foot-candles would be above the light compensation point, whereas a nonacclimatized plant would not. *Source:* C. A. Conover/D. B. McConnell, "Utilization Foliage Plants" in *Foliage Plant Production*, by Jasper Joiner, ed., © 1981, p. 532. Adapted by permission Prentice-Hall, Inc. Englewood Cliffs, New Jersey.

plant will only initially grow in an attempt to convert to a level of acclimatization that will raise it above the light compensation point. It should be noted that had the same two plants been placed under 200 foot-candles, both would have been above the light compensation point, although growth of the acclimatized plant would have been much greater. However, 200 foot-candles is frequently above the level available within interior environments.

Although we have intimated that foliage plants grown under shade were acclimatized, that is not entirely true. Most foliage plants, even if acclimatized, will further increase their level of acclimatization after placement in an interior environment. Thus, light acclimatization is an ongoing process and is not complete until every leaf on the plant has been produced under that growing environment.

NUTRITIONAL ACCLIMATIZATION.

Although nutrition has been shown to direct-

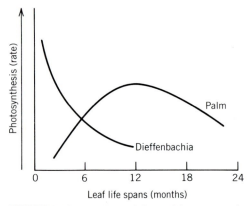

FIGURE 8.1 Leaves have different life spans and levels of efficiency prior to death depending on species.

ly influence the level of acclimatization on some foliage plants, mechanisms of its involvement are generally poorly understood. Levels of nutrition that do not cause plant damage in production areas, but are in excess of need, have been shown to increase interior leaf drop of *Ficus*, *Aphelandra*, and *Brassaia*. It may be that the relationship is solely due to elevated levels of soluble salts that cause water stress within plants and induce leaf abscission under low humidity, or it may be more involved and relate to metabolic processes in respiration. There is no doubt, however, that correct nutritional levels during production and after placement indoors will be very beneficial in aiding a plant to acclimatize to an interior environment. To date, only the effects of nitrogen and potassium on acclimatization are known, with elevated nitrogen levels shown to decrease acclimatization level and potassium shown to have no effect.

For several years, it has been recommended that plants be leached before placement indoors to remove excess fertilizer "salts" from the growing medium. However, recent evidence indicates that this is not always the best procedure, since leaching was only beneficial on *Ficus benjamina* when excess fertilizer was applied. Leaching had no effect on plants grown with proper fertilization levels, but was damaging to plants that were deficient. The process of acclimatization is not completely understood although much is known about changes that occur in both plant anatomy and basic physiology. Within the genetic capabilities of specific plant genera, the process may occur within a few weeks or take several months.

ANATOMICAL AND MORPHOLOGICAL CONSIDERATIONS. Foliage plants grown under high light environments will be different anatomically from plants produced in shade. Major differences include leaf size, thickness, shape, number and organization of leaves, stem caliper, and root system size. Differentiated plant parts obviously cannot be changed during acclimatization, although new leaves, stems, and roots formed during the acclimatization period will be different.

Leaves produced under high light will be smaller than shade leaves. Sometimes, as in the case of *Ficus benjamina*, they will individually have an area equal to one-half or less of shade leaves, whereas with *Dracaena marginata* (red-edge dracaena), the area may be nearly similar, but leaves from high light will be short and wide compared with long, narrow leaves from shade-grown plants. Often, however, total leaf area on a particular foliage plant will be equal for high light plants, since they usually have more leaves than shade-grown plants.

Leaf thickness is also closely correlated with production light intensity. Leaves from plants grown in high light are often twice as thick in cross section as shade-grown leaves (Figure 8.3). This extra thickness is the result of a thickening of the epidermal layer and a lengthening of the spongy mesophyll cells. Cell walls of plants grown in high light are

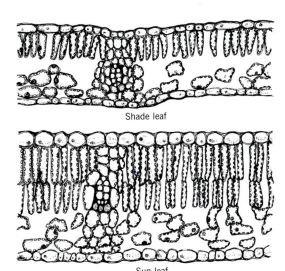

Shade leaf

Sun leaf

FIGURE 8.3 Comparison of leaf structure between leaves grown in shade or sun.

also thicker than those from shade-grown plants.

Leaves from foliage plants grown under high light may also be modified in other ways. On *Ficus*, for example, leaves may be V-shaped rather than flat, whereas with *Aglaonema* or *Dieffenbachia*, leaves will assume a vertical position in high light, while being more horizontal in proper or low light. These modifications appear as methods of reducing surface area subjected to light in high light situations, while maximizing light reception under low light.

Organization of leaves varies also for plants grown in high or low light because of change in internode length. In high light, nodes are close together, so leaves often overlap each other, while in low light, less overlapping occurs since internodes are longer. Overlapping appears to be a protective mechanism for high light plants, but once placed under low light, this becomes a negative factor since it prevents light from reaching interior and lower leaf surfaces.

However, some repositioning occurs on many plants due to changes in light intensity.

Stem caliper for many sun-grown plants is greater than that of shade-grown plants and decreases as light level decreases. With *Ficus*, for example, caliper of plants grown in 60 to 70 percent shade will be 30 to 40 percent less than those grown in full sun. This appears to be due to reduced carbohydrate levels but may also be related to reduced stem stress due to lack of wind movement in shaded greenhouses or shade house environments. This factor does not seem to relate to acclimatization directly but is a reason some producers desire to field-grow plants until desired stem or trunk diameter is achieved. Root systems are also heavier in plants grown in higher light, but this has not been correlated with decreased levels of acclimatization.

PHYSIOLOGICAL CHANGES IN CELLS.

Changes within cells in response to external environmental conditions are tremendously important to plants. The major observed changes occurring in foliage plants are in response to light levels, although other important changes also occur.

Cells containing chlorophyll, as described in Chapter Three, have the capacity to produce food in the form of carbohydrates through the process of photosynthesis. The amount of food produced is proportional to the amount of light energy captured; under interior conditions, this may be very low. Thus, there are several ways foliage plants can regulate their own efficiency in food production. Within cells, chloroplasts have the ability to migrate and, with time, will disperse throughout the cell rather than position themselves near vertical cell walls (Figure 8.4). Dispersal of chloroplasts increases the likelihood of capturing light energy and thus increases the production of food. The rate at which dispersal of chloroplasts occurs is not well documented but

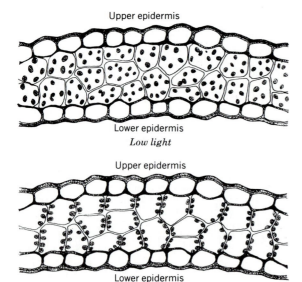

Upper epidermis

Lower epidermis
Low light

Upper epidermis

Lower epidermis
High light

FIGURE 8.4 Comparison of chloroplast arrangement between foliage plants grown under low and high light intensity.

appears to occur over a period of no longer than two to eight weeks.

Another method plants have for regulating photosynthesis is found within the grana, the point at which light energy reacts with chlorophyll. Grana appear dispersed throughout chloroplasts as interconnected stacks of poker chips. Stacks arranged in an upright configuration have limited ability to capture light energy, and this is the configuration commonly found in plants produced under high light. On the other hand, grana with a dispersed configuration (Figure 8.5) have more surface area available for intercepting light energy and are representative of plants adapted to low light environments. Grana have the ability to change configuration in response to light intensity, but the rate of change is unknown.

Finally, it has been shown that chlorophyll levels increase per unit area as a plant's level of acclimatization to low light increases. Increases of as high as doubling of chlorophyll per unit area has been reported for some foliage plants, which greatly increases a plant's ability to produce food (carbohydrates) under reduced light levels of interior living spaces.

TEMPERATURE EFFECTS ON ACCLIMATIZATION. Influence of temperature during production on the ability of a foliage plant to acclimatize to an interior environment is largely unknown. However, it has been shown that acclimatized *Ficus benjamina* moved from a production area to an interior environment during summer were more likely to lose leaves in the new indoor location than similar plants moved during winter. Thus, one could expect more problems with plants that were produced during high temperature periods prior to movement to an interior environment.

Although temperature may not be directly involved, it is likely that it has a strong influence on elevation of respiration rate and, thus, causes increased light compensation

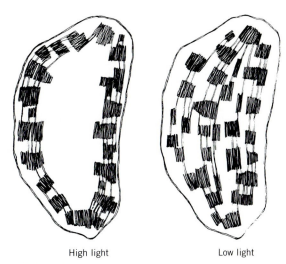

High light   Low light

FIGURE 8.5 Changes in conformation of grana within chloroplasts due to light intensity.

points. These data appear to be borne out with other foliage plants since most are tropical in nature and grow rapidly during high temperature periods, provided other environmental factors are not limiting.

APPEARANCE OF ACCLIMATIZED PLANTS. There are no strict and exact characteristics that can be applied across all foliage plants that indicate whether they are acclimatized or not. However, several items than can be observed on acclimatized or nonacclimatized plants are listed in Table 8.1. Most of these observations relate to whether the plant is light acclimatized. Appearance of nutritional acclimatization and possible tolerance to low humidity usually cannot be observed. However, since light acclimatization usually accounts for more than two-thirds of total acclimatization, these features provide a good measure of the extent of acclimatization.

Plants most highly acclimatized will exhibit several or all of the characteristics listed. It is possible, however, that nonacclimatized plants will have some characteristics listed for acclimatized plants. For example, a *Ficus*

TABLE 8.1 SOME DIFFERENCES THAT CAN BE OBSERVED BETWEEN ACCLIMATIZED AND NONACCLIMATIZED FOLIAGE PLANTS

Acclimatized	Nonacclimatized
Medium to dark green leaves	Yellowish to light green leaves
Large leaves	Small leaves
Flat leaves	Partially folded leaves
Thin leaves	Thick leaves
Leaves widely spaced	Leaves crowded together
Internodes long	Internodes short
Thin to medium stems	Thick stems
Leaf position horizontal or slightly drooping	Leaf position upright
Few new leaves	Many new leaves
Wide branch angles	Acute angles

grown in high light might have large, dark green leaves if heavily fertilized, but it would also have leaves crowded together, short internodes, partially folded leaves, and thick stems, all of which would indicate it was not acclimatized.

Light Acclimatization Pathways

The sequence of occurrences that lead to acclimatization of foliage plants should aid in understanding how a plant becomes light acclimatized. Although solid research is not available to substantiate the importance of each step, or even the order of some steps, the overall results have been proven, as well as the occurrence of each of the changes.

INITIAL RESPONSE. When a foliage plant grown under high light is moved to a low light environment, physiological stress will cause an immediate reduction in photosynthetic rate (food manufacture). Because of a high respiration rate, the plant will immediately start to utilize stored food. Within a short period (one to two weeks), the plant will start to acclimatize to low light with reorientation of chloroplasts and grana, increase in chlorophyll level, and reduction in

respiration rate. The plant will also start to produce new foliage. After two to eight weeks, most reorientation of chloroplasts and grana will have occurred, the respiration rate decreased, and chlorophyll levels increased. The plant will have produced some new foliage and possibly lost many older leaves. At this point, little additional change will occur in chlorophyll level, chloroplast or grana positioning, and respiration level to increase efficiency. If the combination of physiological changes and production of new leaves has raised the plant above the light compensation point, it will probably live. If, on the other hand, it has not, the plant will eventually die, since most stored food would have been consumed after eight to ten weeks.

IMPROVING ACCLIMATIZATION LEVEL. When new plants are first moved indoors, they will undergo considerable stress. One of the best ways to aid plants in making the transition is to reduce by as much as possible the severity of the change in environment. An easy way to accomplish this is to place the plant under a light level that is higher than the final intended location. For example, place a *Dracaena marginata* under 200 foot-candles for four to six weeks and then under 100 foot-candles in its final location. This will reduce utilization of food reserves and aid in reducing stress during the adjustment period. Also, extending the period that light is applied to 12 to 15 hours per day will help. During the transition period, the plant should not be allowed to dry out, nor should it be fertilized.

REVERSE ACCLIMATIZATION. Once foliage plants are acclimatized to their final low light location, it is unwise to move them back to high light situations because severe damage may occur. Foliage produced under low light or on plants adapted to low light will burn and turn brown if the plant is placed under high light. Placement under full sun is not necessary for this to occur as plants from 100 foot-candle locations have been observed to burn when placed under 2000 foot-candles (full sun ranges from 5000–15,000 foot-candles, depending on the season).

Some experts recommend that plants be rejuvenated by placement on patios or even outdoors during warm seasons. This procedure is unnecessary if the plants are healthy and steadily growing in their indoor location. However, if plants are doing poorly because of low light or plants are desired on the patio or in other outdoor locations for aesthetic reasons, it is possible to move them to higher light provided it is not more than five to ten times the original level. For example, a plant growing indoors at 100 foot-candles should not be moved to a location that exceeds 500 to 1000 foot-candles. Plants moved to outdoor locations during warm months will require some reacclimatization when moved back to interior environments, but induced stress will not be severe.

TEMPERATURE

Biological activities are restricted to a very narrow range of temperatures, from 32 to 122°F (0–50°C), and are limited on the lower side by the freezing point of water and on the upper side by denaturization of proteins. The very nature of plants through genetic selection has resulted in plants adapted to both the extremes and midpoint of this range. However, with foliage plants, adaptation to tropical or subtropical regions has resulted in plants generally intolerant of temperatures below freezing and, in some cases, to temperatures below 50°F (10°C). Some foliage plants are fairly tolerant of higher temperatures, even as high as 105°F (40°C) for short periods, but long-term exposure results in decreased food production.

Soil Temperature

Specific soil temperatures most desirable for growing each type of foliage plant are gen-

erally unknown, but plant producers have found that maintenance of soil temperatures between 65 and 90°F (18 and 32°C) is acceptable as long as air temperature is within an acceptable range. Such temperatures are easy to maintain in interior environments, provided extensive energy-saving procedures are not being utilized.

Changes in soil temperature occur more slowly than changes in air temperature due to the soil's insulating ability. Limited research has shown that soil temperatures of 45°F (7°C) or below for extended periods will severely damage plants such as *Ficus*, *Aglaonema*, and others. Such low soil temperatures can result from placement of plants in the ground within a building or a planter along an exterior wall. Other cold climate locations where low soil temperatures may occur are in planters above unheated areas such as garages or crawl spaces.

Even when plant roots are above the point where damage may occur from low temperatures, yet below optimum levels, plant growth will be restricted because uptake of water and nutrients will be reduced. In some cases, the leaf color of foliage plants will also be a lighter green when soil temperatures are below optimum. Suggested soil temperatures for optimum foliage plant growth within interior environments should be 65 to 80°F (18–28°C). These temperatures are easy to maintain in most interior spaces.

Research on crops other than foliage plants has shown that soil at 50°F (10°C) versus 77°F (25°C) resulted in an 80 percent decrease in water absorption. This is thought to be related to several factors such as reduced root elongation, decreased movement of water from soil into roots, decreased cell wall permeability, increased viscosity of protoplasm, decreased vapor pressure of water, and decreased metabolic activity of roots.

Elevated soil temperatures can also influence water relations and root growth in foliage plants. High soil temperatures [90°F (32°C) or above] will restrict growth of roots and also reduce absorption of water. Therefore, it is unwise to place plants on warm surfaces such as radiators, television sets, or other heat-generating equipment.

Air Temperature

Interior spaces utilized for living or work environments generally provide temperature ranges conducive to growing foliage plants. Although there are exceptions, most foliage plants will tolerate a temperature range of 55 to 90°F (13–32°C) and grow well where it is maintained between 65 and 80°F (18–27°C). These ranges are well within those that provide an acceptable and comfortable living environment for humans. Within this temperature range, it is more desirable to provide a higher temperature during the period plants receive light, whether natural or artificial, and a lower temperature during the dark period. This will maximize the photosynthetic rate during the light period and reduce respiration levels during the dark period, thus saving energy.

The major problems with maintaining desired temperatures for foliage plants relate to microclimates within living spaces and our renewed desire to save on heating and cooling energy costs. When temperatures

are set back at night, it is preferable they be set no lower than 60°F (16°C). Even more important is the effect on foliage plants of setting back temperatures for entire weekends or during vacation periods, since plants continue to consume food through respiration even though they may not be able to manufacture food through photosynthesis. Setting back temperatures below 55°F (13°C) or turning heating systems off completely and allowing cooling below 45°F (7°C) may permanently damage some genera such as *Aglaonema*, *Dieffenbachia*, and *Episcia* (Table 8.2). Unlike temperate zone plants, foliage plants can be cold-damaged without freezing, which is referred to as chilling injury. This phenomenon is thought to be caused by reduced membrane integrity, which occurs at higher temperatures in chilling-sensitive tropical plants than in those adapted to temperate zones. Although some hardening occurs in tropical plants due to seasonal influences of light and temperature as days shorten and become cooler, the scope of these changes is not of major importance and has little influence under interior conditions.

Increasing the temperature as with air conditioning during hot months or turning it off entirely may also damage foliage plants. The problem is not related entirely to max-

TABLE 8.2 SOME FOLIAGE PLANTS INJURED BY CHILLING TEMPERATURES BETWEEN 35 AND 50°F (2 AND 10°C) FOR SHORT PERIODS

Botanical Name	Common Name
Aeschynanthus pulcher	Lipstick vine
Aglaonema × 'Silver Queen'	Silver evergreen
Caladium × *hortulanum*	Fancy-leaved caladium
Dieffenbachia maculata	Spotted dumbcane
Dracaena fragrans 'Massangeana'	Corn plant dracaena
Dracaena reflexa	Malaysian dracaena
Episcia cupreata	Flame violet episcia
Fittonia verschaffeltii	Mosaic plant, silver-nerve fittonia
Maranta leuconeura erythroneura	Red-veined prayer plant
Polyscias fruticosa	Ming aralia

imum temperature, since most foliage plants can tolerate temperatures as high as 95°F (35°C) provided they receive adequate water, but to utilization of stored food reserves due to elevated respiration levels.

Temperature as It Affects Plants

Changes in temperature have a strong influence on total plant growth because of its influence on chemical reactions. Specific temperature controlled processes that affect growth of plants indoors include photosynthesis, respiration, and transpiration.

EFFECTS ON PHOTOSYNTHESIS. Because leaf temperatures are generally above ambient temperatures, it is difficult to determine limits of photosynthesis for most plants. However, when low light plants are grown, these temperatures would be close, and for most tropical plants (including foliage plants), it is thought that photosynthesis occurs from about 50°F (10°C) to temperatures as high as 122°F (50°C).

The rate at which photosynthesis proceeds increases as temperature increases up to about 95°F (35°C) for many foliage plants, with some higher and others lower. However, as the temperature nears the upper limit, there is a large decrease in rate with time. This is thought to be due to the damaging effects of high temperature on cell contents. For the most part, however, the foliage plant photosynthetic rate is not usually affected by temperature under interior environments, since light is usually the limiting factor.

EFFECTS ON RESPIRATION. Increasing temperature normally increases respiration rate, the magnitude of which is measured by its Q10 (temperature coefficient). Generally, the Q10 of enzymatic reactions for most plants falls between 2.0 and 2.5; a Q10 of 2 indicates that the rate of reaction doubles with every 18°F (10°C) rise in temperature. Thus, a foliage plant growing at 85°F (29°C) versus 67°F (19°C) would consume twice the level of food in respiration. This can have a

tremendous effect on the long-term growth of foliage plants under low light situations, since excess carbohydrate production is necessary for growth and its absence will result in decreased quality or possible death. Under low light situations, carbohydrate production is low, so reduced respiration rates are necessary to balance the energy budget. During light periods, elevation of temperature above desired ranges will increase both photosynthetic rate and respiration, but they will usually balance unless the temperature is extremely high. During dark periods, however, elevation of temperature has little effect on photosynthesis, but it will increase respiration rate according to the Q10. This relationship is justification for reduced night temperatures, when possible, to reduce respiration and conserve carbohydrates.

EFFECTS ON TRANSPIRATION. Increasing air temperature increases the slope of the vapor pressure gradient through the stomates of plants. This has been shown to be as much as three times greater at 86°F (30°C) than at 68°F (20°C). If we assume that the vapor pressure of the atmosphere at 20°C was half that of a saturated atmosphere at that temperature—8.77 mm Hg—then the excess vapor pressure of the leaf over that of the atmosphere at 20°C was 8.77 mm Hg (17.54 − 8.77). At 30°C, however, the vapor pressure of the intercellular spaces would have increased to about 31.82 mm Hg, whereas the increase in the vapor pressure of surrounding atmosphere would usually be so slight that it can be disregarded. The excess vapor pressure of the intercellular spaces over the atmosphere is now 23.05 mm Hg (31.82 − 8.77) that will result in diffusion of water vapor out of the leaf at a rate nearly three times as fast as at 20°C. Increases of such magnitude will have a large effect on water requirements of foliage plants indoors and, therefore, might necessitate watering two or three times more often if plants are grown at higher temperatures. In the home, this may not be considered a problem, but in commercial installations it would cause increased maintenance costs associated with frequent watering.

TOTAL GROWTH EFFECTS. Temperature controls essentially all the chemical reactions that occur within foliage plants. Therefore, control of temperature within interior environments is an extremely important part of growing foliage plants indoors. Low temperatures will result in lowered respiration but will also result in reduced levels of food production. High temperatures are generally wasteful of energy but may result in increased food production during periods of light, provided the level is not extreme. Overall, best growth of the widest group of foliage plants will be obtained when a temperature range of 65 to 80°F (18–27°C) is provided, with the higher temperature provided during the light period and the lower during the dark period. Figure 8.6 provides a graphic display of the influence of high night temperature on total plant growth. Maintenance of these air temperatures will also provide a satisfactory soil temperature, provided plant containers are not located too

close to a cold or hot surface. Because problem areas can be found within every interior environment, information is provided in Table 8.3 to aid in selection of plants capable of tolerating either low or high temperatures.

LIGHT: NATURAL AND ARTIFICIAL

Light is the ultimate source of energy required by green plants to grow (see Chapter Three). Natural light, for economic reasons, is the light source used to produce commercial crops, although artificial light is often used to supplement natural light for some ornamental crops. Presently, there are even experimental farms where food crops, such as lettuce, are being grown under artificial light.

Those who grow ornamental plants indoors, mainly foliage plants, are the major users of artificial light to grow plants. Because this practice has become so common, one might believe that we know everything there is to know about the subject. However, this is far from true, and every year we learn more about the effects of artificial light on indoor plants. This discussion of light is designed to provide sufficient background on the subject to allow the reader to obtain excellent growth of foliage plants in interior spaces.

LIGHT EFFECTS ON PLANTS. Light affects numerous physiological conditions and processes in plants. Some of these factors are tremendously important to growing plants indoors, whereas others are of little magnitude. Chlorophyll synthesis, for example, only occurs in the presence of light and is vitally important to plant growth, whereas anthocyanin, another type of pigment formation, is more important for outdoor plants but is also important in *Codiaeum* (croton) and other colorful indoor plants. Control of stomates is related to cell turgor and water but is also strongly influenced by light, since stom-

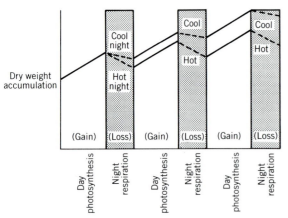

F]GURE 8.6 High night temperatures reduce plant growth because of increased respiration.

TABLE 8.3 SOME FOLIAGE PLANTS CAPABLE OF WITH-STANDING LOW OR HIGH TEMPERATURES FOR PERIODS OF UP TO 12 HOURS ON AN INFREQUENT BASIS

Botanical Name	Common Name
Low Temperature Tolerance of 40 to 50°F (4–10°C)	
Araucaria heterophylla	Norfolk Island pine
Ardisia crenata	Coral ardisia
Aspidistra elatior	Cast iron plant
Beaucarnea recurvata	Ponytail palm
Chlorophytum comosum	Spider plant
Ficus pumila	Creeping fig
Hedera helix	English ivy
Heptaplureum arboricola	Dwarf schefflera
Nephrolepis exaltata	Boston fern
Philodendron selloum	Lacy tree philodendrón
Phoenix roebelenii	Miniature date palm
Pittosporum tobira	Japanese pittosporum
Podocarpus macrophyllus	Southern yew
Rhapis excelsa	Lady finger palm
Sansevieria spp.	Snake plant
Saxifraga stolonifera	Strawberry geranium
Tolmiea menziesii	Piggyback plant
Yucca elephantipes	Spineless yucca
High Temperature Tolerance of 95 to 105°F (35–40°C)	
Araucaria heterophylla	Norfolk Island pine
Beaucarnea recurvata	Ponytail palm
Brassaia actinophylla	Umbrella tree
Cereus peruvianus	Apple cactus
Chamaedorea seifrizii	Reed palm
Codiaeum variegatum	Croton
Crassula argentea	Jade plant
Dracaena marginata	Madagascar dragon tree
Epipremnum aureum	Pothos
Ficus benjamina	Weeping fig
Ficus elastica 'Decora'	Indian rubber tree
Hoya carnosa	Wax plant
Opuntia spp.	Prickly pear
Sansevieria spp.	Snake plant
Yucca elephantipes	Spineless yucca

ates are usually closed when plants are in the dark. Light also exerts considerable effect mainly on leaf temperature, since the level of light energy received has a direct effect on temperature: The more light, the higher the temperature. Light also directly affects physi-ological processes such as the absorption of water and electrolytes, cell permeability, and cellular metabolism. Light levels, sources, and duration can also modify plant appearance, causing either short or tall growth, changes in leaf size and shape, determining color of leaves and stems, and whether the plant will flower. In some cases, light even determines whether seeds will germinate, but this has not been reported for foliage plants.

LIGHT QUALITY. The quality of light refers to its wavelength and thus its color. Within the visible light spectrum is the radiant energy received from a light source that can be seen by the human eye. The total radiant energy spectrum (Figure 8.7) provides an indication of the small portion of light that we are capable of seeing. However, the nonvisible portion also affects our well-being as well as that of green plants. Within the visible spectrum, different light sources provide different levels or amounts of light within the specific range of 390 to 760 nanometers. Natural light supplies high light energy over most of the visible range, whereas other light sources, such as cool-white fluorescent or incandescent lamps, are quite deficient in or overly endowed with certain wavelengths (Figure 8.8).

Plant physiologists have attempted to determine the optimum wavelengths of light for a wide variety of plant processes, sometimes with conflicting results, since there appears to be specific action spectra for different

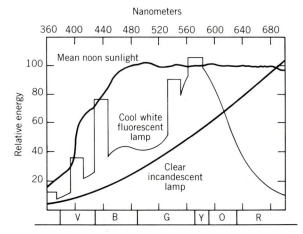

FIGURE 8.8 Comparison of spectral energy curves of natural light with cool white fluorescent and clear incandescent lamps. *Source: Courtesy of GTE Lighting Products.*

plant genera. However, researchers have discovered two action spectra for plants, one for chlorophyll synthesis and another for photosynthesis (Figure 8.9). The maximum rate of photosynthesis occurs near 430 nanometers in the blue range, with a secondary peak near 670 nanometers in the red, whereas the maximum rate of chlorophyll synthesis occurs near 655 nanometers in the red, with a secondary peak near 400 nanometers in the blue. Research has also shown that response to red light is predominantly in carbohydrate production, whereas response to blue light is mainly in accumulation of proteins and other noncarbohydrate substances.

Foliage plants, for the most part, have developed in shaded situations, with light received on a forest floor being quite different from that in open or exposed areas. In exposed locations, plants receive a balance of solar radiation, whereas in shaded locations, leaves receive a greater proportion of light in the green and even some in the blue wavelengths, since these would not be intercepted higher up in the tree canopy.

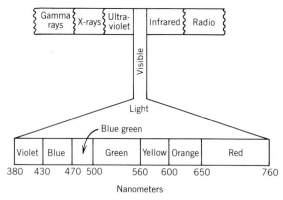

FIGURE 8.7 Wavelengths of visible light and invisible radiation of the electromagnetic spectrum. *Source: Courtesy of GTE Lighting Products.*

Another important factor in considering light requirements of foliage plants is the frequency of cloudy days in the tropical and subtropical regions. On cloudy days, the light intensity will not only be less than on clear days, but it will also be composed of higher levels of blue and green wavelengths. Therefore, it seems probable that foliage plants are environmentally adapted to utilize light energy composed of higher levels of light in the blue wavelengths than red, although probably both are needed.

Within the last decade, the art and science of interiorscaping has developed extensively in locations where little or no natural light was available. In many interior locations, the only source of light had been either fluorescent or incandescent lamps and in each location the foliage plants flourished, provided the correct light intensity and duration was supplied. These successes show that light quality is certainly less important than other factors, but there are subtle changes induced by light source, thus affecting plant growth. This plant response will be discussed in detail in the section on light sources.

LIGHT INTENSITY. Overall, light intensity is the major factor that determines whether indoor plants will grow and be attractive. This is not mentioned to minimize effects of temperature, water, humidity, or even light source on the duration of plant growth, but rather to reinforce the importance of this factor.

During production, foliage plants are usually grown under light intensities that are much higher than those most people are prepared to provide indoors. However, provided foliage plants are acclimatized, they will be able to adjust to indoor lighting if the minimum suggested intensities are provided.

Increasing light intensity increases the rate of photosynthesis, provided some other factor does not become limiting (CO_2, water, temperature, etc.). For the most part, rate of

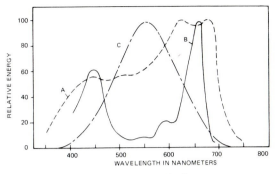

A: Relative response of photosynthesis.
B: Spectral activity of the chlorophyll synthesis process.
C: Visual sensitivity curve (for comparison).

FIGURE 8.9 Action spectra for photosynthesis and chlorophyll synthesis.

photosynthesis is proportional to the light intensity until some maximum level is reached. The maximum rate of photosynthesis is achieved at different light intensities with different foliage plant species. For example, *Ficus benjamina* will grow in full sun and reaches its maximum photosynthetic rate near 10,000 foot-candles, while *Aglaonema* × 'Silver Queen' reaches its maximum near 2000 foot-candles. One might expect that a relationship would exist for foliage plants between the light intensity that provides maximum photosynthetic rate and the lowest light level it can tolerate indoors. However, this does not appear to be the case, since there are numerous foliage plants that grow well in full sunlight (*Dracaena, Brassaia, Sansevieria, Ficus*) that do well indoors under low to medium light, whereas others (*Pilea, Nephrolepis, Gynura*) require shade and yet do not tolerate low light levels.

Foliage plants respond in various ways to extremes of light intensity, either high or low. Plants provided with light intensities above desired levels will have shorter internodes, smaller leaves, reduced levels of chlorophyll, and hence a lighter green color and, when appropriate, increased variegation. In some cases, leaf position also changes such as with *Aglaonema*, in which leaves assume a vertical rather than horizontal position in relation to the light source. Under extremely high light, many shade-requiring foliage plants will be damaged or "burned." This can occur when plants are placed in a sunny window or outside in a sunny location. The process of burning is caused by photooxidation, a process whereby plants consume oxygen in light and use it in oxidation of cell constituents. Very short periods of photooxidation are not damaging, but periods of 30 minutes or more will cause loss of chlorophyll or death of cells. This is the major reason plants grown in low light should not be placed in the sun to "improve" their appearance.

Effects of lower than desirable light intensity for a particular foliage plant may appear as elongation of newly formed internodes (etiolation), elongation and narrowing of leaves or very small leaves, production of few new leaves, loss of older leaves, and a generally sparse appearance.

One major effect of light intensity is phototropism. The way to control this plant response is to provide the same light intensity on all sides or rotate the plant about one-quarter turn every day.

As mentioned previously, providing the proper light intensity for specific foliage plant species is the most important factor in their care. A survey of the literature, including books, magazines, newsletters, and so on, will show that all people "think" they know the best light intensities required for growing plants in interior locations. The problems with the data presented often relate to types of plants observed (acclimatized or not acclimatized), the specific growing conditions—light source, duration, temperature, humidity, fertilization, watering, plant size and age, and so on—and the writer's general feeling about "maintenance" or "growth." All of the factors mentioned affect the light intensity required and ultimate plant quality, but none more than whether we are looking for

maintenance or growth. Maintenance lighting provides sufficient light energy to allow the plant to replace leaves lost through senescence and even add a few extra, whereas growth lighting provides sufficient energy for the plant to produce many extra leaves and grow noticeably indoors. For the most part, growth lighting levels will be at least 50 percent greater than the maintenance lighting levels given in Table 8.4.

The pitfalls of following, without question, many of the recommendations on needed light intensity can be demonstrated by *Ficus benjamina*. Most writers consider this to be a medium to high light-requiring plant and in its nonacclimatized form is definitely such a tree, requiring 300 to 500 foot-candles of light for 12 hours per day. On the other hand, acclimatized trees will adapt well to regimes in which they receive only 150 foot-candles of light and, in time, such trees will further acclimatize down to where they will live for many years at 75 to 100 foot-candles of light for 12 hours per day, provided other growth factors are met. Even lower levels have been reported. The problem for the user or installer relates to requests for extra lighting in the proposed planting location, since one interiorscaper may require a minimum of 300 foot-candles of light before planting a specific foliage plant, whereas another may be content with 100 foot-candles. The difference, of course, is an additional 200 foot-candles of very expensive lighting, which may lose the contract for the interiorscaper requiring the higher light level. One way to improve the potential for plants to acclimatize to a lower light intensity is to purchase acclimatized plants and then hold them in an indoor acclimatization facility where they receive an average of 200 to 250 foot-candles of light for 12 hours per day at plant height for four to six weeks. At the end of this period, those plants that acclimatize will be ready to move to their final location, whereas those with obvious problems (excessive leaf drop, marginal burning, etc.) can be held longer to

TABLE 8.4 FOLIAGE PLANT MAINTENANCE LIGHT REQUIREMENTS
BASED ON LIGHTING FOR 8 TO 12 HOURS PER DAY

Plants for Areas with Low Light Intensity Range 50 to 75 Foot-Candles

Small Plants (Less Than 3 Feet)

Aglaonema commutatum	Silver evergreen
Aglaonema × 'Fransher'	Fransher evergreen
Aglaonema × 'Silver Queen'	Silver queen evergreen
Aspidistra elatior	Cast iron plant
Chamaedorea elegans	Parlor palm
Epipremnum aureum	Pothos
Philodendron scandens oxycardium	Heart-leaved philodendron
Sansevieria trifasciata (cultivars)	Sansevieria (cultivars)

Medium Plants (3–5 Feet)

Howea forsterana	Kentia palm
Schefflera arboricola	Dwarf schefflera

Large Plants (Over 5 Feet)

Chamaedorea erumpens	Bamboo palm
Chamaedorea seifrizii	Reed palm
Rhapis excelsa	Lady finger palm

Plants for Areas with Medium Light Intensity Range 75 to 150 Foot-Candles

Small Plants (Less Than 3 Feet)

Asparagus plumosus	Fern asparagus
Asparagus sprengeri	Sprenger asparagus
Chlorophytum comosum	Spider plant
Cissus rhombifolia	Grape ivy
Cryptanthus bivittatus	Earth star
Dieffenbachia × 'Exotica Perfection'	Dumbcane
Dracaena surculosa	Gold dust dracaena
Ficus pumila	Creeping fig
Hedera helix	English ivy
Hoya carnosa	Wax plant
Maranta leuconeura kerchoviana	Prayer plant
Nephrolepis exaltata 'Bostoniensis'	Boston fern
Peperomia obtusifolia	Oval-leaf peperomia
Pilea cadierei	Aluminum plant
Pteris spp.	Table fern species
Syngonium podophyllum	Arrowhead vine
Zebrina pendula	Wandering jew; inch plant

Medium Plants (3–5 Feet)

Dieffenbachia amoena	Giant dumbcane
Dracaena deremensis 'Janet Craig'	Jane Craig dracaena
Dracaena deremensis 'Warneckii'	Warneck dracaena
Pandanus veitchii	Veitch screw pine
Philodendron selloum	Lacy tree philodendron
Pittosporum tobira	Japanese pittosporum
Pleomele reflexa	Malaysian dracaena
Spathiphyllum 'Mauna Loa'	Mauna loa peace lily

(continued)

TABLE 8.4 (*Continued*)

Plants for Areas with Medium Light Intensity Range 75 to 150 Foot-Candles

Large Plants (Over 5 Feet)

Brassia actinophylla	Umbrella tree, schefflera
Dracaena fragrans 'Massangeana'	Corn plant dracaena
Dracaena marginata	Madagascar dragon tree
Ficus benjamina	Weeping fig
Ficus elastica 'Decora'	Indian rubber tree
Ficus lyrata	Fiddleleaf fig
Ficus retusa	Indian laurel fig

Plants for Areas with High Light Intensity Range 150 to 500 Foot-Candles

Small Plants (Less Than 3 Feet)

Aechmea fasciata	Silver vase
Aphelandra squarrosa	Zebra plant
Begonia rex	Rex begonia
Cordyline terminalis	Ti
Crassula argentea	Jade plant
Dracaena surculosa	Gold dust dracaena
Philodendron scandens × *Citrofortunella mitis*	Philodendron calamondin
Tradescantia albiflora	Wandering jew
Zygocactus truncatus	Christmas cactus

Medium Plants (3–5 Feet)

Codiaeum variegatum	Croton
Coffea arabica	Arabian coffee
Euphorbia tirucalli	Milk cactus
Ficus deltoidea	Mistletoe fig
Ficus triangularis	Triangleleaf fig
Phoenix roebelenii	Miniature date palm

Large Plants (Over 5 Feet)

Araucaria excelsa	Norfolk Island pine
Beaucarnea recurvata	Ponytail palm
Chrysalidocarpus lutescens	Areca palm
Dizygotheca elegantissima	False aralia
Dracaena reflexa	Malaysian dracaena
Ligustrum lucidum	Glossy privet
Podocarpus macrophyllus	Southern yew
Polyscias balfouriana	Dinner plate aralia
Polyscias fruticosa	Ming aralia

allow them to adjust to the interior environment.

LIGHT DURATION. The total number of hours of light received in a given day is considered "light duration" and can be almost as important as light intensity. If the correct light intensity is provided for foliage plants, but the duration is too short, insufficient levels of food will be produced through photosynthesis. Therefore, it is necessary to regulate the period of time foliage plants receive recommended light intensities to maintain desired plant quality.

Most foliage plants are native to the tropics and subtropics, where light duration is fairly constant year-round, and are genetically adapted to daily light durations of 11 to 13 hours per day. Moving northward (or southward) from the equatorial region, large variations in natural light duration occur with the seasons, with as little as 7 or 8 hours received in northern areas in winter to as much as 14 to 16 hours in summer. Reduced light duration combined with reduced intensity is the reason so many foliage plant publications indicate that little growth can be expected from foliage plants during winter months. However, this does not need to be the case, since adjustment of light intensity and duration of its application will allow year-round growth and, contrary to popular belief, so-called "rest periods" are unnecessary.

An interaction exists between light intensity and light duration since higher intensity for shorter duration may be just as effective as lower intensity for longer duration. For example, 200 foot-candles applied for 6 hours produces 1200 foot-candle hours, whereas 100 foot-candles applied for 12 hours also produces 1200 foot-candles. This relationship is useful only when the lower light intensity is above the plants' light compensation points.

Providing the proper light intensity and duration is no more difficult than combining natural with artificial light to obtain the proper intensity and duration. This is covered in the section, "Lighting for Life."

In some commercial installations, such as airports, malls, and hotel lobbies, lights remain on 24 hours a day. Some homeowners also leave security or night lights on in some areas often containing foliage plants. Constant illumination has been shown to damage foliage plants such as *Brassaia*, *Chamaedorea*, *Dieffenbachia*, and others at intensities no greater than 100 foot-candles.

The damage most commonly appears as yellowing of leaves and sometimes even browning of leaf margins. Light intensity during the normal dark period of no more than 25 to 50 foot-candles does not appear to have a damaging effect even if applied 24 hours per day to maintain best plant quality. Therefore, when some type of security or other lighting is necessary on a 24-hour basis, it should be designed so that the intensity can be reduced to less than 50 foot-candles during the normal dark period in areas where foliage plants are growing.

PHOTOPERIODISM. Throughout the world, except in the tropics, day length varies considerably from season to season, depending on the latitude. On the shortest day of the year (December 21st in the Northern Hemisphere), the period from sunrise to sunset is about $9\frac{1}{2}$ hours in Washington, D.C., at about 39°N latitude, whereas in Palm Beach, Florida, at 27°N latitude, it is about $10\frac{1}{2}$ hours. On the equator, at 0°N latitude, the daylength and dark periods are equal at 12 hours each per day. At higher latitudes, the variation in daylength is even greater, since above the arctic circle there is no daylight period on December 21st and it is light continuously on the longest day of the year, June 21st.

The development of plants as conditioned by length and alteration of light and dark periods is known as photoperiodism, whereas the length of the light period is known as photoperiod. Research has shown that different types of plants respond differently to photoperiods of different lengths, with the most observable effect on flowering. As discussed in Chapter Three, some plants flower when days are short and nights are long (short day plants), whereas in others, flowering occurs when days are long and nights are short (long day plants).

Photoperiodism in foliage plants has not been subjected to the in-depth research that characterized examination of most flowering plants, and this could be expected, since most do not produce flowers that are attractive. On the other hand, since most foliage plants are native to tropical or subtropical regions where little daylength variation occurs, one suspects that such adaptation might not have occurred since there is no apparent evolutionary pressure in that direction. Two well-known plants (often classified as foliage plants) grown under interior environments on a year-round basis and known to respond to photoperiod are the Thanksgiving cactus and Christmas cactus. This is a short day plant that grows vegetatively during periods of long light duration and flowers when days become short. Once flowering has been initiated in this plant (it takes six weeks of short days), it will produce flowers in an additional eight to ten weeks. Thus, a plant that is initiated during September or October will bloom in time for Thanksgiving or Christmas, depending on its species. When these cacti are grown indoors, it is possible to keep them vegetative continuously if they are located near a source of artificial light. Therefore, if you want to reflower these plants under an interior environment, it is necessary to locate them somewhere that assures darkness of at least 13 to 14 hours each night. Because this would prevent the use of the room where they may be growing, they can be covered with black cloth to block the light or even be kept in a dark closet at night.

Numerous foliage plants respond to light duration, but this has not been shown to be a photoperiodic reaction. For example, the flowering of *Aphelandra* has been shown to be dependent on total light received (photocumulative). This means that plants will flower after they have received specific light energy that can be obtained with higher intensity for short periods or lower intensity for long durations. Other indoor plants that respond in a similar manner are African violets and *Crossandra*.

Light Measurement

The most common way to measure light intensity is with a foot-candle meter in the area where plants are to be utilized. There are, of course, more technically correct ways of measuring light, as with a quantum/radiometer/photometer, which is designed to measure the actual light energy that falls on a plant within the range of 400 to 700 nanometers. This type of equipment, although technically correct, is beyond the need of those who design interior spaces for plants or grow them indoors. Another light-measuring device utilized by some interiorscapers is a "plant growth photometer," which measures light energy received on a given point within the blue, red, and far-red wavelengths. This piece of equipment is useful for determining the transmission characteristics of glazing materials used for many of the newer skylighted or fully glazed greenhouse-type structures being used to provide interior spaces for tropical plantings. It will also serve as a checkup on the ratio of red:blue light being received from various artificial lamps. Although readings cannot be directly converted to foot-candles from this equipment, an approximation can be made by multiplying by 150 in the blue band and 200 in the red.

THE FOOT-CANDLE. The simplest and traditional method of light measurement in the United States has been the foot-candle. This unit of measurement was originally derived from measuring or estimating the light intensity generated by a "standard candle" one foot from the light source. It should be noted that the foot-candle meter was designed to measure the light seen by the human eye; thus, it is particularly relevant to yellow-green light to which the human eye is most responsive. Plants are, as discussed previously, most responsive to red and blue light, but in spite of this, utilization of a light meter that measures in foot-candles does give us usable information about light intensity.

MEASURING INSTRUMENTS. There are basically two types of light meters, reflectance light meters, which are commonly used by photographers, and incident light meters.

Reflectance light meters measure the light reflected from the surface of an object and indicate light intensity as influenced by the reflective quality of the object and background. A reflectance-type meter must be pointed at the object in the same orientation as light coming from the source. When using a reflectance-type meter, it is necessary to use an 18 percent reflectance test card and a somewhat complex conversion table based on ASA, shutter speed, and diaphram settings to properly measure light intensity in foot-candles. Thus, use of a reflectance-type light meter is impractical for horticultural applications if frequent measurements are required.

Incident light meters are used to measure the light intensity falling on a given object. To obtain readings with an incident meter, it should be placed in the position of the object and aimed toward the light source. The correct way to utilize an incident light meter is to take multiple light intensity readings over the surface of the plant. This requires that multiple measurements be made on all sides as well as the top, middle, and bottom of the leaf canopy. These readings should then be added together and divided by the number of measurements to obtain an average light intensity received over the plant surface (Figure 8.10).

Several incident light meters that may be purchased for less than $100 include General Electric Model 214, Sekonic Model L-246, and Sekonic Studio Delux Model L-28-C2 (this unit measures either incident or reflected light). Each of these units has different sensitivities, but all can be used to measure light intensities found in interior locations. Because of

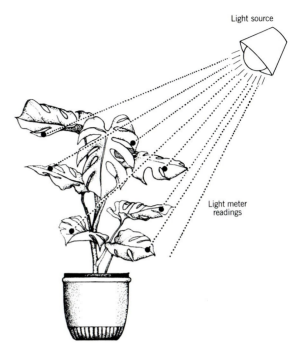

FIGURE 8.10 Measure light intensity with an incident light meter at multiple points over the surface of the plant canopy and average.

ease of use, the General Electric Model 214 has found widest use in the interiorscape industry; the cost at this text's publication was near $50.

When foot-candle light meters are not available, it is possible to obtain an approximation of light intensity by using a camera with an integral light metering system. Set the film speed on the camera at ASA 100 and aim the meter at a reflectance test card located to approximate the leaf surface of the plant (these cards are about 1 foot square). Position the camera so that the card barely fills the viewfinder, but do not block the light falling on the card. Then, set the aperture at f4 and adjust the shutter speed to balance the meter reading. The shutter speed reading obtained approximates the inverse of the light intensity in foot-candles (for example, at f4, a shutter speed reading of 1/500 is equal to approximately 500 foot-candles). As mentioned previously, this method of obtaining light intensity is much less desirable than the use of an incident light meter reading in foot-candles.

The poorest way to measure light is to guess, since the human eye has no reference point as a comparison. However, it is possible to obtain an approximation of light intensity without use of a meter. Such an estimate of light intensity can be obtained by placing a solid object (book, tablet, etc.) between the primary light source and the plant. Place the object 12 inches from the plant and look at the shadow cast by the object on a piece of paper at plant level. If the shadow cast is hard to see and edges are very poorly defined, the light level is from 25 to 75 foot-candles; when the shadow cast is noticeable, but the exact edge is indistinct, the light level is from 75 to 150 foot-candles, and when the shadow is noticeable and the edge distinct, the light level is 150 foot-candles or more. This system is usable only when the light is received primarily from one direction, since indirect lighting will not provide shadows.

When growing foliage plants indoors, it is necessary to know beforehand the light intensity available for plant growth. This measurement is best made with a light meter that reads in foot-candles and averaged for the area as described previously. It is also desirable to consider the light intensity available throughout the day and during different seasons if a major portion of the illumination is natural light. Once you know the average light intensity available for plant growth, selection of foliage plants adapted to the specific location can be made by consulting Table 8.4.

Light Compensation Point
The importance of the light compensation point in relation to acclimatization was discussed previously and was defined as "the point at which food production, through photosynthesis, is equal to food utilization through respiration." However, light compensation points are also tremendously important to the long-term growth and survival of foliage plants under every interior environment. The light compensation points vary for each and every foliage plant cultivar and are related to the genetic constitution of the plant and the native habitat under which it originally developed. Both the production environment and level of acclimatization relate to the light compensation point at the time a plant is moved to an interior environment, but the plant's basic physiology will determine how much lower the light compensation point can drop with further acclimatization under the actual interior environment.

Foliage plants indigenous to the understory of tropical and subtropical rainforests will usually have inherently lower light compensation points than those that developed in full sun. Another factor that affects light compensation points is the level of chlorophyll per unit area. Foliage plants with solid green leaves are likely to have greater chlorophyll levels than those with variegated foliage, although this is not always the factor that decides whether a particular foliage plant will grow under low light environments.

When a foliage plant is placed in a location where light intensity is below the light compensation point, the plant will utilize stored food reserves. Should the plant not acclimatize to the location and reduce its light compensation point below the existing light intensity prior to utilization of stored food reserves, it will deteriorate rapidly and die within a relatively short period. On the other hand, if the plant is able to acclimatize to the light intensity present, it will stop utilizing food reserves and manufacture enought to offset respiration. The information shown in Figure 8.11 shows how light compensation points of several acclimatized foliage plants were further reduced with time after placement under an interior environment. Using *Dracaena* in this figure as an example, one

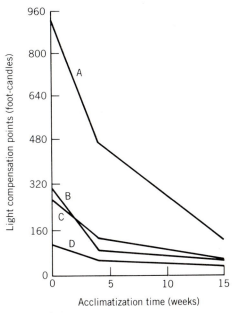

FIGURE 8.11 Relative light compensation point response of four foliage plant species during acclimatization under an interior environment. *Source:* Fonteno, W., and E. McWilliams (revised), "Light Compensation Points and Acclimatization of Four Tropical Foliage Plants," *Journal of American Society of Horticultural Science* 103,56 (January 1978).

A: Dracaena.
B: Epipremnum.
C: Philodendron.
D: Brassaia.

can see that its light compensation point was originally much higher than the other three genera but after 10 weeks under the interior environment had almost decreased to the original level of *Epipremnum* and *Philodendron*. If the light level present in that interior location was only 160 foot-candles, the plant might not have acclimatized in time to survive. However, all of the other genera were 160 foot-candles by the fifth week, and these plants probably would have acclimatized to the new environment since their light compensation points would have been below the available light intensity.

When a foliage plant is growing at its light compensation point, it will eventually die because it will not be producing new leaves and most leaves have only a six-month to two-year life. Therefore, the minimum light intensities necessary for foliage plants are those that will allow sufficient new growth to replace leaves lost due to aging. This means that the light intensity must be sufficiently above the light compensation point to maintain plant quality, but not result in extensive new growth. New growth under low light intensities is often not as attractive as growth under higher light intensities and, thus, extensive new growth is often undesirable. Light compensation points are known for only a few foliage plants and even these have not been obtained under standardized conditions. Therefore, light compensation points are presently not used to determine minimum light intensities for foliage plants.

Lighting for Life

Without light, there can be no life for green plants. Therefore, this section has been designed to aid in the analysis of lighting systems available for plant maintenance and growth. Lighting can be composed of natural light and artificial light, either in combinations or alone. No matter which system is chosen, all parameters of lighting should be considered in the selection of a light source and should include light quality and intensity, energy consumption, fixture cost, and effects on plants, people, and other objects.

NATURAL LIGHT. When applicable, the use of natural light should be maximized, since it is free and also provides light energy over the entire spectrum. When using natural light as a major light source, several limitations must be taken into consideration, including intensity in relation to season and weather, as well as daylength. Even during clear weather, light intensity at northern latitudes will be reduced by nearly 50 percent in winter and even more due to increased cloudiness. Also, at higher latitudes, daylength is much shorter in winter and, thus, foliage plants that depend on natural light may have to exist with 50 percent or less of the light they receive in summer months.

Even though light intensity and duration may be less in winter, the amount of light received by a foliage plant indoors depends on location in respect to windows and the exposure. Figure 8.12 provides an indication of the difference between natural light received in summer versus winter. The inclination of the sun to the earth is less in winter, which allows for further penetration into interior spaces, whereas in summer, it is higher overhead and although greater in intensity, does not penetrate as far. These factors must be considered when using natural light, since sufficient intensity may not be received during certain periods of the year and supplemental artificial light may be required.

Light intensity due to exposure of a window, whether north, east, south, or west, is quite variable and must be determined during different seasons to estimate whether it will be satisfactory for growth of foliage plants. Intensity of light close to windows

will be much greater than at a point just 5 feet away, with decreases of 75 to 90 percent possible in this short distance. Therefore, it is absolutely necessary to determine the light intensity with a light meter to be able to make logical decisions concerning natural or artificial light.

Windows are not the only source of natural light, since skylights are also common in many newer buildings. Most skylights provide diffused light, since they usually have shaded coverings. They are also often located within a light "well" or "shaft," so that light is not evenly distributed within an interior space. Therefore, the intensity of any natural light from these sources should be measured during different periods, as for windows, and considered with the total light available.

ARTIFICIAL LIGHT. Foliage plants can be grown entirely with artificial light or a combination of artificial and natural light, as long as the proper light quantity and quality is supplied for sufficient duration. It is not difficult to find artificial light sources that will provide specific wavelengths of light within specific spectral bands, but the different sources of light do exert subtle changes on foliage plants that need to be considered prior to purchase of lighting fixtures. These changes, or plant responses, to different lamps (light sources) are listed in Table 8.5. Selection of artificial light sources should not be based entirely on plant effects, since energy requirements, fixture cost, aesthetic value, and ease of installation also need to be considered. It should be noted that all lamps used to light interior spaces for human vision are also acceptable for growing plants and means that vision lighting and plant lighting can be combined. For example, if the room lighting level were 75 foot-candles for 8 hours per day, and plants utilized required 125 foot-candles, all that would be required would be the addition of a supplemental lamp over or near the plant to supply

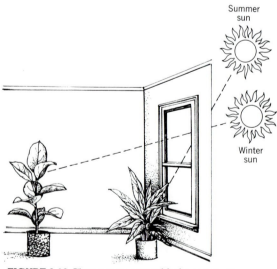

FIGURE 8.12 Changes in natural light penetration occur within interior spaces because of changes in the sun's inclination.

TABLE 8.5 INFLUENCE OF LIGHT SOURCE ON PLANT GROWTH RESPONSES UNDER INTERIOR ENVIRONMENTS

Lamp	Plant Responses
Fluorescent—cool-white and warm-white	Green foliage that expands to parallel to surface of the lamp Stems elongate slowly Multiple side shoots develop Flowering occurs over a long period of time
Fluorescent Gro-Lux and Plant Light	Deep green foliage that expands, often larger than on plants grown under CW or WW Stems elongate very slowly, extra thick stems develop Multiple side shoots develop Flowering occurs late, flower stalks do not elongate
Fluorescent—Gro-Lux-WS, Vita-Lite, Agro-Lite, and wide spectrum lamps	Light green foliage that tends to ascend toward the lamp Stems elongate rapidly, distances between the leaves Suppresses development of multiple side shoots Flowering occurs soon, flower stalks elongated, plants mature and age rapidly
High-intensity discharge— deluxe mercury or metal halide	Similar to CW and WW fluorescent lamps compared on equal energy Green foliage that expands Stems elongate slowly Multiple side shoots develop Flowering occurs over a long period of time
High-intensity discharge— high-pressure sodium	Similar to Gro-Lux and other color-improved fluorescent compared on equal energy Deep green foliage that expands, often larger than on plants grown under H and MH Stems elongate very slowly, extra thick stems develop Multiple side shoots develop Flowering occurs late, flower stalks do not elongate
Low-pressure sodium	Extra deep green foliage, bigger and thicker than on plants grown under other light sources Stem elongation is slowed, very thick stems develop Multiple side shoots develop, even on secondary shoots Flowering occurs, flower stalks do not elongate *Exceptions:* Saintpaulias, lettuce, and impatiens must have supplemental sunlight or incandescent light to insure development of chlorophyll and reduction of stem elongation.
Incandescent and incandescent-mercury	Paling of foliage, thinner and longer than on plants grown under other light sources Stem elongation is excessive, eventually becomes spindly and easily breaks Side shoot development is suppressed, plants expand only in height Flowering occurs rapidly, the plants mature and senescence *Exceptions:* Rosette and thick-leaved plants such as sansevieria may maintain themselves for many months. The new leaves that eventually develop will elongate and not have the typical characteristics of the species.

SOURCE: Adapted from Henry M. Cathey and Lowell E. Campbell, *Foliage Digest 1*, 3 (1978), 10–13.

the additional 50 foot-candles for the plant—the overall room lighting would not have to be raised an additional 125 foot-candles.

Selection of plant lighting based on lamp efficiency is important, but must also be included in all other considerations. Of the two primary sources of light in home environment interiorscapes, fluorescent lamps, especially cool- or warm-white lamps, are much more efficient than incandescent bulbs (Table 8.6). Efficiency in energy use has also been shown to carry over to growth of foliage plants under artificial light, since cool- or warm-white lamps produced more overall increase in growth based on similar energy inputs than the more specialized plant-growth lamps. Several other lamps listed are more efficient than fluorescent or incandescent types, but they are better adapted to commercial installations than home environments.

When selecting lamps for interior growth and maintenance of foliage plants, one must also consider effects on the aesthetic quality of the surroundings. Some factors of importance include the general appearance of the light on neutral colored walls and surfaces, influence on skin color, overall effect or general feeling within a room, and relationships with strong colors that strengthen or weaken their overall effect. Most people are familiar with the effects of incandescent or cool-white fluorescent lighting, but influence of other available lamps on the factors listed above are generally less known. The data provided in Table 8.7 should be used when considering installation of various artificial lighting fixtures.

Final determination of the best artificial lighting type for plants depends also on other factors in addition to those already considered. All lamp types shown in Table 8.8 are used extensively for plant lighting, although each lamp type has its own best use depending on its particular characteristics and its own best usage location. Since each location where plant lighting is needed has its own design parameters, it will be necessary to list these and select lamps that fulfill defined needs. Some of the questions that need to be asked are:

1. Is the area to be lighted of small volume, such as a residence or office space, or a larger volume, such as a bank lobby or mall? This is important since mercury, metal halide, or high-pressure sodium lamps often provide excessive light for limited spaces, whereas incandescent or fluorescent lamps are less useful in larger spaces.

2. Are ceiling heights less than 10 feet or are they greater than 10 feet? When lighting units must be installed on ceilings of 10 feet or greater, the use of fluorescent fixtures is limited since excessive numbers will be needed to elevate light intensity at floor or table level.

3. Is color rendition important within the area to be lighted? If so, the choice is more restricted as to lamp type. Best color rendition can be achieved with incandescent or metal halide lamps and poorest with high-pressure sodium and some of the fluorescent special purpose lamps.

4. Is efficiency of the lamp important, that is, is there concern about operating costs, light output, or heat output in relation to energy

TABLE 8.6 TOTAL LUMENS[a] OBTAINED PER WATT OF INPUT ENERGY FROM DIFFERENT ARTIFICIAL LIGHT SOURCES

Lamp	Lumens per Watt
Incandescent	17
Fluorescent	
Cool-white	70
Warm-white	71
Gro-Lux—Plant Light	20
Gro-Lux-WS	37
Agro-Lite	41
Vita-Lite	47
Mercury deluxe	50
Metal halide	75
High-pressure sodium	100

[a]One lumen per square foot equals 1 foot-candle.
SOURCE: Adapted from Henry M. Cathey and Lowell E. Cambell, *Foliage Digest 1*, 3 (1978), pp. 10–13.

TABLE 8.7 INFLUENCE OF ARTIFICIAL LIGHT SOURCES ON COLOR RENDERING OF PLANTS, PEOPLE, AND FURNISHINGS

Lamp	General Appearance on a Neutral Surface	Complexion (Appearance of Skin)	Atmosphere (General Feeling of Room)	Colors (Improved or Strengthened)	Greyed (Undesirable)
Fluorescent					
Cool-white	White	Pale pink	Neutral to cool	Blue, yellow, orange	Red
Warm-white	Yellowish	Sallow	Yellow to warm	Yellow, orange	Blue, green, red
Gro-Lux— Plant Light	Pink white	Reddish	Purple to pink	Blue, red	Green, yellow
Gro-Lux-WS	Light pink-white	Pink	Warm	Blue, yellow, red	Green
Agro-Lite	White	Pink	Neutral to warm	Blue, yellow, red	Green
Vita-Lite	White	Pink	Neutral to cool	Blue, yellow, red	Green
Discharge					
Mercury (all types)	Purplish white	Ruddy	Cool	Blue, green, yellow	Red
Metal halide	Greenish white	Greyed	Cool green	Blue, green, yellow	Red
High-pressure sodium	Yellowish	Yellowish	Warm	Green, yellow, orange	Blue, red
Low-pressure sodium	Yellow	Greyed	Warm	Yellow	All except yellow
Incandescent	Yellowish white	Ruddy	Warm	Yellow, orange, red	Blue
Incandescent-mercury	Yellowish white	Ruddy	Warm	Yellow, orange, red	Blue

SOURCE: Adapted from Henry M. Cathey and Lowell E. Campbell, *Foliage Digest 1*, 3 (1978), 10–13.

usage? The least efficient light sources are incandescent lamps, whereas high-pressure sodium and metal halide are most efficient. Within limited spaces, cool- and warm-white fluorescent lamps are also efficient. In general, the more efficient lamps have higher light:heat ratios than inefficient ones.

5. Is initial cost of the fixtures important enough to influence design parameters? As could be expected, the more efficient light sources have initially higher installation and fixture costs as related to lower operating costs. Highest fixture costs are associated with high-pressure sodium lamps, whereas

incandescent fixtures are lowest, the reverse of the energy requirements.

6. Does the overall design require plant maintenance or plant growth? If plant maintenance only is desired, primarily blue light lamps will be adequate. If considerable growth is desired, it will be better to use a light source that provides both red and blue light.

7. Does the location of the light fixture make changing lamps difficult or inconvenient? If this is the cse, it will be better to select a light source with long lamp life.

TABLE 8.8 COMPARISON OF VARIOUS TRAITS OF DIFFERENT LAMP TYPES USED FOR PLANT LIGHTING

Trait	Incandescent	Fluorescent	Mercury	Metal Halide	High-Pressure Sodium
Wattage range	6–1500	4–215	40–1000	175–1500	70–1000
Lumens/watt	6.5–22.4	24–84	30–63	68–100	80–140
Lumens/lamp	39–33,620	96–18,000	1200–63,000	11,900–155,000	5800–140,000
Life (hours)	750–8000	9000–20,000	16,000–24,000	1500–15,000	20,000–24,000
Visible radiation (%)	7–11	22	13	20–23	25–27
Invisible radiation (%)	83	36	62	47–54	47
Warm-up time (minutes)	0	0	5–7	2–5	3–4
Color rendition	Excellent	Good to excellent	Good	Excellent	Fair
Concentration	Excellent	Poor	Fair to good	Fair	Fair
Flexibility	Excellent	Poor	Poor	Poor	Poor
Lumen output affected by temperature	No	Yes	No	No	No
Radio interference	No	Yes	No	No	No
Initial cost	Low	Moderate	Moderate	High	High
Operating cost	High	Moderate	Moderate	Low	Low

SOURCE: G. H. Manaker, *American Nurseryman*, Chicago, Ill.: American Nurseryman Publishing Co., 1982, p. 119.

Once consideration is given to the design parameters and other operating constraints, it is possible to select specific lamps to provide needed levels of artificial light. A review of the different types of lamps available follows. More detailed specifications can be obtained by requesting specification sheets from suppliers for each lamp type.

INCANDESCENT SOURCES. Most people are familiar with incandescent lamps because they are commonly found in residences. These lamps have low energy efficiency and short life and produce high heat levels. They also produce light primarily in the red and far-red regions (Figure 8.13). If used as the sole source of light for foliage plants, overall quality will decrease and plants will become unsightly. Therefore, when possible, their use should be combined with natural light or a blue light source

such as fluorescent lamps. As a general rule, plant foliage should not be closer than 4 feet for larger lamps and 2½ to 4 feet for smaller lamps (60–150 watts) to prevent burning of foliage. This is especially true when reflectorized or directed beam lamps are used.

The reasons incandescent lamps are so commonly found in living areas are their excellent color rendition, low installation costs, availability of attractive fixtures with a wide range of wattages, and ability to design creative lighting effects. Their use will continue in residences until such time that other lamp types are made available in more attractive packages, but in the meantime, they can be used for foliage plant lighting as long as their limitations are acknowledged.

FLUORESCENT SOURCES. The most widely used artificial light source for indoor plants is

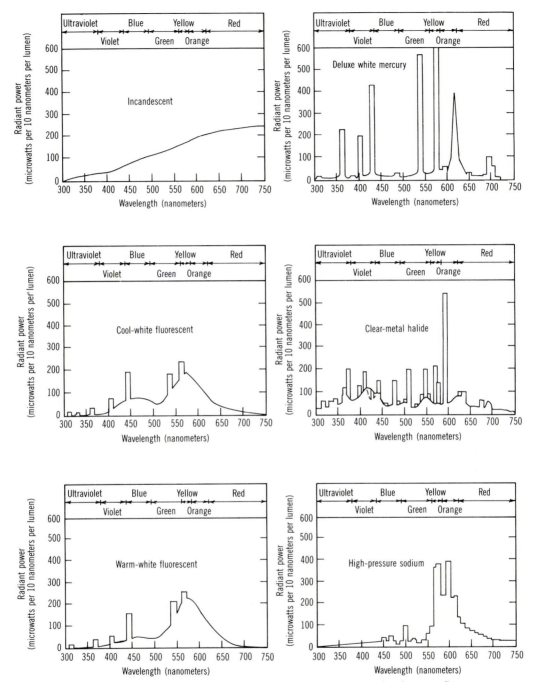

FIGURE 8.13 Spectral energy distribution for various lamps used for interior landscapes. *Source:* Courtesy of GTE Lighting Products.

the fluorescent lamp (tube). These lamps are available in a wide variety of light spectral forms that have been designed to satisfy the demands of almost every potential user. The popularity of fluorescent lamps probably relates to their promotion as excellent light sources for "interior gardens" and the feeling of accomplishment obtained by those who grow vegetables or ornamentals entirely under artificial light.

Fluorescent lamps are in reality mercury vapor-filled tubes coated on the inside with fluorescing phosphorus. Different phosphorus can be used to produce light having different spectral qualities that, in turn, have resulted in the newer types of fluorescent lamps designed for growing plants. Both the cool- and warm-white fluorescent lamps were developed for residential and commercial purposes and have their highest output in the vision range (green–yellow) (Figure 8.13). They are high in blue and low in red light and, thus, are very desirable for growing foliage plants but less desirable for flowering plants under photoperiodic control. The newer types of fluorescent lamps produce greater amounts of light in the red region that is especially beneficial to promotion of flowering, but lamp efficiency is greatly decreased by the addition of red light. Thus, for the same energy input, cool-white or warm-white lamps are still recommended since they are more cost-effective and result in high-quality plants.

Continued popularity of fluorescent lamps is related to their efficiency, long life, and ease of installation. They also burn cool and, thus, can be placed as close as 6 to 18 inches from plants if desired. Only the centrally located ballast emits heat. On the other hand, they can be used at standard ceiling height to supply light when larger commercial fixtures may be undesirable. In comparison to incandescent lamps, fluorescent lamps are a much better source of artificial light for foliage plants but do not provide the convenience and variety of fixtures.

MERCURY LAMPS. Mercury vapor lamps are almost as popular as fluorescent lamps for plant lighting in commercial installations and are an efficient light source. Clear mercury lamps produce very little light in the red band and, thus, produce extremely poor color rendition. Even though the efficiency level of the deluxe white mercury lamp is lower than the clear mercury, it is the best overall mercury lamp for plant lighting, since sufficient light is produced in all bands for plant growth yet provides satisfactory color rendition (Figure 8.13). As with fluorescent lamps, the addition of a phosphor coating increases the amount of red light but also reduces lamp efficiency.

Mercury lamps have an extremely long life and are excellent for ceiling installations or when long life is desirable to reduce maintenance problems associated with lamp changing for inaccessible fixtures. Most mercury lamps require ballasts and large fixtures that are best adapted to commercial situations. Recently, self-ballasted mercury lamps have become available that can be used to replace incandescent flood lamps and are interchangeable in the standard sockets. These lamps have a much longer life (10–12 times) than incandescent lamps and provide a better spectral distribution for plants. However, at the present time, they are expensive and their efficiency is lower than cool-white fluorescent lamps.

METAL HALIDE LAMPS. Efficiency of metal halide lamps is greater than mercury and incandescent lamps and most fluorescent lamps. There are several types of metal halide lamps that produce different spectral characteristics, but the best lamp for plant growth may not be the best lamp for every installation. The I-Line metal halide lamp has the best spectral emission curve, but light color varies between lamps and is dependent on wattage. The standard metal halide lamp does serve well in many plant installations and provides sufficient light in the blue and red ranges for good plant growth (Figure 8.13). Most metal halide lamps are available in wattages from 400 to 1000 and are best adapted to commercial installations. Metal halide lamps do provide better color rendition than mercury lamps and their high efficiency and white light make them very desirable for plant lighting.

HIGH-PRESSURE SODIUM LAMPS. From an efficiency standpoint, high-pressure sodium lamps are superior to all other artificial light sources used for plant lighting. However, the spectral distribution provided by this lamp is not the best since it is strong in the yellow, orange, and red bands. Thus, the general appearance of light from this lamp is yellowish and for this reason it is not commonly used for general lighting purposes in interiors. In larger plant installations in lobbies or other interior spaces, these lamps are often used for extra lighting in off hours (when large numbers of people are not present). They are also quite large and a bit hard to conceive in a "normal" residence.

Only the commonly used and available lamps for interior lighting of plants have been discussed. Each of these lamps has advantages and disadvantages that must be considered for each area needing the addition of artificial light for plant growth. Thus, there is often no right or wrong way to handle a particular job, although best overall results occur when sufficient light can be provided to plants in the proper spectral range while satisfying aesthetic requirements.

Final selection of artificial lighting relates not only to type of plants to be grown and desired feeling within the interior space, but also to ceiling height. Information on light sources and overall aesthetic effects have been provided in Table 8.7 and 8.8. Lamp selection based on ceiling height relates to the ability of a lamp to provide high light intensity at some distance from a plant, since light intensity decreases by the square of distance from the source. Therefore, lamps

TABLE 8.9 LAMP SELECTION BASED ON CEILING HEIGHT

Lamps for Ceilings of 10 Feet or Less
    Incandescent
    Fluorescent

Lamps for Ceilings of 10 to 15 Feet
    Mercury vapor
    Metal halide

Lamps for Ceilings of 15 Feet or More
    Mercury vapor
    Metal halide
    High-pressure sodium

that are of lower wattage or diffused light over a wide distance are not as efficient, where high ceilings exist, as those that direct light to specific areas or have sufficient intensity to light large areas. Table 8.9 provides suggestions on artificial light sources that are best adapted to ceilings of various heights.

Questions always arise as to the efficiency and interchangeability of artificial light from one lamp source to another. Previously, we mentioned that foot-candle meters measured the light that we see, or vision lighting. This, of course, is different from the light perceived by a plant and, more important, to the light energy received by a plant. For this reason, the data provided in Table 8.10 can be used to compare the energy obtained by plants and the variation necessary in foot-candles for a plant to obtain equivalent energy levels from different lamps. The table is based on obtaining 300 foot-candles of light from one 40-watt cool-white fluorescent lamp when a plant is located 15 inches from the lamp. The relationship with other lamps is shown in that conversion to one 40-watt Gro-Lux Plant Light lamp placed 10 inches from the plant would provide equivalent energy, but the foot-candle meter reading would only be 140 foot-candles, yet the energy received by the plant would be similar. Similar comparisons can be made for the other lamps listed as well. Remember, the plant utilizes light energy mainly in the blue

TABLE 8.10 COMPARISON OF FOOT-CANDLE READINGS AT EQUAL ENERGY LEVELS FROM DIFFERENT LIGHT SOURCES

Light Source	Foot-Candle Reading for Equal Radiant Energy	Approximate Lamp Wattage	Lamp Distance for Equal Plant Growth
Sunlight	160	N/A	N/A
Incandescent	100	150	3.5 ft
Fluorescent			
Cool-white (CW)	300	40	15 in.
Warm-white (WW)	300	40	15 in.
Gro Lux—Plant Light	140	40	10 in.
Gro Lux-WS	200	40	13 in.
Agro-Lite	225	40	13 in.
Vita-Lite	240	40	13.5 in.
Mercury	325	400	5 ft
Metal halide	260	400	7 ft
High-pressure sodium	260	400	8 ft

SOURCE: Adapted from Henry M. Cathey and Lowell E. Cambell, *Foliage Digest 1*, 3 (1978), pp. 10–13.

and red wavelengths, while foot-candle meters measure mainly yellow-green light (vision lighting).

Efficiency of uplighting (light source below foliage) as compared to downlighting has not been determined, but rough calculations and experiences of interiorscapers indicate that uplighting is only about 25 percent as efficient as light received from above. Therefore, it should not be considered a replacement for lack of normal lighting, but rather a light supplement, as well as a method of highlighting plant features. One of the advantages of uplighting on larger plant materials such as *Ficus benjamina* or *Brassaia actinophylla* is that light can penetrate into the interior of the foliage mass. Placement of light in this location is usually not possible from above, and thus, benefits are achieved in increased photosynthetic efficiency as well as aesthetic appeal.

Light in nature is obtained from above, and thus, most energy is absorbed through upper surfaces of leaves. Consequently, leaves generally have evolved to achieve greatest photosynthetic efficiency when light (natural or artificial) is received from above. Factors that affect this include higher levels of chloroplasts in palisade parenchyma cells on upper leaf surfaces and lower levels in spongy parenchyma on lower surfaces, as well as reduced cell count on lower surfaces because of intercellular spaces. Although light does penetrate into palisade cells if applied from below, total energy received is much lower since it must penetrate further.

The best artificial light sources for uplighting are incandescent lamps that provide directed light. This source is, of course, strong in red wavelengths, but it is most pleasing to viewers and can be balanced with blue light from above. Uplighting should never be considered as the sole lighting source.

RELATIVE HUMIDITY

The amount of moisture held by air at specific temperatures is defined as relative humidity. Warm air holds more moisture than cool air and if the amount of moisture remains constant, the RH (relative humidity) will be lower at higher temperatures and higher at lower temperatures. Specific ranges for interior plants have not been identified, but most plants do best if RH is above 50 percent.

However, RH as low as 25 percent is not too severe for most interior plants, except for ferns that may be injured. Below 25 percent RH, many indoor plants will be influenced negatively even if they do not appear to be injured.

Effects on Growth

Humidity indoors is usually less than optimal for growth of foliage plants. Plants require gaseous exchange through the stomates to obtain CO_2 necessary for photosynthesis; thus, the guard cells that form stomates must be turgid. However, under extremely low humidity situations, plant roots may not be able to absorb and transport sufficient water to leaves, even if it is available, and stomates may close as the plant experiences water stress. On partial or full closure of stomates, photosynthetic efficiency is reduced and carbohydrate production curtailed. Continued exposure to extremely low humidity levels will prevent indoor plants from producing food necessary for growth and reduce their aesthetic appeal. Low humidity combined with poor watering procedures and low light intensities is lethal for many indoor plants.

INFLUENCE OF APPEARANCE. Low humidity may cause wilting that is usually noticeable but may also cause plants to have dull foliage rather than a normal, bright, fresh appearance. Probably, the most noticeable effect of low humidity is browning of leaf edges on plants with thin leaves or leaflets. Plants extremely susceptible to low humidity include ferns, especially maidenhair and Boston types, and some palms such as areca. Several plant adaptations to low humidity include cupped leaves, hairs on leaves and thick leaves.

RELATIONSHIP TO WATERING. Maintenance of soil moisture is extremely important when foliage plants are grown under low humidity situations. In most instances, adequate soil moisture will partially compensate for low humidity, and in some cases when plants are low growing, evaporation of water from the soil surface will aid in increasing RH surrounding the leaves.

Effects on Air or Water Pollutants

Humidity has been shown to be involved indirectly with effects of air or water pollutants on plants. Foliage plants are no exception and several forms of air and water pollutants may damage plants in an interior environment. Two methods of entry for pollutants into plants through leaves are directly through open stomates or through the cuticle covering the remaining leaf surface. Any factor that aids in maintenance of turgor pressure in the guard cells, such as high humidity, will aid in movement of air- or water-borne pollutants into plants. Smog components such as ozone and peroxyacetylnitrate (PAN) can easily move through open stomates, whereas closed stomates offer some resistance.

Probably, the major factor that governs entry of water-borne pollutants into plants is the length of time the leaf surface remains wet after exposure. High humidity levels, therefore, aid in maintaining water-borne pollutants in a state that can be more easily absorbed through the cuticle or through stomates. One form of water pollution that injures many foliage plants is phytotoxicity (plant injury) from applied pesticides. Even when used at recommended rates, pesticides may cause injury if allowed to remain on foliage for long periods, and they are a primary reason foliage plant producers try to spray in the morning when rapid drying is more likely than in late afternoon or evening when plants may remain wet for longer periods.

Major pollutants that can injure plants include hydrocarbons from automobiles and various types of sulfur dioxides, PAN, and petroleum distillates from industrial wastes. Although these are not common sources of pollutants for foliage plants, there are cases in cities, above parking garages and in industrial areas, where damage has occurred. More commonly, pollutants that cause foliage plant damage under interior conditions include unburned gas from heaters, volatile cleaning fluids, petroleum-based paints, and cigarette or cigar smoke.

Although all the items mentioned can cause damage, problems associated with cleaning materials are probably most common. Not only can volatile compounds saturate the air and cause cell damage through open stomates, but also, cleaning personnel often dump waste water containing these items on the soil or in planters. Symptoms of pollution damage on foliage can include leaf curl and leaf drop as well as other symptoms.

Measuring Humidity

Knowing what the humidity is at any time can certainly be helpful in understanding plant problems and taking corrective action. Instruments that measure humidity are known as hygrometers. There are many relatively inexpensive hygrometers on the market that will indicate humidity within 5 to 10 percent of the actual levels; this level of accuracy is sufficient to aid in growing plants indoors. These can be used during periods when humidity is believed to be low, or when diagnosing plant problems.

Controlling Humidity Indoors

Discussion of humidity control is often easier than actually controlling it within desired ranges. The best system, of course, is to have the heating and cooling system for the interior space engineered for human comfort. This range usually provides 30 to 50 percent RH in properly engineered commercial buildings, although the actual range is often lower during seasons when continuous heating is necessary. In residences where humidity control has been designed into central heating systems, the same goal of 30

to 50 percent RH is desired but rarely achieved. Excess humidity is not a problem for plants indoors, but low humidity (less than 25 percent) should be corrected when possible. Low humidity is not as often a problem during periods of air-conditioning as when interior spaces must be continuously heated.

In residential spaces, the bathrooms and kitchens provide microclimates that often have higher humidities than the rest of the living spaces. When possible, these should be used for plants, such as ferns requiring high humidity provided adequate light levels exist. Humidity within other spaces can be increased by use of portable humidifiers that have the added benefit of making the air feel warmer (increasing humidity decreases the need for higher air temperature for human comfort). Other methods of increasing humidity include ornamental pools, waterfalls, or fountains, grouping plants together on pebble trays, and syringing. Each of these systems has advantages, but their effects are limited to small areas.

Small pools, waterfalls, or fountains will increase humidity considerably within a confined area such as in a garden room or atrium. These are ideal ways to increase humidity and allow growth of ferns or other high humidity-requiring plants in an otherwise low humidity environment.

Pebble trays are commonly suggested as a simple but effective method to improve humidity around small groups of plants (Figure 8.14). When setting up a pebble tray, be sure the water level is below the surface of the pebbles, but close enough to keep the pebbles moist. Water above the pebble surface will be absorbed into the potting medium, possibly keeping it too wet, whereas dry pebbles will do little to improve humidity level. Pebbles, perlite, or a similar material are better than a moist flat surface because they have more surface area for evaporation.

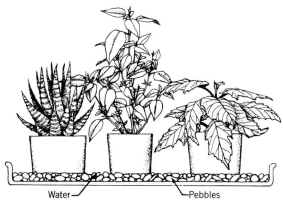

FIGURE 8.14 Pebble trays aid in humidity control.

Crowding plants is not suggested as a normal method of growing but may be useful during periods of particularly low humidity. The reason this system may benefit plants is that transpiration of water from leaves exerts a beneficial effect on nearby plants by raising the humidity, whereas evaporation from the soil surfaces of several pots has the same effect. This system can increase light blockage that may reduce photosynthetic rates sufficiently to cause food production to fall below the light compensation point.

Syringing plants has somehow become a favorite method of improving humidity around indoor plants. This system does work, but it would require keeping foliage wet continuously to really be effective.

Some benefits in humidity control may be obtained by knowing where to place a plant. Areas where plants receive direct air from heating registers will dry them out rapidly and reduce humidity. Other problem areas include plant placement near stoves, fireplaces, television sets, or any heat generator that will not only reduce the humidity imme-

diately around them but also will dry them out more rapidly.

FOR FURTHER READING

Bickford, E., and S. Dunn. *Lighting for Plant Growth.* Kent, Ohio: Kent State University Press, 1972.

Cathey, H., and L. Campbell. "Zero-Base Budgeting for Lighting Plants." *Foliage Digest* (April 1978).

Cherry, E. *Fluorescent Light Gardening.* New York: Van Nostrand Reinhold, 1965.

Fonteno, W., and E. McWilliams. "Light Compensation Points and Acclimatization of Four Tropical Foliage Plants." *Journal of American Society Horticultural Science 103,* 56 (January 1978).

Gaines, R. *Interior Plantscaping: Building Design for Interior Foliage Plants.* New York: Architectural Record Books, 1977.

Hartmann, H., W. Flocker, and A. Kofranek. *Plant Science.* Englewood Cliffs, N.J.: Prentice-Hall, 1981.

Joiner, J. *Foliage Plant Production.* Englewood Cliffs, N.J.: Prentice-Hall, 1981.

Kranz, F., and J. Kranz. *Gardening Indoors Under Lights.* New York: Viking Press, 1971.

Leopold, A., and P. Kriedemann. *Plant Growth and Development.* New York: McGraw-Hill, 1975.

Li, P., and A. Sakai. *Plant Cold Hardiness and Freezing Stress.* New York: Academic Press, 1978.

Manaker, G. *Interior Plantscapes.* Englewood Cliffs, N.J.: Prentice-Hall, 1981.

Manaker, G. "Lighting Techniques for Interior Landscapes." *American Nurseryman* (November 15, 1982).

McConnell, D. *The Indoor Gardener's Companion.* New York: Van Nostrand Reinhold, 1978.

Mudd, J., and T. Kozlowski. *Responses of Plants to Air Pollution.* New York: Academic Press, 1975.

Noggle, G., and G. Fritz. *Introductory Plant Physiology.* Englewood Cliffs, N.J.: Prentice-Hall, 1976.

Poole, R., and C. Conover. "Fertilization of Weeping Fig Before Placement Indoors." *Foliage Digest* (January 1982).

chapter nine
plant disorders*

Indoor gardeners who feel frustrated and disappointed when a favorite plant shows signs of a disorder can take comfort in knowing that no garden is forever problem free. Insects, mites, and diseases, known collectively as **pests,** occur in the greenhouses of public botanic gardens just as they do in the home.

The U.S. Botanic Garden staff answers dozens of inquiries daily on problems affecting house plants. The questions of the past several years indicate that plant loss frequently results from inaccurate diagnosis and improper treatment. It is all too common for an **infested** plant, one that is host to insects or mites, to be treated as if it were **infected,** plagued by a fungus, virus, or bacterial disease. The reverse is also true. But infestations are usually treated quite differently from infections, making an accurate diagnosis imperative for effective control.

The failure to distinguish between pests on the one hand and problems resulting from incorrect cultural practices on the other also results in inappropriate corrective measures. It is not unusual for a Botanic Garden staffer to be presented with a plant recently treated with a variety of chemicals meant to control insects, fungi, or both, but which actually shows a cultural problem such as too much water or lack of light. In addition to the

unnecessary loss of plants, it is distressing to witness the quantity of *potentially hazardous chemicals needlessly introduced into the environment.*

The objectives of this chapter are to help the indoor gardener prevent problems from occurring in the first place, to assist in the proper diagnosis of problems as they arise, and to cure or correct plant maladies effectively and safely.

PROTECTING AGAINST PEST PROBLEMS

Plant disorders cannot be entirely prevented. However, the frequency with which problems occur can be reduced if the indoor gardener routinely follows a few preventive measures. It is far easier to avoid disorders than it is to rid plants of existing pests.

Routine Preventive Measures

Compare your own actions to protect against pests with the suggestions discussed below. If these measures are not included in your routine of house plant maintenance, consider adopting them. A few minutes of time devoted to prevention may save your favorite plant, as well as the headache and expense of elaborate control methods.

*By Karen D. Solit, former Botanist, U.S. Botanic Garden.

CHECK PLANTS BROUGHT INDOORS.
Since one pest-ridden plant can adversely affect an entire collection, it is wise to examine new acquisitions before bringing them into the home. What could be more distressing than to discover a well-established pest on a plant purchased or received as a gift a few days earlier?

ISOLATE PLANTS FOR A WHILE.
Newly acquired specimens may harbor pests that are not at first apparent, despite careful examination. Just to be sure plants are problem free, isolation in a separate room or area for two to three weeks is a good idea. Newcomers can then be placed in the indoor garden.

KEEP THINGS CLEAN.
One of the simplest and most effective pest deterrents is cleanliness. Keeping the growing area, plants, containers, and equipment clean helps avoid pest problems while enhancing the appearance of your interiorscape.

Growing Area. Keep plant shelves clean by wiping them down with soap and water once a month. Remove fallen leaves, flowers, and fruits from soil surfaces and plant shelves regularly to eliminate a potential feeding station for insects and growing medium for disease-causing organisms.

Plants. Cleanliness should also include a monthly plant bath. Regular washing with ordinary tap water will help rid plants of minor infestations that may not be plainly visible. Washing has the added benefit of removing dust and grime that can reduce the amount of light intercepted by leaf surfaces.

Plants can be washed indoors in the sink, tub, or shower by a forceful spray. Naturally, the water should not be turned on excessively strong; this will damage stems or foliage. Special care should be taken to wash the undersides of leaves where most insects and mites feed.

Containers. Cleanliness should also extend to plant containers since unwashed pots and saucers can harbor pests. Wash and scrub all containers in hot water before using and reusing. Unglazed clay pots require a bit more elbow grease to clean thoroughly since they are porous and absorb fertilizer salts, among other unwanted substances.

Never use any container or piece of equipment that has been exposed to **herbicides,** chemicals used to kill unwanted plants. (Some herbicides are selective, killing only certain plants, whereas others kill every plant they contact.)

Equipment. Knives and shears used for propagating and pruning may also harbor disease organisms that can be spread from plant to plant. Equipment should be cleaned with a household disinfectant after each individual use as described in Chapter Five. This is particularly important when propagating plants such as orchids that are highly vulnerable to disease.

Do not forget, hands can also be pest-carriers and should be washed before and between working with plants susceptible to problems. Viruses, mites, and small insects are easily spread by human hands.

USE A FAST DRAINING, STERILIZED POTTING MEDIUM.
Poorly drained soils stay wet too long. Excessive moisture over a prolonged period encourages root rot that can severely weaken a plant, increasing its vulnerability to numerous pests. Such problems often occur when plants are potted directly into soil taken from the garden. Frequently, garden soil contains proportionately large quantities of clay that impedes drainage. In addition, garden soil may harbor insects, their eggs, disease pathogens, and weed seeds.

Topsoil taken from a productive part of the garden can be used successfully if it is sterilized prior to potting and amended with builder's sand or perlite to assure sufficient drainage. (See page 76 of this text for additional information on soil sterilization.)

Many indoor gardeners find it far easier to purchase presterilized, packaged potting soils that are usually pest free and, once amended, drain freely.

NEVER CROWD PLANTS. Leaving space between plants is a precautionary measure that has several advantages but is practiced too infrequently. Proper spacing improves air circulation, allowing water splashed on leaves to dry quickly. This is particularly important when growing plants such as begonias that are subject to foliage diseases encouraged by water remaining on leaf surfaces. It can also be a critical factor when raising African violets and other plants with hairy leaves. Water remaining on the velvety foliage of these plants may cause spotting and discoloration as well as disease problems.

Proper spacing also discourages the easy movement of insects and mites from plant to plant. Another advantage is that problems are more likely to be noticed on well-spaced plants than on those growing, pot to pot, with their leaves intertwined.

TREAT PLANTS GENTLY. Disease organisms can infect plants by entering through wounds caused by careless or rough handling. Extra care should be taken with cacti and other succulents, since once damaged, they heal slowly and are exposed to infection for prolonged periods. Isolating a seriously wounded plant until it heals is a wise precaution.

PROVIDE THE CORRECT ENVIRONMENT. Last, and perhaps most important, care should be taken to provide each plant species with its own special combination of light, water, heat, and nutrition. Healthly robust plants are more likely to survive an infestation or infection than those that have been weakened by inadequate care.

Early Detection of Plant Pests

Despite attention to pest prevention, the frustrating fact is problems still arise. However, early detection often leads to effective control. To catch problems at the outset, a close and careful inspection of all plants about once a week is strongly urged. Disorders that have progressed to the point of easy detection from across the room may be beyond effective corrective measures.

Use a magnifying glass to check for presence of pests. Be on the watch for anything moving as well as for insects that take a fixed position on leaves and stems. Examine all plant parts. Also, look closely at the top layer of potting medium for the presence of soilborne insects. Check for disease by noting yellow or brown blotches or spots on foliage, powdery mold on plant parts, rotting or decaying tissues, discolored streaks, or a yellow and green mosaic pattern on leaf surfaces. If a problem is suspected, immediately isolate the plant. Then, positively identify the specific pest present. (Refer to pages 214–235 of this text for more detailed information on specific plant disorders.)

If the infestation or infection is severe, consider discarding the plant. Experience has shown that this is not popular advice, despite the well-known fact that plant problems can spread rapidly. If the affected specimen is a favorite and the idea of disposing of it is unbearable, at least isolate the plant to protect healthy neighboring specimens while attempting to correct the problem.

PEST CONTROL

There are three general methods for controlling insects, mites, and disease-causing organisms that affect plants growing inside the home: They are mechanical, organic, and chemical.

Mechanical Controls—The Environmentalist's Method

Mechanical controls are by far the safest, least expensive, and most environmentally sound control measures. They involve the physical removal of an insect or mite as well as removal of diseased plant parts. Always try, or at least consider, mechanical controls first. In the discussion of specific pests that begins on page 214, mechanical control measures are provided for each insect and mite described, as well as for diseases, when applicable.

Organic Controls—An Adventure in Pest Destruction

There has been a great deal of discussion in recent years on organic gardening and, in conjunction with it, organic sprays. Such controls, used occasionally on house plants, are intended to repel insects and mites and prevent the spread of some disease-causing organisms.

ODIFEROUS SPRAYS. The types of organic preparations most frequently applied to house plants are homemade from onions, garlic, peppers, marigold stems, scallions, shallots, various herbs, and other plants that have a strong odor. Various combinations of these plants are mixed together in a food blender, passed through cheese cloth or some other type of strainer, diluted with water, poured into an atomizer or mister, and sprayed on the affected plant.

There are a variety of recipes for such organic sprays. Many have appeared in popular magazines on organic gardening and farming. Each preparation is intended to help control one or several pests. A typical recipe, said to control aphids and mealybugs, includes two cloves of garlic, one hot pepper, one-half onion, three bay leaves, and a pint of water.

Such concoctions are messy and may have an unpleasant smell. They are reportedly effective in many instances and may be worth a try. The majority of these recipes have been developed through trial and error. The indoor gardener might find it interesting and worthwhile to experiment with various plant extracts in combination and

test them against a particularly troublesome pest.

SOAPS AND SOAP-BASED PREPARATIONS. Though these products may not be entirely organic in composition and often contain synthetic components, they are included here because of their relative safety.

Use of a soft cloth that has been soaked with soapy water is probably the most common control method for insects and mites that infest house plants. Success with this method is most likely if both leaf surfaces are washed and treatment is repeated weekly until the pest is under control.

There are also soap-based products developed specifically for house plant pest control. One product, Safer Agro-Chem's Insecticidal Soap, has proven very effective in controlling mites on schefflera (*Brassaia actinophylla*), a plant particularly prone to this pest. (It has also been effectively used in the control of mites, aphids, and mealybugs.) Such products are certainly worth trying before more potent chemical pesticides are brought onto the scene. Package instructions explain their use.

Chemical Controls—The Big Guns

Chemicals used to destroy a pest or protect a plant from a pest are called **pesticides**. There are several types. Those most frequently applied to house plants are: **insecticides** that control insects, **miticides** that control spider and other mites, and **fungicides** that control fungi.

USING CHEMICALS EFFECTIVELY, SAFELY, AND LEGALLY. Before purchasing any chemical control product, positively identify the problem. Be sure the plant's symptoms are pest related and not the result of a nutrient deficiency, improper moisture, inadequate light, or some other cultural problem.

After determining that the problem is not cultural, the specific pest should be identified. Often, the wrong type of chemical is applied. Many insecticides, for example, are not effective in controlling spider mites; miticides may not control insects; fungicides will be ineffective on anything other than fungus organisms. Remember also that no pesticide will correct damage caused by improper cultural practices.

Not only are pesticides poisonous to insects and plant pathogens, they are potentially hazardous to the indoor gardener and the plants themselves. Obviously, chemical pesticides should be used as a last resort, after a concerted effort has been made to control pests and diseases mechanically or with the organic preparations previously described. Though a number of pesticides have been tested and can be used safely when applied as directed on the label, it is the responsibility of every indoor gardener to carefully weigh the merits of their use against potential hazards.

According to the Federal Insecticide, Fungicide, and Rodenticide Act (FIFRA), the only pesticides that can lawfully be applied to plants growing indoors are those labeled for use on house plants. If, however, the house plants are moved outdoors for treatment, those products labeled for garden ornamentals may also be used. Since applying pesticides outdoors in the open, away from family members and pets is safest, the law is beneficial in more ways than one.

Whenever spraying pesticides outdoors, note wind direction and be sure to spray as the wind blows. Also, place plants in a shaded spot for treatment; they may be damaged in full sun. As always, note precautions on the label and adhere to the instructions for pesticide use as indicated.

READING THE PESTICIDE LABEL. A pesticide should not be purchased or applied before the label has been read and is fully understood. Take the time to learn all the manufacturer and the U.S. government want known about the product. The majority of pesticide labels include the following information in one form or another. The numbers used below are keyed to the pesticide label reproduced in Figure 9.1.

1. Trade name. Pesticides often have complex chemical names and are usually sold under a trade name. More than one trade name may be used if the product contains a combination of chemicals. Also, the same chemical may be sold under a variety of trade names. Malathion and Kelthane are trade names for frequently used pesticides.

2. Type of pesticide. The label states if the product is an insecticide, miticide, fungicide, or other type of pesticide.

3. Ingredients. The amount of each active ingredient is listed as a percentage of the total quantity of material contained in the package. Inert ingredients may or may not be individually named but their percentage of total content is stated.

4. Signal word. Pesticides are labeled with one of three words: DANGER, meaning the product is highly toxic, WARNING, indicating the pesticide is moderately toxic, CAUTION, meaning the contents have relatively low toxicity.

5. Precautionary statement and statement of practical treatment. This section or sections includes the following types of information: ways in which the product should not be applied; measures for avoiding poisoning; first-aid measures to be taken if exposure occurs; and the types of exposure that warrant professional medical attention. If the person applying a pesticide must be taken to the doctor's office or hospital emergency room, the labeled container should also be taken. The label will provide the physician with appropriate and possibly vital information regarding treatment.

6. Directions for use. This explains pests controlled by the product, the amount of chemical to apply, how to apply, plants on which the product may be safely used, and other related information.

7. Additional information. The manufacturer's name and address, the Environmental Protection Agency's registration number for that product, and information on storage and

HOUSE PLANT SPRAY BOMB [1]

FOR INSECTS [2]

FOR USE ON:
- **AFRICAN VIOLETS**
- **BEGONIAS**
- **CAMELLIAS**
- **CARNATIONS**
- **GERANIUMS**
- **AND OTHER HOUSE PLANTS**
(As Noted On Side Panel)

CONTAINS PYRETHRUM & ROTENONE
Two Naturally Occurring Insecticides

[3] **THIS PRODUCT DOES NOT CONTAIN CHLOROFLUOROCARBONS.**

ACTIVE INGREDIENTS:

	BY WEIGHT
Pyrethrins	0.056%
Rotenone	0.008%
Other Cube Resins	0.016%
Pine Oils	0.900%
Petroleum Distillate	0.406%
INERT INGREDIENTS:	98.614%
TOTAL	100.000%

[7]

EPA Reg. No. 904-122   EPA Est. No. 11561-WV-1

KEEP OUT OF REACH OF CHILDREN
[4] ## CAUTION   CAUCIÓN

PRECAUCION AL USUARIO: Si usted no lee ingles, no use este producto hasta que la etiqueta haya sido explicado ampliamente.

STATEMENT OF PRACTICAL TREATMENT

IF SWALLOWED: Call a physician or Poison Control Center immediately. Do not induce vomiting. Gastric lavage is indicated if taken internally. Aspiration may be a hazard. Do not give anything by mouth to an unconscious or convulsing person.
IF INHALED: Remove victim to fresh air.
IF ON SKIN: Remove contaminated clothing and wash affected area with soap and water. Launder clothing before reusing.
IF IN EYES: Flush with plenty of water. Call a physician.

SEE SIDE PANEL FOR ADDITIONAL PRECAUTIONARY STATEMENTS.

Manufactured For:
[7] **Pratt-Gabriel Division**
MILLER CHEMICAL & FERTILIZER CORPORATION
Hanover, Pennsylvania 17331

NET WEIGHT: 13.5 OUNCES AV.

CONTENTS UNDER PRESSURE

[5] ## PRECAUTIONARY STATEMENTS

HAZARDS TO HUMANS AND DOMESTIC ANIMALS: CAUTION—May be harmful if swallowed or absorbed through the skin. Avoid inhalation of vapors. Avoid contact with skin, eyes and clothing. Wash thoroughly after handling. Wash hands before eating or smoking. Do not contaminate food or feed. Avoid storage near food or feed products. Do not use on humans or household pets. Remove pets, birds and cover fish aquariums before spraying. Do not use on edible crops. In the home all food processing surfaces and utensils should be covered during treatment, or thoroughly washed before use.

PHYSICAL OR CHEMICAL HAZARDS

Extremely flammable. Contents under pressure. Keep away from fire, sparks, and heated surfaces. Do not puncture or incinerate container. Exposure to temperatures above 130° F may cause bursting.

DIRECTIONS FOR USE

It is a violation of Federal Law to use this product in a manner inconsistent with its labeling.

[7] ## STORAGE AND DISPOSAL

Do not contaminate water, food or feed by storage or disposal. **STORAGE:** Store in cool area away from heat and open flame. Store in tightly closed, original container in a locked area away from children and domestic animals. For Disposal, replace cap, and securely wrap original container in several layers of newspaper and discard in trash. Do not incinerate or puncture.

[6] ## DIRECTIONS

Avoid using in bright hot sunshine. Do not use on cyclamen, lantana, maidenhair fern and nasturtium.

1. Shake gently before using.
2. Remove protective cap. Hold can upright, and point nozzle away from you.
3. Press button to spray.
4. Spray plants from a distance of 10 to 12 inches, spraying in short 1 or 2 second bursts.
5. FOR BEST RESULTS: Spraying should begin when insects first appear and should be repeated as needed.

[6] ## GENERAL INFORMATION

This spray may be used on African Violets, Begonias, Camellias, Carnations, Chrysanthemum, English Ivy, Geraniums, Crassula, Kentia Palm, Roses, Rubber Plants, Snapdragons.

Kills the following sucking insects: leaf hoppers, certain aphids, spotted mites, white flies and mealy bugs when sprayed directly on the insects.

LIMITED WARRANTY: Buyer assumes all risks of use, storage or handling of this material not in strict accordance with directions given herewith.

16M MP   Prod. No. 06016

FIGURE 9.1 Sample pesticide label.

disposal precautions are also included on the pesticide label.

PESTICIDE CLASSIFICATION STATEMENT.

Pesticides are intended for either general or restricted use and may be labeled accordingly. General-use pesticides may be sold over the counter to anyone and are usually less toxic than those labeled for restricted use. Restricted-use pesticides can only be sold to and used by certified pesticide applicators or persons under their direct supervision.

Pesticide classifications are determined by the Environmental Protection Agency (EPA). Certification to use restricted-use pesticides is granted by an EPA-approved, state-administered board after the applicant has taken a course in pesticide use and passed a written examination. Information on becoming a licensed user (for commercial users, not home gardeners) of restricted pesticides can be obtained from local Cooperative Extension agents.

PESTICIDE FORMULATIONS.

Pesticides may be classified in several ways including type of formulation. Four types of pesticide formulations commonly used on house plants are emulsifiable concentrates (EC), wettable powders (WP), aerosols (A), and granules (G). **Emulsifiable concentrates** contain the pesticide in a solvent. An emulsifier is added, enabling the product to form a stable mixture when added to water. **Wettable powders** contain a pesticide blended with an inert dust. A wetting agent is added to enable the powder to mix with water and form a suspension. Emulsifiable concentrates and wettable powders are mixed with water, stirred, poured into a sprayer, and applied. (With wettable powders, you must shake the sprayer regularly to keep the mixture homogeneous.) **Aerosols,** often referred to as "bombs" (Figure 9.1), are frequently manufactured specifically for use on house plants. They may contain a combination of chemicals. Although they are convenient to use, most contain a relatively low percentage of active ingredients and are more costly on a unit price basis. **Granules,** relatively large particles of more or less equal size, are ready to use as purchased. They are applied to the soil surface, then watered in.

In the last few years, pesticides labeled for use on house plants have been sold, ready to use, in pump sprays, like those in which window cleaner is sold. Some products are labeled for use on mites, some for whiteflies, others for a combination of pests. They generally contain a small percentage of active ingredients, such as Malathion, Resmethrin, Kelthane, or a combination of chemicals mixed in an inert material. Ready-to-use pump sprays are convenient since no mixing is required and they are easier to target than aerosols. However, like aerosols, they contain a small percentage of active ingredients, thus are sold on a unit price basis.

PESTICIDE MODES OF ACTION.

With insecticides and miticides, the **mode of action,** how the pest is affected by the chemical, is another important classification. The majority of chemical control products are stomach poisons, contact poisons, and/or fumigants. **Stomach poisons** are swallowed by an insect after they have been applied to the plant. Some types of stomach poisons are called **systemics,** that is they are absorbed through the foliage when applied as a spray or through the roots when used as a soil drench. Also, granules are frequently systemic in action. Systemics are transported through the sap of the plant and ingested by the pest as it feeds. **Contact poisons** usually enter through the pest's outer layers or respiratory system. **Fumigants** generally enter through the pest's breathing apparatus. The same pesticide is frequently available in more than one formulation. Regardless of which formulation you use, the product must be labeled for use on house plants.

PESTICIDE TOXICITY.

The toxicity of a pesticide to man is determined by testing it on animals, usually white rats. The test most frequently performed is the LD_{50} oral toxicity test. This procedure determines the dosage of a pesticide at which, when ingested, 50 percent of the experimental animals are killed. Since pesticides also pose a danger when absorbed epidermally, there is also a Dermal LD_{50} toxicity test that indicates the amount of pesticide which in contact with the skin over a 24-hour period will kill 50 percent of the test animals. In both tests, the lethal dosage is expressed in milligrams of pesticide per kilogram (mg/kg) of the animal's body weight. Not only do pesticides pose a danger when ingested or absorbed epidermally, they can also be harmful when their fumes are inhaled.

The higher the LD_{50} for a pesticide, the more it takes to be lethal and the lower the toxicity level. For example, the insecticide Malathion, with an oral LD_{50} of 1000 mg/kg, is more toxic than the fungicide Captan, with an oral LD_{50} of 9000 mg/kg. As in this example, most insecticides and miticides are more toxic than fungicides.

PESTICIDE PHYTOTOXICITY. Pesticides may cause plant damage, even when applied correctly. The injury to plant life caused by a chemical or other agent is called **phytotoxicity** (Figure 9.2). Common symptoms include browning of leaf tips and margins; general yellowing; ring spots; crinkling; yellow, brown, or black spotting; and abnormal growth, especially stunting.

Factors Affecting Phytotoxicity. The possibility of pesticide damage, despite correct use of the product, depends on a combination of factors, including the environmental conditions under which the product is applied, type of formulation, condition of the plant itself, and, in some cases, the species being treated.

Pesticide damage is more likely to occur if air temperatures at the time of application are higher than 85°F or lower than 55°F. The optimum range for applying chemical

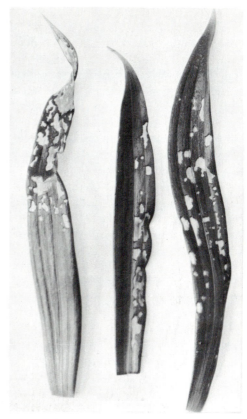

FIGURE 9.2 Phytotoxic damage on lily leaves. *Source: Diseases and Pests of Ornamental Plants,* Pirone, P. P., New York: Wiley, 1978, p. 18. Reprinted with permission.

pesticides is between 65 and 75°F. In addition, some pesticide labels state that relative humidity at the time of application should not be over 45 percent, the smog concentration should be relatively low, and plants should be treated early in the day. These conditions will allow the pesticide to dry rapidly, lessening the likelihood of foliage injury.

In general, sprays made from wettable powders are less likely to be phytotoxic than those made from emulsifiable concentrates that contain potentially damaging solvents and emulsifiers. Aerosols are less likely to cause damage if held farther than 18 inches from the plant being treated. Granules are less likely to cause damage if the material is evenly distributed over the soil surface.

The condition of the plant is also a major factor. The healthier the plant, the less likelihood of pesticide damage. Plants that have outgrown their containers and those in need of water are particularly vulnerable. Plants that have received excessive amounts of fertilizer or were growth under higher than recommended light levels are also candidates for phytotoxic damage.

Obviously, it is not possible to list the specific pesticide products likely to injure particular plant species. However, there are certain plant genera and families especially sensitive to chemical pesticides including *Begonia*, *Brassaia*, bromeliads, *Calathea*, *Crassula*, *Echeveria*, ferns, *Maranta*, orchids, *Peperomia*, and *Sedum*. In addition, the opened flowers of most plants are damaged by pesticides, as are many young plants.

Precautions against Phytotoxicity. When reading the manufacturer's directions on a pesticide label, note which pests are controlled by the product and on which plants the product can be safely used. Also, to be absolutely sure, test the product on a few plants before using it on a wider basis, especially when growing plants listed above. Most important: Follow the label directions and do not exceed the recommended rate of application.

A last word of warning: Phytotoxic effects may be cumulative, appearing only after repeated applications. Therefore, be familiar with the symptoms of phytotoxicity and stay on the lookout. Mistaking pesticide damage for pest damage is a common error. Do not be fooled.

INSECTS AND RELATED PESTS

Before describing the insects and mites that infest house plants, a brief discussion of the classification of these pests, based on their life cycles and modes of damage, is provided.

Classification by Life Stages

Insects and related pests develop through their life stages either by gradual metamorphosis or complete metamorphosis. In **gradual metamorphosis,** the offspring, called nymphs, are almost identical in appearance to the adult insects except they are smaller. In **complete metamorphosis,** the offspring go through four separate and identifiable stages of development during which their appearance is quite different. The process begins with the egg that hatches into a caterpillar, grub, or wormlike larva. The larva changes into a pupa (this may or may not occur inside a cocoon). From the pupal stage emerges the adult. Both types of metamorphosis are depicted in Figure 9.3.

Classification by Mouthparts

Insects and related pests are also classified by their mouthparts that vary considerably in structure to meet particular needs for obtaining food. The pests most frequently found on house plants have **piercing-sucking** mouthparts and feed by inserting a beaklike structure into the plant through which sap is drawn. Other pests have **biting-chewing** mouthparts and feed by tearing and swallowing plant parts, leaving holes in the foliage. Such pests are usually found on plants growing outside in the garden. The indoor plant pests described below exhibit the piercing-sucking characteristic.

Insects and Related Pests Affecting House Plants

Familiarity with the appearance, habits, and life history of an insect or mite is essential for accurate identification. The information provided below is for the insects and mites that most frequently infest plants growing indoors. Figure 9.4 illustrates four common plant symptoms that result from pest infestation.

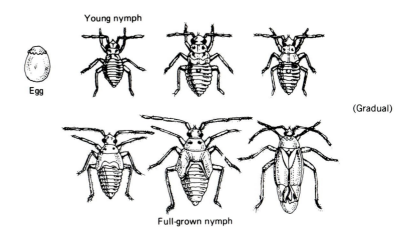

Young nymph

Egg

(Gradual)

Full-grown nymph

FIGURE 9.3 Metamorphosis may be gradual, as illustrated by the life stages of the true bugs (top) or complete (bottom) as exemplified by the beetles. *Source:* Atkins, M., *Insects in Perspective*, New York: MacMillan, 1978, p. 124.

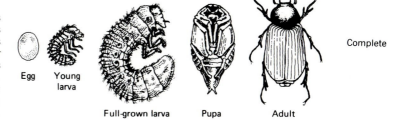

Egg Young larva

Full-grown larva Pupa Adult

Complete

APHIDS. Also known as plant lice, aphids are usually about ¹⁄₁₆ to ⅛ inch long when fully grown. They have soft oval- or pear-shaped bodies and proportionately long legs and antennae. Aphids may be yellow, white, green, gray, brown, black, pink, or red. There are winged and wingless forms though the majority of aphids actively feeding on house plants have no wings (Figure 9.5).

Aphids have a complex life cycle. They undergo gradual metamorphosis and usually, when actively feeding on house plants, give birth to live young who are almost identical to the adults in appearance, only smaller. Aphids reproduce alarmingly fast; one generation being born approximately every two weeks when temperatures are in the 60°F range and more often as tempera-

tures increase. Each parent produces up to 30 offspring, though this figure varies considerably.

Aphids are usually found in clusters or colonies on rapidly growing shoots, the undersides of leaves, and in the vicinity of developing buds. Damage includes a loss of general vigor, malformation of foliage and flowers, yellowing, wilting, destruction of leaf and flower buds and, in the case of severe long-term infestation, death of the plant. Through piercing-sucking mouthparts, aphids remove sap from a plant and excrete the surplus in droplets of a thick sugary liquid known as "honeydew."

Honeydew imparts a sticky feel and unusually shiny appearance to the plant. It may act as an attractant for other insects or support the growth of disease microorgan-

Sucking damage

Chewing damage

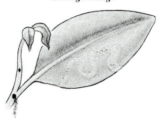

Boring damage

FIGURE 9.4 Some examples of plant damage caused by insects and related pests. *Source:* Courtesy of James F. Gauss.

isms. Since ants, flies, and other pests are attracted to honeydew, their presence on a plant may indicate aphid infestation. In addition, fungi known as black sooty mold may grow on honeydew and, if severe, may interfere with photosynthesis. (Sooty mold is described on page 232).

Susceptible Plants. The list includes *Brassaia, Chrysanthemum, Cineraria, Citrus, Cyclamen, Dieffenbachia, Fuchsia, Gynura, Hedera, Hibiscus, Hoya, Impatiens, Kalanchoe, Nerium,* orchids, palms, *Pelargonium, Peperomia, Sedum, Sinningia,* and others.

Mechanical Controls. For minor infestation, remove aphids with a cotton swab dipped in alcohol. Then, wash the plant with a forceful spray of tap water in the sink or

shower to remove the newborns easily missed with the swab. In warm weather, plants can be taken outdoors and sprayed with a garden hose.

Be sure to spray the undersides of leaves and along stems where aphids usually feed. If infestation is severe, add ½ teaspoon of household detergent to 1 gallon of water and give the entire plant a sponge bath. If this practice is done frequently, cover the soil with aluminum foil to prevent the detergent from contaminating the growing medium. Repeat treatment at weekly intervals for complete control. Keeping humidity high around susceptible plants with the use of a humidity tray is a good preventive measure.

Effective Pesticides. The plant owner should search out aerosols and pump sprays, which should be labeled for aphids and use on house plants; also, properly labeled systemics and emulsifiable concentrates are available.

MEALYBUGS. A type of soft scale insect, mealybugs are one of the most troublesome and frequent house plant pests. Their off-white, oval, flattened bodies, ⅛ to ¼ inch long, are covered with waxy threads that extend from the sides of the insect's body and resemble tiny legs.

One of the most common species found on house plants is the citrus mealybug. It is elliptical in shape with short filaments around the body margin. Another common species is the long-tailed mealybug, very similar in appearance to the citrus mealybug, except that powdery filaments form relatively long threads at the insect's posterior end (Figure 9.6).

Mature female mealybugs deposit hundreds of eggs in a sac that resembles a swab of loose, white cotton. The eggs hatch into tiny nymphs or crawlers, which spread quickly over the plant. The time period from egg to mature female is approximately six to ten weeks, though this figure varies with environmental conditions. Several generations of mealybugs are born during one year indoors.

Mealybugs crawl slowly over the plant, feeding as they go through piercing-sucking mouthparts. They cluster on stems, leaves, in leaf axils, flowers, unopened buds, and fruit. Prolonged infestation results in dwarfing, wilting, early fruit or flower drop and, in extreme cases, death of the plant. This insect produces honeydew that may cause the same problems as described under aphids.

Since mealybugs prefer dark places such as leaf axils, the nymphs, frequently present in far greater numbers than the adults, are difficult to detect. As a result, they are often overlooked without close examination.

In addition to the typical mealybugs that feed on above-ground plant parts, there are

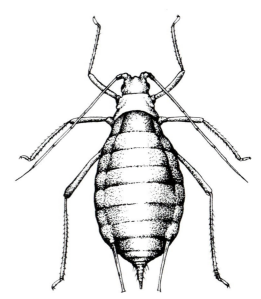

FIGURE 9.5 Aphids generally possess a characteristic pear-shaped body that is about ¹⁄₁₆ to ⅛ inch long.

several smaller species, usually less than ⅛ inch long, that feed on plant roots, resulting in the host's inability to take up sufficient moisture and nutrients. Eventually, infested

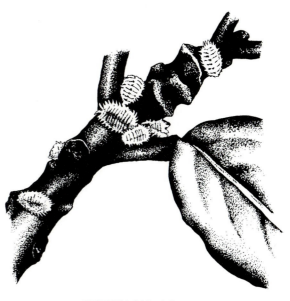

FIGURE 9.6 Mealybugs.

plants are likely to wilt, despite adequate irrigation, turn yellow, become stunted, fail to flower, and lose vigor.

Close inspection of the roots of plants infested with root mealybugs will reveal cottony egg sacs and, if a magnifying glass is used, the insect itself, which may resemble a particle of perlite. You may also see them after watering, either in the drip plate beneath the container or around the base of the stem of an infested specimen.

Since root mealybugs spread easily from plant to plant through container drainage holes, adequate spacing is a wise preventive measure. Also, the placement of several plants on the same tray should be avoided when growing susceptible genera.

Susceptible Plants. The list includes *Anthurium, Aphelandra, Araucaria, Asparagus, Avocado, Begonia,* cactus, *Chrysanthemum, Cineraria, Citrus, Coleus, Codiaeum, Crassula,* cycads, *Dracaena, Echeveria, Euphorbia,* ferns, *Ficus, Fuchsia, Gardenia, Gynura, Hedera, Hoya, Kalanchoe, Lantana, Maranta, Musa, Nerium,* palms, *Pandanus, Sansevieria, Syngonium,* and others.

Mechanical Controls. Foliar mealybugs can be controlled by hand removal with a cotton swab dipped in alcohol. The alcohol helps penetrate the insect's protective waxy coating. Also effective are forceful sprayings with tap water and washing with weak, sudsy water, as described under aphids. Repeat treatment at weekly intervals for complete control.

Root mealybug populations can be reduced, though not eliminated, by cleaning off the soil around the roots of affected plants and cutting out badly infested roots. The treated plant should then be repotted into a fresh, sterilized growing medium.

Effective Pesticides. Foliar mealybugs can be controlled with house plant aerosols and pump sprays recommended for use on house plants and labeled for control of mealybugs; also, properly labeled systemics and

elmusifiable concentrates are available. Insecticidal soaps, discussed on page 209, have also proven effective. (Systemic products may be most effective since contact chemicals do not always penetrate the mealybug's protective waxy coating.)

Root mealybugs are most effectively controlled with granular systemic preparations or one of the emulsifiable concentrates, when used as a soil drench at the concentration recommended on the label. Before using an emulsifiable concentrate as a soil drench, be sure the plant being treated has been well watered to prevent phytotoxic damage.

SCALE INSECTS. These pests fall into two broad categories: soft scales and hard or armored scales. The former are soft bodies and lack a separate scale cover, although some may be obscured by wax; the latter have a hard shelllike covering under which the insect lives. Adult scales are usually ⅛ to ¼ inch long, soft scales being larger than hard scales. Shades of brown predominate, though they may also be white, gray, or black. Adult females are round; males are more elongated.

Female scales undergo gradual metamorphosis. The newly born nymphs, usually referred to as crawlers, are oval, tan, flattened, six-legged, and so tiny they are difficult to detect without a magnifying glass. During the crawling stage, they move about infesting the plant. Then, they settle down, take a fixed position, begin to feed through piercing-sucking mouthparts and, in the case of hard scales, produce a shell. At maturity, females produce up to 1000 eggs during a three-month period, then die.

Scales feed on the leaves and stems of an unusually wide variety of house plants. Infestation weakens the host and results in stunting, yellowing, leaf drop, lack of vigor, and, in severe cases, death of the plant. Scale insects excrete honeydew that introduces the same problems described under aphids.

There are several scale species found indoors. Two soft scales frequently encountered are hemispherical soft scale and brown soft scale. Both are oval, approximately ⅛ inch long, and medium brown. However, the former is convex and the latter flattened. Also, immature hemispherical scales have a notch on the back end that may be seen through a magnifying glass (Figure 9.7). A commonly encountered hard or armored species is the fern scale, so named for one of the many hosts it infests. Females are light brown, about ¹⁄₁₂ inch long, and oval or pear shaped. Males are white, a bit smaller, and narrower (Figure 9.8).

Scales are most effectively controlled during the crawler stage since the shelllike covering, which several species eventually produce, is not easily penetrated by insecticides. Also, once in a fixed position, they are difficult to dislodge by means other than hand picking. This can be a tedious task if infestation is severe, especially since scales often feed in hard-to-reach plant crevices. Regular and careful inspections for the presence of newly hatched scale crawlers cannot be urged strongly enough. Systemics are also an effective treatment and overcome the problem of having to find each scale.

Susceptible Plants. The list includes *Abutilon, Agave, Aloe, Anthurium, Araucaria, Asparagus, Aspidistra, Begonia, Bougainvillea,* cactus, *Chlorophytum, Citrus, Codiaeum,* cycads, *Eugenia, Euphorbia, Fatsia,* ferns, *Ficus, Fuchsia, Gardenia, Hedera, Jasminum, Musa, Oleander,* orchids, palms, *Pandanus, Pelargonium,* and others.

Mechanical Controls. Small populations of adult scales can be scraped off with the fingernail or a blunt knife. As with aphids, crawlers can be removed by washing the plant in 1 gallon of warm water to which ½ teaspoon of household detergent has been added. Treatment with a cotton swab dipped in alcohol is also effective in some cases.

Effective Pesticides. The plant owner

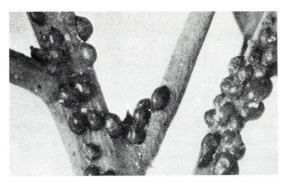

FIGURE 9.7 Hemispherical soft scale on avocado. *Source:* University of California Agricultural Experiment Station.

should look for house plant aerosols and pump sprays labeled for use on scale insects infesting house plants; also, systemics and emulsifiable concentrates that are properly labeled are another possibility.

SPIDER MITES. It is a rare indoor garden that has never been plagued by spider mites. The complaints heard by indoor gardeners concerning this pest outnumber those regarding any other disorder.

Experience has shown that spider mite infestation is frequently misdiagnosed as a cultural disorder, mainly because spider mites are so tiny, about ¹⁄₅₀ inch long. If a plant is suspected of being infested, shake it over a piece of blank white paper where the mites will be easily seen moving about.

Spider mites are oval and have bristle-covered bodies. Females may be red after

FIGURE 9.8 Fern scale greatly enlarged.

feeding; while males are green, black, or yellow, as are females prior to feeding. The species most commonly found indoors is the yellowish two-spotted mite named for the dark spots on its back. Obviously, these spots can only be seen under a magnifying glass (Figure 9.9).

Mites undergo gradual metamorphosis. Minutes after females reach the adult stage, mating occurs. Females lay approximately 80 to 100 eggs over a two- to three-week period. Indoors, the eggs hatch in about 5 to 10 days. Egg-hatch to adulthood takes about 10 to 15 days. It is possible for as many as 17 generations of spider mites to be born in one year under average home conditions.

Spider mites usually feed on the undersides of leaves, though they are sometimes found on tender young stems or other plant parts. They spin silky webs that may cover lower leaf surfaces and extend from leaf to leaf. It is under these webs that the females lay their eggs. Another identifying characteristic of infestation is the presence of tiny, yellow, pinhead-sized spots (stipples) between the veins on the uppersides of the leaves. After prolonged infestation, leaves may pale, turn brown, and drop off.

There are several reasons why mites are among the most serious house plant pests. First, they are difficult to detect because of their size; thus, they frequently go unnoticed until infestation is severe. Second, they reproduce with amazing rapidity. Third, mites have a well-protected respiratory system that makes them resistant to certain contact miticides; their webs also protect them from chemical sprays. Fourth, they infest a wide range of host plants. Finally, mites thrive under the warm dry atmosphere of the home, an ideal environment for their development and reproduction.

Frequent syringing and prompt watering may help discourage infestation. If this pest is a frequent problem or if plants susceptible to mites are being grown, it may help to set specimens on pebble trays (as described on page 204) or place a humidifier in the growing area. Keeping plants clean (as described on page 207) is another preventive measure.

Susceptible Plants. The list includes *Aglaonema, Anthurium, Aphelandra, Asparagus, Araucaria, Aspidistra, Begonia, Brassaia,* cactus, *Calathea, Cissus, Citrus, Codiaeum, Coleus, Cordyline, Dieffenbachia, Dracaena, Fatsia, Fuchsia, Gardenia, Hedera, Hippeastrum, Lantana, Maranta,* palms, *Pelargonium, Peperomia, Polyscias, Saintpaulia, Spathiphyllum,* and dozens of others.

Mechanical Controls. Mite populations can be reduced by forceful spraying with tap water, as described under aphids. This will break up webs and dislodge the mites. However, it may not remove mite eggs. Therefore, plants should be washed several times at weekly intervals to help control the newborns. Be sure to wash the undersides of leaves as well as stems and leaf axils.

Effective Pesticides. The plant owner should search out house plant aerosols and pump sprays labeled for use on spider mites and indoor plants; also, systemic miticides

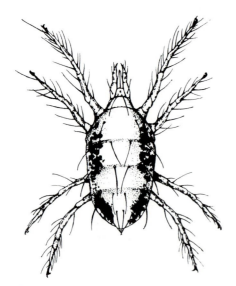

FIGURE 9.9 Two-spotted spider mite greatly enlarged.

and emulsifiable concentrates that are properly labeled may be used. Insecticidal soaps are well worth a try.

WHITEFLIES. These pests appear to be dusted with a white, powdery wax, giving rise to the description "whiteflies." They are tiny insects, about $\frac{1}{16}$ inch long at maturity, with two pairs of wedge-shaped wings (see Figure 9.10).

Whiteflies have a complicated life cycle that includes a pupal stage but which is not considered complete metamorphosis. Females lay at least 20 to 25 pinhead sized eggs; the eggs hatch into minute green or yellow crawlers (nymphs) that are oval and flat on top. The crawlers move about on the foliage for a few days before settling down to feed through piercing-sucking mouthparts. Soon afterward, the insects lose their legs, then feed again for two to three weeks, enter a pupal stage, and finally emerge as winged adults. The time from hatching to maturity is about one month. Whiteflies in all stages of development are frequently present on a plant simultaneously.

Unfortunately, whiteflies often go undetected until the host plant is moved or accidentally jostled, causing the adults to take flight. Soon, however, they return to the host plant or a neighboring specimen and resume feeding.

Whiteflies usually feed on undersides of leaves, especially newly unfurled leaves. They cause foliage to pale, turn yellow, and eventually drop off. Like many other insects that infest house plants, whiteflies excrete large quantities of honeydew that may introduce the same problems described under aphids.

Susceptible Plants. The list includes *Abutilon*, *Begonia*, *Calceolaria*, *Chrysanthemum*, *Cineraria*, *Citrus*, *Coleus*, *Euphorbia*, ferns, *Fuchsia*, *Gardenia*, *Hibiscus*, *Jasminum*, *Lantana*, *Pelargonium*, and many others.

Mechanical Controls. Minor infestations

FIGURE 9.10 Whiteflies on underside of leaf.

may be reduced by forceful spraying, as previously described under aphids. Be sure to spray the undersides of leaves, as well as stems and leaf axils. For best results, repeat treatment every two days until populations have been significantly reduced.

Effective Pesticides. Look for aerosols and pump sprays labeled for use on aphids infesting house plants; also, properly labeled systemics and emulsifiable concentrates are another alternative. For complete control, repeat application every ten days.

Other Nuisances Found on House Plants

There are other crawling pests that infest house plants and they are described below. Though they are encountered less frequently than the organisms discussed above, the indoor gardener should be just as familiar with them so identification can be accurate and control prompt.

ANTS. These familiar and fascinating creatures may be brought indoors during autumn on plants that have been left outside for the summer. Plants infested by honeydew-excreting insects are most likely to be infested. Ants damage plants by burrowing through the soil and causing a disruption of the root system.

Susceptible Plants. Almost all plants are susceptible, especially those vulnerable to honeydew-excreting insects.

Mechanical Controls. Pick off stray ants. Carefully remove as much soil as possible from around the roots of infested plants and repot in a sterilized medium.

Effective Pesticides. Use properly labeled emulsifiable concentrates mixed with water, according to package directions, and poured through the growing medium until they run through the drainage holes in the bottom of the container. To avoid phytotoxic damage, water plants well before treatment.

CYCLAMEN MITES. When fully grown, cyclamen mites are less than $\frac{1}{50}$ inch long, almost transparent, and rarely seen on exposed plant surfaces. As a result, these oval, tan-colored pests are practically impossible to detect without a magnifying glass and are seldom discovered until damage is apparent. Also, cyclamen mites produce no webbing, the tell-tale sign of spider mite infestation (Figure 9.11), but produce great distortion (Figure 9.12).

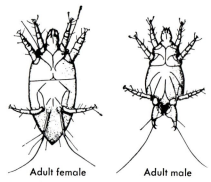

FIGURE 9.11 Cyclamen mites greatly enlarged. *Source:* W. W. Allen, California Agricultural Experiment Station.

Cyclamen mites feed on young leaves as well as developing shoots and buds, especially at the plant's crown. They are usually found in protected places such as the center of an African violet, a plant particularly prone to this pest. The terminal center

FIGURE 9.12 Cyclamen mite injury to dahlia. *Source:* Pirone, P. P., *Diseases and Pests of Ornamental Plants*, New York: Wiley, 1978, p. 229. Reprinted by permission.

leaves of affected plants may eventually become black, distorted in shape, more brittle than normal, and in the case of African violets, more pubescent than usual. Flowers also become deformed, streaked, and may turn purple or black. Occasionally, plants fail to flower or they flower for a shorter than normal period of time.

Susceptible Plants. The list includes *Aphelandra*, *Begonia*, *Crassula*, *Cyclamen*, *Episcia*, *Gynura*, *Hedera*, *Impatiens*, *Pilea*, *Saintpaulia*, and others.

Mechanical Controls. Submerge infested plants and their containers in water that is exactly 110°F for 15 minutes; this is an odd but effective control.

Effective Pesticides. Use aerosols and pump sprays labeled for use on house plants infested by cyclamen mites; miticides, usually sold as emulsifiable concentrates; and properly labeled systemics.

MILLIPEDES. These slow-moving, wormlike animals are 1 to 2 inches long when mature. Although nicknamed "thousand leggers," they actually have up to 200 pairs of legs along their hard, many-segmented bodies (Figure 9.13). Millipedes are readily recognized because they coil when disturbed.

These pests, which favor dark, moist places, feed most actively at night on decaying vegetable matter in the soil. Thus, the removal of fallen leaves, flowers, and fruits from the growing area is an important precaution against infestation. Roots, bulbs, tubers, and above-ground plant parts are also food sources to millipedes that may damage live plant tissues.

Susceptible Plants. Almost all plants are susceptible, especially those potted in soil containing proportionately large quantities of organic matter.

Mechanical Controls. To help reduce populations, carefully remove as much soil as possible from around the roots of infested plants and repot in a sterilized packaged potting soil.

FIGURE 9.13 Millipedes.

Effective Pesticides. Use the same pesticides as for ants.

FUNGUS GNATS. Fully grown gnats are about ⅛ inch long, have one pair of wings, and are dark gray. These insects do not damage plants once they have become adult flies. However, their larvae, known as maggots, can be quite destructive. During this stage, they are soft, wingless, off-white, and about the same size as the adults.

Fungus gnat maggots, found beneath the soil surface, are hatched from eggs layed by the adults. Maggots cause damage by burrowing through the growing medium and feeding on tender plant roots. Infestation results in a gradual decline in the plant's appearance, stunting, yellowing, and leaf drop. Root rot often follows infestation. While in the soil, the maggots pupate, then emerge as winged adults.

Fungus gnats are attracted to most very damp potting media that have a high percentage of decaying organic matter. For this reason, the removal of fallen leaves, flowers, and fruits from soil surfaces and correct watering practices are important preventive measures.

Fungus gnat maggots may frequently be seen in the saucers placed beneath infested specimens or on the soil surface after watering. Since the adults are attracted to light, they are commonly seen hovering around lamps or on window panes.

Susceptible Plants. Almost all plants are

likely targets, especially those potted in mixes containing proportionately large quantities of organic matter.

Mechanical Controls. To help reduce populations, carefully remove as much soil as possible from around plant roots and repot in a sterilized packaged potting soil. Wash saucers beneath infested plants with hot water to destroy the maggots that frequently gather there.

Effective Pesticides. Use the same pesticides as for ants.

THRIPS. Several species of these sliver-thin insects may infest house plants. Adult thrips vary in size from 1/50 to 1/12 inch in length, depending on species, and are usually yellow, tan, or black. They have two pairs of slender wings edged with bristlelike hairs. Mature thrips leap, run, or take flight when infested plants are moved or accidentally jostled.

These pests have a complicated life cycle that is often described as being between gradual and complete metamorphosis. The adults lay eggs that in one week hatch into minute off-white to orange nymphs. The newborns are wingless and may have droplets of black excrement on their backs (Figure

9.14). The nymphs progress through four stages of development prior to reaching adulthood. (During these four stages of development, the nymphs are known as instars.)

Thrips scrape a stem or leaf, then suck the sap that accumulates in the newly made wound. Damage includes the development of silver spots or white speckles with black dots of excrement on leaves, flowers, and stems. Eventually, affected plants become stunted, flowers may be distorted, and leaves turn yellow and drop.

Since thrips are frequently responsible for the spread of viruses, their prompt control is important.

Susceptible Plants. The list includes *Aphelandra*, *Araucaria*, *Ardisia*, *Asparagus*, *Begonia*, *Brassaia*, *Chrysanthemum*, *Citrus*, *Codiaeum*, cycads, *Cyclamen*, *Dieffenbachia*, *Dracaena*, *Epipremnum*, ferns, *Ficus*, *Fuchsia*, *Gardenia*, *Hippeastrum*, orchids, palms, *Peperomia*, *Philodendron*, *Sansevieria*, *Spathiphyllum*, and others.

Mechanical Controls. Minor infestations may be reduced by forceful spraying with water, as described under aphids.

Effective Pesticides. The plant owner should look for aerosols and pump sprays labeled for use on thrips infesting house plants; also, properly labeled emulsifiable concentrates and systemics may be used. The latter may be most effective since thrips may be protected in shoot tips and unfurled leaves.

SLUGS AND SNAILS. One of the most unpleasant experiences associated with indoor gardening is finding a large slug on a house plant, or more likely, on or under its container. Slugs, like snails, are not insects, but mollusks, a group of animals that also includes oysters, clams, and octopuses. Slugs have no protective shell (Figure 9.15). Snails possess the familiar spiral shell within which the animal can retract when threatened.

Slugs make large irregular holes in leaves

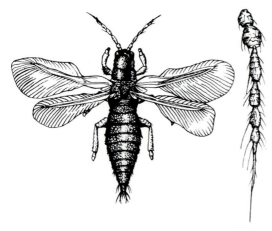

FIGURE 9.14 Thrip anatomy. A female enlarged by 50 diameters and a greatly enlarged antenna.

FIGURE 9.15 Spotted garden slug.

FIGURE 9.16 Variegated cutworm.

and may devour young shoots and seedlings. They exude a mucouslike secretion and leave a shiny "slime trail" that clearly marks their route. A commonly encountered species is the spotted garden slug that is well marked with elongated black spots. It reaches about 4 inches in length and ½ inch in diameter at maturity. There are also smaller species commonly found on potted plants purchased from nurseries and greenhouses.

Slugs and snails feed voraciously at night. During the day, they hide in moist, dark areas such as under pots or flats. Though common in greenhouses, slugs and snails are not usually found in the windowsill garden unless they have been brought inside on plants left outdoors during summer or on newly purchased plants. Check containers carefully before you bring them into the home.

Susceptible Plants. Almost all plants are vulnerable, although *Coleus* and *Pelargonium* are particularly so.

Mechanical Controls. Hand pick the odd slug or snail found beneath or on the sides of a container. A shallow saucer of beer left in the growing area overnight attracts slugs that will drown in the liquid.

Effective Pesticides. Molluscicides, pesticides that controls slugs and snails, may be applied to house plants while they are outside for the summer, if labeled for use on ornamentals.

CUTWORMS. Cutworms, the larvae of certain moths, favor beans, cabbage, corn, and tomatoes and, therefore, are most closely associated with vegetable gardens. However, they may also feed on house plants. Cutworms pose a problem to indoor gardens initially when the moths fly into commercial greenhouses and lay their eggs. These eggs hatch into caterpillars—the cutworms. The cutworms then burrow into potting soil to pupate before emerging as adults. Plants may be unknowingly sent to market infested with cutworm eggs of pupae. Cutworms feed at night, cutting through young stems at ground level. They may also crawl up stems to feed on buds, leaves, and flowers (Figure 9.16).

Susceptible Plants. Almost all plants are vulnerable.

Mechanical Control. Pick off stray cutworms found above ground. Populations may be reduced by removing as much soil as possible from around plant roots and repotting into a sterilized medium.

Effective Control. Pick off stray cutworms. Carefully remove as much soil as possible from around the roots of infested plants and repot in a sterilized medium.

PARASITIC DISEASES—VIRUSES, BACTERIA, FUNGI, AND NEMATODES

This section deals with plant problems caused by viruses, bacteria, fungi, and nematodes. These organisms, which account for the great majority of diseases affecting house plants, are minute in size and are typically parasitic, that is, they depend on the host plant as a source of nourishment. Figure 9.17 compares the symptoms of viruses, bacteria, fungi, and nematodes. The symptoms, susceptible plants, and controls for the parasitic diseases most commonly found indoors are examined below.

Viruses

Viruses are ultramicroscopic organisms that cause a number of plant diseases. There are no sure cures, though plants occasionally recover unaided. Still, it is best to destroy or at least isolate infected plants to save healthy ones.

Realize that viruses can spread to all plant parts including roots, bulbs, and tubers.

Moreover, it is possible for the disease to be present in a plant despite the absence of visible symptoms. Obviously, infected plants must never be asexually propagated since cuttings may be infected. Seed transmission is less probable.

Virus-infected plants typically exhibit one or more of three symptoms: a mottling of the foliage, leaf distortion, and dwarfed growth.

Most viruses are transmitted by insects. Aphids are usually the culprits, though mealybugs, mites, thrips, and whiteflies may also be guilty of spreading virus diseases from plant to plant. (Nematodes may also be carriers.) Thus, prompt control of insects and mites is an essential preventive measure.

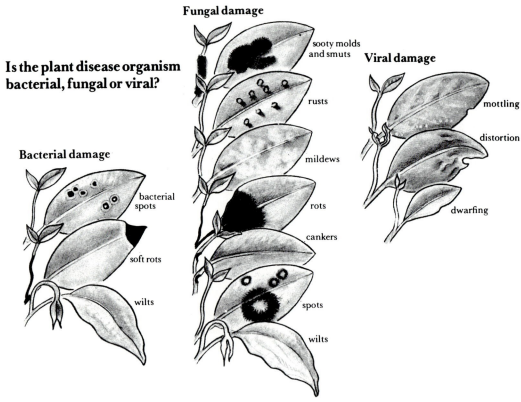

Is the plant disease organism bacterial, fungal or viral?

Bacterial damage — bacterial spots, soft rots, wilts

Fungal damage — sooty molds and smuts, rusts, mildews, rots, cankers, spots, wilts

Viral damage — mottling, distortion, dwarfing

FIGURE 9.17 Some characteristic symptoms of bacterial, fungal, and viral infections of foliage. *Source:* Gauss, J., "Putting Pests in Their Place," *Horticulture 57*, pp. 60–67.

Disease Caused by Viruses

MOSAIC, ALSO KNOWN AS VIRUS LEAF CURL, FLOWER BREAKING. Mosaics are the most common viruses infecting house plants. Distinguishing characteristics include dark and light blotches that give the foliage a mottled or, as the name implies, a mosaic-like appearance. Infected plants may also become stunted; leaves may be curled or puckered; and yellow or white rings and lines may appear on the foliage. Other symptoms include yellowing of the foliage, streaked flowers, and blossoms that fail to open properly.

Mosaics, like all virus diseases, are spread easily from plant to plant. They are often carried by aphids, though mealybugs, mites, and whiteflies may also be vectors for virus organisms. Obviously, it is essential to control insects and mites as soon as they appear, especially on plants susceptible to infection, such as orchids. Garden tools may also be responsible for the spread of viruses and, as previously stated, should be disinfected after each use. Tobacco mosaic virus (TMV) is an extremely infectious type, often spread by the hands of cigarette smokers who must be careful to wash their hands before and between working with plants. Since viruses may be spread through vegetative propagation, familiarity with viral symptoms is important when deciding from which plants to take cuttings.

Susceptible Plants. The list includes *Abutilon, Achimenes, Aglaonema, Aphelandra, Begonia, Bougainvillea, Caladium, Calathea, Calceolaria, Columnea, Chrysanthemum, Cineraria, Coleus, Dieffenbachia, Eucharis, Hippeastrum, Kalanchoe, Maranta,* orchids, *Pelargonium, Peperomia, Philodendron, Pittosporum, Rhoeo, Saintpaulia, Sinningia, Syngonium,* and others.

Mechanical Controls. Destroy infected plants to prevent the virus from spreading to adjacent specimens. Promptly control insect vectors, especially aphids.

Effective Chemical Treatments. None currently exists.

RINGSPOT VIRUS. The symptoms of this viral disease vary considerably. Leaves are usually marked with concentric light-colored rings, a zigzag pattern, or squiggly lines. Leaves may also become distorted; plants may be stunted; yellow or brown spots may appear near or inside the rings or lines; light-colored streaks may appear on petioles and stems; and stem tips may turn completely brown (Figure 9.18).

Thrips, described on page 224, are frequently responsible for the spread of ringspot virus. Therefore, the early detection and prompt control of this pest are essential practices.

Susceptible Plants. The list includes *Abutilon, Begonia, Brassaia, Calceolaria,*

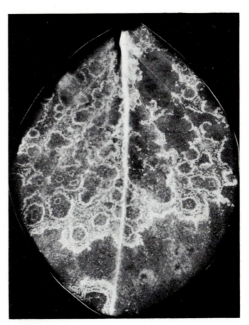

FIGURE 9.18 Ringspot virus on *Peperomia. Source:* Pirone, P. P., *Diseases and Pests of Ornamental Plants,* New York: Wiley, 1978, p. 399. Reprinted by permission.

Chrysanthemum, Cineraria, Fuchsia, Hippeastrum, orchids, *Pelargonium, Peperomia, Sinningia,* and others.

Mechanical Controls. Destroy infected plants to prevent the spread of this disease to adjacent specimens.

Effective Chemical Treatments. None currently exists.

Bacteria

Bacteria are microscopic organisms lacking chlorophyll that, like virus organisms, infest a wide range of species. They frequently enter through wounds caused by insects or rough handling and spread quickly throughout the plant. There are no sure cures and infected plants should be isolated to protect healthy members of a collection. Since bacteria may live for years in potting soil, the growing medium of infected plants should be discarded or sterilized.

Plants infected with bacteria will usually exhibit bacterial leaf spots, soft rots of leaves and stems, or wilting. Occasionally, severe infections will cause **cankers,** that is, a drying and cracking of woody tissues. Because their modes of action are somewhat similar, bacteria and fungi share some similar symptoms, namely, leaf spots, rots, and wilts.

Diseases Caused by Bacteria

BACTERIAL LEAF SPOT. The most distinguishing characteristics of bacterial leaf spot diseases are darkened, water-soaked areas on the foliage that often turn gray, brown, red-brown, or black. The spots may eventually dry and fall out, leaving a "shot-hole" in the leaf. Frequently, the spots have a yellow border; often, they enlarge until the entire leaf is involved. Light-colored streaks on leaves and stems and thin papery areas on the foliage are also common (Figure 9.19).

The heartleaf philodendron, *Philodendron scandens oxycardium,* is particularly susceptible to a form of bacterial leaf spot that causes a yellowing along the leaf margins

FIGURE 9.19 Bacterial leaf spot on geranium. *Source:* New Jersey Agricultural Experiment Station.

beginning at the leaf tip. Infected margins may eventually turn brown or red.

Like other bacterial diseases, leaf spots are difficult to diagnose accurately since their symptoms are similar to those resulting from fungal infections. However, the rapid spread of the symptoms throughout the plant and the absence of a moldlike growth over the infected area help distinguish bacterial from fungal diseases.

Susceptible Plants. The list includes *Abutilon, Aglaonema, Anthurium, Avocado, Begonia,* cactus, *Caladium, Chrysanthemum, Dieffenbachia, Dracaena, Epipremnum, Euphorbia,* ferns, *Gardenia, Hedera, Hibiscus, Monstera, Musa,* orchids, palms, *Pelargonium, Pellionia, Pilea, Spathiphyllum, Syngonium,* and others.

Mechanical Control. Remove and destroy infected plant parts. Maintain dry foliage, to the extent possible, on susceptible specimens.

Effective Chemical Treatments. None currently exists.

ROT. Rot diseases are caused by a variety of bacteria and fungi. The roots, crown, stems, buds, flowers, and leaves of almost all plants are vulnerable to rot. Symptoms are highly variable and include a gradual loss of vigor, accompanied by abnormally small leaves, yellowing, sudden wilting, withering, and leaf curl. Many types of rot are also characterized by mushy, slimy, water-soaked, and putrid smelling plant tissue. A cottony gray mold frequently grows over infected areas (Figure 9.20).

Root rot, generally characterized by severe wilting, is often mistaken for moisture deficiency. When in doubt, knock the plant out of its container to see if the roots are growing vigorously or have decayed. Decaying roots usually smell sour and are darker than normal in color. (If a plant has been repeatedly overwatered, it is likely to have root rot.)

In crown or stem rot, the base of stems may become soft and water-soaked, causing an interruption in the supply of water and nutrients to plant parts above the rotted area. Plants affected by crown or stem rot are usually not salvageable.

Susceptible Plants. Almost all plants are vulnerable.

Mechanical Controls. Destroy infected plants or plant parts.

Effective Chemical Treatments. Properly labeled fungicides, frequently sold as wettable powders, may be effective in the earliest stages of infection.

FIGURE 9.20 Bacterial stem rot of geranium. *Source:* Pirone, P. P., *Diseases and Pests of Ornamental Plants,* New York: Wiley, 1978, p. 394. Reprinted by permission.

WILT DISEASES. Fungi and/or bacteria cause wilt diseases, characterized by wilted foliage, despite an adequate moisture supply. Wilting is caused by clogging of the vessels that conduct water to the stems and leaves of a plant. The vessels may be clogged with the disease organisms themselves, cellular growth triggered by the plant's defense mechanisms, or a gummy substance produced by the plant in response to infection.

Symptoms of wilt include yellow foliage, usually starting at the top of the plant and moving downward, withering, leaf drop, and stunted growth. Prolonged infection often results in the death of the plant. Cutting open infected stems may reveal discolored streaks throughout the vascular system.

Wilt-causing organisms may be soil borne or they may be transmitted by insects. Thus, the use of sterilized potting media and the prompt control of insect vectors are important preventive measures. Wilt diseases are almost impossible to cure because they are systemic in nature, affecting the entire plant.

Susceptible Plants. The list includes *Abutilon, Avocado, Begonia,* cacti, *Calceolaria, Chrysanthemum, Cineraria, Coleus, Codiaeum, Cyclamen, Euphorbia, Fuchsia, Hibiscus, Impatiens, Kalanchoe,* orchids, palms, *Pelargonium,* and others.

Mechanical Controls. Destroy infected plants to prevent the disease from spreading to healthy neighboring specimens.

Effective Chemical Treatments. None currently exists.

Fungi

Most diseases affecting house plants are caused by fungi that, like bacteria, are minute organisms lacking chlorophyll. Fungus diseases can frequently be controlled, if recognized in the earliest stages. However, control is usually difficult once the infection has progressed to the point of ready diagnosis. Therefore, prevention is as important with fungus diseases as it is with viral and bacterial infections.

Unless free water exists on the foliage of plants indoors for eight hours or longer, there will be no new infections. Thus, most problems occur when plants are outdoors or on newly purchased plants.

Fungus-infected plants exhibit a wide range of symptoms including: sooty molds and smuts, dark visible "coatings" of fungal mycelium on leaves or other plant tissues; rusts, reddish-brown spots, usually appearing on leaves; and mildews, light-colored, cottonlike growths on the foliage. Other symptoms are rots, cankers, spots, and wilts.

Diseases Caused by Fungi

BLIGHT, ALSO KNOWN AS BOTRYTIS BLIGHT, GRAY MOLD BLIGHT, LEAF BLIGHT. Blights, more common on plants grown in greenhouses than on windowsill subjects, are usually caused by one of a number of fungal organisms. Symptoms include tan or brown spots that appear on foliage, stems, or flowers. The spots, usually angular in outline, may enlarge over a period of time (Figure 9.21). In addition, flowers are often malformed or rot; affected plant parts may become mushy or slimy; newly rooted cuttings or very young plants may wilt and topple over; and plants often stop growing, then wilt or wither. A fuzzy gray mold, like that seen on strawberries that have stayed in the refrigerator too long, usually grows over infected areas.

A humid, damp, poorly ventilated environment is particularly conducive to the development of blight. To guard against this disease, avoid crowding plants, maintaining an overly humid atmosphere, and splashing water on the foliage.

Susceptible Plants. The list includes *Agave, Aglaonema, Aphelandra, Aralia, Araucaria, Asparagus, Begonia,* cactus, *Caladium, Chrysanthemum, Cineraria, Coleus, Cyclamen, Dracaena, Eucharis, Euphorbia,* ferns, *Ficus, Fuchsia, Gardenia, Hedera, Hibiscus, Hippeastrum, Hoya, Musa,* orchids, palms, *Pilea, Saintpaulia, Sinningia, Yucca,* and others.

Mechanical Controls. Collect and destroy infected plants or plant parts to protect neighboring specimens.

Effective Chemical Treatments. Properly labeled fungicides, frequently sold as wettable powders, may be effective in the early stages of infection.

DAMPING OFF. A number of fungal organisms cause damping off, diseases that can affect the seeds and seedlings of almost all plants. Preemergent damping off causes seeds to rot before they germinate. It is most likely to occur when germination is delayed by overly damp and/or cold soil. Postemergent damping off causes seedlings to rot and topple over soon after they have sprouted.

To guard against damping off, germinate seeds in a sterilized, well-drained medium.

FIGURE 9.21 Leaf blight of *Cattleya* orchid. *Source: Pirone, P. P., Diseases and Pests of Ornamental Plants,* New York: Wiley, 1978, p. 379. Reprinted by permission.

Also, adhere to suggested cultural practices for germinating the particular seeds being grown, including correct temperatures, recommended moisture levels, and adequate spacing. Planting seeds in rows may help to control the spread of infection.

Susceptible Plants. Almost all plants are vulnerable. However, *Aglaonema, Aloe, Anthurium, Aphelandra, Aralia, Ardisia, Begonia, Brassaia, Caladium, Codiaeum, Coffea, Coleus, Crassula, Dieffenbachia, Dracaena, Echeveria, Epipremnum, Fittonia,* *Gynura, Hedera, Hoya, Impatiens, Maranta, Monstera,* palms, *Peperomia, Philodendron, Saintpaulia, Sansevieria, Schlumbergera,* and *Syngonium* are particularly prone to damping off.

Mechanical Controls. Destroy diseased seeds and seedlings as well as the soil in which they are planted.

Effective Chemical Treatments. To help prevent preemergent damping off, dust seeds before planting with an appropriate fungicide according to package directions.

To help prevent postemergent damping off, treat weekly with a fungicide after germination.

FUNGUS LEAF SPOT. The most common plant diseases are leaf spots, caused by a variety of fungi. Symptoms include spots of varying sizes, shapes, and colors on leaf surfaces. There may also be a distinctive margin or "halo" around the spot; often, a series of concentric circles surrounds the affected area. The spot may become covered with a powdery fungus and eventually fall out, leaving a "shot-hole" in the leaf, similar to bacterial infection symptoms. Infected leaves ultimately yellow or wither and drop. Development of this disease is encouraged by wet foliage and an overly humid environment. Fungus disease can be spread by the wind, water, insects, and human hands (Figure 9.22).

Susceptible Plants. The list includes *Acalypha, Acanthopanax, Agave, Aglaonema, Araucaria, Asparagus, Aspidistra, Begonia, Brassaia,* cacti, *Chrysanthemum, Coffea, Coleus, Cordyline, Crassula, Dieffenbachia, Dracaena, Echeveria, Epipremnum, Eugenia, Euphorbia, Fatsia, Ficus,* ferns, *Fuchsia, Gardenia, Gynura, Hedera, Hibiscus, Hoya, Impatiens, Kalanchoe, Monstera, Musa, Nerium,* orchids, palms, *Pandanus, Pelargonium, Peperomia, Philodendron, Pilea, Polyscias, Sansevieria, Sedum, Syngonium,* and others.

Mechanical Control. Collect and destroy infected plant parts.

Effective Chemical Treatments. Use properly labeled fungicides, applied according to package directions.

SOOTY MOLD. Sooty mold, a fungus disease, grows on the honeydew excreted by various insects that infest house plants. Obviously, the control of honeydew-excreting insects is an essential preventive measure. Sooty mold does not invade plant tissue but lives on the honeydew itself. Symptoms include a superficial dark brown or black chalky coating. This substance does not damage plants directly but may prevent light from reaching leaf surfaces, interfering with photosynthesis (Figure 9.23).

Susceptible Plants. The list includes Cacti, *Citrus, Crassula,* ferns, *Ficus, Gardenia, Hedera, Nerium,* palms, *Philodendron,* and others.

Mechanical Controls. Rub off the fungus growth with a damp cotton swab or soft cloth. Pick off and destroy badly disfigured leaves.

Effective Chemical Treatments. Pesticides are not generally required; rubbing the sooty mold off with a damp cloth is sufficient.

Nematodes

Like many fungi, bacteria, and viruses, many types of nematodes are plant para-

FIGURE 9.22 Fungus leaf spot on *Ficus. Source:* Pirone, P. P. *Diseases and Pests of Ornamental Plants,* New York: Wiley, 1978, p. 259. Reprinted by permission.

FIGURE 9.23 Sooty mold on *Osmunda* fern. *Source:* Pirone, P. P., *Diseases and Pests of Ornamental Plants*, New York: Wiley, 1978, p. 261. Reprinted by permission.

sites. They live in soil or on plant tissue. These strange creatures, also known as eelworms and nemas, are worm shaped or threadlike, though some species may become swollen or spherical at maturity. Nematodes are nonpigmented and nonsegmented. They are off-white and often microscopic, rarely exceeding ¹⁄₂₀ of an inch in length (Figure 9.24).

There are numerous nematode species. Many are harmless; others are beneficial by feeding on unwanted pests. Several are destructive. Most nematode species feed from outside plant surfaces, usually on root tissues, producing swellings or galls. After mating, the female nematodes deposit hundreds of eggs within these root galls. The life cycle of a nematode may be as short as a month but is often far longer. (Some types of nematodes damage plants by entering through wounds caused by careless handling. Once inside a plant, these nematodes

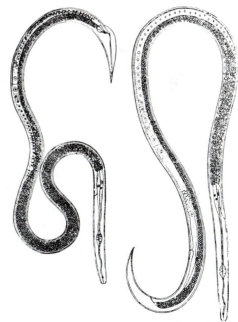

FIGURE 9.24 Nematodes greatly enlarged. *Source:* Pirone, P. P., *Diseases and Pests of Ornamental Plants*, New York: Wiley, 1978, p. 67. Reprinted by permission.

feed in the intercellular spaces and cause collapse of the adjoining cells.)

Damage is easily overlooked because nematodes usually attack beneath the soil surface. Symptoms to watch for include swellings or knots on roots, stunting, yellowing of foliage, sickly appearance, and leaf drop. Plants may also appear as if suffering from lack of or too much water (Figure 9.25). Infestation often results in root rot and wilting. Various fungal or vacterial diseases may enter through the wounds made by nematodes.

If infestation is suspected, and your plant container is large enough to yield a half cup or so of soil, contact your local Cooperative Extension Service. They will provide the address of an area Agricultural Experiment Station where you can send a soil sample. Only a trained professional can accurately diagnose nematodes and distinguish between harmful and harmless species.

Important precautions against nematode infection are the use of sterilized growing media and disinfected tools, as well as implementation of the sanitation procedures described earlier in this chapter.

Susceptible Plants. Almost all plants are vulnerable, particularly: *Aglaonema, Ananas, Ardisia, Asparagus, Begonia, Brassaia, Caladium, Calathea, Calceolaria, Chamadorea, Chrysanthemum, Coleus, Colocasia, Cyclamen, Dieffenbachia, Dizygotheca, Echeveria, Euphorbia, Ficus,* ferns, *Fuchsia, Gardenia, Hibiscus, Hippeastrum, Impatiens, Jasminum, Maranta, Monstera, Musa,* orchids, *Pelargonium, Philodendron, Saintpaulia, Sansevieria, Sempervivum, Sinningia,* and others.

Mechanical Controls. Collect and destroy infected plants and the soil in which they are potted.

Effective Chemical Treatments. None is recommended for use on house plants.

FIGURE 9.25 Nematode symptoms on fern frond. *Source:* Pirone, P. P., *Diseases and Pests of Ornamental Plants*, New York: Wiley, 1978, p. 30. Reprinted by permission.

PHYSIOLOGICAL DISORDERS

When a plant is growing poorly but no symptoms of infestation or infection are present, the disorder is likely to be cultural. The symptoms of physiological disorders resulting from incorrect cultural practices are frequently mistaken for the presence of fungi, viruses, or bacteria. The yellowing of leaves, for example, often results from insufficient water.

An example of how mistakes in diagnosis occur follows: It is very common to get into the routine of watering a plant once a week; yet as the plant grows and its roots fill the container, more frequent irrigation is required, especially during summer. If the gardener is unaware of this change, the plant will be under severe moisture stress and may start to turn yellow. Obviously, the problem is a cultural one.

Distinguishing between cultural and pest-related disorders requires an experienced eye. Sometimes, no matter how long we have been gardening, we mistake one for the other and treat for disease when the problem is a nutrient deficiency or improper soil pH. Fortunately, these mistakes lead to increased horticultural expertise and enable a more accurate diagnosis of plant problems in the future.

Table 9.1 lists common symptoms of physiological disorders and their probable causes. The table will, it is hoped, help you distinguish between pests and cultural problems.

TABLE 9.1 SYMPTOMS AND CAUSES OF SOME COMMON PHYSIOLOGICAL DISORDERS

Symptoms	Possible Cause
1. Stems leggy; internodes elongated; new leaves undersized; foliage light green	Insufficient light
2. Yellow or brown leaf spots on plant parts closest to sunny windows; leaves pale and thick; temperatures and light intensity high	Too much light
3. Leaves and stems wilt; leaves drop; soil feels dry to the touch	Insufficient water
4. Stems abnormally soft; lower leaves yellow and drop; new leaves abnormally small; plant lacks vigor and grows slowly; soil continuously soggy; water moves through the soil slowly	Too much water, poorly drained soil
5. Leaves hug container; foliage color abnormally dark; leaves and stems more brittle or leathery than normal	Temperatures too low
6. Leaves wilt, despite proper soil moisture; plants bear few or no flowers; plant lacks vigor and grows slowly	Temperatures too high
7. Leaves yellow, wilted, and abnormally small; plant lacks vigor; fertilizer not applied during the growing season; plants growing in a soilless mixture or in the same container for an extended time period	Nutrient deficiency
8. Leaves yellow but veins normally green	Iron deficiency (chlorosis)
9. Plant produces few or no flowers; foliage growth abundant and healthy; high-nitrogen fertilizer applied often or balanced fertilizer used more frequently than recommended	Nutrient excess
10. Crust forms on pot rims and sides of container; leaves touching rim wilt and wither	Buildup of fertilizer salts
11. Leaf edges and tips brown; plants lack vigor and grow slowly	Insufficient humidity
12. Yellow streaks or spots on leaves of gesneriads and other fuzzy-leaved plants	Cold water remained on foliage too long
13. New growth abnormally small; roots growing through drainage holes; water runs through soil faster than normal; soil dries rapidly between watering	Plant has outgrown container; check to see if it is root bound

CONCLUSION

Each insect and disease pathogen affects each plant species in a slightly different way. We may be used to recognizing fungus leaf spot on rex begonias but have difficulty distinguishing it from fertilizer burn on ficus. The more familiar we are with specific plant maladies, the more likely we are to recognize problems at the outset, on all the plants in our collection, and to control them effectively.

As millions of people invest more time and money in indoor plant collections, there is an increased interest in keeping plants trouble free. To witness a thoughtfully amassed collection of lady slipper orchids succumb to tobacco mosaic virus is heartbreaking for anyone. However, if the symptoms of this insidious disease are recognized early, the purchase of infected plants can be avoided and the isolation of healthy specimens, before they too become infected, can be timely enough to save them.

Keeping abreast of new chemical control products introduced into the market can also be essential. Pests often become resistant to products they have been exposed to for prolonged periods. Keeping an eye out for new pesticides labeled for use on house plants may save the day. Also, pesticides are constantly being reviewed for safety. Old standbys may be taken off the list of general-use products and become restricted, available only to licensed pesticide applicators. Knowing of more than one effective pesticide for problems affecting your collection is obviously important.

Once a pest takes hold, control can be expensive, time consuming, and frustrating. It is always hard to throw in the towel and toss out a once-favored plant. Remember: The easiest route to a problem-free indoor garden is prevention—frequent checkups, cleanliness, proper cultural practices, and most of all, a keen eye.

FOR FURTHER READING

Barmby, B. A., and A. J. Pate. "Foliage Plant Problems Diagnosed By Commercial Growers Clinic—A Three-Year Summary." *Foliage Digest* 3, 1, p. 7.

Biamonte, Richard L. "Diagnosing Plant Problems Indoors." *Foliage Digest* 2, 5, p. 12.

Borel, Mike. "Ornamental Pesticide Toxicity Values." *Foliage Digest* 2, 10, p. 16.

Chase, A. R. "Common Bacterial Diseases of Foliage Plants." *Foliage Digest* 4, 8, p. 10.

Chase, A. R. "Common Viral Diseases of Foliage Plants." *Foliage Digest* 4, 9, p. 9.

Chase, A. R. "Disease Control Basics—Alternatives to Chemicals." *Foliage Digest* 3, 10, p. 13.

Conover, Charles A. "Foliage Plant Problems." *Foliage Digest* 1, 12, p. 14.

Cravens, R. H. *Pests and Diseases.* Alexandria, Va.: Time-Life Books, 1977.

Fitcher, G. S., and H. S. Zim. *Insect Pests.* New York: Golden Press, 1966.

Hamlen, Ronald A. "Pesticides—Do You Know Where We Are Today?" *Foliage Digest* 2, 2, p. 3.

Hamlen, R. A., and R. W. Henley. "Using the No-Pest Strip Insecticide for Pest Control on Indoor Ornamental Plants." *Foliage Digest* 3, 9, p. 11.

Insects. The Yearbook of Agriculture. Washington, D.C.: U.S. Dept. of Agriculture, 1952.

Insects and Related Pests of House Plants. Home and Garden Bulletin #67. Washington, D.C.: U.S. Dept. of Agriculture.

Isely, D. *Methods of Insect Control.* Parts I and II. Ann Arbor, Mich.: Braun-Brumfield, 1957.

Joiner, J. N. *Foliage Plant Production.* Englewood Cliffs, N.J.: Prentice-Hall, 1981.

Metcalf, C. L., W. P. Flint, and R. L. Metcalf. *Destructive and Useful Insects: Their Habits and Control.* New York: McGraw-Hill, 1962.

Osborne, L. S., and R. W. Henley. "Evaluation of Safer Agro-Chem's Insecticidal Soap for the Control of Mites in the Interior Environment." ARC—A Research Report RH-82-2.

Pesticide Applicator Training Manual. CORE Manual. Northeastern Regional Pesticide Coordinator, 1977.

Pirone, P. P. *Diseases and Pests of Ornamental Plants.* New York: Wiley, 1978.

Poole, R. T., R. H. Hamlen, A. R. Chase, and B. A. Barmby. "Foliage Plant Problems Diagnosed in Commercial Grower's Clinic. *Foliage Digest* 3, 6, p. 8.

Richards, O. W., and R. G. Davies. *Imms' General Textbook of Entomology.* New York: Wiley, 1977.

Short, D. E., and R. W. Henley. "Insect, Mite and Related Pest Control on Commercial Foliage Crops—1981." *Foliage Digest 4*, 12, p. 3.

Shurtleff, M. D. *How to Control Plant Diseases.* Ames, Iowa: Iowa State University, 1962.

Simone, Gary W. "Disease Control Pesticides for Foliage Production—1980." *Foliage Digest 3*, 10, p. 3.

Thomson, W. T. *Agricultural Chemicals*, Books I and IV. Thomson Publications, 1967.

Yepen, R. B. *Organic Plant Production.* Emmaus, Penn.: Rodale Press, 1966.

chapter ten
care and maintenance of established plants

In concluding Part Two of this text, several topics need attention to complete our understanding of proper indoor plant culture. We have investigated the container, the growing medium, fertility, climate, and plant disorders. Each of these considerations plays an important role in establishing plants successfully.

Our discussion now turns to several important cultural considerations as plants are nutured over time. We begin first with a practice that accounts for more plant injury and death than any other—watering. Second, we move into grooming practices that ensure an attractive plant appearance as growth develops. This growth also necessitates moving plants into larger containers as the root system expands; our third topic, repotting, explains the methods and principles behind performing this function correctly.

In considering our fourth topic, seasonal changes, we address another culprit of sudden death among indoor plants. Recognizing seasonal cycles and properly caring for plants during vacations and other times of absence can mean the difference between success and failure in maintaining healthy plants. Finally, we discuss "holiday visitors," those bright plants that arrive from the florist or garden center for special occasions. Some last only several weeks; others can become a

continued source of pleasure with proper care.

WATERING: NO SIMPLE MATTER

In reading research and production literature on indoor plants, it does not take long to discover that watering practices are of extreme importance. In fact, no other production factor accounts for more loss of quality and plant death. One of the reasons for this critical nature of watering is that water relations affect many other aspects of plant growth, such as soil aeration and disease incidence. On the other hand, many factors influence water relations: plant species, relative humidity, soil constitution, and container type, for example. All these variables determine how and when water should be applied to plants.

Our discussion of this important topic is designed around the sequence of events involved in watering plants: (1) the water source, (2) watering methods, (3) water within the growing medium, (4) uptake and use of water by the plant, (5) when and how much to water, and (6) the stress associated with improper watering.

The Water Source

Does it matter where a plant's water comes from so long as it is relatively clean and nontoxic? In terms of immediate harm, usually not. Over the long run, however, water quality can have a varying and profound effect on plant performance.

Accessible water is rarely pure. Many parts of the United States, for example, have hard water, that is, water that has relatively high concentrations of calcium, magnesium, or other minerals. Hard water is usually treated with a water softener, which substitutes sodium for the minerals contributing to the original hardness. Chlorine, an element used in municipal water purification systems, and fluorine, added to impede tooth decay, can also contribute to plant problems over time (Table 10.1). Of course, well water may contain iron, copper, or other elements dissolved from the earth.

These "foreign" elements are usually present in water as partial molecules, called *ions*, that have an electrical charge due to the loss or gain of one or more negatively charged electrons. These ions join together in water, positive attracting negative, to form **soluble salts.** These salts include not only the minerals and elements already mentioned but fertilizer salts as well.

Soluble salts are perfectly normal in the potting medium of healthy plants and necessary for proper growth. When they reach high levels of concentration, however, they can be harmful to the plant, even to the point of death (Figure 10.1). It is of the utmost importance, therefore, that the level of soluble salts within the potting soil remain within acceptable limits. The most reliable way for

TABLE 10.1 RELATIVE SENSITIVITY OF FOLIAGE PLANT SPECIES TO FLUORIDE CONTAINED IN SOIL AMENDMENTS

Species	Common Name	Family	Sensitivity to Fluoride
Aspidistra elatior	Cast-iron plant	Liliaceae	Suspected
Calathea spp.	Calathea	Marantaceae	Moderate–slight
Calathea insignis	Rattlesnake plant	Marantaceae	Moderate–slight
Calathea makoyana	Peacock plant	Marantaceae	Moderate–slight
Chamaedorea elegans	Parlor palm	Palmae	Slight
Chamaedorea seifrizii	Seifrizii palm	Palmae	Slight
Chlorophytum comosum	Spider plant	Liliaceae	Moderate
Chrysalidocarpus lutescens	Areca palm	Palmae	Moderate–slight
Cordyline terminalis 'Baby Doll'	Baby doll ti	Liliaceae	Severe
Ctenanthe sp. 'Dragon Tracks'	Dragon tracks	Marantaceae	Slight
Dracaena deremensis 'Janet Craig'	Janet Craig	Liliaceae	Severe
Dracaena deremensis 'Warneckii'	Warneckii	Liliaceae	Severe–moderate
Dracaena fragrans 'Massangeana'	Corn plant	Liliaceae	Moderate–slight
Dracaena marginata	Marginata	Liliaceae	Suspected
Dracaena sanderana	Belgian evergreen	Liliaceae	Suspected
Dracaena thalioides	Pleomele	Liliaceae	Suspected
Maranta leuconeura erythroneura	Red nerve	Marantaceae	Slight
Maranta leuconeura kerchoviana	Prayer plant	Marantaceae	Slight
Spathiphyllum spp.	Peace lily	Araceae	Slight
Spathiphyllum cannifolium	Peace lily	Araceae	Slight
Yucca elephantipes	Spineless yucca	Liliaceae	Moderate

SOURCE: Conover, C., and R. T. Poole, "Fluoride Analysis of Materials Commonly Available as Nutritional Soil Amendments," *Foliage Digest* 4, 10 (1981).

FIGURE 10.1 Distilled water, available at grocery stores, is one method of reducing soluble salt concentrations in the soil solution.

the home gardener to assess the soluble salt concentration is through soil tests that are usually obtainable through the Cooperative Extension Service. Instruments are available for analyzing soluble salts, but are too expensive for home use.

The conventional wisdom in watering plants has been to allow about 20% of the applied water to exit through the drainage holes. This practice continually leaches or flushes soluble salts from the container, thus preventing a detrimental buildup. Recent research, however, stimulated by rising fertilizer costs, scarcity of water supplies, and contamination of ground water with chemicals and fertilizers, concludes that this practice is neither necessary nor desirable among indoor plant producers. If water and fertilizer are applied in correct measure, the need for leaching no longer exists.

In larger operations where precise testing is a must, this "zero leaching" recommendation is sound. For the indoor gardner at home, however, the "20% rule" will ensure that unsuspected buildups do not occur. We will see shortly why it is important to control the level of soluble salts.

SALTS AND pH. Soluble salts also play an important role in determining the pH of water. Some salts generate acids, thus lowering the pH, whereas the presence of calcium will raise the pH to more alkaline levels. Ideally, a range of 5.5 to 6.5 is most desirable for indoor plant growth. The home gardener can test for pH levels in water or soils through the use of litmus strips which, when inserted into solution, change color to indicate pH level.

Because of the importance of proper pH and soluble salt levels to plant performance, use water as free from salts as possible when watering. You might ask at this point why plants outdoors are not particularly bothered by these factors. Rain water is essentially distilled water; it is basically devoid of ions. Also, a much larger soil volume and frequent leaching action moderate extremes of pH or salt concentration.

Collected rain water, distilled water, and deionized water are the ideal types to use on plants. When these are not practical, well water and hard water are desirable in descending order of preference. In some areas of the country such as the Pacific Northwest, tap water is nearly equivalent to distilled water in salt content.

Proper Methods of Watering

Watering correctly is not an operation independent of other gardening principles. Potting, for example, should be carried out with watering requirements in mind. The composition of the potting mix, the plant container, and the location of the container will affect when and how watering must be performed. We touched on these subjects in Chapter Five.

Proper watering imitates a good rain. The purpose is to drench the soil thoroughly without erosion, bringing it to field capacity (see Chapter Six), and to utilize water, fertilizers, and time efficiently.

WATERING FROM ABOVE VERSUS BELOW.

Effective watering must also take into account whether the plant is watered from above or below; each method has separate considerations. Water applied from above should not contact the leaves except when cleaning is intended. Periodic splashing of water onto foliage will create unsightly mineral residues, particularly with hard water. Take care also to avoid forceful streams of water that will either flush soil out of the pot or erode a hole, leaving the plant's roots exposed to air. Potting plants with the soil level ½ to 1 inch below the pot's rim makes watering much easier; water can be filled to near the rim and allowed to percolate slowly through the soil mass. By placing a collection saucer under each pot, the plants can

be watered from above while remaining in their permanent location.

Watering from below involves placing the pot in a container of water, causing capillary action to draw the water up into the soil mass. This method is used when it is difficult to avoid wetting the plant leaves during watering, such as with the African violet. Watering from below also prevents soil surface compaction and ensures complete saturation of the soil mass. Since plants must be taken to a water basin for soaking, this procedure takes more time than surface watering, although the process can be hastened through the use of a deep soaking reservoir (Figure 10.2).

COPING WITH SOIL SHRINKAGE. A common problem with watering, particularly when the soil mix has a clay constituent, is shrinkage of the medium away from the pot wall. Plants watered in this condition often drain quickly through the side void, preventing the water from soaking throughout the

FIGURE 10.2 Bottom watering takes less time to perform when a deep reservoir, such as the dishpan at left, is used.

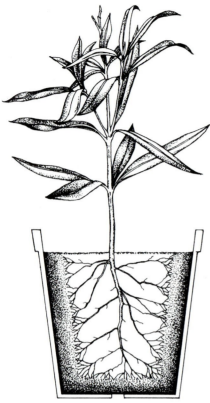

FIGURE 10.3 Plants growing in soils containing clay are apt to suffer root damage from internal soil dryness.

soil mass (Figure 10.3). Consequently, the interior root system can be damaged from drought even though watering may be relatively frequent. This problem is best prevented through limiting or eliminating clay in the soil mix.

WATERING ALTERNATIVES. Other means of watering are constantly surfacing on the market. The use of a wick, one end inserted into the soil and the other end in a water source, can be useful for keeping plants alive during extended absences such as vacations. Another version of this technique, capillary matting, is commonly used by plant producers. The greenhouse bench is covered with a mat similar to cotton flannel that is kept saturated with water. As the pots set on the bench with their soil touching the wet mat through the drainage holes, water is pulled into the soil through capillary action.

Chapter Six addresses the new container systems that utilize hydroponic or capillary watering. Both techniques are proving fruitful with proper attention to soil characteristics.

WATERING CONTAINERS WITH NO DRAINAGE. Since many decorative containers have impervious walls and lack drainage holes, watering technique is particularly critical. The greatest difficulty is finding the proper balance between over-and under-watering. Applying too much water will create stagnant conditions in the bottom of the container. Too little water will cause drying, and, of course, soluble salts are more apt to build up in these poorly drained conditions and be more harmful.

Containers of this type probably should have a generous layer of drainage material, such as gravel, under the soil mass where excess water can stand without keeping the soil saturated. As we pointed out in Chapter Five, however, not all horticulturists favor this addition of drainage material. Since the soil is only able to lose water through its surface, longer periods of time must pass between waterings than with conventional containers of similar size. Occasionally, these types of containers should be watered thoroughly, tilted on their side, and allowed to drain. Repeating this procedure a couple of times will rid the soil of soluble salt accumulations. In general, watch plants of this type closely for signs of loss in leaf turgor, then water promptly and moderately. As we shall see shortly, sometimes loss of turgor may be associated with too much water.

Do not overlook the possibility of making drainage holes in ceramic containers. Most ceramic materials can be slowly drilled without cracking the container. A shallow layer of water around the point of drilling will prevent the drill bit from overheating.

When drainage holes are impractical to create, calibrating the container prior to actual planting is helpful. Fill the container with potting soil and determine how much water must be applied to achieve the desired moisture level. Empty the container, dry the soil, and pot the plant. Now, you will be able to determine approximately how much water to apply when watering. Because the lower soil area will usually remain moist, you will rarely need to apply the entire calibrated amount of water.

Water within the Growing Medium

Once water is applied to the plant, an interesting set of circumstances develops. If we assume a soil of good texture and structure and watering is from the top, a chain reaction of water and air movement down through the pot takes place. As water works its way down through the soil, air is both forced out through the drainage holes and bubbled to the soil surface up through the water. The water fills, momentarily at least, each pore in the soil, both large and small. The force of gravity pulls the water down through the soil so that eventually each of the larger pores drains, creating a suction effect that pulls fresh air into these drained pores from the soil surface. This benefit, replacing old soil air high in carbon dioxide with fresh, oxygenated air, is one of the most beneficial, but overlooked, aspects of the watering process (Figure 10.4).

A common term in describing the cultural requirements of plants is that they prefer a "well-drained soil." This description refers to the relative proportion of macropores in the soil that drain readily following watering; it is not a description of the total amount of air space in the soil. A soil heavy in clay, for example, has more total air space than a typical commerical indoor plant potting soil, but it will hold much more water since each

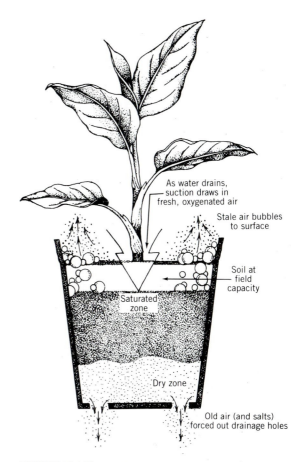

As water drains, suction draws in fresh, oxygenated air

Stale air bubbles to surface

Soil at field capacity

Saturated zone

Dry zone

Old air (and salts) forced out drainage holes

FIGURE 10.4 The watering process sets up a chain reaction of beneficial circumstances.

small particle space will retain water. The potting soil, on the other hand, because of the presence of large pores, will allow water to drain through relatively quickly. Let us look at why this characteristic is so important to proper plant growth.

FORMS OF SOIL WATER. Once field capacity is reached (see Figure 6.6), water is stored in the soil as liquid, vapor, or a "quasi-solid"; only water in the liquid state is available to the plant roots. This liquid form of water is held through the adhesion of water to the soil particles and the cohesive attraction of water to other water molecules. These forces of adhesion and cohesion are stronger than the pull of gravity, thus holding over 90 percent of the water in the soil as available liquid for plant use. Water vapor is found in the macropores that drain shortly after watering. The "quasi-solid," or hygroscopic water, behaves much like ice in that it is so tightly held by the soil particles that it is unavailable for use by plants.

Uptake and Use of Water by Plants

A common misconception about terrestrial plants in containers is that the soil primarily supports the plant and provides moisture to its roots and that the plant absorbs the gases it requires through the foliage. The weakness in this belief is that roots also must respire, thus requiring a constant supply of oxygen. Since the roots give off carbon dioxide in the respiration process, the oxygen-carbon dioxide ratio in the soil air changes to the plant's detriment. A plant in poorly aerated soil is equivalent to our trying to breathe inside a paper bag; we might be able to function, but not at the optimum level. When we look at water-related stress in plants later in this section, we will discuss this aeration issue in more detail.

WATER AVAILABILITY. Having established the importance of aeration to root development, let us investigate how water is utilized. The soil moisture available to the plant is not constant; it varies according to the forces that work to overcome the osmotic attraction of plant roots to water. There are two of these forces.

Matrix Suction. First, as the soil moisture is pulled away by gravity, the level of suction exerted on the remaining soil moisture increases as the drying process continues. This adhesion pressure mounts, finally making the remaining soil moisture generally unavailable (as we explained in Chapter Six), at the wilting point. Because of its origin in the soil matrix, this tension is called **matrix suction.**

Osmotic Suction. The second force that pulls water away from plant roots, osmotic suction, is related to the concentration of salts in the soil solution. A characteristic of osmotic pressure with respect to plant membranes is that if two solutions differing in salt concentration are placed on different sides of plant membranes, water will flow, through osmosis, to the side of higher salt concentration. At the cellular level, differences in salt concentration can cause water to move from root cells if the salt concentration is greater outside the root in the soil solution (Figure 10.5). If the difference in salt concentration is great enough, for instance in cases of over-fertilization, the movement of water from the cells can be so rapid that death of the cells, and ultimately the root, will result. This phenomenon is generally referred to as burning the roots, although heat is not a factor.

It is interesting to note that in both matrix suction and osmotic suction, situations that are depriving the root system of adequate water, water is present, sometimes in abundance, in the soil.

WATER UPTAKE BY ROOTS. How, then, does the root system take in water? Let us look at the two forces that move water from the soil into the plant.

First, since moderately transpiring plants do not exert a strong pull from cohesion (see Chapter Three), water moves into the root cells through osmosis. Ions are secreted from the root cells into the xylem. The xylem sap, because of its increasing salt concentration, attracts water from surrounding cells. A positive pressure, called **root pressure,** develops in the xylem, resulting in a push of water and ions up the xylem. Thus, water is made available to the shoot system by a passive and purely chemical process. Often, this principle results in the water of guttation (described in Chapter Five) that may be found as droplets on leaf margins early in the day.

The second means by which water enters

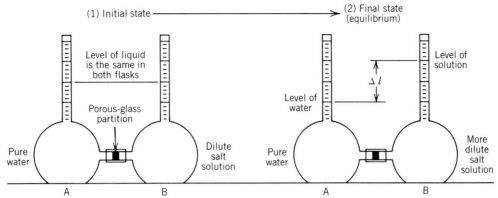

FIGURE 10.5 A typical laboratory experiment demonstrating osmotic pressure. *Source:* Quagliano, J., and L. Vallarino, *Chemistry*, Englewood Cliffs, N.J.: Prentice-Hall, 1969, p. 429. Reprinted by permission.

the root system likely accounts for almost all water movement into the roots. Usually occurring under higher rates of transpiration than the first method of water entry, this method—the cohesion-adhesion-tension mechanism—is marked by tension in the xylem sap. Transpirational loss of water creates a pull of water through the plant, reducing the salt accumulation in the xylem sap of the root. Consequently, most osmotic movement decreases. Water is brought into the roots, which become passive absorbing surfaces, because of the water pull exerted by the transpiring foliage. Drinking water through a straw employs a similar principle (Figure 10.6). Chapter Five describes the movement of water and nutrients within the plant.

Watering: When and How Much?

Unfortunately, there is no standard formula for determining when plants need water. As we have seen, soils differ in their ability to retain water based on texture and structure, organic matter content, and container shape. Soil drying rate varies with different containers, atmospheric conditions, plant use, air movement, temperature, soil constitution, sunlight, and plant size. And, of

course, plant species differ in their need for water. Some species, such as ferns, perform best in constantly moist soil conditions. At the other extreme, plants such as cacti that inhabit arid regions tolerate dry soils; in fact, these dry-natured species are often quite

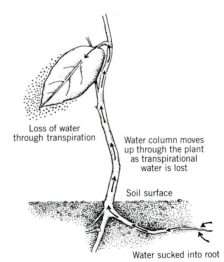

Loss of water through transpiration

Water column moves up through the plant as transpirational water is lost

Soil surface

Water sucked into root

FIGURE 10.6 Unlike diffusion of water into root cells through osmosis, the cohesion-adhesion-tension mechanism pulls water into the plant by suction as the foliage loses water through transpiration.

susceptible to rots when moisture is too prevalent. Most plants are best watered to field capacity, then allowed to dry near, but not to, the permanent wilting point.

DETERMINING THE NEED TO WATER.
How does one evaluate whether to water? The following testing methods, either individually or in combination, are helpful in maintaining a proper watering schedule.

Testing by Turgor. For most plants, the level of soil dryness can be determined by feeling the foliage to determine the beginnings of turgor loss. In other words, the foliage feels somewhat flaccid rather than firm. Allowing plants to reach a slight level of wilting usually causes no permanent damage. Noticeable wilting, on the other hand, may cause the lower leaves to drop from the plant. Although the plant may survive the trauma, an attractive appearance is difficult to regain.

Testing by Feeling. Plants in containers with drainage holes and well-drained soil can be checked for moisture by digging a finger ½ to 1 inch below the soil surface. Dry soil at that level indicates a need for water. With poorly drained soil or impervious containers, soil at the surface may be dry while water stands in the container's base. In these circumstances, water should be added to prevent damage to the shallow root zone, but the container should be turned on its side to allow excess water to escape. It is important to note that soil color can indicate relative dryness, but only at the surface. For this reason, we recommend scratching below the surface.

Inserting a toothpick into the soil gives a rough idea of soil moisture. If it comes out with soil particles clinging to it, the soil is still somewhat moist. If it comes out clean, the soil is dry enough to need watering.

Testing by Weight. Since water is a relatively heavy material, its presence in containers changes their weight noticeably.

With practice, the relative moisture level can be roughly determined by picking up the container. Although a rough estimate, this method can be used to confirm indications of turgor loss or subsurface feeling.

A visual Check. Another accurate method, if we assume the soil mass is well established and matted together with roots, is to remove the soil mass from the container and inspect it. A visual check of the entire soil unit is a most reliable method, although this should not be done on a regular basis.

Technology. Although several instruments have been developed that are designed to indicate moisture levels in soils, little data are available to indicate their merits (Figure 10.7). Perhaps a reason for this is that their reliability, convenience, and handiness cannot match a finger scratched into the soil. Any reliance on instruments of this type should be backed by empirical evidence that the indications are accurate. The best use for these instruments is with difficult-to-determine moisture relations in large and impervious jardinieres.

Time. An unreliable but commonly used method of determining dryness is time. Seeking convenience and consistency, indoor gardeners often base watering decisions on how much time has passed since last watering. The problem with this method is that it does not account for variables in environment, such as seasonal changes, that can radically affect the drying rate of soil. This method is best used as confirmation of more reliable techniques. It is helpful, for example, it there is a question about whether watering is appropriate to remember when the last watering occurred. A more appropriate use of the time method is to determine when a check, rather than watering, is necessary. For instance, if a plant typically requires watering every 10 days, it would be reasonable to begin checking the plant by feel after a week or so. In any case, an inspection by feel or another reliable check

FIGURE 10.7 Two of the numerous instruments that have appeared on the market for testing soil moisture levels in potted plants.

should be the ultimate determinant of the need for watering.

DETERMINING HOW MUCH WATER TO APPLY. As we mentioned earlier, the amount of water applied to plants has traditionally been enough to create a 15 to 20 percent loss through the drainage holes. Because of variables, though, this rule of thumb can be misleading. If the soil has shrunk away from the pot side, for example, water may quickly exit the draining holes, giving a false impression. What about plants with no drainage holes? Will seasonal changes affect the amount of water applied?

Almost without exception, the soil should be completely saturated with each watering.

The issues with watering, since saturation is almost always appropriate, are how often to water and how to avoid oversaturation. These subjects were discussed in the previous section.

The only real concern with the amount of

water applied is to balance the leaching possibility with the soluble salt buildup possibility. Although professional viewpoints differ on this question, we recommend the "15 to 20 percent rule," keeping in mind that saturation of the entire soil mass is essential, even if additional water must be applied. Since overfertilization and excessive salts are more probable than the alternatives, we feel that moderate leaching with each watering provides a desirable margin of cultural safety.

Water-Related Plant Stress

As indicated, water mismanagement accounts for a substantial percentage of failures in plant cultivation, a fact not surprising when one considers the importance of water to plants. The average indoor plant's weight consists of over 90 percent water. This would lead one to expect that a plant utilizes most of the water it absorbs from the soil, but that is not the case. A typical foliage plant incorporates into its structure only about 1 percent of the water it absorbs; it transpires or otherwise loses the other 99 percent.

Why then, with such a large demand for water, do plants develop so many water-related difficulties? The answer, ironically, is that most water-related disorders or stresses actually deprive the plant of water, even overwatering. This will become apparent as we investigate the major stresses on plants related to watering.

POOR AERATION OF ROOTS. Overwatering plants will drown them much in the same sense as humans drown. As water enters the human lungs, their ability to absorb oxygen and disperse it through the body ceases. Consequently, death occurs through lack of oxygen.

Overwatering plants forces the oxygen from the soil (Figure 10.8). This can occur by watering relatively well-drained soils too frequently or through the poor drainage characteristic of inferior soils, particularly those heavy in clay content.

The tendency of soils to retain water, and thus exclude oxygen, is a variable process

FIGURE 10.8 Ironically, a plant that dies from overwatering usually displays drought symptoms. The roots, devoid of oxygen, are unable to supply water to the shoot system.

dependent on soil structure, microorganism activity, environmental factors, and temperature. Consequently, a constant weekly supply of a certain amount of water on a particular plant may be optimum some weeks but too much or too little other weeks.

In addition to excluding oxygen, high levels of water can favor the buildup of carbon dioxide in the soil through various biological and chemical reactions. This development adversely affects the growth of roots and favors the growth of soil organisms, common to stagnant soils, that produce toxic substances.

Roots that malfunction due to aeration problems reduce and perhaps eventually cut off water flow to the upper plant. The visual symptoms may appear to be a nutrient deficiency at first, developing into yellowing, stunting, burning, or wilting of foliage. By the time these symptoms have progressed noticeably, the root damage is usually beyond the point of correction. Some of the typical responses to these symptoms are more water and more fertilizer, both of which hasten the demise of the plant.

SALT STRESS. As we mentioned previously, plant roots can be deprived or depleted of water when the salt concentration of the soil solution is higher than solutions within the root. Under these conditions, the root is unable to take in water through osmosis. Problems of this nature occur most frequently through soluble salt buildup and over-fertilization.

A related problem caused by acid-forming fertilizers is the reduction of the bacterial organisms that transform ammonia into usable nitrogen fertilizers. The continued presence of ammonia in the soil solution will either kill or damage plants.

UNDERWATERING. Although the previous stress conditions generally occur under conditions of adequate moisture, available water in the soil may be below the plant's required level. Although water may be present in the soil, most of it may be held tightly by the soil particles as hygroscopic water. This condition often has similar visual symptoms to the previous three stress situations since all ultimately lead to reduced water available to the above-ground plant structure. Note that this is the only one of the ture. Note that this is the only one of the stress conditions discussed here that is solved through the addition of water, with the exception of soluble salt problems that can be rectified through leaching. Both overwatering and disease problems are generally aggravated with additional irrigation.

It is interesting that plants have natural, almost instinctive responses to water stress. Some plants develop a general dullness or grayness in foliage color as water is withheld. Others tend to point their leaves upward in order to lessen the drying effect of sunlight striking the leaf surface. More generally, water stress and high salts produce similar symptoms—nutrient deficiencies such as chlorosis (lack of nitrogen or iron), marginal burning, stunting, and eventual leaf drop.

TEMPERATURE-RELATED WATER STRESS.
In certain circumstances, the soil temperature may be significantly less than the air temperature around a plant's foliage. This can occur during winter when warm air from a heat source warms the foliage while the soil mass, having lost heat during the cool night, remains chilled. Watering plants with cold water, especially during winter, can have a similar effect. Because of the warm foliage and cool root system, the roots cannot absorb moisture as quickly as the foliage demands it. The resultant rapid transpiration from foliage and slow absorption through the roots can cause wilting even though the soil mass is sufficiently moist.

PLANT GROOMING
Living organisms brought into "civilization" must be managed differently than those re-

maining in the wild. Since most indoor plants have less growing room than their outdoor counterparts, their size must often be restrained and their form altered. Without the periodic rainfall that plants in nature enjoy, leaves and other plant structures accumulate dust indoors. In order to cultivate these inhabitants of wild environments, therefore, the indoor gardener must perform certain functions periodically to maintain a satisfactory level of sanitation and appearance. These procedures fall under two headings: shaping and cleaning.

Shaping
The size and shape of many indoor plant species, such as the African violet, are satisfactory indoors with very little human intervention. Most plants, however, require the removal of stems or foliage to restrict size, improve overall form, increase compactness, or simply to remove old, damaged, or diseased plant parts. The removal of these structures, depending on the extent, is termed either pinching or pruning.

PINCHING. Because of the succulent nature and small size of most indoor species, pinching is by far the most commonly used shaping technique. As the name implies, **pinching** is removing the tender growing tips of plant stems using the thumb and forefinger.

Pinching interferes with apical dominance and encourages the development of additional buds in order to increase the number of stems, leaves, and flowers that the plant will bear. This encouragement of bushiness also reduces the overall height and size of the plant, making it more suitable for restricted indoor spaces (Figure 10.9).

Timing. When to pinch is almost as important as the actual technique. Pinching should be performed in *anticipation* of desirable growth, rather than delayed until a substantial amount of plant tissue must be removed to achieve the desired results. An old saying among nurserymen is that pruning (pinch-

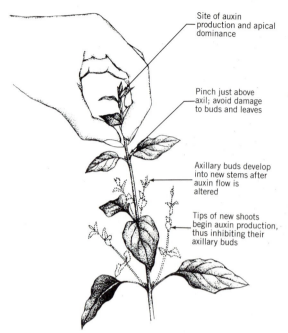

Site of auxin production and apical dominance

Pinch just above axil; avoid damage to buds and leaves

Axillary buds develop into new stems after auxin flow is altered

Tips of new shoots begin auxin production, thus inhibiting their axillary buds

FIGURE 10.9 Pinching removes the supply of auxins to the stem, allowing axillary buds to develop.

growers often remove several young, inner leaves to give the emerging flower structures more room for initial development.

Proper pinching removes the desired tissue without damaging the remaining tissue. Several points are important in accomplishing this objective. First, the pinch should be made ¼ inch above a node, leaving no unsightly internode stubs. Since these stubs would eventually decay, their removal minimizes the possibility of disease infection. Second, use care in pinching to avoid inadvertantly breaking off axillary buds or leaves. This is best accomplished by aligning the axis of the thumb and forefinger perpendicular to the leaf and bud axis during the pinch (Figure 10.10). Third, try to time pinching so that as little tissue as possible

ing) must be performed "from the ground up." This simply means that pruning and pinching should be promptly performed from the time a plant is very small.

With vigorous indoor plants such as *Coleus* and *Plectranthus*, pinching is needed after two or three nodes are developed so that the plant will produce several stems near its base. These, in turn, produce more new stems with later pinching. The amount of pinching necessary on a plant depends on its growth rate, as well as the ultimate size and branching pattern. Plants that produce flowers at the ends of the stems, for example, need frequent pinching during their development to encourage numerous flowering sites.

Technique. Pinching does not have to be performed only with the fingers, but this method is usually easiest. Nail clippers or small scissors can also be used. Pinching is also used for purposes other than creating bushiness. With African violets, for example,

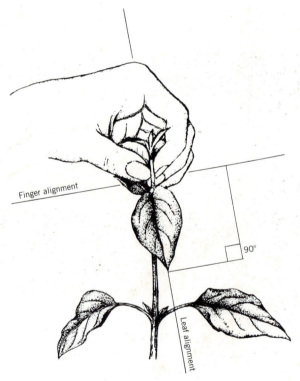

Finger alignment

90°

Leaf alignment

FIGURE 10.10 Aligning fingers perpendicular to the leaf/bud axis below the pinch minimizes plant damage. New, self-branching cultivars are being released that eliminate the need for pinching altogether.

must be removed. If three or four well-developed extended nodes must be removed in properly locating the pinch, the pinch is coming too late. And fourth, be sure the apical meristem is included in the removed tissue. On some plants like the wandering Jew, the leaf petioles project beyond the apical meristem at the stem tips. By removing too little of the stem tip, the pinch may miss the meristem, thus thwarting the effectiveness of the operation. Attention to these four points will ensure that the pinching operation is both timely and efficient.

PRUNING. Pruning is the removal of plant parts or stems so fully developed that pruning tools are required. This usually occurs when a plant has outgrown its space or when improper culture or lack of pinching has resulted in poor overall form. In these circumstances, removal of large amounts of plant structure is necessary to rejuvenate the plant to an attractive form or satisfactory size.

Pruning may be performed with scissors, pruning shears, or a sharp knife. Shears with small blades are more satisfactory for indoor use than those with larger, heavy-duty construction.

Pruning Principles. Adhering to accepted pruning principles during general shaping will prevent a "butchered" appearance. First, make cuts ¼ inch above nodes. Second, if numerous cuts are to be made, make them at different heights, giving the plant a more natural outline. Third, notice the direction of the bud or buds below the pruning cut. These buds will probably develop strongly and will determine the direction of the new stem axis. If possible, cut above nodes where the bud is not directed toward the center of the plant. And fourth, try to avoid pruning by pinching plants on a regular basis and providing sound cultural cut.

Placing Pruning Cuts Correctly. A common mistake in pruning is making cuts too far out onto the branches. As with pinching,

pruning must anticipate the desired growth effect. Cutting a plant back to the height it should be is a mistake; cut it back to a point well below the desired height and let it grow back, perhaps pinching as growth occurs to increase compactness (Figure 10.11).

This principle is especially true with plants whose form has become too straggly, too tall, or too unattractive due to loss of lower leaves. In most cases of this type, the best option is to cut the plant back within a couple of inches of the soil line. This results in fast growth because of the existing mature root system. Some plants, however, do not respond well to this treatment.

Herbaceous vines such as wandering Jew will not recover well from severe pruning. The best strategy with these plants is to pinch them regularly as they develop, exercise consistent and sound culture to avoid leaf drop, and occasionally start new plants from cuttings in order to replace older, declining specimens.

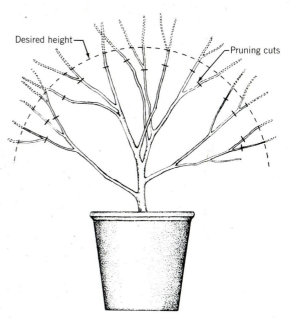

FIGURE 10.11 Reducing a plant to a smaller size should be performed by cutting back, using cuts at varying stem positions, to points an inch or two below the desired height.

With some plants, such as *Ficus*, *Dieffen-bachia*, and *Aglaonema*, severe pruning may be performed in conjunction with prop-agation techniques. *Ficus* may be air-lay-ered before the plant is severely pruned back to rejuvenate the basal portion. *Dief-fenbachia* and *Aglaonema* species may be air-layered and the stem may be sectioned into cuttings. Of course, the roots and lower trunk may be allowed to send out new branches, as well.

APICAL DOMINANCE. We have mentioned that proper pinching throughout a plant's life can eliminate the need for pruning. On plants that exhibit strong apical dominance, however, pinching is futile because only one, or perhaps two, new shoots will emerge after pinching is performed. Thus, with the rubber plant, for example, there is little use in trying to pinch back the terminal bud because branching is very difficult to initiate. Other plants, like the palms, should not be pruned because of their growth habit and form.

It is important to realize these differences in plants before either pinching or pruning. Some plants respond readily to pinching; others do not. The discussions of individual species in Part Five will indicate whether plants have peculiarities regarding pinching and pruning. When pinching is needed, improved plant quality and form are well worth this occasional maintenance need. When pinching is ineffective in stimulating compactness, group planting is an alternative.

ROOT PRUNING. Though rare, root pruning is necessary in some situations, particularly with respect to pot binding. When a plant's roots have encircled the pot in which it is growing, failure to prune the root system can reduce the growth potential after repotting. This procedure can be performed by pulling the encircling roots away from the soil mass and cutting them back to an inch or two of the soil. An easier method that proves just as

satisfactory is to make three or four vertical cuts 1 inch deep into the soil mass. Both techniques stimulate the development of new, vigorous feeder roots (Figure 10.12).

Root pruning may also be used to reduce the growth rate of certain species. The orien-tal practice of bonsai, growing miniature plants, depends largely on this practice of selective root pruning to restrict growth. By removing the soil mass from the container, larger plants may be slowed from rapid growth by judiciously removing feeder roots. This should be done in several operations, taking selected roots each time, in order to avoid a situation in which the root system is imbalanced with the plant's top. Removing too many roots too abruptly can damage the plant's growth potential significantly.

WHEN TO CUT. Since pinching and pruning should be performed in anticipation of plant growth, these operations are best performed in the spring before active growth of most species begins. This timing not only prevents the plant from standing in a weakened con-

FIGURE 10.12 Root pruning of root-bound specimens is essential to optimum growth after repotting. Here, the roots have been pulled away from the soil mass and cut back to within 1 inch of the soil to stimulate new root growth.

dition over an extended period of time, but it also minimizes the duration of the after-pruning appearance. Light pinching may be performed at any time of year and is particularly recommended during the season of active growth. In general, pinching should occur once a stem has developed two to four nodes. Since pruning is a more drastic operation than pinching, its seasonal timing is somewhat more critical than the timing of pinching.

MANAGING PHOTOTROPISM. In addition to inhibiting lateral bud development, auxins also help plant tissues orient themselves toward the light source. A plant placed in a bright window, for example, will eventually turn its stems toward the window. This natural mechanism ensures that leaf surfaces are turned toward the light, thus allowing efficient illumination of the surfaces. This phenomenon, known as **phototropism,** helps plants adapt to changing light availability as they grow and compete with other vegetation (Figure 10.13).

Phototropic responses can have an even more dramatic impact on plant form than pruning practices. Although pinching or pruning can be used to offset the effects of phototropism somewhat, a more desirable approach is to turn the plant a quarter turn every few days. This treatment will change the direction of the light source and provide a more even distribution of auxin on all sides of plant stems. The net result will be a more uniformly shaped and proportioned plant.

TOPIARY. For centuries, beginning with the ancient Romans, man has enjoyed pruning plants into unusual shapes. This practice, known as **topiary,** fashions plants into geometrical shapes, such as spheres, cubes, and abstract forms, as well as recognizable shapes such as animals. Topiary has historically been performed on plants outdoors where high light intensity stimulates rapid and dense growth. Although the practice is more challenging on indoor plants topiary is

FIGURE 10.13 Phototropism, if allowed to continue too long in one direction, can result in a fixed curvature of mature tissue. An undesirable plant form can result.

nevertheless possible inside by purchasing several components and practicing careful culture and pinching (Figure 10.14).

Making inside topiaries consists of training a vining plant such as *Ficus pumila* 'Minima' or *Hedera helix* over a preformed frame filled with tightly packed sphagnum moss. The procedure is rather simple. Pack the frame tightly with moistened sphagnum moss that is held in place with clear monofilament line. The root systems of several small plants are planted into the sphagnum moss, watered and fertilized frequently, placed in bright light, and pinched often to encourage dense growth. Several months of this culture and occasional clippings to refine the shape will create the effect of your choice.

Cleaning

All indoor plants need periodic cleaning to remove dust from leaf surfaces. This procedure is typically done by wiping individual leaves with a soft cloth, spraying the foliage, or brushing. The best method is based more on convenience than plant considerations. It

FIGURE 10.14 Topiary is an interesting and imaginative diversion from typical plant culture indoors.

is difficult, for example, to move a large floor specimen to a location where spraying can be performed; wiping the leaves is usually more convenient. Some plants, however, do have certain characteristics that must be respected. African violets, for example, can be damaged by spraying with cold water, and botrytis blight may occur if the flowers are moistened. Since the leaves are pubescent, brushing is often the most practical approach (Figure 10.15). Excepting these types of considerations, the cleaning method employed is not as important as the fact that leaves are cleaned periodically.

WHY IS CLEANING NECESSARY? Dust creates shade on plant surfaces, reflecting light that would otherwise be used for photosynthesis. Dust on lower leaf surfaces may also clog stomates, inhibiting gas exchange within the leaf. Along the leaf margins, water of guttation may cause an accumulation of salts that can result in leaf burning unless these salts are periodically removed

FIGURE 10.15 Plants such as the African violet whose leaves are hairy and prone to cold water damage are best cleaned with a soft brush.

through cleaning. And finally, dust on leaves dulls their normal coloration and finish, thus lessening plant value.

PLANT POLISHES. Garden centers and plant shops market numerous plant shine products or polishes that are designed to remove dirt, pesticide spray residues, mineral deposits from water spots, and to increase the surface gloss. These products have been shown by research to create different effects on various plant species. For example, a particular product may create an even glossy finish on one species while looking less glossy and spotty on another species. In general, though, the products demonstrate little difference in their performance or effect.

The question, then, is whether these products are necessary or desirable. Since they do not damage plants, there is little harm in using them. One's decision to use or not use these products should, financial considerations aside, be based on the level of glossiness desired. Some gardeners prefer such materials as milk or mineral oil as an alternative to these commercial polishes. As with pruning, the method is probably not as important as the consistency of cleaning. Using the commercial products over long periods of time, however, can result in a buildup of polish. Some horticulturists do not recommend them at all for this reason. Keep in mind, also, that plant polishes are best used on foliage with a waxy cuticle layer, rather than on pubescent or rough-surfaced leaves where application would be difficult or uneven.

REPOTTING PROCEDURES

As living and growing organisms, plants must occupy more and more space in their environment. Outdoors, plants are able to compete both for increased aerial and underground space. When a tree's nutrient supply becomes inadequate, for instance,

the root system may extend into newer and more fertile soils.

Confined to a fixed-boundary container, an indoor plant is totally dependent on the confined soil mass in which it grows. The plant is ultimately dependent on the indoor gardener who is responsible for the proper care and adaptation of the growing medium. One purpose in this section is to investigate fully this subject—one that we addressed briefly in Chapter Five—describing the why, how, and when of repotting.

Why Transplant?

By moving an existing plant into a larger container, we provide fresh potting mix, more root space, and an expanded ability for water and nutrient uptake. Although this procedure is usually beneficial to the plant, it must be performed at the right time, under the necessary conditions, and with certain limitations.

WHEN TO TRANSPLANT. Since transplanting disturbs the root system somewhat, the operation should be performed just before or during active growth of the plant. It is important that the root system initiate active growth after transplanting to reestablish soil contact by the roots and root hairs. Also, the sooner the new roots occupy the fresh and expanded soil volume, the less opportunity there is for soil erosion as a result of watering over an extended period.

DETERMINING THE NEED FOR TRANS-PLANTING. Scrutinizing a plant visually can give clues regarding the need for transplanting. If the plant appears "top heavy," that is, the foliage mass looks out of proportion to the container size, transplanting to a larger container is probably in order. Some plants, such as the snake plant (*Sansevieria*), establish more and more shoots from the soil as time passes. Ultimately, the pot is packed with shoots emerging from the soil. Hence, the plant simply outgrows its container. Plants of this type must be divided and repotted as individuals or in smaller clumps to allow growth to continue. A third visual indicator that transplanting is needed occurs at the container's drainage holes. If roots are protruding through these holes, the root system has probably become what is termed **root bound;** the root system has outgrown the soil volume of the container. The container should be inverted and the soil mass gently tapped out of the pot exposing the root system. If the roots encircle the soil mass, root binding has indeed occurred and transplanting is necessary (Figure 10.16).

Other indicators of the need for transplanting are less visible. A plant that requires watering much more frequently, for example, has probably also become root bound. A visual inspection of the soil would be in order in these circumstances. In some cases, the first symptom may be stunted growth; this indicator is the most subtle to detect.

Finally, soil characteristics may suggest transplanting. If the soil appears packed, devoid of organic matter, and generally depleted, or if a watered plant needs an extended period to drain, repotting should occur quickly.

Failure to repot promptly and correctly

1. Plant appears "top-heavy."

2. The plant fills the container with new shoots arising from the soil.

3. Roots are emerging through the pot's drainage holes.

FIGURE 10.16 Visual indicators of the need for repotting.

probably accounts for a majority of physiological disorders. It is an extremely important procedure to undertake periodically.

Preparing for Transplanting

Anticipating transplanting, the indoor gardener should water plants accordingly. The soil of most plants should be neither overly wet nor overly dry at the time of repotting. This condition allows the soil mass to remain intact if that is desirable or to be easily reworked if a more substantial overhaul is needed. Some plants, such as cacti and succulents, that normally require dry conditions should be allowed to dry out prior to repotting. This procedure creates a less favorable opportunity for the introduction of disease organisms into the newly repotted specimens.

Since repotting is a somewhat messy operation involving numerous materials, assemble and organize all necessary materials before commencing. The repotting site should be a place where spilled soil can be easily cleaned up. Although the kitchen sink may be a tempting spot, the introduction of soil into drains can quickly clog them. Either choose another location or place a filtering material over the drain inlet.

The necessary materials include fresh pots that are approximately 1 or 2 inches larger in diameter than the old containers. Other materials include the plants to be repotted, an adequate supply of potting medium, drainage materials to be placed in the bottom of the new container, tools, and newspaper or plastic on which to work. This preliminary organization will save much time and inconvenience.

The Potting Procedure

The first step in repotting is to remove the old plant from its container. If the plant has grown there for an extended period or is seriously root bound, it may be difficult to extricate. The first method is to tap the edge of the inverted container on the edge of the

working table, while holding the soil mass and top with one hand. A plant that is slightly moist will release easier than one that is either too dry or too wet. If this method fails, running a work knife around the perimeter of the soil mass will release the adhesion.

ROOT TREATMENT. On removal, examine the root system for both color and density. Roots that are dark and mushy indicate that the plant has been kept too wet. Healthy roots should appear white and covered with root hairs (Figure 10.17). If the roots are substantially encircling the soil mass, this condition will have to be corrected before repotting. Either pull the roots away from the soil mass and prune them back somewhat or make 2 or 3 ½-inch deep vertical cuts down the side of the soil mass. Either method will stimulate new secondary roots to develop after transplanting.

SELECTING THE CONTAINER AND MEDIUM. Keeping in mind that the plant should be repotted at its original depth, select a new container that will allow a couple of inches of drainage materials and new soil at

FIGURE 10.17 Healthy roots appear white and covered with root hairs (left); unhealthy ones are dark in color and mushy.

its bottom and ½ to 1 inch of new soil around the perimeter. Do not use containers any larger than this rule of thumb. Plant roots grow through the new soil and then grow along the pot surface. Since the absorptive root hairs are near the root tip, most of the "feeding" eventually occurs near the outer surface of the new soil. Adding more than a 1-inch thickness of new soil will simply add weight and bulk, while not effectively increasing the root system's ability to intake water and nutrients.

The potting medium should reflect the nature of the plant being repotted. The medium for plants requiring dry conditions should contain additional aggregate to facilitate drainage. Those needing constant moisture, such as ferns, should contain additional organic matter as a means of increasing water retention. In any case, the soil should be loose, friable, and well drained. Chapter Six examined the growing medium in detail.

STEPS IN REPOTTING. The first material put into the new pot should be the drainage material. This may be broken pot shards, commercial pot "chips" that are placed over the drainage hole or holes, or any other coarse material that will prevent soil erosion through the drainage holes. An inch or so of potting medium should be placed over the drainage material and gently firmed in. The plant is then placed into the center of the pot so that the top of the original soil mass rests at least an inch below the pot rim. This allows for a temporary reservoir during subsequent watering. Additional potting medium is then placed around the perimeter of the root ball and compressed gently with the thumbs periodically during filling. Little or no soil should be placed atop the old root mass if the original soil was left intact. Plants repotted deeper may suffer from rot occurring at the crown or from reduced aeration of the upper root system (Figure 10.18).

SOIL SURFACE CONFIGURATIONS.
The soil surface may be shaped to affect

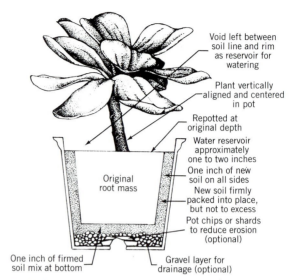

Void left between soil line and rim as reservoir for watering

Plant vertically aligned and centered in pot

Repotted at original depth

Water reservoir approximately one to two inches

One inch of new soil on all sides

New soil firmly packed into place, but not to excess

Pot chips or shards to reduce erosion (optional)

Original root mass

One inch of firmed soil mix at bottom

Gravel layer for drainage (optional)

FIGURE 10.18 Cross section of a plant properly repotted.

moisture in the vicinity of the plant crown. A concave shape, with the crown at the base of the depression, will extend the drying time at the crown. A mounded configuration, on the other hand, will dry quickly in the crown region. The latter procedure can be helpful with plants that are particularly susceptible to crown rot. Either practice should be very exaggerated since both slopes will flatten over time and watering.

In general, though, a flat configuration is adequate.

STAKING. Taller plants, those with a reworked soil mass, and plants such as some orchids that require very light soil mixes should be staked after repotting. Staking adds additional support to the top, thus increasing stability and reducing stress on the newly establishing root system. Stakes may be purchased from florists or garden centers, or they may be simple materials available at home. They typically consist of a simple stick inserted into the soil and secured to the plant with twist ties. Tying should be done loosely to avoid girdling the plant stem. More sophisticated stakes are available at garden centers that clip onto the pot's edge for a more secure anchoring. These are commonly used with orchids.

AFTERCARE. Since newly repotted plants need time to reestablish contact of their roots and root hairs with the soil, they are at some growth disadvantage. Consequently, the normal light intensity, watering, and fertilization should be reduced for a few weeks until active growth is again apparent. Plants should be kept away from direct sunlight, but in indirect light for continued photosynthesis. Since the root system contains wounds, reduced watering lessens the chances of disease problems. The reduced growth rate indicates a lower need for nutrition. This aspect of transplanting probably leads to more failure than any other part of the process.

Transplanting Seedlings or Cuttings

The principles involved in transplanting seedlings and cuttings are similar to those outlined above, but on a smaller scale. Since there is no easily identified pot size from which these are transplanted, more judgment is needed in determining the new container's size.

SEEDLING TRANSPLANTING. Seedlings are usually transplanted from a very loose material, such as vermiculite. They should be transplanted when the first two true leaves are fully developed. To remove new seedlings from the growing medium, grasp either a cotyledon or true leaf (not the fragile stem!) and pry up the root system from underneath with a flat label or stick. A small pot or container, approximately 2 inches or so in size, should be waiting with a small amount of potting medium in the bottom. The seedling is positioned in the new container with the top of the root system about ½ inch below the pot rim. While holding the seedling in position with one hand, fill the pot with potting medium with the free hand. The container should be filled level with potting medium,

then gently firmed in with the thumbs. The firming process will leave watering reservoir space in the top of the pot (Figure 10.19).

TRANSPLANTING CUTTINGS. Cuttings should be removed from the propagation bench or pot when roots are 1 to 1 ½ inches long. Pry them up in a similar fashion to seedlings, but the more durable stem of cuttings may be held rather than a leaf. Place into the new pot in a similar fashion to the procedure outlined for seedlings.

AFTERCARE OF SEEDLINGS AND CUTTINGS. Both newly transplanted seedlings and cuttings should be treated like transplanted established plants. Light, water, and fertilization rates should be reduced until the new plants are well established. Do not, however, allow them to dry out. Simply avoid overwatering. After the acclimation process is completed, move the new plants back into their normal light intensity, establish a watering regime, and fertilize gently at first. Fertilization applied at one-third to one-half rate will help prevent burning the young plants' tender root system.

SEASONAL CONSIDERATIONS

The successful culture of plants over a period of years requires a recognition of both plant and human annual cycles. Most foliage plants, being of tropical origin, respond to a wet/dry seasonal cycle. The monsoon season brings heavy and constant rainfall over a period of several months, followed by long periods of hardly any rain. During the dry season, tropical plants enter a dormancy similar to that of temperate region plants during the winter season. Cultural care of indoor plants, then, must respect this natural cycle of plant activity, as well as the temperate seasonal cycle in which the plants have been placed. Additionally, vacations and the seasonal habits of people necessitate appropriate changes in plant care. Let us look first at the plant requirements, then at

(a) Removal from seed bed. Grasp by leaves or cotyledons. Pry up roots with wood label.

(b) Potting. Hold seedling with crown one-half inch below pot rim. Fill in soil with free hand. Firm gently with thumbs.

FIGURE 10.19 Proper procedure for transplanting seedlings.

how we can accommodate seasonal human events.

Respecting Plant Cycles

CULTURE DURING INACTIVE GROWTH.

Many tropical, Southern Hemisphere plants respond to the stimuli of wet/dry climatic seasons, whereas the cycles of temperate Northern Hemisphere plants are triggered by warm/cold seasonal changes. Tropical plants, consequently, often exhibit a winter/ summer cycle in reverse of our temperate patterns. In other words, they undergo dormancy during our spring and summer and active growth during our fall and winter. In spite of this natural tendency, most indoor plants eventually convert to the temperate cycle, responding to the reduced light, lower temperatures, and shorter days of autumn and winter.

Plant growth does not stop during the dormant period; it simply slows down. Recalling the theory of limiting factors that we discussed in introducing Part Two, you will remember that the rate of growth can only be as rapid as the most limiting factor. Because the overall rate of growth is reduced by environmental factors during dormancy, watering and fertilization must be reduced accordingly. Failure to recognize this requirement can result in the noticeable decline or death of a plant.

The dormancy period will be characterized by slow growth and little initiation of new vegetative tissue. This phase of growth generally arrives gradually as the shorter, cooler days of autumn approach.

CULTURE DURING ACTIVE GROWTH.

As spring arrives, bringing longer days, higher temperatures, and brighter light conditions, active growth will usually resume. This may be determined by flushes of new vegetative growth or perhaps flowering. Because of the more advanced level of growth and the increased need for nutrition and water, cultural practices should reflect these needs. It is important to note that a plant entering active growth, but located in less than optimal environmental conditions, still will not benefit from optimum fertilization and watering. Cultural care should reflect the conditions of growth, as well as the season.

A common and beneficial practice early in the growing season, once outside temperatures have warmed sufficiently, is to place foliage plants outside for fresh air, additional light, and natural rainfall. They lend attractiveness to decks and patios as well. Like any abrupt change, however, this one may have severe consequences unless the transition is gradual. Even though a plant might have spent the winter on a southern window sill soaking up direct sunlight much of the day, the glass of the window has protected the plant from ultraviolet rays. Like humans, plants can sunburn from ultraviolet radiation until the foliage is acclimated. Placing plants directly outside into unfiltered sunlight will usually result in severe ultraviolet burning of the foliage. Consequently, plants must be moved outside gradually. This may be accomplished by exposing the plants to small amounts of light at first, gradually increasing the exposure, or by placing the plants in shady locations, gradually moving them into brighter spots (Figure 10.20).

In placing indoor plants outdoors for the summer, respect their natural cultural requirements. A plant that requires indirect sunlight, for instance, cannot endure full sun even during the beautiful days of spring. Place it in an area where the light conditions match its preferences. Pots containing indoor plants may be sunken into planting beds to stabilize the pot and to reduce the soil drying rate. It is best to fill planting beds intended for this purpose with clean, sharp sand to lessen the chances of exposing the root system to soil-borne organisms. Of course, the good drainage provided by the sand is a typical preference of most indoor species.

FIGURE 10.20 Sunburning plants through improper exposure to direct sunlight can put a fast end to attractive appearance.

A final consideration in moving plants outdoors for the summer is their heightened exposure to pests and diseases, particularly when they are located close to landscape plant materials. Prior to moving plants back indoors for the winter, a close inspection and a ten-day isolation period is desirable to spot pest or disease problems before they are brought into the proximity of other indoor plants.

Caring for Plants in Absentia

Several times a year, plants must be left on their own or in the care of someone other than the owner. Most people must be away from home, at least for a day or two, during the course of a year. These absences, even though short, can create circumstances in which the condition of a plant collection declines rapidly, nullifying months of conscientious care.

USING A CARETAKER. In leaving plants under the care of others, select someone who has as much knowledge of plant care as possible. The simple ability of a friend to determine when to water, for example, can mean the difference between healthy and declining plants on your return. Regardless of the qualifications of the attendant, leave written instructions for care and request daily checks. Your instructions might indicate which plants need particular attention with respect to watering, insect problems, or other requirements.

Prior to leaving, fertilize and water your plants if necessary so the caretaker at least will not have to fertilize. Misunderstandings of fertilizer rates or application techniques can either be disastrous or innocuous.

Also check for pest or disease symptoms before leaving home. Since another person may be less attached to the plants involved than the owner, he or she may not spot a problem as it develops. By the time you return, the infestation could have spread to

FIGURE 10.21 Wicks from a single source may water several plants.

several specimens in your collection. In general, it is best to simply leave watering in the hands of a friend, and even then, under clear and specific instructions.

LEAVING PLANTS UNATTENDED. This method can work satisfactorily for short periods of time if proper precautions are taken. Watering may be made "automatic" through the installation of wicks into the soil mass that draw water from a bucket or other container. Experiment with this watering technique prior to leaving home to ensure that it performs satisfactorily (Figure 10.21). Move plants to a less bright location, in order to reduce their water requirements, but not into so much darkness that leaf drop occurs.

Grouping all your plants together in one location, such as in the bathtub if light is sufficient, will raise the humidity and slow the soil drying rate. Do not invite rots and leaf spot problems by enclosing the collection in plastic to increase humidity. Also, be sure to inspect all plants for insects and diseases prior to clustering.

COMMERCIAL OPTIONS. An ideal though expensive method of vacation maintenance is to locate a commercial greenhouse that rents space for plant storage. These "plant hotels" are available, though many greenhouse owners do not want to bring in home plants because of the danger of introducing insects or diseases into their collections. On the other hand, visit a willing greenhouse to determine whether insect infestations are present that might be transferred to your plants.

Proper attention to seasonal variations and appropriate maintenance during times of absence can have a significant impact on the quality of an indoor collection. Particularly in situations where the plant specimens in question are numerous and large, the time and money spent on seasonal planning are wise investments.

FOR FURTHER READING

Bachman, T. "Maintenance Programs for Interior Gardens." Proceedings from the Symposium on the Use of Living Plants in the Interior Environment, Society of American Florists, 1975.

Conover, C., and R. Poole. "Fluoride Analysis of Materials Commonly Available as Nutritional Soil Amendments." *Foliage Digest 4*, 10 (1981).

Gaines, R. *Interior Plantscaping.* New York: Architectural Record Books, 1977.

Henley, R. "Tips for Growing Potted Ornamental Plants on Capillary Mats." *Foliage Digest, 4,* 12 (1981).

Joiner, J. *Foliage Plant Production.* Englewood Cliffs, N.J.: Prentice-Hall, 1981.

Kramer, P., and T. Kozlowski. *Physiology of Woody Plants.* New York: Academic Press, 1979.

Manaker, G. *Interior Plantscapes.* Englewood Cliffs, N.J.: Prentice-Hall, 1981.

Moody, E. "Water Relations in Ornamentals Affect Root Rot Diseases." *Foliage Digest 3*, 4 (1980).

Moore, R. "Watering Your Mix." Proceedings of the 1977 National Tropical Foliage Short Course, Florida Foliage Association.

Nebergall, W., F. Schmidt, and H. Holtzclaw, Jr. *General Chemistry.* 4th ed., Boston: D. C. Heath and Co., 1972.

Neel, P. "Soil and Water Relationships." Proceedings of the 1977 National Tropical Foliage Short Course, Florida Foliage Association.

Poole, R. "Leaching of Potting Media." *Foliage Digest 5*, 2 (1982).

Poole, R. "Soluble Salts Interpretation." *Foliage Digest 4*, 6 (1981).

Poole, R., and C. Conover. "Foliage Plant Cosmetics." *Foliage Digest 1*, 6 (1978).

Poole, R., and C. Robinson. "Moisture Stress of Foliage Plants." *Foliage Digest 4*, 6 (1981).

Quagliano, J., and L. Vallarino. *Chemistry.* Englewood Cliffs, N.J.: Prentice-Hall, 1969.

Raven, P., R. Evert, and H. Curtis. *Biology of Plants.* Worth Publishers, 1981.

Rayle, D., and L. Wedberg. *Botany: A Human Concern.* New York: Saunders College Publishing Holt, Rinehart and Winston, 1980.

Taylor, J. *Growing Plants Indoors.* Minneapolis, Minn.: Burgess, 1977.

PART THREE

USING PLANTS TO CREATE PLEASING INTERIORS

We now turn our attention from the technical aspects of growing indoor plants to the aesthetic considerations of using them effectively and attractively indoors. We begin with a chapter on interior design, written by landscape architect Robert McDuffie, who presents the elements of design and plant function in both an interesting and informative manner. The chapter concludes with instructions for carrying out your own design process, a consideration of special environments in which plants might be used, and a case study showing the steps of planning indoor plants as part of the interior environment. Chapter Twelve looks at design from a smaller viewpoint, emphasizing plant gardens that can be constructed as an accent feature indoors. The various types of plant gardens are discussed, with particular attention to their design and construction.

The discussion then turns to terrariums, that special type of enclosed garden, which can serve both as an attractive feature indoors as well as an educational laboratory. Building one can be as interesting as watching the completed project!

Then finally, Chapter Twelve looks at the host of plants that have become established gift ideas for particular seasons. Here, we examine the most popular gift plants and how, on receiving one of these, we can be successful in enjoying it to the fullest.

chapter eleven
plants and interior design*

Plants make people feel special. We feel good about a plant sprouting new leaves or just coming into bloom. Although harsh concrete may be all around us, its harshness is tempered at the sight of healthy green plants. Life may be hectic, but there sits the plant: a perfect example of peace, tranquility, and patient growth.

History is rich with examples of cultures bringing plants indoors. From the orangeries of Europe and Colonial America, to the modern indoor mall, from the single-family residence to the high-rise apartment, from every walk of life, everyone who enjoys nature has at some time attempted to bring it inside in the form of plants. In clay pots, old buckets, or paper cups, plants are an added dimension to interior design; they are living design elements. With these living organisms, however, comes the challenge of using them effectively. Because they are living and growing, they must be given special consideration.

Even the most experienced indoor gardeners struggle between satisfying a plant's innate cultural requirements and placing it in just the right place-to achieve a pleasing effect. That is the purpose of this chapter—to give insight into using plants in interior de-

*By Robert F. McDuffie, Associate Professor of Horticulture, Virginia Polytechnic Institute & State University.

sign, to consider environmental conditions with respect to their placement, and to provide helpful suggestions to you in creating an interior garden. The chapter concludes with an explanation of the design process and a look into a few common but special environments.

WHY USE PLANTS IN INTERIOR DESIGN?

Plants are used in interior spaces for a variety of reasons, ranging from the very functional, like screening views or articulating space, to that almost intangible feeling one gets from just being around plants. We will explore the uses of indoor plants in these two broad categories: (1) uses that appeal most to our aesthetic sense (those intangibles) and (2) functional uses.

Aesthetic Uses

Plants have qualities that are often difficult to express. J. Heriteau in *The Office Gardener* says it like this:

When there's new growth bursting out all over, everything fresh, green, and flourishing, the plants are little rockets of success going off every time you look at them. They make up for crowded elevators, crotchety bosses, grumpy partners, and mistakes somebody thinks you made. They even make up for mistakes you really did make.

Plants have a certain aesthetic appeal that most people find welcome. However, if you were to ask most people why they like plants, they would have difficulty explaining. Our exploration of the aesthetic uses of plants investigates why we enjoy plants so that we will be better equipped to use them effectively indoors.

PLANTS AND PEOPLE. J. Heriteau further suggests that plants act as equalizers in an environment. As our society has become more urban and space on the ground has become more limited, people have become increasingly separated from nature. On entering a city, the number of green plants in the landscape diminishes. Grasses, trees, and most other familiar plant life play a lesser role in the look of the cityscape as one moves farther downtown. As the green disappears, our desire for it intensifies. In homes, offices, and commercial establishments, plants have been brought inside to compensate for their absence outside (Figure 11.1).

A strong bond exists between plants and people. From plants comes our sustenance. Directly or indirectly, plants represent our only food source. The air we breathe contains the oxygen released by plants. On the other hand, they themselves benefit from the carbon dioxide that we exhale. The many facets of this mutually beneficial relationship are the basis for much of our love of nature and the underlying reasons why many people grow indoor plants.

DESIRE FOR THE EXOTIC. The plants that we bring indoors must be able to adapt to a warm, dry, and relatively dark environment. Thus, these plants are typically native to tropical regions. In general, as one draws closer to the equator, the foliage of plants becomes more interesting. The leaf sizes may be larger, their shapes more complex, the colors more exotic, and the texture more expressive.

People enjoy possessing the different, the

FIGURE 11.1 Because the number of outdoor plants rapidly diminishes as one travels farther downtown, people have made up for the loss by bringing them inside, such as in this indoor mall.

exotic. Historically, gardeners have prized unusual plants. In selecting plants for indoor use, therefore, there is a bonus: The plants that survive and flourish in the indoor environment are from regions that boast a substantial variety of colors, textures, and forms. The addition of plants to the indoor environment satisfies this basic desire to collect the unusual, the exotic (Figure 11.2).

SUBSTITUTION FOR LAND. As our society becomes more urban, an individual who has the desire to work with plants must, out of necessity, often live where there is little or no access to land. Since apartments and condo-

FIGURE 11.2 Plants from regions close to the equator are more foreign in appearance than those of more northerly climates. This is a delight to collectors who seek the unusual and the exotic.

miniums represent a substantial portion of today's housing, this separation of people and the land is solved, psychologically at least, by having one's own indoor garden. A person who normally would be outside working in the soil can find pleasure and enjoyment in working with plants indoors.

SEASON-FREE GARDENING. Many indoor plants can also be used outside, but only for a season. This is true for many bedding plants. To enjoy the blossoming effects of plants all year round, bring them inside. Because the climate indoors is a rather stable one without drastic seasonal changes, a

select number of plants will brighten up a house or office by the extension of their blooming season (Figure 11.3).

Another effect of the indoor climate that works to the advantage of the indoor gardener is that of forcing dormant bulbs into full bloom. When everything is gray outside, a room can be full of the bright colors and fragrant scents of spring.

THE SOOTHING BENEFITS OF GREEN. Finally, any indoor environment benefits aesthetically by the addition of the green color of plants. No matter what the color scheme is, plants will be a welcome addition to the design simply because of their green color.

Scientists have long agreed that green is a soothing color, and that it can have profound effects on the moods of people. In *Color,* edited by H. Varley, green is spoken of in the following terms:

Green is a most ambivalent hue. The colour of mould and decay, it is, nonetheless, the colour of life itself. Despite its traditional negative associations with nausea, poison, envy, and jealousy, on this green planet it is the colour of foliage, of rebirth in spring, of the silent abiding power of nature.

. . . Belief in green's beneficial effects on the eye has manifested itself down the ages from ancient Egyptian times, when green malachite was used as a protective eyeliner, to the green colour of twentieth-century office steno pads. Theatres since 1678 have afforded the customary backstage sanctuary called the Green Room to actors awaiting call or entertaining friends. The colour of the decor was thought to relieve the actors' eyes from the glare of stage lights.

Green is the most restful colour to the eye. The lens of the eye focuses green light almost exactly on the retina. In daylight, when the majority of colour receptor cells in the eye are working together, they are most sensitive to yellowish green light.

Perhaps the association of this colour with

FIGURE 11.3 Many plants that usually grow outside may be brought indoors to extend the length of flowering.

the qualities of stability and security stem from its ease of perception.

Functional Uses of Plants

Beyond aesthetic considerations, plants play an important role in the function of indoor spaces. They may act as ceilings to enclose spaces, or walls to open or restrict views and direct foot traffic. In general, they perform the duties of architectural elements such as wood and steel, and yet, as they carry out these functions, they retain their aesthetic grace and the softness for which they are matchless. Some of the functional uses of plants are outlined below as an aid in developing a design.

ENCLOSURE. Enclosure is a secure and private condition in which a person is surrounded on two or more sides by some kind

of barriers. An enclosure can be made in a large room by using plants as walls that partition off a section of the room (Figure 11.4). It is important to assess the degree of enclosure desired. Should it be a very tight space created with dense trees or hanging baskets? Or should the space be loosely defined with airy plants simply implying the enclosure? In either case, the degree of enclosure will affect the degree of privacy and the feeling of separation from adjacent areas. Plants are a means of creating private enclosures where people can enjoy their solitude and feel comfortable enough to read a good book or just relax.

ENLARGEMENT. Although plants can enclose a small private space in a large room, they also can make a small room seem larger by creating the illusion of increased

FIGURE 11.4 Here, plants act as walls to provide a quiet, secluded enclosure among larger, more open spaces.

striking plant is placed along the intended path to attract attention, the guest will require no other encouragement or direction and will take the intended route (Figure 11.5).

VIEW CONTROL. Controlling views has long been a technique of landscapers in outdoor situations. When an especially offensive view exists, they use plants to block it, or if there is an especially interesting one, they frame it to highlight its effect. The same can be accomplished inside. By closing off views into the kitchen, for example, with plants, an undesirable view is replaced with the view of an attractive plant. Framing a good view

space. By breaking up the room into parts, using plants to partition areas or obscure views, the room appears larger. A room without furniture always seems smaller until the furniture arrives. By adding plants to a room, the plants take up space and act as implied walls, giving the illusion of increased room.

DIRECT FOOT TRAFFIC. In a home or office, there is often a place where the traffic flow through a room just does not work well. It may be that guests on entering a home have a natural inclination to proceed straight, when the host would prefer they turn to the right. Plants can function well here to direct their movement. The judicious placement of the proper plant material successfully redirects the flow of traffic via the more desirable route. The end result has been accomplished in an unobtrusive, pleasant way. Furthermore, if a particularly

FIGURE 11.5 Indoor plants can be used to direct foot traffic. Here, they clearly mark the intended route, preventing one from being disoriented.

of the interior, or framing the view out a window that sports an interesting vista, will enhance any home. Be careful that the plants used to frame views are "neutral" visually. Plants with especially interesting foliage or spectacular blossoms will distract the attention from the view itself (Figure 11.6).

CLEAN AIR. In considering the functional uses of indoor plants, it would be regrettable to omit the role that plants play in refreshing the air we breathe. As a part of their life processes, plants take in carbon dioxide and expel oxygen in greater quantities than they themselves require. What a perfect combination! While our bodies are hard at work making the air stuffy, our plants are just as laborously working to make it fresh again.

ACOUSTICAL CONTROL. Plants absorb and buffer undesirable sound. Plants, drapes, and other acoustically absorbent materials reduce the noise in a household substantially. Although their impact alone may not be great, plants used in combination with other materials can aid in reducing noise.

REDUCE HARSH ENVIRONMENT. Modern construction techniques often leave us with surroundings that are less than personal. Offices and institutions frequently have bare, uninteresting walls and stark floors. Here is where plants can have an especially noticeable impact on the quality of our surround-

FIGURE 11.6 Plants are used here to frame and therefore enhance an already spectacular view. Note that the plants do not themselves demand attention, but rather focus attention on the view beyond.

FIGURE 11.7 A room that might often be cold and uninviting now appears more hospitable with the appropriate use of plants.

ings. By introducing rich color and textural variety, plants can "warm up" the visual coldness of glass, chrome, and concrete. This softening of indoor spaces creates a more conducive environment for people (Figure 11.7).

THE ELEMENTS OF DESIGN

A group of elements exist that are the essence of all design. Whether it is the design of a musical composition, the design of a building complex or the design of interior spaces using plants, these elements are present. In this section, we will explore these elements as they apply to plants in interior design and give suggestions on their practical use.

Texture

Indoor plants are often referred to as foliage plants. The reason for this is that their beauty lies principally in their foliage, rather than in their ability to produce fruit or flower. One of the more distinctive characteristics of foliage plants is the variety of textures available (Figure 11.8).

The word **texture** is derived from the Latin word *texere*, meaning to weave. Immediately, we see the correlation between textures and textiles and consequently the connection between textures and surface qualities. Textures are to be felt, but we often see textures instead, so our mind instantaneously "feels" the surface for us. It is a rather complex process: Seeing textures is something that causes a mental reaction and we take notice.

The usual description of texture is simply fine, medium, or coarse. Unfortunately, this is a rather weak description system because there are many other aspects to note. F. Bell Robinson offers five distinctive factors in *Planting Design:* (1) size of the leaves, (2) spacing of the leaves, (3) shape and division of the leaves, (4) surface quality of the leaves, and (5) length and stiffness of the petioles.

SIZE OF THE LEAVES. The size of the leaf is the factor on which our usual description of fine, medium, or coarse is based. Those plants with larger leaves are said to have a coarse texture; those with small leaves have a fine texture. The smaller the individual leaf, the finer the texture. With foliage plants, leaf size can vary from several feet in length to fractions of an inch. This is one of their more fascinating aspects: In northern latitudes where leaf size outside becomes smaller and smaller in evergreen plants, inside leaves may grow to be 10 or 20 times the size of their native relatives outside.

Coarseness and fineness are also relative. If one is close to a plant with large leaves, it appears to have a coarse texture. On the other hand, distance creates an appearance of fineness (Figure 11.9).

SPACING OF THE LEAVES. Although the leaves of two different plants may be identical in size, other factors come into play in creating textural quality. One of these is the spacing or density of the leaves. Some plants have larger voids or gaps between leaves than others. The distinction that smaller gaps, for example, create is due in part to the shadows from the leaves, causing darker areas within the plant, thereby accentuating the lighter leaf surfaces through contrast. Often, the density of the leaves will depend on the amount of light available for the plant. If a plant is placed in a location where it receives less than its optimum light requirement, but the amount of light is still within its range of tolerance, the plant may compensate by producing less leaves and, consequently, a more open texture.

SHAPE AND DIVISION OF THE LEAVES. The shape and division of the leaves is perhaps the most expressive characteristic of leaf texture and is often simply referred to as **textural expression.** Each leaf has a distinctive shape. The line of the edge of the leaf may be straight or circular, toothed or

FIGURE 11.8 The variety of textures in indoor plants is almost endless, providing solutions to almost any design problem.

FIGURE 11.9 Up close these plants have a relatively coarse texture. When viewed from a distance, however, they appear to be quite fine textured.

FIGURE 11.10 The expressive nature of this plant's texture is evident in the subtle geometric patterns created by the pattern of the leaves.

smooth, or any number of different shapes and combinations of shapes. As one sees the entire plant, the interplay of the lines created by the leaves may appear to be geometric or even freeform. In many plants, the essential design character of the entire plant is expressed in these lines. If the plant has very narrow and long leaves, its textural expression is quite different than one with short, round leaves (Figure 11.10).

SURFACE QUALITY OF THE LEAVES. The fourth factor, the surface quality of the leaves, refers to the topographic features of the leaves: dull versus shiny, smooth versus

rough. This characteristic affects how noticeable a plant is. In most cases, plants with shiny or glossy leaves tend to stand out. Their surface catches one's eye much like the reflective surface of water. Those plants with surfaces that are not reflective are better suited as background plants or subtle accents (Figure 11.11).

LENGTH AND STIFFNESS OF THE PETIOLES. The last factor of texture has to do with how the leaves react to air or other movement, indicating a special quality of texture. If the plant has rather stiff petioles, the textural appearance is not as soft in the

FIGURE 11.11 Notice how the plant with the shiny leaves catches one's eye: The plants with duller leaves serve as background plants.

wake of air movement as in a plant with flexible petioles, exhibiting movement of the leaves at the slightest breeze.

In summary, texture is more than a simple matter of coarse, medium, or fine. Understanding the role of the size, spacing, shape, and surface quality of the leaves along with the stiffness of the petioles gives the designer a greater appreciation of plant textures and opens doors to more effective design possibilities. Once familiar with these factors, the designer can begin to make some basic decisions about using different textures. Below are a few suggestions.

USE PLANTS IN MASS. Using the same species in a mass enhances the effect of an individual plant's texture. Unless a single plant has ample foliage to give enough expression to the texture, more than one plant should be used. This is especially critical if the plants are to act as a backdrop for more spectacular plants or other important accessories. The decision to use plants in mass or as individuals rests on whether there is enough space and the role for which the plant texture is intended: either for a background or as a focal point.

PLANTS AS FOCAL POINTS. A focal point based solely on texture can be easily achieved by choosing plants whose textures contrast. Backgrounds are usually served better by small-leaved specimens, whereas coarser textures function well as focal points (Figure 11.12). For the best effect, choose textures for focal points and backgrounds from opposite ends of the textural spectrum. In general, as the distance between two plants on the textural spectrum increases, the more obvious the focal point will be.

TEXTURES AND ROOM SIZE. Small rooms are not well suited to coarsely textured plants. On the other hand, plants with fine textures can create the illusion of increased space in a small room. Our eyes do not notice individual leaves but rather perceive a mass of leaves much like the effect created by intricately patterned wallpaper. Conversely, wallpaper with large figures can dwarf a small room, as can coarsely textured plants.

ARCHITECTURAL CLUES. Our final suggestion concerning the use of plant textures is to take clues from the architecture involved. If the room seems heavy and cold because of the materials used, add plants with textures that are light and warm. Look at the surroundings. When some element in the room is extreme and overpowering, balance it with a texture from the other extreme. Walls of stone or concrete deserve nothing less than a plant with a light, airy texture (Figure 11.13).

FIGURE 11.12 Notice how the plant with the coarse texture stands out among those with finer textures. The contrast creates an interesting focal point.

FIGURE 11.13 These fine-textured plants provide just the right contrast with the coarseness and heaviness of the surrounding walls, achieving a welcome balance.

Color

Just as there is an unlimited variety of textures among foliage plants, so it is also with color. The array of colors found in foliage plants would rival the palette found in any art museum. There are so many variations, not only in green, but also in other hues, that having so many choices may be more of a problem than a solution. In designing interiors, four principles are important in the use of color: (1) color to achieve focal points, (2) color as a unifying element, (3) color to create or enhance a mood, and (4) color of plants with other furnishings.

COLOR TO ACHIEVE FOCAL POINTS.

Since focal points have only been discussed briefly, a closer look at what a focal point is and how it functions is warranted. One of

the best ways to define focal point is to look at a photograph for only a few seconds and then turn away. Try to recall what you have seen. Most people will then state the first thing that their eyes focused on. That initial item recalled will be the primary focal point in that photograph.

The way we perceive focal points in photography is the same as for interior design. When a person comes on a scene indoors, there should be something in the scene that immediately captures the attention. There may be more than one focal point in a scene, but they should be in some order of prominence. That is, one point should dominate and then lead the eye to the next point, and it in turn should lead the eye to the next, and so on. Studies have shown that the eye movements of visitors in art galleries take on certain patterns when viewing works of art. The viewer's eyes are first attracted to the strongest point of a painting, then move to the next point of interest, and then to the next, until the cycle is complete. Good design using plants should take on similar characteristics.

Color, texture, and form can all be the means of establishing a focal point, but color is the most effective method of focusing our attention. We must be cautious, therefore, in our use of color. A common tendency is to put the most spectacularly colored plants in one room or scene. Unfortunately, this leads to visual confusion because too many rival focal points have been established, making it difficult for our eyes to pick up any pattern or hierarchy of order. Work for one principle focal point, with others being of less importance.

COLOR AS A UNIFYING ELEMENT. Here is where foliage plants have their greatest impact on interior design. Because the majority of indoor plants are predominantly green, plants may serve as unifying elements in any room. They act as a background for a variety of other color schemes, since the green of plants is a rather neutral color. Another method of using plants as unifying elements is to splash a particular color throughout the design. It may be a subtle red, used in some spots as the blossom of a plant and in other places as a part of the foliage color.

COLOR TO CREATE OR ENHANCE A MOOD. Research on color theory indicates that colors affect our emotions to the point of transporting us into different moods. Michael Doyle in *Color Drawing* addresses the issue of color enhanced moods. Although his comments are directed toward drawings, they are nonetheless applicable to interiors. He states that:

Many general moods have commonly accepted color equivalents. When designing some-thing functional, such as a public environ-ment, you can begin to establish a direction for your color composition by eliminating colors that are not appropriate. You proba-bly would not allow dark, weak . . . colors to dominate a room intended to feel cheerful and airy, for example.

Contrasts in hue, value, and chroma will also help determine the mood of the com-position. Strong contrast, especially in the values and chromas of the colors used, tends to be more stimulating and exciting, while subtle contrasts seem to impart a more soothing, quiet atmosphere.

Taking advantage of the ability of color to create mood is of primary concern in the use of indoor plants. Choose plant material that reflects the mood established by the furnish-ings of the room or generate a mood based solely on the color of the plants.

COLOR OF PLANTS WITH OTHER FURNISHINGS. It is important that plants used in interiors have the appearance that they "fit" into the overall color scheme of a room. If the plants chosen for a particular room have colors that are entirely foreign to the colors already in the room, they will look as though they do not belong. Plant color must complement the furnishings of a room but not necessarily duplicate it. For example, if the sofas in an office or home are dark green, a poor choice of plant color would be more dark green. A better choice would be a color that provides an interesting contrast but still relates to the dark green back-ground.

Foliage plants offer unlimited variety of color and color combinations. The problem lies in choosing colors that promote harmony and create the intended mood. Proceed with caution. Too much variation in the color scheme may spell disaster. Create strong focal points and back them up with ample supporting elements. Strive for color to strengthen unity and enhance the mood of the room. Remember that poorly chosen colors often compete with one another, resulting in a disturbing, rather than settling effect.

Form

The architect's motto of "form follows function" implies that the form, or the composition of an object, should relate to its function. Form has many of the connotations of shape and the terms are often used interchangeably. References to physically attractive people may make mention of their form. Form in music is usually based on a sequence of melodic material occurring at different points in time. Form in a painting is based on a two-dimensional interpretation of three-dimensional objects. Form has many meanings and facets, all of which are not totally applicable to the use of indoor plants in interior design. The reason for this is that, in most cases, indoor plants are treated as accessories, certainly important accessories, just as are lighting, floor coverings, and other aspects of interiors. We will discuss form as it relates to individual plants, groupings of plants, and finally the overall design of plants in a room. Along the way, we will touch on some of the areas related to form, such as balance, line, and scale.

INDIVIDUAL PLANT FORM. Nature has provided us with unlimited variety in the form of individual plants, just as she did with texture and color. As one can readily see from examples of plant forms in silhouette, the possibilities are endless, and because plants are living and growing, their forms are constantly in a state of change.

The three plant form groups based solely on size are: (1) trees, (2) shrubs, and (3) groundcovers. These classifications are the same for landscape plants since indoor plants in their native region are landscape plants.

Although most homes and offices have limitations as to the size of trees used, there are many occasions on which small trees may be used. If the ceiling height is ade-

FIGURE 11.14 Trees create a dramatic impact on a room. Here, for example, the trees make the room seem more comfortable despite the very high ceilings.

quate, very large trees can be employed. The effect of a single, large tree inside is very dramatic. On the other hand, a small tree can also have a profound effect on a room of more limited size (Figure 11.14).

Shrubs or plants that range in size from about 1 ½ feet to 4 or 5 feet make up another category. Often, a tree in its early stages of growth functions as a shrub. Shrubs can act as room dividers or simply as focal points, to be seen and admired, but on a smaller scale than trees.

Those indoor plants that function as groundcovers by far get the most use. Vines or plants that grow less than a foot in height are categorized as groundcovers. Because they take the shape of their container or the shape of the object over which they grow, the potential for creative forms is virtually endless (Figure 11.15).

FIGURE 11.15 The plants in these hanging baskets would be categorized as groundcovers. However, they can mimic the effect of a tree without losing precious floor space.

COLLECTIVE PLANT FORM. Many plants are attractive and function well standing or hanging alone. The size of the room will dictate, to a great extent, the size of the plants used. In a smaller room, a scattering of solitary plants throughout the room may be very appropriate (Figure 11.16). But often, when space allows, it is advantageous to use more than one plant in a group. Recalling the discussion of the functional uses of plants, in order to accomplish a certain function such as screening out views or dividing up a room, it may be necessary to use multiple plants (Figure 11.17). In such cases, here are some suggestions in approaching the design.

Choosing Plants. The·choice of plants for a composition may be difficult. Here are two suggestions for making initial decisions. First, avoid too much variety in the group.

FIGURE 11.16 In this room, because of its limited size, strategically placed plants create a subtle, but important, effect.

FIGURE 11.17 In order to accomplish the function desired, more than one plant was necessary. Now individual plants in the group diminish in importance, whereas the importance of the group increases.

FIGURE 11.18 The sameness of container unifies the composition of these plants. Containers that are the same or similar can serve as a background element, thereby accentuating the plants in them.

Too many spectacular plants will draw attention away from the composition and bring back the problem of too many focal points. Choose plants that relate to each other. The leaf shapes may be similar but with marked differences in leaf size. Or they may be similar in color but with contrasting textures. Try not to have plants that contrast in every aspect.

The second suggestion is to be bold in using multiples of the same plant in a group. These plants may act as a background for other contrasting plants. A large splash of a distinct color or texture is always welcome.

Often, we become too concerned with the plants and are remiss about their settings. Since most indoor plants live in pots, we cannot forget about the pots as design elements. In designing a composition of many plants, sometimes the pots should take a less dominant role. Having all the plants in a composition in the same kind of pot or basket yields importance to the plant, providing a background for the composition. The con-

tainer then serves as a unifying element in the design (Figure 11.18).

The Group of Plants Should Take on the Form of Its Intended Function. Again, form should follow function, and it is easier to create a functional form with several plants than it is with just one. Using more than one plant lends more flexibility to the collective shape of the group. Consequently, the group will be able to perform its intended function more efficiently. Another advantage of groupings versus individuals is that the group can be employed to handle a bigger job. And finally, the plants in a group are valued aesthetically not only for their individual forms, but for their collective effect as well (Figure 11.19).

Take Care in Designing with Trees. This is not to say that trees are inappropriate in a design. Quite the contrary, trees are often the most important element of the composition. But because they are in comparatively small pots, trees may appear to be top-heavy and out of balance. If the crown

FIGURE 11.19 This composition of plants is designed to function in a situation in which a large mass is required. The composition also is designed to be appealing aesthetically, lending attention to the composition itself rather than the individual plants in it.

of the tree hangs to one side, the imbalance may even be exaggerated. The solution is to balance out the top by adding more visual "weight" at the bottom. By using ground-covers or small shrubs around the base of the tree, thus giving the composition a stronger visual base, there is enough mass to counterbalance the top and provide a pleasing composition.

The Role of Individual Plants in a Composition. An artist, beginning a new painting, begins with a general concept of what the finished work will be. Rough sketches are usually the first step, outlining the placement of figures and objects on the canvas. The individual figures are less important than how they appear together as a group. The painting must be evaluated for its compositional beauty, rather than for

each individual part in it. So it is with groups of plants; they must be visualized as a group, rather than as individuals. Each plant's beauty becomes less important individually and more important as part of the beauty of the whole. Our final suggestion concerning the design of plants collectively, then, is to create interest through collective composition of focal points, background elements, and relationships between individual parts. Avoid a design dependence on individual plants.

THE PROCESS OF DESIGN WITH INDOOR PLANTS

Think for a moment of an indoor place with many plants that you have visited recently. The plants did not overwhelm you; instead, they seemed to blend in just right. You felt comfortable, not crowded, and you had a good feeling because all the plants seemed to be thriving. Such a situation is not always easily achieved, but by following some basic guidelines, you will be able to duplicate this comfortable atmosphere. In this segment, we will outline three simple design steps to follow and then explain how it is done in an example. The steps to follow are these: (1) decide what you want to accomplish with plants in the room, (2) determine possibilities the room has for plants, and (3) choose plants that will both fit your purpose and thrive.

Conceptualizing the Design

The first step is deciding what is to be accomplished in the room with the use of plants. With eyes closed, try to visualize what the room could look like with plants. This exercise should be an aid in coming up with an idea or concept about what the room will feel like. Will it project a warm and intimate feeling? Will it have clean and crisp lines? Is the room to be full of light and spacious? Do the plants dominate, or are they a subtle part of the room's design? These questions and others will help in formulating a basic concept about what kind of atmosphere the room will exude.

The process of formulating a concept may be better understood through illustration. Suppose the room to be designed with plants is a home library. The atmosphere is comfortable and inviting. The colors of the room are rich and warm, but subdued. In this room are found the crisp lines of book shelves, and the seating is comfortable but not casual. Having examined the room to arrive at these conclusions, you next decide the role that plants are to play.

In formulating a basic design concept, the role that plants play in the design is of paramount importance. The following analogy will be helpful in this important step. In most classical and popular music, one usu-

ally finds a combination of two elements: melody and accompaniment. The accompaniment acts in a supportive role. It does not drown out the melody, but adds excitement and interest. On the other hand, the melody should be easily heard and recognizable above the accompaniment. So it is with plants. In a given room, each plant must function as part of either the melody or the accompaniment. Should plants dominate the scene like a melody, placing all the furniture and accessories in a subordinate role, or should they simply be the accompaniment, providing an interesting background for the artwork or furniture? The former is a good solution for people on tight budgets. Among sparse furniture, plants fill in the gaps and make up for a lack of furnishings. In most cases, however, plants will be used as accessories and should fit into the overall scheme for the room.

So then, in formulating a concept about the library, the design attempts to complement the atmosphere already established. The role of the plants will be purely supportive. The number of plants, their placement, and the actual plants chosen should relate to the concept. A delicate plant with lacy pink blossoms obviously does not fill the bill. Perhaps dark foliage is more appropriate with fine and loose textures and a regular repetition of line in the leaves. These qualities better accentuate the room's geometry and soften the mood.

As part of forming a concept, look for the functions that a plant or group of plants could perform. Is there a problem area that needs hiding? Are there traffic patterns that do not fit into the overall scheme? In the segment on functional uses of plants, we outlined other considerations. Look for any problems that can be solved by using plants.

Examining the Environment

The second step is to examine the possibilities that the room itself presents for plant survival and growth. Assess the amount of light available, either natural or artificial. Practically all other factors such as soil and moisture can be altered at little expense. Light, however, is dependent on the existing architecture. The inclusion of artificial lighting as a light source is possible, but can be costly.

In some cases, especially larger areas such as indoor shopping malls, it is wise to look for sources of water. Is the nearest hose bib 100 yards away? A water source that is too far will make watering difficult and time-consuming.

Consider also the human factor. Will the plants be handled often and, if they are, will the frequent movement be detrimental to their health? Using the information from Chapter Eight, "The Climate Indoors," you should be able to pinpoint areas in the room that will support specific foliage plants.

Blending Concept with Environment

With some idea as to what the room is to look like and what functions are to be reinforced by plants, as well as outlining the room's limitations, the final step is to choose plants. By examining the functions to be performed, answer these questions: Should the plants be short or tall, in pots on the floor, or in hanging baskets? Once this has been decided, begin looking for plants with texture, form, and color that relate to each other and the furnishings of the room.

The final decision about the choice of plants involves the environmental conditions where the plants are to be placed. If there is sufficient light and other conditions are correct, the design is complete. If the plant cannot remain healthy because of low or even high light conditions, return to the drawing board and find one that will. Consider the process of designing with indoor plants to be cyclical, in that each step along the way depends on the other steps. If one step cannot be resolved, the previous steps should reflect a change.

Case Study

The following example will aid in your understanding of the process of designing with plants. The setting is a typical townhouse apartment. As Figure 11.20 indicates, the house is oriented such that sunlight enters from both the front and the back: The front receiving morning sunlight, whereas the back receives the majority of light in the afternoon. In the front yard are several shade trees, so that the amount of light entering is much less than from the backyard that has no interfering trees. The amount of sunlight available is shown in a diagram in Figure 11.21.

The design of the living room has several major flaws. There are access points from each of the four corners of the room. In a small room, this creates some major obstacles to arranging furnishings. In the front are the main entrance and the entrance to the upstairs. In the rear of the room, there is access to the dining room and kitchen, and in the other corner are three doors: one to a hall closet, one to a downstairs bathroom, and finally one to the furnace area. Because of these access points, the alternatives are limited as far as room arrangement is concerned. Figure 11.22 shows that there are three major paths through the living room: one from the front door to the stairs, one from the dining room to the stairs, and one from the front door to the dining room. These major routes, as well as the required access to the corner closets and bath, present an obstacle to creating a living room that provides family members a close, enclosed space or a comfortable place to entertain guests. The essence of the problem is that major traffic patterns divide up the room into too many small, unmanageable spaces.

The other facts relating to the physical setting are the existing furniture, which includes a couch, loveseat, two end tables, oriental chest, piano, and lighting (three

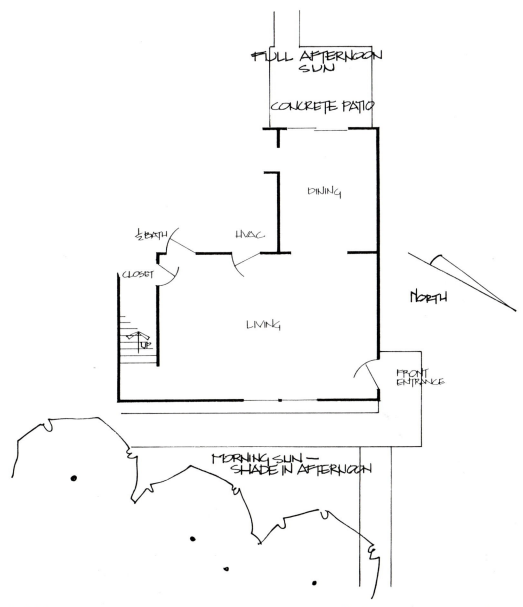

FIGURE 11.20 Note how the physical setting around the house, as well as the house's orientation, affect the use of plants inside.

lamps). The style of the furniture is oriental, with the couch and loveseat having bright earth tone figures set on a black background. With all this in mind, we have enough information to begin making some primary decisions about the design of the room and the role of plants in that room.

The first step in the process is to develop a concept for the room and the role of plants in it. Because the furnishings are oriental with

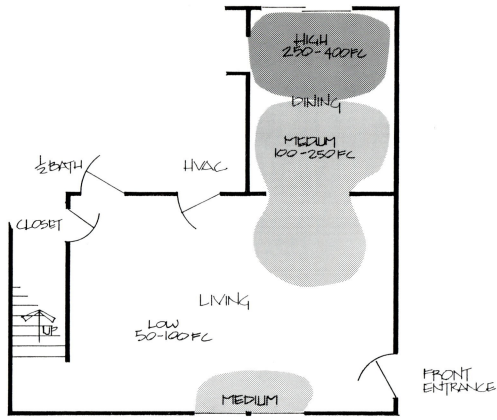

FIGURE 11.21 The drawing here shows the amount of sunlight in foot-candles available for the plants.

bright patterns in the couch and loveseat, the plants must reflect the reserved and delicate qualities of oriental art and design. The plants will be finely textured and the colors will be subdued and muted, to avoid overpowering the pattern in the seating. Perhaps if screening is needed at eye level, a small tree with delicate branching could be utilized to reflect the oriental qualities of the room as well as to function as a screen.

Once the concept has been firmly established, the next step is to examine the functional aspects of the room. In light of the apparent problems of access, it appears that the solution lies in an arrangement of furniture that would appear somewhat unconventional. Figure 11.23 shows how the

furniture is arranged to provide easy access routes and still allow the living space to function as a semiprivate, partially enclosed conversation space. The piano is placed to one side, providing enough room for a person to play and another person to walk past. Figure 11.23 also reveals how the room now has two principle spatial units: a corridor leading from the front door to the dining room and a larger space that is actually the living space.

In order to reinforce the division of the space, plants will be placed strategically to aid in defining the living space and to partially screen off the dining room, thereby yielding more privacy. In addition to the plants used for screening and spatial defini-

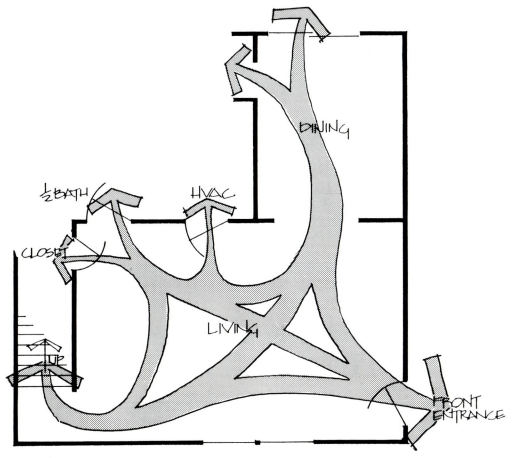

FIGURE 11.22 The required circulation paths are indicated in the diagram above. Note the number of different paths and their route.

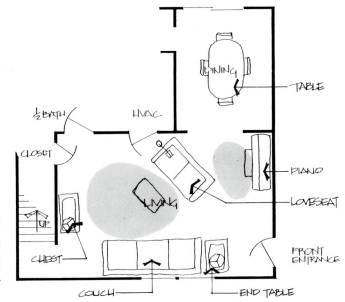

FIGURE 11.23 Here, the importance of furniture arrangement is demonstrated with respect to the room's function. Notice how the room is now divided into two distinct spaces.

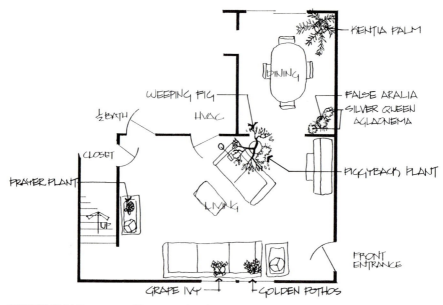

FIGURE 11.24 Represented here are the choices of plants for the townhouse.

tion, other plants will be scattered about the room as background plants. The color of foliage for these plants will be a subtle dark green so that they do not outshine the existing furnishings. Because the furnishings are in bright colors, plant color is critical: The plants must complement rather than detract from the ornate furnishings.

The final step is to choose specific plants for specific locations. Figure 11.24 indicates our choices, which not only fit the functions desired, but also aesthetically complement the decor of the room.

SPECIAL ENVIRONMENTS

The way that plants are used indoors will vary in every setting because the factors that govern their use in each place are unique. We can, however, categorize to a certain extent some settings that deserve special consideration. These are (1) homes, (2) offices, and (3) commercial establishments. Each environment has its own particular requirements for the choice, placement, and growth of plants that make it possible to address the environment as a group.

Plants in the Home

The home environment best demonstrates the many reasons why people like plants. Used in a home, plants can offer much in return for little time given them. For some people, they are a hobby, whereas other people enjoy them simply for their beauty. What is it that makes using plants in a residence different from other environments? On the following pages, we will discuss some of the reasons that make the home a special place for plants and also the reasons why the home places limitations on their use.

PERSONALIZED ATTENTION. The most overriding factor that makes the home one of the best environments for plants is that once in a home, they become prized possessions. People have a natural tendency to take just a little better care of the things they own. And because of this, plants at home receive the most personalized care and attention. To many people, plants are a hobby. They collect as many different kinds as will grow in the space available.

BETTER GROWING ENVIRONMENT. Besides the personal care available, the home also has greater flexibility in creating a more suitable environment for plants. The relative humidity can be altered more readily than in an office or a store, and because of the architectural differences between offices, stores, and residences, the quality of light is better. The fact that the growing environment is better is a boon to the collector. Not only does the home provide a setting suitable for better care of plants, it provides an environment favorable to a greater variety of plants.

The home is also more conducive to bringing unhealthy plants back to their original state and provides the opportunity to propagate new plants. In fact, a good idea is to designate a certain window location as a propagation area.

UNIFIES INTERIOR WITH EXTERIOR. Bringing plants inside may provide the occasion to enhance the unity between the interior of a home with its surroundings. If the house is located on a forested lot, for example, the inclusion of plants indoors creates a visual connection to plants outside. The home is perhaps the best place where nature can be "brought" indoors visually.

POISONOUS PLANTS. Special problems may arise in a residence that would not be a problem for plants elsewhere. First, some tropical plants have foliage or other plant -parts that are poisonous (see Chapter Twelve). This is a hazard especially to young children. Another problem limited to the home is that of plants versus pets or vice versa. In the first case, the plants may poison the pet, whereas in the second case, the pet may abuse the plants. Plants will often suffer by household animals climbing in them or

eating the foliage. While the solution lies in proper training of the pet, the indoor gardener should be aware of the potential difficulties.

ARCHITECTURAL LIMITATIONS. In the home, it is often difficult to grow plants of significant size unless the architecture lends itself to them. The average home today has 8-foot ceilings and the top of most doors and windows never exceeds 7 feet in height. If the sole source of light is natural sunlight from windows and doors, plants may never reach above 6 feet.

Skylights, one solution to this problem, are finding their way into many homes. Skylights allow sunlight into many locations in the house where only artificial light was available before. One room that has traditionally been very limited in terms of plant selection is the bath. A most favorable environment for plants with respect to humidity, a bath with a skylight in it offers good lighting and high humidity, the two growth factors that are most difficult to manipulate.

CONSIDER THE OCCUPANTS. When designing with plants in a residence, it is important to consider who the plants are for. What kind of family unit is it? How many children and what are their ages? Because the plants must be maintained, will there be someone to take charge of the task? Are there areas that do not function well that could be improved by judicious placement of plants? These and other questions must be considered in order to make decisions about placement and choices of plants for the home environment.

The Office Environment
The role of plants in an office is a rather complex one because of the diversity of office sizes and decors. Office environments also present problems to plants because of their lower light levels, often limiting the choices of plants. In any office environment, however, there is a place for plants to carry out

FIGURE 11.25 This office environment is a better place to work and do business because of the plants. What can often be a sterile environment is made more pleasant with the addition of plants.

specific functions and add life to the space (Figure 11.25).

The one kind of office decor that genuinely requires the extensive use of plants is a so-called open system. Spaces are defined only by partitions that are usually about 5 feet tall. Functions are centralized. For example, file cabinets may be in only one location. Plants are used in the open system as functional elements to screen views, to define and soften spaces, and ultimately to add life to what can often be a sterile environment.

There are unique problems that accompany office environments that must be taken into consideration. A list of suggestions follows for designing with plants in the office environment.

USE PLANTS TO REINFORCE THE EFFECT OF EXISTING PARTITIONS. In a large office, low partitions function well when employees are sitting. But when one stands up, an ocean of these partitions may be visible.

Strategically placed plants can break up the large space into smaller units. They also add welcome variety from the repetition of many similar partitions.

USE PLANTS TO UNIFY. An office is often a hodgepodge of different styles and colors of furnishings, leading to visual chaos. Using the same plants throughout the space helps to tie everything together visually, thereby unifying the look of the office.

PLANTS FOR TRAFFIC CONTROL. In many offices, the traffic patterns may be ill defined because of the open environment. In order to minimize the number of paths through the office or to direct the routes of paths, plants can serve as obstacles, thus directing movement and ultimately defining where people can feel free to walk.

TAKE ADVANTAGE OF CEILING HEIGHTS. Offices often have higher ceiling heights than the traditional 8-foot residential height. If light levels permit, the opportunity may present itself for the use of trees. The impact of a tree in such an environment is significant.

LOWER LIGHT LEVELS. Typically, many offices not only have lower light levels, but also the quality of light is inferior to that of natural sunlight. Use care in obtaining correct information about the amount of light available and choose plants that will flourish in such an environment.

HEATING SCHEDULES. In many large office buildings, the heat is turned down at night and on weekends. This condition will affect the choice of plants, since many common varieties are susceptible to damage from even moderately low temperatures.

Commercial Environments
In recent years, shopping has taken on an entirely different posture. All over the country, indoor shopping malls have sprung up. These temperature-controlled commercial gi-

FIGURE 11.26 In this temperature-controlled shopping mall, plants are used in much the same way they would be used outside as landscape plants. The trees, shrubs, and groundcovers make shopping an experience that the customer will want to repeat many times over.

ants have revolutionized the way we shop. Because they are totally indoors, however, these malls must be made more pleasant and more conducive to shopping. The solution is obvious: Bring the outside inside. Now, most indoor malls integrate plants as part of their design (Figure 11.26). Plants are the equalizers, the means of making people feel comfortable. In the shopping mall, we see at play all the aesthetic reasons for using plants, as well as many of the functional ones.

Designing these large areas is very similar to designing with plants outdoors. One has the same set of elements to work with: trees, shrubs, and groundcovers. Reexamine the section on the functional uses of plants to review how they can be used.

Unfortunately, the commercial environment is not one that is especially hospitable to plants. It has many of the problems of an office environment plus a few more. Even though the architecture is currently being designed to produce a better plant environment, in most cases the heavy traffic is taking a toll on the plants. Coffee poured in the soil, children (or adults) picking leaves, or shopping bags placed on top of plants are commonplace in any mall. The solution cannot lie in making the users more careful, but rather in using plants that can withstand this kind of punishment. Obviously, given these prerequisites, the field of plants to choose from is narrowed.

The most important difference between plants in commercial environments as opposed to the others mentioned is that commercial plants must be durable, being able to withstand almost any kind of abuse.

SUMMARY

Plants have played and will continue to play an essential role in making indoor spaces more pleasant for living, working, and shopping. An appropriate composition of plants enhances the livability of a room and affects each person's mood in a positive way. Plants not only have an aesthetic appeal that is almost universal, but also they can be used to make indoor spaces more functional. All of this, however, depends on a logical process of design that can be followed by homeowners and professional interior plantscapers alike.

FOR FURTHER READING

Gaines, R. L. *Interior Plantscaping.* New York: Architectural Record Books, 1977.

Halpin, A. M. *Encyclopedia of Indoor Gardening.* Emmaus, Penn.: Rodale Press, 1980.

Heriteau, J. *The Office Gardener.* New York: Hawthorn Books, 1977.

Hunter, M., and E. H. Hunter. *The Indoor Garden.* New York: Wiley, 1978.

chapter twelve
indoor gardens and seasonal visitors

In this chapter, we deal with the "celebrities" of the indoor plant world. To create special effects with plants, we either combine them creatively into plant gardens or we use species that exhibit some spectacular characteristic. Because of the wide variety of foliage color and flower exuberance among indoor plants, the possible combinations are plentiful in this regard. Having covered the cultural aspects of plants, including their requirements of light, humidity, temperature, and soil, we can turn our attention to the creative display of plants.

In the previous chapter, we discussed how any interior use of plants must consider the artistic principles of interior design. Such things as color coordination, textural compatibility, and the use of focal points will remain an integral part of our discussion here. The use of dish gardens or seasonal plants for special display will require adherence to the principles of interior landscape design in order for their impact to be most effective.

We begin by looking at the special types of plant gardens that have gained acceptance and popularity—dish gardens, cactus gardens, and terrariums. We will then turn to the fascinating subject of forcing bulbs indoors for winter display before concluding the chapter with a look at the "seasonal

visitors," those plants that are purchased as gifts or for seasonal interest.

PLANT GARDENS

Making Indoor Gardens Effective

We have seen that plants can be combined in beautiful ways to create striking visual effects. In this section, we discuss the typical ways that plants are combined in the *same container*. The first order of business is to investigate how these gardens can be used to full advantage.

CONSIDER THE POINT OF VIEW. Ideally, it is best to know where a dish garden will be placed before its construction. Knowing its probable location allows us to design the planting arrangement within the container based on the directions from which the container will be viewed. For example, a plant garden situated on a coffee table should be attractive from all sides. Larger plants should be located near the center of the container, with smaller specimens located around the perimeter. A garden to be located on a table against a wall, on the other hand, needs only to be appealing on the side toward the room. Consequently, the larger plants should be placed toward the rear of the container, with smaller ones occupying the foreground (Figure 12.1).

Certainly, these arrangements of plants are not the only ones that can be used, but they demonstrate the principle. Some plant gardens utilize figurines, stones, or other objects associated with relatively few plants. The design, however, should still reflect the points of view from which the container will be seen.

DISTANCE AND SPEED OF VIEW. In planting schemes outdoors, we vary the degree of plant massing, textural contrast, and color based on what is called the "design speed." The plantings along a highway, for example, would be employed in greater masses and with less textural variety than those located near a patio. As the distance and speed of viewing diminish, the detail interest offered by plantings should increase.

The same principle holds true with indoor gardens. A plant garden that is viewed as one is walking through the house or from a distance should utilize bolder texture with less foliage variety. The plant garden located on a coffee table, which will be viewed at close range for an extended period, should provide the viewer with an interesting combination of texture, color, and pattern.

BLEND WITH THE SURROUNDINGS. The plants in a plant garden should relate both to their container and the surrounding conditions. Let us look at the container first.

A colorful, splashy variety of plants in a plant garden should be combined with a relatively simple container. When the plantings offer less "splash," the container might provide a little more zest. Basically, the container characteristic should take its lead from the plants. An ornate container under a vivacious plant grouping can easily cause an uncomfortable sense of visual business. If the plants take a leading role, let the container play a supporting role.

Arranged for viewing from the right

Arranged for viewing from all sides

FIGURE 12.1 The arrangement of plants in a dish garden is determined by the directions from which the garden will be viewed.

Not only should the plants fit the container, but the garden itself should correspond to the surroundings of its location. First, the plant colors and textures should blend with the character of the room. Again, a busy planting arrangement in a busy room is usually a mistake. In a more contemporary setting, however, a bold plant might be used as an accent (Figure 12.2).

In like fashion, the container should accentuate the room. Perhaps its color picks up the color of the carpet or curtains. Or perhaps its textural qualities are based on the textures found in the furniture or wall fabrics.

FIGURE 12.2 The level of design complexity in a dish garden should complement the complexity of its surroundings.

In any case, there are two levels of compatibility that must be addressed with plant gardens. First, the plants must match the container and second, the plant garden as a whole must relate to the design of the room.

IS THE GARDEN A FOCAL POINT? A dish garden can either be an accent piece that provides a flavor of festivity for the room, or it may simply be a subdued element that adds interest but does not detract from some other main feature. Design the plant garden accordingly. Perhaps a featured garden might include such flamboyant plants as croton or the ti plant. A supporting garden might include plants such as a green philodendron or peperomia, simply providing a splash of green.

Within the garden itself, there should usually be a place to which the eye is drawn.

In a subdued planter, perhaps one specimen has an unusual texture or variegation. In a more exuberant planting, perhaps the focal point is a green plant, since all the other materials might display more color. In any case, do not just fill the container with colorful or interesting plants. Think about where you want the viewer's eye to be directed first and plant your most interesting plant in that location. The other plants that follow should be placed in such a way that they support the focal point you have initially established (Figure 12.3).

CULTURAL FACTORS. As we have said before, the cultural aspects of indoor plants can rarely be separated from their visual characteristics. A plant garden that is either constructed or located improperly will not provide the desired visual effect.

Periodic Health Checks. Probably no sight related to indoor plants is sadder than a sickly plant garden. The prevention of this condition begins with the selection of a location for the plant garden. If the garden is to be situated in a dark area, select low light plant materials. If the garden is destined for a sunny windowsill, select plants that are at home in higher light levels. It is extremely important to select plant types that are ap-

FIGURE 12.3 Note how one plant captures interest, whereas the others serve as an interesting background.

propriate for the location and compatible with each other.

Every House Has Its Microclimates. In every house, there are spots that are cooler, brighter, and more humid than others. The plants selected for a particular plant garden should recognize this range of conditions. Various kinds of ferns, for example, might be used if the garden is to be placed in a humid area of the home. Plants that like reduced soil moisture should be selected if a south window is the spot. Never combine plants that have differing cultural requirements in the same plant garden. Since each plant of the grouping will share the same location, the same temperatures, and the same soil conditions, they must be selected accordingly.

Proper Drainage. Commercial dish garden containers that are available through garden centers may be selected with an eye toward proper drainage. A deeper container, for example, is probably more appropriate for plants requiring frequent watering. Since overwatering is apt to occur, the deeper soil column will stimulate the movement of water down through the soil. Also, ½ inch of standing water is less detrimental in the bottom of a deeper container than in a shallow dish. Most cactus garden containers, on the other hand, are fairly shallow because the root systems of these species are shallow.

It is a good idea to avoid standing water in the base of plant gardens altogether. This can be accomplished through purchasing containers with drainage holes or carefully drilling holes in the bottom of the container that has no holes. Even ceramic containers can be drilled if the drill bit is kept flushed with water where it contacts the container. The water helps to minimize the chances of overheating the drill bit.

RECOGNIZE THE END. Since most plants eventually grow larger than the space allotted in a typical plant garden, they usually do one of two things eventually: become stunted from root restriction or die a slow death. It is important to recognize when the useful life of a plant garden has expired. Perhaps the plants have become too leggy, or perhaps they have become so crowded that the effect is one of chaos rather than compatibility. Be aware, beginning with the time you plant a plant garden, that its usefulness is relatively short lived. The garden will eventually need to be replanted, and the removed plants will need to be repotted and allowed to grow to a larger mature size or discarded. Plants are dynamic. Do not allow them to remain constricted in the plant garden so long that they become an interior landscape liability rather than an asset.

Dish Gardens

Dish gardens, a popular gift item sold at florist shops and garden centers, are also called **planters.** Dish garden seems to be a more precise term because planters range from small sizes all the way up to those big enough to support trees. As mentioned earlier, a dish garden is distinguished by the presence of two or more plants, rather than a single specimen as is typical with most indoor plant containers.

The dish garden container is generally a typical pottery or glass dish, usually 3 inches or more deep. Containers may also be constructed of plastic or wood and covered with decorative materials such as fabric, straw, or other textural elements.

TYPES OF DISH GARDENS. Generally speaking, dish gardens may be tropical, woodland, cacti, or succulents, although we will be treating cactus gardens as a separate topic. Gardens are generally classified this way because the plants of these groups have similar characteristics. We noted earlier that the plants of dish gardens should be quite similar in their environmental requirements.

A woodland dish garden consists of young plants indigenous to the forest floor. The benefit of collecting such a group of plants is not only that they can create a very interesting exhibit indoors, but also the exercise of collecting the plants opens one's eyes to the vast variety of small plant life that grows among the forest giants.

The tropical dish garden is easy to initiate. The small foliage plants necessary for the garden are readily accessible at plant shops and garden centers. Many foliage plants are right at home in a dish garden. Table 12.1 lists some foliage plants that are often found in dish garden settings.

PREPARATION FOR PLANTING. Having all the materials at hand greatly expedites the planting of a dish garden. The materials needed are the container, soil, drainage material, and the plants.

The soil selected for a dish garden should not be excessively fertile in order to slow the growth rate of the plants and extend the life of the garden. The soil should be well drained and porous, thus facilitating aeration and preventing compaction. A commercial blend of vermiculite and peat moss is a good choice, as well as a mixture of equal parts soil, sand, and peat moss. Since all three components of the latter mixture can vary in their individual characteristics, experimental blending of the components in several ratios

may be necessary to ensure the proper overall porosity.

Moisture content of the soil is very important in the construction of the dish garden. Soil that is too dry is difficult to work with because it will not hold its shape, making it more difficult to keep the plants in position as they are placed. Soil that is too wet adheres to the fingers and becomes less aerated as it is worked and packed. It is a good idea to moisten the soil to the proper level a while prior to the potting process. Dry soil that has just been watered is difficult to work with because there are invariably portions that are too dry and too wet. The proper soil moisture level can be determined by balling up a small portion of soil, then crumbling the ball. If the ball is difficult to make, the soil is too dry. If the ball does not break apart easily, the soil is too moist. This is obviously a rough determination but sufficient for general use.

DRAINAGE. There are probably as many ideas about how to prepare a dish garden for overwatering as there are dish garden designs. Some people like to include a thick layer of gravel with soil on top. Others like gravel, then sand, then soil. Others like gravel, then charcoal, then soil. The list goes on and on. Personally, we prefer a thin (½

TABLE 12.1 SOME OF THE COMMON FOLIAGE PLANTS USED IN DISH GARDENS

Aglaonema spp.	*Cissus rhombifolia* (grape ivy)
Pilea cadierei (aluminum plant)	*Hemigraphis alternata* (red ivy)
Pilea microphylla (artillery plant)	*Crassula argentea* (jade plant)
Asparagus spp. (asparagus fern)	*Pellionia* spp.
Soleirolia soleirolii (baby's tears)	*Peperomia* spp.
Brassaia actinophylla (Australian umbrella tree)	*Philodendron* spp.
Bromeliads	*Epipremnum aureum* (pothos)
Dieffenbachia spp. (Dumbcane)	*Tolmiea menziesii* (pick-a-back plant)
Dracaena spp.	*Plectranthus* spp.
Hedera helix (English ivy)	*Podocarpus macrophyllus* (southern yew)
Episcia spp. (flame violet)	*Sansevieria* spp.
Dizygotheca elegantissima (false aralia)	*Saxifraga stolonifera* (strawberry geranium)
× *Fatshedera lizei* (aralia ivy)	*Syngonium* spp.
Ferns	

inch) layer of coarsely ground charcoal covered with the soil medium. The charcoal not only serves as a small drainage basin for free water, but also helps prevent the soil from developing an odor with age (Figure 12.4).

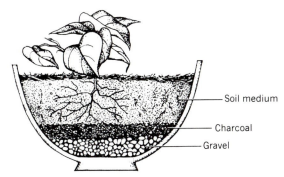

FIGURE 12.4 Cross section of a dish garden, showing proper placement of components.

WATERING. Proper watering should eliminate the need for drainage material in the bottom of a dish garden. Perhaps the best way of watering is to immerse the dish garden until air no longer escapes from the soil. Following immersion, the garden should be placed on its side for a sufficient time to let all excess water run out. Unfortunately, many people like to water dish gardens without ever giving them a chance to drain. Even though they may never create a free water situation in the bottom of the container, the chances are excellent that the soluble salt content of the soil continues to increase with each watering. Eventually, the plants deteriorate because of the elevated salt level. If heavy watering followed by draining is impractical for some reason, distilled water or rain water will help prevent the buildup of soluble salts.

It is important to maintain a fairly consistent level of soil moisture with dish gardens because too much water as well as too little will damage the plants. If wilting occurs, the lower leaves are apt to be dropped. Although less convenient, it is better to gauge the need for watering by some indicator, such as scratching a finger into the soil, rather than some predetermined time schedule. As temperature and humidity conditions change in the home due to seasonal fluctuations outdoors, the appropriate time period between waterings may vary.

Another advantage of moving the garden to a sink for immersion is that, with time, you will be able to judge by the weight of the container whether watering is necessary.

PLANTING THE GARDEN. Before planting, organize all the necessary materials on a work table. Place all the plants you intend to use into the empty container and arrange them in a satisfactory design. Remember to consider whether the container will be viewed from one side or all sides. Remove the plants from the container, remembering the arrangement you have selected.

After placing the drainage material and a shallow layer of soil in the bottom of the container, build up the soil so that each plant's original soil surface is about ¼ to ½ inch below the rim of the container. If the plants were grown in peat pots, remove the peat pots, or at least break away the rims so that the peat cannot extend above the new soil level. Exposed above the soil, the peat pot rim will act as a wick and remove water from the soil. The plant in the exposed peat pot, consequently, will dry faster than the others in the container.

Remember that watering will help compact the soil around the root systems of the plants. It is not necessary to do more than gently firm the soil around the roots. Too much packing will reduce the future aeration available to the root systems. Some people, florists in particular, enjoy "surfacing" or mulching the dish garden with moss. This is not a bad practice except when the moss is mounded to the point it is even or above the rim of the container. The problem is that dry moss tends to shed water, thus diverting it downslope and over the side of the container. Remember to leave a reservoir at the top of the container to facilitate water retention and soil soaking.

UPKEEP OF THE PLANT GARDEN. A tropical plant garden does not require a lot of care, but the little attention that is necessary is important. First, do not be afraid to pinch back plants that are fast growing. This will help improve their density, as well as reduce their height. A half-strength fertilizer is beneficial occasionally, with application frequency determined by the relative growth rate of the plants. Plants growing in low light and relatively unfavorable environmental conditions will not need very much fertilizer, if any.

Another advantage of watering by immersion is that the foliage of the garden can be washed during the watering process. Insects can also be physically removed during the washing process, thus minimizing the need for application of commercial chemicals.

Like metals and glass, dish gardens should be recycled. A typical life span is about six months. At that time, take a critical look at your creation and decide whether it might need to be replanted. In this vein, consider the dish garden as a small indoor nursery, providing the necessary early-growth conditions for future indoor specimens that will grow up happily planted in their individual containers.

Cactus and Succulent Gardens

Gardens of this type create a vastly different design mood than tropical or woodland dish gardens. Cacti, in particular, because of their prominence in arid regions of the world remind us of those types of places. Because these plants have adapted to an environment lacking in water, they have typically sacrificed lushness for survivability. Cacti are essentially stem tissue with leaves converted to spines for protection. This configuration not only saves water through the elimination of typical leaf structures, but also creates fascinating textural effects. Other

typical succulents, on the other hand, have retained their leaves but usually as fattened structures that lack the airy qualities of thinner, more typical leaf structures.

In the interior setting, therefore, a cactus garden should be viewed more as a special accent with strong sculptural qualities. Because these plants usually have such dynamic forms, they must be combined with care. It is easy with cactus gardens, for example, to create too much variety among the plants. The result is a situation in which each plant relates poorly to the other specimens in the dish. Keeping in mind the principles outlined previously regarding developing one focal point will help immensely. Consider, for example, using one plant with exceptional characteristics—perhaps a tall, branched plant or one with colorful spines—and use it among several other plants with similar characteristics. Ideally, there should be some aesthetic connection such as color or texture, which relate the focal point plant to the others.

Whereas a tropical dish garden can easily reflect the dense lushness of the tropical forest, the cactus garden should reflect the spaciousness between plants characteristic of arid regions. Also with cactus gardens, because of the nature of their inhabitants, the design concept of verticality is important to utilize. The varying heights of cacti with similar structure creates an interesting design opportunity (Figure 12.5).

ASSEMBLING A CACTUS OR SUCCULENT GARDEN. First, decide which types of cactus should be included in the garden. A review of the cactus family in Chapter Thirteen will give you information regarding the typical types. In assembling and planting cacti that have spines, no matter how small, handle the plants with protected fingers or tongs. Cacti with fuzzy spines will often not inflict pain during handling but will leave fiber-glasslike particles in the skin, causing festering at a later time.

FIGURE 12.5 Because of their natural forms and growing conditions, cacti and succulents should be used with strong measures of vertical variety and space.

The soil mix for cacti and succulents should be more aerated that that used for tropical or woodland dish gardens. A good mixture is one part sand and one part peat, if we assume that the peat is not overly decomposed. Root rot is the major problem to fear in cactus gardens, so soil preparation and proper watering are particularly important. Since the western soils where many cacti originate tend to be alkaline, ground limestone may need to be incorporated into the soil mix to raise the pH.

Proper watering requires some knowledge of the typical life cycle of a cactus or succulent. Generally in nature they receive rain only during brief periods; the beginning of the growth cycle is associated with a rainy period. It is extremely important, therefore, to recognize that cacti and succulents go through a rest period during winter, followed by growth beginning in the spring. Watering must respond to this cycle. During active growth, the plants should be watered, allowed to drain well, and watered again only

when the soil becomes relatively dry. As active growth is subsiding in the fall, the watering frequency should be reduced, finally to a level of about once or twice per month during the winter, depending on the level of relative humidity. Most will tolerate slight shriveling due to water stress.

The planting preparation and procedure is identical to that described for the tropical dish garden above. Two essential differences are the need for finger protection during the handling of cacti and the availability of pure sand that may be used as a "mulch" on top of the peat and sand mixture. The pure sand makes the garden seem more desertlike in appearance. For even truer authenticity, include small pieces of driftwood.

OVERCOMING FALLACIES REGARDING CACTI AND SUCCULENTS. Somehow, perhaps because of misunderstandings about the desert, several misconceptions have arisen regarding the culture of these fascinating plants. The first is that all succulent plants are cacti. The fact is that the cactus family, *Cactaceae*, represents only one group of succulent plants. Succulents are plants that have the enhanced ability to store water. This may be through modified stems as in cactus; through thicker and fleshier leaves as with the jade plant; or through special structures, such as the leaf vases of bromeliads.

A second fallacy is that all succulents grow in the desert. Some succulents grow in temperate regions, for example, such as Spanish moss that is a member of the bromeliad family. Spanish moss is found over much of the southeastern United States. A related fallacy is that all succulents grow in full sunlight. This belief perhaps arises because of the succulents' association with the desert, but some succulents do prefer less than full sun exposure.

A final set of misconceptions have to do with the soil and water requirements necessary for succulents. Again because of the desert association, some people believe that all succulents must grow in pure sand. Related beliefs are that cacti can only be watered at the base, because water may damage the above-ground parts, and that all succulents can live without water. As we have already noted with the recommended soil mix and water instructions, none of these is true, but together they represent exaggerations of the extreme environmental conditions that these amazing plants can tolerate.

CONTAINERS. Of course, any typical dish garden container can be used for cacti and succulents. A popular technique, however, has been to use clay pottery containers because of the heavy use of this material in hot, arid regions. Water is often kept in these vessels because of the porous walls that provide evaporative cooling. Because of the lack of wood in these regions, earthenware is a particularly important element of the lifestyle. Consequently, clay pottery seems to fit with the plants indigenous to these regions.

A danger of using clay containers as opposed to glazed dishes is that the porosity can be a disadvantage if certain precautions are not taken. Because moisture will escape through the walls and bottom of clay containers, a saucer must be used beneath the container if the furniture below is susceptible to water damage. This is true even when the container has no drainage holes. An alternative to saucers when water staining is not a concern is the use of inverted pots that both elevate the container and minimize potential water damage.

TEMPERATURE. Many people do not realize that although arid regions can be excessively hot during the day, they can be quite chilly at night. In fact, during the winter rest period, succulents may suffer if night temperatures do not fall below 60°F. With some succulents, such as the Christmas cactus, flower initiation is dependent on cool temperatures and other factors. During the growing season, succulents respond best to night temperatures between 60 and 70°F. Generally, the lowest acceptable temperature is around 40°F; colder conditions can cause chilling damage.

AVOIDING PROBLEMS. Much of the disease and insect prevention with cacti and succulents occurs at the time of purchase. Unfortunately, cacti and succulents are susceptible to disease and insect problems in spite of their climatic toughness. Mealy bugs, scale insects, spider mites, and aphids, to name a few, may be found on these plants. It is essential at the time of purchase to carefully inspect each plant before buying it, looking for insect or disease symptoms. Mealy bugs and scale insects, in particular, are sometimes difficult to spot on cacti because they blend with the pads or areoles, or are obscured by the spines.

Whether tropical, woodland, or succulent, a dish garden can be a striking and enjoyable element of the interior landscape. Careful preparation and design can provide a great deal of enjoyment for several months. By following the steps outlined here, you are more assured of creating a healthy and well-designed attractive setting.

TERRARIUMS: A WORLD OF THEIR OWN

Consisting of a group of plants growing within a transparent container, a **terrarium** is perhaps the most fascinating of all indoor plant gardens. Because of its enclosed state, the terrarium consists not only of plants and soil, but also of the basic cycles involved in the functioning of our earth. Within a totally closed terrarium, for example, we see the hydrological cycle that occurs as water vapor leaves the plant stomates through transpiration and the soil surface through evaporation, eventually collecting as droplets that return to the soil. In addition, the nutrients required by the plants are recycled by means of the nitrogen and carbon cycles.

In effect, the terrarium is a microcosm of the same cycles that nurture life on our planet.

We spoke earlier in this text of the harshness of the indoor environment as it relates to indoor plants. The major advantage of a terrarium is that it creates controlled, favorable environmental conditions for the plants it houses. The humidity level can be readily controlled by adjusting the ventilation of the container. Soil moisture can be maintained at a rather steady level through the proper application of water.

Temperature changes are buffered by the container, and the impact of drafts on tender plants is greatly minimized. Maintenance is reduced because of the exclusion of dust and insects; even physical threats to plants, such as those posed by children, are also reduced.

Another great advantage of terrarium gardening is that small, delicate plants can be grown that otherwise would not survive the typical indoor environment. A terrarium offers the further advantage of portability, even with sensitive plants, since the container can be moved to various locations without creating microclimatic problems, provided that the changes in light level and temperature are not detrimental (Figure 12.6).

For those who travel frequently or are otherwise away from home for extended periods, but who still like plants nevertheless, terrariums are an ideal solution. With proper construction and watering, a terrarium may be closed and allowed to stand for months without any outside interference. It is important, however, to underscore the need for proper construction and water level. After building a terrarium, for example, a period of time is required to "fine tune" the moisture relations within the container. We will see how this is done shortly.

HISTORICAL DEVELOPMENT OF THE TERRARIUM. The development of the terrarium is generally credited to Dr. Nathaniel Ward, an English physician, in 1836. In trying to

FIGURE 12.6 Terrariums offer the opportunity of growing humidity-loving plants that could not otherwise be grown successfully indoors.

hatch a moth in a bottle containing soil, he noticed that small plants were thriving under the moist conditions.

During the time that Ward made his discovery, England was in strong pursuit of ornamental plants worldwide. English gardeners had begun growing plants in elaborate greenhouses and were "bedding-out" plants for outdoor displays at the beginning of the growing season. Consequently, a vast demand arose for exotic plants, and many nurseries were underwriting long voyages to bring back plants from all parts of the world. Unfortunately, many of these plants were lost because of the exposure to the elements and salt spray during the extended period of the journey.

Ward's discovery led to the inclusion on ships of large, covered glass cases known as

Wardian cases. These ship-borne terrariums greatly enhanced the flow of exotic plants into the British Isles.

As glass became more available to the English after the 1850s, the practice of displaying ornamental, miniature Wardian cases became widespread. These parlor cases, as they came to be called, became ever more elaborate and complex. In various parts of Europe, the cases were employed for the propagation of scarce seeds, displaying miniature scenes, and creating an interesting habitat for small animals. Of course, many were used simply for the display of plants in an interesting fashion. Although we may never see another period of history in which terrariums are so faddishly displayed, they continue to provide great intrigue and enjoyment.

CONTAINERS SUITABLE FOR TERRARIUMS.

Any transparent container that is big enough to house plants, small enough to fit comfortably indoors, and attractive enough to enjoy is suitable for constructing a terrarium. Many prefabricated containers are offered commercially for this purpose, and many interesting configurations have been devised by imaginative individuals. Perhaps the most commonly used vessel is a 5- or 10-gallon aquarium. Because of the availability now of strong glues, an aquarium suitable for terrarium use should be glued at the intersections rather than held by metal corners. Corners glued with transparent adhesives allow almost unimpeded viewing.

Most garden centers offer various containers—domes, spheres, pyramids, squares, and mushroom shapes in both glass and plastic. Many of these are equipped with a suitable base; others may be hung in strategic locations with macramé or other decorative hangers. More ornate containers are available in the form of stained glass, coffee tables, and other furniturelike configurations. Self-made containers should be constructed of heavy-duty glass or plexiglass

because of the stresses imposed by the weight of the growing medium. As we shall see shortly, there is no need for drainage holes in a terrarium.

PLANTS FOR TERRARIUMS.

Terrariums have been used historically as excellent structures for the propagation of seeds and cuttings. Their high humidity level is quite conducive to plant growth; consequently, most plants thrive under terrarium conditions. In planning the plant list for a terrarium, consider those plants that would be very difficult to grow outside the protected confines of an enclosed container.

Insectivorous Plants. A popular group for this purpose is the insectivorous species such as the Venus fly-trap (*Dionaea*), pitcher plants (*Darlingtonia* and *Sarracenia*), butterworts (*Pinguicula*), and sundews (*Drosera*). Because these plants often inhabit soils low in nitrogen and phosphorus, they have become adapted to the entrapment of insects for their nutrient requirements. The Venus fly-trap, for example, grows only in certain boggy areas of North Carolina and requires relatively high humidity to thrive. The ends of its leaves have been modified into hinged traps lined with spines. The inside areas of the traps become bright red in sunny conditions, thus luring insects. When the insect touches two of several bristly triggers called **trichomes** located on the inner surfaces of the trap, the jaws of the trap snap shut, entrapping the victim. Over a period of several days, the insect is digested by means of juices secreted by the trap tissue. The resulting nutrients are absorbed by the plant.

Insectivorous plants use both active and passive means to entrap their prey. Sundews utilize movement but in a different fashion from the Venus fly-trap. Sundew leaves are covered with bristles tipped with a droplet of sticky liquid that glistens like dew in the sunlight. The unsuspecting insect who lights on the leaf becomes mired in the droplets, and additional bristles bend toward the entrapped insect, adding their portion of stickiness to the entrapment. Another group of insectivorous plants called the butterworts are covered with a butterlike substance that also adheres to insects. Butterwort movement involves a rolling of the leaf blade enveloping the insect until digestion is complete.

Pitcher plants, on the other hand, use no movement but rather an interesting pitcher-shaped leaf structure into which insects may fly, crawl, or fall, but from which escape is quite difficult. The upper portion of the leaf is covered with hairs that point toward the opening of the pitcher, making walking difficult for the insect in any direction but toward the opening. Once inside the opening, the walls of the pitcher become waxy and slick, causing the insect to lose its footing among the hairs, falling into the reservoir of water and digestive juices that stay in the lower portion of the pitcher.

Sundews and pitcher plants present a variety of plant forms and sizes among the various species. A collection of insectivorous plants not only provides fascinating conversation, but also displays a beautiful array of textures and forms. One should be aware, however, that the collection of these plants from the wild may be regulated by law.

Other Plants. Many species of plants offer miniature types that work quite well in a terrarium setting. A great number of miniature orchids, for example, are available through orchid nurseries. These plants offer a phenomenal variety of flower forms and colors and perform quite well in the high humidity of the terrarium. Bromeliads also offer many possibilities for terrarium culture and can provide a brilliant floral display as well. Members of the African violet family and ferns should be considered. Chapter Thirteen and Part Five give more specific information on the flowering requirements of some of these plants.

Other plants, such as succulents, which do not require the high humidity terrariums can provide, may also be used, so long as some ventilation is provided that will prevent excessively humid conditions.

Since the space within terrariums is limited, some restraint should be used in including plants whose mature size is over 12 inches in height. Vines and other aggressive plants should be avoided, unless one is prepared to prune occasionally to inhibit growth.

DESIGN CONSIDERATIONS. Two design themes seem to predominate terrariums. One is the lushness of growth found in humid areas, such as with the ferns along streams or the tropical rain forest. Unless you are displaying plants with striking forms, some jostling among the plants is probably appropriate with the "lushness" theme.

The other common theme is the miniaturized landscape. These types of plantings sometimes include natural features such as lakes, as well as small figurines of animals, stones, or people.

Since a glass container somewhat obscures the view to plants within because of reflections, the use of strong contrasts in plant forms, textures, and colors is beneficial. Such techniques as including white sand areas, saltfree driftwood, and colorful species help in this regard. Also, a variety of plant heights helps enhance the visual interest of the planting.

The primary detraction from an attractive terrarium is usually the exposed soil seen through the front of the terrarium. Several methods exist for minimizing the impact of the soil. Containers are now available with opaque bases that hide the soil area. For containers with transparent bases, consider keeping the soil quite shallow in the front of the terrarium, sloping it up toward the back of the container. Moss may be used to line the front and sides of the terrarium so that its greenness shows through the glass where soil would ordinarily be seen. Another method is to use individual potted plants, concealing the pots with moss or creeping plant materials. Another once-popular method of disguising the soil is through designs of colored sand built up next to the glass as the soil is added. This creates a colorful display, adding interest to the terrarium's appearance, but may distract from the beauty of the plants.

PREPARATION FOR PLANTING.

Tools. The nature of the terrarium to be planted will determine the selection of tools to have on hand. A container with a wide opening through which planting can be performed by hand will necessitate very few tools. A water syringe is useful for cleaning the inside of the glass after planting and scissors are handy for pruning, but beyond those two items, very little is needed.

More elaborate tools are necessary for small-mouthed vessels such as bottles. A dowel for positioning plants and soil, a long stick with a flat end for tamping, a wire loop for raising and lowering plants, a baster tube for adding and removing water, and a funnel for adding soil make the job much easier. As you work with small-mouthed containers, you will undoubtedly "invent" new tools to enhance your ability to position and plant the individual species.

Of course, you should have the proper soil mix, small gravel, and charcoal on hand, as well. A long-handled brush is used for cleaning the glass and the foliage once planting is complete. A final useful item is tape that can be applied beneath the terrarium, indicating the planting date and other pertinent information.

The Planting Medium. The soil for planting a terrarium should be appropriate for the plants anticipated. Most foliage plants do quite well in a typical soil-less commercial medium or a typical potting soil.

For epiphytic plants, such as certain members of the African violet family, orchids, and bromeliads, a soil containing one-third fir bark is recommended. Mixing ground char-

coal with the soil mix for any planting will help to inhibit the development of unpleasant odors.

The soil level in a terrarium should be kept quite shallow. Remember that the plants are in a very favorable environment, so they can tolerate less soil than one might expect. Since the growth of plants should be inhibited in a terrarium, the soil should be relatively low in nutrients as well. If a plant has a soil mass deeper than the soil in the terrarium, gently break up the plant's soil mass and spread the roots until it will fit into the soil available in the terrarium.

Fertilizer. The best way to fertilize terrariums is to watch for signs of deficiencies; fertilize only as needed. Remember that there is no drainage provided in a terrarium, so salts can build up very quickly. The best means of fertilizing in a terrarium is to mix a soluble fertilizer one-quarter strength and apply the liquid with an atomizer or baster tube to prevent soil disturbance. Again, keep in mind that you are sustaining the plants, not stimulating them.

Light. Because enclosed glass containers build up heat very quickly when exposed to direct sunlight, terrariums should never be placed in that position. An exception to this guideline is cacti. They can tolerate direct sun, provided that ventilation is present so that damaging temperatures will not be reached.

As with fertilizer, do not stimulate the growth of the plants by providing as much light as possible. Maintain the plants in a healthy state; any additional stimulation will only shorten the time before the plants outgrow the terrarium.

THE PLANTING PROCESS. Before beginning the planting process, assemble all the necessary equipment on an appropriate working surface. Then place the plants you intend to include in the terrarium and formulate your planting arrangement. Noting the final arrangement, remove the plants from the terrarium and make sure that the glass surfaces are as clean as possible. As you plant, try to avoid touching or smudging the glass surfaces since cleaning is more difficult after the plants are installed. Since you will probably smudge the glass somewhat during the planting process regardless of how careful you may be, it is a good idea to use soil as dry as possible so that the water used in cleaning will bring the soil to the proper moisture level rather than overwet it.

The first step of planting is to place a very thin layer of small gravel in the bottom of the container. This layer should be no more than ½ inch thick. Then, the soil mix should be added, charcoal included, so that the soil level is shallow in front and deeper to the rear. Generally, a maximum soil depth of 1 or 2 inches is adequate.

Beginning with the smallest plants, position each specimen in its preselected location, firming the soil gently around its root system. Try to avoid allowing the foliage to touch either the soil or glass surface. The points of contact will remain moist and function as a site for disease growth. When all the plants have been planted, look over the entire grouping and prune where necessary to remove dead foliage, improve the plant composition, or reduce size. Be sure to remove all excess foliage from the container. If a mulch is to be added to the soil surface, it should be done at this point. The final step is to clean the inside of the glass, if necessary, with either a brush or a water syringe.

WATERING. The most critical aspect in the success or failure of a terrarium is the watering. A newly planted terrarium should have only enough water added to moisten the soil, with very little water allowed to collect in the gravel drainage layer. If water is inadvertently added, the terrarium should be left open so that the water can evaporate or the excess moisture should be drawn off with a baster tube. It is far better to underwater a terrarium than to overwater it.

Prior to watering a dry terrarium, check the foliage and glass surfaces to see whether any cleaning is necessary that might involve adding water. Do not make the mistake of watering the terrarium, only to realize that additional water is needed to do the cleaning. Remember that a terrarium cannot be tilted to remove excess water!

Rainwater or distilled water is ideal for terrarium use. Tap water may elevate the level of soluble salts rather quickly, depending on the hardness of the water used. The need for watering can usually be determined by the soil color, initial wilting, or simply feeling the weight of the container or the leaves of the plants. Generally, a little wilting is not harmful unless it progresses to a more severe state.

It is generally advisable to try to reach an equilibrium of water relations in a terrarium. This is done by covering the terrarium and watching for condensation on the side of the container. When condensation occurs, allow a little ventilation until the condensation evaporates. Continue this process in small steps until no condensation appears. The container has then reached a moisture equilibrium that will allow the container to remain closed for an extended period of time. Once this fascinating level of permanency with a terrarium is reached, the effort involved in planning and planting the terrarium pays off. In terms of maintenance-free indoor gardening, the terrarium is difficult to match.

Forcing Bulb Gardens For Winter
Most indoor planting projects yield immediate results. Planting a dish garden or a terrarium, for example, provides immediate gratification. In order to enjoy the winter splendor of bulbs flowering indoors, an investment of time is necessary between the planting and the fulfillment.

It is this planning ahead, as well as the exuberant color of spring bulbs, that make forcing these plants into flower so gratifying.

As winter wears on and the bleakness grows old, a colorful splash of daffodils, tulips, or other bulbous plants can lift the spirits and brighten the season.

THE CONCEPT OF FORCING BULBS. Most bulbs used for indoor forcing flower naturally during the spring. The bulb, an over-wintering storage organ for the plant, is typically planted in the fall. During the winter months, the bulb develops a root system and fulfills its cold requirement prior to flowering in the spring. The flowering process is triggered by the warming temperatures of spring.

Forcing bulbs, then, is simply a matter of duplicating these necessary steps, but in a shorter period of time. Although a bulb lies below ground all winter, it does not need that entire length of time to produce its roots and fulfill the cold requirement.

PREPARATION FOR PLANTING. A basic requirement of successful bulb forcing is to begin with healthy material. Bulbs should be firm and devoid of any basal rots that might be apparent in the basal plate area.

Small abrasions or a loose skin (tunic) are not harmful to the future development of the plant, but one should certainly strive for the best quality possible. There is, incidentally, a correlation between the size of the bulb and the size of the flower it will produce. Generally, the larger bulbs demand higher prices.

Almost any plant container is appropriate for forcing bulbs into bloom indoors. One essential requirement is one or more holes for drainage of excess water.

Since bulbs must go through a storage process, they might suitably be planted in what could be called "utility containers." These might be standard bulb pans or other makeshift containers that will be placed in more attractive containers during flowering. This method avoids tying up attractive containers during the storage period.

Bulbs are not as selective regarding their soil requirements as cacti. Any loose, friable soil mix is appropriate. Generally, however, it is a good idea to avoid reusing pasturized soil for bulb forcing because of the increased likelihood of disease.

An ideal soil for bulbs should be sufficiently fertile to support growth, yet not so heavily fertilized that burning may occur. The soil must also be firm enough to support the top-heavy flower in full development. A mix of equal parts soil, peat moss, and sand is recommended. Since the bulb has stored all the necessary food for flowering during the preceding growing season, there is no need to add fertilizer to the soil mix.

THE POTTING PROCEDURE. The potting of bulbs is not a delicate practice but should be handled somewhat carefully to avoid damaging the base of the bulbs. After covering the drainage holes with broken pot shards or other materials to prevent soil erosion, partially fill the container with the soil mixture. The fill level will be determined by the bulb height, based on placing the bulb nose or tip at the same level as the rim of the container. Gently firming the bulbs into the soil, allowing them to almost touch one another, fill the pot with as many bulbs as possible. This will ensure a more pronounced effect when flowering occurs. Make sure the soil filters down between the bulbs during filling and that the tips of the bulbs protrude about ½ inch above the soil surface. A thorough watering should follow, preferably by soaking. By allowing the water to soak up through the soil medium, there is less chance of soil disturbance.

An essential element of the forcing process is accurate record-keeping. In each container planted, place a label that notes the proper name of the bulb, the flower color, and the date planted.

THE COOLING. Most spring flowering bulbs require cold conditions to develop properly. Generally, bulbs must be chilled for at least 12 weeks. A typical tulip or daffodil will need

14 weeks of cooling, and some varieties need as much as 15 or 16 weeks.

The temperature in the storage area should be between 41 and 48°F. Lower temperatures will lengthen the rooting period, and temperatures above 50°F will inhibit rooting and insufficiently stimulate flowering.

Three basic options exist for cooling bulbs for forcing. The first is to place the planted containers into a refrigerator for cooling. Unless a second refrigerator is available, usually one's kitchen refrigerator will not provide enough space for this purpose.

The second option is placing the bulbs in a cold, dark indoor location. This might be a cellar, crawlspace, garage, or shed that does not freeze hard. The containers should be covered to keep them dark if the storage area is lighted. The third option is the digging of an outdoor pit somewhat deeper than the tallest container. Cover the base of the pit with sand or vermiculite to keep the container bases clean. After positioning as many containers in the pit as possible, cover the group with 1 or 2 inches of sand, vermiculite, or other clean, similar materials to protect the emerging shoots. A 6-inch layer of soil is then placed on top of the sand layer.

Water the bed thoroughly to eliminate air pockets and provide water for rooting. Since water should not stand in the pit, thus rotting the roots, digging the perimeter of the pit somewhat deeper than the center is an advantage. Also consider an area of sand on the side of the pit through which you can dig down and remove containers from the side during winter without disturbing the covering over the bed.

When the cold weather develops, protect the bed with a layer of straw, leaves, or mulch. This will keep the pit at a more even temperature and inhibit the development of frost.

CHECKING THE BULBS. After the prescribed time of cooling, check a couple of the containers for roots protruding through drainage holes and 2-inch tall shoots. If you do not see roots outside the container, remove the container gently to see whether the root system is enveloping the soil mass. If the roots are not sufficiently developed, return the container for another couple of weeks of cold treatment. Continue to check every two weeks until the proper root development has occurred.

Following rooting, move the container to a warm, bright location not exceeding 72°F. The plants should be kept out of direct sunlight and away from radiators or heating vents. Some bulbs, such as daffodils and minor bulbs, require a cooler temperature of between 60 and 65°F.

It is important to remember that bulbs cannot be forced until their roots are sufficiently developed. Bringing the plants into warm conditions before adequate root development has occurred will result in disappointing flowering (Figure 12.7).

FIGURE 12.7 Consider using a variety of bulbs to create a fascinating display. Ensure that the container remains in cold storage long enough to satisfy the requirements of all the bulbs.

BULBS FOR FORCING. Although most bulbs are suitable for forcing, several enjoy the greatest popularity.

Tulips. An interesting characteristic of the tulip is that a large leaf develops consistently on one side of the flower. Fortunately, this leaf emerges on the flat side of the tulip bulb, so positioning that flat side toward the rim of the pot will ensure a symmetrical foliage appearance.

Tulip shoots should be at least 3 inches tall before being brought into warmer, lighter conditions. This ensures proper elongation of the flower stem.

Tulips are available in many varieties, offering numerous colors and flower configurations. As with all bulbs to be used for forcing, check with your local garden center to determine the newest available varieties. Since different varieties will require different cooling periods, they may be brought into bloom on a continuing basis without having to stagger the planting sequence.

Hyacinths. An advantage of hyacinth is that its flower is showy enough to allow one bulb per container. They are also very easy to force. The bulbs, for multiple plantings, should be set closely together.

Garden centers offer precooled hyacinth bulbs that can be forced immediately. Hyacinth glasses are available that may be partially filled with water up to a point that barely touches the base of the hyacinth bulb. The vase is then placed in a cool, dark area until the roots are fully developed and the flower bud is protruding about 4 inches from the neck of the bulb. Flowering will occur shortly after the vase is brought into the light, if we assume the water level remains slightly below the base of the bulb.

Daffodils. Daffodils also offer a variety of flower configurations and colors; the trumpet types are most often used for forcing. These are forced in the same way as described for the previous bulbs.

This group, however, includes the "paper white" narcissus that can be forced into flower without a cooling period. The bulbs are placed in a shallow container and half covered by pebbles. Add enough water to keep the pebbles moist and place the containers in a dark room for about a week. Gradually, move the plants to a location with filtered light and temperatures around 60°F. An added benefit of the yellow, white, or cream-colored flowers is their delightful fragrance.

Other Suitable Bulbs. Smaller bulbs such as crocus, muscari, scilla, and iris create interesting small-flowered arrangements. As a general guideline, plant two bulbs per inch of container diameter.

THE HOLIDAY VISITOR

Plants have been given as gifts for centuries, particularly as a beautiful holiday gesture. This tradition has been so strong that some plants are associated with holidays, such as the poinsettia with Christmas. The Easter lily, another example, even bears the name of its associated time of year. Other showy plants, though not associated with a particular season, are nevertheless selected for special occasions.

Most of the plants in this gift category are showy at one particular time before fading to a dormant cycle or less attractive form. They lack the year-around foliage appeal of the plants included in Part Five.

Each year, the florist industry introduces new possibilities for green gifts. Our intent here is to consider those plants that are well established and most likely to appear year after year. We will discuss the peculiarities of each type, pointing out the potential and pitfalls of culturing these plants after their beauty of flower or fruit has passed. Plants such as the begonias that are important both as house plants and gift plants are included in Chapter Thirteen or Part Five, rather than here.

Amaryllis

This popular winter-flowering bulb, belonging to the genus *Hippeastrum* of the Amaryllis family (Amaryllidaceae), is only popularly known as amaryllis (pronounced am-ah-RILL-us). It differs from the true, but less well-known, *Amaryllis* genus in very minor ways, such as hollow verus solid flower stalks (scapes) and the lack of leafy bracts on the scapes.

Though noted for its large, star-shaped flowers that appear during the winter months, amaryllis is usually purchased as a dormant bulb that is potted and brought into flower. The bulbs, quite large compared to other common bulbs, commonly weigh as much as 2 pounds and measure 4 to 6 inches across. In general, larger bulbs produce larger or more flowers; consequently, their value varies proportionately.

The flowers are borne as a grouping of trumpets, each 6 to 10 inches across, atop the thick 1- to 2-foot-tall flower stalk. Often, a second flower shoot will follow the first,

FIGURE 12.8 The large amaryllis flowers herald the end of dormancy.

extending the duration of flowering. The straplike leaves, approximately 2 inches wide and a couple of feet long begin to emerge following the first flower stalk (Figure 12.8).

Amaryllis bulbs can be kept indefinitely. It is better to invest in cultivars rather than seedlings labeled only as white, orange, red, or another color. Cultivars have been selected for their superiority of color and include pinks, salmons, oranges, reds, scarlets, whites, and various stripes. Even though cultivars may cost somewhat more, the bulbs last indefinitely, producing more and bigger flowers each year.

Amaryllis bulbs are generally purchased while dormant with roots attached. The bulbs should be planted in a container only 1 inch larger than the diameter of the bulb and can be left in the same pot for three or four years before repotting is necessary. Unlike most plants, the amaryllis thrives in a confined root space.

The bulb should be held in the container with its "nose" or point just above the rim of the container. A well-drained potting soil should be worked in around the root system, gently firming the soil so as to avoid breaking the sometimes brittle roots. The soil should only come about half way up onto the bulb. After repotting, watering should be sparse to prevent rotting the establishing roots. When the flower bud begins to protrude from the bulb's nose, watering and monthly fertilization may begin. This initiation of growth may occur immediately or after several months. The plants prefer temperatures in the 70s (farenheit) during active growth, but the flowers last longer if shade and cooler temperatures prevail during flowering. Amaryllis produce offset bulbs that can be severed from the parent bulb and potted individually. Since these offsets are formed asexually, their genetic character will be identical to the parent. Thus, new members of the cultivar can be established.

Following flowering, when danger of frost is past, amaryllis plants can be placed outdoors in a spot with several hours of direct sunlight, although they will grow in full sun or heavy shade. The bulb is producing food for next year's flower during this time; proper watering, fertilization, and light will pay dividends in larger or more flowers next year. In the fall, watering and fertilization should stop, the yellow leaves removed close to the top of the bulb, and the pot moved indoors to prevent freezing. Thereafter, place in a warm spot and commence watering and fertilizing once new growth is evident.

Azalea

This group of shrubby, profusely flowering plants, pronounced ah-ZAY-le-a, belong to the acid-loving heath family (Ericaceae) along with rhododendrons. Both azaleas and rhododendrons are popular as colorful landscape shrubs in much of the United States, particularly the Northwest and Southeast. Noted for the prolific and vibrant spring flowers that cover them, azaleas have inspired several southeastern localities to conduct celebrations known as Azalea Festivals.

Azaleas flower naturally outdoors, usually in May, with colors including white, reds, oranges, pinks, and many combinations of these (Figure 12.9). Although azaleas may be either deciduous or evergreen, most gift plants are the evergreen type. Consequently, they may be used effectively year after year with proper care.

Azaleas, like other members of the heath family, prefer evenly moist and well-drained soil (preferably very high in peat moss), cool temperatures, and bright filtered sunlight. Kept too warm, they develop spindly growth and flower poorly in low light conditions.

By manipulating temperatures, growers can force azaleas into bloom at will; most are marketed during the late fall to spring. Plants are best purchased when the flower buds are just beginning to open. After flowering, the spent flowers and developing seed structures should be removed, as well as any stems whose lengths are unattractively long. Since the flowers usually fade on gift azaleas during the late winter or early spring, the timing is right for repotting into a slightly larger pot.

Azaleas prefer an acidic medium of either 100 percent sphagnum or other peat moss, or an equal mixture of peat moss and coarse sand, both of which provide sufficient drainage.

A common problem with azaleas is the unintentional raising of the pH with alkaline tap water, thus making the iron in the medium chemically unavailable for use by the plant roots. Interveinal chlorosis, a lightening of the foliage color while leaf veins remain dark green, results from this iron deficiency and must be corrected. Either the pH can be lowered by watering with a solution of one ounce of iron sulfate in two gallons of water or by using iron chelate sprinkled on the soil according to package directions. Either method should restore the chlorotic leaves to a dark green color.

When the danger of hard freezes is over in the spring, azaleas may be set outside in a spot with filtered shade. Sinking the pot in

FIGURE 12.9 Although their foliage and form are attractive, azaleas are most noted for their colorful and prolific flowers.

garden soil retains moisture and provides a constant, cool soil temperature.

Be sure, however, that the garden soil is well drained or prepare a bed of sand and peat moss for the purpose. Azaleas are prone to root rot in poorly drained soils. Although spider mites may appear on plants either indoors or outdoors, thorough washing or spraying of the foliage periodically will usually prevent a significant buildup. Bring the plants back indoors prior to freezing temperatures in the fall. By providing these few essential requirements, the indoor gardener can expect years of colorful satisfaction.

Caladium

These beautifully colored natives of tropical America may be purchased from plant retailers either as a potted plant or a dormant tuber. Most of the plants seen nowadays are the hybrid "Fancy-Leaved Caladiums" (C. × hortulanum), named in reference to their large arrow-shaped leaf blades marked with attractive and bright combinations of green, red, white, pink, salmon, and silver (Figure 12.10). The slender petioles arise directly from the underground tuber, elevating the leaves to a height of about 15 inches. In typical aroid (Araceae) fashion, the flower is composed of spathe and spadix but is not particularly attractive. Consequently, the flower is usually taken off to prevent the removal of energy from the vegetative growth. Fortunately, flowers arise near the end of the growth cycle.

Being herbaceous tuberous plants, caladiums must be given a rest each year. The plant will usually initiate this on its own about six to eight months after the growth period begins. The leaves begin to wither and continue until the entire set dies. The tubers should then be removed from the soil, dusted with a fungicide and insecticide, and stored at about 60°F in a dry, sterile material such as peat moss or vermiculite. After a rest of three to four months, place the tubers 2 to

FIGURE 12.10 In spite of their beauty, caladium leaves are toxic if ingested. (Refer to "Plants with Harmful Characteristics" near the end of Chapter Thirteen.)

3 inches deep in moist sphagnum or peat moss for sprouting, kept at 70 to 80°F until roots and perhaps leaves appear. At that point, plant the tubers 1 inch deep outside after the soil temperature reaches 68°F, or pot into a light soil mix with ample organic matter and drainage.

Caladiums prefer a 75 to 85°F day temperature and bright semishaded light conditions. Full sun, particularly at midday, will scorch the foliage, whereas poor light will result in rank growth and less spectacular foliage color. Keep the soil evenly moist and fertilize every two or three weeks during active growth. Average home humidity is tolerable but may cause tip or marginal burning on the leaves if inordinately low. Caladiums are also very intolerant of cold drafts, such as from outside doors or air-conditioning. Cool, nonfreezing temperatures will surely damage or kill their foliage. foliage.

Propagation is by dividing the tubers just prior to sprouting, incorporating two or more buds into each section. Sterile cutting tools and sprouting medium are critical in avoiding rots after propagation by division. Seeds may also be used but will generally not perpetuate a clone and not resemble the parents at all.

Calceolaria

More popularly known as pocketbook flower, calceolaria (cal-cee-oh-LAIR-ee-uh), unlike the previous three plants, is best enjoyed in flower and then thrown away.

Native to a cool mountainous region of South America, these members of the figwort family (Scrophulariaceae) require cool temperatures during the day and substantially cooler temperatures at night. This sensitivity to climate makes them too tempermental for the ability of most indoor gardeners.

Calceolaria is a popular group, in spite of this peculiarity, because of the colorful and unusual flowers. Shaped like pouches or oval balloons, the flowers range from various shades of red and maroon to yellow and orange. Most are spotted with rust-colored markings. Though delicate in appearance, the flowers will last approximately one month (Figure 12.11).

While the flowers are being enjoyed, the soil should be kept fairly moist. It is also a good idea to water from the bottom, keeping moisture off the foliage to prevent leaf rot.

Chrysanthemums

Like azaleas, chrysanthemums (chris-AN-thuh-mums) are noted for their bright and colorful floral displays outdoors. Unlike azaleas, however, chrysanthemums belong to the compositae family and offer a wide variety of flower shapes and are usually thrown away after the flowers have faded (Figure 12.12).

Commonly grown outdoors as plants that provide color in the fall, chrysanthemums are forced into flower year-round by growers for the gift market. Plants that fade in early spring may be pruned severely, divided into individual plants, and placed in the garden for fall flowering. Generally, though, chrysanthemums will not endure the winter months since most cultivars sold as flowering

FIGURE 12.11 The pocketbook flower (*Calceolaria*) produces one of the most colorful and interesting flowers among plants sold by florists.

FIGURE 12.12 Chrysanthemum is a familiar and boldly flowered favorite among sellers of gift plants.

plants are not the hardy types that are normally planted in the landscape.

Chrysanthemums are best purchased when the buds are just opening. Buying a plant in full flower deprives the owner of the full enjoyment of flowering. Purchasing plants in the very early bud stage, however, is also somewhat dangerous since temperature changes can inhibit flower opening.

Chrysanthemums that are produced widely spaced on the greenhouse bench will have a broader, more attractive appearance than those grown close together that develop spindly and without leaves near their base. Use care in purchasing this plant to make the distinction.

Unfortunately, chrysanthemums attract aphids and mealy bugs and are often sold with these stowaways on-board. Inspect plants prior to purchase or avoid initially placing them with other plants in order to prevent the possible infestation of your other plants.

Cineraria

Though it sounds like a generic name, cineraria (sin-er-AIR-ee-uh) is actually a common name for a group of conspiciously flowering plants derived as varieties and cultivars of *Senecio cruentus*, a member of the compositae family. Though incorrectly listed as annuals in some references, cinerarias are perennial plants that require much sun and quite cool temperatures. Consequently, they are generally treated as annuals among home owners who cannot meet their stringent requirements.

Florists sell both large- and small-flowered cinerarias, generally throughout the cold months of the year. Somewhat like daisies in appearance, the flowers range from 2 to 5 inches across and display many vibrant shades of blue, red, and white, including combinations. The velvety appearance of the flower and the profusion of flowering creates a dramatic seasonal effect (Figure 12.13).

Somewhat like *Calceolaria*, the foliage of

FIGURE 12.13 The daisylike quality of cineraria generates a festive feeling.

cineraria is large and densely packed, necessitating care in watering to prevent wetting the foliage and creating stem and leaf rots. The plant should be kept in full sun in a cool location, ideally around 50°F.

A gift of cineraria should be viewed as a winter bouquet of color to be thrown away on its passing. Newly acquired plants should be checked carefully for aphids, a common intruder on this species.

Citrus

The *Citrus* genus is well known to most people because of the fruit of its various species—orange, lemon, lime, tangerine, and grapefruit. Who has not watched citrus seedlings grow in pots on the windowsill as a child?

In spite of their ease of propagation from seeds, citrus plants are best purchased rather than propagated to obtain dwarf plants more suited for indoor spaces.

The most popular indoor citrus, the calamondin orange, is a hybrid between the genus *Citrus* and *Fortunella* (a relative of citrus). Generally given as a gift when the miniature, tangy oranges are present, the

FIGURE 12.14 Calamondin oranges are miniature, but more tartly flavored, replicas of the popular edible orange.

calamondin orange (× *Citrofortunella mitis*) provides both year-round fruiting and foliage (Figure 12.14).

The small, white, and fragrant flowers borne individually at the twig tips are followed by developing green oranges that later turn to a deep, rich orange and develop to 1 ½ inches in diameter. Under optimum cultivation, flowers and fruit often appear on the same plant, since the fruit is slow to develop and to deteriorate when ripe.

The primary cultural requirement is sun, at least 4 hours or so daily. As a tropical plant, warm temperatures of the home are no problem. The plant should be watered well, then allowed to dry slightly prior to the next watering. Fertilization should occur several times annually, and periodic inspections for mealy bugs and spider mites will prevent pest problems.

Growing naturally to a height of about 10 feet, the calamondin orange must be pruned each year to maintain a suitable size for the home. This is best done just after new growth develops. As the plant ages, even if its size is kept in check, occasional repotting with

fresh, well-drained potting soil and into a larger container will be necessary.

Cyclamen

Among the most striking of flowering plants, cyclamens (SY-kla-mens) are a popular and interesting addition to the home during the winter months. They are members of the primrose family (Primulaceae). The graceful, almost windblown-looking flowers stand erect above the dense mat of grey-green foliage and continue to develop over a long period of time. The flowers are delicately scented but are more noted for their hues of pink, white, crimson, and delicate lavender. For flower and foliage effect, cyclamens are difficult to upstage (Figure 12.15).

Their beauty, however, comes with a cultural price. Native to the Mediterranean

FIGURE 12.15 Cyclamen, flowers and foliage add great beauty to the home. Beauty has a price, however, as cyclamens have exacting cultural requirements.

region and preferring shade, the cyclamen needs as much sunlight as you can provide in the home and quite cool temperatures, preferably around 40 to 50°F. The plant should be kept constantly moist; periods of drought will endanger the developing flower buds.

Many people purchase or receive cyclamens, enjoy their flowering season during the fall and winter, and dispose of them in the spring. Since the foliage and flowers arise from a corm, the plant can be cultured indefinitely with proper summer care. This is a challenge, however, since most will not reflower. After flowering, the plant should be allowed to dry out and kept out of the sun. In early summer, repot the corm in fresh potting soil, placing it at the depth at which it previously grew. In later years, as the corm grows, it will be planted only halfway into the soil. Water sparingly to retain the existing foliage. As new foliage begins to develop, step up watering and fertilization to strengthen the plant for flowering and to stimulate foliage development.

Easter Lily

With flowers as triumphant as the season they commemorate, the Easter lily is an inspirational plant at any time of the year. Florists and growers purchase precooled bulbs in order to force Easter lilies into flower at the appropriate season (Figure 12.16). Otherwise, they create an excellent effect outdoors. These majestic plants belong to the lily family (Liliaceae).

Unless you plan outdoor planting of the bulb after it flowers inside, throw the plant away when the flowers decline.
When forced a second time indoors, the plant's performance is disappointing.

These plants should be placed in bright indirect light, kept cool at night and no warmer than the mid-60s (farenheit) at day. Keep the soil moist. The flowers will last approximately a week indoors, so do not

FIGURE 12.16 The Easter lily proudly proclaims the good news of the Easter season.

count on a particularly long visit by this species. Removing the anthers soon after the flowers open will prevent pollination and extend the life of the flowers, as well as keep the pure white petals clean and bright.

Erica

Another member of the acid-loving heath family (Ericaceae), *Erica* (ER-ih-ka) is a dense, shrubby evergreen with minute leaves and a profusion of small, delicately colored flowers.

The most commonly used species for indoor use is *Erica melanthera*, the Christmas heather, named for its gift popularity at that time of year. A small plant staying under 2 feet tall, the Christmas heather is loaded with minute pink flowers during the winter and spring. The overall plumelike quality of the plant provides a unique textural effect (Figure 12.17).

In spite of its beauty, this plant is not as widely offered by florists as other plants listed here. On purchasing or receiving one, treat it culturally much like azalea that belongs to the same family. Like azalea, *Erica* will not thrive in various parts of the country

FIGURE 12.17 In areas where florists include *Erica* species in their inventory, these plants make for an unusual departure from the usual selection of flowering plants.

FIGURE 12.18 Gardenia flowers are both lovely and extremely fragrant.

outdoors, but wherever it does survive, will provide years of beauty.

Gardenia

The most fragrant of all indoor flowering plants, the gardenia (gar-DEEN-ya) is native to China with a long history of use in this country, particularly in the warm Deep South. It belongs to the madder family (Rubiaceae). Its glossy, dark green leaves and large white flowers up to 3 inches across enhance its fragrance with attractiveness (Figure 12.18).

Culturally, bright sun and cool nights are a must for flower production. If gardenias are placed where they receive less than half a day of sun and night temperatures over 70°F, flower buds will not appear. They also like acidic and constantly moist soil that is well drained. As with azaleas, iron sulfate can help to keep the soil pH at a desirable acidic level. The leaves are good indicators of soil needs. The presence of chlorosis indicates a lack of iron caused by a high pH. If the veins are not darker than the other leaf areas, but there is a general foliar yellowing, the problem is probably nitrogen deficiency.

Mealybugs, aphids, and whiteflies are the primary pests to watch for; they infest the leaves and leaf axils. Periodic inspections will prevent a buildup.

The buds from which gardenia flowers come are extremely tempermental, falling at the slightest provocation—low humidity, improper watering, improper fertilization, and drafts. The most common problem is the shock of the home's dry humidity, following the humid production greenhouse. Keeping the newly acquired plant in a moist area and misting it frequently will help to acclimate it to the new surroundings.

Geranium

The garden geranium (*Pelargonium hortorum*), also called the zonal geranium (ger-RAIN-ee-um) because of the circular darkened zone that appears on each rounded leaf, is one of the more difficult plants to grow indoors. Geraniums belong to the geranium family (Geraniaceae). As the "garden geranium" name implies, the plant enjoys the full sun of the garden; in fact, it demands it. Except under the brightest of conditions, geraniums kept indoors eventually stop flowering and become leggy, unattractive specimens. Although they flower continuously under greenhouse conditions, they will only flower during seasons of long days indoors.

The geranium's soil should be allowed to dry between waterings to prevent stem or root rots. The plant should be fertilized frequently during its active growth.

Geraniums are available throughout the year, but most commonly in late winter and early spring. Their flower colors range from red and pink to white, with some cultivars having variegated foliage as well (Figure 12.19).

Garden geraniums are best kept outdoors during the warm months. Cuttings propagated during the summer can grow into attractive plants before cold weather. Trying to carry garden-grown plants over winter indoors will usually lead to disappointment. Many growers now produce garden geraniums from seed. These are of high quality and free of virus disease, which can be carried on into new plants through cuttings.

Of recent popularity is the hanging geranium (*Pelargonium hastatum*). In spite of its graceful hanging growth habit and attractive flowers, the hanging geranium is even more difficult to culture indoors than the garden geranium. The plant's tendency to produce long internodes causes a leggy quality when light is inadequate. Hanging geraniums are best purchased early in the growing season and grown outdoors during summer.

Another group in this genus, the scented geraniums, emit various fragrances from the leaves or stems when they are rubbed. Plants can be obtained that smell like mint, lemon, nutmeg, ginger, apricot, peppermint, apple, lime, or other scents. These plants generally have foliage much more lacy in appearance than the garden geranium and typically exhibit a spindly growth habit; they are more interesting for their scent than for their form or flowers.

FIGURE 12.19 Geraniums provide colorful beauty after purchase but will continue to do so only in full sun.

Gloxinia

This beautiful but fragile plant was first discovered as a chance seedling in Scotland during the mid-nineteenth century. Years of selection have led to today's flower colors of red, blue, white, purple, and other pastels (Figure 12.20).

A "cousin" to the popular African violet (Gesneriaceae), gloxinia (glox-IN-ee-uh) needs similar growing conditions: bright, indirect light; warm night temperatures; and frequent feedings. Watering is critical. Soil should be kept slightly moist at all times, but slight overwatering can precipitate crown rot. Unlike the African violet, though, gloxinia (*Sinningia speciosa*) goes through pronounced periods of dormancy after flowering. When the flowers fade, reduce watering gradually and stop fertilization. The leaves will eventually deteriorate as

FIGURE 12.20 With proper attention to dormancy requirements, the indoor gardener can enjoy gloxinia flowers year after year.

watering is withheld. After several months, the plant will again generate new growth, indicating the need for repotting in a rich, well-drained soil and the renewal of watering and fertilization. After the foliage is again established, flowering will commence.

Also like the African violet, the foliage of gloxinia is quite fragile. Since the leaves are big and overhang the rim of the pot, they are easily damaged during movement of the container. Use care in this regard, since one of these large leaves lost can leave a size-able void in the foliage pattern. With proper care and attention to the dormancy cycle, gloxinia can provide years of velvety, trumpet-shaped flowers. In addition, the number of plants can be easily increased through leaf cuttings. The petiole is inserted into a well-drained propagation medium; the plants that arise, if cared for properly, will reach flowering size in six to eight months.

Hydrangea

The popular bigleaf hydrangea (*Hydrangea macrophylla*) is one of the few plants in cultivation that changes flower color accord-

ing to soil pH. A somewhat acid soil will produce lavender-colored flowers. If the pH rises above 6.2 (moderately acid), the flower color becomes increasingly pink. On the other hand, a pH of less than 5.5 will result in blue flowers because of the aluminum made available to the plant in acidic soils. Bigleaf hydrangea (hi-DRAN-gee-uh) can be cultured in soils of various pH to manipulate the flower color, but attempts to change the flower color from pink to blue, or vice versa, once the color is showing will result in an unattractive mixture. More successful is to enhance the inherent color through increasing the acidity or alkalinity, as appropriate, with iron sulfate or ground limestone, respectively (Figure 12.21).

Because of this interesting color characteristic and the large, cushion-shaped flower head, the bigleaf hydrangea has been popular for centuries in Europe as a potted plant. Growing into a shrub in warmer parts of this country, the plant will quickly outgrow a suitable size indoors. Consequently, periodic pruning, moving the plant outdoors, or prop-

FIGURE 12.21 Hydrangea is one of the few flowers that offers two attractive flower colors, depending on soil pH.

agating new plants through stem cuttings is necessary.

Hydrangeas do well indoors for short periods. They "enjoy" the typical household temperature. The soil should be kept constantly moist and watered frequently because of rapid water transpiration through the large leaves. The individual flowers in the showy clusters are sterile and will last for up to six weeks. White varieties are available that do not change color with pH variations. Several cultivars with superior flower color and form are available. The hydrangea is a member of the saxifrage family (Saxifragaceae).

Jerusalem Cherry

Related to the well-known potato and tomato as a member of the nightshade family (Solanaceae), the Jerusalem cherry (*Solanum pseudocapsicum*) is best known for its fruit closely resembling cherry tomatoes (Figure 12.22). Unfortunately, this fruit, unlike the tomato, is reported to be poisonous, a definite disadvantage in homes with small children. The plant is typically sold during the Christmas season because of its red fruit color and contrasting dark green foliage. There is a less well-known, yellow-fruited variant. The small white flowers appear in late summer.

This plant is a perennial and can be carried over for future years but generally produces disappointment because of a straggly growth habit and poor fruiting due to insufficient pollination. It is best used for its interesting fruiting effect during the Christmas season, then discarded.

Because of its profusion of thin leaves, the plant requires watering constantly. Keep it moist and in as much sun as possible. Its primary drawback indoors is the need for low night temperatures (around 50°F). Yellowing leaves indicate that conditions are too warm. Because of the need for frequent watering, plant growth will be enhanced if fertilization is frequent also.

Whiteflies are particularly attracted to this plant. Ensure during purchase or receipt of the plant that no whiteflies are present by brushing the foliage and watching for the small flying gnats.

Kalanchoe

Pronounced kal-an-KOE-ee or, less preferably, ka-LAN-choe, this succulent genus in

FIGURE 12.22 The attractive fruit of Jerusalem cherry creates a red Christmas display.

FIGURE 12.23 The vivacious kalanchoe is best treated like cut flowers—enjoyed, then discarded.

Indoor Gardens and Seasonal Visitors **319**

the orpine family (Crassulaceae) contains around 100 species of plants. The most popular, the Christmas kalanchoe, is derived as cultivars and hybrids from *Kalanchoe blossfeldiana* (Figure 12.23). Like several other gift plants we have discussed, this one is best enjoyed while it flowers, then grown as a foliage plant or thrown away. Because of its high light and mainly photoperiodic (short day) requirement for flowering, subsequent attempts to induce flowering usually prove futile.

Plants and flowers should be given all the sun you can provide. Allow the soil to dry thoroughly between waterings to discourage rots and withhold fertilization. Typical home temperatures are satisfactory.

The flowers of the Christmas kalanchoe are profuse clusters that literally cover the top of the plant. As a result of the general interest in its cultivation over the years, numerous flower colors are now available including red, orange, yellow, white, and pink.

Poinsettia

This popular holiday plant (*Euphorbia pulcherrima*) was named after a U.S. ambassador to Mexico during the early nineteenth century. Poinsettia (poin-SET-ee-

FIGURE 12.24 Bracts, not flowers, provide the brilliant burst of color so noted among poinsettias.

uh) is strongly associated with the Christmas season. Ironically, the colorful "flowers" for which it is noted are not flowers at all, but rather bracts, leaflike structures that turn from green to another attractive, bright color—usually red. The actual flowers are the yellow cluster at the center of the colorful bracts (Figure 12.24).

Through the years since its introduction into this country from its origin as a Mexican wildflower, the poinsettia has continued to be improved. The colorful bracts are now found in various colors ranging from red to white. Quite recently, plants were developed that held their lower leaves for months following the holiday season; previously, it was not unusual to have bracts atop naked stems just several days after Christmas. As a member of the euphorbia or spurge family (Euphorbiaceae), the poinsettia has a characteristic milky sap. This sap, called **latex**, is also quite sticky. The poinsettia is related to the genus *Hevea*, the most important source of natural rubber.

Poinsettias enjoy much sun and no drafts, particularly cold ones. In colder parts of the country, florists who deliver poinsettias must protect them from the cold on the short trips to and from the truck. Otherwise, the cold will initiate leaf drop. The ideal cultural temperature is reminiscent of Mexican nights near 60°F or slightly below and days in the 70s. The soil should dry between watering.

With some care, poinsettias can be maintained year after year, and even planted outdoors in southern California and Florida. When the plant passes its peak of attractiveness, cut back each stem to two or three buds and repot. Cultivate outdoors with plenty of fertilization, light, and water, but allow drying between waterings. Even though the bracts are not flowers, their coloration develops concurrently with flowering. Since the poinsettia is a short-day plant, it must have long nights to initiate flowering. Therefore, around the middle of September,

subject the plant to at least 14 hours of darkness each night for six weeks. Any interruption in darkness, such as momentarily turning on a closet light where the plant is located, will prevent flowering. After flower initiation occurs around the end of October, long days are no longer required.

Additional plants can be propagated by cuttings.

FOR FURTHER READING

Bradford, R., and Luciano. *Terrariums and Aquariums.* New York: Hidden House/Flash Books, 1975.

Bulbs. Handbook #31. Brooklyn Botanic Garden, New York.

Miniature Gardens. Handbook #58. Brooklyn Botanic Garden, New York.

Bulbs. Alexandria, Va.: Time-Life Books, 1971.

Cacti and Succulents. Alexandria, Va.: Time-Life Books, 1971.

Evans, C. M., and R. L. Pliner. *The Terrarium Book.* New York: Random House, 1973.

Fitch, C. M. *The Complete Book of Terrariums.* New York: Hawthorn Books, 1974.

Genders, R. *Bulbs: A Complete Handbook of Bulbs, Corms and Tubers.* London: Robert Hale and Co., 1973.

Grounds, R. *Bottle Gardens.* Chicago: Henry Regnery Company, 1976.

Grubman, B. J. *Introduction to Terrariums, A Step by Step Guide.* New York: Popular Library, 1972.

Kramer, J. *Bottle Gardens.* New York: Lancer Larchmont Books, 1973.

Kramer, J. *The Complete Book of Terrarium Gardening.* New York: Scribner's, 1974.

Lamb, E., and B. Lamb. *Colorful Cacti of the American Deserts.* New York: MacMillan, 1974.

Lewis, G. *Terrariums: The World of Nature Under Glass:* Waukesha, Wisc.: Outdoor World, 1973.

Martin, N. J., P. R. Chapman, and H. A. Auger. *Cacti and Their Cultivation:* London: Faber and Faber, 1971.

McConnell, D. B. *The Indoor Gardener's Companion.* New York: Van Nostrand Reinhold, 1978.

Poincelot, R. P. *Gardening Indoors with House-plants.* Emmaus, Penn.: Rodale Press, 1974.

Synge, P. M. *The Complete Guide to Bulbs.* New York: E. P. Dutton, 1962.

Van Nass, M. *Cacti and Succulents—Indoors and Outdoors.* New York: Van Nostrand Reinhold, 1971.

Wilson, C. L. *The World of Terrariums.* Middle Village, N. J.: Jonathan David Publishers, 1975.

PART FOUR

PLANT GROUPS
OF SPECIAL INTEREST

Up to this point in the text, we have talked about the variety of considerations involved in growing indoor plants successfully. No doubt as we have used various plant examples to illustrate the many principles of plant growth and culture, the reader has begun to develop an appreciation of the marvelous variety of color and texture found in the plants we use indoors.

In spite of this grand variety, certain groups of plants have proven over the years to be the most durable and popular specimens for indoor use. Because these plant groups have proven to be so important, they are best considered as units, rather than as individuals treated solely in the encyclopedic section that follows. We have not, however, limited plants of these groups exclusively to this chapter. Some of the members of these groups are so valuable indoors that they cannot be overlooked as part of the top 150 plants. Consequently, we have discussed those plants as part of the "Top 150" that follows and have covered their family characteristics, as well as subordinate species, here in Chapter Thirteen.

Concluding the chapter is a section describing those plants that have harmful characteristics of which we should be aware. Some plants, for example, are toxic if ingested and can cause a severe reaction. On the other hand, in a more positive light, we

have classified the most popular 150 indoor
plants according to their aesthetic value and
uses. This concluding table of Chapter Thirteen will assist the reader in determining the
best methods for using particular plants
indoors.

chapter thirteen
major
plant groups

In spite of the overwhelming individuality of indoor plants, certain families or groups of plants have established themselves as particularly important. Members of these families typically exhibit superior foliar quality, flowering interest, unusual form, or ease of cultivation.

Our purpose in this chapter is to introduce these prominent groups, presenting their (1) common and unique qualities, (2) world distribution, (3) botanical characteristics, (4) significant genera, and (5) cultural properties. Several of these groups have spawned plant societies that promote knowledge and utilization of the plants. Consequently, we will present the significant aspects of these plants here, leaving the reader to contact the appropriate plant society to acquire further information.

Many of these societies, such as the African Violet Society of America, publish periodical journals or magazines that offer timely and instructional articles. Additionally, most have local chapters that conduct periodic meetings, offer educational programs, and sponsor shows.

The plant groups under consideration in this chapter will be aroids, begonias, bromeliads, cacti, ferns, gesneriads, orchids, and palms. Following these discussions, we turn our attention to grouping plants on a functional basis. Here, we offer lists of plants based on the following criteria: flower effect, ornamental fruit, colorful foliage, hanging quality, climbing capability, and large size. The chapter concludes on a more solemn note—plants that must be used with care because they bear thorns, are poisonous, or possess other potentially harmful traits.

ARACEAE: THE AROIDS OR ARUM FAMILY

Common and Unique Qualities
Although we are arranging these eight important families or groups alphabetically, our discussion begins with the most indispensable group. Araceae consists of 50 genera and about 2000 species and a massive quantity of cultivars and variants. They are long-lasting and well adapted to the indoor environment. The growth habits of these terrestrial, aquatic, or epiphytic plants include stemless herbs and climbing vines with aerial roots. An unusual feature of this monocot family is that many members lack parallel venation that typifies most monocots.

The underground storage structures of several aroid genera are used for subsistence food in a number of tropical areas. Many contain calcium oxalate crystals, but baking or boiling destroys these, making the starchy substance edible.

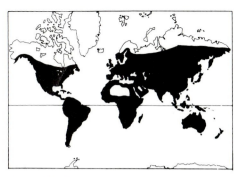

FIGURE 13.1 Distribution of Araceae. *Source:* Heywood, V., *Flowering Plants of the World*, New York: W. H. Smith Publishers, 1978, p. 307. Reproduced with permission of Gallery Books an imprint of W. H. Smith Publishers.

World Distribution

Although aroids inhabit most tropical regions of the world, some species, such as the well-known jack-in-the-pulpit (*Arisaema triphyllum*), are found in temperate regions. Members of the family cover the globe excluding northern Canada, northern Asia, the Arctic, and Antarctica region. The only other significant region lacking aroids is the Sahara Desert in northern Africa (Figure 13.1).

Botanical Features

FOLIAGE. Leaves of some species arise in rosettes from underground corms or rhizomes, whereas other species produce alternate leaves along a stem. Although the leaf shapes vary dramatically and range from entire to greatly dissected, the common denominator of aroid foliage is the long, membranous basally sheathing petioles. The leaves and other tissues of many aroid genera contain a milky sap, known as latex, and calcium oxalate crystals. The genus *Dieffenbachia*, the dumbcanes, contain these crystals and, if chewed, cause painful swelling of the mouth.

In many genera, the juvenile leaves of young plants are shaped differently than those of adult or mature plants. With some of the *Monstera* species, for example, the young plants resemble *Philodendron*, whereas the adult foliage becomes heavily perforated. In fact, the juvenile *Monstera deliciosa* is frequently labeled and sold as *Philodendron pertusum*.

FLOWERS. Aroids characteristically produce a thick, fleshy spike, called the **spadix**, bearing bisexual or unisexual flowers. Although the spadix is usually not particularly conspicuous, the large bract that subtends it gives the inflorescence a prominent and attractive appearance.

This bract, called the **spathe**, may surround the base of the spadix, as with *Anthurium* species, or it may envelop the spadix, as in the *Spathiphyllum* genus (Figure 13.2).

In most genera, the flower display is an attractive feature; in the colorful caladium, however, the flowers are normally removed before full development occurs to reduce their impact on the plant's vigor (see Chapter Ten).

Though not common, the inflorescence of some aroids emits an unpleasant odor that in

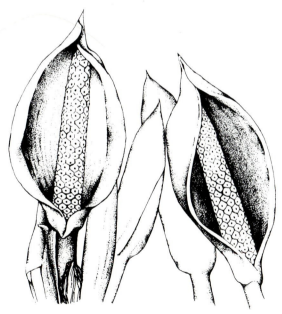

FIGURE 13.2 The aroid inflorescence, showing spathe and spadix.

nature attracts flies for pollination. One such plant is skunk cabbage (*Symplocarpus foetidus*), which inhabits the temperate eastern seaboard of the United States. As one might expect, the plants valued indoors do not exhibit this odiferous trait.

FRUIT. The fruit is a berry, sometimes brightly colored, that contains one or many seeds. These are borne on the spadix. One of the better aroid genera for fruiting attractiveness is *Aglaonema*.

ROOTS. Aroid roots are adventitious (occurring other than in the usual places) and are of two types: (1) roots that are not influenced by gravity and grow away from the light, adhering firmly to surface irregularities of the support or tree, and (2) those that develop water-absorbing tissue over their surface and grow downward toward the soil. In nature, aroids may be planted by birds up in trees and these roots may eventually reach down into the ground. On indoor species, aerial roots can either be tucked into the container or removed without harm.

Significant Genera

As presented in Table 13.1, the aroids represent a significant portion of the top 150 plants described in Part Five. The brightly colored caladium is discussed as a "holiday visitor" in Chapter Twelve. In addition to the thorough treatment given to aroid genera in Part Five, we will include three other genera here that are of interest.

ACORUS. Variegated grassy-leaved sweet flag (*Acorus gramineus* 'Variegatus') is the most individualistic aroid of the group. Its

leaves are linear and 12 inches long, much like grass. They are arranged fanlike and are light green with white variegations. A water lover by nature, this plant is excellent for terrariums or aquatic settings.

ALOCASIA. The most common species is *Alocasia macrorrhiza*, commonly known as pai or taro. Growing to 15 feet in its native habitat, the plant produces huge 3-foot-long leaves. There are several other species, smaller in size than pai, that possess interesting and colorful leaf patterns.

ZANTEDESCHIA. This genus, known as calla or calla lily, is a rhizomatous group of plants with a showy, almost circular funnel-shaped spathe (Figure 13.3). Perhaps best known as a florist-cut flower, dormant calla rhizomes are planted in early fall and grown indoors in full sun. They need high humidity, warm temperatures, and a rich well-drained potting soil that is kept constantly moist.

FIGURE 13.3 The graceful inflorescence of *Zantedeschia*, the calla lily.

TABLE 13.1 ARACEAE GENERA INCLUDED IN PART FIVE

Aglaonema	*Monstera*
Anthurium	*Philodendron*
Dieffenbachia	*Scindapsus*
Epipremnum	*Spathiphyllum*
	Syngonium

Culture

ENVIRONMENTAL FACTORS. Aroids inhabit a great percentage of American homes because of their ability to endure warm temperatures, low light, and low humidity. Ideally, they should be given relatively high humidity conditions, with bright indirect sunlight for full leaf development and flowering, moderately warm temperatures during the growing season, and soil and watering conditions that match their native conditions. Because of the diversity of native habitat, Part Five should be consulted to determine cultural characteristics for a particular genus. In general, though, philodendrons are among the easier plants to culture indoors.

PROPAGATION. Most popular aroids are climbers, which are easily propagated from tip cuttings, stem cuttings, or leaf-bud cuttings. Chapter Four discusses these cutting methods in detail. A number of species produce tubers, rhizomes, or corms that may be propagated by dividing the structure with a knife before planting. Most aroids can be easily produced from seeds if they are sown fresh onto a sterile medium and maintain moist conditions and temperatures in the high 70s (farenheit).

PESTS AND DISEASES. In residential culture, aroids are relatively free of insects and diseases, although mealybugs, scale, thrips, and mites are possibilities. Disease problems would include leaf spots and rots, particularly in over-humid conditions or as a result of overwatering. Some genera are particularly susceptible to virus and bacterial diseases, neither of which can be effectively controlled in the home.

BEGONIACEAE: THE BEGONIA FAMILY

World Distribution

The begonia family, containing three genera, consists of over 1000 species, almost all of which belong to the *Begonia* genus. These fascinating plants heavily inhabit the tropical and subtropical regions of the world. Their range includes all of Central America, the northern half and southern tip of South America, the southern two-thirds of the African continent, southern and southeastern Asia, and the Philippines. These monoecious, perennial herbs or shrubs may be climbing, procumbent, or shrublike.

Since the first species was discovered in Central America in 1690, the group has continued to grow in stature and popularity. The American Begonia Society, Inc. publishes a monthly journal entitled *The Begonian*, which contains instructional and promotional articles. To date, over 10,000 hybrids and cultivars are recorded. Few other plant families include a more varied palette of growth and foliage characteristics than this one.

Botanical Features

FOLIAGE. It is this one aspect of begonias that makes them so unique among indoor plants. Figure 13.4 illustrates the vast array of leaf types and shapes. Leaf sizes range from less than an inch to over 2 feet long. Characteristically, the leaves are alternate, two-ranked, asymmetrical, and bear large deciduous stipules at their base. As Figure 13.4 also demonstrates, begonia leaves are excellent impostors of other plants, including maples, grapes, ivy, and elms.

FLOWERS. Arising in axillary cymes, the unisexual flowers are white, pink, red, orange, yellow, or variations of these hues. Typically standing above the foliage, the flowers are an attractive and conspicuous addition.

FRUIT. Capsules typically follow flower maturity, producing many dustlike seeds. These capsules are not ornamental.

FORMS OF GROWTH. Various authorities classify begonias into specific groups accord-

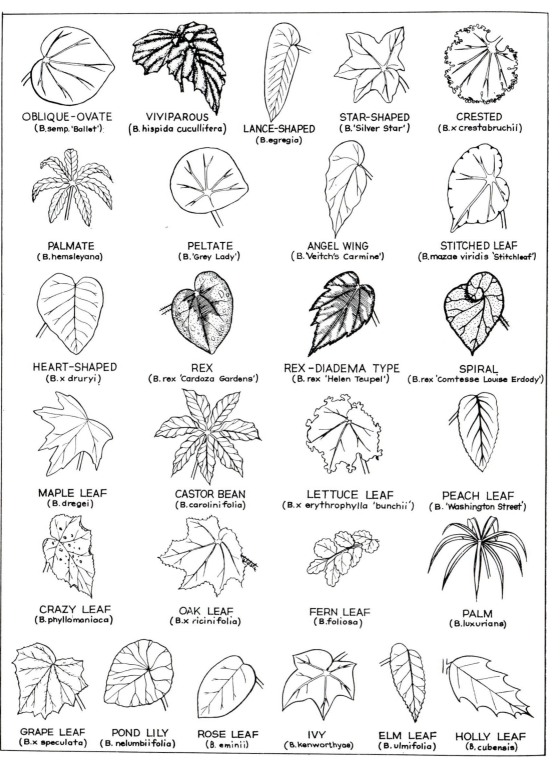

OBLIQUE-OVATE
(B. semp. 'Ballet')

VIVIPAROUS
(B. hispida cucullifera)

LANCE-SHAPED
(B. egregia)

STAR-SHAPED
(B. 'Silver Star')

CRESTED
(B. × crestabruchii)

PALMATE
(B. hemsleyana)

PELTATE
(B. 'Grey Lady')

ANGEL WING
(B. 'Veitch's Carmine')

STITCHED LEAF
(B. mazae viridis 'Stitchleaf')

HEART-SHAPED
(B. × druryi)

REX
(B. rex 'Cardoza Gardens')

REX-DIADEMA TYPE
(B. rex 'Helen Teupel')

SPIRAL
(B. rex 'Comtesse Louise Erdody')

MAPLE LEAF
(B. dregei)

CASTOR BEAN
(B. carolinifolia)

LETTUCE LEAF
(B. × erythrophylla 'bunchii')

PEACH LEAF
(B. 'Washington Street')

CRAZY LEAF
(B. phyllomaniaca)

OAK LEAF
(B. × ricinifolia)

FERN LEAF
(B. foliosa)

PALM
(B. luxurians)

GRAPE LEAF
(B. × speculata)

POND LILY
(B. nelumbiifolia)

ROSE LEAF
(B. eminii)

IVY
(B. kenworthyae)

ELM LEAF
(B. ulmifolia)

HOLLY LEAF
(B. cubensis)

FIGURE 13.4 The typical leaf shapes of Begoniaceae. *Source:* Graf, Dr. A. B., *Exotica*, East Rutherford, N.J.: Roehrs Co., 1976, p. 294.

ing to growth characteristics. One method is based on growth habit, describing the plants as canelike (stems generally stout, straightened, and jointed at the nodes), shrublike, thick-stemmed, semperflorens (wax begonias), rhizomatous, Rex, tuberous, and trailing scandent.

A more simple and widely utilized method is based on their root stock characteristics: fibrous-rooted, rhizomatous, and tuberous (Figure 13.5). We shall see a similar method of classification for Gesneriaceae.
The fibrous-rooted begonias include the wax begonia group, the cane types, and species with wooly leaves. This group is valued both for flower and foliage effect. Those species with rhizomes include the Rex group and a variety of other types; this group has the least ornamental flowers of the genus. And finally, the tuberous-rooted begonias include various plants useful for summer landscaping, hanging baskets, and greenhouse culture during cold weather. This group is grown predominantly for its flowers. Tuberous-rooted begonias normally have a distinct dormancy period during which the foliage declines and resprouting must occur.

Major Species
The begonia family is an overwhelming group of plants from which to select the most important genera. Many contain hundreds of cultivars and variants exhibiting various forms, leaf shape and color, and flower color. One of the most common fibrous-rooted types, the wax begonia, is discussed fully in Part Five.

Let us consider the various genera according to the eight classifications of growth habit.

The **cane-stemmed** begonias, also called

FIGURE 13.5 The three groups of begonias based on root stock characteristics: fibrous rooted (wax begonia), tuberous (tuberous begonia), and rhizomatous types (maple-leaf begonia).

angel wing begonias, have bamboolike stems with wide internodes. The leaves are dramatically oblique, looking much like wings. Perhaps the best known species is *Begonia corallina*, with glossy green leaves that are red below and white spotted above. The canes grow to a height of 8 to 10 feet in nature. *Begonia* 'Lucerna' is one of the older cultivars in this group with *B. corallina* parentage. 'Lucerna' has larger, more olive green leaves than *Begonia corallina* and the spots are silver. The bright red flowers droop in large clusters.

The **shrublike** begonias are perhaps the least common commercial type. The stems are much less stout and vigorous than those of the cane type. An example of this growth habit is *Begonia suffruticosa*, the maple-leaf begonia. The specific epithet "suffruticosa" means shrubby.

Thick-stemmed begonias are somewhat like the cane stemmed, but they are usually even more stout. Of the numerous cultivars on the market, *Begonia* 'Perle de Lorraine' is one example.

The fibrous-rooted **wax** begonias (*Begonia × semperflorens-cultorum*) are discussed in Part Five. A relatively new begonia with red to orange-red flowers larger than wax begonias, but smaller than the flowers of the tuberous begonia is *Begonia × Rieger*, the Rieger begonia. These colorful additions are gaining in popularity as gift plants.

Rhizomatous begonias include numerous plants with a wide variety of leaf shapes. Two of the more important species in this group are *Begonia masoniana*, the iron-cross begonia (Figure 13.6), and *Begonia × erythrophylla*, the beefsteak begonia.

Rex begonias (*Begonia × rex-cultorum*) represent the highest fashion among this family. These spectacular plants have multicolored and variously textured leaves that reach lengths of 1 foot. These plants are extremely variable from seed, so are propagated vegetatively by rhizome division in which genetic consistency is necessary.

FIGURE 13.6 *Begonia masoniana*, the iron-cross begonia.

Tuberous begonias are often bought simply as dormant tubers, sprouted, then potted into hanging baskets or containers for a showy display of flowers (Figure 13.7). The single or double flowers come in a wide variety of colors. *Begonia × hiemalis*, winter-flowering begonias, are the most notable group. Another one, *Begonia × tuberhybrida*, produces camellia- or carnationlike flowers up to 6 inches across in shades of white, pink, red, orange, and yellow.

The **trailing-scandent** types are best suited for hanging baskets in which their slender, pendulous canes can hang gracefully. The flowers are borne in clusters, primarily at the stem tips. Although there are many, a well-known cultivar is *Begonia* 'Florence Carrell' with light green leaves and light coral flowers.

Any attempt to spotlight the most outstanding group of begonias is ultimately futile. So many outstanding species and cultivars must be omitted that those included represent only the tip of the iceberg. *Hortus Third*, for example, includes 12 pages on begonia species, a treatment that includes only a few of the thousands of variants.

FIGURE 13.7 The showy and graceful display of the tuberous begonia.

Culture

ENVIRONMENTAL FACTORS. Although the wide variety of plant types in Begoniaceae creates some cultural diversity, typically begonias enjoy moist, warm conditions. Night temperatures should stay above 65°F and not surpass 80°F during the day. Because of their susceptibility to mildew, good air circulation is necessary, particularly when humidity levels are high.

Soil for begonias should be light and well drained, as well as rich in organic matter. Most species like even moisture at their roots, but some types, such as the wax, cane-stemmed, and velvety types, should dry somewhat between waterings.

For dense foliage development and profuse flowering, filtered sunlight is important, particularly for the wax and cane-stemmed types. Most should be placed in full winter sunlight to maintain a compact form. Fertilization should be frequent, but at half strength during active growth and withheld during the dormant period.

PROPAGATION. Although most begonias can be produced readily from seed if dustlike seed procedures are followed, some of the hybrids, such as the Rex begonias, will not reproduce the appearance of the parent from seed. These may be planted experimentally, however, to produce new and unusual color combinations. Some species produce axillary bulbs that may be removed and planted to form new offspring. Most stem-type begonias can be propagated easily from stem or tip cuttings using partially matured tissue. The wax begonia, for example, can be rooted easily in water.

The rhizomatous types are started from rhizome sections buried horizontally in the propagation medium. Rex, rhizomatous, and other begonia species with heavy leaves may be started with whole-leaf cuttings or leaf wedges that include a vein. This method is slower than stem or rhizome cuttings and produces new plantlets at the base of the vein.

PESTS AND DISEASES. Only a few pests and diseases are serious on begonias, but those that show up must be dealt with promptly. Perhaps the most troublesome, because of its insidious nature, is the root-knot nematode. These microscopic creatures infest the root system of the plant, causing swellings and the inability of the root to take in water. Droopy foliage is the first symptom, but often it appears after the damage is done. Occasional checks of the root system are necessary to spot swollen roots early. Unfortunately, one of the best remedies is to simply discard the plant before the nematodes spread to other specimens. Mealybugs, both foliar and root, can also occur.

The most troublesome disease, mildew, is fortunately easy to manage with diligence. Allowed to develop, mildew will quickly destroy foliage. Occasional sprays with fungicide, particularly during damp weather conditions or in places with little air circulation, are effective. The same treatment is recommended for botrytis, another fungal infection that will attack the succulent foliage, particularly on species like *Begonia × rex-cultorum*, which have a thin cuticle layer.

BROMELIACEAE: THE PINEAPPLE FAMILY

Common and Unique Qualities

Bromeliads (bro-MILL-ee-ads), the common designation for members of the pineapple family, are a unique and diverse group of about 45 genera including over 2000 species.

Most members of this family are herbaceous plants with short stems and rosettes of stiff leaves, often formed into water-holding vases. Their level of specialization varies. The least specialized members are terrestrial dwellers with unexpanded leaf faces and leaf hairs that only function to reduce transpiration. A more specialized group are the tank-root types (pineapple, for example) that have few true roots. The overlapping leaf faces form a reservoir for water and humus that are absorbed by adventitious roots growing up between the leaf faces. A still more specialized tank type has larger leaf faces that are lined with absorbent specialized leaf hairs (**trichomes**) rather than by the roots. Most genera belong to this group. The most specialized plants (Spanish moss, for instance) are strictly epiphytic, having roots only as young seedlings and lacking the leaf vase reservoir. These plants absorb atmospheric moisture through specialized trichomes (Figure 13.8).

World Distribution

With the exception of one African species, bromeliads range from as far north as coastal Virginia to the southern tip of South America.

FIGURE 13.8 Spanish moss, one of the more specialized of the Bromeliaceae genera.

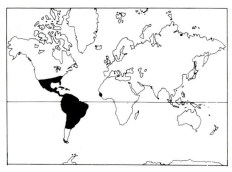

FIGURE 13.9 The natural range of Bromeliaceae. *Source:* Heywood, V., *Flowering Plants of the World*, New York: W. H. Smith Publishers, 1978, p. 294. Reproduced with permission of Gallery Books an imprint of W. H. Smith Publishers.

They are particularly prevalent in Mexico, the Antilles, Costa Rica, eastern and southern Brazil, and the Andes of Columbia, Peru, and Chile. These habitats represent almost every climatic extreme. Many grow in tropical rain forests characterized by high temperatures and luxuriant rainfall, whereas others have climbed mountains to exceedingly high altitudes, enduring cold and windy conditions. Some species grow in xerophytic areas, such as deserts, often associated with cacti (Figure 13.9).

Classification

Because of these water retention characteristics, bromeliads are sometimes classified as succulents—plants that have adapted the ability to retain water. This is not a universally accepted view, however. Plants with fleshy leaves and stems, such as cacti, form the typical succulent image.

The distinct differences among bromeliad genera have resulted in a division of the group into the following three subfamilies.

PITCAIRNIOIDEAE. This group, consisting of about one-third of the species, primarily contains terrestrial xerophytes. Other distinctions are made according to flower and seed characteristics. The primary genera are *Pitcairnia*, *Puya*, and *Dyckia*.

BROMELIOIDEAE. This group of terrestrial and epiphytic forms accounts for almost two-thirds of the family members. The included genera are *Aechmea*, *Ananas*, *Billbergia*, and *Bromelia*.

TILLANDSIOIDEAE. The members of this group, entirely epiphytic, are the genera *Tillandsia* and *Vriesea*.

Botanical Features

FOLIAGE. The leaves of bromeliads range from less than 2 inches in length on Spanish moss (*Tillandsia usneoides*) to the large, thick lancelike leaves of the pineapple (*Ananas comosus*). As we have seen above, the foliage has developed various degrees of specialization depending on the genus and habitat. The leaves are typically stiff and marginally spined and most frequently arranged in the water-holding rosette. Various species, such as the pineapple, produce fibers that are used for making cloth and cordage. The rigidity of Spanish moss foliage is demonstrated by its past use as a substitute for horse hair in stuffing upholstery.

FLOWERS. The spike, raceme, or panicle inflorescence typically arises from within the foliar rosette, usually followed by the death of the plant. Suckers are typically produced before death, however, allowing for reproduction.

Bromeliad flowers are characteristically brightly colored with vivid shades of yellow, white, red, purple, and related hues. The individual flowers are borne in the axils of often brightly colored bracts (Figure 13.10). On some species such as *Guzmania*, *Tillandsia*, and *Neoregelia*, the upper leaves (actually bracts) become vividly colored during and following flowering. On *Neoregelia*, for example, this central coloration can last

FIGURE 13.10 Bracts equal the importance of flowers in creating the striking effect of bromeliad inflorescences.

up to six months. Although many bromeliads are grown for their interesting form and foliage quality, the flowers of many species, including *Aechmea*, *Vriesea*, *Guzmania*, and *Tillandsia*, are particularly spectacular.

FRUIT. Of course, the most notable fruit of this family is the pineapple, a fusion of individual fruits that forms a multiple fruit. In other species, the fruit is a berry or capsule and not nearly as prominent as the pineapple fruit.

NATURAL PECULARITIES. The vases of bromeliads have been studied substantially to determine their significance other than as water sources for the plants. Various types of fauna and flora, including tree frogs, inhabit the vases of these plants in nature. In dryer tropical areas, these water-holding tanks facilitate the breeding of mosquitoes that carry malaria. Since mosquito larvae can be controlled in open expanses of water, the presence of bromeliads has slowed the elimination of malaria in some parts of the world.

Significant Genera

Part Five discusses individually several of the outstanding bromeliad genera: *Aechmea*, *Ananas*, *Cryptanthus*, and *Neoregelia*. Several remaining genera can provide interesting foliage and flower effects, as well as admirable durability.

BILLBERGIA. Commonly known as vase plants or queen's tears, *Billbergia* is an epiphyte with rosettes of broad or straplike convex leaves that form a water-holding reservoir. They are noted for their colorful foliage, which may be banded, striped, mottled, or spotted, and their graceful inflorescence that protrudes from the vase, extending above the foliage or hanging gracefully to one side. Although the inflorescence is short-lived, it displays bright rose-colored bracts and colorful flowers.

BROMELIA. This large terrestrial bromeliad is armed with hooked spines along its leaf margins; consequently, it is one of the less desirable species for the home. Nevertheless, its characteristic trait of developing brilliant red leaves with flowering makes it an attractive specimen. The inflorescence bracts are red and the principal flowering attraction.

GUZMANIA. This genus of epiphytic rainforest dwellers is considered by some authorities to be the most beautiful of all bromeliads (Figure 13.11). The straplike foliage is often banded, somewhat like the snake plant, and the flowers arise from the central vase with a spectactular splash of brilliant color ranging from white to yellow or red. Because of their natural habitat, these plants require more humidity, shade, and warmth than most other members of the family.

NIDULARIUM. Another group of rainforest inhabitants, these bird's nest bromeliads are characterized by flaring, straplike leaves that are thinner than the leaves of most other

FIGURE 13.11 Guzmania species offer both flower and foliar beauty. Shown here is *Guzmania musaica*, the mosaic vase.

FIGURE 13.12 *Tillandsia* species offer a finer textural quality than other Bromeliads.

genera. Characteristically, they are often mottled or variegated and display metallic or purple coloration. As a shade lover, *Nidularium* is relatively easy to cultivate.

TILLANDSIA. Like their most famous member, Spanish moss, *Tillandsias* normally have narrow, grasslike foliage tinted silver (Figure 13.12). Although most are epiphytes of the subtropical and tropical Americas, this genus is the most widely distributed of the family. The silvery foliage color is caused by fuzzy scales that cover the plant and absorb atmospheric moisture, holding it for absorption by the living plant cells. The flowers are colorful spikes on some species. *Tillandsia* prefers cool temperatures and occasional mistings to facilitate its natural means of acquiring water.

VRIESEA. One of the more hybridized members of the family, this genus offers numerous attractions in foliage and flower. Most are epiphytes with smooth, leathery foliage and spikes arising from the vase, typically into a brushlike configuration of red and yellow. The species *Vriesea × mariae* (the painted feather) is a well-known stalwart of this genus (Figure 13.13).

Culture

ENVIRONMENTAL FACTORS. Bromeliads can endure a wide variety of climatic conditions. They perform best in filtered sunlight and warm places. Depending on the epiphytic or terrestrial nature, they may be grown in standard potting soil (terrestrial) or in a fast-draining organic mix (epiphytes) that will keep the roots moist but not wet.

Watering of most bromeliads amounts to keeping their central vase full and their soil moist. A dilute fertilizer can be added to the foliar basin about once a month. They require about half the fertilizer of other indoor plants.

The epiphytic, vase types can usually

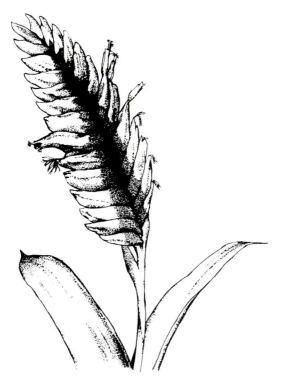

FIGURE 13.13 *Vriesea × mariae*, the painted feather.

thrive mounted on driftwood. Their central vases supply all their water and nutritional needs.

FLOWERING. A unique quality of bromeliads is that their flowering can be stimulated earlier than the plant would naturally flower. This is accomplished by exposing the cells at the base of the vase where the flower arises to either acetylene or ethylene gas. Several methods are possible. An easy one is to place eight to ten pea-sized pellets of calcium carbide into 1 quart of water, then fill the base of the plant with this solution. The acetylene gas that is released influences the normal plant growth regulation system and stimulates the plant into flowering.

A simpler method is to empty the central vase, place a ripening apple on the soil surface, and seal a plastic bag around the plant and container for five to seven days (Figure 13.14). The ethylene gas given off by the ripening apple will trigger the same reaction as the acetylene gas from calcium carbide.

FIGURE 13.14 Proper method of exposing bromeliads to the ethylene gas of a ripening apple. Empty plant vase of water before sealing.

After these treatments, flowers should appear within four weeks for *Billbergia*, six weeks for most *Aechmea* species, and eight weeks for *Vriesea*. If young flower structures are not apparent by those dates, the plant: (1) has already flowered, (2) is not mature enough to flower, or (3) has been treated incorrectly (water stood in the vase during the apple treatment, for instance). Main stems often die slowly after flowering but produce several basal offsets.

PROPAGATION. The easiest and most successful method of propagation is through suckers rising from the base of the plant. When the offsets are about 8 inches tall, they are severed at their base and repotted into individual containers. Seeds may also be used, though they are not practical in most home situations. They germinate on wet, sterile Kleenex tissue in an enclosed container under indirect light and conditions of 65 to 70°F.

Pineapples may be propagated by offsets or by removing the leafy crown of the fruit, allowing it to dry several days, and placing it into a well-drained and sterile propagation medium. The fruit stalk may also be sectioned and placed into a propagation medium.

PESTS AND DISEASES. The most prevalent invader is either soft or black scale. These may be treated with appropriate pesticide or an oil solution (see Chapter Nine). Since the scales are hard and impermeable, they should be scraped off prior to control treatment.

CACTACEAE: THE CACTUS FAMILY

Common and Unique Qualities

The cactus story is one of conquest—a tale of victory over hot, dry, and hostile regions. The family is a large one, including as many as 220 genera and 2000 species of xerophytic trees, shrubs, and vines.

Living in dry climates, these plants adapt to harsh conditions. Their leaves, in order to conserve water, are small or nonexistent. The stems are enlarged to store water and carry out the process of photosynthesis. Characterized by thick or milky sap, the ribbed or flattened plant structure never directly confronts the harsh heat of the sun. And for protection from natural enemies of the animal kingdom, these plants are armed with spines for defense. Because of this specialized and unique environmental relationship, cacti come in every conceivable shape and growth habit. Some are even epiphytic.

World Distribution

Cacti are native to the warm, dry semideserts of North, Central, and South America. A few are scattered in other parts of the world, but not to a significant extent.

Botanical Features

STEMS. As mentioned above, stems are the primary means through which cacti survive the drought of their native habitats. The stems of most species are green, carrying out the food manufacturing process of photosynthesis, but with age they become corky. The arborescent species develop a woody, spineless trunk much like conventional tree species. Even on some indoor species, such as the Christmas cactus, older plants develop a noticeable corkiness on the older stem tissue.

The stems are round, flattened, or triangular in cross section and may be jointed, ribbed, or tubercular (with small rounded projections). They may be simple or branched. A distinguishing feature of all cactaceae stems are the small cushions called **areoles,** which are ranged in an orderly fashion along the raised ribs or positioned singly on tubercles. In essence, these cushions are compacted lateral branches; they give rise to leaves (if present), spines, and branches. Glochids, tufts of short barbed hairs, may also arise from the areo-

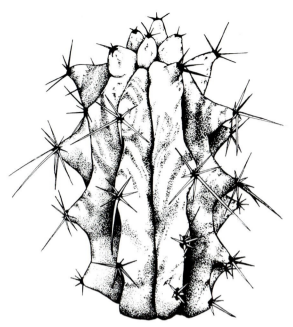

FIGURE 13.15 Areoles serve to accentuate the form of many cacti. *Source:* Kramer, J., *Cacti and Other Succulents*, Harry N. Abrams, 1977, plate 114, p. 94.

FIGURE 13.16 The cactus flower, though short lived, provides a vivid splash of form and color.

les. Their typically light color contrasts with the darker stem tissue, giving them a distinct and often attractive appearance (Figure 13.15).

FOLIAGE. Except for a few cactus species, such as the lemon vine (*Pereskia aculeata*), the great majority of plants have either no foliage or greatly reduced leaves. The stem typically takes over the photosynthetic process, since the leaves have been dropped to conserve moisture.

FLOWERS. Cactus flowers are usually short lived, but they rank highly among other plants with respect to spectacular beauty (Figure 13.16). The petals radiate daisylike and display vibrant shades of red, orange, yellow, white, and purple. In most species, they emerge at the end of a dormant period. Indoors, most cactus species must have direct sunlight in order to pop into bloom.

FRUIT. The juicy berry, which is typical of many species, is occasionally colorful and extends the period of interest during flowering. On other species, the berry may be leathery and dry, splitting at maturity to release the seeds.

ROOTS. The root system of cactus species absorbs water rapidly near the soil surface. Generally, the larger the species, the wider spreading is the root system.

Classification of Cacti

Because of their distinct growth habits, members of cactaceae are classified into three subfamilies:

PERESKIOIDEAE. Leaves are present, glochids are absent, and the seeds are black and lacking an aril. *Pereskia* is the primary genera of interest represented here (Figure 13.17).

OPUNTIOIDEAE. Both leaves and glochids are present, and the seeds are winged or covered with a pale aril. *Opuntia* is the primary genus of indoor interest.

CACTOIDEAE. The leaves are absent or quite small, glochids are absent, and the

FIGURE 13.17 *Pereskia aculeata*, the lemon vine, is one of the few cacti with expanded foliage.

dark seeds are enclosed with an aril. This group, which accounts for most of the Cactaceae genera, is divided into the following two tribes.

Cereeae. These are columnar plants predominantly, usually with stems sparsely ribbed and jointed. Flowering arises from the old areoles. Some of these plants flower only at night. *Cereus* and *Echinopsis* are the two most important indoor genera.

Cacteae. These are dwarf plants with non-jointed, liberally ribbed stems, with flowers arising from the new areoles. *Schlumbergera*, *Mammillaria*, and *Notocactus* are examples of this group.

Significant Genera

Because of the inherent durability and variety among Cactaceae members, a list of possible plants could fill the remainder of this text. Our purpose here is to select some of the easier-to-grow and popular cacti, including a variety of forms and growth habits.

The more serious student can make inquiries of the Cactus and Succulent Society of America, Inc., which publishes the *Cactus and Succulent Journal*, a bimonthly educational publication. Part Five covers three cactus genera: *Cereus*, *Opuntia*, and *Schlumbergera*.

We should mention here that many succulent plants are similar in appearance to cacti and are frequently confused with them. It is true that all cacti are succulents, but not all succulents belong to the cactus family. The collection of cacti and succulents has become a popular pastime for many serious amateur horticulturists.

APOROCACTUS. The rattail cactus (*Aporocactus flagelliformis*), a Mexican native, is the most popular member of this genus. A creeping or trailing plant with 1-inch-thick stems up to six feet long, it produces showy crimson-pink flowers similar in form to those of the Christmas cactus. The flowers are followed by small red berries.

ASTROPHYTUM. Called the star cacti collectively, these plants are easy to grow, rounded plants with unusual form (Figure 13.18).

FIGURE 13.18 *Astrophytum* offers some of the more unique cactus forms.

The most noted species are *Astrophytum myriostigma*, the bishop's cap (an 8-inch globe with five prominent ribs and large yellow flowers); *Astrophytum asterias*, the sea-urchin cactus or sand-dollar (a flattened globe speckled with white; eight shallow, spineless ribs; and yellow flowers); and *Astrophytum capricorne*, the goat's horn cactus [a green globe with seven or eight prominent ribs, each giving rise to several contorted spines, its flowers are yellow with a red center]. On all of these species, the flower sets prominently atop the globe.

ECHINOPSIS. The sea-urchin cacti are globose or oblong with prominent ribs. *Echinopsis longispina* has 25 to 50 ribs, with each areole giving rise to 10 or 15 spines up to 3 inches long. *Echinopsis multiplex*, the barrel cactus, produces spiny 8-inch-high stems that are 6 inches across. The flowers are rosy-red and nocturnal.

FEROCACTUS. These are rounded or oblong plants heavily covered with spines that are flattened and hooked, making their removal from flesh painful and difficult. The flowers arise near the apex of the stem in shades of yellow to orange.

LOBIVIA. This genus is quite similar in appearance to *Echinopsis*, but with shorter flowers that bloom during the day.

MAMMILLARIA. One of the most popular genera, these plants provide a variety of growth habits and spine configurations. Commonly known as pincushion or strawberry cacti, *Mammillaria* are often quite small. The have no ribs, but produce protuberances that are spine-tipped. The flowers range in shades of white, yellow, pink, and bright reds. They often are followed by bright red berries (Figure 13.19).

MELOCACTUS. Known commonly as the turk's cap cactus, this genus distinguishes itself by a velvety caplike pad that is perched atop mature plants. Flowers emerge from

FIGURE 13.19 *Mammillaria*, the pincushions, are one of the easier cactus groups to grow.

this area. This group has strong ribbing with spiny areoles lining the ridge of each rib.

NEOPORTERIA. This group has small, ribbed cacti with large flowers ranging from red or pink to yellow. Most are globular when young, but become more cylindrical with age. This group, known collectively as the ball cacti, are noted by some authorities as the best, easiest to grow, and most reliable flowering among the family. Flowering when small and maintaining a round shape for several years, these plants will produce yellow or red flowers on sunny windowsills.

PARODIA. This is another genus that flowers after only a couple of years. Called the Tom Thumb cacti, these plants are small flattened spheres with colorful spines. The flowers arise from the top of the sphere in clusters, ranging in color from yellow to rich red.

PERESKIA. As the most primitive of the cacti, this genus has large, ovate leaves and woody stems. The flowers are white, pink, or yellow and are similar in appearance to small single roses. The lemon vine (*Pereskia aculeata*) is shrublike when young but becomes a vine with age (see Figure 13.17). Its yellow, spiny fruit gives rise to the common name.

REBUTIA. These are small, globular cacti that differ from most other species in that the prolific flowers emerge from the sides and base of the plants. A free-flowering genus, these plants produce multitudes of bright red or yellow flowers in adequate sunlight. They are commonly known as the crown or pigmy cacti.

RHIPSALIS. These tropical epiphytes are leafless and lovers of moisture and warmth. Naturally perching on trees, their pendulous, leafless stems hang gracefully; hence, their best use indoors is in hanging baskets, potted into humus, fast-draining media. Because of an unusual appearance, these bear such common names as wickerware cactus, chain cactus, mistletoe cactus, and willow cactus (Figure 13.20).

FIGURE 13.20 Epiphytic cacti, such as *Rhipsalis,* offer graceful variety among a mostly terrestrial family.

Culture

ENVIRONMENTAL FACTORS. Keeping in mind that most cacti live in unbearable heat during the day and frigid conditions at night, one can see that the home is a relatively moderate climate for these durable specimens. As indoor plants, cacti are much more likely to be loved to death than destroyed by neglect. Without water, they simply become thinner and stop growing. Too much shade will distort the normal growth and coloration, but the plants will continue to live indefinitely.

Ideally, cacti should have direct sun as much as possible. This is necessary for proper photosynthesis, growth habit, and flowering. During the active growing season, which begins in the spring, the plants will absorb water; watering and fertilization will need to be rather frequent. During the winter, watering should be withheld as the plant goes through its dormancy period. Keeping the plant dry prevents root rots, and cool temperatues in the high 40s help stimulate flower bud initiation.

The potting medium should be exceptionally well drained. A combination of sand, potting soil, and humus is ideal for most species.
most species.

The epiphytic cacti, such as *Rhipsalis,* will need more shade, warmth at night, and water than their xerophytic relatives.

PROPAGATION. Since cacti produce berries containing viable seeds, this form of propagation is quite common. Fresh cactus seed has a high percentage of germination if handled properly. Placed on a porous propagation medium with an optional dusting of limestone, the seed will germinate within a few weeks for most species if the medium temperature is kept in the 80s. Watering by soaking will help prevent disturbance of the germinating seed.

Most species of cacti are also easily propagated by joint cuttings. A cutting of several joints, severed at a joint, should be air-dried for several days prior to placing it into the propagation medium. Attention to sanitation and adequate drainage is necessary to prevent rotting during propagation.

Many cactus species are grafted for various reasons. Some of the colorful cacti are slow growing or unable to survive alone, so they are grafted onto more vigorous root stocks. Some are grafted for effect. Most garden centers and plant shops carry colorful globe cacti grafted onto a more upright understock (Figure 13.21). The techniques used are flat grafts (two flat surfaces are joined), the side graft (two 45° cuts are joined), the cleft graft (a wedge-shaped cut at the base of the scion is inserted into a longitudinal split at the top of the understock), and the stab graft (a wedge-shaped

scion base is inserted into a stab wound in the understock).

PESTS AND DISEASES. Mealybugs can be a particular problem on cactus since they are hidden so well among the areoles. Scale insects can also nestle down among the ribs and spines, making physical removal difficult. Thrips and red spiders may cause discoloration of the stem. Root mealybugs can be a pest of cactus species as well.

Most disease problems, such as stem rots, are related to overwatering, particularly during periods of inactive growth.

A WORD ABOUT HANDLING CACTI. In transplanting, cleaning, or grafting cactus species, use a paper towel or similar material to handle the plants. The spines of most species can cause painful puncture wounds to naked fingers. Species without spines often have small, fiberglasslike bristles that enter the fingers unnoticed during handling, later causing swelling and irritation. Only species that have no spines or bristles, such as the Christmas cactus, should be handled without some protection.

FERNS

Common and Unique Qualities

Unlike most other species of indoor interest, ferns are nonflowering plants, a group collectively known as Cryptogams. Rather than producing flowers or seeds, ferns bear **spores,** one-celled microscopic structures characteristic in the reproduction of algae, fungi, and mosses. Ferns, though, are separated from these three lower plant groups by the fern's large, true leaves and their specialized vascular tissue that accounts for the taller growth of ferns.

The great majority of indoor ferns belong to the family Polypodiaceae, a group with an erect underground stem or creeping rhizomes. Most other ferns are found in five other families, including climbers, aquatics,

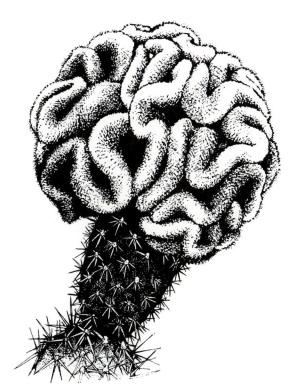

FIGURE 13.21 Grafting of cacti requires a minimum of knowledge to be successful.

and tree ferns. It was the prehistoric tree ferns that first forested the earth and provided the vegetative mass necessary for the formation of coal. The Polypodiaceae alone accounts for about 180 genera and 7000 species.

World Distribution

This mammoth plant group, unlike most other plants, inhabits various elevations worldwide. Although some ferns are xerophytic, most flourish in shade, moderate temperatures, and moisture. Their environmental prferences range from the Arctic to the equator. In size, they include tree ferns over 80 feet tall and minute, creeping, mosslike members. Very few plant groups have adapted themselves to more locations and conditions than the ferns.

Uses of Ferns

Through the centuries, ferns have contributed a number of myths and uses to civilization. The most interesting myth, perhaps, is the ancient view that the possession of fern seed would allow one to become invisible; since ferns do not produce seeds, the theory has never been disproven. Medicinally, ferns have treated lunacy and snake bites. Spiritually, ferns have been the means of placing curses on an enemy, protecting oneself from goblins, and bringing rain. More current medicinal uses of some species are for liver, kidney, and heart problems; whooping cough; colds; and sensitive teeth.

In northeast North America, the emerging leaves called **fiddleheads** of the ostrich fern (*Matteuccia*) are valued as a culinary delight much like asparagus. Unfortunately, there are now suspicions that carcinogenic compounds may be present in various ferns.

The American Fern Society is a reliable source of further information on this interesting group of plants.

Botanical Features

Ferns are superficially recognized by their finely divided leaves, called **fronds;** as a result, we frequently refer to "ferny" plant textures (Figure 13.22). Although this is generally true, all ferns are not "ferny," nor are all such plants ferns. In spite of its look-alike qualities, the asparagus fern (*Asparagus* spp.) belongs to the lily family. Fern leaves may be simple or palmate but are most commonly pinnate or bipinnate. The fronds are typically borne on wirelike petioles that arise from underground stems or rhizomes.

The fronds play an important role in reproduction, serving as sites for sporangia and the buds, bulbils, or plantlets that form on some species. This will be discussed in more detail under propagation.

FIGURE 13.22 The finely divided fronds of ferns give most members of the genus an airy texture.

Significant Genera

ASPLENIUM. This group of terrestrial or epiphytic ferns is most commonly represented indoors by *Asplenium nidus*, the bird's nest fern, an epiphytic plant with bright green, 4-foot-long and 8-inch-wide fronds arising funnellike from a short, erect rhizome. The fronds are oblanceolate with wavy margins and a darkened midrib. Propagation is from spores borne in linear sporangia on the back of the fronds. This is a popular species indoors, though its large size and coarse texture make it useful only in certain situations. Evenly moist soil, warm temperatures, and freedom from drafts are necessary to maintain attractive growth (Figure 13.23).

Asplenium bulbiferum, the hen-and-chickens fern is another notable member of the genus, similar in size to the bird's nest fern but with feathery, bipinnately, or tripinnately compound fronds. Unlike the bird's nest fern, this species produces bulblets or plantlets on the upper leaf surfaces.

CIBOTIUM. These members of the family Dicksoniaceae, true tree ferns, are slow growers with fine, tripinnately compound foliage. It is the trunk sections of this rough-trunked, Hawaiian species that are used as the familiar totem pole stakes for climbing indoor species.

DAVALLIA. This genus of ferns is known for its stout wooly rhizomes, which give rise to the rabbit's foot fern's common name. These epiphytic ferns have finely divided fronds and are grown as hanging basket specimens or fern balls with plants placed into wire forms filled with sphagnum moss.

PELLAEA. These small, rock-loving ferns, commonly known as cliff brakes, perform best in moderately cool locations. The most notable species is *Pellaea rotundifolia*, the button fern, that as a young plant produces round, evenly spaced leaflets, giving the plant a dramatic patterned texture. These plants are best used as small pot plants or terrarium specimens (Figure 13.24).

PHYLLITIS. Unlike most ferns, *Phyllitis* produces strap-shaped fronds that are up to 18

FIGURE 13.23 The bird's nest fern, *Asplenium nidus*.

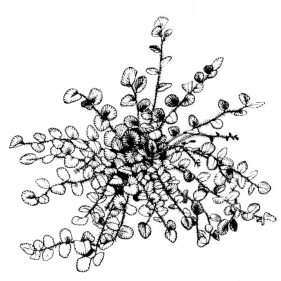

FIGURE 13.24 The button fern, *Pellaea rotundifolia*.

inches long and 3 inches wide. The most well-known species is *Phyllitis scolopendrium*, heart's tongue fern. Numerous cultivars have been named, including those with crisped or divided margins, as well as dwarf types. This genus enjoys cool temperatures and moist soil.

POLYPODIUM. The genus from which the polypody family is named, this group of epiphytic, rhizomatous ferns offer a variety of foliage qualities. Although the fronds of most are pinnately compound, one of the more well-known species, *Polypodium aureum*, is the origin of several variants that have simple, lobed fronds. Because of its stout brown and wooly rhizomes, *Polypodium aureum* is also referred to commonly as the rabbit's foot fern. This genus is one of the easier fern groups to cultivate indoors, although they do best with at least moderate humidity.

RUMOHRA. Probably the most widely recognized fern because of its popularity as greenery in flower arrangements, the leather fern (*Rumohra adiantiformis*) also produces the unusual "rabbit's foot" characteristic, but without fur, of *Davallia* and *Polypodium aureum*. Another durable fern, *Rumohra* tolerates a moderately wide range of temperatures and performs best as a potted plant when the finely cut leaves can be shown to best advantage.

Table 13.2 lists ferns that have potential indoors.

Culture

ENVIRONMENTAL FACTORS. Depending on their native habitat, ferns enjoy either warm or moderately cool temperatures. The terrestrial ferns should be potted into a standard potting mix, but the epiphytic types need a fast-draining medium. Since most like shady conditions naturally, the indoor environment is suitable in terms of light. Humidity, however, is usually uncomfortably low for ferns in the typical home. Techniques to raise the relative humidity, such as misting, grouping plants together, and water and gravel trays beneath the plants will help, as will locating ferns in moist areas of the home.

Regardless of culture, some ferns vary in appearance depending on their age. Some *Pteris* species are compact and attractive when young, but become more straggly with age. Typically, however, most ferns that are marketed exhibit attractive characteristics at any age.

PROPAGATION. Ferns can be started by spores, division, buds, or plantlets that form on the fronds of some species.

Spore propagation involves two phases of growth as illustrated in Chapter Three. The propagation process involves using fresh, dried spores that are sown onto a humus, sterilized medium. The developing plants are quite susceptible to damping-off; preliminary sterilization of containers and other germination equipment is extremely important. After spreading the spores onto the moist, lightly packed soil, glass should be placed just above the soil surface until the surface begins to turn green, usually in two or three weeks. During the next month, the light intensity is gradually increased by using newspaper and other translucent materials until reaching a level of about 150 foot-candles. Various genera take different lengths of time to germinate.

Keeping the soil and plants moist is critical, since the fertilization process depends on water for transport of the sperm cells. Water by bottom soaking until the first small fronds appear. When humidity is crucial to survival (e.g., *Dicksonia*), the fronds will brown at the tips unless the relative humidity is increased.

During the germination process, the light source should remain constant and the temperature should range between 65 and 85°F. Once the small plantlets appear, transplant them individually or in small clumps into 2-inch pots (Figure 13.25).

TABLE 13.2 A LIST OF FERNS SELECTED FOR INDOOR POTENTIAL

Old Standbys, Just as Good Now as for the Future

Adiantum raddianum cv. Fritz Luthii	Fritz Luthii maidenhair
Adiantum raddianum cv. Pacific Maid[a]	Pacific maid maidenhair
Adiantum hispidulum	Rosy maidenhair
Asplenium nidus	Bird's nest fern
Cyrtomium falcatum cv. Rochfordianum[a]	Rochford holly fern
Davallia fejeensis	Fiji davallia
Dicksonia antarctica	Tasmanian tree fern
Nephrolepis cordifolia	Tuber sword fern
Nephrolepis exaltata cv. Dwarf Boston[a]	Dwarf Boston fern
Nephrolepis exaltata cv. Fluffy Ruffle	Fluffy ruffle
Nephrolepis exaltata cv. Rooseveltii	Roosevelt sword fern
Pellaea rotundifolia	Button fern
Polypodium aureum	Rabbit's foot fern
Polypodium aureum cv. Mandianum	Manda polypody, mandianum
Pteris cretica	Cretan brake
Pteris ensiformis var. Victoriae[a]	Victorian brake
Rumohra adiantiformis (*Polystichum capense*)	Leatherleaf fern
Sphaeropteris cooperi (*Alsophila australis* of trade)	Australian tree fern

Worth Trying If You Have Not Done So

Adiantum capillus-veneris	Southern maidenhair fern
Adiantum raddianum cv. Pacottii	Double maidenhair
Adiantum raddianum cv. Triumph	Triumph maidenhair
Aglaomorpha coronans	
Aglaomorpha sp. (*Aglaomorpha* 'Roberts')	
Arachniodes aristata (*Polystichum aristatum*)	East Indian holly fern
Arachniodes standishii (*Polystichum standishii*)	
Asplenium bulbiferum	Mother fern
Asplenium nidus, new variants	Bird's nest fern
Cibotium glaucum (*Cibotium chamissoi* of trade)	Hawaiian tree fern
Davallia solida	Polynesian davallia
Davallia trichomanoides	Squirrel's foot fern
Didymochlaena truncatula	
Dryopteris erythrosora	Autumn fern
Dryopteris filix-mas	Male fern
Humata tyermannii	Bear's foot fern
Lastreopsis microsora spp. *pentangularis* (*Ctenitis pentangularis*)	
Lygodium japonicum	Japanese climbing fern
Microlepia platyphylla	
Microlepia strigosa	
Pellaea falcata	Australian cliff brake
Pellaea viridis var. *viridis* (*Pellaea hastata*)	Green cliff brake
Platycerium bifurcatum[a]	Common staghorn fern
Polypodium polycarpon	
Polypodium polycarpon cv. Grandiceps	Climbing bird's nest fern

(continued)

Table 13.2 (*Continued*)

Polypodium subauriculatum	Jointed polypody
Polypodium subauriculatum cv. Knightiae	Knight's polypody
Polystichum munitum	Western sword fern
Polystichum polyblepharum (*Polystichum setosum* of trade)	
Polystichum setiferum, various cultivars (*Polystichum angulare*)	Shoft shield fern
Pteris cretica cv. Childsii	Child's brake
Pteris cretica cv. Parkeri	Parker's brake
Pteris multifida (*Pteris serrulata*)	Spider brake
Pyrrosia lingua	Japanese felt fern, Tongue fern
Rumohra adiantiformis, the variant from Brazil (*Polystichum capense*)	Leatherleaf fern
Todera barbara	

Little Known Ferns with Future Trade Potential

Belvisia mucronata

Elaphoglossum, various species

Microlepia firma

Microlepia speluncae cv. Corymbifera (*Microlepia pyrimidata* of trade)

Polypodium formosanum

Polypodium menisciifolium (*Polypodium fraxinifolium* of trade)

Polypodium viellardii

Quercifilix zeilanica

Schyphularia pentaphylla (*Davallia pentaphylla*)

[a]Included in Part Five.

SOURCE: Hoshizaki, B., "Ferns with a Future," in *Proceedings* of the 1978 National Tropical Foliage Short Course, W. Henley and R. Biamunte, Eds. Foliage Education and Research Foundation, Inc., Apopka, Fla., pp. 187–191. Reprinted with permission.

FIGURE 13.25 Young ferns, propagated from spores, ready for transplanting.

PESTS AND DISEASES. An interesting aspect of ferns is that their healthy root system looks quite similar to the roots of other indoor plants that have been overwatered and poorly aerated. The roots are usually dark in color with a lighter growing tip; realize this is normal and not a disease symptom. Rotting, however, will sometimes occur when overwatering or overly humid conditions prevail.

The most predictable insects on ferns are aphids, scales, mealybugs, and thrips. Descriptions and control of these pests was covered in Chapter Nine.

Ferns are frequently diagnosed by amateurs as having scale problems after spore development occurs. Since the **sori** or spore cases are typically brown dots on the back side of fronds, they appear much like scale insects. Sori can be distinguished, however, by the fact that scale insects do not organize themselves in the neat, orderly fashion characteristic of sori.

Ferns are particularly sensitive to damage from spray materials. Read pesticide directions carefully before applying chemicals to ferns. Since emulsions contain oil that can damage fern foliage, use dusts or sprays from wettable powders whenever possible. Commercial growers often apply as little as 10 to 15 percent of the manufacturer's recommended rate to avoid burning their fern crops. It is advisable to spray one or two fronds with an untested chemical prior to treating the entire plant.

GESNERIADS: THE AFRICAN VIOLET RELATIVES

Common and Unique Qualities
One of the larger indoor plant groups, gesneriads (guess-NER-ee-ads) number about 125 genera and over 2000 species. Added to this number are innumerable hybrids and mutations that also account for much of the family's popularity. Almost all the members are hairy herbs or subshrubs, with a few species becoming shrubs, vines, and trees. The gesneriads are generally attractive, displaying velvety foliage and conspicuous wheel-, bell-, or tube-shaped flowers. Extensive variety exists among the members of this group.

World Distribution
Mostly terrestrial or epiphytic in nature, gesneriads occupy expansive regions of the tropics, although a few species inhabit temperate areas. Their geographical range includes Central America, most of South America, southern Europe, west and southeastern Africa, southeastern Asia, eastern Australia, Japan, Polynesia, Madagascar, and a small portion of China (Figure 13.26).

Botanical Features

FOLIAGE. The leaves are typically opposite or whorled in a basal rosette, though rarely alternate or completely lacking. They are simple, either entire or toothed, and possess no stipules at the petiole base. Foliage color and texture are extremely variable.

FLOWERS. The flowers may be borne alone, in racemes, or in cymes. Five sepals and petals are characteristic, each set typically taking on a tubular configuration.

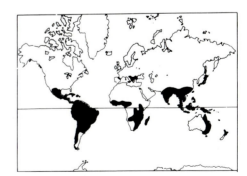

FIGURE 13.26 The world distribution of gesneriads. *Source:* Heywood, V., *Flowering Plants of the World,* New York: W. H. Smith Publishers, 1978, p. 246. Reproduced with permission of Gallery Books an imprint of W. H. Smith Publsihers.

Many gesneriads depend on bird pollinators, particularly hummingbirds in the Americas. Bees, bats, butterflies, moths, and flies also facilitate natural pollination, being attracted to the often colorful leaves and plant hairs.

FRUIT. The typical fruit of most species is a round or elongated capsule, although fleshy berries are characteristic of several popular indoor species. The seeds produced at fruit maturity are exceptionally small, being dust-like in character.

FORMS OF GROWTH. Gesneriads are conveniently divided into three major groups based on three distinct modes of growth: tuberous, scaly rhizomes, and fibrous roots (Figure 13.27).

Tubers. As we saw in Chapter Four, a tuber is an expanded underground stem for food storage during the dormant dry season. The most common genus with a tuberous growth habit is *Sinningia*, more commonly known as gloxinia.

Scaly rhizomes. Several species, most notably *Achimenes*, produce an underground rhizome that is covered with modified leaves or scales. Looking somewhat like a pine

Scaly rhizome (*Kohleria*)

Fibrous rooted (*Saintpaulia*)

FIGURE 13.27 The three modes of growth of Gesneriads.

cone, these scaly rhizomes range from several inches in length to less than an inch. Occasionally, small rhizomes appear higher up on the plant in leaf axils or flowers.

Fibrous Roots. Most of the gesneriads commonly used indoors are fibrous rooted. Conveniently, these plants may be classified into two groups, those with two stamens and those with glands. Since gesneriaceae is characterized by five flower parts, those species with only two stamens represent a distinct group. The well-known African violet (*Saintpaulia*), as well as *Streptocarpus*, fall into this category.

The second group of fibrous rooted gesneriads are even more unique. These plants, including *Alloplectus*, *Columnea*, and *Episcia*, bear glands that secrete sticky materials. These glands may be located on leaves, stems, flower stalks, or petals, but most characteristically are at the back and bottom of the ovary. The gland-bearing gesneriads are also unique in that the fruit is a fleshy berry, in contrast to the typical capsule of other species. As a group, these plants are easily damaged by temperatures that fall below the mid-50s.

Significant Genera

Table 13.3 lists the gesneriad genera that are discussed at other points in this text. Aside from these members of the group, there are two other genera that may be grown indoors.

ACHIMENES. The tubular flowers whose five petals flare into a pansylike shape are responsible for the numerous common names:

monkey-faced pansy, orchid pansy, and magic flower. The wide variety of flower colors includes white, blue, pink, red, orange, and various combinations. Numerous species and cultivars of *Achimenes* are now available and because of their trailing stems that bend upward at the tip, provide graceful displays in hanging baskets. They spread by means of a scaly rhizome.

ALLOPLECTUS. These fibrous-rooted members bear large leaves similar to the florist gloxinia. The leaves are borne opposite in typical gesneriad fashion, but the pairs are usually unequally sized. This climbing plant eventually develops almost woody stems and a straggly growth habit; consequently, new cuttings should be rooted periodically to replace old plants.

COLUMNEA. These fibrous-rooted, epiphytic plants may either be shrubby or creeping. The opposite leaves are often neither shaped nor sized alike. The flowers may be red, yellow, orange, or pink, their shape giving rise to the common generic name of goldfish plants (Figure 13.28).

FIGURE 13.28 The "goldfish" flower of *Columnea*.

TABLE 13.3 GESNERIAD GENERA INCLUDED IN CHAPTER TWELVE OR PART FIVE OF THIS TEXT

Aeschynanthus (Part Five)
Episcia (Part Five)
Sinningia (Chapter Twelve)
Saintpaulia (Part Five)
Streptocarpus (Part Five)

These plants, because of their epiphytic nature, thrive best in a well-aerated, fast-draining medium. Many hybrids and cultivars are now registered with the American Gloxinia Society, Inc.

NAUTILOCALYX. These tropical American herbs bear a slight resemblance to some species of *Impatiens*. These plants have elliptical, quilted leaves borne opposite on upright stems that require frequent pinching to inhibit the tendency toward lankiness. Root cuttings must be taken periodically to replace older plants.

The yellow or ivory flowers appear in the leaf axils, resulting in a much less conspicuous display than on most other gesneriads.

Culture

ENVIRONMENTAL FACTORS. Gesneriads enjoy bright, diffused sunlight, rich, well-drained soil, and moisture, both at their roots and in the atmosphere. As warmth loving plants, their nights should get no cooler than 65°F, and days should average around 70 to 75°F.

Most gesneriads indicate improper lighting by physical changes. Dark green color and lanky growth indicate that light is sufficient. Long-stalked and widely spaced leaves indicate that light is lacking. Blistering and crispy brown leaves are being damaged by too much sun.

Since most species need to be kept evenly moist but are susceptible to root and stem rots, the soil should be rich both in water-holding organic matter and in drainage materials such as sand or perlite. Soil mixes are available commercially that are specifically designed for African violets and their relatives. An additional environmental requirement is a relative humidity range of 40 to 60 percent.

DORMANCY. After gesneriads complete their heavy flowering, particularly those that bear underground storage structures, they enter a resting period. Once the flowering has ended and growth subsides, tubers should be kept barely moist in 60°F conditions until new sprouts emerge several months later. Repotting when new growth begins will prepare the plant for successful subsequent growth. On entering dormancy, gesneriads with fibrous roots take on a declining look, lose their lower or all leaves, or, as with the African violet, begin a more upright growth tendency. Normal watering and fertilization should be reestablished with active growth.

PROPAGATION. Five alternatives exist for starting new gesneriads. The dustlike seeds of most species will produce flowering plants within a year. Leaf and stem cuttings produce new plants quickly, as well. Older plants may be divided, and tubers can be cut into sections before replanting. Although the individual scales of rhizomes can be rooted, larger sections usually yield faster results. And, finally, some species such as *Episcia* cupreata produce runners or stolons that root and produce new plantlets along their axis (Figure 13.29).

FIGURE 13.29 The plantlets borne on *Episcia* stolons may be layered (rooted while still attached to the parent plant) or severed prior to propagation.

PESTS AND DISEASES. The most trouble-some aspects of growing most gesneriads are mealybugs, root mealybugs, and mites, particularly the cyclamen mite that causes distortion of young foliage. In conditions of poor drainage or too frequent watering, root and crown rots may also occur. With these few exceptions, gesneriads provide a color-ful and carefree subject for indoor gardening.

ORCHIDACEAE: THE ORCHID FAMILY

Common and Unique Qualities

There are an estimated 600 to 800 genera of orchids and 17,000 to 30,000 species, not to mention thousands of variants and cultivars. The group is considered to be the largest and most advanced flowering plant family in terms of species number.

Of all the plants covered in this text, per-haps no other has reached the level of specialization of the orchid. The most notable trait is the beautiful and exotic flower of many species. Varying greatly in structure, these delicate organs have specialized them-selves to facilitate certain pollinators, thus ensuring proper cross-pollination. The plant's physical structure is adapted to a wide range of geographic locations and climates.

As we look at the various configurations of orchids and the unique morphological adap-tations that family members have under-taken, you will find them to be a fascinating group of plants. Serious students may refer to the American Orchid Society, Inc. as a means of acquiring additional information. The *American Orchid Society Bulletin*, pub-lished monthly, is an excellent vehicle for learning orchid culture and identification. The flowers of numerous orchid species— *Cattleya, Cymbidium, Oncidium,* and *Pha-laenopsis,* among others—have been staples among florists for corsages and bouquets. Aside from the flowers, orchids are of little commercial value, with one exception. The vanilla orchid, *Vanilla planifolia,* provides the familiar extract from its long, fleshy seed pods.

World Distribution

Orchids are found worldwide, except in des-ert regions. They are particularly prevalent (about 85 percent) in tropical zones.

Orchids may grow terrestrially or as epi-phytes, occupying specialized soils and habitats. In North America, they are com-monly found in cool bogs, although they also inhabit sandy plains, moist grasslands, and woodlands. The epiphytic orchids are basi-cally confined to the tropics including parts of Florida, growing attached to trees or other support.

Botanical Features

FOLIAGE. Orchid leaves fall into one of two categories: (1) **plicate** or (2) **conduplicate.** Plicate leaves are ribbed longitudinally and are thin and membranous in texture. Typi-cally lasting only one growing season, they resemble the leaves of lilies. Plicate leaves are not involved in water retention. They are found on primitive members of the family, such as *Cypripedium,* the lady's slipper.

Conduplicate leaves, on the other hand, are typical of epiphytic orchids. They are leathery or fleshy, V-shaped in cross section, and are strengthened by thick-celled walls and fibers. The thick epidermis and the stomates (confined to the lower leaf surface) help control water loss from the plant. These leaves are found on the more specialized genera such as *Cattleya.*

FLOWERS. Flowers are the most interesting and specialized structures of orchids. They are borne singly or on inflorescences. Morphologically, orchid flowers have a reduced number of parts that are fused together and a petal that has been devel-oped into a lip. Typically, orchid flower

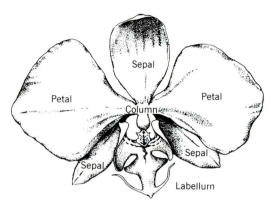

FIGURE 13.30 Close-up of *Phalaenopsis* flower showing floral parts.

parts occur in groups of three. The three sepals are frequently colorful and indistinguishable from the petals. This is true in most cultivated orchids. The three segments of the corolla are of two types: (1) two petals located on either side of the upper (dorsal) sepal and (2) a lip or **labellum**, which is usually expanded in size and three-lobed (Figure 13.30). Serving as a landing platform for pollinating insects, the lip may be flat, pouch-shaped, tasseled, or otherwise ornate and colorful.

An interesting aspect of orchid flowers is that the lip is located at the top of the flower bud; it obtains its ventral position through a 180° rotation of the flower during maturity. Orchid flowers have long been studied for their interesting attraction of pollinators. Orchid pollination is highly species specific, with each orchid species usually being pollinated by one specific organism. Insects and hummingbirds are the two most common pollinators.

The sexual components of orchid flowers are greatly reduced in number and fused, uniting the male and female reproductive organs into one structure called the **column**. This configuration is a great departure from the morphology of other monocotyledonous plants. Also unusual is the pollen structure. Rather than forming as the dustlike pollen typical of other plants, orchid pollen is in masses known as **pollinia**, numbering from two to eight per flower depending on the species.

Most genera have a small beaklike structure called the **rostellum** that separates the pollinia from the stigma and assists in the transfer of pollen by pollinators.

FRUIT. The ovary of orchids, being inferior, lies beneath the point of attachment of the sepals. After fertilization, the ovary develops into a capsule that produces several million dustlike seeds that are basically few-celled embryos. At maturity, the capsule splits along three sutures, dispersing the seeds by wind currents. As we shall see under the propagation section, growing orchids from seeds is a very demanding practice.

ROOTS. Orchid roots may be of two types: (1) those that anchor the plant to its support and (2) those that absorb water and salts. Terrestrial orchids have roots that are sparsely branched and densely hairy, enabling the root system to absorb water more efficiently in dry locations. Epiphytic orchids, on the other hand, are distinguished by the presence of a shiny, buff to gray outer covering called the **velamen**. This layer serves to anchor the roots to support, quickly absorb water and nutrients, and protect the interior tissues of the root from cold, dry, or physical damage (Figure 13.31).

Because epiphytic orchids live in trees where the water and mineral supply is erratic at best, these plants have the ability to live through long periods of drought. Orchids are quite unusual among plants in that their roots are photosynthetic. On most species, this photosynthetic region can be observed at the green growing tip. In some leafless orchids, the roots are flattened and leaflike, taking over the role of food manufacture for the plant.

In nature, orchids often live in specialized soil conditions and a symbiotic relationship with specific fungi called **mycorrhizae**.

FIGURE 13.31 Detail of an epiphytic orchid root, showing the light-colored velamen.

The orchid roots provide a dwelling for the fungus, and the fungus helps the orchid meet its nutritional needs. Since the fungus must also have the correct environment, native orchids are difficult to transplant to new locations or grow from seed at home.

FORMS OF GROWTH. Terrestrial orchids, in order to survive winter in temperate zones and drought in the tropics, grow from tubers or rhizomes that store food during dormancy. In plants of this type, the stem is short and the leaves form a basal rosette. The flowers arise from the apex of the short stem.

In epiphytic orchids, two growth forms are typical. Sympodial growth is characterized by a horizontal rhizome that creeps along the soil surface of potted specimens. Each new shoot arises from the base of the preceding one. With this type of growth, inflorescences may occur as a terminus of growth or may arise from lateral axes. Since most orchids with sympodial growth are epiphytes living in tree canopies and are subjected to rigorous environments, their stems have developed into specialized structures called *pseudobulbs*. These are water storage organs, formed as a swelling of internodes (Figure 13.32). Seven typical pseudobulb shapes are recognized, ranging from globose to cylindrical (long and slender).

FIGURE 13.32 Comparison of the sympodial (right) and the monopodial (left) form of growth in orchids. Note the pseudobulbs beneath the leaves on the plant at the right.

Each shoot formed in sympodial orchids is determinate—it flowers once and eventually dies. Since this death occurs after a succession of new shoots have been developed, the plant lives indefinitely.

Monopodial orchids, on the other hand, produce leaves and stem from an apical growing point indeterminately. These plants continue to grow upward, often forming a long axis, and bear axillary inflorescences and adventitious roots at the nodes. Some modopodial orchids, such as *Phalaenopsis* (moth orchids), have a short axis, bearing only several leaves at any one time.

Significant Genera

A vast array of orchid genera could be presented here. Our purpose, however, is to provide insight into the major members that have indoor potential and are relatively easy to acquire locally.

CATTLEYA. These epiphytic, rhizomatous orchids are best known for their use as corsage flowers (Figure 13.33). Probably the showiest of all orchids, cattleyas produce large flowers with spreading, colorful petals. Thousands of cultivars, including many from intergeneric hybridization, are available. The leathery, straplike leaves are perched atop elongated pseudobulbs. They perform best in higher humidity and require bright indirect sunlight for flowering. The flowers will last for weeks on maturity, as long as they are not pollinated. Culturally, these orchids are in the intermediate class (see culture).

CYMBIDIUM. These cool (see culture) orchids are florist favorites during the spring season, particularly around Easter. Growing both as terrestrials and epiphytes, cymbidiums produce long, linear leaves on top of elliptical pseudobulbs. The waxy blooms are long-lasting and include colors of white, pink, red, yellow, and green (Figure 13.34).

HAEMARIA. The gold lace orchid, *Haemaria discolor*, is unusual in that it is valued for its foliage. The ovate leaves are three-six in a basal rosette and are about 3 inches long. The leaf color is a dark reddish-green interlaced with reddish veins. The flower is an erect raceme of small white flowers that

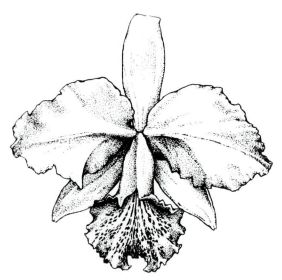

FIGURE 13.33 The graceful *Cattleya* flower, a long-time favorite among florists.

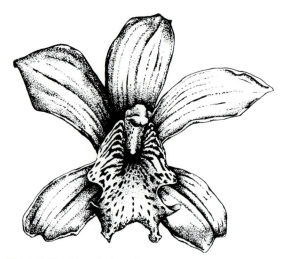

FIGURE 13.34 *Cymbidium* flowers are prominent in corsages during the spring.

ascends from the apex of the short stem. Culturally, gold lace orchids require warm temperatures, high humidity, and a humus, fast-draining potting mix.

MILTONIA. These "pansy orchids" are small epiphytes with round, flat blooms and a large rounded lip. The flower color ranges from white, cream, and yellow to pink and very dark reds. Miltonias often produce six flowers on each of two spikes, remaining in flower for many weeks. These are typically cool orchids, but Brazilian species are more tolerant of warmth.

ONCIDIUM. These orchids are noted for their branching sprays of fragrant flowers. The individual flowers are small with a rounded, enlarged lip and somewhat linear sepals and lateral petals. Called dancing dolls or butterfly orchids commonly, these easy-to-grow plants flower mostly in hues of yellow and brown. An intermediate orchid culturally, oncidium is valued in Europe as a cut flower.

PAPHIOPEDILUM. The famous lady slippers are distinguished by a pouch-shaped lip, a larger than normal dorsal sepal, and spreading horizontal petals that may be linear and pendulous. These small orchids are available with various temperature preferences and a wide variety of flower qualities. Many have beautifully mottled or spotted flowers, while others have interesting striping and shades of green, red, white, and yellow (Figure 13.35). These are considered one of the easier orchids for beginners to grow.

PHALAENOPSIS. The moth orchids are without pseudobulbs and are characterized by expanded petals and sepals, as well as a small, brightly colored three-lobed lip. Available in pink, yellow, white, and other shades, these flat blooms are popular in bridal bouquets. As warm orchids, these plants grow well with cattleyas but require less light to flower. (Refer to Figure 13.30.)

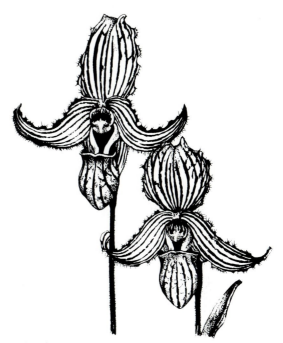

FIGURE 13.35 The lady slipper, *Paphiopedilum*, is noted for its pouchlike labellum.

Culture

ENVIRONMENTAL FACTORS. Temperature is probably the most immediate critical factor in raising orchids. Orchid authorities have grouped species into three temperature ranges, depending on their requirements for both night and day temperatures. They are as follows.

Warm Orchids. These require night temperatures between 60 and 65°F with daytime temperatures between 75 and 80°F.

Intermediate Orchids. These species require night temperatures between 50 and 60°F and daytime temperatures in the high 70s. The greatest number of orchid species fall into this category.

Cool Orchids. These require a night temperature of 50 to 55°F and a daytime temperature of around 70°F.

Since most orchids that are grown indoors are epiphytic plants, they should be potted into osmunda or coarsely shredded fir bark, with peat moss or perlite added to improve water retention.

Watering should be carried out daily during active growth, less during rest periods. Poor drainage will result in root rots. A monthly fertilization with nitrogen during the growing season will improve the foliage color and growth rate. Terrestrial orchids perform best in humus soil or sphagnum moss.

A common problem with most orchid types grown indoors is low humidity. The ideal range would be around 50 percent, but homes, especially in winter, drop down to the 10 to 20 percent range. Occasional mistings or water/gravel trays will aid to some extent, as will keeping the plants away from heat sources. Most orchids need considerable light, in some cases direct sunlight, to stimulate vigorous flowering. Placing them outdoors during the warm months, subjected to their preferred level of light, will promote active growth and flower bud initiation.

DORMANCY. Orchids generally require a rest of several months prior to flowering. During this dormancy, the plant initiates flower buds and prepares physiologically for the process of flowering. During this time, reduce watering and fertilization.

PROPAGATION. Orchids are propagated by seeds, tissue culture, and division.

Seeds are extremely difficult to germinate because of their small size and few-celled structure. They must be grown in sterile conditions and on a complex nutrient medium. They are not practical for germination at home.

Unlike other indoor plant species, the germinated seeds of orchids have an intermediate stage prior to seedling development. After germination, the seed enlarges into a multicelled structure called a **protocorm** that can be divided, recultured, and developed into numerous seedlings. Orchid growers have found that by rotating these cultured

protocorms on a motorized wheel, root and shoot formation is thwarted, thus continuing protocorm multiplication. Although this technique proved beneficial in producing many young plants, there was no way of predetermining whether the seedling would be of commercial value genetically. In recent years, some growers have undertaken techniques of tissue culture, extracting very small parts of the meristem tissue and culturing it on a nutrient medium. Originally designed as a technique for acquiring virus-free plants, tissue culture was found to develop protocormlike bodies much like a germinating seed. These bodies, when rotated, multiply much like protocorms. Consequently, this technique duplicates particular plants in great numbers while maintaining genetic identity. Because the technique perpetuates a clone, it is called **mericloning.** Plant stores and garden centers now carry young plants propagated with this technique that are guaranteed to replicate the physical qualities of the parent (Figure 13.36).

Orchids bearing pseudobulbs can be divided by cutting the horizontal rhizome at

FIGURE 13.36 Mericloned seedlings, growing in sterile culture.

the desired point. Overgrown orchids, such as cattleya species, that have grown to the edge of the pot can be divided into several clumps and repotted. Some orchids, such as *Phalaenopsis*, produce plantlets at the nodes of the flower stalks following blooming. Their flower stems may also be sectioned, each with a node, and placed on nutrient culture.

PESTS AND DISEASES. A considerable number of fungal pathogens infect orchid leaves. It is rare to find orchids without some blemish of foliar leaf spot. Fungal rots are another almost universal problem with orchids. These devastating organisms cause dark, soft lesions that can spread throughout the plant if left unchecked. Orchids are also notorious for picking up virus diseases, so particular care should be given to sterilization of tools during multiple divisions.

Insect pests include scale, mealybugs, aphids, and spider mites. Consult Chapter Nine for pest and disease control measures.

ARECACEAE: THE PALM FAMILY

Common and Unique Qualities

Symbols of warm, tropical regions, the palms are a majestic, unusual, and ancient assortment of treelike woody plants. The group is commercially important and well-known worldwide. It is one of eight plant families that is still frequently called a botanical family name (Palmae) without the -aceae ending.

Although most palms are treelike, some are climbers or shrubby. Some reach great heights; others are quite small. Generally, the trunk is unbranched, but in at least one species, forking may be extensive. Unlike most other woody trees, the palm has one terminal growing point that, if destroyed by cold or physical damage, will result in the death of the plant. As we shall see, palms are quite different morphologically in a number of ways from other woody plants. These evergreen monocots have been rever-

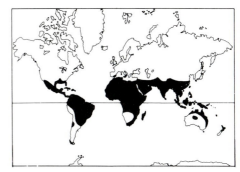

FIGURE 13.37 The world distribution of Palmae. *Source:* Heywood, V., Flowering Plants of the World, New York: W. H. Smith Publisher, 1978. Reproduced with permission of Gallery Books an imprint of W. H. Smith Publishers.

ed throughout history, being named "principes," the "princes of plants."

World Distribution

Palms account for about 210 genera and nearly 3000 species that occupy much of the tropical world (Figure 13.37). Ten genera are native to the United States, with most living in Hawaii and Florida. California, Arizona, Texas, and other warm states have spotted representation. Worldwide, they are found in great quantities in South America and the eastern tropics and less profusely in Africa and the Indian Ocean islands, such as Madagascar. One species, *Chamaerops humilis* (European Fan Palm), is a native of Europe.

Economic Uses

Without question, palms are the most economically significant plants of indoor usefulness. This value dates back to civilization's beginning; one of the most hostile acts of war among the Babylonians was to cut down the enemy's date palm trees. These provided food, thatching material, building materials, and fibers for various uses.

Today, the coconut palm and the African oil palm are two of the world's most important cultivated plants, providing industrial vegetable fats. As in days of old, palms provide fruit, sugar and starch, beverages, fiber for brushes and ropes, materials for building and furniture, and leaf tissue for thatching, basket making, and other purposes. In addition, the palms represent one of the more important plant groups for interior decoration.

Botanical Features

FOLIAGE. The graceful airiness and arching quality of palm leaves, perched atop a tall, slender trunk, have become the primary image of the tropical landscape. Although these leaves vary greatly in their size and design, they fall into two relatively distinct categories: (1) the "feather palms" with pinnately compound leaves and (2) the "fan palms" with palmate leaves. A few palm species are difficult to classify into one of these two groups; thus, their identification requires a more careful look at flowers and fruit characteristics.

Palm leaves may also be distinguished as induplicate (∧-folded) or reduplicate (∧-folded). Induplicate leaves never possess an apical leaflet, whereas reduplicate leaves always have one. Most of the fan leaves are reduplicate. (See Figure 13.38.)

STEMS. Palm trunks are distinctly different in appearance and growth characteristics from other woody trees. The first unique quality is the presence of only one growing point at the apex of the plant. Protected by leaf bases, spines, or poisonous tissues, the apical bud is the "heart" of the palm. Its death or removal marks the death of the plant.

A second difference is that palm trunks typically do not grow thicker with age, although some do. A seedling plant builds up an inverted trunk cone, reaching full width before growth commences; the trunk never widens beyond this point. Unlike woody trees, palms have no cambium layer that adds thickness to the trunk as the plant matures.

FIGURE 13.38 Cross-sectional view of palm leaf segments, showing induplicate folding.

Third, the vascular system of palms is a network of numerous, small, separate vascular bundles, each encased in a hard fibrous sheath. These may be evenly spaced throughout the trunk or more commonly concentrated into an exterior layer around a spongy interior. In the latter configuration, the outer "wood" is extremely hard.

The surface texture of palm trunks ranges from a relatively smooth surface marked by leaf scars to a rough texture of residual leaf bases.

FLOWERS. Fortunately, because palm flowers are not showy, palms grown indoors are usually in the juvenile, nonflowering phase of growth. It is rare to find indoor

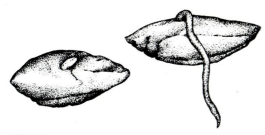

FIGURE 13.39 Date fruits are single-seeded drupes. The pits may be germinated easily; the new root and shoot emerge through a hatchlike structure.

TABLE 13.4 PALMS INCLUDED IN PART FIVE, ACCORDING TO LEAF TYPE

Feather

Caryota mitis	Burmese fishtail palm
Chamaedorea elegans	Parlor palm
Chrysalidocarpus lutes-cens	Areca palm
	Sentry palm
Howea forsterana	Miniature date palm
Phoenix roebelenii	

Fan

Chamaerops humilis	European fan palm
Rhapis excelsa	Bamboo palm

palms, except those in conservatories, that flower. Palm inflorescences vary from spikes to complex panicles, sometimes yielding in nature as many as 250,000 flowers on one species. Floral parts are typically in threes; plants may be monoecious, dioecious, or polygamous.

FRUIT. Because of the commercial importance of date palms and coconut palms, many people think immediately of fruit when palms are mentioned. Palm fruits are usually one-seeded berries or drupes that vary greatly in size among species. Coconut flesh is the endosperm contained within a thin endocarp; the husk is mesocarp tissue. The date fruit is a single-seeded drupe (Figure 13.39).

Significant Genera

As with the other seven families we have discussed in this chapter, palms also have numerous members that are suitable indoors. See table 13.4 for the palms included in Part Five that have superior promise indoors. We will discuss a few additional plants here, referring more in-depth pursuit to The Palm Society, which publishes a journal entitled *Principes*.

ACOELORRHAPHE. This fan palm is a water lover, being native to swampy coastal areas. A noted species is *Acoelorrhaphe wrightii*, known commonly as the everglades palm or silver saw palm. This useful tub plant has nearly round leaves up to 3 feet across.

The foliage is green above and silvery below and deeply divided into 40 or more segments.

ARECASTRUM. A feather palm, *Arecastrum* is usually represented indoors by the queen palm, *Arecastrum romanzoffianum*. The queen palm has dark green, glossy leaflets arranged on arching or drooping leaves with a long petiole. Although the plant is quite shade tolerant, it only holds a few leaves at a time indoors and has a heavy "thirst."

LIVISTONA. The most common indoor member is *Livistona chinensis* var. *chinensis*, the Chinese fan palm. This is one of the hardier species in the genus and has large, glossy, and broad leaves up to 6 feet wide in nature. Each leaf has a central undivided area with numerous segments at the perimeter that are again split near their apex, hanging like a fringe. Because of the large size, they need lots of growing room, enjoy warm conditions, and need much water.

PTYCHOSPERMA. The macarthur palm (*Ptychosperma macarthurii*) is the most common member of this genus. It has pinnately compound leaves with 40 to 50 pinnae on either side of the rachis. Its characteristic of constantly sending up additional shoots from the soil helps it develop and maintain a

FIGURE 13.40 The macarthur palm (*Ptychosperma macarthurii*) develops a compact form as a result of its suckering habit.

pleasant compactness indoors (Figure 13.40). The soft, glossy leaflets are green, about 1 foot long and jagged tipped.

VEITCHIA. These feather palms are represented indoors by *Veitchia merrillii*, the Manila palm or Christmas palm. It has ascending leaves up to 6 feet long with 50 or 60 leaflets on each side of the rachis. The leaflets extend almost to the base of the petiole and are bright green, leathery, lanceolate, and scaly. The slender trunk is prominently encircled with narrowly spaced leaf scars. Plants in the adult phase produce pendulous clusters of bright red fruit during the winter months. This palm can tolerate the environmental stress typical of indoor locations but prefers high light levels.

Culture

ENVIRONMENTAL FACTORS. Palms prefer bright indirect light indoors, but some species will tolerate very low light levels. Depending on the species, particularly those that are nonsuckering, palms may tend to be sparse in growth habit unless several plants are placed into a container. Fortunately, tolerance to crowding is an asset for palms. They perform relatively well when the root system is somewhat crowded in the container.

This tolerance to crowding affects other aspects of palm culture. Root crowding slows down the growth rate and ultimate size and helps prevent overwatering. Palms should be potted into a well-drained soil generously amended with organic matter and kept constantly moist. It is important that palms not be overwatered, yet constant moisture is critical to prevent killing the small feeder roots, and thus the plant. A secret in this is allowing the plant to grow in smaller containers than normal. Under these conditions, the root to soil ratio is altered so that drainage is improved.

Repotting, then, should be undertaken only when a reduction in vigor is noticed, and only during spring or summer when root development is occurring. During warm weather, palms may be taken outside, but they should be situated so that their exposure to sunlight is similar to that encountered indoors.

Fertilize palms during active growth with monthly feedings of a dilute general-purpose plant food.

PROPAGATION. Most palms are propagated easily from seed in temperatures around 70 to 80°F. Relatively high humidity and a well-drained propagation medium kept constantly moist are beneficial to germination. Smaller seeds, such as those from dates, may be covered with ½ inch of medium, whereas coconuts should only be half-buried with the husk left intact.

A few species can be propagated by division of offshoots from the parent plants. *Phoenix* and *Rhapis* are two genera for which this method is possible.

One genus, *Chamaedorea*, may be air-layered once it becomes unattractively leggy in late maturity. The top can be replanted as a small specimen once sufficient adventitious rooting has occurred.

PESTS AND DISEASES. The most troublesome pests of palms are spider mites, mealybugs, and scale insects. Since palms are rather easy to inspect and treat because of their sparseness of growth, syringing or hand picking and scrubbing are easier than with many other plants.

Various diseases may occur in palms such as bacterial blights and fungal problems such as leaf spots and rots. These diseases are more prevalent under production conditions than indoors, but they may occur. The lethal yellowing disease, of virus origin and attacking landscape palms in Florida, has not become a significant problem indoors.

PLANTS WITH HARMFUL CHARACTERISTICS

Like most things in life, some indoor plants must be used with care. Unfortunately, the physical attributes of a plant often give little warning of its dangerous nature. This section will address those plants that are poisonous or possess physical structures that can be injurious if handled improperly.

Poisonous Plants

Because of the attractive appearance and easy access of indoor plants, children and occasionally adults will ingest plant fruit, foliage, or other tissue. Direct skin contact with plant foliage occurs rather frequently. It is important, therefore, to recognize those plants that can either cause gastrointestinal poisoning or skin irritation, such as dermatitis. Most indoor plants are benign; the poisonous or irritating ones, however, are often popular, colorful, and apt to be handled.

FALSE ASSUMPTIONS CAN BE DEADLY. The rule for adults with respect to eating plant parts is to eat nothing unless you are absolutely sure it is safe. Take nothing for granted, since general rules and logical associations do not always hold true. For example, a common belief is that milky sap is poisonous; some is, but there are many exceptions. Fruit harmlessly ingested by animals or birds is not always safe for human consumption. And quite important, do not assume that relatives of edible plants or plants named after edible plants are safe to eat. A prime example is the Jerusalem cherry, *Solanum pseudocapsicum*. The leaves and unripe fruit of this popular Christmas ornamental contain the substance solanine, which causes gastrointestinal, respiratory, and central nervous system poisoning. Since the fruit looks like small tomatoes, which belong to the same family, and the fruit is called a cherry (a misnomer), many people are led to believe that it is edible. Its attractive red fruits are especially tempting to small children. Though most plants do not have such misleading common names and family associations, the Jerusalem cherry illustrates well the danger of making incorrect assumptions.

Most of the poisonings treated by the various Poison Control Centers around the United States occur in children under five years old. Plants are the seventh most prevalent source of poisoning. Keep all plants with known poisonous or harmful characteristics well away from young children.

WHAT TO DO IF POISONING OCCURS. Most symptoms of poisoning will appear within 4 hours of ingestion. If ingestion has occurred at least 12 hours before discovery, as with a child, and no symptoms have appeared, chances of poisoning are slim.

As soon as possible after ingestion of poisonous plant material, the following steps should be followed.

1. Note when the poisonous material was

TABLE 13.5 POISONOUS PLANTS: THEIR CHARACTERISTICS AND TREATMENT

Plant	Poisonous Part(s)	Symptoms	Treatment
Aroids (*Alocasium, Anthurium, Caladium, Dieffenbachia, Monstera, Philodendron, Scindapsus,* and *Syngonium*)	Leaves and roots (calcium oxalate crystals)	Burning sensation and swelling of mouth and throat tissue; can inhibit breathing; dermatitis; nausea, salivation, vomiting, and diarrhea also possible	Induce vomiting if breathing is normal; administer egg whites, milk of magnesia, or milk to counteract poison
Azalea spp.	Toxic resin containing andromedotoxin; found in leaves, twigs, flowers, and pollen	Slow pulse, lowering of blood pressure, lack of coordination, convulsions, paralysis, and death	Gastric lavage (flushing) or vomiting
Burmese fishtail palm (*Caryota mitis*)	Berries	Dermatitis	Wash juice from skin with soap and water
Coffee (*Coffea*)	Fruit contains caffeine, a teratogen	Congenital abnormalities	None
Croton (*Codiaeum* spp.)	Seed contains croton oil, a purgative; seeds rarely develop on plants sold in the United States	Burning pain in mouth and stomach, rapid heartbeat, bloody diarrhea, and coma; can be fatal	Empty stomach through lavage (flushing); milk as demulcent; treat other symptoms
Date palm (*Phoenix dactylifera*)	Pollen	Hay fever, bronchial asthma	Prevent plant from flowering
English ivy (*Hedera helix*)	Leaves and berries contain heteragenin	Excitement, difficult breathing, vomiting, diarrhea, nervous depression, coma, dermatitis	Gastric lavage or vomiting; oxygen and artificial respiration; symptomatic treatment
Euphorbia spp. (crown of thorns)	Sap contains complex esters, carcinogens	Dermatitis; severe poisoning; severe irritation of mouth, throat, and stomach	Wash sap from skin with soap and water; gastric lavage or vomiting
Fig (*Ficus* spp.)	Sap	Dermatitis	Wash sap from skin with soap and water
Japanese poinsettia; Redbird cactus (*Pedilanthus tithymaloides*)	Sap	Dermatitis, severe poisoning	Wash sap from skin with soap and water; gastric lavage or vomiting; symptomatic treatment
Jerusalem cherry (*Solanum pseudocapsicum*)	Leaves and unripe fruit contain solanine, a poisonous alkaloid	Gastrointestinal symptoms, convulsions, respiratory and central nervous system severe depression	Gastric lavage or vomiting; wash sap from skin with soap and water
Pineapple (*Ananas comosus*)	All parts possess the enzyme bromelian	Dermatitis	Wash juice from skin with soap and water
Sago palm (*Cycas revoluta*)	Plant tissue contains mutogenic and teratogenic cycasin, a known carcinogen and liver toxicant	Alterations in reproductive cells, congenital abnormalities	None

SOURCE: Adapted from Driesbach, R., *Handbook on Poisoning*, Lang Medical Publications, 1980; Arena, J., *Poisoning: Toxicology, Symptoms, Treatments*, 4th ed., C.C. Thomas, 1979.

TABLE 13.5 A PLANTS WITH HARMFUL CHARACTERISTICS

Name	Mode of Action
Agave spp.	Sharp leaf tips
Aloe spp.	Marginal teeth on leaves
Asparagus spp.	Spines
Bromeliad spp.	Occasional sharp leaf tips, spines on leaf margins
Cactus spp.	Spines, irritating bristles
Crown of thorns (*Euphorbia milii*)	Spines
European fan palm (*Chamaerops humilis*)	Thorny leaf bases
Euphorbia spp.	Spines
Phoenix spp. (date palms)	Spiny leaf bases
Sensitive plant (*Mimosa pudica*)	Slightly spiny stems
Screw pines (Pandanus spp.)	Spiny leaf margins
Yucca spp.	Sharp leaf tips, rough leaf margins

ingested. This information can be of help to doctors treating poisoned patients.

2. Note what symptoms have appeared. Typical symptoms of plant poisoning are nausea, vomiting, and diarrhea. In rare circumstances, elevated temperature, flushed skin, dilated pupils, and weakened breathing may be observed. In extreme cases, shock may also be a factor.

3. Determine as closely as possible what was eaten. Try to identify the plant in question, and take it, if possible, to the hospital with the victim.

4. Try to determine what type of plant tissue and how much was eaten. Often, plants have certain parts that are poisonous and other parts that are not.

5. If the conditions of plant poisoning are unknown, induce vomiting with syrup of ipecac, repeating the procedure in 15 minutes. Fortunately, most poisonous plant substances are not caustic to human tissue so vomiting can be induced without harmful effects. Furthermore, there are few specific antidotes for plant poisons, so treating the symptoms is more important than identifying the plant.

In any case, try to arrange for medical help as soon as possible, either by rushing the victim to the nearest hospital or by calling 1-800-642-9999, the national Poison Control Center toll-free telephone number.

Although numerous plants are listed in Tables 13.5 and 13.5A, relative danger varies widely. Some, in fact, may rarely be involved in actual poisoning situations. The charts are included to create a more informed student, rather than to condemn the use of these plants. The choice of their use will depend on the individual circumstances of each reader.

AESTHETIC VALUE AND USES OF THE TOP 150 INDOOR PLANTS

Having concluded our discussion of these eight major families and anticipating the individual plant discussions of Part Five, we present here a reference table that indicates the aesthetic value and uses for the top 150 plants in Part Five.

The table includes both the botanical and common name for the plant; its aesthetic value, considering flower, fruit, and unusual foliage coloration; and appropriate uses. These uses include small specimens for window sill or table top, larger shrubby plants more suitable for floor use, plants that pro-

TABLE 13.6

Botanical Name/Common Name	Aesthetic Value			Uses				
	Flowers	Fruit	Unusual Foliage Coloration	Small Pots or Containers for Windowsill or Table	Floor Plant	Indoor Tree	Hanging Basket	Climber
Acalypha wilkesiana Jacob's coat, copperleaf			X	X	X			
Adiantum raddianum Delta maidenhair fern				X	X		X	
Aechmea fasciata Urn plant, silver vase	X		X	X				
Aeschynanthus pulcher Scarlet basket vine, lipstick plant	X			X			X	
Agave victoriae-reginae Queen agave			X	X	X			
Aglaonema commutatum Silver evergreen	X	X	X	X	X			
Aglaonema commutatum maculatum Silver evergreen			X	X	X			
Aglaonema commutatum 'Fransher' Fransher evergreen			X	X	X			
Aglaonema commutatum 'Pseudobracteatum' Golden evergreen			X	X	X			
Aglaonema commutatum 'Silver King' Silver king evergreen			X	X	X			
Aglaonema commutatum 'Treubii' Ribbon aglaonema			X	X				
Aglaonema costatum Spotted evergreen			X	X				
Aglaonema crispum Painted drop-tongue				X	X			
Aglaonema modestum Chinese evergreen	X			X				
Aloe barbadensis Barbados aloe, medicinal aloe, burn plant			X	X				
Ananas comosus Pineapple	X	X		X	X			

Table 13.6 (Continued)

Botanical Name/Common Name	Aesthetic Value			Uses				
	Flowers	Fruit	Unusual Foliage Coloration	Small Pots or Containers for Windowsill or Table	Floor Plant	Indoor Tree	Hanging Basket	Climber
Anthurium × cultorum Flamingo lily	X			X				
Aphelandra squarrosa Zebra plant, saffron spike	X		X	X				
Araucaria heterophylla Norfolk Island pine					X	X		
Ardisia crenata Coralberry, spiceberry	X	X		X	X			
Asparagus densiflorus 'Sprengeri' Sprenger asparagus, sprengeri fern	X	X		X			X	
Asparagus densiflorus 'Myers' Plume asparagus				X			X	
Asparagus setaceus Asparagus fern, lace fern				X			X	X
Aspidistra elatior Cast-iron plant, barroom plant, parlor palm					X			
Beaucarnea recurvata Ponytail palm, elephant foot tree				X	X			
Begonia × semperflorens-cultorum Bedding begonia, wax begonia	X		X	X			X	
Begonia × erythrophylla Beefsteak begonia	X			X				
Begonia masoniana Iron-cross begonia	X		X	X				
Begonia × rex-cultorum Rex begonia	X		X	X				
Brassaia actinophylla Australian umbrella tree, octopus tree				X	X	X		
Caryota mitis Burmese fishtail palm, clustered fishtail palm				X	X	X		
Cereus peruvianus Peruvian apple, column cactus	X			X	X			

(continued)

Table 13.6 (Continued)

Botanical Name/Common Name	Aesthetic Value			Uses				
	Flowers	Fruit	Unusual Foliage Coloration	Small Pots or Containers for Windowsill or Table	Floor Plant	Indoor Tree	Hanging Basket	Climber
Ceropegia woodii Rosary vine, string of hearts, heart vine	X		X	X			X	
Chamaedorea elegans Parlor palm				X	X			
Chamaerops humilis European fan palm				X	X	X		
Chlorophytum comosum Spider ivy, spider plant	X			X			X	
Chlorophytum comosum 'Vittatum' Variegated spider ivy	X		X	X			X	
Chrysalidocarpus lutescens Areca palm, yellow palm				X	X	X		
Cissus rhombifolia Grape ivy, venezuela treebine				X			X	X
Cissus antarctica Kangaroo vine				X			X	X
Cissus rotundifolia Arabian wax cissus				X			X	X
Codiaeum variegatum pictum Garden croton			X	X	X			
Coffea arabica Coffee				X	X	X		
Coleus × *hybridus* Garden coleus			X	X				
Cordyline terminalis Good-luck plant, Hawaiian ti			X	X	X	X		
Crassula argentea Jade plant, jade tree	X			X	X			
Crassula argentea 'Tricolor' Tricolor jade plant	X		X	X	X			
Cryptanthus bivittatus Earth-star	X		X	X				

Table 13.6 (Continued)

Botanical Name/Common Name	Aesthetic Value			Uses				
	Flowers	Fruit	Unusual Foliage Coloration	Small Pots or Containers for Windowsill or Table	Floor Plant	Indoor Tree	Hanging Basket	Climber
Cryptanthus × 'Tt' Color-band cryptanthus	X		X	X				
Cuphea ignea Cigar flower, cigar plant, firecracker plant	X			X				
Cycas revoluta Sago palm, conehead, funeral palm				X	X			
Cyperus alternifolius Umbrella plant, umbrella palm	X			X	X			
Cyrtomium falcatum Holly fern				X				
Dieffenbachia amoena Giant dumbcane, charming dumbcane			X	X	X			
Dieffenbachia exotica Exotic dieffenbachia			X	X	X			
Dieffenbachia exotica 'Perfection' Perfection dumbcane			X	X	X			
Dieffenbachia maculata Spotted dumbcane			X	X	X			
Dieffenbachia maculata 'Rudolph Roehrs' Yellow-leaf dumbcane			X	X	X			
Dizygotheca elegantissima False aralia			X	X	X			
Dracaena fragrans 'Massangeana' Corn plant			X	X	X	X		
Dracaena deremensis 'Janet Craig' Janet Craig dracaena				X	X			
Dracaena deremensis 'Warneckii' Striped dracaena			X	X	X			
Dracaena goldieana Queen of dracaenas			X	X	X			
Dracaena marginata Madagascar dragon tree, red-edged dracaena			X	X	X			

(continued)

Table 13.6 (Continued)

Botanical Name/Common Name	Aesthetic Value			Uses				
	Flowers	Fruit	Unusual Foliage Coloration	Small Pots or Containers for Windowsill or Table	Floor Plant	Indoor Tree	Hanging Basket	Climber
Dracaena sanderiana Belgian evergreen, ribbon plant			X	X				
Dracaena surculosa Gold dust dracaena, spotted dracaena			X	X				
Epipremnum aureum Pothos, golden pothos			X	X	X		X	X
Episcia cupreata Flame violet	X		X	X			X	
Euphorbia milii splendens Crown of thorns	X			X	X			
× *Fatshedera lizei* Aralia ivy				X	X			
Fatsia japonica Japanese fatsia				X	X			
Ficus benjamina Benjamin tree, weeping fig				X	X	X		
Ficus deltoidea Mistletoe fig		X		X	X			
Ficus elastica 'Decora' Wideleaf rubber plant					X	X		
Ficus elastica 'Variegata' Variegated rubber plant			X	X	X	X		
Ficus lyrata Fiddle-leaf fig					X	X		
Ficus pumila Creeping fig				X			X	X
Fittonia verschaffeltii Red-nerve plant, mosaic plant	X		X	X			X	
Fittonia verschaffeltii argyroneura Silver-nerve plant			X	X			X	
Gibasis geniculata Tahitian bridal veil	X			X			X	

Table 13.6 (Continued)

Botanical Name/Common Name	Aesthetic Value				Uses			
	Flowers	Fruit	Unusual Foliage Coloration	Small Pots or Containers for Windowsill or Table	Floor Plant	Indoor Tree	Hanging Basket	Climber
Gynura aurantiaca 'Purple Passion' Purple-passion vine	X		X	X			X	
Hedera helix English ivy				X			X	X
Hemigraphis alternata Red ivy	X		X	X			X	
Heptapleureum arboricola Dwarf schefflera				X	X			
Howea forsterana Sentry palm, kentia palm				X	X	X		
Hoya carnosa Wax plant, honey plant	X			X			X	
Hoya carnosa 'Krinkle Kurl' Hindu rope	X			X			X	
Hypoestes phyllostachya Polka-dot plant, freckle-face	X		X	X				
Iresine herbstii Beef plant, chicken-gizzard, beefsteak plant	X		X	X				
Kalanchoe daigremontiana Devil's backbone	X			X				
Maranta leuconeura leuconeura Prayer plant, ten commandments	X		X	X				
Maranta leuconeura erythroneura Red-nerve plant, red-veined prayer plant	X		X	X				
Maranta leuconeura kerchoviana Rabbit's foot, rabbit's track	X		X	X				
Mikania ternata Plush vine			X	X			X	
Mimosa pudica Sensitive plant, touch-me-not	X			X				
Monstera deliciosa Swiss-cheese plant, breadfruit vine				X	X			X

(continued)

Table 13.6 (Continued)

Botanical Name/Common Name	Aesthetic Value			Uses				
	Flowers	Fruit	Unusual Foliage Coloration	Small Pots or Containers for Windowsill or Table	Floor Plant	Indoor Tree	Hanging Basket	Climber
Neoregelia carolinae 'Tricolor' Striped blushing bromeliad	X		X	X				
Nephrolepis exaltata 'Bostoniensis' Boston fern				X			X	
Nephrolepis exaltata 'Fluffy Ruffles' Fluffy ruffles fern				X			X	
Opuntia microdasys Rabbit ears	X			X	X			
Pandanus veitchii Veitch screw pine			X	X	X			
Pellionia pulchra Satin pellionia, rainbow vine			X	X			X	
Peperomia obtusifolia Baby rubber plant, pepper-face	X			X				
Peperomia obtusifolia 'Variegata' Variegated peperomia			X	X				
Peperomia argyreia Watermelon begonia	X		X	X				
Peperomia caperata Emerald-ripple peperomia	X			X				
Peperomia scandens Philodendron peperomia	X			X			X	
Philodendron scandens oxycardium Heart-leaf philodendron				X	X		X	X
Philodendron bipennifolium Horsehead philodendron				X	X			X
Philodendron domesticum Spade-leaf philodendron, elephant's ear				X	X			X
Philodendron × 'Emerald Duke' Emerald king philodendron				X	X			X
Philodendron × 'Florida' Florida philodendron				X	X			X

Table 13.6 (Continued)

Botanical Name/Common Name	Aesthetic Value			Uses				
	Flowers	Fruit	Unusual Foliage Coloration	Small Pots or Containers for Windowsill or Table	Floor Plant	Indoor Tree	Hanging Basket	Climber
Philodendron × 'Majesty' Majesty philodendron				X	X			X
Philodendron × 'Red Duchess' Red princess philodendron				X	X			X
Philodendron scandens micans Velvet-leaf philodendron				X	X		X	X
Philodendron selloum Tree philodendron, saddle-leaf philodendron					X			
Phoenix roebelenii Miniature date palm				X	X	X		
Pilea cadierei Aluminum plant	X		X	X			X	
Pilea microphylla Artillery plant				X				
Pilea 'Moon Valley' Moon valley pilea				X				
Pilea nummulariifolia Creeping charlie				X			X	
Pilea 'Silver Tree' Silver-tree panamiga			X	X				
Pittosporum tobira Japanese pittosporum, Australian laurel, mock orange				X	X			
Platycereum bifurcatum Common staghorn fern							X	
Plectranthus australis Swedish ivy	X			X			X	
Podocarpus macrophyllus Southern yew, Japanese yew, Buddhist pine				X	X	X		
Polyscias fruticosa Ming aralia, Chinese aralia, parsley aralia				X	X	X		
Pteris ensiformis 'Victoriae' Victoria brake fern, silver-leaf fern			X	X				

(continued)

373

Table 13.6 (Continued)

Botanical Name/Common Name	Aesthetic Value			Uses				
	Flowers	Fruit	Unusual Foliage Coloration	Small Pots or Containers for Windowsill or Table	Floor Plant	Indoor Tree	Hanging Basket	Climber
Rhapis excelsa Bamboo palm, slender lady palm				X	X	X		
Rhoeo spathacea Purple-leaved spiderwort, moses in the cradle	X		X	X			X	
Saintpaulia ionantha Common African violet	X			X				
Sansevieria trifasciata Snake plant, mother-in-law tongue	X			X	X			
Sansevieria trifasciata 'Hahnii' Bird's nest sansevieria				X				
Sansevieria trifasciata laurentii Variegated snake plant	X		X	X	X			
Saxifraga stolonifera Strawberry geranium, strawberry begonia, creeping sailor, mother of thousands	X		X	X			X	
Saxifraga stolonifera 'Tricolor' Magic carpet saxifraga	X		X	X			X	
Schlumbergera bridgesii Christmas cactus	X			X			X	
Scindapsus pictus 'Argyraeus' Satin pothos			X	X	X		X	X
Sedum morganianum Burro's tail, donkey's tail, lamb's tail			X	X			X	

Table 13.6 (Continued)

Botanical Name/Common Name	Aesthetic Value			Uses				
	Flowers	Fruit	Unusual Foliage Coloration	Small Pots or Containers for Windowsill or Table	Floor Plant	Indoor Tree	Hanging Basket	Climber
Senecio mikanioides German ivy, parlor ivy	X			X			X	
Senecio macroglossus 'Variegatum' Variegated wax vine	X		X	X			X	
Senecio rowleyanus String of beads, bead vine	X			X			X	
Soleirolia soleirolii Baby's tears				X			X	
Spathiphyllum 'Clevelandii' White anthurium, peace lily	X			X				
Spathiphyllum 'Mauna Loa' Mauna loa peace lily	X			X	X			
Streptocarpus saxorum False African violet	X			X			X	
Syngonium podophyllum Nephthytis, arrowhead vine				X			X	X
Tolmiea menziesii Pickaback plant, piggyback plant	X			X			X	
Tradescantia fluminensis Wandering Jew	X			X			X	
Yucca elephantipes Spineless yucca, bulb stem palm-lily				X	X	X		
Zebrina pendula Wandering Jew	X		X	X			X	

vide a treelike quality, those that trail and are suitable for hanging baskets, and finally, those that are able to climb by twining, clinging tendrils, or aerial roots.

A number of plants are suitable for various purposes or have multiple aesthetic effects. In addition, a plant may be suitable for a small container early in its life but require a larger container with maturity. In these circumstances, both categories, the small container and floor specimen columns, for example, would be checked.

It is our hope that this table will not only provide a quick reference to the plants listed in Part Five but also will serve as a handy reference key throughout the years you own this book.

FOR FURTHER READING

Arena, J. *Poisoning: Toxicology, Symptoms, Treatment.* 4th ed. Springfield, Ill.: Thomas, 1979.

Bechtel, H., P. Cribb, and E. Launert. *The Manual of Cultivated Orchid Species.* Boston: The MIT Press, 1981.

Driesbach, R. *Handbook on Poisoning.* Lang Medical Publications, 1980.

Graf, A. *Exotic Plant Manual.* East Rutherford, N.J.: Roehrs Co., 1970.

Graf, A. *Exotica.* East Rutherford, N.J.: Roehrs Co., 1976.

Hardin, J., and J. Arena. *Human Poisoning from Native and Cultivated Plants.* Duke University Press, 1974.

Heywood, V. *Flowering Plants of the World.* New York: W.H. Smith Publishers, 1978.

Hoshizaki, B. *Fern Growers Manual.* New York: Alfred A. Knopf, 1975.

Innes, C. *Cacti and Succulents.* Ward Lock Limited, 1977.

Kramer, J. *Cacti and Other Succulents.* Harry N. Abrams, Inc., 1977.

Liberty Hyde Bailey Hortorum. *Hortus III.* New York: MacMillan, 1976.

Lewis, W., and M. Elvin-Lewis. *Medical Botany.* New York: Wiley, 1977.

Mickel, J. *The Home Gardener's Book of Ferns.* New York: Holt, Rinehart, and Winston, 1979.

Mulligan, W. *Cacti and Succulents.* New York: Grosset and Dunlap, 1975.

Northern, R. *Miniature Orchids.* New York: Van Nostrand Reinhold, 1980.

Rouh, W. *Bromeliads.* Blandford Press, 1973.

Reinikka, M. *A History of the Orchid.* Coral Gables: University of Miami Press, 1972.

Rittershausen, B., and W. Rittershausen. *Orchids.* Blandford Press, 1979.

Schulz, P. *Gesneriads and How to Grow Them.* Diversity Books, 1967.

Wurthman, E. "Best of the Bromeliads." *Foliage Digest 2,* 4 (1979).

PART FIVE

A GUIDE TO THE IDENTIFICATION AND CULTURE OF THE TOP 150 INDOOR PLANTS

INTRODUCTION

No group of plants represents a broader range of physical appearance or geographical distribution than that which we culture indoors. Some grow naturally as trees, while others creep along shaded forest floors. Certain species inhabit arid regions of the world while others literally stand in water at the edge of streams or lakes. Some stand alone, while others must depend on other species for support. Although most occupy tropical regions, their total geographical expanse spans the globe.

This encyclopedic section considers each of these diverse plants individually, providing the student with the necessary information to understand, cultivate, and enjoy each one. In order to simplify the wide variety of cultural requirements these specimens demand, each genus contains four cultural "keys" that simply and accurately define the required characteristics of light, water, temperature, and humidity. Following is a specific explanation of each category within these four cultural categories.

Light

As we discussed in Chapter Eight, light is best measured for our purposes in foot-candles. Under this system, plants need one of three light conditions.

Low Light: Requiring a range of 50- to 1000-foot candles during daylight hours.

Bright indirect: Requiring a range of 1000- to 3000-foot candles during the daylight hours, but never being exposed to full sunlight.

Full Sun: Requiring light in the range of 4000- to 8000-foot candles during the daylight hours; as much direct sun as possible.

Water

Chapter Ten discusses the aspects of watering in full detail. There are the three general types of watering.

Dry: During active growth, the soil mass is drenched with each watering and allowed to dry fully between waterings; during inactive growth, water should be withheld, applying infrequent moistenings only when the soil becomes quite dry.

Normal: During active growth, the plant should be watered well and allowed to approach, but not reach, the wilting point prior to watering again; during inactive growth, use similar timing, being careful not to water before drying to near the wilting point has been accomplished.

Evenly Moist: During active growth, water by thorough saturation and allow only moderate drying between waterings; during inactive growth, allow more drying between waterings, but never to the wilting point. This category should not be construed as "evenly wet"; very few plants enjoy standing in water all the time.

Temperature

As a general rule, these temperature ranges are for seasons of active growth. During inactive growth, lessen the ranges by 10°F.

Cool: Night temperatures from 40 to 60°F; days at least 10° warmer.

Moderate: Night temperatures between 50 and 65°F; days at least 10° warmer.

Warm: Night temperatures 60 to 80°F; days at least 10° warmer.

Humidity

Since relative humidity is the amount of water vapor in the atmosphere related to the air temperature, specific humidity recommendations are difficult to establish.

In general, though, we can outline ranges in which the humidity might fall for best growth of certain plants. Consequently, we offer the following relative humidity standards, conceding that varying temperatures and air movement conditions can drastically influence their effect on plant growth.

Arid: Relative humidity between 10 to 25 percent.

Moderate: Relative humidity between 25 to 60 percent.

High: Relative humidity above 60 percent.

A WORD ON PLANT SELECTION

Determining the 150 most important indoor plants is difficult at best. Unfortunately, very little information exists that allows a precise determination, and that which is available suffers from being out-of-date. Consequently, we have determined the top 150 plants (those accompanied by a drawing) through our teaching experience, consultation with authorities familiar with the indoor plant industry, other publications, and, to a minor extent, predictions of future popularity. Because of the wide range of species that can be grown indoors and the large number of cultivars that continue to enter the indoor plant market, we have limited our list to those that we feel are commercially important enough to be included in academic collections.

AN ALPHABETICAL LISTING, BY GENUS, OF THE TOP 150 INDOOR PLANTS

BOTANICAL NAME: *Acalypha wilkesiana*
(uh-CAL-ih-fa wilkes-ee-AY-na)

COMMON NAME: Jacob's coat, copperleaf

FAMILY: Euphorbiaceae (Spurge)

ORIGIN: Pacific Islands

With its broad elliptical to ovate leaves and multicolored foliage—bronze-green, mottled with red, copper, or purple—this species resembles the colorful coleus. In addition to easy culture and propagation, Jacob's coat sports 8 inch long or so slender reddish flower spikes. A fast grower, it is used as a hedge plant in its native area, growing to a height of 15 feet. Provides good contrast to other green plants.

Culture   Grow in good potting soil and fertilize regularly in good growing conditions. If leggy form develops, cut back severely or start new plants from cuttings. Keep night temperature above 60°F; avoid cold locations with this one.

Propagation   Quite easy by cuttings at any time of year.

Related Plants

A. hispida "Chenille plant." Similar in size and appearance to *A. wilkesiana,* but with green foliage and red or purple female spikes that are up to 18 inches long, fuzzy, and hang gracefully.

Typical Problems   Spider mites are the most serious pest, particularly in dry, hot locations.

Water		
DRY	NORMAL	**EVENLY MOIST**

Temperature		
COOL	MODERATE	**WARM**

Light		
LOW	BRIGHT INDIRECT	**FULL SUN**

Humidity		
ARID	**MODERATE**	HUMID

BOTANICAL NAME: *Adiantum raddianum*
(ah-dee-ANT-um rad-ih-AN-um)

COMMON NAME: Delta maidenhair fern

FAMILY: Polypodiaceae (Polypody)

ORIGIN: Brazil

Known collectively as maidenhair ferns, this genus is noted for its airy and graceful fronds with dark, wirelike petioles and small, fan-shaped pinnules. The delta maidenhair, somewhat easier to grow indoors than other species, still requires careful attention to culture in order to remain lush. It is distinguished by pinnule veins that terminate at a marginal sinus and grows to a 12- to 15-inch size with fronds gracefully arching. The fronds, rosy in color when young, mature to a fresh light green. A good plant for terrariums and hanging baskets.

Culture This fern requires high humidity, wet soil during growth, and moist soil in winter and should stay out of direct sun. Soil should be high in organic matter to retain moisture and drain well. Avoid wilting, which does irreparable frond damage, and cold drafts.

Typical Problems Mites, mealybugs, scale insects, and occasional leaf spot diseases.

Propagation Easily by spores, as described in Chapter Thirteen, or by dividing the horizontal rhizome in late winter after removing the foliage.

Related Plants
A. capillus-veneris (Southern M.F.). Similar in appearance to *A. raddianum,* but somewhat larger, more difficult to grow, and with veins ending at the marginal teeth.

A. tenerum 'Farleyense' (Farley M.F.). Large pinnules deeply cut and crisped, giving a fluffy and coarser appearance to the foliage.

Water

DRY	NORMAL	EVENLY MOIST

Temperature

COOL	MODERATE	WARM

Light

LOW	BRIGHT INDIRECT	FULL SUN

Humidity

ARID	MODERATE	HUMID

BOTANICAL NAME: *Aechmea fasciata*
(EEK-me-uh fas-see-AH-tuh)

COMMON NAME: Urn plant, silver vase

FAMILY: Bromeliaceae (Bromelia/Pineapple)

ORIGIN: Brazil

With broad, spiney, straplike leaves, the urn plant holds water in storage until it is needed. White on black horizontal stripes across the deep green leaves create a distinctive color scheme.

The flower structure, composed of spiney pink bracts and petals changing from blue to red, arises from the central vase and lasts for months. After flowering and offset production, the plant dies. Grows naturally as an epiphyte up in trees; can be grown indoors in pots or anchored to wooden structures reminiscent of its natural habitat.

Culture The soil, providing primarily support to this naturally epiphytic plant, must be well-aerated. Sphagnum moss, fir bark, or osmunda fibre are good constituents for abundant aeration.
Keep night temperature above 60°F. Keep vase filled with water, spiked occasionally with a few drops of liquid fertilizer. Feed through the soil also.

Typical Problems Scales, mites, basal rot, and leaf diseases occur. Also, since soil should be light and loose, staking of larger, newly potted plants is often needed until roots are anchored.

Propagation Naturally propagates through production of offsets that may be severed when 10 inches tall or so, by tissue culture, or seed that takes several years to yield flowers.

Related Plants

A. chantinii Similar in form and size to *A. fasciata,* but with silvery white leaf markings and yellow flowers.

Water		
DRY	NORMAL	EVENLY MOIST

Temperature		
COOL	MODERATE	WARM

Light		
LOW	BRIGHT INDIRECT	FULL SUN

Humidity		
ARID	MODERATE	HUMID

BOTANICAL NAME: *Aeschynanthus pulcher*
(es-shih-NAN-thus PULL-cher)

COMMON NAME: Scarlet basket vine, lipstick plant

FAMILY: Gesneriaceae (Gesneria)

ORIGIN: Java

Noted and named for the rich red developing flower that protrudes from the green, waxy calyx, this somewhat straggly epiphyte flowers throughout the year with adequate light. The ease of flowering, even in lower light exposures, makes it a rewarding plant to grow.

A cousin to the African violet, the lipstick plant is sometimes called basket vine because of its trailing habit. The waxy, ovate leaves are borne in an opposite configuration. Use in a hanging basket or where the graceful form and rich red tubular flowers can be enjoyed.

Culture Prune straggly stems after flowering subsides. Provide warmth, keeping night temperatures over 60°F. Pot into a humus-potting mix and fertilize monthly during active growth.

Typical Problems Leaf blights and spots, stem cankers (rots), mites, and scale insects.

Propagation Stem cuttings.

Related Plants

A. speciosus. Similar to *A. pulcher* but with orange flowers that are yellow at the base.

Water

DRY	NORMAL	EVENLY MOIST

Temperature

COOL	MODERATE	WARM

Light

LOW	BRIGHT INDIRECT	FULL SUN

Humidity

ARID	MODERATE	HUMID

BOTANICAL NAME: *Agave victoriae-reginae*
(a-GAH-vee vik-TORE-ee-ah RET-in-ee)

COMMON NAME: Queen agave

FAMILY: Agavaceae (Agave)

ORIGIN: North Mexico

As a group, Agaves are known as century plants because of their need of ten to fifty years to flower. After flowering once, they die and offsets usually carry on. The queen agave is a small species that is suitable for indoor use. The larger species listed below may quickly outgrow their usefulness in the home. The queen agave is a small mound of dark green, 6-inch leaves that are white and horny on the margin and spined at the apex. The inflorescence is a 4-foot-tall cluster of greenish flowers. The tough, fibrous nature of the agave leaf is demonstrated by the fact that one species provides us with sisal hemp for rope.

Culture   The most important cultural consideration is to avoid overwatering that can create root rots and the death of the plant. A loamy soil with a generous sand constitutent provides good drainage. Fertilize only during active growth and then only every two months. Repot every two to three years or when overcrowding occurs.

Typical Problems   Leaf yellowing may occur with too frequent watering. Also, the leaf axils may be sites for mealy bug or scale infestation.

Propagation   Most species are propagated by seed or through cultivation of offsets. The queen agave, however, should be started by seeds since it will form no or few offsets.

Related Plants   Over 100 species exist. *A. americana.* "Century plant", "American aloe." A large gray-green specimen that can be grown indoors when small. The cultivar 'Marginata,' the variegated century plant, has yellow leaf margins.

A. angustifolia 'Marginata.' "Variegated Caribbean agave." Similar to *A.a.* 'Marginata,' but with white leaf margins.

A. fernandi-regis. "King agave." A small species similar in size and appearance to the queen agave, but with fewer leaves and a more open growth habit.

Water		
DRY	NORMAL	EVENLY MOIST

Temperature		
COOL	MODERATE	WARM

Light		
LOW	BRIGHT INDIRECT	FULL SUN

Humidity		
ARID	MODERATE	HUMID

BOTANICAL NAME: *Aglaonema commutatum*
(ag-lay-oh-NEE-muh com-yew-TA-tum)

COMMON NAME: Silver evergreen

FAMILY: Araceae (Arum/Aroids)

ORIGIN: Philippine Islands

The popularity of this genus in commercial plantings reflects a superior tolerance to low light conditions and a general ease of culture. This species is typical of the group in that it spreads slowly by a rhizome, producing thickened stems that sprawl with age. The foliage is elliptical and elongated, 12 inches long by 4 inches wide, and dark green with gray-green variegation along the major veins. The durability and beauty of this species have led to the development of several popular cultivars and varieties through the years. Bears a pale green spathe; later, clusters of 1-inch berries on the spadix that turn yellow, then bright red.

Culture These slow growers can endure extremely low light levels, cool drafts, and erratic watering regimes. In fact, they can be cultured in water to some extent. The leaves turn upward in bright locations. Keep night temperature above 65°F.

Typical Problems To a moderate extent, mealy bugs, mites, and a variety of blights and rots occur, but not often in indoor culture if proper care is provided.

Propagation Large plants may be multiplied by division of the rhizome, tip or cane cuttings, or fresh seed.

Water

DRY	NORMAL	EVENLY MOIST

Temperature

COOL	MODERATE	WARM

Light

LOW	BRIGHT INDIRECT	FULL SUN

Humidity

ARID	MODERATE	HUMID

Related Plants   Listed here are the more popular variants of *A. commutatum*, as well as other species that are recognized commercially as important members of the group. All require similar culture and possess the durability of *A. commutatum*.

AGLAONEMA COMMUTATUM VARIANTS

A. c. maculatum. "Silver evergreen." Leaves marked with four to six silvery white, irregular bands along lateral veins.

A. c. elegans. "Silver evergreen." Similar markings to *A. c. maculatum;* valued for its ability to endure very low light levels.

A. c. 'Fransher.' "Fransher evergreen." The long, slender leaves are generally cream-colored with green margins and irregular green bands along lateral veins. The leaf petioles are also ivory in color.

Aglaonema commutatum maculatum

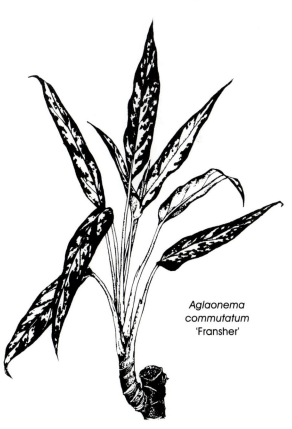

Aglaonema commutatum 'Fransher'

A. c. 'Pseudobracteatum.' "Golden evergreen." Known originally as 'White rajah,' this plant is similar to 'Fransher,' but with broader leaves, a white stem structure, and with richer green tones in the leaf.

A. c. 'Silver King.' "Silver king evergreen." The elongated dark green leaves are heavily marked with silver along each lateral vein, leaving a zone of green between veins. The plant grows to a 30-inch height.

A. c. 'Silver Queen.' "Silver queen evergreen." Similar coloration to **A. c.** 'Silver King,' but with narrower leaves and a maximum height of 24 inches.

A. c. 'Treubii.' "Ribbon aglaonema." As its name implies, **A. c.** 'Treubii' has quite narrow leaves only 2 inches wide that are marked with three or four large irregular pale green patches.

Aglaonema commutatum
'Pseudobracteatum'

Aglaonema commutatum
'Silver King'

OTHER SPECIES OF AGLAONEMA

A. costatum. "Spotted evergreen." The broad, almost heart-shaped leaves are blackish green with a white midrib and varying densities of prominent white spots. Shorter than most other species.

A. crispum. "Painted drop-tongue, pewter evergreen." Known formerly as **A. roebelinii,** this showy and darkness-tolerant plant has grayish green leaves with a pair of silvery patches on each side of the midrib that run the length of the leaf.

A. modestum. "Chinese evergreen." The original **Aglaonema** offered by florists, this species is the oldest and most basic member of the commercially important group. The foliage is a consistent waxy green with an undulate margin. The fruit color is orange.

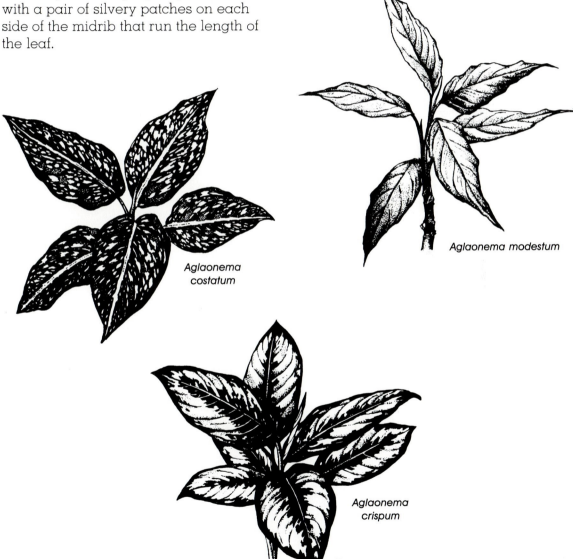

Aglaonema costatum

Aglaonema modestum

Aglaonema crispum

BOTANICAL NAME: *Aloe barbadensis*
(al-OH-ee bar-buh-DEN-sis)

COMMON NAME: Barbados aloe; medicinal aloe; burn plant

FAMILY: Liliaceae (Lily)

ORIGIN: Mediterranean Region

Interestingly, the scientific name "aloe" has three syllables as shown, but the common name has only two (Al-lo). This stoloniferous plant forms clumps of upright, lanceolate leaves 1 to 2 feet long that are white-spotted and have whitish teeth on the margin. The sap, known now as aloe vera, has been used for soothing burns and cuts since ancient times. Occasionally in winter, yellow 1-inch flowers appear on a 3-foot-high raceme. Confused with agaves, aloes have juicier and more tender leaves than their tough, fibrous counterparts.

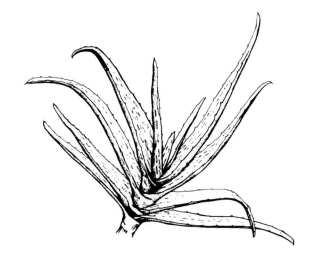

Culture   This durable plant only needs fertilization every six months to annually. Repot as needed, never setting the plant deeper than it originally grew. A loamy soil, heavy on the sand, will provide the necessary good drainage.

Typical Problems   Mealy bugs may infest the leaf axils and scale may appear on the undersurface of the leaves.

Propagation   Most easily from the offsets that arise at the base of older plants. Seeds may also be used.

Related Plants   Over 200 species are in existence, a number of which are cultivated.

A. nobilis. "Golden-tooth aloe." An 18-inch-tall plant with yellowish teeth on the margins and back of the thick green leaves.

A. variegata. "Partridge-breast." One of the smallest of the aloes, forming a 9-inch mound of triangular blue-green leaves in three rows. The oblong white spots on the leaves give rise to the common name.

Water

DRY	NORMAL	EVENLY MOIST

Temperature

COOL	MODERATE	WARM

Light

LOW	BRIGHT INDIRECT	FULL SUN

Humidity

ARID	MODERATE	HUMID

BOTANICAL NAME: *Ananas comosus*
(ah-NAN-us ko-MO-sus)

COMMON NAME: Pineapple

FAMILY: Bromeliaceae (Bromelia/Pineapple)

ORIGIN: Tropical America

Somewhat large (3 to 4 feet across) and spiney for many home situations, particularly those with children, the pineapple creates an attractive and striking effect where appropriate. The reddish flowers, which may have to be induced with ethylene as described in Chapter Thirteen, are upstaged by the familiar fruit that ascends to a prominent position above the foliage. It is from this species that the important Hawaiian fruit cultivars are derived.

Culture   Provide well-aerated and humus soil to this terrestrial bromeliad, rather than a mix suitable for an epiphyte such as *Aechmea.* To do well, the plants must get at least four hours of full sun daily. Night temperatures should be above 60°F.

Typical Problems   Scales, mites, root rots, and leaf diseases are reported.

Propagation   Propagate by the leafy crown above the fruit, offsets from the plant's base, or by "slips" that are borne along the stalk below the fruit. Before

sticking rootless materials into a propagation medium, allow them to dry for several days to reduce the chance of rotting.

Related Plants

A. bracteatus 'Striatus.' "Variegated wild pineapple." Leaves with broad, white stripes on the margins and coarser teeth than *A. comosus;* the fruit bracts and leaves margined with red.

Water		
DRY	NORMAL	EVENLY MOIST

Temperature		
COOL	MODERATE	WARM

Light		
LOW	BRIGHT INDIRECT	FULL SUN

Humidity		
ARID	MODERATE	HUMID

BOTANICAL NAME: *Anthurium* × *cultorum*
(an-THUR-ee-um the hybrid species cul-TOR-um)

COMMON NAME: Flamingo lily

FAMILY: Araceae (Arum/Aroids)

ORIGIN: Hybrid from species native to tropical America

As a group, anthuriums offer both spectacular and unusual "flowers" and stunning foliage. The most conspicuous aspect of this species is the bright red, waxy, and heart-shaped spathe that surrounds the base of the protruding light-colored spadix. Related species offer more colorful and interesting foliage, resembling philodendron, but are distinguished by the swelling at the petiole base and a vein that runs parallel to the leaf margin. Without high humidity, these plants are difficult to flower.

Culture   Humidity is the key to success with this plant. As with other epiphytes, pot in a coarse, well-aerated mixture, such as fir bark and unmilled sphagnum moss. Keep moist, feed at least monthly and continue pulling medium onto the plant crown as it rises above the soil line.

Typical Problems   Spider mites, particularly in dry locations; scale insects and mealy bugs may appear, as well as various leaf spots and rots.

Propagation   Most easily by removing the small offsets (and the attached roots) that develop. This method ensures genetic duplication, as do stem cuttings and division. Fresh seeds may be germinated in warm conditions.

Related Plants

A. clarinervium. A small plant with 5-inch-long heart-shaped leaves that are emerald green in color with prominent white veins. The leaves rest atop petioles of equal length.

A. cubense. Similar in appearance to the bird's nest fern, this plant has linear leaves 2 feet long and 8 inches wide, broader at the tip than at the narrowed base.

A. scherzeranum. "Pigtail anthurium." A plant with 9-inch-long lanceolate leaves and an attractive scarlet spath. The spadix is twisted, rather than the typical straight configuration, hence the common name.

Water

DRY	NORMAL	EVENLY MOIST

Temperature

COOL	MODERATE	WARM

Light

LOW	BRIGHT INDIRECT	FULL SUN

Humidity

ARID	MODERATE	HUMID

BOTANICAL NAME: *Aphelandra squarrosa*
(a-fell-AN-druh square-OH-suh)

COMMON NAME: Zebra plant, saffron spike

FAMILY: Acanthaceae (Acanthus)

ORIGIN: Brazil

The zebra plant is grown both for its large ovate dark green leaves with white veins and for its showy yellow flower spike that rises from the apex of the plant in the fall of the year. Because of these two features, **Aphelandra** was a favorite plant of the Victorian era. The showy bracts of the inflorescence, incidentally, have the fortunate characteristic of lasting about six weeks. The plant usually remains about 12 to 18 inches tall in the home. Although quite attractive, the zebra plant is not particularly easy to grow in the home since rapid environmental changes or stresses may cause leaf drop, bud and flower drop, and reduced plant vigor.

Culture   Prune in the spring to promote lateral branching and bushy form; taking cuttings at this time will serve a dual purpose. The roots must not be allowed to dry out. Allowing the plant to become pot-bound will help initiate flowering. Low humidity is its biggest enemy in the home. Fertilize every month during flowering and active growth, less during rest periods.

Typical Problems   Excessive soluble salts, poor light, or improper watering will cause dropping of the lower leaves.

Scale insects, mealy bugs, and aphids attack the leaves and stems. Fungal leaf spot creates round brown or black spots on the foliage. Avoid wounding the plant, as this allows leaf spot fungus to enter the plant.

Propagation   By stem cuttings taken in the spring. Air layering can be used on older plants or those with a leggy form.

Related Plants

A. s. 'Dania.' A popular stocky Danish introduction with excellent vein-leaf contrast, robust growth, and yellow-orange flower spike.

A. s. 'Leopoldii.' Vigorous variety with short-lived yellow and red flower spikes.

A. s. 'Louisae.' A popular form with excellent white-vein, dark-leaf contrast, and yellow-gold flower spikes. 'Louisae Compacta' is smaller, similar to 'Dania' but with darker leaves.

A. s. 'Uniflora Beauty.' A slow, compact form with small leaves.

Water

DRY	NORMAL	EVENLY MOIST
		■

Temperature

COOL	MODERATE	WARM
		■

Light

LOW	BRIGHT INDIRECT	FULL SUN
	■	

Humidity

ARID	MODERATE	HUMID
		■

BOTANICAL NAME: *Araucaria heterophylla*
(are-uh-CARE-ee-uh het-er-oh-FILL-uh)

COMMON NAME: Norfolk Island pine

FAMILY: Araucariaceae (Araucaria)

ORIGIN: Norfolk Island, a minute island
in the South Pacific

This tree grows to a height of 200 feet in its native habitat. Grown indoors in its juvenile form with formal tiers of branches evenly spaced up a central trunk, the symmetrical form makes it a favorite plant, especially at Christmas. The specific epithet *heterophylla* means "many-leaved" in reference to the profusion of small, medium-green needles. This tree, under proper cultivation, increases in beauty and size each year and will usually achieve a maximum height of about 10 to 12 feet indoors.

Culture   The Norfolk Island pine tolerates cultural abuse rather well, but the form may suffer under such conditions over time and pruning will usually do more harm than good to the appearance. Fertilize every two to three months and provide full sun, if possible, and less water during winter. Repot every three to five years.

Typical Problems   Needle drop and burning can occur in arid conditions, as well as fast infestations of spider mites that, left unchecked, can severely damage the foliage appearance. Over-

watering can occur in winter months or where environmental conditions are impeding normal vigor.

Propagation   By seeds and rooting cuttings of vigorous, upright shoot tips. The lateral branches will propagate a misshapen specimen. Propagation is difficult at home. Taking cuttings may adversely affect the form of the original plant.

Related Plants   The related species *A. bidwillii,* the "bunya-bunya" or "bunya-bunya pine" is also used indoors. Its long, glossy needles are sharp, giving the plant a more vicious appearance than *A. heterophylla.*

Water

DRY	NORMAL	EVENLY MOIST

Temperature

COOL	MODERATE	WARM

Light

LOW	BRIGHT INDIRECT	FULL SUN

Humidity

ARID	MODERATE	HUMID

BOTANICAL NAME: *Ardisia crenata*

(ar-DIZ-ee-uh cren-AH-ta)

COMMON NAME: Coralberry, spiceberry

FAMILY: Myrsinaceae (Myrsine)

ORIGIN: Japan to northern India

Grown natively as a 6-foot evergreen tree, this plant is noted indoors for its elliptical, leathery, and shiny dark green leaves, but more importantly, for its abundant crop of bright red berries borne during winter. A slow grower, the plant can be used when young as a small pot plant, then moved into more significant settings as it grows.

Culture   A relatively easy plant to grow but one that requires bright conditions for strong flowering and fruit set. Night temperatures over 55°F are needed for proper development. Pot into a rich potting mix and feed moderately, primarily during active growth and flowering. In keeping the plant moist, watch for symptoms of rots.

Typical Problems   Scale insects, nematodes, and mites occasionally, as well as various leaf spots and rots.

Propagation   Either by stem cuttings or cleaned seed sown during late winter.

Related Plants   None.

Water		
DRY	NORMAL	EVENLY MOIST

Temperature		
COOL	MODERATE	WARM

Light		
LOW	BRIGHT INDIRECT	FULL SUN

Humidity		
ARID	MODERATE	HUMID

BOTANICAL NAME: *Asparagus densiflorus* 'Sprengeri'
(uh-SPARE-uh-gus den-sih-FLOOR-us SPRING-er-eye)

COMMON NAME: Sprenger asparagus, sprengeri fern

FAMILY: Liliaceae (Lily)

ORIGIN: South Africa

Although truly a relative of the edible asparagus, this plant is an imposter in that it is not a true fern. Furthermore, what appears to be foliage are small leaflike branchlets known as cladodes; the leaves are small and scalelike, located at the base of the cladodes and sometimes modified as spines. Spring brings small greenish or white flowers that in fall yield bright red berries. The "foliage" is needlelike, wispy, and arching to form a spreading, graceful plant that is excellent for hanging basket use. It usually reaches a height of 1 to 2 feet, but may spread or trail up to 3 to 4 feet. Sprenger asparagus is excellent in combination with other plants due to its fine textural quality.

Culture Unlike true ferns, this plant should be allowed to dry somewhat between waterings, especially in periods of reduced growth. Cutting back older "foliage" will stimulate new, vigorous growth. A loamy soil is preferable, with fertilization every one to two months during active growth. In contrast to ferns, asparagus can tolerate drier air and requires a larger pot to accommodate the root system.

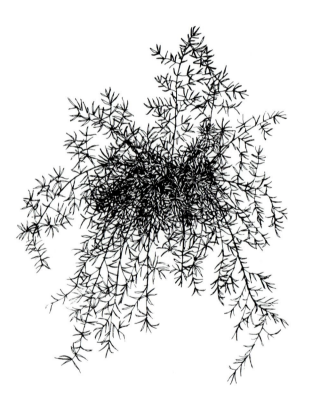

Water

DRY	NORMAL	EVENLY MOIST

Temperature

COOL	MODERATE	WARM

Light

LOW	BRIGHT INDIRECT	FULL SUN

Humidity

ARID	MODERATE	HUMID

Typical Problems   By far the most common cultural difficulty is leaf loss due to low humidity. Leaf yellowing and loss can also occur through poor lighting or improper watering to either extreme. Spider mites are the most likely pest to infest this plant, although aphids will occasionally appear. This species is sensitive to some chemical sprays.

Propagation   The roots, although tuberous, are not generally used for propagation. Seeds germinate easily if sown prior to drying out, or they may be soaked overnight before planting. Also, clumps may be divided into several new plants. Division can occur anytime, although spring is preferable. Cut back the old foliage severely when dividing plants to stimulate new growth.

Related Plants

A. d. 'Myers.' "Plume asparagus" often misspelled "Meyers," this cultivar produces many erect, compact, carrot-shaped branches up to two feet high.

A. d. 'Sprengeri Nanus.' A dwarf cultivar similar to 'Sprengeri.'

A. setaceus "Asparagus fern, lace fern." The feathery foliage is commonly used in floral arrangements. Requires more warmth than 'Sprengeri.'

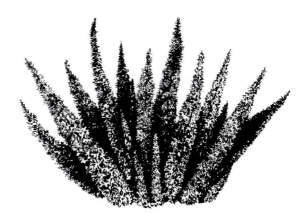

Asparagus densiflorus 'Myers'

Asparagus setaceus

BOTANICAL NAME: *Aspidistra elatior*
(as-pih-DISS-tra ee-LAY-tih-or)

COMMON NAME: Cast-iron plant, barroom plant, parlor palm

FAMILY: Liliaceae (Lily)

ORIGIN: China and Japan

Cast-iron plant, as the name implies, is one of the most durable and easily cultivated of all indoor plants. Although it will survive the most difficult of indoor environmental conditions, it will, with proper care and placement, reach a height of 2½ to 3 feet (hence *elatior* that means taller). The leathery, dark green, and glossy leaves arise from a rhizome that creeps at or below the soil surface. The inconspicuous flowers, brown-purple and borne near the soil level, are further obscured by the foliage. A favorite plant in Victorian parlors.

Culture   A loamy soil mix with some organic matter and aggregate added, such as peat moss and perlite, is ideal. Fertilize monthly from spring through fall and withhold food at other times.

Typical Problems   One of the few indoor plants that is typically free of diseases, pests, and environmentally induced disorders.

Propagation   By division of the rhizome. A length of rhizome containing one or several leaves and the associated roots will quickly develop into a respectable plant.

Related Plants

A.e. 'Variegata.' "Variegated cast-iron plant." Leaves longitudinally striped with bands of green and white in variable widths.

Water		
DRY	NORMAL	EVENLY MOIST

Temperature		
COOL	MODERATE	WARM

Light		
LOW	BRIGHT INDIRECT	FULL SUN

Humidity		
ARID	MODERATE	HUMID

BOTANICAL NAME: *Beaucarnea recurvata*
(bow-CAR-nee-uh ree-cur-VAH-ta)

COMMON NAME: Ponytail palm; elephant foot tree

FAMILY: Agavaceae (Agave)

ORIGIN: Mexico

This slow-growing, graceful native to a hot-dry climate is a durable and interesting specimen. Its common names refer to its "mane" of weeping, slender foliage arising from the stem apex and the water-storing bulbous swelling, resembling an elephant's foot, at the stem base. Growing to 30 feet in its homeland, the ponytail palm typically stands 2 to 3 feet indoors. Excellent for small planters when young; develops into large specimen slowly over the years.

Culture   Each spring, preceding new growth, fertilize and repot if growth stimulation is desired. Keep in as much sun as possible, but ease into sunny locations from shady ones gradually to prevent scorching. Their temperature tolerance ranges from the 40s into the 90s (F).

Typical Problems   Rare, but mites, mealy bugs, and scale are reported. Various rots also occur, particularly when watering is heavy-handed.

Propagation   From seeds.

Related Plants   None.

Water

DRY	NORMAL	EVENLY MOIST

Temperature

COOL	MODERATE	WARM

Light

LOW	BRIGHT INDIRECT	FULL SUN

Humidity

ARID	MODERATE	HUMID

BOTANICAL NAME: *Begonia × semperflorens-cultorum*
(bee-GONE-ee-uh the hybrid species
sem-per-FLOR-ens cul-TOR-um)

COMMON NAME: Bedding begonia, wax begonia

FAMILY: Begoniaceae (Begonia)

ORIGIN: Hybrid from several species, mostly from South America

This begonia is prized indoors and out for its waxy foliage and abundance of colorful flowers. Both the foliage and flowers are available in various colors. As fibrous-rooted begonias (see Chapter Thirteen for generic description), these plants will flower continuously if provided with adequate light. Most will thrive in bright indirect light, but variegated and colored-leaf types need even greater illumination.

Culture   Feed frequently and repot during the spring before summer growth begins. Drying between waterings is necessary to avoid fungal-related problems, and frequent pinching is needed to discourage legginess.

Typical Problems   With age or inadequate brightness, wax begonias become leggy. In order to maintain continuity with this plant, propagate cuttings to develop new plants. More prone to leaf spots and various rots than the occasional mites and scale that sometimes visit.

Propagation   Older plants can be cut back severely and divided into sections for repotting. Cuttings are a quick and reliable method, but seeds are quite satisfactory if they are cultivated properly.

Related Plants
B. × erythrophylla. "Beefsteak begonia." A rhizomatous type with round, thick, and glossy foliage; red below. Pink flowers ascend above the foliage in profusion with good cultivation.

Water

DRY	NORMAL	EVENLY MOIST

Temperature

COOL	MODERATE	WARM

Light

LOW	BRIGHT INDIRECT	FULL SUN

Humidity

ARID	MODERATE	HUMID

B. masoniana. "Iron-cross begonia." The oblique heart-shape and wrinkled texture of the bright green leaves contrast against the dark brown, starlike markings that follow the primary veins. The flower clusters are reddish in color.

B. × rex-cultorum. "Rex begonia." Breeding interest over the years has produced many variations of this plant, all with brilliantly colored and patterned foliage in shades of green, red, brown, silver, and other colors. Hundreds of named cultivars have been registered in this group.

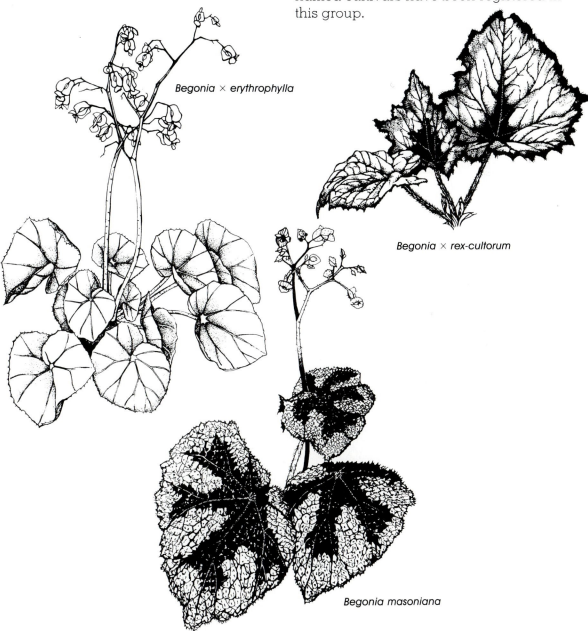

Begonia × erythrophylla

Begonia × rex-cultorum

Begonia masoniana

BOTANICAL NAME: *Brassaia actinophylla*

(brass-SAY-uh ak-tin-oh-FILL-uh)

COMMON NAME: Australian umbrella tree, octopus tree

FAMILY: Araliaceae (Aralia)

ORIGIN: Queensland, New Guinea, Java

This tree is more popularly, but incorrectly known as **Schefflera actinophylla.** Growing to a height of 100 feet in its homeland, it is used in large sizes in commercial spaces and in small sizes in the home. It may be maintained as a multistemmed, bushy specimen by cutting it back occasionally. The palmately compound leaves, composed of glossy green leaflets 4 to 12 inches long, form an umbrellalike crown. The purple flowers are rarely seen indoors. One of the best and most durable trees for indoor use. Can be used as an outdoor tubbed plant in warmer climates.

Culture   Pot in a loam/peat/sand or perlite soil mix and fertilize monthly during active growth. Will tolerate, but does not prefer, low light. Exposure to cold drafts may cause leaf yellowing and burn.

Typical Problems   Spider mites and scale insects are the most likely bother, but mealy bugs will occasionally infest the plant. Leaf spot, in the form of round, brown spots on leaves, elongated patches on stems, or small swellings under leaves that change to reddish-brown patches, may be restrained by keeping the leaves dry and ensuring good air circulation.

Water

DRY	NORMAL	EVENLY MOIST

Temperature

COOL	MODERATE	WARM

Light

LOW	BRIGHT INDIRECT	FULL SUN

Humidity

ARID	MODERATE	HUMID

Propagation Easily started from fresh seeds, but they lose viability quickly in storage. Air-layering and stem cuttings are the two most common asexual techniques.

Related Plants

Heptaplureum arboricola "Dwarf schefflera." A compact, dark green form with smaller foliage than **B. actinophylla.** Not listed in Hortus III, but gaining wide popularity.

Heptaplureum arboricola

BOTANICAL NAME: *Caryota mitis*
(car-YO-ta MY-tis)

COMMON NAME: Burmese fishtail plam, clustered fishtail palm

FAMILY: Palmae (Palm)

ORIGIN: Burma to Malay Peninsula, Java, and the Philippine Islands

This attractive palm, distinguished from others as the only palm with bipinnately compound leaves, derived its common name from the toothed, obliquely tipped fan-shaped pinnules that look strikingly like fishtails, even to the point of being droopy. This plant suckers freely, adding to the denseness already present due to the numerous broad pinnules. Hence, it is useful as both a potted specimen when small and a floor specimen or screen plant in larger sizes. On maturity, green or purple flowers develop progressively down the plant axis, finally resulting in the death of the plant.

Culture   Among the palms, this species is noted as being somewhat tempermental, needing bright light, a warm environment, and high humidity. Low light situations and dry air may cause browning of the leaf tips.

Typical Problems   Root damage occurs if plants are kept overly damp and cool during inactive growth.

Propagation   By division of suckers and from seeds.

Related Plants   Other palms

Water		
DRY	NORMAL	EVENLY MOIST

Temperature		
COOL	MODERATE	WARM

Light		
LOW	BRIGHT INDIRECT	FULL SUN

Humidity		
ARID	MODERATE	HUMID

BOTANICAL NAME: *Cereus peruvianus*
(SER-ee-us per-u-vee-AN-us)

COMMON NAME: Peruvian apple, column cactus

FAMILY: Cactaceae (Cactus)

ORIGIN: Southeastern South America

The Peruvian apple is native to the drier tropical regions, needing sun and warmth. The green, 4-inch-diameter stems are leafless and lined with 6 to 8 prominent scalloped ribs with spined areoles positioned between the scallops about 1 inch apart. Growing as a column and branching with age, this cactus produces white funnel-shaped flowers that open at night, followed by yellow or reddish fruit 2½ inches in diameter. May be used alone in its stark uprightness, or among other arid plants to create a desert effect.

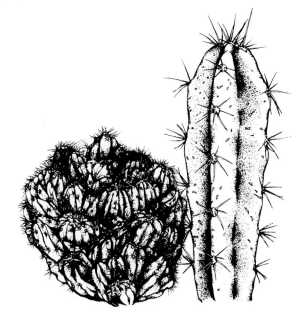

Culture   Although these plants naturally enjoy full sun and warmth, they will tolerate very low light levels indoors, provided that watering and feeding are quite sparse, particularly during inactive growth. Night temperatures should stay above 55°F. Pot in a sandy, well-drained potting medium.

Typical Problems   Scale insects are the only typical pest, but difficult to spot because of the camouflaged effect among the areoles. Overwatering or excessive humidity will induce rots and blights.

Propagation   By fresh seeds or cuttings stuck into warm sand after dipping into charcoal and drying for a few days.

Related Plants

C. p. 'Monstrosus'. "Giant-club, curiosity plant." Similar in form to the species, but with 12 or so irregularly formed and pronounced ridges, giving the plant an appearance similar to a heavily waxed candle.

Water

DRY	NORMAL	EVENLY MOIST

Temperature

COOL	MODERATE	WARM

Light

LOW	BRIGHT INDIRECT	FULL SUN

Humidity

ARID	MODERATE	HUMID

BOTANICAL NAME: *Ceropegia woodii*
(sir-oh-PEE-gee-ah WOOD-ee-eye)

COMMON NAME: Rosary vine, string of hearts, heart vine

FAMILY: Asclepiadaceae (Milkweed)

ORIGIN: Southern Rhodesia to South Africa

Known by a variety of common names, this plant is unique with its succulent, heart-shaped leaves and tubercular nodes (like beads on a rosary). The leaves are opposite, marbled dark green and white above, and purple below. The 3 foot long stems usually arise from a rounded tuber that lies near the soil surface. Tiny purplish brown flowers occasionally appear, but are not the plant's primary attraction since they blend with the foliage color. Its trailing growth habit makes it exceptionally good for hanging basket use.

Culture   The most important cultural aspect is to avoid overwatering this succulent plant, particularly in the fall and winter. If not fatal, overwatering will reduce the vigor and coloration of this plant. A humus, well-drained soil is best. Fertilize twice a month during the spring and early summer with a half-strength fertilizer.

Typical Problems   Very rarely bothered with pests or diseases. Mealy bugs are the only pest that occasionally appears.

Propagation   By stem cuttings, planting the tubers that form at the nodes or at the base of the plant, and rarely seeds.

Related Plants   None.

Water		
DRY	NORMAL	EVENLY MOIST

Temperature		
COOL	MODERATE	WARM

Light		
LOW	BRIGHT INDIRECT	FULL SUN

Humidity		
ARID	MODERATE	HUMID

BOTANICAL NAME: *Chamaedorea elegans*

(kam-e-DOR-ee-uh EL-e-gans)

COMMON NAME: Parlor palm

FAMILY: Palmae (Palm)

ORIGIN: Mexico and Guatemala

Known formerly as **Neanthe bella,** the parlor palm is one of the more familiar palms and one of the easiest to grow. Its foliage typically extends no taller than a couple of feet; the leaves bearing 11 to 20 elliptical pinnae on either side of the rachis, giving the plant a somewhat coarser texture than the areca palm. This palm is useful as a terrarium or dish garden plant as a seedling, later becoming useful as a distinctive, midsize floor plant.

Culture   Pot into a well-drained sandy mix, keeping the plant away from drafts and cold air. Feed monthly during active growth and provide as much indirect light as possible to maintain the dense form. Potting several plants together overcomes the natural sparseness of the plant. Keep these plants pot-bound. A periodic rinsing under warm water will physically remove spider mites, as well as clean the foliage.

Typical Problems   Spider mites are the most troublesome pests, particularly in dry situations.

Propagation   By seed.

Related Plants

C. erumpens. "Bamboo palm." A species of palm resembling bamboo, with a suckering habit that creates natural denseness. The pinnae are short, broad, and drooping.

C. seifrizii. "Reed palm." Similar in form to the bamboo palm, but with more pinnae per leaf that are also more straight, stiff, and narrow than the bamboo palm's.

Water		
DRY	NORMAL	EVENLY MOIST
		■

Temperature		
COOL	MODERATE	WARM
		■

Light		
LOW	BRIGHT INDIRECT	FULL SUN
	■	

Humidity		
ARID	MODERATE	HUMID
	■	

BOTANICAL NAME: *Chamaerops humilis*
(KAM-e-rops hew-MILL-is)

COMMON NAME: European fan palm

FAMILY: Palmae (Palm)

ORIGIN: Mediterranean Region of Europe and North Africa

This unusual palm, the only one native to Europe, can either be grown as a single, stemmed tree reaching 15 feet indoors, or as clumps if suckers are allowed to mature. The tough, dull green, fan-shaped leaves are 2 to 3 feet across, stiff and pleated, and coarser in appearance than the foliage of many other palms. The mature trunk is covered with dry and thorny leaf bases. The durability of this palm outweighs its attractiveness. Useful as a tub plant for cooler locations where other palms might want for more warmth.

Culture   Though not particular about its soil, performs best in rich potting soil. Night temperatures ideally should be in the 50s F, and leaves should be removed as they age and begin to deteriorate.

Typical Problems   In providing constant soil moisture, watch for symptoms of overwatering or rots.

Propagation   Seeds of this palm germinate quickly and easily, requiring fertilization to stimulate growth. Suckers may also be removed from the plant's base and potted individually or in clumps of several.

Related Plants   Several cultivars exist, but are not commercially important.

Water		
DRY	NORMAL	EVENLY MOIST

Temperature		
COOL	MODERATE	WARM

Light		
LOW	BRIGHT INDIRECT	FULL SUN

Humidity		
ARID	MODERATE	HUMID

BOTANICAL NAME: *Chlorophytum comosum*
(chlor-oh-FIGHT-um koe-MOE-sum)

COMMON NAME: Spider ivy, spider plant

FAMILY: Liliaceae (Lily)

ORIGIN: South Africa

One of the more commonly grown and easily propagated plants for indoor use, spider ivy is popular because of its arching, linear leaves and its prolific plantlets that develop and cluster on the suspended panicles after the small, white flowers decline. The production of flowers and plantlets is photoperiodic in response, that is, they are stimulated by short days (long nights). The plantlets can be left attached for years, eventually creating a suspended abundance of foliage. Because of its durability and tolerance of abuse, spider ivy has been a favorite plant for many years.

Culture   Requires no pruning except removal of dead leaves and large plantlets. The rapid growth and fleshy root system necessitate repotting annually using a standard loamy soil mix with 50 percent organic matter. Fertilize every two or three months. A durable plant, it can tolerate temperatures as low as 35 to 40°F without damage. Poor flowering and plantlet production occur with poor lighting.

Typical Problems   Spider ivy is very sensitive to the fluoride in most public water supplies, as well as low humidity.

Both result in a browning of the leaf tips. Also, scale insects may occasionally infest the plant (in large numbers if left unchecked), particularly under the leaves and along the flower stalks. Spider mites and white flies are also known to occur.

Propagation   This plant forms many crowns that can be divided, each with a portion of the fleshy root system. The most common method is to remove the plantlets borne on the cascading

Water		
DRY	NORMAL	EVENLY MOIST

Temperature		
COOL	MODERATE	WARM

Light		
LOW	BRIGHT INDIRECT	FULL SUN

Humidity		
ARID	MODERATE	HUMID

Chlorophytum comosum 'Vittatum'

panicles. Since these plantlets attain a relatively large size and form a number of roots while still attached to the parent plant, they can be grown into a large plant rather quickly.

Related Plants

C. bichetii. "St. Bernard's lily." A dwarf species with turflike green and yellow striped leaves about 8 inches long.

C. c. 'Mandaianum.' A dwarf cultivar with a yellow strip in the center of dark green leaves.

C. c. 'Picturatum.' Leaves with a central yellow stripe.

C. c. 'Variegatum.' Leaves with white margins.

C. c. 'Vittatum.' Leaves recurved with a central white stripe.

BOTANICAL NAME: *Chrysalidocarpus lutescens*
(krih-sal-ih-doe-CAR-pus lew-TES-sens)

COMMON NAME: Areca palm, yellow palm

FAMILY: Palmae (Palm)

ORIGIN: Madagascar

This graceful, arching palm that grows to 30 feet in its homeland will reach a 15- to 20-foot height ultimately indoors. Producing an ever-expanding clump of stems arising from the soil, this tree maintains itself in a constant state of rejuvenation. The leaves ascend, curving outward at their tips, attractively displaying 40 to 60 neatly aligned narrow pinnae on each side of the rachis. Useful when young as small dish garden or container plants and developing into floor specimens.

Culture   Warm temperatures are imperative since this palm is less cold-tolerant than some others. Yellowing foliage occurs following overfertilization; it is advisable to leach newly acquired plants to reduce the level of fertilization.

Requiring evenly moist soil, these plants are apt to be over-watered by too frequent applications or poorly drained soil. Keep somewhat pot-bound.

Typical Problems   Mites, mealy bugs, and scale insects, particularly in dry atmospheric conditions.

Propagation   Most easily reproduced through division of the clump. Propagation from seed is possible, though uncommon.

Related Plants   None.

Water

DRY	NORMAL	EVENLY MOIST

Temperature

COOL	MODERATE	WARM

Light

LOW	BRIGHT INDIRECT	FULL SUN

Humidity

ARID	MODERATE	HUMID

BOTANICAL NAME: *Cissus rhombifolia*
(SIS-us rom-bih-FOE-lee-uh)

COMMON NAME: Grape ivy, Venezuela treebine

FAMILY: Vitaceae (Grape)

ORIGIN: Northern South America, West Indies

At one time, plants belonging to **Cissus** were classified in the **Vitis** or grape genus because of the grapelike, coiling tendrils the plants use for clinging. However, most do not need to climb to be attractive. **C. rhombifolia** has trifoliate leaves with, as the name implies, rhomboid-shaped leaflets that are dark glossy green. New shoots and the underside of older leaves are covered with a brown pubescence. Generally speaking, **Cissus** grows somewhat slowly in the

home and requires frequent pinching to prevent straggly growth. Grape ivy is considered one of the best vining plants for indoor use, especially in hanging baskets.

Culture   Fertilize every month during active growth and about every other month at other times. A loam soil is appropriate, as well as a slight drying of the soil surface between waterings.

Typical Problems   Mealy bugs may infest the leaf nodes and axils, and spider mites will cause leaf mottling.

Propagation   Stem cuttings will root at any time of the year, but application of a rooting hormone will speed up initiation. Cuttings will root in time even in plain water. Started less frequently, but occasionally, by seeds.

Water		
DRY	NORMAL	EVENLY MOIST

Temperature		
COOL	MODERATE	WARM

Light		
LOW	BRIGHT INDIRECT	FULL SUN

Humidity		
ARID	MODERATE	HUMID

Related Plants

C. antarctica. "Kangaroo vine." A species with simple, ovate, bright green leaves with coarsely toothed margins. Similar in growth habit to **C. rhombifolia. C. a. minima,** a dwarf form, is available.

C. discolor, "Trailing begonia" or "begonia treebine." A climbing species with simple leaves similar to the rex begonia.

C. rotundifolia. "Arabian wax cissus." A climbing plant with fleshy, round leaves similar to those of *Peperomia obtusifolia.*

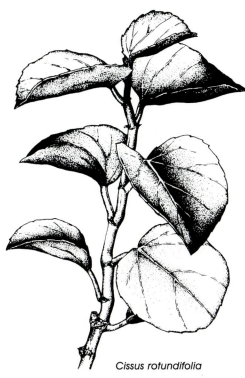

Cissus rotundifolia

Cissus antarctica

BOTANICAL NAME: *Codiaeum variegatum pictum*
(KOE-dih-EE-um var-ih-GOT-um PIK-tum)

COMMON NAME: Garden croton

FAMILY: Euphorbiaceae (Spurge)

ORIGIN: Southern India, Ceylon, and Malaya

C. variegatum pictum, among the more difficult house plants to grow in the typical home, is a quite variable plant group with glossy, leathery leaves and inconspicuous white drooping racemes. Over 100 forms are in existence, each primarily cultivated for its leaf shape, ranging from linear or ovate to lobed, and for its coloration. Most types are variegated in shades of green, white, yellow, orange, and red, with oranges and reds more typical of older leaves. In nature, crotons grow as tall as 6 feet and are bushy in form. Indoors, they are usually 2 to 4 feet tall and bushy if grown under sufficient light conditions. Fortunately, they are fast growers. For individuality and foliage interest, crotons are difficult to surpass, in spite of their tempermental cultural nature.

Culture   Although most well-drained potting mixes will suffice, crotons demand high light, warmth, and humidity for good coloration and bushiness. They need pruning occasionally for shaping and size control and should be fertilized every two or three months during active growth. Repotting should occur about once every one or two years preferably during the spring.

Typical Problems   The most common cultural problem is leaf drop due to drafts and poor lighting. Spider mites and scale insects are the most likely pests to be found on crotons, usually on the undersurface of leaves, although mealy bugs may occasionally infest the leaf axils and lower leaf surfaces as well.

Water

DRY	NORMAL	EVENLY MOIST

Temperature

COOL	MODERATE	WARM

Light

LOW	BRIGHT INDIRECT	FULL SUN

Humidity

ARID	MODERATE	HUMID

Propagation   Seeds may be used, but usually yield variable offspring.

To maintain the characteristics of the parent plant, propagate vegetatively by stem cuttings taken from newly matured growth or by air-layering, especially on leggy specimens. Application of a root-promoting substance to cuttings and layers will speed rooting.

Related Plants   A few of the more common forms are the following.

C.v.p. 'Bravo.' "Bravo croton." Young leaves elliptical with gentle lobing, yellow veins, and green color changing to red veins on maroon background with age.

C.v.p. 'Craigii.' "Craig's croton." Leaves three-lobed and fine-textured, with yellow veins on green background.

C.v.p. 'Norwood Beauty.' "Oakleaf croton." Small three-lobed leaves with yellow veins and a rosy margin around a bronze to dark red background color.

C.v.p. 'Punctatum Aureum.' "Gold dust croton." Small dark green elliptical leaves spotted with yellow.

BOTANICAL NAME: *Coffea arabica*

(KOF-ee-uh ah-RAB-ih-ka)

COMMON NAME: Coffee

FAMILY: Rubiaceae (Madder)

ORIGIN: Tropical Africa and Latin America

Though an excellent conversation plant because of its famous product, the coffee plant can also be attractive under the right conditions. Unfortunately, a conservatory does the best job of this. The 6 inch glossy, dark green leaves are elliptical and arranged opposite one another along the stem. The fragrant white flowers that precede the slow-maturing fruit are an asset, as well as the mature red berries containing the coffee "beans." The flower and fruit clusters are borne at the base of the leaves.

Culture   A heavy transpirer of water, the plant requires high humidity and constantly moist soil. Leaf browning occurs with dryness or through leaf contact by passers-by. Bright indirect sunlight is required for desirable dense growth. Feed at least monthly, more frequently during active growth. Repotting to larger quarters is necessary annually to prevent root binding.

Typical Problems   Watch for leaf spots and various rots, particularly in light of the need for constant moisture and humidity. Mealy bugs, scale insects, and whiteflies are a possibility.

Propagation   Best reproduced by stem cuttings from mature, upright growing tips, since side branches produce less desirable form. Seeds are used commercially, but are impractical indoors since they remain viable only a short time after ripening.

Related Plants   None.

Water		
DRY	NORMAL	EVENLY MOIST

Temperature		
COOL	MODERATE	WARM

Light		
LOW	BRIGHT INDIRECT	FULL SUN

Humidity		
ARID	MODERATE	HUMID

BOTANICAL NAME: *Coleus × hybridus*

(KO-lee-us the hybrid species HY-brid-us)

COMMON NAME: Garden coleus

FAMILY: Labiatae (Mint)

ORIGIN: Hybrid species of African and Indonesian parentage

Numerous cultivars of this popular plant are used as bedding plants for shady locations outdoors and for colorful houseplants. Membership of coleus in the mint family may be easily determined by the square succulent stems. The leaves are ovate and toothed, and beautifully colored in reds, greens, golds, creams, browns, and many other colors. These plants are striking accent plants while they remain dense, compact, and colorful; they develop a straggly appearance, however, with age or poor light conditions.

Culture Bright indirect light is necessary to maintain rich foliage color, and frequent pinching avoids legginess. Grow under warm conditions with minimum night temperatures of 60°F. Pot into rich soil.

Typical Problems The succulent tissue of coleus is attractive to caterpillars, mealy bugs, mites, slugs, whiteflies, and scale insects, although the plant structure makes detection and control easy. The need for constant moisture also makes coleus susceptible to blights and rots. Keeping water off the foliage except for an occasional washing is helpful.

Propagation For genetic continuity, stem cuttings or leaf-bud cuttings are easy and fast to root. Seeds are also easy to germinate, but only a certain percentage of seedlings will reflect the quality of the parents. Seedlings, however, can produce some interesting new color combinations.

Related Plants Over 200 named cultivars of coleus are on the market.

Water		
DRY	NORMAL	EVENLY MOIST

Temperature		
COOL	MODERATE	WARM

Light		
LOW	BRIGHT INDIRECT	FULL SUN

Humidity		
ARID	MODERATE	HUMID

BOTANICAL NAME: *Cordyline terminalis*
(kor-dih-LYE-nee ter-men-AL-iss)

COMMON NAME: Good-luck plant, Hawaiian ti

FAMILY: Agavaceae (Agave)

ORIGIN: East Asia: India, Polynesia, Malaysia

Used in Hawaii for thatch roofs and hula skirts, the leaves of this plant are oblong, medium green, and up to 3 feet long and 4 inches wide. The plant can reach a 6-foot height indoors, and the leaves generally cluster at the top of the plant, exposing a gray, canelike trunk. With bright light, the yellow or rose flower panicles may appear, followed by red berries. This plant is frequently offered for sale as 2- to 4-inch stem lengths that can be sprouted rather easily. *Cordyline terminalis* is often mistaken for a *Dracaena.*

Culture   Although tolerant of average home humidity, this plant prefers a high level for best growth. Requires much water during active growth, but benefits from less moisture during slow growth periods. Grows in water if given sufficient light. Prune back severely at any season and feed every three months.

Typical Problems   Lower leaves often are shed from colored-leaf types in late winter after new foliage color peaks. Tip and margin browning indicates too low humidity or fluoride damage from use of tap water. Occasional infestation by mealy bugs, scale insects, and spider mites. Avoid wetting foliage in order to prevent leaf spot.

Propagation   Most commonly by cane cuttings placed horizontally in propagation medium. When shoots develop 4 to 6 leaves, cut them off with part of the original stem attached and root in medium. Also by 6 to 8 inch long leafy stem tip cuttings, air-layering, and 2-inch root cuttings placed horizontally in the medium.

Water

DRY	NORMAL	EVENLY MOIST

Temperature

COOL	MODERATE	WARM

Light

LOW	BRIGHT INDIRECT	FULL SUN

Humidity

ARID	MODERATE	HUMID

Related Plants

C.t. 'Baby Doll.' A colorful, dwarf cultivar with green, red, and maroon variegations.

C.t. 'Madame Eugene Andre.' "Flaming dragon tree." Dark coppery or maroon leaves edged with red. New foliage, appearing in early winter, is a vivid pink color.

C.t. 'Negri.' "Black dracaena." Leaves large and very dark coppery or maroon.

C.t. 'Tricolor.' "Tricolored dracaena." Variegated red, green, and pink.

BOTANICAL NAME: *Crassula argentea*
(KRASS-u-lah ar-JEN-tee-uh)

COMMON NAME: Jade plant, jade tree

FAMILY: CRASSULACEAE (Orpine, stonecrop)

ORIGIN: South Africa

One of the most commonly grown house-plants, the jade plant grows literally for decades indoors, forming stouter and stouter stems and a treelike form less than 2 feet tall. The leaves are succulent, displaying red margins in full sun; thus, the plant needs drying between water-ings. This plant is useful when young in dish gardens and is an excellent spec-imen for an oriental decor. As slow grow-ers, jade plants can be controlled in their size by allowing pot-binding to occur. Repotting can be done at any time.

Culture Bright indirect light or full sun is necessary for strong and full stem and foliage development, although the plant can survive at very low levels. Watering is critical; water normally during active growth, allowing the plant to remain generally dry during the winter months. Fertilize several times per year.

This plant is not particularly temperature-sensitive, but nights above 50°F are pre-ferable.

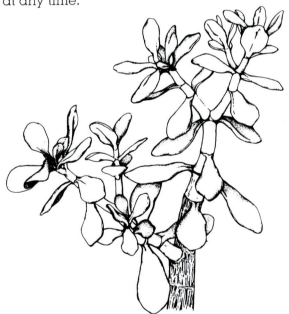

Water

DRY	NORMAL	EVENLY MOIST

Temperature

COOL	MODERATE	WARM

Light

LOW	BRIGHT INDIRECT	FULL SUN

Humidity

ARID	MODERATE	HUMID

Typical Problems   The major invader is the mealy bug, which likes to nestle into the leaf axils. Prompt eradication is necessary to prevent the difficult task of eliminating a generous infestation.

Propagation   Stem cuttings rooted either in water or propagation medium. Leaf-bud cuttings propagate easily, but leaves without the bud will simply root, forming no shoot.

Related Plants

C. a. 'Tricolor.' "Tricolor jade plant." Leaves variegated with deep green and clear white, giving a more distinctive appearance than the cultivar 'Variegata.'

C.a. 'Variegata'. "Variegated jade plant." Similar form to the species, but with leaves marked longitudinally with green, grayish, and cream to orange-yellow.

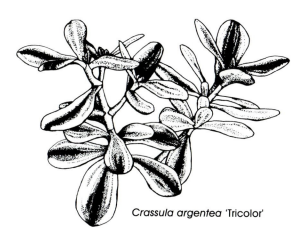

Crassula argentea 'Tricolor'

BOTANICAL NAME: *Cryptanthus bivittatus*
(krip-TAN-thus bih-vih-TA-tus)

COMMON NAME: Earth-star

FAMILY: Bromeliaceae (Bromelia/Pineapple)

ORIGIN: Brazil

These small (6 to 18 inches across) terrestrial bromeliads are noted for their neat rosette of colorful leaves. This species, parent of several interesting variants, has lanceolate leaves that are longitudinally striped with greenish brown and reddish pink. The leaves are stiff, toothed and wavy at the margins, and arched. Fortunately, the ill-smelling flowers are rare. These plants are colorful table specimens or additions to drier dish gardens.

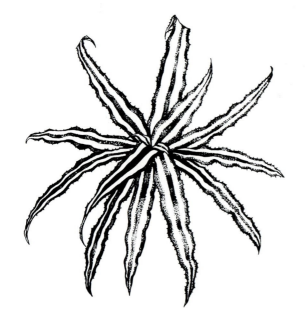

Culture   These undemanding plants endure poor light, but develop better color in bright conditions. The night temperature should remain above 60°F. Plant weakness or rotting can develop from overwatering or excessive humidity. Feed three or four times per year, particularly during active growth.

Typical Problems   Rots, wilts, molds, and leaf spots occur in moist conditions. Mealy bugs and scale insects may appear in the leaf axils.

Propagation   Offsets develop between the leaves as flowering ends. These may be rooted in a suitable propagation medium.

Related Plants

Cryptanthus × 'It.' "Color-band cryptanthus." Reaches a width of up to 16 inches. Leaves are coppery green with pink-tinted ivory and prominently wavy margins.

Water

DRY	NORMAL	EVENLY MOIST

Temperature

COOL	MODERATE	WARM

Light

LOW	BRIGHT INDIRECT	FULL SUN

Humidity

ARID	MODERATE	HUMID

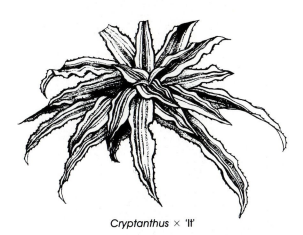

Cryptanthus × 'It'

C. b. 'Minor.' "Dwarf rose-stripe star."
Similar in size to the species, the green
leaves are evenly divided by two longitudinal cream stripes with bronze-pink
tint.

C. b. 'Minor Pink Starlite.' "Pink starlite."
Leaves bright pink except for dark green
midrib bordered by two lighter green
stripes.

C. b. 'Minor Starlite.' "Starlite." Leaves
with two ivory stripes between pink midrib and dark green margins.

BOTANICAL NAME: *Cuphea ignea*
(KOO-fee-uh IG-knee-uh)

COMMON NAME: Cigar flower, cigar plant, firecracker plant

FAMILY: Lythraceae (Loosestrife)

ORIGIN: Mexico and Jamaica

As the common names imply, this is one of the more interesting flowering plants for indoor use. In addition, the flowering period is a year-round attraction if cultural requirements are met. Each flower is actually a ¾ inch long, bright red tubular calyx (fused sepals) with a white tip—there are no petals on this flower. The oblong or lanceolate leaves are an attractive medium green background to the flowers. Overall, the plant has a spreading, upright form and usually reaches about a one foot height.
The cigar flower is also used outside as a bedding plant. Pinching is necessary indoors and out to avoid legginess.

Culture Most important, give full sun to stimulate flowering. The plant will maintain itself under lower light, but flowers less and becomes more spindly. Pinching is necessary regardless of light conditions. Also, avoid water stress since this plant is fast to wilt. A loamy soil with organic matter incorporated is best. Fertilize every month during active growth.

Typical Problems The most common problem is poor flowering due to too little light. In this case when possible, move the plant to higher light conditions.

Spider mites may give the plant a white or yellow speckled appearance, especially in hot, dry locations.

Propagation Easily grown from seeds that produce flowering plants in five months under good conditions. Stem cuttings, 4 to 5 inches in length, quickly root and produce new plants that flower about twice as quickly as seedlings.

Related Plants

C. i. 'Firefly.' A dwarf cultivar.

C. hyssopifolia. "False heather; elfin herb." A plant similar in form to the cigar flower, but with smaller, more linear leaves and small, profuse white or lavender flowers with petals.

Water

DRY	NORMAL	EVENLY MOIST

Temperature

COOL	MODERATE	WARM

Light

LOW	BRIGHT INDIRECT	FULL SUN

Humidity

ARID	MODERATE	HUMID

BOTANICAL NAME: *Cycas revoluta*
(SIGH-kas reh-voe-LOO-tuh)

COMMON NAME: Sago palm, conehead, funeral palm

FAMILY: Cycadaceae (Cycad)

ORIGIN: Southern Japan

The sago palm, with its pinnately-compound leaves and revolute (rolled down) leaflet margins, is one of the very few cycads used indoors. Cycads are among the most primitive of living seed plants. Though not a true palm, the sago palm can reach a 10-foot height and a 6 to 8 foot width indoors with its 5-foot-long leaves that are so tough and stiff they resemble plastic fern fronds. A very hardy plant (tolerant of temperatures as low as −10°C), the sago palm is one of the most durable house plants and the most widely used cycad. One of the slower growing house plants, producing only a few leaves each year.

Culture A plant that requires no pruning except to occasionally remove a declining older leaf. Fertilize every three to six months during the spring and summer when growth is active. Avoid keeping the soil overly moist. A loamy, well-drained soil with high organic matter content is preferable. Repot rootbound plants in early spring. During watering, avoid wetting the fur-covered terminal bud area at the base of the leaves.

Typical Problems Scale insects will infest the leaves and the scaly trunk of the plant.

Propagation Seeds should be sown on the surface of the medium, not buried. The young shoots that arise from the base of the plant may be severed during dormancy and rooted in a suitable medium. Also, a woody scale and its associated bud may be removed and propagated.

Related Plants

C. circinnalis. "Fern palm." A faster growing and fuller plant than sago palm, with leaflets that have flattened rather than revolute margins.

Water

DRY	NORMAL	EVENLY MOIST

Temperature

COOL	MODERATE	WARM

Light

LOW	BRIGHT INDIRECT	FULL SUN

Humidity

ARID	MODERATE	HUMID

BOTANICAL NAME: *Cyperus alternifolius*
(SY-per-us al-ter-nih-FOE-lee-us)

COMMON NAME: Umbrella plant, umbrella palm

FAMILY: Cyperaceae (Sedge)

ORIGIN: Madagascar

This unusually structured and attractive aquatic herb is a close relative of the Egyptians' papyrus, used for papermaking. The umbrella plant can reach a 4-foot height, but usually only 2 to 3 feet indoors. The ribbed stalks rise from fibrous roots to terminate in a rosette of grasslike, food-producing bracts that subtend terminal clusters of inconspicuous flowers. The true leaves are reduced to sheaths. The umbrella plant creates a striking accent as a container plant or may be used at pool edges or planted in shallow aquariums.

Culture   One of the few indoor plants that thrives in wet feet; keep them in saucers of water. If tops die from drought, the roots may send up new shoots if watered quickly enough. Repot annually and fertilize frequently, particularly during active growth.

Typical Problems   Mealy bugs, scale insects, thrips, and whiteflies are reported. Various blight, leaf spot, and rot diseases are reported among producers, but are less bothersome in residential settings. Remove any foliage immediately that appears to be developing disease.

Propagation   As a suckering plant, the clump of stalks may be divided with age. Also, the rosettes may be removed, the bracts trimmed back to an inch or so and submerged into propagation medium or water. New shoots and roots will arise from the bract axils. Seed propagation is also possible.

Related Plants

C. a. 'Gracilis.' "Dwarf umbrella plant." A miniature of the species, growing only to about 12 inches and rarely flowering.

C. albostriatus. "Broad umbrella palm." Similar in form to *C. alternifolius,* but with broader bracts that give the plant a coarser appearance.

Variegated variants are available for both species listed here.

Water		
DRY	NORMAL	EVENLY MOIST

Temperature		
COOL	MODERATE	WARM

Light		
LOW	BRIGHT INDIRECT	FULL SUN

Humidity		
ARID	MODERATE	HUMID

BOTANICAL NAME: *Cyrtomium falcatum*
(sir-TOE-mee-um fal-KATE-um)

COMMON NAME: Holly fern

FAMILY: Polypodiaceae (Polypody)

ORIGIN: Asia, South Africa, and Polynesia

The leathery dark green and ovate pinnae of the 2½-foot fronds create a more coarse texture than on other ferns. The durable foliage, however, makes this one of the better ferns for low light cultivation, provided that watering and fertilization are restrained to reflect the reduced growth level.

Culture   Tolerates low light and occasional drying, but prefers bright indirect light, evenly moist rich potting soil, and good ventilation.

Typical Problems   Scale insects and mealy bugs are the only reported pest or disease problems. This fern, like others, is susceptible to damage from pesticides.

Propagation   Easily propagated from spores (see Chapter Thirteen). Older plants may be reproduced through division of the rhizome.

Related Plants
C. f. 'Rochfordianum.' "Japanese holly fern." The pinnae margins are coarsely fringed, giving the plant a more fluffy textural appearance.

Other cultivars with various pinnae configurations are 'Fluffy,' 'Holly,' 'Mayi,' and 'Leather.'

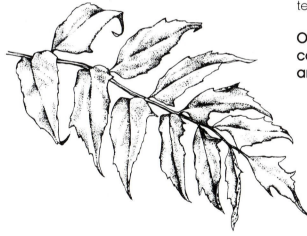

Water

DRY	NORMAL	EVENLY MOIST

Temperature

COOL	MODERATE	WARM

Light

LOW	BRIGHT INDIRECT	FULL SUN

Humidity

ARID	MODERATE	HUMID

BOTANICAL NAME: *Dieffenbachia amoena*
(dee-fen-BAK-ee-uh uh-MEE-na)

COMMON NAME: Giant dumbcane, charming dumbcane

FAMILY: Araceae (Arum/Aroids)

ORIGIN: Tropical America

Another work horse genus of the indoor plant world, *Dieffenbachia* contributes numerous forms of color and durability to interior spaces. The uncomplimentary dumbcane designation refers to the calcium oxalate crystals found in the plant tissue. Chewing this plant leaves one painfully and temporarily speechless. The best aesthetic description of dumbcanes is that they provide "splash."

The huge elliptical leaves arching gracefully from the upright stem require space and a larger room to look proportionate. The popularity of these plants stems from this appearance as well as their durability in warm, dark places. The giant dumbcane displays dark green leaves up to 18 inches long that are streaked with creamy white markings along the lateral veins.

Culture   Excellent plants in hot and dry rooms with low light. Maintain night temperatures above 60°F and keep away from cold drafts. Pot into a rich potting soil. Dry somewhat between waterings, particularly during inactive growth.

Typical Problems   Mites, mealy bugs, and thrips occur, plus various leaf spot and rot organisms. The Achilles heel of this group is overwatering.

Propagation   Overly mature dumbcanes can be air-layered and multiplied by stem cuttings incorporating a leaf scar and associated bud. Plants will root in time if placed horizontally in propagation medium with the bud up. Suckers may also be divided from the parent and potted individually.

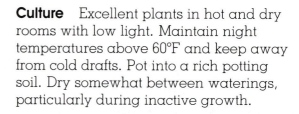

Water

DRY	NORMAL	EVENLY MOIST

Temperature

COOL	MODERATE	WARM

Light

LOW	BRIGHT INDIRECT	FULL SUN

Humidity

ARID	MODERATE	HUMID

Related Plants   Listed here are other important *Dieffenbachia* variants and species important to the foliage industry

D. a. 'Tropic Snow.' Similar in growth habit to the species, but with darker green leaves and more general interior coloring of cream-yellow.

D. × *bausei.* "Bause Dieffenbachia." Leaves 12 inches long and broadly sword-shaped and colored yellow-green, with a few large irregular green blotches and white spots.

D. exotica. "Exotic Dieffenbachia." One of the smaller and better species for home use, the exotic dieffenbachia has bright leaves marbled with green and white.

D. exotica. 'Perfection.' A compact plant with deep green leathery leaves that are variegated with greenish ivory markings.

D. maculata. "Spotted dumbcane." Attractive elongated leaves heavily spotted white and with numerous lateral veins.

Dieffenbachia exotica

Dieffenbachia exotica 'Perfection'

Dieffenbachia maculata

*Dieffenbachia
maculata
'Rudolph Roehrs'*

D. m. 'Rudolph Roehrs.' "Yellow-leaf dumbcane." A two-tone type with new leaves bright yellow contrasting with rich green midrib and margin. The yellow turns to pea green with age.

D. × *memoria-corsii*. Oblong green leaves irregularly marked along the midrib with grayish silver.

D. *oerstedii*. A small dumbcane with leathery dark green leaves 10 inches long and an off center midrib.

D. *o. variegata*. Same as species, but with prominent creamy white midrib.

BOTANICAL NAME: *Dizygotheca elegantissima*
(dih-zee-go-THEE-kah ell-ih-gan-TISS-ih-ma)

COMMON NAME: False aralia

FAMILY: Araliaceae (Aralia)

ORIGIN: New Caledonia, Polynesia

Often mistaken for the marijuana plant (**Cannabis sativa**), the false aralia has similar palmately compound leaves with 6 to 10 fingerlike, green-brown, toothed leaflets. In good form, the plant is truly "most elegant," the meaning of *elegantissima*. The stems are mottled with a cream color. When the adult stage of growth is reached, the leaf character changes from the slender juvenile form to a much broader, lanceolate form. Formerly known as *Aralia elegantissima,* this tree reaches a height of 25 feet in its native habitat.

Culture Prune back occasionally to encourage bushy growth. Adverse culture, such as low humidity, high soil salts, poor watering, or drafts will aggravate the tendency for lower leaves to drop. Fertilize every month during active growth.

Typical Problems Mealy bugs are the most common pest, inhabiting leaf axils and the intersection of leaflets. Spider mites may also occur. Moving the plant into the arid confines of the tpyical home usually causes considerable dropping of the lower leaves.

Propagation Primarily by seeds or air-layering, but stem cuttings can be propagated under mist or humid conditions.

Related Plants None.

Water

DRY	NORMAL	EVENLY MOIST

Temperature

COOL	MODERATE	WARM

Light

LOW	BRIGHT INDIRECT	FULL SUN

Humidity

ARID	MODERATE	HUMID

BOTANICAL NAME: *Dracaena fragrans* 'Massangeana'
(dra-CEE-na FRA-grans ma-san-gee-AN-uh)

COMMON NAME: Corn plant

FAMILY: Agavaceae (Agave)

ORIGIN: Upper Guinea

Dracaena contributes numerous species and variants as mainstays in the foliage plant industry. The members of this group range in size from trees to small, slow-growing shrubs. All of them are noted for their adaptability to difficult interior circumstances; hence, their immense popularity in shopping malls, offices, and other commercial settings. The corn plant, the most popular variant of *Dracaena fragrans,* sports long corn-like leaves embellished with a central yellow stripe. Useful as a small potted plant when young, it quickly matures into a large specimen, spreading 3 or 4 feet and reaching a height of up to 10 feet indoors.

Culture   Dracaenas enjoy warmth and a constantly moist medium; in fact, most types may be propagated from cuttings and grown in water. Under low light conditions the corn plant will lose its yellow variegation and broadness of leaf.

Typical Problems   Leaf-tip browning can be caused by fluoride toxicity, and marginal burning from pesticide application. Mealy bugs, mites, and thrips occur, as well as various rots, blights, and leaf spots, particularly in overly humid circumstances.

Propagation   Typically dracaenas can be propagated by cuttings, air-layering, and stem sections. Most are not typically propagated by seeds.

Related Plants   Listed below are the various dracaenas that are well-known and heavily used in the industry.

Water

DRY	NORMAL	EVENLY MOIST

Temperature

COOL	MODERATE	WARM

Light

LOW	BRIGHT INDIRECT	FULL SUN

Humidity

ARID	MODERATE	HUMID

D. arborea. "Tree Dracaena." A less utilized member, this large tree forms a dense head of green, lanceolate, and twisted leaves atop a smooth, light trunk.

D. deremensis 'Janet Craig.' "Janet Craig dracaena." A dark, glossy green specimen with arching leaves. Growing to a height of 10 feet or so and 3 to 4 feet wide indoors, this plant needs space. Keeps well indoors, but eventually becomes elongated and spindly in poor light. Using a water source high in fluoride will cause tip burn.

D. d. 'Warneckii.' "Striped dracaena." Leaves similar but more narrow than those of 'Janet Craig,' but lined with two white narrow stripes that give a distinctive touch of contrast.

D. draco. "Dragon tree." A less common dracaena whose dark red sap was believed to be dragon's blood by ancient superstition. The 2-foot-long gray-green swordlike leaves are perched on an unusually thick stem.

D. goldieana. "Queen of dracaenas." As indicated by the name, considered by some authorities to be the most spectacular dracaena in cultivation. Its broadly elliptical 9-inch leaves have cross bands of gray and bright green. Though beautiful, not as widely cultivated as others.

D. marginata. "Madagascar dragon tree, red-edged dracaena." Perhaps the most popular of all dracaenas because

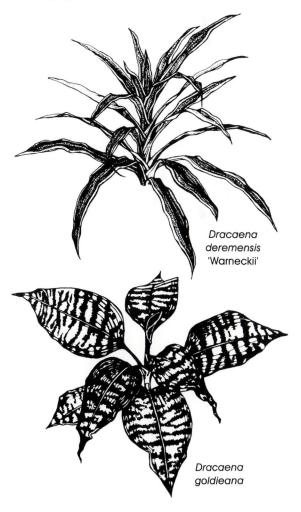

Dracaena deremensis
'Warneckii'

Dracaena deremensis
'Janet Craig'

Dracaena goldieana

of its slender narrow deep green leaves edged in red that form a rosette atop a long slender trunk. Tending to grow twisted and crooked, the stems of these plants are often used in variously shaped combinations to create interesting multiple stem effects. A very tolerant species to low light conditions. Useful as a potted table plant when young.

D. sanderiana. "Belgian evergreen, ribbon plant." An attractive and durable rosette of 9-inch-long milky green leaves with wide marginal stripes of white. Commonly used in dish gardens and small planters; with age the plant becomes unattractively top-heavy.

D. surculosa. "Gold-dust dracaena, spotted dracaena." The only dracaena among the group listed here with white spots on a green, elliptical leaf. Unlike the other species, this plant forms a shrubby habit and thin, wirelike stems.

Dracaena sanderiana

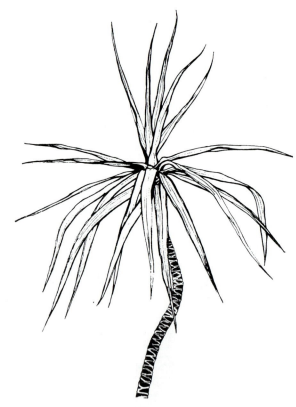

Dracaena marginata

Dracaena surculosa

BOTANICAL NAME: *Epipremnum aureum*

(eh-pih-PREM-num AR-ee-um)

COMMON NAME: Pothos, golden pothos

FAMILY: Araceae (Arum/Aroids)

ORIGIN: Solomon Islands

Once known as *Scindapsus aureus,* this plant is a very common and durable vine for hanging baskets and totem pole planters. Its heart-shaped leaves are predominantly rich green and glossy, and marbled with streaks of cream. This form is the juvenile growth habit that will usually remain as long as the plant is used hanging. In upright situations, the leaves continue to enlarge, finally becoming cut, somewhat like *Monstera,* as they reach the adult phase of growth. Because of the variegated leaf quality, the plant needs bright indirect light to maintain good foliage color.

Culture   With night temperatures above 65°F, adequate humidity, and protected from direct sun, these plants are easy to grow and maintain. Pinching frequently is desirable to maintain a thick habit. Fertilize two or three times a year and allow the soil to dry somewhat between waterings. This plant grows well in water.

Typical Problems   The most serious are water-related, such as molds, rots of stem and root, and leaf spots. Mealy bugs can damage both the root system and above-ground tissue. Scale insects and thrips also occur occasionally.

Propagation   Easy to root as stem cuttings or leaf-bud cuttings. Seed propagation is possible if a source of seed can be located.

Related Plants

E. a. 'Marble Queen.' "Marble queen pothos." Similar in growth habit to the species, but leaves mostly white-variegated, with green spotting and patches.

E. a. 'Tricolor.' "Tricolor pothos." Leaves are medium green and marbled spotted with pale green, cream, and yellow.

Water

DRY	NORMAL	EVENLY MOIST

Temperature

COOL	MODERATE	WARM

Light

LOW	BRIGHT INDIRECT	FULL SUN

Humidity

ARID	MODERATE	HUMID

BOTANICAL NAME: *Episcia cupreata*
(e-PIS-see-uh kew-pree-AH-ta)

COMMON NAME: Flame violet

FAMILY: Gesneriaceae (Gesneria)

ORIGIN: Columbia and Venezuela

The flame violet, a close relative of the African violet, is noted for its quilted leaves of subdued, rich color. The leaves are also broadly elliptical and velvety to the touch. As low-growing, perpetually flowering, creeping terrestrial herbs that produce stolens bearing new plantlets, the flame violet is excellent as a ground cover or hanging basket specimen.

Culture   The fleshy leaf quality of this plant demands drying between waterings during inactive growth. Top-water with tepid water to flush salts down and avoid leaf damage. Warmth and humidity are the essential requirements, although plants may revive following dormancy stimulated by cold conditions.

Typical Problems   The foliage easily burns from cold water exposure or contact with a soil surface laden with high salt concentrations. Root rot is the most serious potential problem although mealy bugs, nematodes, and mites may also appear.

Propagation   Most easily from the new plantlets produced from runners and from stem cuttings. Leaf cuttings may also be used, but are slower and more susceptible to rotting.

Related Plants   Many cultivars are available exhibiting a variety of foliage markings and colors, as well as flower colors. Here are a few.

E. c. 'Acajou.' Large dark mahogany leaves with silver-green; large orange-red flowers.

E. c. 'Metallica.' "Kitty episcia." Large coppery leaves with silvery green centers and metallic pink margins. Orange-scarlet flowers.

E. c. 'Tropical Topaz.' "Canal Zone yellow episcia." Bright yellow flowers and plain green leaves.

E. c. 'Reptans.' "Flame violet." Brownish green leaves marked with silvery green; flowers deep red outside and pink inside with fringed lobes.

Water

DRY	NORMAL	EVENLY MOIST

Temperature

COOL	MODERATE	WARM

Light

LOW	BRIGHT INDIRECT	FULL SUN

Humidity

ARID	MODERATE	HUMID

BOTANICAL NAME: *Euphorbia milii splendens*
(you-FOUR-be-ah MILL-ee-eye SPLEN-dens)

COMMON NAME: Crown of thorns

FAMILY: Euphorbiaceae (Spurge)

ORIGIN: Madagascar

The crown of thorns, not from biblical lands as the name implies, is an imposter in yet another way—it looks like a cactus, but is not. The succulent, gray stems and the prolific spines give the plant a rugged appearance, especially when the small, obovate leaves drop during resting periods. The small red flowers stand above the foliage in clusters and are present most of the year in good conditions. Use this plant with care around children because of the sharp spines and the supposedly poisonous sap. A 2-foot height is typical indoors.

Culture   This succulent should be allowed to dry between waterings, but not to the extent of cacti and other succulents without leaves. Reduce watering during the resting period. Fertilize monthly during active growth. A loamy, well-drained potting mix is essential. Repotting should occur at the beginning of active growth.

Typical Problems   Low humidity may cause leaf drop, but this is harmless to the plant. Older plants may require staking.

Propagation   By stem cuttings. Because of the white sap that flows freely on cutting the stem, allow cuttings to sub-erize for several hours prior to placement in the medium.

Related Plants   Several forms of *E. m. splendens* are available, with flower color ranging from off-white to yellow to red.

E. fulgens, "Scarlet plume." Profuse flowers similar to those of *E. m. splendens*, but with thin, arching branches and narrow, lanceolate leaves.

E. lactea. "Mottled spurge, candelabra cactus, dragon bones." A three-foot, leafless plant, candelabra-like in structure, that has triangular stems with milky white markings on each side and spines lining the three angles.

E. pulcherrima. "Poinsettia." This popular Christmas plant is discussed in Chapter Ten.

Water		
DRY	NORMAL	EVENLY MOIST

Temperature		
COOL	MODERATE	WARM

Light		
LOW	BRIGHT INDIRECT	FULL SUN

Humidity		
ARID	MODERATE	HUMID

BOTANICAL NAME: × *Fatshedera lizei*

(the hybrid genus fats-HEAD-er-uh LIZ-ee-eye)

COMMON NAME: Aralia ivy

FAMILY: Araliaceae (Aralia/Ginseng)

ORIGIN: Hybrid genus between *Fatsia* and *Hedera*

Accidentally discovered in France around 1940, aralia ivy displays the upright growth habit of Japanese fatsia and the leave-lobing qualities of English ivy. It will grow to a height of 6 feet or so if supported, but can be pruned into a denser shape. Its cultivation is similar to fatsia, although it prefers temperatures somewhat more temperate than fatsia. The leathery and shiny foot-wide leaves are palmately lobed more reminiscent of English ivy. Works best indoors where its tendency to grow tall can be exercised.

Culture   As with fatsia, keep this plant in cooler surroundings, no less than 50°F at night. Keep the soil evenly moist, but be aware of any disease symptoms that might arise; reduce watering during inactive growth and in poor light situations.

Typical Problems   Spider mites, scale insects, aphids, and mealy bugs, as well as various rot and leaf spot organisms may appear.

Propagation   Reproduced primarily by stem cuttings; this maintains the plant's genetic identify.

Related Plants   See *Fatsia* and *Hedera*.

Water		
DRY	NORMAL	EVENLY MOIST

Temperature		
COOL	MODERATE	WARM

Light		
LOW	BRIGHT INDIRECT	FULL SUN

Humidity		
ARID	MODERATE	HUMID

BOTANICAL NAME: *Fatsia japonica*
(FAT-see-uh ja-PON-ih-ka)

COMMON NAME: Japanese fatsia

FAMILY: Araliaceae (Aralia/Ginseng)

ORIGIN: Japan

A glossy green evergreen in Japan, fatsia creates a striking appearance with its 10- to 15-inch wide, deeply cut leaves into 7 to 11 toothed lobes. Since the leaves are big and held generally horizontally, the plant's texture is dense and orderly in spite of the coarse foliage. Another fatsia species, **F. papyrifera,** is the source of Chinese rice paper. *Fatsia japonica* is an excellent house plant with a striking appearance and rich green color that blends well with other colors. The peppy growth rate and large leaf size make fatsia most suitable as a container specimen for uncrowded spaces.

Culture   Fatsia can tolerate various temperature ranges, but excels in coolness. It needs to be kept constantly moist, but it can suffer either from overwatering or dryness. Feed about three times a year.

Typical Problems   Leaves will drop in poor light or drought conditions. The attractive large size of the leaves will be lost as new leaves develop. Aphids, spider mites, mealy bugs, scale, and thrips are known to infest this plant. Diseases include rots and leaf spots, particularly in overly wet conditions.

Propagation   Fatsia can be started from cuttings, seeds, or root cuttings. Air-layering is also possible on larger plants.

Related Plants   See × *Fatshedera.*

Water

DRY	NORMAL	EVENLY MOIST

Temperature

COOL	MODERATE	WARM

Light

LOW	BRIGHT INDIRECT	FULL SUN

Humidity

ARID	MODERATE	HUMID

BOTANICAL NAME: *Ficus benjamina*
(FY-cus ben-ja-MINE-uh)

COMMON NAME: Benjamin tree, weeping fig

FAMILY: Moraceae (Mulberry)

ORIGIN: India, southeastern Asia, Malay Archipelago, and northern tropical Australia

The Benjamin tree is a durable and well-known plant, both as a small container specimen, as well as a large tree, up to 15 or 20 feet in public spaces. It represents one among many species of fig that have earned an important niche among indoor plants for their durability and wide variety of foliage and growth habits. The common fig, *F. carica*, produces the edible fruit. The Benjamin tree is a graceful, densely twigged tree with somewhat weeping branches and lustrous rich green leaves 3 to 4 feet long. It is valued for its fine texture and airy appearance. As members of the mulberry family, *Ficus* species have milky sap; most produce aerial roots as well.

Culture   It is important here to purchase acclimated plants that have been exposed to shade prior to home use. Otherwise, the tree will shed its leaves, replacing them with shade-tolerant ones. The plant enjoys warm temperatures and bright indirect light for optimum leaf production, but will stand the more stringent conditions of less desirable spots. Pot into a rich soil and allow drying, particularly during the winter months, between waterings.

Typical Problems   Relatively disease-resistant, but several pests are a possibility, including mealy bugs, whiteflies, scale insects, and foliar chewers.

Propagation   Typically by stem cuttings. Air-layering is a common method for most species of ficus.

Related Plants   The following species and variants are commercially important types of Ficus

F. b. 'Exotica.' "Exotic fig tree." Branches droop more noticeably than the species; leaves with long and twisted tips.

Water		
DRY	NORMAL	EVENLY MOIST

Temperature		
COOL	MODERATE	WARM

Light		
LOW	BRIGHT INDIRECT	FULL SUN

Humidity		
ARID	MODERATE	HUMID

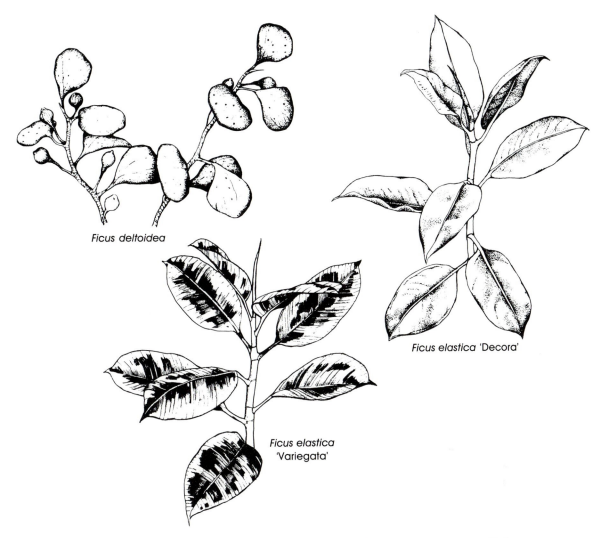

Ficus deltoidea

Ficus elastica 'Decora'

Ficus elastica 'Variegata'

F. deltoidea. "Mistletoe fig." An attractive shrubby plant with broadly obovate or rounded leaves up to 3 inches long that are cinnamon-green below. The attractive fruit, ½ inch yellow figs are held conspicuously in view on long peduncles arising from the leaf axils.

F. elastica. 'Decora.' "Wideleaf rubber plant." The familiar plant with waxy elliptical leaves borne on a straight ascending stem. The leaves are abruptly pointed at the apex, have a white midrib above, and a red petiole and midrib below. This plant enjoys all the sun it can get, but will tolerate very low levels. This cultivar holds its lower leaves much better than older types. Propagate by air layering or leaf-bud cuttings.

F. e. 'Abidjan.' A striking plant with dark maroon foliage and contrasting bright red upper veins.

F. e. 'Doescheri.' A variegated plant with patches of green, gray, cream, and pink in varying proportions.

F. e. 'Variegata.' Leaves light green, bordered by a white or yellow margin.

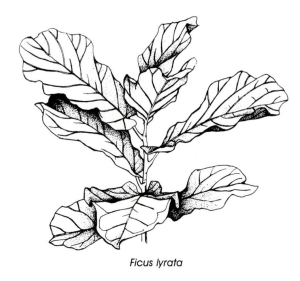

Ficus lyrata

Ficus pumila

F. lyrata. "Fiddle-leaf fig." An unusually textured plant with leaves up to 15 inches long, broadly obovate and rounded (somewhat like the shape of a violin), and rich green in color with lighter green veins. This species tends to be upright, branching, and slow growing.

F. pumila. "Creeping fig." A vine of dense small leaves that clings to walls with aerial roots. A vigorous grower and a durable plant. The three cultivars available are 'Minima'—small leaves; 'Quercifolia'—pinnate lobing on leaves; and 'Variegata'—leaves green and white.

F. retusa. "Indian laurel." A tree similiar in texture to the Benjamin tree, but the broader leaves give a coarser texture. The dark green, waxy leaves are borne on ascending branches that become more weeping with age.

F. retusa nitida is an upright form commonly used for pruning into formal shapes.

F. sagittata. "Rooting fig." A vine, similar in growth habit to the creeping fig, but with lanceolate leaves. A variegated cultivar, 'Variegata,' is available with prominent white margins.

BOTANICAL NAME: *Fittonia verschaffeltii*
(fit-TONE-ee-uh ver-shaf-FELL-tee-eye)

COMMON NAME: Red-nerve plant, mosaic plant

FAMILY: Acanthaceae (Acanthus)

ORIGIN: Columbia to Peru, South America

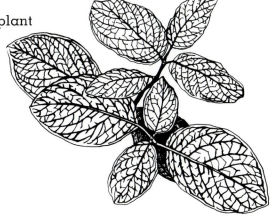

The egg-shaped leaves of the red-nerve plant are dark green and netted with deep-red veins. A groundcover plant in nature, it grows flat to form a blanket of foliage. Fittonias love warmth and humidity, making them particularly suitable for terrariums and greenhouses. If underwatered, they wilt rapidly, but recover with a prompt drenching.

Culture Fittonia responds well to soil with generous amounts of organic matter and aggregate material to aid drainage. Repot any time the plants become overcrowded. Fertilize carefully; about once a month with one-half strength solution. Do not fertilize newly repotted plants for eight weeks.

Typical Problems Marginal burning of leaves occurs with low humidity conditions. Mealy bugs occasionally infest the areas of leaf-stem intersection.

Propagation Stem cuttings (3 to 4 inches long) and by division of larger plants. Stems of the plant often root on soil contact; these may be severed, uprooted, and transplanted to another container.

Related Plants

F.v. argyroneura. "Silver-nerve plant." Rich green foliage color and attractively netted white veins.

F.v. argyroneura 'Nana.' Same as above variety, but with smaller foliage (× ½) and stature.

F.v. pearcei. "Snake-skin plant." The foliage is larger and thinner than the species and of a glaucous olive-green color with carmine veins.

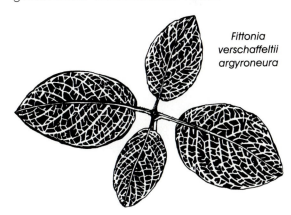

Fittonia verschaffeltii argyroneura

Water

DRY	NORMAL	EVENLY MOIST
		■

Temperature

COOL	MODERATE	WARM
		■

Light

LOW	BRIGHT INDIRECT	FULL SUN
	■	

Humidity

ARID	MODERATE	HUMID
		■

BOTANICAL NAME: *Gibasis geniculata*
(ji-BAS-is ge-nih-ku-LA-ta)

COMMON NAME: Tahitian bridal veil

FAMILY: Commelinaceae (Spiderwort)

ORIGIN: Tropical America

This dense, finely textured trailer or creeper becomes a mat of glossy dark green with maturity. The leaves are broadly lanceolate and approximately 1 inch long; underneath they are quite purple. Accounting for the bridal veil label, the flowers are delicate white clusters, reminiscent of baby's breath, that stand gracefully above the foliage in a veillike fashion. Grown as a hanging basket specimen in adequate light, with proper attention to moisture and pinching, this plant is a most versatile specimen.

Culture Although this plant should be allowed to dry between waterings, drought can quickly damage the foliage irreparably. Pot into a standard potting soil and provide as much light as possible, since low levels will result in a sparse habit and little flowering. Pinching is necessary every few weeks during the growing season to maintain good density.

Typical Problems Aphids can appear, as well as gray mold on dead foliage, that can spread to healthy tissue under humid conditions. A proper watering regime is critical to prevent death by dryness or overwatering.

Propagation Use pinched materials from pruning as stem cuttings, putting several in one small container to enhance early compactness. These plants root at the nodes, thus making cutting propagation quick and easy.

Related Plants None.

Water

DRY	NORMAL	EVENLY MOIST

Temperature

COOL	MODERATE	WARM

Light

LOW	BRIGHT INDIRECT	FULL SUN

Humidity

ARID	MODERATE	HUMID

BOTANICAL NAME: *Gynura aurantiaca* 'Purple Passion'
(guy-NOOR-ah aw-ran-tee-A-ca)

COMMON NAME: Purple-passion vine

FAMILY: Compositae (Composite or Sunflower)

ORIGIN: Java; origin of this cultivar is unknown

The purple-passion vine is a twining, fast-growing plant with ovate leaves that are serrate and covered with prominent violet or purple hairs and deeper colored veins. The flowers, although attractive orange discs, smell quite offensive and should be removed in the bud stage. Frequent pinching of the shoot tips will discourage the plant's tendency to become straggly. The unusual foliage coloration is best on the newer foliage and in high light conditions.

Culture   Will grow well in plain water. Prefers a loamy soil such as equal parts of loam, peat, and sand. Fertilize once a month during active growth. Poor light conditions will result in quite straggly growth and more subdued coloration.

Typical Problems   Whiteflies, aphids, and mealy bugs are the most common difficulties with this plant.

Propagation   Easily started by stem cuttings taken any time of the year.

Related Plants   None.

Water		
DRY	NORMAL	EVENLY MOIST

Temperature		
COOL	MODERATE	WARM

Light		
LOW	BRIGHT INDIRECT	FULL SUN

Humidity		
ARID	MODERATE	HUMID

BOTANICAL NAME: *Hedera helix*
(HEAD-er-uh HEE-licks)

COMMON NAME: English ivy

FAMILY: Araliaceae (Aralia)

ORIGIN: Europe, Western Asia, and North Africa

Known well as a garden vine and ground cover, English ivy offers many leaf forms and other good qualities for indoor use. It likes coolness and fits well into energy-saving interiors with low thermostats. Since the stems sprout clinging aerial rootlets, this plant can be used in a number of climbing configurations. Outside, the plant will flower in the adult phase of growth, but rarely does it flower inside. Unfortunately, many of the cultivars are mutations that frequently revert back to the original three or five-lobed leaf form with age.

Culture English ivy can be grown in plain water, but thrives in a loamy soil rich in organic matter. Pinch occasionally to break apical dominance and induce bushiness. An excellent plant for areas with cool drafts and air-conditioning.

Typical Problems Spider mites are particularly troublesome in warm, dry conditions. Broad mites distort the new growth. Aphids and scale insects also attack plants occasionally. Crown rot, a rotting of the stems at the soil level, and bacterial leaf spot, small water-soaked spots under the leaves, also occur on damp and poorly ventilated foliage.

Propagation Easily started from stem cuttings. However, they require several months to get established and initiate active and rapid growth.

Related Plants Many cultivars are offered, differing primarily in leaf shape. Among the best are 'Glacier' (small leaves variegated with pink and white margins), 'Needlepoint' (five-pointed, starlike leaves), 'Hahn's Selfbranching' (branching and bushy, the leaves borne close together on the stem), 'My Heart' (leaves heart-shaped), and 'Buttercup' (leaves yellow). Related species: *H. canariensis.* "Algerian or canary ivy." A species with much larger foliage 4 to 6 inches), as well as several interesting cultivars, 'Variegata' being the most popular.

Water

DRY	NORMAL	EVENLY MOIST

Temperature

COOL	MODERATE	WARM

Light

LOW	BRIGHT INDIRECT	FULL SUN

Humidity

ARID	MODERATE	HUMID

BOTANICAL NAME: *Hemigraphis alternata*
(him-ih-GRAF-is al-ter-NA-ta)

COMMON NAME: Red ivy

FAMILY: Acanthaceae (Acanthus)

ORIGIN: Malay Archipelago

As its common name implies, the leaves of red ivy are an unusual metallic violet above and reddish purple below. Generally heart-shaped and borne opposite one another on the stems, the leaves are bullate or puckered, bluntly toothed, and roughly resemble those of Swedish ivy. The small white flowers arise in terminal clusters. Used in southern Florida as ground cover and basket plants; the latter is most appropriate indoors.

Culture   Warmth and protection from overly bright light are the two essential components of culture, although growth may become rank in quite dim locations. Reduce the watering level during seasons of inactive growth. Plant into a general all-purpose potting mix.

Typical Problems   Most problems with red ivy relate to failure to provide proper cultural requirements.

Propagation   This plant tends to layer naturally as a ground cover; propagation by cuttings is fast and easy.

Related Plants   None.

Water		
DRY	NORMAL	EVENLY MOIST

Temperature		
COOL	MODERATE	WARM

Light		
LOW	BRIGHT INDIRECT	FULL SUN

Humidity		
ARID	MODERATE	HUMID

BOTANICAL NAME: *Howea forsterana*
(HOW-ee-uh for-ster-AN-a)

COMMON NAME: Sentry palm, kentia palm

FAMILY: Palmae (Palm)

ORIGIN: Australia

This stately palm grows to a height of 60 feet or more in its natural habitat. Grown originally indoors as large specimens in European public places; now grown in southern California landscapes. Suited as container plants or floor specimens with age, sentry palms have graceful ascending pinnately compound leaves with dark green leathery pinnae arranged mostly horizontal and drooping at the tips. This slow-growing and durable palm is one of the best for cooler and darker environments. Potting a clump of several plants enhances the density and attractiveness of this species.

Culture Pot into a well-drained medium, keeping the plant somewhat pot-bound and evenly moist, drier during inactive periods. Liking night temperatures in the 50s (F), sentry palms do well in air-conditioning. Excellent keeping qualities, withstanding low light better than most plants. Do not prune except to remove dead or damaged leaves.

Typical Problems Poor water relations, either too dry or too wet, will cause leaf tip browning. Otherwise, tolerant of normal environmental variations. The most likely pest is the spider mite, particularly in low humidity.

Propagation By seed.

Related Plants None.

Water

DRY	NORMAL	EVENLY MOIST

Temperature

COOL	MODERATE	WARM

Light

LOW	BRIGHT INDIRECT	FULL SUN

Humidity

ARID	MODERATE	HUMID

BOTANICAL NAME: *Hoya carnosa*
(HOY-yuh car-NO-suh)

COMMON NAME: Wax plant, honey plant

FAMILY: Asclepiadaceae (Milkweed)

ORIGIN: Southern China to Australia

The wax plant derives it common name both from its waxy, succulent, ovate leaves and from its attractive flowers that are waxy, fragrant, pinkish white, and borne in clusters. Produced annually on spurs on the previous year's and older growth, the flowers should be allowed to drop naturally to avoid injuring the spurs. Also, the slightest movement or change in environmental conditions may cause the flower buds to drop. This plant is an excellent climbing vine or hanging basket specimen due to its clean habit and attractive appearance.

Culture For flowering, sufficient light is the most important consideration. Otherwise, watering is critical since root rots are common among overwatered Hoyas. Pot into a loamy, well-drained soil. Reduce watering during slow growth periods. Fertilize every two to three months during active growth.

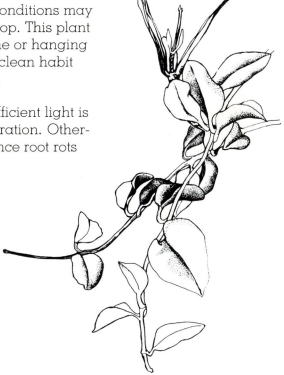

Water

DRY	NORMAL	EVENLY MOIST

Temperature

COOL	MODERATE	WARM

Light

LOW	BRIGHT INDIRECT	FULL SUN

Humidity

ARID	MODERATE	HUMID

Typical Problems   A general wilting or shriveling of the foliage indicates over-watering. Flowering does not occur in too little light. Mealy bugs and scale insects may occur.

Propagation   Easily started by stem cuttings, leaf-bud cuttings, or layering.

Related Plants   A number of species and cultivars are now on the market. Among them are the following.

H. bella. "Miniature wax plant." A dwarf species with white and dark crimson flowers.

H.c. 'Krinkle Kurl.' "Hindu-rope." Leaves folded and curled, as well as crowded on the stem.

H.c. 'Variegata.' Leaves with a white margin.

H. purpurea-fusca. "Silver pink wax plant." Leaves like the wax plant, but with pinkish silver blotches.

Hoya carnosa 'Krinkle Kurl'

BOTANICAL NAME: *Hypoestes phyllostachya*
(high-poe-ESS-tes fill-oh-STACK-ee-uh)

COMMON NAME: Polka-dot plant, freckle-face

FAMILY: Acanthaceae (Acanthus)

ORIGIN: Madagascar

An upright, fast-growing plant with interesting rich green leaves spotted with prominent lavender-pink markings. A height of 3 feet is possible, but not common in the home environment. The leaves are ovate and arranged on the stem in an opposite configuration. With its tendency to become straggly, this plant is good for about a year before it needs replacing. Pinching out the developing small lilac flowers will retard the plant's deterioration. Often frequently and incorrectly known as *H. sanguinolenta.*

Culture   Provide this plant with a soil rich in organic matter such as peat moss or leaf mold. Pinch frequently to maintain a full, bushy habit of growth. Avoid placement in areas susceptible to cold drafts to prevent leaf drop and curling.

Typical Problems   Improper light will usually result in legginess and poor coloration of the spots (too dark) or scorching of the foliage (too bright). Whiteflies are also a problem.

Propagation   Easily started from seed or from stem cuttings.

Related Plants
H.p. 'Pink Brocade' and *H.p.* 'Splash.' These two cultivars are considered superior to the species, having more and larger pink spots on the foliage.

Water

DRY	NORMAL	EVENLY MOIST

Temperature

COOL	MODERATE	WARM

Light

LOW	BRIGHT INDIRECT	FULL SUN

Humidity

ARID	MODERATE	HUMID

BOTANICAL NAME: *Iresine herbstii*
(eye-re-SEEN-ee HERB-stee-eye)

COMMON NAME: Beef plant, chicken-gizzard, beefsteak plant

FAMILY: Amaranthaceae (Amaranth)

ORIGIN: South America

The graphic common names of this species refer to the radiant purplish red foliage that is accented with lighter red veins. The round leaves, notched at the tip and sized up to 2½ inches across, create a most unusual effect among foliage plants. Widely used in warm parts of the United States as a bedding plant or border edging, the beef plant is best used indoors where light can enhance its color and compactness. The wooly flower heads are not showy, but interesting against the colorful background of the foliage. *Iresine herbstii* is cultivated much like coleus.

Culture   Light is the primary requirement for attractiveness, as noted above.

Thrives well in any general-purpose potting mix and responds to frequent fertilization during rapid growth, but both fertilization and water should be reduced during the colder months. An easy plant to cultivate.

Typical Problems   Scale insects and aphids are the most likely pests; root rot and leaf spots are also reported.

Propagation   Easy to propagate from stem or tip cuttings.

Related Plants

I.h. 'Aureo-reticulata.' Leaves greenish red with yellow veins.

Water

DRY	NORMAL	EVENLY MOIST

Temperature

COOL	MODERATE	WARM

Light

LOW	BRIGHT INDIRECT	FULL SUN

Humidity

ARID	MODERATE	HUMID

BOTANICAL NAME: *Kalanchoe daigremontiana*
(kal-an-KOE-ee deh-gre-mon-tee-A-na)

COMMON NAME: Devil's backbone

FAMILY: Crassulaceae (Orpine, stonecrop)

ORIGIN: Madagascar

This interesting plant is valued as a propagation curiosity more than an attractive indoor plant. The devil's backbone is an easy-to-grow, upright succulent plant that can reach 3 feet in height. Its fleshy lanceolate leaves are cupped upward and brownish green in color. Reaching lengths up to 8 inches, the leaves are decorated with crenelated margins that bear adventitious buds at every crease. Mature leaves develop young plantlets from these buds that drop from the plant and root whenever conditions are suitable for growth. Used primarily as an interesting potted specimen that quickly outgrows attractiveness.

Culture   Grown in general-purpose potting soil and given adequate light, this plant grows exceedingly well. If rapid growth is desirable, fertilize every month during the growing season.

Typical Problems   Diseases and pests cause very few problems, with the exception of occasional mealy bugs, but the young plantlets can cause "weed" problems in greenhouse culture. Falling among other nearby plants, the offspring can create a literal groundcover effect.

Propagation   Most efficiently propagated by pegging expanded leaves onto propagation medium. New plantlets will arise at each crease along the leaf margin, quickly rooting down and growing. On more mature plants, the plantlets can be collected from the leaves and placed onto propagation medium. Stem cuttings are also an alternative.

Related Plants

K. tomentosa "Pussy ears, panda plant." A short (10 inches) plant with dense leaves and an overall velvety texture. Leaf margins spotted with brown near the apex. An attrative succulent during its youth. See *Kalanchoe* under "Seasonal Visitors" in Chapter Ten.

Water		
DRY	NORMAL	EVENLY MOIST

Temperature		
COOL	MODERATE	WARM

Light		
LOW	BRIGHT INDIRECT	FULL SUN

Humidity		
ARID	MODERATE	HUMID

BOTANICAL NAME: *Maranta leuconeura leuconeura*

(ma-RAN-ta loo-koe-NOOR-uh loo-koe-NOOR-uh)

COMMON NAME: Prayer plant, ten commandments

FAMILY: Marantaceae (Maranta or Arrowroot Family)

ORIGIN: Brazil, South America

The prayer plant is so named because of the noctural vertical folding of its leaves. During the day, the leaves revert back to a flat or horizontal position. The species is found less in cultivation than the several popular varieties listed below. An interesting aspect of these plants is the formation of thick, starchy roots. One species of *Maranta* is the source of arrowroot, a cooking starch. The inflorescences of the varieties below are racemes, standing above the foliage and composed of several dainty white flowers with reddish spots.

Culture   Hold back on watering during the winter months when growth is slow. Prune occasionally to maintain a bushy form. Soil should be high in organic matter and fertilized only every two to three months to avoid soluble salt buildup.

Typical Problems   Marantas are very sensitive to fluoride and soluble salt accumulation in the soil, exhibiting dying tissue along the leaf margins under such conditions. Avoid the use of tap water if possible. Spider mites also cause a

Water

DRY	NORMAL	EVENLY MOIST

Temperature

COOL	MODERATE	WARM

Light

LOW	BRIGHT INDIRECT	FULL SUN

Humidity

ARID	MODERATE	HUMID

speckling and curling of the leaves. Mice enjoy the starchy roots.

Propagation Stem cuttings are easily rooted, and the numerous crowns of old plants may be divided and potted individually.

Related Plants

M. l. erythroneura. "Red-nerve plant, red-veined prayer plant." Leaves with bright red parallel veins superimposed over an olive and bright green background. Prefers a humus soil. An excellent *Maranta* for indoor use.

M. l. kerchoviana. "Rabbit's foot, rabbit's tracks." Named for the five pairs of dark green or brown spots that line each side of the midrib and overlay a gray-green background.

Maranta leuconeura erythroneura

Maranta leuconeura kerchoviana

BOTANICAL NAME: *Mikania ternata*
(mih-KAN-ee-uh ter-NA-ta)

COMMON NAME: Plush vine

FAMILY: Compositae (Composite/ Sunflower)

ORIGIN: Southern Brazil

This unusual hanging basket plant is one of the few indoor plants with palmately compound leaves. Arranged opposite on the brown stems, the leaves have usually five and sometimes seven variously shaped leaflets, up to 1½ inches long, that are dark gray-green above and covered with short light hair. The leaves are purple below, giving an interesting color contrast to the plant. The plush vine is an excellent specimen to use as background color for the more spectacular foliar "stars." On its own, the plush vine's interesting texture and graceful form make it an attractive addition indoors.

Culture *Mikania* should be pinched frequently to encourage denseness of growth, particularly in poor light. Withhold watering during the less active winter months; fertilize frequently during active growth. Pot into a soil mixture rich in humus and keep night temperatures above 55°F. Bright indirect light is necessary for good foliar density.

Typical Problems Relatively trouble-free except for rust that may occur under humid conditions. Aphids, whiteflies, and mealy bugs are also occasional visitors.

Propagation Easily reproduced by tip or stem cuttings placed into propagation medium or plain water.

Related Plants None.

Water

DRY	NORMAL	EVENLY MOIST

Temperature

COOL	MODERATE	WARM

Light

LOW	BRIGHT INDIRECT	FULL SUN

Humidity

ARID	MODERATE	HUMID

BOTANICAL NAME: *Mimosa pudica*
(mih-MOE-sa PU-dih-ka)

COMMON NAME: Sensitive plant, touch-me-not

FAMILY: Leguminosae or Fabaceae (Pea)

ORIGIN: Tropical America; a widespread weed

The sensitive plant is included here as an educational curiosity rather than an attractive specimen. It grows to a height of 20 inches and bears wiry stems with feathery bipinnate leaves. Under sufficient light, a puffy spherical flower head of purple arises during active growth. A curiosity to both adults and children, this plant, on being touched, folds up its pinnae as the petioles droop. After awhile, the plant is back into its normal configuration once again. This unusual reaction is thought to occur as a response to heat. Because of its spindly growth, pinching from an early age is recommended. Use as a container specimen and place where its interesting qualities are easily accessible.

Culture   Pot into a rich general-purpose soil and fertilize monthly during active growth. The primary requirement is as much sun as possible for compact growth and flower production. A rather easy plant to grow.

Typical Problems   Rarely bothered by pests or diseases.

Propagation   Typically propagated by seeds. Germination percentage is often disappointing, but several seeds planted in a small container will yield at least one or two plants.

Related Plants   None.

Water		
DRY	NORMAL	**EVENLY MOIST**

Temperature		
COOL	MODERATE	**WARM**

Light		
LOW	BRIGHT INDIRECT	**FULL SUN**

Humidity		
ARID	MODERATE	HUMID

BOTANICAL NAME: *Monstera deliciosa*

(mon-STER-uh dee-LISH-ee-o-suh)

COMMON NAME: Swiss-cheese plant, breadfruit vine

FAMILY: Araceae (Arum/Aroids)

ORIGIN: Mexico and Central America

Young plants of this species resemble philodendrons, a close relative, and are often sold as *Philodendron pertusum,* an improper name. Reaching adulthood, Monstera develops fenestrated (perforated with holes and deep sinuses) foliage resulting in the swiss-cheese association. As natural climbers, these plants are usually trained onto a stake or slab to which the stout aerial roots will eventually attach. Since this plant will not branch well, even when pinched, it continues to grow in one direction—up. Consequently, after a few years when the lower leaves drop, monstera should be rejuvenated by air-layering or severe pruning. Best used as a floor specimen with several plants to a container. Somewhat like dumbcane, monstera tissue contains some calcium oxalate crystals that can irritate human tissues.

On larger plants, the yellow spathe and edible pineapple-banana-flavored fruit also create interest.

Culture   Monsteras are quite easy to cultivate, provided the lighting is sufficient to produce large leaves and short internodes. Growth will subside when night temperatures dip below the low 60s (F). Fertilize two or three times a year, particularly as active growth be-

gins. Pot into any commercial potting soil, repotting as necessary into larger containers.

Typical Problems   Aerial roots may create a straggly appearance; either cut off or direct them into the soil for additional support and nourishment.

Poor leaf development and rank growth may result from poor light, overwatering, or high soluble salts. Mealy bugs, mites, and scale insects are the most common pests. Various leaf spots and tissue rots are reported.

Propagation   Air-layering, leaf-bud cuttings, tip cuttings, and seed.

Related Plants

M. d. borsigiana. Smaller, less perforated leaves than the species.

M. friedrichsthalii. Leaves narrow, thin, and entire, with two or three internal perforations on either side of the midrib. Not as common as *M. deliciosa.*

Water		
DRY	NORMAL	EVENLY MOIST

Temperature		
COOL	MODERATE	WARM

Light		
LOW	BRIGHT INDIRECT	FULL SUN

Humidity		
ARID	MODERATE	HUMID

BOTANICAL NAME: *Neoregelia carolinae* 'Tricolor'
(nee-o-ree-JEEL-ee-uh care-o-LIN-ee TRY-cul-or)

COMMON NAME: Striped blushing bromeliad

FAMILY: Bromeliaceae (Bromelia/Pineapple)

ORIGIN: Brazil

This epiphytic bromeliad is a neat rosette of straplike leaves, each up to 16 inches long and 1½ inches wide. The 'Tricolor' cultivar is so named because of the leaf coloration that is primarily longitudinal light ivory stripes (that develop a rose tint in bright light) and rich green leaf margins that are toothed. The blushing nickname of this cultivar comes from the unusual tendency for the inner leaves of the rosette to turn a brilliant shade of red in association with flowering, a fortunate thing since the violet or lavender flowers only protrude slightly above the water level in the central "vase" of the foliage. This plant is an excellent house plant particularly when the light intensity is sufficient to produce flowering and leaf coloration. See Chapter Thirteen for information regarding flower stimulation.

Culture   Like most bromeliads, this form is a durable specimen and tolerant of the dry atmospheric conditions of interior spaces. Pot into a fir bark or similar mix that will give adequate support and the abundant root aeration required by epiphytes. Fertilize once a month or so, particularly as flowering begins, using a more diluted than normal rate. Add to the water-holding vase and the roots.

Typical Problems   Scale insects are the most likely pests. Avoid treating scale insects on bromeliads with oil sprays that are sometimes recommended because the oils can damage the food-absorbing basal areas of the leaves.

Propagation   By separating the offsets from the parent plant and potting separately, or by seed.

Related Plants   Other bromeliads.

Water

DRY	NORMAL	EVENLY MOIST
		■

Temperature

COOL	MODERATE	WARM
		■

Light

LOW	BRIGHT INDIRECT	FULL SUN
	■	

Humidity

ARID	MODERATE	HUMID
	■	

BOTANICAL NAME: *Nephrolepis exaltata* 'Bostoniensis'
(neh-fro-LEP-is ex-al-TA-ta bos-ton-ee-EN-sis)

COMMON NAME: Boston fern

FAMILY Polypodiaceae (Polypody)

ORIGIN Tropics of both hemispheres

Known collectively as sword ferns, *Nephrolepis* is a widely spread inhabitant of the tropics and indoor climates. Gaining in popularity during the Victorian era, the Boston fern was found in most parlors on a pedestal. Now, it is used both on stands and in hanging baskets. The large, erect fronds are pinnately compound, fresh green in color, and may extend 2 to 5 feet in length. With age, they arch over, developing a pendulous character. Consequently, they will develop into a large specimen, but one that adds a refreshing grace to the indoors.

Culture Being a fern, *Nephrolepis* prefers constantly moist conditions and somewhat shaded light, but is tougher than most ferns. For best results, allow the night temperatures to drop to the 55° to 60°F level. Allowing root binding to occur will reduce the chances of soil stagnation from frequent watering. Pot into a potting soil rich in humus. Avoid drafts, but good temperate circulation is beneficial.

Typical Problems Suffers easily from pesticide exposure and foliage fungus under wet conditions, although it prefers higher humidities. Scale insects (white and brown), whiteflies, and mealy bugs may appear, particularly in low humidity.

Propagation Most easily propagated by rooting the plantlets developed at the

Water

DRY	NORMAL	EVENLY MOIST

Temperature

COOL	MODERATE	WARM

Light

LOW	BRIGHT INDIRECT	FULL SUN

Humidity

ARID	MODERATE	HUMID

end of the small rhizomes running from the plant crown. Care should be exercised, however, because some cultivars produce variants in these cases that are not genetically identical to the parent. Tissue culture is now being used as well. The cultivars of this species do not produce viable spores.

Related Plants   Fifty-five cultivars of *N. exaltata* are listed in Hortus Third. The more widely used, aside from 'Bostoniensis,' are: 'Bostoniensis Compacta' —"Dwarf Boston Fern"; 'Fluffy Ruffles'— an upright grower with dark green fronds about 12 inches long; 'Rooseveltii'—similar form to the Boston fern, but with wavy lobed pinnae; 'Verona'— a type with lacy pinnae, giving the plant a feathery appearance; and 'Whitmanii' "Lace Fern"—similar to 'Verona', but with shorter fronds.

N. biserrata 'Furcans.' "Fishtail fern." Similar in appearance to the Boston fern, but with coarser foliage and forked pinnules.

Nephrolepis exaltata 'Fluffy Ruffles'

BOTANICAL NAME: *Opuntia microdasys*
(o-PUN-tee-uh my-kro-DAS-is)

COMMON NAME: Rabbit ears

FAMILY: Cactaceae (Cactus)

ORIGIN: Northern Mexico, Texas

This group of cacti is distinguished by flattened, padlike stem sections that are fleshy and loosely jointed. In the case of *Opuntia microdasys,* these padlike structures stand erect much like rabbit ears, hence the common name.
An important distinction between opuntias and other cacti is the presence of glochids, sharp and irritating bundles of barbed bristles that are easily detached from the areoles. Handle these plants with care! The short-lived flowers are pale yellow. This plant creates an interesting effect among other cacti in dish gardens where the desert effect is desired.

Culture   This plant is especially sensitive to rot, so should be kept quite dry. Plant into a sandy, well-drained mix and provide as much light as possible. Feed infrequently, perhaps once or twice per year associated with active growth.

Typical Problems   Rots are the primary worry, although mites and scales may also appear. Scales may be difficult to spot camouflaged among the areoles.

Propagation   Reproduce from joint cuttings, allowing the sections to dry several days before placing into propagation medium.

Related Plants

O. m. 'Albispina.' "Polka-dot cactus." Similar in form to the species, but with neater pure white, more well-defined tufts on the neatly rowed areoles.

O. vilis. "Little tree opuntia." Club-shaped stem segments on a spreading small plant with brilliant, red flowers.

Water

DRY	NORMAL	EVENLY MOIST

Temperature

COOL	MODERATE	WARM

Light

LOW	BRIGHT INDIRECT	FULL SUN

Humidity

ARID	MODERATE	HUMID

BOTANICAL NAME: *Pandanus veitchii*
(pan-DAN-us VEETCH-ee-eye)

COMMON NAME: Veitch screw pine

FAMILY: Pandanaceae (Screw Pine)

ORIGIN: Polynesia

Named for the spiraled arrangement of the foliage on a central trunk, the screw pine is one of our more durable plants indoors. Its leaves are variegated with white stripes near the margins.
The leathery recurving leaves can reach 3 feet long and 3 inches wide. Its most unusual habit is the development of stiltlike roots that can give the plant the appearance of floating above the soil level. Because of the small spines on the margins and lower midrib, the plant is not comfortable to the touch. The length of the foliage requires that screw pine be given adequate room to grow; in planters when young and in floor planters with age are the best uses of this species.

Culture   The variegated nature of this screw pine requires bright indirect light and adequate water to remain impressive. Pot into a rich potting soil and feed monthly or less depending on growth rate and environmental conditions. Occasional leaf cleaning is necessary to maintain the attractive lustrous surface of the leaves.

Typical Problems   Relatively pest- and disease-free.

Propagation   By offsets that develop at the base of the plants and seed.

Related Plants   None.

Water		
DRY	NORMAL	EVENLY MOIST

Temperature		
COOL	MODERATE	WARM

Light		
LOW	BRIGHT INDIRECT	FULL SUN

Humidity		
ARID	MODERATE	HUMID

BOTANICAL NAME: *Pellionia pulchra*
(pell-lee-ON-ee-uh PULL-kruh)

COMMON NAME: Satin pellionia, rainbow vine

FAMILY: Urticaceae (Nettle)

ORIGIN: Vietnam

A creeper with obliquely oval leaves mottled grayish-green and brown. The purplish stems with the horizontally oriented leaves either creep along the soil surface or hang from a planter, making *Pellionia* excellent as a groundcover in a larger planter or as a hanging plant. The leaves are so close together on the stem that, under ideal cultural conditions, they overlap one another.

Culture *Pellionia* prefers a loamy soil mixture and a high relative humidity. Warmth and moisture, characteristic of Vietnam, are its key cultural requirements. Frequent pinching of the growing tip is necessary for dense form. Fertilize every one or two months and repot about every two years.

Typical Problems Brown leaf edges may indicate low humidity, whereas yellowing of leaves suggests too frequent watering. Spider mites cause a light speckling of the foliage.

Propagation By 3 to 5-inch-long stem cuttings or removing layered (rooted) stems from established plants. Older plants may be divided. Several cuttings should be started in one pot for faster effect.

Related Plants

P. daveauana. "Trailing watermelon begonia." Similar in form to the satin pellionia, but with light green leaves marked by a dark green margin.

Water		
DRY	NORMAL	EVENLY MOIST

Temperature		
COOL	MODERATE	WARM

Light		
LOW	BRIGHT INDIRECT	FULL SUN

Humidity		
ARID	MODERATE	HUMID

BOTANICAL NAME: *Peperomia obtusifolia*

(pep-er-OM-ee-uh ob-tus-ih-FOL-ee-uh)

COMMON NAME: Baby rubber plant, pepper-face

FAMILY: Piperaceae (Pepper)

ORIGIN: Tropical America and southern Florida

This genus of about 1000 small, succulent plants contains some of the more popular and attractive plants available indoors. The most widely known, perhaps, is the baby rubber plant, so named for its waxy, dark green leaves that are almost round and about 2 to 3 inches in diameter. These attractive leaves are held horizontally on stout brown stems. The flowers are borne on single or paired spikes that ascend vertically 6 inches or so. These plants are commonly found as small tabletop specimens or as members of dish gardens and terrariums. The distinctive leaf shapes and markings of peperomias make them an attractive addition to almost any decor.

Culture   The primary requirement of peperomias in general is freedom from wet feet; stem and leaf rots can be devastating. Pot into a sterile, well-drained potting mix and fertilize monthly during active growth. Leggy growth will occur under conditions of poor light. Pruning of overly tall stems can produce leaf and stem cuttings for propagation. Remove any declining foliage right away to prevent rotting.

Typical Problems   Reported pests are mites, mealy bugs, and thrips. Moisture-associated diseases, such as leaf spots and various rots, are the most troublesome aspect, particularly when soil moisture is kept at a high level.

Propagation   Stem cuttings and leaf cuttings are the typical methods.

Related Plants

P. o. 'Albo-marginata.' "Silver-edge peperomia." The gray-green leaves are surrounded with a silvery border.

Water

DRY	NORMAL	EVENLY MOIST

Temperature

COOL	MODERATE	WARM

Light

LOW	BRIGHT INDIRECT	FULL SUN

Humidity

ARID	MODERATE	HUMID

Peperomia obtusifolia 'Variegata'

Peperomia argyreia

Peperomia caperata

P. o. 'Minima.' A compact version of the species.

P. o. 'Variegata.' "Variegated peperomia." Leaves are marked with a gray and green central blotch with irregular, wide ivory-colored margins.

P. argyreia. "Watermelon begonia, watermelon peperomia." The ovate leaves, with petiole attaching within the leaf area, are marked by alternating, radiating stripes of gray and dark green. The 3- to 5-inch-long leaves resemble the end of a watermelon. This plant was formerly known as **P. sandersii.**

P. bicolor. "Silvery velvet peperomia." A ten-inch tall peperomia with broadly elliptical olive gray leaves marked with a broad silver stripe at the midrib, as well as silver margins and lateral veins.

P. caperata. "Emerald-ripple peperomia." A short, dense mat of heart-shaped, dark green leaves that are deeply grooved and held aloft by reddish petioles. One of the more striking peperomias for textural effect. Also available in a variegated form.

P. glabella 'Variegata.' "Variegated wax privet." A small six-inch plant with

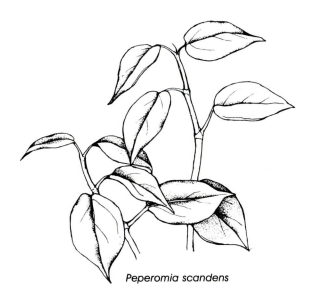

Peperomia scandens

elliptical leaves that are about 2 inches long and broadly margined in creamy white around a light green center.

P. incana. "Felted pepper-face." A durable, heat-loving plant with succulent, gray leaves to 2 inches long.

P. scandens. "Philodendron peperomia." A sparse, trailing peperomia with reddish stems and petioles contrasting with the waxy, rich green leaf color. Similar to but larger than **P. serpens.**

P. verschaffeltii. "Sweetheart peperomia." A dense mass of extended heart-shaped leaves alternately striped with bluish green and silver.

BOTANICAL NAME: *Philodendron scandens oxycardium*
(fill-oh-DEN-dron SCAN-dens ox-ee-CARD-ee-um)

COMMON NAME: Heart-leaf philodendron

FAMILY: Araceae (Arum/Aroids)

ORIGIN: Eastern Mexico

The heart-leaf philodendron is one of the earliest and most widely recognized stalwarts of the indoor plant industry. Like most philodendrons, its juvenile stage leaves (4 to 6 inches long) are smaller than its adult stage leaves (up to 1 foot long). Philodendrons are typically epiphytic plants either climbing by means of aerial roots, as this species does, or "self-heading," developing a cluster of foliage atop a single trunk. Philodendrons offer a wide variety of foliage shape and size; most species have rich green waxy foliage. Philodendrons display excellent durability under poor light conditions and are used as ground covers, totem pole plants, small potted plants, hangers in baskets, or as large self-heading or climbing specimens.

Culture   Leaf size is reduced in poor light, overly wet soil conditions, or in excessively high salts. Pot into a rich, well-drained potting soil and locate in a warm, humid area. Prune back vigorous shoots using the severed material for cuttings if desired.

Typical Problems   The most important concern should be prevention of the various blights, leaf and stem rots, leaf spots, and other organisms that can affect philodendrons, particularly in wet circumstances. Mealy bugs, thrips, mites, and scale insects may also occur.

Propagation   Philodendrons are multiplied by terminal cuttings, air-layering, stem sections with several leaves attached, or fresh seed.

Related Plants

P. bipennifolium. "Horsehead philodendron, fiddle-leaf philodendron." A scandent species with dark olive-green, glossy foliage that is leathery in texture. The leaves can reach an 18-inch length under excellent conditions, but 12 inches is more normal indoors. As the common name implies, the foliage looks like a horse's head, with two hastate basal

Water

DRY	NORMAL	EVENLY MOIST

Temperature

COOL	MODERATE	WARM

Light

LOW	BRIGHT INDIRECT	FULL SUN

Humidity

ARID	MODERATE	HUMID

Philodendron bipennifolium

Philodendron domesticum

lobes forming the ear, two intermediate lobes forming the eye region, and an elongated oblanceolate terminal lobe, half as long as the entire blade, resembling the horse's nose. If lighting is poor, the leaf shape becomes less distinct. On a support, the plant can climb up to 4 to 6 feet.

P. domesticum. "Spade-leaf philodendron, elephant's ear." One of many types with an elongated, triangular leaf shape. In this case, the 2 foot leaves are rich glossy green in contrast to the lighter veins. The wavy leaf margins taper to a point at the apex and form (hastate) lobes at the base. The petioles are as long as the blades. One of the more striking philodendrons in flower, this species produces a 7-inch green spathe on a 6-inch peduncle. Inside, the spathe is cherry red with a green border and encloses a darker red spadix. This scandent plant will climb as high indoors as desired, usually needing pruning eventually to keep it at a particular height. A variegated form is named *P. d.* 'Variegatum,' its leaves irregularly blotched with light green, yellow, and off-white.

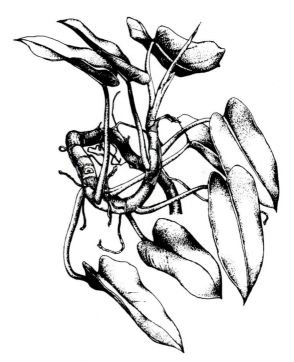

Philodendron × 'Emerald Duke'

P. 'Emerald Duke.' "Emerald duke philodendron." One of the many variants introduced by Mr. Robert McColley of

Bamboo Nurseries in Florida, a well-known foliage plant breeder. This hybrid has large 1-foot cordate leaves with a rich green color and thick glossy texture. It may be grown with or without support.

P. × 'Emerald King.' "Emerald king philodendron." A McColley hybrid similar in growth habit to 'Emerald Duke,' but with more pointed, spade-shaped leaves like *P. domesticum.* Generally trained onto a support, this hybrid is regarded as more disease-resistant than the spade-leaf philodendron.

P. × 'Emerald Queen.' "Emerald queen philodendron." A compact, vigorous climber with elongated, cordate leaves on short petioles. The deep green foliage forms a consistent textural effect due to its uniformity of size. This hybrid is particularly resistant to fungal and bacterial rots.

P. × 'Florida.' "Florida philodendron." An unusual hybrid similar in appearance to the horsehead philodendron, but with more deeply cut sinuses between the five lobes. In this case, the lobes are also lobed at their apex. The foliage color is an attractive dark glossy green above and red-brown below. The petioles are long and slightly warty in texture. Trained on a totem pole or other support, this plant can reach 4 to 6 feet in height. *P.* × "Florida Compacta' is offered as a nonvining or slowly vining form that needs no support.

P. × 'Majesty.' "Majesty philodendron." Another McColley hybrid with 10 to 12 inch, dark reddish green, spade-shaped leaves borne on darker stems and petioles. The aerial roots and leaf sheaths are a lighter shade of red. This hybrid

Philodendron × 'Florida'

can be grown without support, or it can be supported for additional height.

P. × 'Prince Dubonnet.' "Prince dubonnet philodendron." A McColley hybrid that is self-supporting or climbing depending on its training. A slow grower with aerial roots, it has dark greenish red leaves that are spade-shaped, 8 to 12 inches long, and borne on long dark red petioles. In addition, the leaf undersides are also dark red and the plant is quite tolerant of low light levels.

P. × 'Red Duchess.' "Red princess philodendron." A scandent McColley hybrid with large cordate leaves (8 to 10 inches) borne on red petioles. Like 'Prince Dubonnet,' the leaf undersides are red, but this hybrid must have support.

P. × 'Red Emerald.' "Red emerald philodendron." Similar to the preceding cultivars, but with larger, glossy green, cordate to spade-shaped leaves (12 to 15

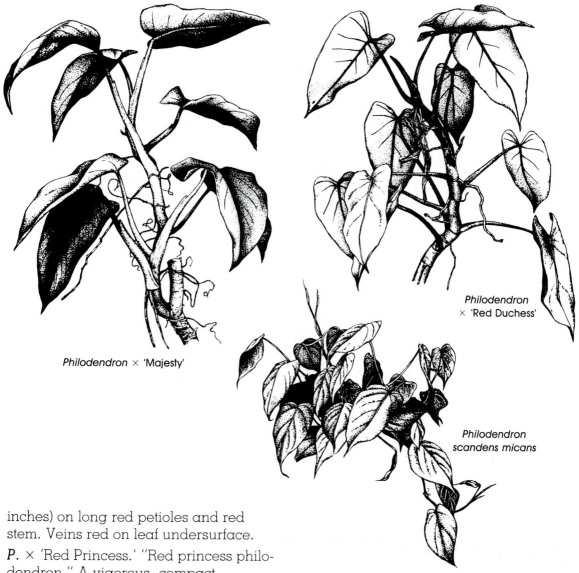

Philodendron × 'Majesty'

Philodendron × 'Red Duchess'

Philodendron scandens micans

inches) on long red petioles and red stem. Veins red on leaf undersurface.

P. × 'Red Princess.' "Red princess philodendron." A vigorous, compact, climbing hybrid needing staking. The mature dark green leaves, first emerging coppery maroon in color, are spade-shaped, 8 to 12 inches long, and supported by red petioles and stem. A Bamboo Nurseries introduction.

P. × 'Royal Queen.' "Royal queen philodendron." A McColley hybrid similar to 'Majesty' but more compact. This self-supporting specimen has glossy, dark green leaves, supported by rich red petioles and stems, that are ovate, red below, and emerge with a bronze color.

P. scandens micans. "Velvet leaf philodendron." A form of the species with the juvenile leaves red below and the upper surface dark green with a silky sheen.

P. selloum. "Tree philodendron, saddle-leaf philodendron." A fast-growing self-header that is an excellent accent plant with bold texture. Reaching an indoor height of four feet and a spread up to six feet, the plant needs the scale of a large space. The deeply cut 18-inch-long leaves resemble those of *Monstera*.
A climbing epiphytic plant by nature, it will produce large aerial roots near the base of the plant. These can be removed if desired in the early stages of development.

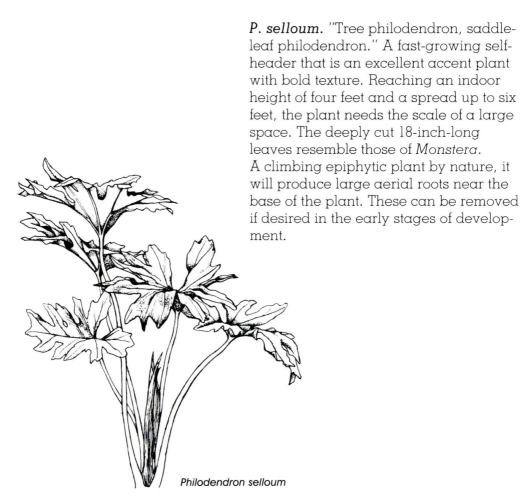

Philodendron selloum

BOTANICAL NAME: *Phoenix roebelenii*
(FEE-nix row-buh-LEEN-ee-eye)

COMMON NAME: Miniature date palm

FAMILY: Palmae (Palm)

ORIGIN: Laos

Among the ancient Babylonians, one of the most severe acts of war was cutting down the enemy's date palms because of their importance for food, fiber, and other necessary products. Growing indoors to a height of up to 12 feet, the miniature date palm is an exceptionally graceful, durable, and popular decorative plant throughout the world.
The pinnately compound leaves, borne atop a trunk roughened with old leaf bases, are recurving and bear about 50 ten-inch-long and ⅜-inch-wide pinnae on either side of the rachis. The pinnae are neatly arranged into rows. This species is useful either as a small pot plant or as a single-stemmed or clustered small tree. Handle with care; thorny barbs are found on the inside leaves.

Culture   Like most palms, ***Phoenix*** is a thirsty species needing constant moisture and frequent fertilization, preferably once a month during its growing season. Bright indirect light is ideal, but it is tolerant of low light conditions, although some problems in appearance may eventually arise in excessive darkness. It prefers warmth, but will fare well in air-conditioning.

Typical Problems   Spider mites are the most likely pest to occur. Dying foliage at the base of the crown is normal; remove these leaves as they deteriorate, but do not prune otherwise.

Propagation   Phoenix palms are grown from seed.

Related Plants   None.

Water

DRY	NORMAL	EVENLY MOIST

Temperature

COOL	MODERATE	WARM

Light

LOW	BRIGHT INDIRECT	FULL SUN

Humidity

ARID	MODERATE	HUMID

BOTANICAL NAME: *Pilea cadierei*
(py-LEE-uh ca-DEER-ee-eye)

COMMON NAME: Aluminum plant

FAMILY: Urticaceae (Nettle)

ORIGIN: Vietnam

These small herbaceous plants are either shrubby or trailing. The aluminum plant grows to about a 10-inch height, has quilted 3-inch-long leaves with silvery bands between the coppery maroon veinal areas, and has opposite leaves on the stem. *Pilea* foliage is minute in some species, a few inches long in others. The variety of color, pattern, and form has made the genus a popular inhabitant of indoor hanging baskets, desk containers, dish gardens, and terrariums. Although a member of the nettle family, *Pilea* causes no pain like its stinging cousins.

Culture   Keep moist, humid, and away from extreme temperature drafts to prevent wilting. Pot into a rich general-purpose soil and provide bright light; otherwise, rank growth will result. Pinch overly vigorous stems back to just above the node.

Typical Problems   Mealy bugs and whiteflies are reported, as well as several types of rots and leaf spots.

Propagation   Stem or tip cuttings root easily, even in water. Creeping species can be divided into new plants.

Related Plants

P. c. 'Minima.' "Miniature aluminum plant." A reduced version of the species.

P. involucrata. "Panamiga, friendship plant." A species with wooly, quilted leaves that are about 1½ inches long and purplish below. The higher the light levels afforded this plant, the more reddish
brown will be the leaves. Small red flower clusters will appear in bright conditions.

P. microphylla. "Artillery plant." Named for the small staminate flowers that puff a cloud of pollen when shaken or mature. This plant is a freely branching, upright, shrubby specimen with small fresh green leaves crowded along the green succulent stem. Grows to a one foot height.

P. 'Moon Valley.' "Moon valley pilea." A dark green, quilted leaf with lighter and toothed margins. One of the best textural focal points for dish gardens, terrariums, and small planters.

Water		
DRY	NORMAL	EVENLY MOIST

Temperature		
COOL	MODERATE	WARM

Light		
LOW	BRIGHT INDIRECT	FULL SUN

Humidity		
ARID	MODERATE	HUMID

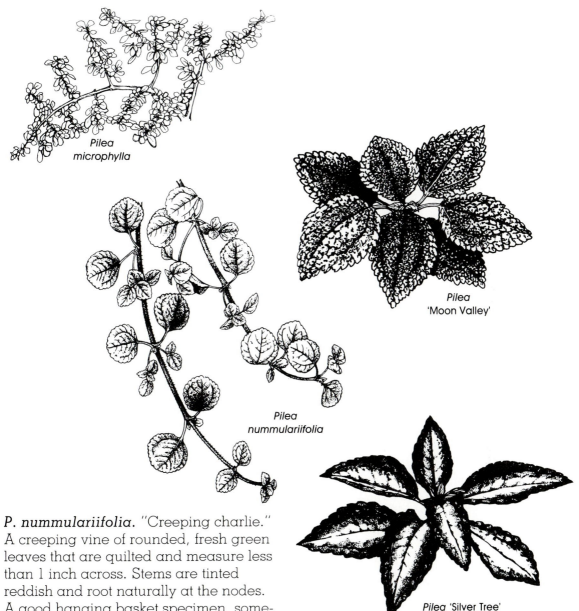

*Pilea
microphylla*

*Pilea
'Moon Valley'*

*Pilea
nummulariifolia*

Pilea 'Silver Tree'

P. nummulariifolia. "Creeping charlie."
A creeping vine of rounded, fresh green
leaves that are quilted and measure less
than 1 inch across. Stems are tinted
reddish and root naturally at the nodes.
A good hanging basket specimen, somewhat like **Plectranthus** in appearance,
but smaller.

P. repens. "Black-leaf panamiga."
With dark, coppery brown foliage in
bright light, **Pilea repens** is a low,
spreading plant with brown stems and
ovate, quilted leaves just over an inch
long.

P. 'Silver Tree.' "Silver tree panamiga."
A branching herb with quilted bronzy
green leaves marked with a silver band
along the midrib. A good small plant for
dish gardens, terrariums, and small
containers.

BOTANICAL NAME: *Pittosporum tobira*
(pit-oh-SPORE-um toe-BEER-uh)

COMMON NAME: Japanese pittosporum, Australian laurel, mock orange

FAMILY: Pittosporaceae (Pittosporum)

ORIGIN: China, Japan

An excellent landscape and seaside plant in the southern United States, Japanese pittosporum has obovate, dark lustrous green leaves arranged in pseudowhorls at the ends of the twigs. During the spring under good conditions, small ivory-white flowers appear at the branch tips and produce an excellent fragrance (hence the mock orange common name). The plant can reach a 10- to 15-foot height outside, but usually remains at 2 to 3 feet as a typical house plant. As a durable, attractive specimen and a plant that can endure chills and cold drafts, pittosporum is one of the best.

Culture If needed for shaping, pruning should occur in late winter before new growth occurs. Lower leaves drop under poor light or if top growth is too dense. Use a loam soil, fertilize every three to four months, and repot only when root-binding occurs.

Typical Problems Scale insects, aphids, and mealy bugs will infest occasionally, and leaf spots may develop, especially when the foliage is moistened frequently. Leaf wilt and marginal browning may indicate excessive soluble salts.

Propagation Seeds or cuttings taken from newly matured growth in midsummer. Air-layering can be practiced at any time of the year.

Related Plants

P. t. 'Variegata.' "Variegated mock-orange." Leaves grayish green and unevenly margined with creamy-white. This cultivar prefers a more filtered light than the species.

P. t. 'Wheeleri.' "Dwarf pittosporum." Smaller size and more compact growth habit than the species.

Water		
DRY	NORMAL	EVENLY MOIST

Temperature		
COOL	MODERATE	WARM

Light		
LOW	BRIGHT INDIRECT	FULL SUN

Humidity		
ARID	MODERATE	HUMID

BOTANICAL NAME: *Platycereum bifurcatum*
(plat-ih-SIR-ee-um by-fur-CA-tum)

COMMON NAME: Common staghorn fern

FAMILY: Polypodiaceae (Polypody)

ORIGIN: Australia and Polynesia

The staghorn fern is one of the more unusual ferns in that it has two entirely different types of fronds. One is somewhat like a cabbage leaf: rounded, fleshy or parchmentlike, and sterile. These enclose the root system and attach this epiphytic fern to its tree or support. The fertile fronds resemble antlers and may reach a length of 3 feet. Their tendency to weep and bear brown spore cases makes them even more interesting. Staghorn ferns are usually grown attached to the bark side of a slab or in baskets of sphagnum moss and osmunda. One of the more unusual and dramatic indoor species, staghorn ferns are well worth the extra effort their unusual culture requires.

Culture   Keep these plants evenly moist by dunking their root system and container into water, periodically including liquid fertilizer. Like many ferns, they prefer cool night temperatures down into the 50s (F) for best development. Withhold fertilization and reduce watering frequency during the winter months. It is critical that the potting medium be extremely well-drained and humus.

Typical Problems   The fern scale is the most likely pest to show up on this species, although mealy bugs are a possibility as well. This species is found naturally in various climates, in some cases tolerating cold as low as 15°F. Consequently, it will tolerate coolness and drafts, as well as neglect, better than many ferns.

Propagation   Most easily reproduced by separating the suckers that arise at the tips of roots once they are large enough to handle. This and other species have been successfully tissue cultured.

Related Plants

P. b. 'Netherlands.' "Regina Wilhelmia staghorn." A Dutch cultivar with shorter and more lobing fertile fronds that spread in all directions and are bright green and velvety.

Water

DRY	NORMAL	EVENLY MOIST

Temperature

COOL	MODERATE	WARM

Light

LOW	BRIGHT INDIRECT	FULL SUN

Humidity

ARID	MODERATE	HUMID

BOTANICAL NAME: *Plectranthus australis*
(plek-TRAN-thus aus-TRA-lis)

COMMON NAME: Swedish ivy

FAMILY: Labiatae (Mint)

ORIGIN: Southeastern Australia

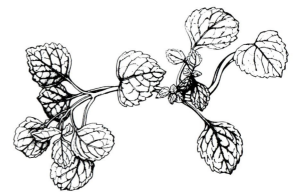

A good confidence builder for novices, Swedish ivy quickly and easily grows into a substantial specimen with a minimum of care. This member of the mint family, as evidenced by its square stems and opposite leaves, forms a mass of rounded, glossy green, bluntly toothed leaves. In sufficient light, its white flower clusters ascend above the foliage, creating a graceful effect. Swedish ivy is an excellent hanging basket plant where its graceful habit will be best shown to advantage. It is also good as a dish garden or terrarium plant, but grows so quickly that it soon finds itself in cramped quarters. Although the leaves and stems are green, pinching (which is necessary for dense growth) leaves one's fingers with an orange, easily removed stain.

Culture *Plectranthus* grows best in bright indirect light protected from the direct rays of the sun. Pot into a rich potting soil and fertilize according to how fast growth is desired. This plant root binds quickly because of its rapid growth and will need repotting occasionally. Also, it will eventually become unattractive as its stems become more woody. Keep new plants coming by propagating several cuttings to a pot as mature plants begin to decline.

Typical Problems The only pest problems are occasional mealy bugs, nematodes, and whiteflies.

Propagation Easily started from tip or stem cuttings, leaf-bud cuttings, and seeds.

Related Plants

P. coleoides 'Marginatus.' "Candle plant." Resembling its close relative coleus, the candle plant has irregular, creamy margins surrounding a matte green center.

P. oertendahlii. "Brazilian coleus, prostrate coleus." A low, freely branching plant with reddish stems and green leaves with silvery veins. The leaf margins, the underside of older leaves, and the petioles are purplish. The light pink flower clusters rise above the foliage.

Water

DRY	NORMAL	EVENLY MOIST

Temperature

COOL	MODERATE	WARM

Light

LOW	BRIGHT INDIRECT	FULL SUN

Humidity

ARID	MODERATE	HUMID

BOTANICAL NAME: *Podocarpus macrophyllus*
(poe-doe-CAR-pus mack-row-FILL-us)

COMMON NAME: Southern yew, Japanese yew, Buddhist pine

FAMILY: Podocarpaceae (Podocarpus)

ORIGIN: China

Although reaching a 40-foot height in China, southern yew normally achieves no more than 4 to 5 feet indoors since it is easily pruned. It is a dense, coniferous tree with dark green linear needles and fine texture. A tough plant, it endures cold drafts after new growth matures, as well as years of life in the same pot. If conditions are good, *Podocarpus* will last indefinitely and can be sheared into numerous configurations.

Culture   Pruning should be done before new growth starts in the spring. Care should be taken to avoid overwatering. Too little light will cause lower needles to drop. A loamy soil is appropriate and fertilization should occur every three to six months. Repot only when rootbinding is apparent.

Typical Problems   Scale insects, if present, are usually brownish clusters on the needles and stems. With enough infestation, they may cause mottling of the foliage.

Propagation   By seeds or stem cuttings taken in the fall.

Related Plants

P. m. maki. The branches of this variety are more upright than the species, and the plant form is more dense and compact. The needles are smaller than those of *P. macrophyllus.*

Water		
DRY	NORMAL	EVENLY MOIST

Temperature		
COOL	MODERATE	WARM

Light		
LOW	BRIGHT INDIRECT	FULL SUN

Humidity		
ARID	MODERATE	HUMID

BOTANICAL NAME: *Polyscias fruticosa*
(poe-LISS-ee-us frew-tih-KOE-suh)

COMMON NAME: Ming aralia, Chinese aralia, parsley aralia

FAMILY: Araliaceae (Aralia or Ginseng)

ORIGIN: India to Polynesia

As the generic name indicates ("polys," many; "skias," shade), the ming aralia has many feathery compound leaves that resemble the texture of parsley. The plant usually grows into a 5- to 6-foot specimen with contorted multiple trunks. The fine texture of the foliage is quite attractive and useful among the other foliage plants with bolder lines. This is one of the better choices for use in oriental decors and may even serve as a bonsai specimen. Select plants from a reputable dealer who has provided care to acclimate the plants to indoor use, or leaf drop may occur on moving the plant to a darker, drier home.

Culture   In keeping this plant evenly moist, water liberally when watering to avoid buildup of soluble salts that may cause leaf drop. Also, avoid cold drafts that may have the same effect. Use a loamy, well-drained soil high in organic matter, fertilizing every three to four months. Repot in spring as overcrowding dictates.

Typical Problems   This is one of the most sensitive plants to air pollution, dropping its leaves in such conditions. Keep it

away from ripening fruit, because the resulting ethylene gas is toxic to this plant. Browning of leaf edges and margins implies low humidity, whereas a white or yellow speckling may indicate spider mites. Scale insects may also attack the stems and leaf undersurfaces.

Propagation   Most commonly by 4- to 6-inch stem cuttings taken from the top of the plant or from the suckers or side shoots that arise at the base of the plant. Air-layering may also be used, as well as cane cuttings or root sections.

Water

DRY	NORMAL	EVENLY MOIST

Temperature

COOL	MODERATE	WARM

Light

LOW	BRIGHT INDIRECT	FULL SUN

Humidity

ARID	MODERATE	HUMID

Related Plants

P. balfouriana. "Balfour aralia." A bushy, 3-foot plant with trifoliate leaves and 2 to 4 inch, orbicular, cordate-based, and crenate leaflets. Requires the same culture as *P. fruticosa.*

P. b. 'Marginata.' "Variegated balfour aralia." Gray-green leaves with a white margin.

P. b. 'Pennockii.' "Pennock's aralia." Cupped, light green leaves edged with dark green.

P. f. 'Elegans.' Compact form of the ming aralia with dense, dark green foliage.

BOTANICAL NAME: *Pteris ensiformis 'Victoriae'*
(TER-is en-sih-FORM-is vik-TOR-ee-uh)

COMMON NAME: Victoria brake fern, silver-leaf fern

FAMILY: Polypodiaceae (Polypody)

ORIGIN: Eastern Asia, Malay Peninsula, and Australia

This group of ferns, also known as table ferns, are typically short with interesting frond shapes and colors arising from a short rhizome. Although these ferns are small, being quite useful for dish gardens and terrariums, they are robust and can endure some neglect. Drought, if allowed to progress too far, will result in dead foliage. The Victoria brake fern is graced with bipinnately compound fronds. The coarsely lobed pinnae are etched with prominent white markings.

Culture   These ferns are not particularly fussy about soils, but they perform best with well-drained, evenly moist soils and bright indirect light. Fertilize during active growth monthly, but reduce watering frequency, temperature, and fertilization during the winter months. Repot occasionally to maintain plant vigor.

Typical Problems   Foliar, leaf, and bud nematodes and scale insects are the most likely pests, although mealy bugs and whiteflies may appear as well. Leaf spot and blights are the most likely diseases, particularly under overly humid or wet conditions.

Propagation   Propagated by spores and division of mature plants.

Related Plants

P. cretica. "Cretian brake fern." A species of brake ferns with more linear pinnae than the Victoria brake fern. A number of cultivars are on the market, including types with white markings, lacy or divided pinnae, or larger size.

Water

DRY	NORMAL	EVENLY MOIST

Temperature

COOL	MODERATE	WARM

Light

LOW	BRIGHT INDIRECT	FULL SUN

Humidity

ARID	MODERATE	HUMID

BOTANICAL NAME: *Rhapis excelsa*
(RA-pis ex-SELL-sa)

COMMON NAME: Bamboo palm, slender lady palm

FAMILY: Palmae (Palm)

ORIGIN: Southern China; introduced into cultivation from Japan

This slow-growing and durable palm will reach an ultimate height of 5 to 10 feet indoors. Its leaves are dark glossy green, divided into three to ten segments that are palmately arranged and up to a foot long. Each segment is terminated abruptly with a shallow, oblique tooth at the apex. The segments are up to 3 inches wide and cross-wrinkled. The bamboo palm is used in the major oriental countries as a durable floor specimen. The bold leaves and linear texture make it an ideal component of either a contemporary or oriental decor.

Culture   This palm has a tempermental reputation, probably because it needs constant moisture, but should be kept on the dry side until the root system is well-established in a container. Feed it every month or two during active growth; less during winter. It prefers cool nights down into the 50s (F), but will tolerate warmer situations. Pot into a humus soil that is well-drained. The form will suffer under extremely low light.

Typical Problems   Mites, mealy bugs, and scale insects may appear, particularly in dry atmospheric conditions.

Propagation   Multiply by seed or dividing mature clumps.

Related Plants

R. e. 'Variegata.' "Variegated lady palm." The leaf segments are banded longitudinally with alternating green and ivory stripes.

A number of other cultivars have been developed for this species.

Water		
DRY	NORMAL	EVENLY MOIST

Temperature		
COOL	MODERATE	WARM

Light		
LOW	BRIGHT INDIRECT	FULL SUN

Humidity		
ARID	MODERATE	HUMID

BOTANICAL NAME: *Rhoeo spathacea*
(REE-oh spa-THAY-see-uh)

COMMON NAME: Purple-leaved spiderwort, Moses in the cradle

FAMILY: Commelinaceae (Spiderwort)

ORIGIN: West Indies, Mexico, and Guatemala

Probably no other indoor plant carries as many common names as this species, the only one in the **Rhoeo** genus. Most of these names refer to the small white flowers enclosed in boat-shaped bracts that arise in the leaf axils, creating an unusual if not conspicuous effect. Arranged in a rosette fashion, the foot long leaves are rigid, fleshy, waxy, and lanceolate, reaching a width of up to 3 inches at their widest point. The leaf color is a dark metallic green above and rich glossy purple below. Tolerant of most home conditions, this plant is an excellent table-top container or hanging plant in which its flowers can be viewed at close range.

Culture   Pot *Rhoeo* into a standard potting soil, keeping it constantly moist during active growth. It performs best and reaches its full potential of foliage color under sunny conditions. Keep the night temperatures above 55°F in order to maintain active growth. Does not require pruning; fertilize four or five times per year, primarily during the summer months.

Typical Problems   Most typically stem rot, leaf spot, and anthracnose are the most likely disease candidates, particularly under excessive humidity or moisture conditions. Mealy bugs and mites may also infest this plant.

Propagation   Start new plants from seed or the offsets that arise from the base of the plant.

Related Plants

R. s. 'Variegata.' Equivalent to the species in form, but with leaves longitudinally striped with light yellow on the upper side.

Water

DRY	NORMAL	EVENLY MOIST

Temperature

COOL	MODERATE	WARM

Light

LOW	BRIGHT INDIRECT	FULL SUN

Humidity

ARID	MODERATE	HUMID

BOTANICAL NAME: *Saintpaulia ionantha*
(saint-PAUL-ee-uh eye-on-AN-tha)

COMMON NAME: Common African violet

FAMILY: Gesneriaceae (Gesneria)

ORIGIN: Coastal Tanzania

These east African plants are probably the most popular flowering indoor plants in the United States. First discovered in 1892, the common African violet has now led to thousands of variants and cultivars through the years. The intense interest in hybridizing and finding new sports has led to double-flowered, bicolored, and variegated forms. Though the flowers are typically violet to blue, many additional shades are now available. African violet leaves are dark green and cordate to round and are borne horizontally, radiating from a central crown. With adequate light, most cultivars will flower year-round.

Culture   Bright indirect light is required for flowering and proper leaf development. Too little light will cause petiole elongation, small dark leaves, and up-turned leaves. Too much light will bleach the leaves and burn the flowers. Pot into a well-drained soil mix or one commercially available for African violets. Water with tepid water, only wetting the leaves when washing is desired. Cold water will damage the leaf surfaces. Use a brush to remove dust from the fuzzy leaf surfaces. Fertilize once or twice per month during flowering.

Typical Problems   Cyclamen mites that curl the young foliage, aphids, and mealy bugs are the most probable pests. African violets are also susceptible to crown rot and *Botrytis* blight. Avoid salt buildups in the soil; leaves and petioles are damaged by contact with soil or pot surfaces high in salt concentrations.

Propagation   African violets are easily propagated with leaf-petiole cuttings. When placed into the proper medium, the petiole base will give rise to a small cluster of new plants. Older plants may be propagated by division of the crowns.

Related Plants   The African Violet Society of America, Inc. has registered thousands of cultivars.

Water

DRY	NORMAL	EVENLY MOIST

Temperature

COOL	MODERATE	WARM

Light

LOW	BRIGHT INDIRECT	FULL SUN

Humidity

ARID	MODERATE	HUMID

BOTANICAL NAME: *Sansevieria trifasciata*
(san-seh-VEER-ee-uh try-fas-see-AH-tuh)

COMMON NAME: Snake plant, mother-in-law tongue

FAMILY: Liliaceae (Lily)

ORIGIN: Southern Africa

This and other species of **Sansevieria** are among the most durable foliage plants in the world; hence, their prolific use. Growing as a rosette of long, upright, straplike leaves, the snake plant is the most commonly grown species of the group. Like other species, it spreads by short rhizomes that send up more rosettes. The inflorescence, a raceme of greenish white flowers, is moderately attractive and fragrant. These plants are excellent for situations that normally would stress other plants. They are oblivious to poor light, improper watering, lack of humidity, and blasts of hot or cold air.

Culture   The most common cultural requirement is repotting every three years or so as the plants become overcrowded. Watering should be reduced during the winter months. Fertilize every two or three months during active growth. Soil should be loamy with organic matter incorporated.

Typical Problems   Overwatering may cause leaf yellowing. Little else can phase this plant.

Propagation   Two methods predominate: (1) leaf sections about 3 inches long, severed with a V-cut to indicate proper polarity and (2) division of the rhizomes into individual rosettes of foliage. *S. t. laurentii* should be propagated by division since leaf sections yield green offspring.

Water

DRY	NORMAL	EVENLY MOIST

Temperature

COOL	MODERATE	WARM

Light

LOW	BRIGHT INDIRECT	FULL SUN

Humidity

ARID	MODERATE	HUMID

Related Plants   There are several cultivars and varieties that are commercially important.

S. t. 'Hahnii.' "Bird's nest sansevieria." With short, four-inch long leaves in a spreading rosette.

S. t. 'Golden Hahnii.' "Golden bird's nest." Like 'Hahnii,' but with cream-colored or yellow bands along the margin.

S. t. laurentii. "Variegated snake plant." Form like the species, but with cream or yellow band on the margin.

Other species, such as *cylindrica, ehrenbergii,* and *suffruticosa,* offer varying forms and leaf shapes, but the same cultural toughness.

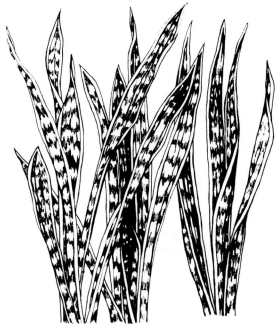

Sansevieria trifasciata laurentii

Sansevieria trifasciata 'Hahnii'

BOTANICAL NAME: *Saxifraga stolonifera*

(sacks-uh-FRAY-ga stow-lun-IFF-er-uh)

COMMON NAME: Strawberry geranium, strawberry begonia, creeping sailor, mother of thousands

FAMILY: Saxifragaceae (Saxifrage)

ORIGIN: East Asia

The name *stolonifera* means "stolon-bearing," in reference to the numerous stems that trail out of older plants and have young plantlets at their tips. An obsolete name still in common use is **S. sarmentosa,** meaning "runner-bearing," which implies incorrectly that these specialized stems are runners rather than stolons. The trailing stolons, as well as the showy, erect panicles of white flowers, make the plant excellent for hanging baskets. The leaves are 4-inch discs and are dark green above with silvery marking, and red below. Incidentally, it is neither a geranium nor a begonia, but is so-named because of the resemblance only.

Culture Easy to grow, even outside in the southeastern United States. Avoid overwatering that can cause root rot to occur. A loamy soil mixture with good drainage is essential. Fertilize every two or three months and repot every year or when plants become crowded in the container. One of the few plants that does not need pinching.

Typical Problems Leaf yellowing may indicate too frequent watering. Wetting the foliage may cause *Botrytis* blight on the growing tips. Spider mites, white flies, and mealy bugs will occasionally infest this plant.

Water

DRY	NORMAL	EVENLY MOIST

Temperature

COOL	MODERATE	WARM

Light

LOW	BRIGHT INDIRECT	FULL SUN

Humidity

ARID	MODERATE	HUMID

Propagation Started by severing plantlets at the end of stolons and propagating them, layering in which the plantlets are placed in medium and propagated prior to severance from the parent plant, and division of crowded, overgrown plants.

Related Plants

S. s. 'Tricolor.' "Magic-carpet saxifraga." Leaves variegated with dark green and gray-green, creamy white, and flushed with rose.

S. cotyledon. "Jungfrau saxifrage." Leaves pubescent and spatulate, forming 4-inch rosettes. White flowers fragrant and very conspicuous, borne in 1- to 2-foot upright panicles.

Saxifraga stolonifera 'Tricolor'

BOTANICAL NAME: *Schlumbergera bridgesii*
(schlum-BER-jer-uh BRIH-jes-ee-eye)

COMMON NAME: Christmas cactus

FAMILY: Cactaceae (Cactus)

ORIGIN: Brazil

This epiphytic cactus is distinguished by its flattened, green, and branching stems that bear no leaves; the stems are the food-producing organs for the plant. Spreading in all directions and arching gracefully, the foot long and one-half to one inch wide stems are divided into 2-inch long joints with two or three crenations per joint margin. More conspicuous, though, are the bright cerise flowers that are up to 3 inches long and arise at the ends of the stems. These are usually borne around Christmas, their development being influenced by temperature and day length (see Chapter Three). These plants make excellent moderately sized container or hanging basket plants.

Culture The Christmas cactus should be given two rest periods with lower temperatures and less moisture, one for

Water		
DRY	NORMAL	EVENLY MOIST

Temperature		
COOL	MODERATE	WARM

Light		
LOW	BRIGHT INDIRECT	FULL SUN

Humidity		
ARID	MODERATE	HUMID

two months after flowering and the other in early fall to prepare for flowering. Direct sunlight will yellow the leaves, whereas dark conditions during active growth will create rankness of growth. Pot into a humus soil with excellent drainage and keep moist during active growth, dry during rests. Fertilize every two to four weeks during active growth, very little during rest periods. These plants flower best when the root system is pot-bound; repot after several years if flowering reduction is noticed.

Typical Problems   Various rots will destroy the plant tissue, particularly if watering is heavy during rest periods. Mites, scale insects, and mealy bugs are also occasionally found on this species.

Propagation   Typically reproduced by cuttings containing three to five joints, stuck into a well-drained propagation medium. This plant is often grafted onto *Pereskia,* the leaf cactus, resulting in a treelike form.

Related Plants

S. truncata. "Crab cactus, Thanksgiving cactus." A fall-flowering species similar in form to **S. bridgesii,** but with two or four sharp serrations on each joint margin. Flowers are similar to those of **S. bridgesii.**

BOTANICAL NAME: *Scindapsus pictus* 'Argyraeus'
(skin-DAP-sus PIK-tus ar-gy-REE-us)

COMMON NAME: Satin pothos

FAMILY: Araceae (Arum/Aroids)

ORIGIN: Malay Archipelago and Indonesia

The satin pothos is from a genus of plants that climb high, attaching themselves for support by aerial rootlets. Their leaf size usually gets bigger and their shape more interesting as the adult phase of growth is reached. Thought by some authorities to be a juvenile form of the species, the satin pothos has 3 inch long, cordate leaves that are a satiny blue-green with margins and prominent spots of silver. This plant is suitable for use as either a hanging basket specimen or trained onto a totem pole; small plants are also used in dish gardens and terrariums.

Culture   Satin pothos does its best in warm, humid conditions, but will tolerate the dry environment of the typical home relatively well. Pot into a humus soil, keeping it barely moist at all times. Fertilize three or four times per year and pinch back the stem tips frequently to encourage branching and more compact growth.

Typical Problems   Bothered most by water-related diseases, particularly leaf spots and rots. Mealy bugs and scale insects are the two most frequently reported pests.

Propagation   The satin pothos is normally propagated by either single or double eye cuttings that can be conveniently made during pruning operations. Since this plant may decline in vigor with age, keeping new plants developing is a beneficial practice.

Related Plants   See *Epipremnum aureum* that, until recently, was classified as a species of this genus.

Water		
DRY	NORMAL	EVENLY MOIST

Temperature		
COOL	MODERATE	WARM

Light		
LOW	BRIGHT INDIRECT	FULL SUN

Humidity		
ARID	MODERATE	HUMID

BOTANICAL NAME: *Sedum morganianum*
(SEE-dum mor-gan-ee-A-num)

COMMON NAME: Burro's tail, donkey's tail, lamb's tail

FAMILY: Crassulaceae (Orpine, Stonecrop)

ORIGIN: Mexico

As one might expect from the name, burro's tail has trailing stems closely packed with succulent, football-shaped leaves that are covered with a bluish material called bloom. Culturally, the plant is durable, but its placement must be away from traffic or other potential disturbances because the leaves drop from the stem with the greatest of ease. The flowers, rose-pink terminal clusters, are rarely produced in lower light conditions.

Culture   Pot the burro's tail in a loamy soil with very good drainage. Fertilize only two or three times per year during active growth. Reduce watering to the subsistence level during rest periods. Repot only when absolutely necessary.

Typical Problems   Underwatering will cause leaves to shrivel and drop, whereas overwatering will generate root rot problems.

Propagation   Most commonly by leaves partially stuck, base down, into a propagation medium. Stem cutting will root, but is difficult to prepare and pot without knocking off numerous leaves.

Related Plants   About 600 species are known; only several receive much indoor use.

S. divergens. "Old man's bones." A cascading species with green, clublike leaves that, like burro's tail, fall with the slightest disturbance. Hence, the common name.

S. pachyphyllum. "Many fingers, jelly beans." A weak, shrubby succulent with densely arranged, club-shaped, bluish leaves that curve upward.

S. sieboldii. "October daphne, October plant." A creeping plant with unbranched stems and whorls of three round, 1 inch, fleshy leaves.

Water		
DRY	NORMAL	EVENLY MOIST

Temperature		
COOL	MODERATE	WARM

Light		
LOW	BRIGHT INDIRECT	FULL SUN

Humidity		
ARID	MODERATE	HUMID

BOTANICAL NAME: *Senecio mikanioides*
(sin-EE-she-oh mih-can-ee-OY-dees)

COMMON NAME: German ivy, parlor ivy

FAMILY: Compositae (Composite or Sunflower)

ORIGIN: South Africa

German ivy is easily confused with English ivy, except for the brighter green color and the softer, fleshier leaves that are five- to seven-lobed. The vining growth habit allows the plant to be grown as a trailing hanging basket specimen or in an upright trellised fashion. In good light conditions, clusters of yellow, disc-shaped inflorescences may appear. The parlor ivy designation refers to its popularity in times past when parlors (formal sitting rooms) were prevalent in homes.

Culture   Pinching the plant frequently, especially in reduced light, is the most necessary task. Due to the thinner leaves, it will not stand infrequent watering as well as string of beads (**S. rowleyanus**). Pot in a loamy, well-drained mix and fertilize every one to two months during active growth. Repot about every two years.

Typical Problems   Mealy bugs may infest the leaf axils, and aphids may appear, especially on the tender new growth.

Propagation   Very easy to start by stem cuttings placed in water or another propagation medium. Leaf-bud cuttings and seeds may also be used.

Water

DRY	NORMAL	EVENLY MOIST

Temperature

COOL	MODERATE	WARM

Light

LOW	BRIGHT INDIRECT	FULL SUN

Humidity

ARID	MODERATE	HUMID

Related Plants

S. _macroglossus_ 'Variegatum,' "Variegated wax vine." Similar in growth habit to German ivy, but with cordate-based triangular leaves that are medium green bordered with cream.

S. × _hybridus_. "Cineraria." The popular and colorful florist plant. A compact plant that covers itself with daisylike flowers in a wide range of rich colors.

S. _rowleyanus_. "String of beads, bead vine." Leaves are bright green and round like pearls, each with a narrow translucent line. Stems hang two feet or more.

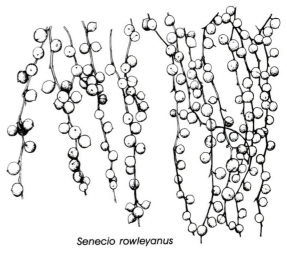

Senecio rowleyanus

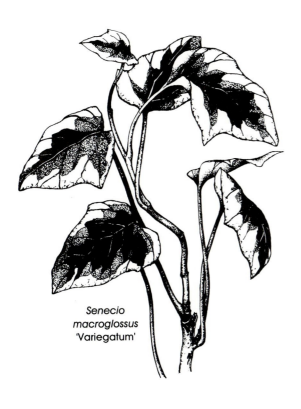

Senecio macroglossus 'Variegatum'

BOTANICAL NAME: *Soleirolia soleirolii*
(SOE-lih-ROLL-ee-uh soe-lih-ROLL-ee-eye)

COMMON NAME: Baby's tears

FAMILY: Urticaceae (Nettle)

ORIGIN: Western Mediterranean Islands and Italy

This creeping, matlike plant is generally used as either a greenhouse or terrarium ground-cover because of its high humidity requirement, although with care and proper placement, it may do well in the home. The leaves are round and quite small (¼ inch across) and the ¼ inch flowers, appearing only in conditions of bright light, are greenish and rather inconspicuous. If given the chance, it will trail attractively from an elevated container. Although baby's tears is the most common name, there are many others, including peace in the home, and mind your own business!

Culture   The most critical factors are sufficient water and humidity; without these the plant quickly wilts, browns, and dies. Fertilize every two to four months and pinch to thicken the foliage mass and keep the plant in bounds. Use a humus soil mix that is very high in organic matter.

Typical Problems   Browning of the leaf tips and margins indicates too low humidity.

Propagation   Quickly started by severing and potting some of the lower stems that have rooted on contact with the soil, or by rooting stem cuttings in water or another medium. Larger plants may also be divided.

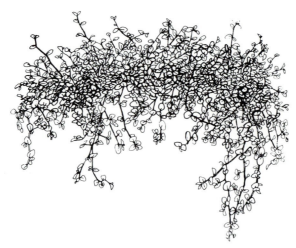

Water		
DRY	NORMAL	EVENLY MOIST

Temperature		
COOL	MODERATE	WARM

Light		
LOW	BRIGHT INDIRECT	FULL SUN

Humidity		
ARID	MODERATE	HUMID

BOTANICAL NAME: *Spathiphyllum* 'Clevelandii'
(spa-thih-FILL-um klev-LAND-ee-eye)

COMMON NAME: White anthurium, peace lily

FAMILY: Araceae (Arum/Aroids)

ORIGIN: Tropical America

Spathiphyllum is a heavily used genus in commercial interiorscaping; this group can not only tolerate low humidity and poor lighting, but will continue to flower, as well. The cultivar 'Clevelandii' is a form that flowers freely. The leaves are 1 foot long, over 2 inches wide, and elliptical. The glossy dark green leaves arise on long petioles from a very short stem at the face of the plant. The white flowers, 4- to 6-inch spath and white spadix, are borne several inches above the foliage. With proper care, these plants will become quite dense since they keep sending up new leaves from the base. Plants of this genus are used both as small container plants when young and as floor specimens as they mature to larger sizes. Because of their rich green color, consistent texture, and low height, this plant is often used commercially as "facing" plants in front of groupings of larger specimens.

Culture "Spaths" are among the best indoor plants available; they tolerate very low levels of light with minimal detriment to the foliage quality and the flower proliferation. Although they prefer warm temperatures, they stand air-conditioning well. Pot into a general, well-drained soil and keep constantly moist. The only required pruning is the removal of dying or damaged leaves and spent flowers. Keep night temperatures above 55°F to maintain growth.

Typical Problems Not typically bothered by pests, but mites, mealy bugs, and scale insects are a possibility. Under heavy watering or humid conditions, leaf spots, blight, and anthracnose are apt to occur.

Propagation Multiply by dividing clumps or germinating seed. Tissue culture is used commercially as well.

Water		
DRY	NORMAL	EVENLY MOIST

Temperature		
COOL	MODERATE	WARM

Light		
LOW	BRIGHT INDIRECT	FULL SUN

Humidity		
ARID	MODERATE	HUMID

Related Plants

S. cannifolium. A slightly taller species than 'Clevelandii,' but with leaves somewhat shorter. The thick, leathery leaves are dark green and oblanceolate.

S. floribundum. "Snowflower." A small one foot tall compact plant with flat finished, satiny leaves that are leathery and broadly elliptical. Noted for its small but prolific flowers with a 2- to 3-inch white spathe.

S. 'Mauna Loa.' "Mauna loa peace lily." This popular and easy-to-grow specimen is thought to be a hybrid between **S. floribundum** and a Hawaiian hybrid. Like **S. floribundum,** it is floriferous, but with white spathe up to 5 inches long. It needs, however, bright indirect light to flower.

S. 'Wallisii.' This species, which is not listed in **Hortus Third,** is similar to 'Clevelandii,' but smaller overall.

Spathiphyllum 'Mauna Loa'

BOTANICAL NAME: *Streptocarpus saxorum*
(strep-toe-KAR-pus sax-OR-um)

COMMON NAME: False African violet

FAMILY: Gesneriaceae (Gesneria)

ORIGIN: East Africa

The false African violet closely resembles **Saintpaulia** but has characteristics uniquely its own. The growth habit is a prostrate one with the branches upright at first, but later spreading and hanging. The short, 1-inch-long leaves are succulent, bright green, and pubescent. The delicate violetlike flowers extend above the foliage, generating a conspicuous display of white and pale lilac. Arising from the leaf axils, the flowers extend over several months under sufficient light. Best used as a small container plant when young and as a hanging basket specimen with age.

Culture The false African violet requires bright indirect light, high humidity, and a humus, well-drained soil to perform at its best. Fertilize monthly during active growth and pinch when young to encourage compact growth.

Typical Problems Occasional problems with whiteflies, aphids, and mealy bugs.

Propagation Easily started from seed, stem cuttings, leaf cuttings, and division of larger plants.

Related Plants

S. × *hybridus.* "Hybrid cape primrose." A hybrid group with several parents that produce elongated, quilted leaves and prolific flowers ranging in color from white to orchid, blue, and purple.

Water

DRY	NORMAL	EVENLY MOIST

Temperature

COOL	MODERATE	WARM

Light

LOW	BRIGHT INDIRECT	FULL SUN

Humidity

ARID	MODERATE	HUMID

BOTANICAL NAME: *Syngonium podophyllum*
(sin-GON-ee-um po-do-FILL-um)

COMMON NAME: Nephthytis, arrowhead vine

FAMILY: Araceae (Arum/Aroids)

ORIGIN: Mexico to Panama

These easy-to-grow climbing vines are typically grown indoors as juvenile plants. During this growth stage, the foliage is arrow-shaped and attractively variegated; in adulthood, the leaves become green and palmately divided. In general, these plants are characterized by leaves on long petioles, aerial roots forming at the joints and milky sap. During juvenile growth, stem extension is slow, thus keeping the foliage in clusters. The small plants may be grown in containers or dish gardens and trained against slabs of wood for upright growth when the plant's size increases. The nephthytis common name refers to the previous classification of these plants under the **Nephthytis** genus.

Culture   These plants may easily be grown in either water or all-purpose potting soil. They prefer evenly moist soil and warm temperatures, ideally over 65°F overnight. Pinch back periodically if vining growth is not desired.

Typical Problems   More problems result from disease than from pests, although mealy bugs, scale, and thrips may occur. Rots, leaf spots, and blight are a production problem where humidity and watering regimes are high. Though not so bothersome in indoor culture, these diseases may appear.

Propagation   Easily started by tip, stem, or leaf-bud cuttings; roots are often

Water

DRY	NORMAL	EVENLY MOIST

Temperature

COOL	MODERATE	WARM

Light

LOW	BRIGHT INDIRECT	FULL SUN

Humidity

ARID	MODERATE	HUMID

already developed at the joint when cuttings are taken. Propagation is easy in either water or more conventional medium.

Related Plants   Variants of *Syngonium podophyllum* include the following.

S. p. 'Albovirens.' "Cream nephthytis." Compact foliage with creamy-yellow veinal markings and dark green border.

S. p. 'Emerald Gem.' "Emerald gem nephthytis." Compact plant growing to about 24 inches with dark, glossy green foliage.

S.p. xanthophilum. "Greengold nephthytis." Juvenile leaves yellowish green and shield-shaped with two flaring basal lobes.

S. angustatum 'Albolineatum.' Juvenile plants variegated with white along the midribs and lateral veins, often with only the leaf margins green. Leaves soon dividing into three or five distinct narrow lobes.

S. macrophyllum. Juvenile leaves heart-shaped with velvety, emerald green upper surface.

S. wendlandii. Leaves soon becoming three-parted with ashy gray to silver veins and midribs contrasted against velvety deep green leaves.

BOTANICAL NAME: *Tolmiea menziesii*
(TOLL-me-uh men-ZEE-see-eye)

COMMON NAME: Pickaback plant, piggyback plant

FAMILY: Saxifragaceae (Saxifrage)

ORIGIN: Western North America

The pickaback plant is unusual in that it is one of the few plants that produces new plantlets from its still-attached leaves (hence the common names). The plantlets arise at the point of petiole attachment on top of leaves that are 4 inches across and lobed similar to maple leaves. Also, the plant is unusual among the house plants in that it originates in the United States and Canada rather than the tropics. The inflorescence, an erect raceme with small greenish flowers, is not spectacular. Overall, *Tolmiea* reaches a height of 6 to 8 inches and a width of 12 to 15 inches.

Culture A standard loamy soil is proper, with fertilization occurring about every one or two months. The older leaves should be pinched off on occasion to encourage new growth and compactness. Excessive elongation of the leaf petiole is an indication of poor lighting.

Typical Problems Too low humidity will cause the leaf margins to turn brown. Spider mites and aphids prey on this plant, as well as mealy bugs that infest the leaf axils. Frequent inspections will prevent severe infestations.

Propagation Leaves with plantlets attached, or large leaves with no plantlet apparent, may be propagated by inserting about 2 inches of petiole into the medium. The leaf base should contact the medium and may need some weighting or pinning down to establish good contact. Seeds are used less commonly.

Related Plants None.

Water

DRY	NORMAL	EVENLY MOIST
		■

Temperature

COOL	MODERATE	WARM
	■	

Light

LOW	BRIGHT INDIRECT	FULL SUN
	■	

Humidity

ARID	MODERATE	HUMID
	■	

BOTANICAL NAME: *Tradescantia fluminensis*

(trad-es-KAN-tee-uh flew-men-IN-sis)

COMMON NAME: Wandering Jew

FAMILY: Commelinaceae (Spiderwort)

ORIGIN: South America

These durable, but short-lived, trailing plants have been exchanged among friends through cuttings long before they gained commercial importance; hence, they are named after the many European Jews who, before Israel was established, had no homeland. This common designation extends also to **Zebrina** species as well. Also called inch plants because of their rapid growth through short stem segments, **Tradescantia** species are easy to cultivate indoors. They may be acquired in either green or in various types of variegation, the coloration varying greatly even on the same plant. After a year or so of growth, these plants need to be restarted with cuttings because they lose their lower leaves with maturity, causing a straggly appearance. These plants are excellent potted specimens when young, becoming more appropriate for hanging baskets after a few months.

Culture *Tradescantia* performs best in bright light that will allow dense growth and large leaves. Allow to dry between waterings to prevent rotting and fertilize once or twice a month during active growth. Keep night temperatures above 50°F for best growth. Pinch frequently, being careful to remove the stem's growing tip that may be deep within the cluster of terminal leaves.

Water

DRY	NORMAL	EVENLY MOIST

Temperature

COOL	MODERATE	WARM

Light

LOW	BRIGHT INDIRECT	FULL SUN

Humidity

ARID	MODERATE	HUMID

Typical Problems   Mealy bugs, scale insects, and nematodes occur occasionally, as well as rots, leaf spots, and blight. Proper watering helps to control disease incidence.

Propagation   Cuttings of *Tradescantia* are so easy to root that four or five may be stuck directly into a pot of loamy potting mix and rooted in place. They are also easily rooted in water.

Related Plants

T. f. 'Variegata.' "Variegated wandering Jew, speedy Henry." Shiny ovate leaves to 1½ inches long with leaves variously variegated with green and yellow or ivory-white. Needs bright indirect light to maintain good variegated color.

T. albiflora. "Wandering Jew." A plant with leaves 2 or 3 inches long, compared to 1½ inches long on *T. fluminensis.* Often confused in the trade with *T. fluminensis.*

Cultivars include 'Albovittata' (leaves with white stripes); 'Aurea' (leaves yellow); 'Laekenensis' (leaves light green, striped with white, and banded with purple); and 'Variegata' (leaves striped with yellow and white).

BOTANICAL NAME: *Yucca elephantipes*
(YUH-ka el-e-phan-TIP-es)

COMMON NAME: Spineless yucca, bulb stem palm-lily

FAMILY: Agavaceae (Agave)

ORIGIN: Mexico

Species of yucca are among the toughest of plants, both outdoors and indoors. Sometimes sold as *Y. gigantea,* spineless yucca is named for its large 3-inch-wide leaves that extend 4 feet. They are soft and leathery, fresh green, and have rough margins and a soft tip. The white flowers are borne on a large inflorescence at the top of the plant. Yucca is primarily used as a floor specimen with a striking rosette of foliage. Its strong form may be used alone or blended with other textures and colors.

Culture This tough plant is insensitive to typical indoor extremes of heat, light, and humidity. It performs best under full sun, but can tolerate very dark areas as well. No pruning is necessary except to remove occasional declining older leaves on the developing woody stem. Fertilize two or three times per year, particularly during active growth.

Typical Problems Scale insects and root mealy bugs are a possibility, as well as various leaf spots and blights, although all of these are uncommon.

Propagation From seeds, rooting the occasional branches that develop, and basal suckers.

Related Plants

Y.e. 'Variegata.' "Giant variegated palm-lily." Leaves bordered with an ivory band.

Water

DRY	NORMAL	EVENLY MOIST

Temperature

COOL	MODERATE	WARM

Light

LOW	BRIGHT INDIRECT	FULL SUN

Humidity

ARID	MODERATE	HUMID

BOTANICAL NAME: *Zebrina pendula*
(zee-BRIN-uh PEN-du-la)

COMMON NAME: Wandering Jew, inch plant

FAMILY: Commelinaceae (Spiderwort)

ORIGIN: Mexico

Sharing the wandering Jew and inch plant common name with *Tradescantia*, *Zebrina* is similar in that it is a popular, attractive, and relatively fast-growing plant. Suitable for small containers during its first few months of growth, it grows into a trailing specimen for hanging baskets or pedestals. *Zebrina pendula* is one of the more colorful foliage plants on the market; its 2-inch-long leaves are deep green and purple with two wide silver bands on the upper surface. The leaf under sides are bright purple. The flowers are rosy pink clusters that are upstaged by the foliage. Like *Tradescantia*, *Zebrina* loses its lower leaves after a year or so and must be restarted from cuttings.

Culture Pinch *Zebrina* frequently to promote dense growth, but be sure to remove the stem's growing tip that is obscured by the terminal cluster of leaves. Pot into a general potting mixture, keeping evenly moist but avoiding overwatering. Keep night temperatures above 50°F to maintain active growth. Fertilize once or twice per month during the growing season.

Typical Problems Leaf spots and rust occasionally; mealy bugs, scale insects, aphids, and nematodes also may appear.

Propagation Tip cuttings (which may be collected during pruning) root easily in water or a loamy soil mix. Plant four or five unrooted cuttings directly into a container of loose soil; the plants will root and grow without requiring transplanting. Cuttings may also be rooted easily in plain water.

Related Plants

Z. p. 'Purpusii.' Leaves consistently dark red or reddish green.

Z. p. 'Quadricolor.' Metallic green leaves striped with green, red, and white.

Water		
DRY	NORMAL	EVENLY MOIST

Temperature		
COOL	MODERATE	WARM

Light		
LOW	BRIGHT INDIRECT	FULL SUN

Humidity		
ARID	MODERATE	HUMID

index

Throughout the index the following notations are used: 1) **boldface** numbers identify pages where concepts are defined in the text proper; 2) *italicized* numbers identify plants discussed in parts four and five of the text; 3) numbers followed by "t" identify tables; those followed by "f", figures.

Amaryllis, *see Hippeastrum*
Ananas, 31, 84, 234, 334, 335, 364t, 366t, *389*
Angiosperms, **18**
Anions, **156**
Annuals, **43**
Anther, **55**
Anthurium, 31f, 326, 327t, 364t, 367t, *390*
　　disorders of, 218, 219, 220, 228, 231
Aphelandra, 147t, 175, 188t, 190, 367t, *391*
　　disorders of, 218, 220, 223, 224, 227, 230, 231
Apical dominance, **90**
Aporocactus, 340
Arabian wax cissus, *see Cissus*
Arachniodes, 347t
Aralia ivy, *see ×Fatshedera*
Araucaria, 19, 20t, 27t, 37, 57, 183t, 188t, 367t, *392*
　　disorders of, 218, 219, 220, 224, 230, 232
Ardisia, 33, 183t, 367t, *393*
　　disorders of, 224, 231, 234
Areca palm, *see Chrysalidocarpus*
Arecastrum, 361
Areoles, **338**
Arisaema, 326
Aroids, 325–328, 364t
Arrowhead vine, *see Syngonium*
Artillery plant, *see Pilea*
Asexual cycle, **39**
Asparagus, 22t, 187t, 296t, 344, 365t, 367t, *394–395*
　　disorders of, 218, 219, 220, 224, 230, 234
Aspidistra, 27t, 33, 36, 99, 183t, 187t, 239t, 367t, *396*
　　disorders of, 219, 220, 232
Asplenium, 345, 345f, 347t
Assimilates, **66**
Astrophytum, 340, 340f, 341
Atoms, **156**
Aucuba, 37t, 57
Australian cliff brake, *see Pellaea*
Australian laurel, *see Pittosporum*
Australian tree fern, *see Sphaeropteris*
Australian umbrella tree, *see Brassaia*
Autotrophic, **155**
Autumn fern, *see Dryopteris*
Auxin, **68,** 85–87
Avocado, 33, 218, 230
Axillary or lateral buds, **25**
Azalea, *see Rhododendron*

Baby rubber plant, *see Peperomia*
Baby tears, *see Soleirolia*
Balfour aralia, *see Polyscias*
Bamboo palm, *see Chamaedorea; Rhapsis*
Banana, *see Musa*
Bark, **66**
Barrel cactus, *see Echinopsis*
Barroom plant, *see Aspidistra*

Basic, **160**
Bead vine, *see Senecio*
Bear's foot fern, *see Humata*
Beaucarnea recurvata, 34, 183t, 188t, 367t, *397*
Bedding-out, **5**
Beef plant, *see Iresine*
Beefsteak plant, *see Iresine*
Begonia, 19, 19t, 20t, 21, 22, 37t, 44, 57, 84, 85, 91, 99, 147t, 188t, 308, 320, 320f, 325, 328–333, 367t, *398–399*
　cane-stemmed, **330**
　disorders of, 214, 218–221, 223, 224, 227, 228, 230–232, 234, 236
　rex, **331**
　rhizomatous, **331**
　shrublike, **331**
　thick-stemmed, 331
　trailing-scandent, **331,** 331f
　tuberous, **331**
　wax, **331**
Belgian evergreen, *see Dracaena*
Belladonna lily, *see Amaryllis*
Beloperone, 147t
Belvisa, 348t
Benjamin tree, *see Ficus benjamina*
Berry, **33**
Biennials, **43**
Bigleaf hydrangea, *see Hydrangea*
Billbergia, 334, 335, 338
Bipinnately compound (leaves), **26**
Bird's nest fern, *see Asplenium*
Bishop's cap, *see Astrophytum*
Bloodleaf, *see Iresine*
Bolt, **43**
Boston fern, *see Nephrolepis*
Bougainvillea, 219, 227
Brake ferns, *see Pteris*
Brassaia, 22, 26f, 28, 28f, 36, 175, 183t, 185, 188t, 189, 193f, 202, 209, *400–401*
　disorders of, 214, 216, 220, 224, 228, 231, 232, 234
Brazilian Coleus, *see Plectranthus*
Breadfruit vine, *see Monstera*
Bromelia, 334, 335
Bromeliads, 36, 48, 98, 146t, 147t, 214, 296t, 299, 303, 304, 325, *333–338,* 365t
Buddhist pine, *see Podocarpus*
Bud sport, **82**
Bulb, **99,** 146t, 306, 307, 307f, 309, 310
　forcing, 305–308
　scales, **99**
Bulblets, **99**
Bulbstem palm-lily, *see Yucca*
Bunya-bunya, *see Araucaria*
Burmese fishtail palm, *see Caryota*
Burn plant, *see Aloe*
Burro's tail, *see Sedum*